CLARENDON LAW S

Edited by

PAUL CRAIG

CLARENDON LAW SERIES

Personal Property Law
(4th edition)
MICHAEL BRIDGE

The Idea of Arbitration
JAN PAULSSON

The Anthropology of Law
FERNANDA PIRIE

Law and Gender
JOANNE CONAGHAN

The Conflict of Laws (3rd edition)
ADRIAN BRIGGS

The Concept of Law (3rd edition)
H.L.A. HART

With a Postscript edited by
Penelope A. Bulloch and
Joseph Raz
With an Introduction and Notes by
Leslie Green

Land Law (2nd edition)
ELIZABETH COOKE

Administrative Law (5th edition)
PETER CANE

Discrimination Law (2nd edition)
SANDRA FREDMAN

An Introduction to the Law of Trusts
(3rd edition)
SIMON GARDNER

Natural Law and Natural Rights
(2nd edition)
JOHN FINNIS

Introduction to Company Law
(2nd edition)
PAUL DAVIES

Employment Law (2nd edition)
HUGH COLLINS

International Law
VAUGHAN LOWE

Civil Liberties
CONOR GEARTY

Intellectual Property
MICHAEL SPENCE

Policies and Perceptions of Insurance Law
in the Twenty-First Century (2nd edition)
MALCOLM CLARKE

Philosophy of Private Law
WILLIAM LUCY

Law in Modern Society
DENIS GALLIGAN

An Introduction to Tort Law (2nd edition)
TONY WEIR

Equity (2nd edition)
SARAH WORTHINGTON

Atiyah's Introduction to the Law of
Contract (6th edition)
STEPHEN A. SMITH,
P.S. ATIYAH

Unjust Enrichment (2nd edition)
PETER BIRKS

An Introduction to Family Law
(2nd edition)
GILLIAN DOUGLAS

Criminal Justice
LUCIA ZEDNER

Contract Theory
STEPHEN A. SMITH

Public Law
ADAM TOMKINS

Personal Property Law (3rd edition)
MICHAEL BRIDGE

Law of Property (3rd edition)
F.H. LAWSON AND
BERNARD RUDDEN

An Introduction to Constitutional Law
ERIC BARENDT

Resulting Trusts
ROBERT CHAMBERS

Legal Reasoning and Legal Theory
NEIL MACCORMICK

Labour Legislation and Public Policy
A Contemporary History
PAUL DAVIES AND
MARK FREEDLAND

LAW AND VALUES IN THE EUROPEAN UNION

STEPHEN WEATHERILL

Jacques Delors Professor of European Law
and Fellow of Somerville College at the University of Oxford

OXFORD
UNIVERSITY PRESS

OXFORD
UNIVERSITY PRESS

Great Clarendon Street, Oxford, OX2 6DP,
United Kingdom

Oxford University Press is a department of the University of Oxford.
It furthers the University's objective of excellence in research, scholarship,
and education by publishing worldwide. Oxford is a registered trade mark of
Oxford University Press in the UK and in certain other countries

First Edition published in 2016

Impression: 1

Published in the United States of America by Oxford University Press
198 Madison Avenue, New York, NY 10016, United States of America

British Library Cataloguing in Publication Data
Data available

Library of Congress Control Number: 2016933502

ISBN 978–0–19–955726–4 (hbk.)
ISBN 978–0–19–955727–1 (pbk.)

Printed and bound by
CPI Group (UK) Ltd, Croydon, CR0 4YY

PREFACE

More than twenty years ago I wrote a book entitled *Law and Integration in the European Union*: it was published in OUP's Clarendon series in 1995. This book, *Law and Values in the European Union*, is in a sense its successor, but not a single sentence, not even a single sub-clause, has survived unscathed. The project of European integration has mutated and its examination demanded that I start again from scratch. The ambition of this book is not so different—I want to convey now, as I did then, the dynamic, evolving character of EU law against a background of fluctuating political, economic, and social pressures—but the way to realize that ambition has changed a lot. So this is a completely new book.

I hope the non-lawyer might read the introductory Chapter 1 and the concluding Chapter 8, which are designed to explore the objectives of the EU and the extent to which it has a values-driven vocation, and be tempted to dip into the more detailed legal examination conducted in the chapters in between. But this is primarily a book for lawyers written by a lawyer. I try to develop a thematic explanation that the EU is founded on an institutional architecture that is not based on the model of a State, but which rather seeks to reflect the interests of States and of their peoples in an environment of deepening transnational activity that tends to push the effective site for problem-solving in some areas (such as climate change, migration, security, economic reform) beyond the State. In such circumstances the legitimacy of the process must be somehow secured, albeit unavoidably not by the orthodox patterns of democracy and accountability that are familiar within a State. The abiding thematic tension lies between designing institutions with sufficient autonomy to pursue *effective* problem-solving while also ensuring that those institutions are subject to adequate *control*. Moreover, the EU is built on a constitutionalized legal order, which aims to sustain effective policing of agreed rules not only at supra-State but also at national level while also protecting individual rights. This is international treaty law, but it is more than international treaty law. Most of all I portray the EU as a site to manage the interdependence of States. As I explain in the concluding chapter, the EU could be abolished tomorrow, but the problems to which it is an intended solution would not vanish and would generate an urgent construction of bilateral and multilateral arrangements to address them (which would quite likely be a lot less effective and more intransparent than those found right now in the EU itself).

So States exercise their sovereignty through membership of the EU. States give up a degree of power to act unilaterally so that they may participate in the deployment of a collective problem-solving capacity that is a great deal more effective. Resources of power are not finite: acting through the EU expands the sum of State powers so it becomes greater than its parts. The EU 'adds value' to its Member States. Moreover, the EU also serves as a means to impose constraints on States, to 'tame' their historically toxic capacity to cause harm to each other. The EU's rules and institutions do not replace, still less suppress, the several different locations political authority to be found across Europe, but instead lock those locations into a credible set of reciprocally undertaken commitments designed to make real promises to solve problems their citizens expect to see solved and by preventing them inflicting external harm. The failure of the Treaty establishing a Constitution is explained at Chapter 1.4, but its lost motto for the EU, 'United in diversity', deserves to live on as a worthy aspiration. The EU aims to supplement the claims of its Member States to be effective democratic and legitimate actors in an interdependent world, but it does not and should not pretend to suppress the diversity that is Europe's most cherished richness. The EU aims to accommodate that diversity within a managed framework. It seeks not to replace States, but rather to achieve a better management of their interdependence.

And yet what if the EU does too much? And what if it does what it does badly? The EU's geographical and functional expansion is a major theme of this book: this is in part a heroic story but it brings severe pressures too. The EU, as its impact has increased, needs to address questions of democracy, accountability, respect for fundamental rights and for national and local diversity. It should not be measured against the same benchmarks of legitimacy as a State, as it will always fail, but it does need to achieve legitimacy. It needs, in short, values. And its Treaties aspire to grant it values. I vividly remember, a child of the InterRail generation, looking out over the dusty, dirty, wind-blown wasteland of Berlin's Potsdamer Platz in September of 1980. There was no 'Europe'. Never did I feel luckier to have been born in the West. Today there is 'Europe': democracies (more or less) stretch from the Atlantic Ocean to the Baltic and the Black Sea. But today Europe is faced by new cleavages and new affronts to justice. Migrants drown in the Mediterranean, razor-wire fences are hurled at human distress, minorities are blamed, democracy suddenly looks horribly fragile in some parts of Europe. The rise of intolerance and austerity mocks the 'values' to which the EU is constitutionally committed and on which I focus in this book's concluding chapter. This book's final sentence is gloomy. I hope I mis-read the mood. I hope the EU will be able to live up to its values.

TABLE OF CONTENTS

TABLE OF CASES

ALPHABETICAL

NUMERICAL

TABLES OF LEGISLATION

TREATIES AND CONVENTIONS

Regulations

Directives

OTHER JURISDICTIONS

1

WHAT IS THE EUROPEAN UNION FOR?

1.1 THE LOGIC OF THE EUROPEAN UNION

A State decides to build a new power plant. It locates it on its coast, far away from any of its cities, where the prevailing winds will blow polluting fumes and other toxic material away from its territory and towards the densely populated territory of a neighbouring second State. That second State is home to a small and not very successful producer of cars, which lobbies the government to introduce new product specifications which have the effect of excluding from the market cars of a different design imported from a third State, which is home to several large producers of cars previously popular among, but now unavailable to, the consumers of the second State. The third State introduces repressive measures against a minority group and many members of that group flee its territory, forcing a neighbouring fourth State to set up large refugee camps to accommodate them. The fourth State has lately cut its tax rates applicable to companies and has also abolished many rules setting health and safety standards for the workplace, as well as repealing laws setting a minimum wage. A neighbouring fifth State finds that several firms based on its territory have chosen to move their headquarters to the fourth State where their operating costs are consequently much lower. The fifth State has introduced strict new laws designed to ensure secrecy in the banking sector. A neighbouring sixth State fears that this has made it much easier for criminals operating on its territory to conceal the pathways through which they transmit their ill-gotten gains, thereby making the detection of crime much harder. That sixth State has a fixed exchange rate for its currency which the government decides is far too high, and so it decides to devalue the currency. In consequence its exports become much cheaper and traders in a seventh State find that they are rapidly losing market share to goods produced in and exported from the sixth State.

And so on. One may readily add extra States and imagine further flashpoints and disputes. Each of these cases has its own nuance but the core common problem is that each State fears that a neighbouring State's policies are causing it harm, while it stands accused of inflicting harm on a neighbour.

In each case the State is exercising its sovereignty—to locate the power plant, to set product specifications, to repress minorities, to tax companies, and so on. And in each case the State is a victim of the sovereignty exercised by one of its neighbours—it suffers pollution, it finds export markets are closed, it must deal with an influx of refugees, it suffers corporate flight, and so on. This is the reality of State sovereignty when States are interdependent. Its exercise creates victims. All the States are victims.

There is accordingly a case for co-operation. If agreement replaces unilateral action, then polluting power plants can be sited where they will harm the fewest number of people, irrespective of which State they happen to live in. Product specifications can be agreed which are apt to keep markets open, allowing producers to compete and thereby to enhance consumer choice. Perhaps States will agree common standards or perhaps they will agree to recognize each other's different standards. A consensus can be pursued on the protection of minority rights or at least to share the burdens of sudden population migration. And so on. Under this model a State surrenders the right to act unilaterally and thereby to impose costs on other States, but by choosing instead to co-operate that State gains by being able to participate in a decision-making process which restrains other States from acting unilaterally and imposing costs on it. Still more broadly, many problems that beset States today are problems that are faced in common—climate change, security, migration, and so on—and it is plausible that they are more likely to be solved in an effective manner by action taken in common. All States are able to gain once they are locked into a mutually agreed framework for addressing such issues: each gives up a degree of autonomy but in return knows that all other participants have made precisely the same concession.

The case for co-operation is not uncontested. One might argue, for example, that competing, rather than co-operating, on tax rates or labour standards or currency valuation is an expression of autonomy: to the winner the spoils, to the loser the inducement to change policy. There are clearly politically sensitive questions to address about *how much* co-operation should be pursued among States. However, as a minimum, the point is that one State's decisions exert an impact on other States and that therefore there is no independence from external pressure. States are *inter*dependent. The issue is only how to respond to and manage such interdependence, not to ignore or, worse, deny its existence.

This is the logic of the European Union.

Twenty-eight Member States, comprising the majority of States and the majority of the population in Europe that stretches west from Russia to the shores of the Atlantic Ocean, have agreed a dense network of co-operative relationships, under the foundational authority of the two key Treaties which, have since the entry into force of the Treaty of Lisbon in 2009, governed the modern European Union. These are the Treaty on European Union (TEU) and the Treaty on the Functioning of the European Union (TFEU). So TEU and TFEU—two Treaties, one, the TEU, comprising fifty-five Articles, the other, the TFEU, stretching over 358 Articles, and buttressed by important Protocols attached to both. These are the foundational texts of EU law. The EU is an international organization founded on a set of Treaties entered into by its Member States. What is involved *in detail* is the subject matter of this book.

The basic purpose is the management of interdependence.

The initial impulse for the modern European Union was the Second World War. This was the harm inflicted across national frontiers that provoked the quest to devise a basis for a more intensely co-operative relationship among States. The destructive scale of that catastrophe was such that it impelled a search for radically new arrangements for engineering a post-War reconstruction of Europe and, according to the chosen design, progressively to *deepen* that interdependence. Participating States were at first limited to *western* Europe—the looming presence of the Soviet Union not only prevented the involvement of the States of eastern and central Europe but also strengthened the sense of need among Europe's luckier States to stand together. The six founding States—France, Germany, Italy, the Netherlands, Belgium, and Luxembourg—began by creating a common framework for the management of their coal and steel industries. These sectors were chosen in part because of the perceived need to strip those materials, the very foundations of war-making, out of an exclusively national grip. But this first step, the establishment of the European Coal and Steel Community (ECSC) under the Treaty of Paris with effect from 1952, also counted as the 'limited but decisive point' on which initial political agreement could be secured, to borrow the terms of the transformative 'Schuman Declaration' of 1950, proclaimed by Robert Schuman, then Foreign Minister of France. The assumption was that such initial practical steps would be only the start of a process of deepening community which would become significantly more politically ambitious over time. So the ECSC Treaty begins not with reference to opencast mining or the Bessemer Converter, but rather with the declaration that 'world peace can be safeguarded only by creative efforts commensurate with the dangers that threaten it'.

In similar vein, the much broader and more ambitious European Economic Community (EEC) Treaty, which entered into force by virtue of the agreement on the Treaty of Rome among the same six original States in 1958, begins with the expression of determination 'to lay the foundations of an ever closer union among the peoples of Europe'. Some of this was doubtless frothy rhetoric and hyperbole and no doubt some politicians of the time had little, if any, commitment to such transformative design: making European States more prosperous made plenty of political appeal as an end in its own right, and the *detail* of the system instituted by the Treaty of Rome was largely concerned with economic integration. Moreover, the more aggressively political plan to create a European Defence Community launched at the same time as that to create the Coal and Steel Community, which would have established a European army and would have entailed close co-ordination of foreign policy, faltered and collapsed by 1954 for want of adequate national, especially French, support. But even after stripping out any false assumption that a misty-eyed stairway to political unity was ever the dominant narrative of the founders, some politicians did pursue a wider vision, beyond the quest for solid economic growth. And the experiment, once set in motion as an overtly economic, not political exercise, gathered its own momentum. This, once the EEC had begun in 1958, was sufficient to propel the process of integration 'from within' for some thirty years, and it was as late as 1987, on the entry into force of the Single European Act, that the original Treaties were the subject of any major formal revision. That initiated a cycle whereby revision of the Treaties has become relatively common: the Maastricht Treaty (1993) altered the creature's name to the European Union while expanding the scope of co-operation under the so-called 'three pillar' system; the Amsterdam Treaty (1999) and the Nice Treaty (2003) made relatively technical adjustments; and, in the final act of this incremental process (so far), the Treaty of Lisbon (2009) injected further reform, including the final abandonment of the term 'Community' and the collapse of the three pillars in favour of a single European Union. But the European Economic Community Treaty, the Treaty of Rome, put in place in the 1950s foundation stones that remain recognizably the modern EU's method of functioning.

None of this vision could be credibly pursued without a commitment to operate within a framework promising more intense co-operation than mere intergovernmental bargaining. The ambition to transcend a system based on inter-State consensus, which had failed miserably to prevent the ghastly excesses of the Second World War, required a concrete readiness to equip institutions 'beyond the State' with a degree of autonomy from the unilateral expression of partisan State interests. As early as 1949 a group of ten (today forty-seven) States had embarked on the process of piecing together co-operation and means to safeguard their common principles and ideals from the debris of the post-War terrain, but that initiative, the creation of the Council of Europe from which in 1953 emerged the European Convention on Human Rights, was relatively conventional in its institutional and constitutional form. The EU was and remains a much bolder enterprise, reflecting an appetite for institutional support apt to drive deeper political aspiration. The institutional and constitutional character of the EU has conventionally been seen to rest on a balance between the 'intergovernmental' and the 'supranational'. Broadly, this refers to the necessary reliance on both the (intergovernmental) control exercised by the Member States, reflecting the need for authorization by politically legitimate sources, and the effectiveness that is delivered by institutions that have some degree of (supranational) autonomy from partisan State interests and are therefore enabled to transcend such blockages. Chapter 3 of this book explores in detail these institutional arrangements, which go to the character of the EU as a uniquely sophisticated international organization. It has—and it has always had—three principal political institutions which also lie at the heart of the legislative process. The Commission is an institution which is formally independent of the Member States, and it is charged with the responsibility to devise and to propose legislation and to ensure that the law of the EU is enforced. Its autonomy is vital to secure progress by cutting through partisan State interests—its absence of accountability is the reason why it does not make law, but rather only proposes it and, once made, secures its enforcement. The adoption of legislation is the preserve of the Council and the Parliament. The Council comprises representatives of the governments of the Member States, typically made up of Ministers dealing with the particular subject matter under discussion, while the Parliament, directly elected since 1979, represents the peoples of Europe, and sits and typically votes by party affiliation, not by nationality. That legislation is made both by an institution representing States and one representing people and, moreover, only (in almost all instances) on the initiative of an independent institution, the Commission, is central to the EU's claim to have established a system that is qualitatively different from that found in a typical international organization—and also one that is quite distinct from that found within a State. The addition of a judicial institution, the Court of Justice, which enjoys compulsory jurisdiction and which has a direct channel of co-operation with the national courts via the preliminary reference procedure, distances the EU's institutional character still further from possible international or national comparators. The Court of Justice, based in Luxembourg, has not only fulfilled the orthodox judicial task of legal interpretation of relevant texts; it has also driven an ambitious constitutional re-imagining of the very nature of EU law. The Court made early choices of a constitutionally spectacular manner, fashioning a 'new legal order' and making claims about its practical day-to-day relationship with national law which transcend those made by orthodox international law. This is a process of 'constitutionalization': a Treaty-based legal order has been expanded into one that in important respects functions *as if* it is arranging the constitutional relationship between different levels of governance within a polity, and which, more generally, contains judicially enforceable principles constraining the exercise of public power. Chapter 4 examines this story.

The vision of the EU as a means to manage interdependence among the States of Europe is not simply a matter of crafting rules and institutions at EU level that are apt to tame States and to solve problems faced in common. This is, after all, a rather mundane technocratic vision. The aspiration that motivated some, though certainly not all, of the politicians and public officials involved in the post-War birth of the modern European Union was to craft a system that would manage interdependence among the Member States according to an assumption that further functional co-operation and closer political ties would follow. But it is important to appreciate that there is also a *democratic* element to the case in favour of building governance structures beyond the State. Take the example of the polluting power plant. The citizens of the State which chooses to locate the plant where its emissions will harm only people in another State have a voice in the decision. Under the political practices which apply locally, the decision-maker is accountable to local voters. By contrast those citizens who are directly affected, living in the territory of the neighbouring State receiving the cross-border pollution, have no voice or vote at all. This is a perversion of democracy: those (in the neighbouring State) affected by the decision are denied representation in its making, and the decision-maker bears not a shred of accountability to them. Meanwhile the voters in the first State determine where the plant shall be located, yet are blithely unaffected by the consequences of that choice. They have shoved the cost on to external victims. This is exactly the problem which arises where democratic structures based on the State come up against the reality of cross-border effects and mutual interdependence between States.

A strong case may accordingly be made that the introduction of rules by a supra-State authority which compel all affected States to operate under a system which takes account of the full range of affected interests comes closer to meeting legitimate democratic aspirations than one which treats each State as a wholly autonomous political unit. EU rules—on siting power plants, on product specifications, and so on—are ways to give some expression to the *democratic* anxiety about the implications of a decision taken internally within a single State without reference to those externally affected. In this sense the EU serves as a means to address and correct the democratic failings of States. Moreover, that perception of the EU as means to secure an *enhancement* of State political legitimacy can be taken further by embrace of the perception that States alone do not simply cause harm by imposing external costs (and so need to be 'tamed'), but also that they are incapable of meeting their citizens' aspirations through unilateral action, simply because so many problems today are transnational and can be solved only by transnational action. Matters such as climate change, migration, and security, as well as the rise of hugely powerful corporations and the influence of mobile capital, are pressing concerns for citizens but no European State acting solo can devise solutions that are remotely likely to satisfy voters. So using the EU as a site to agree, implement, and enforce rules that apply in common is a means to improve the legitimacy of political decision-making beyond that which can be achieved by unilateral action taken at State level.

1.2 THE LIMITS OF THE EUROPEAN UNION

Such a heroic tale! This broad account cannot, of course, provide a satisfying or comprehensive explanation for every intricate feature of the EU's chosen design or for the shape of every single conferred competence, still less for the detail of particular EU legislative texts or decisions of the Court of Justice. It does, however, point in the general direction of the EU properly portrayed as a system of virtues and vices that demands assessment alongside the virtues and vices of its Member States—and it makes claims for symbiosis, in the sense that the EU may be able to provide a forum for solving problems that Member States acting alone cannot, while the Member States may be able to provide the underpinning of democracy and legitimacy that eludes the EU as a non-State actor with no stable constituency of people who treat it as 'their' polity. But the limits of this logic demand appreciation. The sustainability of the EU's claim to exercise legitimate political and legal authority is not infinite. This agenda of 'taming' States to prevent them harming their neighbours, allied to a capacity for collective problem-solving, counsels for the European Union's role to be *limited* to matters where it is able to fulfil those expectations. Shaping the EU's scope of action must pay attention and respect to the enduring claims to political authority legitimately made by Member States.

Moreover, it is important to avoid over-inflation of the democratic case for a system of governance 'beyond the State' in the abstract and for the EU as a particular instance of such institutional innovation. States acting unilaterally suffer from deficits in their claim to act democratically because of the effects their actions cause externally, as the example of the power plant reveals, and more broadly States acting alone cannot effectively address all the problems their citizens expect to be tackled, from climate change to migration and security. The EU is apt to soothe these frictions. It *adds* to the claims of States to be responsible democratic and legitimate actors in an interdependent world. But the EU does not and should not aspire itself to become a State, because, like its States, it too suffers from serious—though different—flaws when judged from the perspective of democratic legitimacy. A major blockage to treating the EU as a State-in-the-making is that there is in short no European '*demos*': most people in Europe do not think of their political identity as primarily 'European'. Instead most find their primary sense of political allegiance within the State of which they are citizen—whether as a citizen of that State (French, British, German, and so on) or as a citizen of a nation or a region within that State (Scottish, Basque). This is how the EU has grown: its founding reliance on economic integration as its method of action neither demanded nor expected the generation of any fund of loyalty or allegiance among the peoples of Europe. One cannot exclude that a 'European *demos*' may develop over time, but the generation of such revolutionary change seems highly improbable in the absence of necessary catalysts. Politics is typically national, not EU-wide; the media is largely national, not EU-wide; and so on. The absence of a 'European public space' means that the type of solidarity and readiness to accept redistribution of resources which is treated as normal in principle, if contested in detail, *within* a State is missing at EU level. The case for equipping the EU with ever wider competences and powers on the basis that it is better at the job than its Member States acting unilaterally eventually encounters serious objection where citizens believe that the job in question is one that *should* be done at State level. The more politically and culturally sensitive the job—tax and spend, defence, criminal justice—the louder the protest about the EU's involvement. The political authority of the EU is and should be limited.

A deeper critique would hold anyway that any such shifts in favour of a stronger EU, and still more a European State (of some kind), are undesirable. To re-shape the State(s)-based pattern that has served Europe so ill for centuries as a bigger, grander, and quite probably still nastier single State is to betray the far more subtle post-War ambition that launched the EU. So this is to argue that the EU, as an international organization founded on international Treaties, co-exists with its Member States, and should not supersede them.

From this perception of the EU's limited popular identification with the exercise of legitimate political authority flow a number of important consequences. Whatever authority the EU claims—to 'tame' States, to solve problems in common, and more generally to address the flaws in States' claims to act democratically and legitimately under conditions of interdependence—must be rooted in a grant made to it by the Member States, as the principal site of recognized political authority in Europe. And, provided this is maintained, the Member States come to the rescue of the EU by supplying it with the political legitimacy to act which on its own it lacks. This has consequences both for determining what the EU should do—what should be its scope of action in common and what should instead be left to be dealt with according to national preference?—and for deciding how should the EU do it—what constitutional and institutional arrangements should govern its capacity for law- and policy-making?

That the EU's powers and competences go no further than those granted to it by the Member States according to the Treaties is constitutionally fundamental, and is examined more fully in Chapter 2 of this book. This is where the EU claims its legitimacy—in the mandate freely agreed by the Member States and authorized according to the constitutional procedures employed for the ratification of international treaties according to local practice. That means that where the EU trespasses beyond that Treaty mandate it subverts the legitimating role played by the Member States at times of Treaty revision, and tends to tip the EU towards illegitimate over-reach. That, however, is more easily asserted in principle than guaranteed in practice. The EU's mandate is broad and, as part of the design of a flexible system apt to solve unforeseen problems as they emerge, it is not tied down by detail. There is, moreover, a substantive element to this friction. Probably there would be general agreement that the EU is an apt site for addressing matters with obvious cross-border rhythms, such as pollution, electronic data transfer, or conservation of fisheries. Probably there would be general agreement that there is no need for the EU to lay down common rules on dog licensing or school uniforms. But much lies in between where agreement on the appropriate level of decision-making will be elusive. The most conspicuous elements of the narrative in the early post-war years of European integration were the delivery of economic growth across the EU, focusing in particular on the project to complete the internal market, but the more recent rise of the single currency within the Eurozone has loaded extra and heavier management tasks on the EU. Once the EU moves beyond technical problem-solving and engages in policies with authentic contested political or cultural resonance, in particular where those policy choices have distributional implications for individuals and for States, its legitimacy is shaky. Within a polity bound together by a common *demos* there is a greater readiness to share burdens than would be found in a looser community. A transfer of wealth from rich areas (Bavaria, south-east England) to poorer areas (Saxony, north-east England) is part of the very nature of living in a modern State. Agreeing to a transfer between Germany and Greece is immediately a far greater stretch. The ties of solidarity are far looser, perhaps non-existent. So there are limits to the load the EU should be asked to bear, for fear that its activities come to be seen as illegitimate. This might mean that even where the EU is better at performing a particular task than its Member States acting unilaterally, it nevertheless should *not* do so because there is not enough popular support for the very notion that the EU, rather than the national level, is the right place to make the relevant decisions. At the same time a conclusion that the EU should not carry out a particular function because of such strain on its legitimacy should not be reached without close examination of just what sort of a job a State can do in tackling that problem through unilateral action. There is likely to be a necessary trade-off between practically superior problem-solving, where the EU is comparatively better, and politically legitimate problem-solving, where States are comparatively better. The economic crisis that exploded in 2008 and its continuing repercussions provide a vivid illustration of the choices at stake, while also posing existentially challenging questions about the durability of the EU model. A logic informed by recognition of the State as the primary site of political allegiance might urge retreat to national-level decision-making about economic and monetary policies as a means to improve a sense of ownership among citizens, but as a solution this makes some implausible assumptions about the ability of States acting in a more fragmented way to the challenges they face in common. The *more* the Member States do in common in order to address problems they face in common, the more the EU's legitimacy as the site for such common action is contested given the absence of a European *demos*, and yet it is that very absence which blocks the feasibility of simply replicating at EU level the democratic and accountable institutions familiar at State level; whereas the *less* the Member States do in common, the greater the risk that problems will be left inadequately addressed, with the result that the democratic and accountable institutions familiar at State level will be emptied of useful purpose.

The key insight is that the EU and the Member States acting in combination can achieve a great deal more than could be achieved if only the EU or only the Member States existed. The EU should not be seen as a zero-sum game: it is not a question of EU *or* Member States but rather EU *and* Member States. Converting this abstract insight into a convincing and detailed prescription for the optimal distribution of competences and powers between the EU and the Member States is the most pressing of all constitutional tasks.

The EU's institutional design is also conditioned by this understanding that there are limits to the EU's proper role. This means in this context that the blessing conferred by States must be secured not only by their acceptance of the basic Treaty texts but also by a heavy State involvement in the daily operation of the EU. The blend of both the (intergovernmental) control exercised by the Member States and the effectiveness that is delivered by institutions that have some degree of (supranational) autonomy from partisan State interests is the EU's basic working system. This is, as explained in Section 1.1 and as amplified in Chapter 3, central to the EU's claims to house a uniquely sophisticated form of international architecture, within which the expression of State interests (through the Council) co-exists with the direct democratic claims of the directly elected European Parliament, alongside the Commission and the Court which, in different ways, owe allegiance to the textual mandate of the Treaty rather than to any immediate source of political power to which they are accountable. There is a balance of sorts in the EU's institutional architecture. A plea for more *effective* institutions tends to generate fears about their control and their accountability, for making the EU's institutions more independent of State interests exposes them to criticism aimed at their lack of sensitivity to voters. A plea for more *accountable* institutions tends to generate fears about their autonomy as problem-solvers, for making the EU's institutions more subject to control runs the risk that they be stripped of capacity to promote a common European interest in preference to partisan interests. Finding a system that blends effectiveness of decision-making at EU level and control over its trajectory is the most pressing of all institutional tasks.

1.3 FUNCTIONAL AND GEOGRAPHIC EXPANSION

The smouldering end of the Second World War is remote in time now and the idea of soldiers' blood once again soaking deep into Flanders fields has become inconceivable. But the notion that European States are interdependent—that they can harm each other and, more positively, that they can likely address problems in common more effectively than unilaterally—is not only enduring; it has in fact become ever more pressing.

The two central questions that dominated the planning of the adventure of European integration from the very beginning continue to dominate it. First, *what should the EU do*? And second, *how should the EU do it*? These questions have forced their way with increasing urgency on to the debate about the role and future of the EU's place, because the situation does not remain static. If interdependence among States deepens, as is highly likely under the influence of economic and technological development, then the question is how much *more* should the EU do. That challenges the stability of the division of competence between EU and Member States and in turn, in so far as a heavier load is placed on the EU, it asks whether the associated institutional arrangements are up to the task.

As early as the 1950s important decisions were taken about the character of the EU which have proved enduring. But the EU has undergone an astonishing cycle of functional and geographical expansion over time. It operates across a far wider field of activity than could ever have been envisaged in the early years; and the territory on which its law runs stretches across most of the European continent. These patterns of growth have sometimes been the result of Treaty revision, sometimes the product of more subtle pressure and internal momentum. But functional and geographical expansion has brought with it tension and friction and, most of all, existential challenge to the EU's legitimacy.

In particular, the pressures of *functional and geographic expansion* have sharpened concerns about competence definition and the politicization of the EU's tasks and about institutional design. And the EU has been groping for satisfying answers for some time now.

'Functional expansion' refers to the fact that the EU is engaged in a great many more activities than it was in its early years. An aim is to create a single European market across the territory of the twenty-eight Member States, but not to create a single European State. In truth, however, the European Union is engaged with much more than the establishment of a market. In part this is because of the unavoidable need to adopt important policies in common at EU level and to convert them into legal rules in order to transform markets fragmented along national lines by diverse regulatory choices. But, more broadly, today the project nowadays goes far beyond the economy—affecting liberty, criminal justice, asylum policy, and so on. Each successive round of Treaty revision has typically extended the scope of EU action. The current Treaties are the (several times) amended versions of the Treaties of Paris and Rome which over fifty years ago established what we now know as the 'European Union'. Each amendment—by the Single European Act, which entered into force in 1987, the Maastricht Treaty (1993), the Amsterdam Treaty (1999), the Nice Treaty (2003), and the final act of this incremental process, the Treaty of Lisbon (2009)—possessed its own particular driving motivation and each is in detail different, but, in the matter of competence, each revision was thematically aligned by the attribution of more competences and powers to the EU. So too, albeit once again in different ways and to different extents at the level of detail, each round of Treaty revision has typically made it easier for the EU to legislate, most of all by adapting the voting rules in Council to shrink radically the areas where States enjoy a veto power, while also increasing the influence of the most conventionally democratic institution, the directly elected Parliament.

Given the depth of interdependence among States in Europe, accelerated by economic and technological change, it is no great surprise that more has come to be tackled in common, and that less is left to unilateral national choice. Part of that pattern of co-operation involves adoption and enforcement of a historically informed reciprocal set of rules for preventing States inflicting harm on each other—typically involving legal prohibitions against pernicious practices such as unjustifiably protectionist inter-State trade barriers. Part of it involves acting in common to solve problems collectively, where the problem is better (or even only) capable of resolution at a transnational rather than a national level—consider matters such as terrorism, asylum, climate change. Here the EU needs to be able to adopt its own common rules, not merely to forbid its States from acting in ways that may harm each other. Part too involves projecting European power on a global scale in a way that States alone cannot hope to achieve. All this is housed within an understanding that one State is willing to tolerate giving up 'sovereignty' in order to participate in arrangements that equally and reciprocally involve toleration of confinement of the harm-causing sovereignty of its fellow participants; and that, in shaping patterns of acting together rather than unilaterally, the EU is a venue whereby the sum of Member State action is permitted to exceed the individual parts.

The EU is, in the modern but ugly phrase, a 'force multiplier'. It supplements and strengthens its States' capacity for action. It does not propose to replace them. 'Managing interdependence', as a rationale for the EU's very existence, stretches far and wide across many functional activities, much more so than would have been envisaged in the dawn of the project in the 1950s.

This functional expansion is accompanied by the geographical expansion of the EU. The EU today comprises twenty-eight Member States, stretching from the shores of the Atlantic to the Black Sea, from Scandinavia to the waters of the Mediterranean. States joined at periodic intervals for reasons largely associated with appreciation that their ability to get the best for their citizens was enhanced by joining the EU club—that whatever they gave up in the currency of independence was exceeded by what they gained in opportunities to manage *inter*dependence. The narrative embraces the economic advantage secured as a member of the EU, but also covers desire to provoke and sustain social reform that would be blocked in a purely domestic setting and, in cases such as Greece, Spain, Portugal, and many of the States of central and eastern Europe, the immediate post-War quest to find a transnational means to entrench the resumption of democratic politics found a fresh late-twentieth-century expression. In particular the astonishingly quick collapse of the Soviet Union in 1989 allowed the EU to become a truly European enterprise. And the EU became the obvious and easy way to provide for the reintegration of these historic lands into the mainstream of European democratic tradition.

The pattern of the early years, rooted in achieving trade integration among six Member States, has long been overtaken by this narrative of accelerating functional and geographical expansion. What is, however, open to question is how far this increasing burden of tasks can be suitably fulfilled by the EU. Subsidiarity is the most commonly invoked catchphrase. Examined in Chapter 2, it is designed to provoke reflection on the competing claims of centralization and preservation of local autonomy. The decline in the uniform application of EU law—the rise of opt-outs and differentiated integration—is another part of this trend to question the ability of a functionally and geographically expanded EU to operate according to its orthodox working method. This is examined in Chapter 5. The core questions ask whether the room allowed to Member State action has been shrunk to such an extent that the notion of the EU as a place for States to breathe legitimacy into the EU and vice versa is no longer plausible. Should this be so, the EU's social legitimacy is imperilled. This means, in short, that it can expect to encounter popular resistance. Increasingly it has done so.

1.4 THE CHALLENGE OF LEGITIMACY

From a formal perspective, the legitimacy of the process of European integration is guaranteed by the requirement that Treaty revision be conducted with respect for the domestic constitutional arrangements of each Member State and with the support of all of them. The procedure is today mapped out in Article 48 TEU. In principle nothing happens at EU level unless it complies with the anchoring ground rules that have been agreed and authorized by all the Member States. In the 1950s, when the system was first built, what this in fact meant was the agreement of the *governments* of the Member States. This largely remained true at the time of periodic revisions of the Treaty system, which were typically conducted through the convening of an *intergovernmental* conference at which political élites would hammer out bargains at EU level that could then be formally ratified at national level. The nature of the EU as a creature of international law is most vividly demonstrated at times of Treaty revision. But legitimacy has dimensions that stretch beyond the formal. The intergovernmental conference is on the one hand the means of conferring formal State approval on the shaping of the Union, but it is on the other hand a powerful statement to citizens that the trajectory of the Union is, in short, none of their business. What is largely missing from an account rooted in formal legitimacy is *people*.

The Court of Justice from an early stage re-branded the EU legal order as one with a much deeper attachment to the individual citizen than is found in conventional international Treaty regimes. It was, the Court asserted soon after the founding of the system, a new legal order which did not simply bind States but also served as a source of legal rights for individuals enforceable before national courts. This story is told in Chapter 4. Moreover, legislative initiatives had been openly aimed at investing the EU with a 'human face', reaching beyond the emphasis on trade liberalization. The 'Paris Summit' of 1972 set in motion a process that nurtured EU environmental and consumer protection. However, the EU's working method was largely stealthy. It did not engage in high politics. It did not go close to powers to tax and spend, which were jealously guarded at national level. The EU's early years were an exercise in relatively technical market-making. And although Treaty revisions, agreed intergovernmentally, could come into effect only once all Member States had completed the ratification process, there was in practice little engagement with domestic politics. There were no significant formal revisions of the Treaty until as late as 1987 and that text, the Single European Act, attracted little popular attention. It was as late as the beginning of the 1990s that it first became apparent that the EU might find it impossible to survive as a project propelled by Treaty revision struck by intergovernmental bargain, an executive-driven process unattached in any practical sense to national political or constitutional constraints. Ratification of the Maastricht Treaty stumbled as the Danes, required to approve ratification by referendum as a matter of national law, voted first 'no', and only subsequently 'yes'. That they *did* ultimately vote 'yes', so the Treaty duly came into force in 1993, suggests that the momentum of the EU project is hard to resist, but this was a key moment at which for the first time the process of Treaty revision was shown to be contested and not simply in the gift of governments.

There was a certain peculiarity that the rise of popular dissent occurred in connection with a Treaty which was the first to recognize the place of subsidiarity as a general principle of EU law apt to modify the thirst for centralization, but the truth is doubtless that the Danish hesitation was not aimed at any detailed aspect of the Maastricht Treaty but was rather a more general protest about the poorly explained trajectory of élite-driven integration. And the troubled process of ratification of the Maastricht Treaty was accompanied by another new and critical voice, that of national constitutional courts, most of all Germany's *Bundesverfassungsgericht*. Chapter 4 will explore its reservations in detail, but the key point was that it made clear in a ruling of great significance delivered in 1993 that German ratification of the Maastricht Treaty, and indeed of any future revising Treaty, was not simply a governmental or even Parliamentary choice, but rather fell to be checked against the limits set by German constitutional law. Like the people of Denmark, the judges of Karlsruhe were ultimately persuaded to give the green light to their State's ratification of the Treaty, but the lesson was the rise of veto players. Governments could not simply direct their preferred pattern of European integration from on high. Instead they needed to persuade their voters, where a referendum on ratification was offered or required (a matter determined by national law), and they needed to satisfy the judicial guardians of the State constitution.

The Amsterdam Treaty entered into force in 1999 without having to cross any awkward obstacles, but the Nice Treaty generated a similar 'first no, then yes' pattern to that visible at the time of Maastricht—this time not in Denmark but in Ireland, where similarly ratification by referendum was required. No doubt this too was not based on objection to the Treaty of Nice itself, a pale and inoffensive document, but rather reflected a much wider set of points of discontent, including but not limited to the evolution of the EU.

The EU's geographical and functional expansion meant that integration by stealth was no longer a viable strategy. Deeper popular engagement was required. The EU's attempts to respond to these challenges in recent years have proved extraordinarily clumsy. Efforts to invest the Union with a greater degree of social legitimacy have been astonishingly unsuccessful, to the point where popular disenchantment with what is done in the name of the EU—or at least what is perceived to be done in the name of the EU—is a serious restraint on what is plausibly to be achieved via the EU.

The Nice Treaty, signed in 2001 and entering into force in 2003, was intended to be the last in the line of incremental Treaty revisions driven by intergovernmental processes. The Convention on the Future of Europe, established under the Chairmanship of Giscard d'Estaing, former President of France, was composed of a wider range of actors than the traditional intergovernmental conference. The overt intention was to generate a more inclusive discussion about how best to develop further the EU. It began its work in February 2002 and was completed in July 2003. Its Draft Treaty establishing a Constitution for Europe was not accepted in every single respect by the Member States but its broad intent and key features were accepted and in June 2004 agreement on a gently revised text was reached.

The Treaty establishing a Constitution for Europe was signed in Rome on 29 October 2004. Rome was no accident. This was intended as a re-imagining of the project initiated by the Treaties of the 1950s, most of all the Treaty of Rome. The document was in legal form a Treaty, which would, if ratified, have served as another instrument of revision, and one which in fact would have brought about relatively little substantive change, albeit that it would have moved beyond the incremental design of previous patterns of revision and would have created a single Treaty based on four parts to govern the whole EU. But the *political* message was clear from the use of the label 'Treaty establishing a Constitution for Europe'. This was intended as something fresh—something of *constitutional* weight. The EU would gain a flag and a motto, a commitment to fundamental rights, and other attributes too that were intended to change the way the EU should be viewed. This was a calculated attempt to make a big leap beyond élite-driven incrementalism and to deepen the EU's social legitimacy.

And the project failed.

Referendums in France and in the Netherlands held in the middle of 2005 were negative. In the face of rejection by a clear margin in two of the EU's founding Member States there was no appetite to try again, and the ratification process across the Union was briefly put on ice and then abandoned completely. The Treaty establishing a Constitution for Europe was killed off by public disdain.

Attention turned instead to what became the Lisbon Treaty. It was agreed in 2007. The Lisbon Treaty is not the same as the Treaty establishing a Constitution. It is simply one more incremental amending Treaty. So, unlike the Treaty establishing a Constitution, it is in its own right utterly unreadable, because it is simply a very long collection of amendments to the pre-existing texts. A consolidated version of the Treaties, as amended periodically since the 1950s, must be consulted to make sense of the accumulated pattern of serial Treaty revisions folded eccentrically on top of each other. And though it was a Treaty, just as the Treaty establishing a Constitution was a Treaty, it was aggressively presented as *only* a Treaty, and one stripped of the symbol-laden pretensions of its shamed predecessor. It was announced in the Conclusions of the European Council Presidency in June 2007 that 'the constitutional concept which consisted in repealing all existing treaties and replacing them by a single text called Constitution is abandoned'. There is no motto, there is no flag. Stripped of lavish rhetorical decoration, the Lisbon Treaty, though in substance sharing much in common with the Treaty establishing a Constitution at a detailed level, was presented as something much more modest.

Even the scaled-down ambition of the Lisbon Treaty did not ensure it an easy passage. In most Member States, even (and perhaps especially) those which had offered or promised to offer a referendum to their citizens on whether to ratify the Treaty establishing a Constitution, it was brazenly proclaimed that the more modest ambition—in truth, the more modest labelling and presentation—removed the need for such appeal for approval. Only in Ireland was a referendum offered. In 2008 the people of Ireland said no. But in 2009, they changed their mind. Ireland ratified the Treaty. It also had to survive inspection by more than one constitutional court, and that of the German *Bundesverfassungsgericht*, delivered in June 2009 and examined in Chapter 4, was the most high-profile. But the

Treaty ran the gauntlet of this growing crowd of veto players and entered into force on 1 December 2009, almost a year later than planned.

As a result of the amendments made by the Lisbon Treaty with effect from 1 December 2009, the EU is built on two founding Treaties. The Treaty on European Union (TEU), recognizably an updated version of material first introduced by the Treaty of Maastricht with effect from 1993, contains a set of common provisions which govern the EU system's operation and also detailed provisions on the EU's common foreign and security policy. The Treaty on the Functioning of the European Union (TFEU), an enlarged and much amended version of the original Treaty of Rome which set up the European Economic Community in the 1950s, contains a mass of complex material governing the substantive law of the EU—the control it exercises over public authorities and private actors, its legislative competences, its scope to adopt common policies, and so on, in intricate detail. This is the EU today—this is EU law today.

Tension is created by rising sensitivity about whether the EU's functional and geographical expansion places too heavy a load on the EU. That is probably a fair summary of some of the anxieties of 'no' voters in national referendums; it is easily traceable too in the judgments of constitutional courts which, though sometimes as hard to decipher as the motivations of voters in referendums, tend to draw attention to fears that the extended reach of the EU might impoverish the vitality of democratic processes and checks within national political culture. The problem is in part perception and should not be over-inflated. It is sobering to recall the EU's tiny budget and absence of autonomous tax-raising powers and, even if one properly appreciates that the incremental increase in the EU's influence over the years means that few areas of national social, political, and economic life are *wholly* untouched by EU law, most of the key structural, organizational, and budgetary decisions taken in matters of education, health care, social welfare, and so on belong at national level. Most of all, the EU is in no sense divorced from the influence of national political life: through the Council most conspicuously but also through the Parliament it is tethered to it.

However, even if much resentment is based on misperception rather than reality, that is in itself a problem that is real. It corrodes the EU's legitimacy. It is plain that the EU—'Brussels', as it is frequently pejoratively and misleadingly labelled—is commonly portrayed as an alien top-down intrusion on national practice. The governance of the Eurozone has emerged as the strongest challenge to the claim that the EU is a proper site for addressing problems that face States in common.

The economic crisis that struck in 2008 might have arisen in some form even had the EU not created a monetary union, but it would certainly have been different and it would probably have been more limited in impact. The creation of a single currency, founded on the attribution of exclusive competence to the EU to decide monetary policy for the States in the Eurozone, was a political choice, not an economic necessity, and it quickly led to serious strains because of the ability of States to borrow imprudently. The EU's fingerprints were on the project and policy failures therefore attach to the EU and harm its claims to serve as an effective problem-solver. The current arrangements for managing the 'Eurozone', initially crafted under the Maastricht Treaty, refined since and now exposed as inadequate, have forced political élites to resume the search. The looming nightmare, tracked in Chapters 3 and 8, is of executive-driven solutions placed ahead of any quest for popular consent.

1.5 MANAGING INTERDEPENDENCE

The EU is a place to manage the interdependence of States in Europe. This mission is underpinned by a democratic understanding, in the sense that the EU restrains States from taking decisions that impose costs on nationals of other States who have no political voice in the first State's decision-making process, as well as a more crude sense that Europe operating collectively is able to exert influence and power that exceeds the sum of its parts. And the EU seeks not to deny and still less to replace the varying aspirations of peoples in Europe, but rather to accommodate and respect that diversity within a managed framework. It is not designed to suppress difference, but rather to suppress an insular refusal to acknowledge when the assertion of difference or at least of autonomy might inflict external costs on neighbours and rob a State acting unilaterally of effective problem-solving capacity.

The major questions that confront the EU do not ask whether the States of Europe require frameworks within which to manage their mutual interdependence. They clearly do. The abiding questions surround how much should be done in common rather than left to State autonomy, and whether the patterns for doing whatever is decided should be done in common which were established in the immediate post-War period and relatively little modified since remain suitable for a geographically and functionally expanded EU.

And so to the detail.

2

WHAT DOES THE EU DO?

2.1 INTRODUCTION: COMPETENCE AND POWERS

The question 'may the EU act in this area of law- and policy-making?' is always answered by 'well, it depends on whether the Treaties so provide'. This is the question of *competence*—is the EU constitutionally competent to act? And then even if the answer, after inspection of the Treaty texts, turns out to be 'yes! The EU may act because it has been granted competence by the Treaties', a more detailed examination must be made of the associated institutional arrangements specified by the Treaties. One must grasp exactly how the institutions may exercise their *powers*. This chapter addresses primarily *competence*; the next deals with *powers*.

It is constitutionally fundamental that the EU may do no more than its Treaties permit. Its competence is *limited*—limited to that conferred on it by the Treaties. The purpose of this chapter is first of all to explain what the Treaties *do* permit. What is at stake here is both the negative dimension of the EU's role—the legal rules that forbid action by public authorities and private actors that is hostile to the EU's objectives—and also the positive dimension of the EU's conferred competence—the range of its legislative capacity. This reflects the quest mapped in Chapter 1 to create arrangements at EU level that are apt to 'tame' the ability of States to inflict harm on each other while also delivering solutions to problems that confront Member States in common. This is the essence of managing interdependence among States in Europe.

This chapter then explains how *in practice* the notion that the EU's activity is ring-fenced by the limits imposed by the Treaties is a good deal less reliable and appealing than it appears at first sight *in principle*. This is one of the most awkward tensions in the design of the EU: at what point should its competence to restrain Member State action and to adopt rules at EU level stop? Competence should not seep away indefinitely towards the EU at the expense of the Member States, yet at the same time the EU requires a flexible set of competences and powers to address problems as and when they arise. Designing rules and institutions that meet the competing demands of control (by the Member States) and empowerment (of the EU) is an enduringly delicate process, both legally and politically. The rise of the principle of subsidiarity and the enhanced political monitoring role allocated to national Parliaments, examined in this chapter, are part of the attempt to improve the EU's ability to confine its centralizing tendencies to circumstances where they are justified. However, as is plain by reference to *any* political system within which powers are divided between different levels, there is no silver bullet that provides a wholly satisfying and static answer to the core question 'who does what?'.

2.2 THE COMPETENCE OF THE EU: THE PRINCIPLE OF CONFERRAL

The constitutionally fundamental point that the EU does *not* enjoy a general regulatory competence, but rather that it must operate within the limits set by the Treaties, is formally designated the *principle of conferral.* That is an inelegant label for a matter of the highest constitutional significance, but nevertheless it captures the basic concept, if prosaically: the EU operates on the basis of the competences *conferred* upon it by its Member States pursuant to the founding Treaties. The term *principle of conferral* was an innovation of the Treaty of Lisbon and so it has been part of the system under that label since 2009, but the basic point that outside the boundaries defined by the Treaties the EU has no valid basis for action has always been the constitutional starting-point.

Article 5(1) TEU provides that the limits of Union competences are governed by the principle of conferral. Article 5(2) TEU explains that this means that 'the Union shall act only within the limits of the competences conferred upon it by the Member States in the Treaties to attain the objectives set out therein'. The issue here is whether a Union competence *exists.* Article 5(1) TEU adds that the use of Union competences is governed by the principles of subsidiarity and proportionality. This relates to the logically subsequent issue of the conditions governing the *exercise* of a Union competence, once it is shown to exist. Subsidiarity and proportionality are considered later in this chapter (Section 2.11).

The corollary to the principle that the Union's competences are limited to those listed in the Treaties and conferred by the Member States is that competences which are *not* conferred upon the Union belong to the Member States. This is made explicit in Article 4(1) TEU and the second sentence of Article 5(2) TEU, and the point appears yet again in Declaration 18 attached to the Treaty. These are all provisions introduced with effect from 2009 by the Treaty of Lisbon, but in fact they change nothing. It has always been clear, and is perfectly logical, that competences which the Member States have chosen not to confer on the EU remain with the Member States.

The decorations added at Lisbon reveal a concern to increase the legitimating rhetoric of *control* exercisable by the Member States over the process. The root of EU rule-making is the consensual processes of domestic politics which have generated a decision to ratify over time the several Treaties which make up the EU's foundational texts. In short, what the EU does, it does because all its Member States have authorized such action. Any slippage by the EU beyond its Treaty mandate is a slippage which in one way or another deprives Member States of autonomy in circumstances where authority for the shift is lacking. This is theft: it robs the EU of a legitimate basis for claiming authority for its action.

The principle of conferral dictates that the EU does not possess the competence to extend its own competence: that lies in the gift of the Member States acting unanimously at times of Treaty revision, when the EU system lays bare its roots in international law. How far this principle is respected *in practice* is a thematically important question addressed in this chapter. This is one source of tension. A distinct question asks which body has the competence to decide whether the EU has exceeded its competence. If there is theft, who blows the whistle? The Court of Justice considers that this competence lies with it alone. National courts do not all agree. This, explored more fully in Chapter 4, injects further tension at the scene of the—alleged—crime. More broadly still, a major source of difficulty lies in the nature of some of the EU's competences. Some lack precision, some lack sharp edges. Endemic to the EU system is the *functional* character of much of its conferred competence. Accordingly, determining just where the reach of the EU's conferred competence stops and where the areas that belong to the Member States start is a ready source of controversy, and it concerns both detailed questions about the validity of the EU's rules and more profound inquiry into the quality of claims to legal authority.

This chapter shows how the principle of conferral is hard to apply in practice and how as a result the limits of EU competence are less reliably controlled than the Treaty texts might seem to promise. The story is an insight into the virtue and the vice of the EU system. It is crafted according to an institutionally and constitutionally dynamic pattern that grants it a character that is distinct from an orthodox Treaty-based system and yet which may *as a consequence* subvert the very basis of its creation, the consensual but limited grant of competence made by the Member States.

2.3 CATEGORIES OF COMPETENCE

Article 5 TEU expresses the principle of conferral at an abstract constitutional level, but it does nothing to put flesh on the bones. What *are* these conferred competences? What subject matter is involved? And what is their nature—in particular, what is their relationship with State competence in the same field?

Article 1(1) TFEU states that 'This Treaty organises the functioning of the Union and determines the areas of, delimitation of, and arrangements for exercising its competences.' The place to go is Title I of Part One of the TFEU. This is entitled *Categories and Areas of Union Competence* and it occupies Articles 2–6 TFEU. Article 2 TFEU defines the several types of competence which are conferred on the Union. There are three principal types:

exclusive competence (Article 2(1) TFEU), which entails a reservation to the Union of competence to legislate. Member States may act only if empowered by the Union;

shared competence (Article 2(2) TFEU), which involves both the Union and the Member States enjoying a competence to legislate. Member States shall exercise their competence to the extent that the Union has not exercised its competence, and Member States shall 'again' exercise their competence to the extent that the Union has decided to cease exercising its competence;

Supporting or co-ordinating competence (Article 2(5) TEU), whereby the Union is competent 'to carry out actions to support, coordinate or supplement the actions of the Member States'. Here, then, the Member States retain primary responsibility and it is made explicit that Union legislation in areas of supporting or co-ordinating competence shall not entail harmonisation of national laws.

Two other sector-specific competences are allocated their own governing sub-paragraph but are not of enough general significance to deserve more than brief mention here. Article 2(3) TFEU grants the Union a competence to provide arrangements for Member States to co-ordinate their economic and employment policies. Article 2(4) states that the Union has competence to define and implement a common foreign and security policy, but the details of this, which have little in common with the orthodox system under the TFEU, are housed separately in the TEU. And Article 5 TFEU, also not here explored further, concerns the co-ordination of Member State economic policies, employment policies, and social policies.

So Article 2 TFEU sets out the types of competence, of which there are three principal types: exclusive, shared, and supporting. Then the TFEU allocates particular areas of activity to each of the available categories.

Article 3 TFEU declares that the Union has *exclusive competence* in five areas—customs union, the establishment of the competition rules necessary for the functioning of the internal market, monetary policy for the Member States whose currency is the euro, the conservation of marine biological resources under the common fisheries policy, and the common commercial policy. In addition a special reference is made in Article 3(2) TFEU to exclusivity in the case of conclusion of an international agreement in defined circumstances. This seems a rather odd assortment of areas for which the EU is entitled to assert exclusive competence: the explanation is that Article 3 TFEU, which is a product of the Treaty of Lisbon reforms, is not a fresh start, but rather is drafted with reference to the Court's accumulated case law in this area.

Article 4 TFEU lists areas of *shared competence*—and by specifying that this is the governing type of competence for areas which do not fall within Articles 3 or 6 TFEU, it is thereby ensured that this is the residual 'catch all' category. 'Shared competence' governs the internal market; social policy; environment; consumer protection; energy; the area of freedom, security, and justice; and so on. Both Member States and the Union may act in these areas. The need for conflict rules will arise in so far as they try to cover the same subject matter but in different ways. This is examined further in Section 2.4.

Article 6 TFEU identifies seven areas in which the Union enjoys *supporting, coordinating, or supplementary competence.* These are the protection and improvement of human health; industry; culture; tourism; education, vocational training, youth, and sport; civil protection; and administrative co-operation.

What are now Articles 2–6 TFEU did not exist at all prior to the entry into force of the Lisbon Treaty in 2009. It was then necessary to trawl through the whole Treaty to gather the scattered batch of provisions conferring explicit legislative competences on the EU. That was messy and deeply unsatisfactory. Today Articles 2–6 TFEU package the basic rules on competence much more helpfully than before. But it is packaging: the *substance* was little changed in 2009. And in order to discover how each of these legislative competences actually operates in practice it remains necessary to work one's way through the dense undergrowth of the TFEU, provision by provision, to assemble and understand all the relevant authorizations for legislative action by the EU. At a more detailed level, the powers of the individual institutions are limited and they too are defined in and by the Treaties. Just because the EU is equipped with a competence to act in a particular area does not mean that the inquiry into the precise manner in which they may act is at an end. One must understand the detailed nature of the powers attributed to each institution, political and judicial. There is no hiding from the fact that this demands a dogged mental attitude.

2.4 THE EU'S COMPETENCES UNDER THE TFEU

One would certainly be left bemused if one tried to rely on Articles 2–6 TFEU alone to understand the nature of the competences available to the EU *in particular areas*. Social policy, for example, is blandly listed as a shared competence in Article 4 TFEU. But one has to pore over Articles 151–161 TFEU to grasp precisely what this entails at the boundaries between Union and State competence. In particular, Article 153(2) TFEU envisages the adoption of measures designed to improve co-operation between Member States in the fields of social policy listed in Article 153(1), while expressly excluding harmonization of national laws; and also the adoption by Directive of minimum rules governing *some* but *not all* of the fields of social policy listed in Article 153(1). And, adding to the complexity, Article 153(2) separates out the several relevant fields of social policy by subjecting *some* to the ordinary legislative procedure and *others* to a special procedure requiring unanimous support in Council. A similar and complex sector-by-sector inquiry is needed to understand the exact nature of the EU's legislative competences conferred across a wide range of areas by the TFEU.

The particularly awkward question of the extent to which an EU legislative act may set aside State competence demands a similarly intricate engagement with the body of the TFEU. In the matter of shared competence, Article 2(2) TFEU stipulates that the Member States shall exercise their competence to the extent that the Union has not exercised its competence. Competence is shared for research, technological development, and space, and for development co-operation and humanitarian aid, and it is explicitly provided in Article 4(3) and 4(4) that in these areas the exercise of Union competence shall not result in Member States being prevented from exercising theirs. One might therefore assume that for all other areas of shared competence the consequence of the exercise of Union competence is that Member States are prevented from exercising theirs. But that would be a major alteration compared with practice prior to the entry into force of the Treaty of Lisbon in 2009 and, moreover, it would contradict sector-specific provisions such as Article 153(4), Article 169(4), and Article 193 TFEU which envisage that Union measures on social policy, consumer protection, and environmental protection respectively shall set *minimum* EU rules only. Article 2(2) TFEU's definition of shared competence is at best unhelpfully lacking in nuance, at worst simply incompatible with the several distinct versions of shared competence to be found scattered throughout Part Three TFEU. Chapter 5 will look again at this matter in the wider context of review of EU law's fragmented application.

There are many more instances of the need to reckon with detailed provisions buried deep in the TFEU, but there is no call here to plod through them exhaustively. The point is only that none of this detail can be satisfactorily gleaned from Articles 2–6 TFEU alone. So the impression of clean lines governing categories of competence which is conveyed in the early part of the Treaty is misleading. Articles 2–6 TFEU are a good *starting-point* for those seeking to grasp the scope and nature of the EU's conferred competences, but they cannot be treated as the last word.

Even after reading and absorbing Articles 2–6 TFEU, one has acquired only a partial view of the reach of EU law. What is at stake in these foundational provisions is the *legislative* competence of the EU. But the EU reaches far beyond the package of competences which authorize legislative intervention. The Treaty contains a set of 'negative' rules: rules which forbid particular types of practice which are hostile to the achievement of the objectives mapped out by the Treaty. Most prominent are the core rules of EU internal market law—those which prohibit restrictions on the free movement of goods, persons, services, and capital (albeit in all cases admitting the possibility that such restrictions may be justified) and those which control anti-competitive practices. The prohibition against discrimination based on nationality is another example of a powerfully important prohibition embedded in the Treaty. These are not *legislative* competences but they are foundationally important to understanding the scope of application of EU law. Public bodies and private parties are (in different ways, to differing extents: see Chapter 6.2.3) subject to these basic rules telling them what they may *not* do. And these core rules operate across the whole sphere of activity covered by the Treaty, which is extremely broad—broader than the scope of legislative competence.

So, as Article 2(6) TFEU makes explicit, the detailed arrangements governing the exercise of the EU's legislative competences are found scattered throughout the TFEU. As Article 2 TFEU does *not* make clear, there are a host of relevant prohibitions also scattered throughout the Treaty. It takes a hard, long read to grasp exactly what is the scope of the legislative competences and the applicable institutional powers, combined with appreciation of the scope of the governing prohibitions in EU internal market law. The place to go is Part Three of the TFEU, entitled *Union Policies and Internal Actions*. It is huge, containing twenty-four Titles, and stretching from Article 26 to Article 197 TFEU. So, since there are 358 Articles in the TFEU, Part Three is home to almost half of them. Here lie the nuts and bolts of what the EU is competent to do, with what aims and through which procedures. Absorb this material and you are a well-educated EU lawyer.

The two dozen titles which comprise Part Three TFEU cover: The Internal Market; Free Movement of Goods; Agriculture and Fisheries; Free Movement of Persons, Services and Capital; Area of Freedom, Security and Justice (which is the most institutionally and procedurally atypical); Transport; Common Rules on Competition, Taxation and Approximation of Laws; Economic and Monetary Policy; Employment; Social Policy; European Social Fund; Education, Vocational Training and Sport; Culture; Public Health; Consumer Protection; Trans-European Networks; Industry; Economic, Social and Territorial Cohesion; Research and Technological Development and Space; Environment; Energy; Tourism; Civil Protection; Administrative Cooperation.

The EU does not possess a general regulatory competence: that is forbidden by the principle of conferral. But the scope of its competence, though in principle limited, is plainly wide-ranging. As mentioned in Section 2.3, few of the EU's activities are carried out under a claim to *exclusive* competence, so the reality is that in this wide sweep of activity the EU acts alongside its Member States, thereby creating a complex and dense network of multi-level rule-making.

Some of these Treaty Articles contain rules of a precision that is sufficient to allow their immediate application (by the Court of Justice and by national judges). Part Three TFEU is home to free movement law and to competition law, which are good examples of provisions which operate to control practices falling within the scope of EU law largely without the need for legislative amplification, in part because of their typically unconditional textual character but also, as elaborated in Section 2.9, sometimes because of the Court's predilection for maximizing judicial application. Other provisions in Part Three TFEU are drafted in schematic and broad fashion and therefore require elaboration through EU secondary legislation, which in the case of Directives in particular requires implementation at national level. Such Treaty provisions act as a framework. The shaping of detailed policy therefore depends first on the applicable procedures for law-making and the powers that are made available to the EU institutions, and then on the detailed and sometimes politically controversial process of law-making (Chapter 3). Because of the constitutional principles of direct effect and supremacy (Chapter 4), the former types of rule—those susceptible to immediate judicial application—are capable of much more vigorous application than the latter, in particular by private parties before national courts who are able to police defaulting Member States. There is a certain bias here, which tends to favour the enforcement of deregulatory rules over those that (re-)regulate the EU market, a matter explored more thoroughly in Chapters 4 and 6.

The intended design holds that compliance with these foundational rules should be ensured *ex ante* by assiduous regard to them in the law-making process by the political institutions of the EU and, should the required restraint be found wanting, the Court stands ready to review the validity of adopted legislation *ex post facto* (whether through actions brought directly before it, most obviously in an action for annulment under Article 263 TFEU, or in a preliminary reference triggered by a challenge before a national court to the validity of an adopted EU act). The difficulties arise in translating these principles into an operationally useful system of *ex ante* and *ex post* supervision. In short, the accusation, explored throughout this chapter, is that the principle of conferral has minimal bite in practice, with the consequence that EU influence tends to inflate over time.

2.5 THE BROADENING OF EU COMPETENCE

To pin down the *limits* of EU competence involves, first, survey of the general picture painted by Articles 2–6 TFEU and then, second, a more challenging wrestle with the intricacies of Part Three TFEU. But the competence of the EU, though *limited*, is not *static*. It has broadened.

The Court declared in the early 1960s that 'the Member States have limited their sovereign rights, albeit within limited fields';[1] in 1991 it was able knowingly to update its observation to describe the States as having 'limited their sovereign rights, in ever wider fields'.[2] In principle the Treaty does not 'self-extend'. It is the Member States themselves that have extended the scope of EU law by amending the Treaty and adding extra competences to the list of those conferred on the EU. In each instance of periodic revision, albeit to varying degrees, expansion in the scope of the Treaty has been among the most prominent thematic features. New provisions have been gradually added (such as environmental protection in 1987, consumer protection in 1993, energy in 2009) and existing provisions widened. And such extension in the scope of EU law affects not only legislative competence; it also carries with it the unavoidable implication

[1] Case 6/64 *Costa* v *ENEL* [1964] ECR 585; Case 26/62 *Van Gend en Loos* [1963] ECR 1.

[2] *Opinion 1/91* [1991] ECR I-6079.

that the prohibitions in free movement law and competition law and rules against discrimination 'bite' in ever wider areas.

The EU has tended to be an arena in which the direction of migration of competences is from State level to EU level. Naturally so—the starting-point in the 1950s was unilateral State power. The extension of competence conferred on the EU, which has been a leitmotif of most of the periodic rounds of Treaty revision, is no threat in principle to the principle of conferral, for the EU still operates within limits. The point is simply that those limits are cast wider. In practice, however, this matters a great deal. Increasingly the clamour has grown for a more circumspect approach to the expansion in the scope of EU competences. The causes and manifestations of these tensions and sensitivities are several and varied and certainly cannot be treated as a single phenomenon. However, what lies at the heart of the increasingly anxious debate about competence of recent years is the perception that the *principle* that the EU operates within the confines of the principle of conferral tends to be obscured by an open-handed reading of the matter *in practice*. The Treaty mandate has been extended, by the Member States acting at times of periodic Treaty revision, but the critical issue is whether the legislative and political institutions operating *within* the EU's system play fast and loose with the principle of conferral. Is there self-extension of EU competence *in practice*? The problem is neatly captured by the catchphrase: *competence creep*.[3]

So, the complaint runs, the *practice* in this matter of competence definition and competence control is a good deal less clear and a good deal more subversive than the straightforward account based on the text of Article 5 TEU suggests. In part the problem attaches to the nature of the rules themselves, which in many cases are not conducive to, and are not designed to be conducive to, yielding a clear answer to the question mentioned at the start of this chapter, 'may the EU act in this area of law- and policy-making?'. In part the issue is the institutional context in which the rules are applied, *ex ante* and *ex post*, politically and judicially. In different ways the EU's institutions enjoy a degree of autonomy from control—from voters, from States—and although grant of autonomy is necessary to permit them to discharge their tasks effectively, it may also permit them to invade constitutionally shaky territory without fear of protest or, still less, sanction. The Council

[3] For relatively early inquiry see J. Weiler, 'The Transformation of Europe' (1991) 100 Yale LJ 2403; M. Pollack, 'Creeping Competence: The Expanding Agenda of the European Community' (1994) 14 Journal of Public Policy 95. More recently S. Weatherill, 'Competence Creep and Competence Control' (2004) 23 YEL 1; L. Azoulai, *The Question of Competence in the EU* (OUP, 2014).

is designed to represent national interests but may in practice represent the interests of the executive or, in particular sectoral Councils, the interests of one part of the executive. It is notorious that the EU level of rule-making may be exploited precisely because it provides a means to circumvent the obstacles rooted in the national political infrastructure. And although the Court is supposed to preserve the proper limits of the principle of conferral, for some critics it is more part of the problem than reliable solution because of its tendency to interpret EU law broadly and flexibly.

This is a narrative that is familiar to all students of federal or quasi-federal systems. The several components of this debate, which now fall for examination, have become increasingly central to designing an EU that is able to meet the challenges of geographical and functional expansion while also preserving cherished aspects of local autonomy from over-hasty centralization.

2.6 THE 'SOFT' NATURE OF THE RULES GOVERNING CONFERRED COMPETENCE

The EU operates according to the principle of conferral, but this means in practice that the Treaty proceeds to set out where the EU is competent to act—not where it is not. There are no bright-line rules which allocate specific functions to the Member States, nor are there comprehensive rules that place areas of activity off-limits to the EU. Even the very few Treaty provisions that tend in this direction—such as Article 345 TFEU, which explicitly declares that the Treaties 'shall in no way prejudice the rules in Member States governing the system of property ownership'—have not been read in a way that is protective of State autonomy. The Court typically does not question the *existence* of property rights but it does assert the control of EU free movement and competition law over their *exercise*.[4] This characteristic approach provoked Koen Lenaerts to a vivid and oft-cited observation that 'there simply is no nucleus of sovereignty that the Member States can invoke, as such, against the' Union.[5] Seen from the other direction, this approach serves as a 'vehicle for the totalization of the process of integration'.[6]

The EU is in principle granted only limited competences, but the location of those limits lacks a reliable map. Would EU law affect dog licensing?

[4] Eg Case 119/75 *Terrapin* v *Terranova* [1976] ECR 1039; Joined Cases C-105/12 to C-107/12 *Essent* judgment of 22 October 2013.

[5] In 'Constitutionalism and the Many Faces of Federalism' (1990) 38 AJCL 205.

[6] L. Azoulai, 'The "Retained Powers" Formula in the Case Law of the European Court of Justice: EU Law as Total Law?' (2011) 4 EJLS 192.

Yes, it would require that a migrant national of an EU Member State be charged no more for a licence than a local resident. Even though cases sporadically emerge in which the subject matter is found to lie beyond the reach of EU law, these tend to be ad hoc. It is very hard to identify *in principle* any area of exclusive national autonomy. So, for example, *Kremzow* involved an Austrian national tried for murder in Austria, and the Court found that although deprivation of liberty may impede the exercise of a right to free movement, the prospect *in the case* of any such restriction was purely hypothetical and so the matter had no connection with EU law.[7] But the injection of an actual or potential cross-border element would immediately have brought EU law into play and subsequently the Court, relying on the Treaty provisions governing citizenship which are examined later in Chapter 7.5, has even extended EU law into such 'internal' situations where there are consequences for the individual's right to remain on the territory of the EU.[8]

Similarly, in *Society for the Protection of Unborn Children Ireland* v *Grogan* the Court refused to permit a students' union in Dublin to rely on EU free movement law when, in reaction to the strict controls over abortion in Ireland, they published information about how to secure an abortion in London.[9] The challenge to which they were subject before Irish courts did not involve EU law because they, as students' unions, had no economic connection with the provider of the service, and so the matter fell for resolution under Irish law alone. But this did not mean that *in principle* abortion services fell outwith the scope of EU law: it merely meant that this particular litigant could not rely on EU law for want of commercial motivation. Moreover, even where a matter is plainly beyond the scope of EU law the Court will still provide an interpretation of EU law where national law has chosen to pursue the same solution as EU law.[10] As a means to reduce regulatory complexity this is an increasingly attractive solution at national level, but its effect is to extend still further the practical influence of EU law.

The Treaty does not envisage the ruthless depletion of national autonomy to regulate markets or, more broadly, to choose a different path from that set at EU level, but its typical model is to assert a broad scope for EU law and to place control of that diversity *within* the EU legal order. Free

[7] Case C-299/95 *Friedrich Kremzow* [1997] ECR I-2629.

[8] Case C-256/11 *Dereci* [2011] ECR I-11315.

[9] Case C-159/90 [1991] ECR I-4685.

[10] Eg Case C-583/10 *Nolan* judgment of 18 October 2012; Case C-313/12 *Giuseppa Romeo* judgment of 7 November 2013.

movement law does not guarantee absolute rights to trade across borders. Instead national obstacles to trade may be justified (Chapter 6.3). But that justification must be rooted in and recognized by EU law. And the very notion of an obstacle to trade, which triggers the requirement to demonstrate justification, is itself broadly interpreted (Chapter 6.2). In similar vein, legislative action by the EU does not necessarily preclude State action in the same area, but the grant of permission comes from the EU's founding constitutional texts and/or the detailed provision made in its secondary legislation (Chapter 5). More broadly still, Article 4(2) TEU provides that the Union shall respect the 'national identities' of the Member States, as well as their 'essential State functions'. This is a form of 'soft' protection of Member State choices, apt to test EU legislation and to guide assessment of Member State derogation from free movement and/or competition law. But much depends on the institutional context in which such ambiguous phrases are shaped, interpreted, and applied. There is nothing here that allows a Member State to make a constitutionally clean and compelling argument that a particular sector is immune in principle from EU intervention.

So, what remains wholly untouched and untouchable by the requirements of EU law? Not much! This is the nature of the Treaty design. There are no useful provisions that would provide the basis for a claim that national practices are *in principle* beyond the reach of EU law. Moreover, important elements of EU law are defined with reference to functionally broad objectives, most of all the internal market, with the consequence that such limits as they possess are wide and hard to fix. This is true in particular of Articles 114 and 352 TFEU among the legislative competences and so too of the provisions governing free movement and competition, which are so important that they deserve and receive dedicated examination in Sections 2.7 and 2.8. EU law, limited in principle to the competences conferred by the Treaties, is in practice broad and contained by ambiguous borders.

2.7 LEGISLATIVE COMPETENCE

The EU's legislative competences range from the sector-specific to the broad and functionally driven.

2.7.1 Sector-specific competences

The EU's sector-specific legislative competences elaborate rules and impose limits which are attuned to the particular characteristics of the sector in question. This is true of environmental policy, energy policy, agricultural policy, and so on. These Treaty provisions, especially those added incrementally in recent years at times of Treaty revision, are typically drawn carefully and narrowly. For example, EU action in the fields of culture and public health is defined by Articles 167 and 168 TFEU respectively as supplementary to State action. Harmonization of laws pursuant to these provisions is explicitly excluded. Articles 193, 153, and 169 TFEU, governing competence to legislate in the fields of environmental protection, social policy, and consumer protection respectively, contain stipulations that national measures that are stricter than the agreed Union standard are permitted. Just because the EU is competent to act in a particular area does not mean that State action in that area is excluded. In fact, exclusive EU competence consequent on legislative action is here very much the exception, not the rule. Moreover, there are micro sector-specific bars to EU intervention. For example, Article 153(5) TFEU declares that the legislative competence created in the field of social policy 'shall not apply to pay, the right of association, the right to strike or the right to impose lock-outs'. This plainly reflects an anxiety to preserve national autonomy in such areas, although, as will be examined more fully in Section 2.8, this provision is apt to curtail the EU's legislative ambition but not the scope of application of the Treaty's free movement provisions.

So, as promised by the principle of conferral, the EU's legislative competence is limited. However, this is to address some but not all of the anxiety about competence creep. The Treaty generally is driven by a functional logic, and two Treaty provisions in particular challenge the vitality in practice of the principle of conferral. These are Articles 352 and 114 TFEU.

2.7.2 Articles 352 and 114 TFEU: functionally driven competences

Article 352 grants the EU, in the shape of the Council acting unanimously, a competence to legislate where necessary to attain one of the objectives set out in the Treaties where the Treaties have not otherwise provided the necessary powers. Article 114 grants the EU, in the form of action by the Parliament and the Council acting in accordance with the ordinary legislative procedure, the competence to adopt measures harmonizing national laws in order to promote the establishment and functioning of the internal market. In accordance with the principle of conferral, both provisions have limits—in short, a tie to attaining the EU's objectives under Article 352 and a tie to market-making under Article 114. But Articles 352 and 114 are profoundly different from the sector-specific legislative competences in the sense that they, as provisions tied to objectives, not particular sectors, are both strikingly broader and more ambiguous. They are therefore conducive to an environment within which legislative competence 'creeps' beyond the limits set by the Treaty.

These two Articles grant the EU an enviable functional flexibility, allowing legislative action to address unforeseen challenges, while at the same time imperilling the autonomy of Member State action. 'Effectiveness' is in friction with 'control'. They have long been recognized as the Treaty's 'problem cases'. Writing in 1992, John Usher referred to them as the 'terrible twins',[11] while the perils of (what are now) Articles 352 and 114 TFEU were recognized in the European Council's Laeken Declaration on the Future of the European Union of 2001, which mentions these two Treaty provisions *and no others* in the context of stimulating the re-thinking of the pattern of EU competence allocation that eventually led, via the failed Treaty establishing a Constitution, to the modest reforms made by the Lisbon Treaty.

2.7.3 *Article 352*

What is now Article 352 TFEU has always, in its several guises, allowed the EU to legislate to achieve objectives set by the Treaty where no specific legislative provision is available. In principle this 'gap-filling' function could not go so far as to extend the scope of Union powers or objectives, for that would constitute an impermissible amendment of the Treaty 'from within' and therefore constitute a violation of the principle of conferral,[12] but the practical reality of such control was relatively rare. In particular in the early years the provision was ruthlessly exploited to extend EU rules into areas not explicitly addressed in the original Treaties, such as environmental protection.[13] However, the Court has always made clear that what is today Article 352 TFEU must yield to other Treaty provisions which supply a subject-specific competence.[14] Since one of the most significant features of periodic Treaty revision has been precisely the addition of an increasing range of sector-specific legislative competences (such as environmental protection, added in 1987), it follows that

[11] J. Usher, 'The Continuing Development of Law and Institutions' in Academy of European Law (ed), *Collected Courses of the Academy of European Law* (Kluwer 1992), p 146.

[12] Eg Opinion 2/94 [1996] ECR I-1759; Case C-249/96 *Grant* v *South West Trains* [1998] ECR I-621; Cases C-402/05P and C-415/05P *Kadi and Al Barakaat* v *Council* [2008] ECR I-6351.

[13] On past practice, see R. Schütze, 'Organized Change towards an Ever Closer Union: Article 308 EC and the Limits to the Community's Legislative Competence' (2003) 22 YEL 79.

[14] Eg Case 45/86 *Commission* v *Council* [1987] ECR 1493.

Article 352 is correspondingly diminished in scope. The Lisbon Treaty is simply the latest piece in this jigsaw, as it added specific legal bases in areas such as energy and intellectual property which had previously been, but no longer should be, the subject of legislative attention pursuant to Article 352. Moreover, Article 352(4) directs that Article 352 may not be used to pursue the objectives of the common foreign and security policy, which in fact absorbs an earlier decision of the Court,[15] and, by virtue of another Lisbon innovation, it is explicitly declared in its third paragraph that Article 352 shall not be used to establish rules that harmonize national laws in areas where the Treaties exclude such harmonization.

So anxiety to assert *control* over Article 352's use is prominent. However, the requirement for unanimity in Council is at least as significant a control as the carefully crafted constraints written into the Treaty. The requirement to assemble unanimity in Council in order to rely on this Treaty provision was in the early years part of the problem, for if there *was* unanimity the Council tended to act with disdain for constitutional niceties associated with 'competence creep'. Today unanimity is much more of a controlling device than a facilitator, given that securing agreement among all twenty-eight Member States is intensely arduous. Moreover, part of the internal deal leading to German ratification of the Lisbon Treaty involves much tighter (internal) control over German approval of use of Article 352,[16] while in the UK an Act of Parliament is required in some but not all cases before a Minister may commit to a proposal advanced under Article 352.[17] Although in principle the limits of EU competence are defined by textual interpretation rather than political reality, in practice, as a motor of competence creep, Article 352 has been drained of most of its poison.[18] The same cannot be said of Article 114.

2.7.4 *Article 114*

Article 114 TFEU is driven by the functional project of completing the internal market, as defined in Article 26 TFEU. This is of its very nature wide-ranging. Article 114 is accordingly much more conspicuous for its *breadth* than for its constitutional *limits*. Any type of national practice which has the requisite impact on the project of market-making—by

[15] Cases C-402/05P and C-415/05P *Kadi and Al Barakaat* v *Council* [2008] ECR I-6351.

[16] On this 'German problem' see P. Kiiver, 'The Lisbon Judgment of the German Constitutional Court' (2010) 16 ELJ 578.

[17] Section 8 European Union Act 2011.

[18] Cf T. Konstadinides, 'Drawing the Line between Circumvention and Gap-Filling: An Exploration of the Conceptual Limits of the Treaty's Flexibility Clause' (2012) 31 YEL 227.

impeding the free movement of goods or services or by causing an appreciable distortion of competition—may be subjected to the discipline of harmonization. It does not matter what is the content or purpose of the national laws in question, save only that Article 114(2) TFEU excludes harmonization of fiscal provisions, those relating to the free movement of persons and those relating to the rights and interests of employed persons. Otherwise, provided the necessary market-making element is present, anything is fair game for the discipline of harmonization pursuant to Article 114 TFEU, which, moreover, since it attracts the ordinary legislative procedure, is subject to qualified majority vote in Council (plus also Parliamentary approval). There is no State veto.

The Court will not accept legislative harmonization consequent on 'a mere finding of disparities between national rules'.[19] Nor is harmonization permissible where the measure has only the incidental effect of harmonizing market conditions within the Union.[20] There is no 'general power to regulate the internal market', for that, as the Court has made explicit, would be incompatible with the principle of conferral set out in Article 5 TEU, which insists that the powers of the Union are limited to those specifically conferred on it.[21] But in a series of cases the Court has crafted a formula which is a good deal more apt to empower rather than to restrict the EU. It considers that the EU is competent to intervene to establish harmonized standards pursuant to Article 114 'where there are differences between national rules which are such as to obstruct the fundamental freedoms and thus have a direct effect on the functioning of the internal market... or to cause significant distortions of competition' or where 'the aim is to prevent the emergence of such obstacles to trade resulting from the divergent development of national laws', provided the emergence of such obstacles is likely and the measure in question is designed to prevent them.[22]

The threshold is low. Regulatory divergence between Member States' treatment of products will be perfectly common and easy to find in an EU of twenty-eight Member States. True, the Court's formula insists that

[19] Eg Cases C-154/04 and C-155/04 *Alliance for Natural Health* [2005] ECR I-6451, para 28.

[20] Eg Cases C-70/88 *Parliament* v *Council* [1991] ECR I-4529, para 17; Case C-209/97 *Commission* v *Council* [1999] ECR I-8067, para 35.

[21] Case C-376/98 *Germany* v *Parliament and Council* [2000] ECR I-8419, paras 83, 106–7.

[22] Case C-58/08 *Vodafone, O2* et al v *Secretary of State* [2010] ECR I-4999, paras 32, 33. Similarly Case C-491/01 *R* v *Secretary of State ex parte BAT and Imperial Tobacco* [2002] ECR I-11543; Case C-380/03 *Germany* v *Parliament and Council* [2006] ECR I-11573; Cases C-154/04 and C-155/04 *Alliance for Natural Health* [2005] ECR I-6451; Case C-66/04 *UK* v *Parliament & Council* [2005] ECR I-10553; Case C-398/13P *Inuit* judgment of 3 September 2015.

there must be a *direct* effect on the functioning of the internal market or a *significant* distortion of competition or a *likely* emergence of obstacles, but since these phenomena are hard to measure, it is hard for objectors to prove their absence. This mirrors the general structural point about EU law's principle of conferral—it is hard to find a reliable benchmark for proving it has been violated.

A good example is provided by *Vodafone, O2* et al v *Secretary of State.*[23] The so-called 'Roaming Regulation', Regulation 717/2007, was based on Article 95 EC, which is today, after amendment, Article 114 TFEU. It addressed the problem of the high level of prices payable for use of mobile telephone networks when travelling abroad within the EU on the basis that Member State authorities were under pressure to act (in doubtless divergent ways), and put in place harmonized EU rules to control prices. Its validity was challenged before the English courts, and the matter was referred to the Court of Justice. Advocate General Maduro did *not* think the Court's criteria for valid 'preventive harmonisation' were satisfied, but he did wish to uphold the Regulation's validity on the basis that it addressed the actions of private actors which directly involved cross-border activity and were apt to exert unfavourable effects thereupon. But, in more orthodox fashion, the Court found the measure valid as 'preventive harmonisation'. It accepted that there was pressure for Member States to take measures to address the problem of the high level of retail charges for EU-wide roaming services, and so it was, the Court agreed, 'likely' that diverse national measures would be adopted.[24] Harmonization was designed to forestall measures which would 'probably' have been taken by the Member States.[25] This was enough to permit the use of Article 114.

Part of the problem is that the threshold requirements of likelihood and probability are imprecise and very hard to measure. In the case the Court agreed they were met because, as it observed, the Regulation's Preamble said they were, and the Commission had confirmed that to be the case at the oral hearing in the case before the Court. The Court also felt confirmed in the finding of 'likely' divergence in national action by citing the explanatory memorandum to the proposal for a regulation and the supporting impact assessment. But these were hardly impartial sources! The Court, asked to review the validity of the measure, checked its compliance with the principle of conferral by reference to the very texts that it was supposed to be subjecting to an objective standard of constitutional review. Moreover, the Court ignored the powerful argument that, far from being 'likely' to

[23] Case C-58/08 note 22. [24] Para 45. [25] Para 46.

act, Member States had incentives *not* to regulate their own markets to cap the cost of roaming, because they would have the perverse effect of harming the competitive position of companies based on the regulator's territory while protecting only out-of-state consumers.[26] Regrettably, this compelling twist was completely ignored in a judgment which tamely took at face value the claims of the EU legislature.

In a small number of cases the Court has identified circumstances in which reliance on Article 114 TFEU or its predecessors may *not* be justified. This has arisen where what is being created is a new free-standing EU-level entity or system, which cannot come within the notion of 'harmonization' of national laws. It is not always easy to determine when this line is crossed[27] but when it is, which is when the EU measure 'leaves unchanged the different national laws already in existence... but has as its purpose the creation of a new form... in addition to the national forms', it is Article 352, not Article 114, that must be used.[28] But the most high-profile example of the Court resisting legislative over-ambition is the first *Tobacco Advertising* case—more properly, *Germany* v *Parliament and Council*.[29]

Directive 98/43 on the advertising of tobacco products had been adopted as a measure of harmonization directed at integrating goods and services markets and was based on provisions which are now, in amended form, Articles 114, 53 and 62 TFEU. Germany had opposed the measure but had been outvoted in Council. Here, then, was the bite of qualified majority voting. But Germany persuaded the Court to annul the Directive. The Court insisted that a measure of harmonization must actually contribute to eliminating obstacles to the free movement of goods or to the freedom to provide services, or to removing appreciable distortions of competition. The challenged 'Tobacco Advertising' Directive was not regarded as a valid exercise of the competence to harmonize laws because much of its content was directed at the suppression of advertising on products such as ashtrays, billboards, and parasols for use in street cafés, where the contribution to the establishment and functioning of an internal market was minimal. The implication of the Court's analysis was that the measure was

[26] M. Brenncke, 'Annotation' (2010) 47 CMLRev 1793, esp 1804–6.

[27] Case C-270/12 *UK* v *Council and Parliament* judgment of 22 January 2014 provides a good example: AG Jääskinen believed Art 114 TFEU could *not* be used to create a power vested in the European Securities and Markets Authority to intervene in short selling (Art 28 Reg 236/2012), but the Court disagreed.

[28] Case C-436/03 *Parliament* v *Council* [2006] ECR I-3733 para 44. In fact the measure was valid because Art 308, now Art 352, *had* been used.

[29] Case C-376/98 [2000] ECR I-8419.

in truth concerned with public health protection, and that even though the Treaty grants a competence in that field, the relevant provision, which is now Article 168 TFEU, expressly excludes harmonization of laws. It would not have been, and still is not, constitutionally sturdy enough to support such a wide-ranging Directive.

Germany, having lost the political debate in Council, was able to persuade the Court that it should assert its role to preserve the constitutional limits of EU legislative competence against attempts by the majority of the Member States allied with the Commission and the Parliament to subvert them. However, for all the glowing tributes that one might pay to the Court's protection of the constitutional structure created by the Treaties and in particular the principle of conferral, the reality is that this is an exceptional decision, which reflects more a one-off instance of legislative carelessness than a vigorous and enduring judicial restraint of legislative over-ambition.

Vodafone, examined earlier in this section, shows that it is relatively straightforward for the EU's legislative institutions to construct their texts in such a way as to satisfy the Court that they meet Article 114 TFEU's threshold requirements, but in fact the consequences of *Tobacco Advertising* itself already revealed the limits of judicial control. After Directive 98/34 was annulled in *Tobacco Advertising* the legislature responded by adopting Directive 2003/33 on the harmonisation of laws relating to advertising and sponsorship of tobacco products.[30] This was a slimmed-down version of the annulled Directive, focusing on harmonized bans on the advertising of tobacco products in periodicals, magazines, and newspapers. Its validity too was challenged by Germany, but this time without success. This is the so-called second *Tobacco Advertising* case, more properly *Germany* v *Parliament and Council*.[31] Directive 2003/33 passed the Court's test, where Directive 98/34 had failed it in the first *Tobacco Advertising* case, because, the Court concluded, prohibiting the advertising of tobacco products in periodicals, magazines, and newspapers improved the functioning of the internal market as the elimination of regulatory diversity among the Member States opened up the market for these press products. Deleting treatment of ashtrays, billboards, and parasols brought the measure within the scope of Article 114 TFEU as a service to the internal market. But the Court's green light was no surprise. In the first *Tobacco Advertising* case the Court had explicitly declared that a Directive prohibiting the advertising of tobacco products in periodicals, magazines, and newspapers could

[30] OJ [2003] L152/16.

[31] Case C-380/03 [2006] ECR I-11573.

be validly adopted with a view to ensuring the free movement of press products.[32]

This has become the norm. It is not that since the first *Tobacco Advertising* case the Court's teeth have become less sharp; rather, the EU legislature has been able to absorb the Court's vocabulary and readily present its initiatives as consistent with the rather wide scope of Article 114. The mistake which led to annulment in the first *Tobacco Advertising* case was largely one of drafting: the legislature had carelessly failed to present its text in the shape of an internal market measure.[33] It has learned.

It is improbable that the Court will invalidate measures that faithfully adopt the appropriate but vague vocabulary: it is hard to imagine how, other than in cases of legislative absurdity, one could deny a claim that distortion of competition caused by diversity between national laws is 'appreciable' or that Member State action is 'likely'. There is no violation of the principle of conferral here, but there is in practice a great difficulty in determining just where the limits of EU activity lie and, in particular, limited practical possibility to police them. It is a gap between principle and practice. There are real constitutional risks for Member State regulatory autonomy and for individual legal protection where the EU is able to act so broadly in the name of the 'market'.[34] But the Court should be absolved of some, and perhaps all, blame. It is not the Court that created Article 114 as a functional competence driven by the broad and ambiguous notion of the 'internal market'. By conferring on the EU legislative competences of this type, the Treaty itself is structured in such a way as to make it hard for opponents of EU legislative initiatives to pin down specifically *constitutional* objections. The debate is therefore dominated by majoritarian politics, carrying a centralizing tendency. In principle it is precisely the Court's job to prevent violation of the constitutionally central principle of conferral but, in the matter of Article 114, the Treaty has given it a dull-edged instrument.

In conclusion, Article 114 is well designed if one's aim is to maximize the flexibility entrusted to the EU law- and policy-making process. Article 114 is a powerful example of how in general the EU is deficient in *hard* rules and procedures for restraining legislative 'creep'. It is plain that

[32] Case C-376/98 note 29, paras 98–99.

[33] See S. Weatherill, 'The Limits of Legislative Harmonisation Ten Years after *Tobacco Advertising*: How the Court's Case Law has Become a "Drafting Guide"' (2011) 12 German Law Journal 827.

[34] See eg A. Somek, *Individualism: An Essay on the Authority of the European Union* (OUP, 2008).

a Member State acting unilaterally cannot readily control the direction of movement, and this simply betrays the extent to which the EU—quite deliberately—is constructed to allow its institutions a degree of autonomy from State control. The EU, as an incomplete contract, could not function without institutions that enjoy a degree of distance from political élites within the Member States. It is in this vein the Commission and the Court which come most obviously into view, but the Council, when it acts by qualified majority voting (QMV) rather than unanimity, is also protected from a brake pressed by an *individual* Member State, except in the rare circumstances where the constitutional limits of Article 114 are shown to be transgressed. In a sense 'competence creep' is the pejorative label for a phenomenon that is loaded into the EU's DNA, and it is more benevolently treated as an instance of allowing room to find solutions for newly emerged collective problems.

2.7.5 Article 114, competence, and the 'dual function' of harmonization

There is more to this narrative about the wide-ranging sweep of the harmonization programme. The Court in the first *Tobacco Advertising* case did *not* deny that public health policy and concern for consumer protection may legitimately inform the shaping of the harmonization programme. Quite the reverse: the Court insisted that such concerns form a constituent part of the EU's other policies, including market-making pursued in the name of harmonization.[35] The Court has made clear that provided that the conditions for recourse to Article 114 TFEU as a legal basis are fulfilled, the EU legislature 'cannot be prevented from relying on that legal basis on the ground that public health protection is a decisive factor in the choices to be made'.[36] In fact there is no bar to any other concern recognized by EU law serving as such a 'decisive factor', provided only the internal market condition for reliance on Article 114 is met. This is confirmed by the directions in favour of policy integration found scattered across the Treaty and the Charter. Articles 11, 12, 167(4), and 168(1) TFEU and Articles 37, 38, 22, and 35 of the Charter direct that environmental protection, consumer protection, culture, public health, and consumer protection respectively shall inform the definition and implementation of other EU policies. Creating an internal market is one such policy.

It logically follows that the EU is able, by harmonization, to adopt a re-regulatory standard that restricts or even forbids particular forms

[35] Case C-376/98 note 29, paras 78, 88.

[36] Eg Case C-380/03 note 22, para 39; Cases C-154/04 and C-155/04 note 22, para 30.

of practice throughout the territory of the EU.[37] A harmonized ban on unsafe products creates an internal market for safe products.[38] A harmonized ban on unfair commercial practices creates an internal market for fair commercial practices.[39] The internal market is not built only on the basis of market freedoms unfettered by regulatory prohibition. In *Tobacco Advertising* the problem was not that the Directive banned advertising on products such as ashtrays, billboards, and parasols for use in street cafés, but rather that it did so without opening up the market for any other kind of product. Once a (harmonized) ban is placed within a broader framework which contributes to market-making there is no objection to legislative reliance on Article 114. So in the second *Tobacco Advertising* case the ban on tobacco advertising was directed at newspapers, magazines, and periodicals as a means to level the regulatory landscape applicable to those products and therefore to integrate the market for such products.

Article 168(5) TFEU confers a competence on the EU to act to protect and improve human health but it expressly excludes the possibility of harmonization. This in turn has the effect of blocking any use of Article 352 TFEU to establish common EU rules in that field, since Article 352's third paragraph makes plain that it may not be used in cases where the Treaties exclude harmonization. But Article 168(5) has no bite at all where Article 114 comes into play. Provided the necessary market-making threshold is crossed, which, as demonstrated in Section 2.7.4, is remarkably easy, reliance on Article 114 disarms sector-specific restraint written in elsewhere in the Treaty, while also causing Article 114 itself to be inflated by the policy concerns expressed elsewhere in the Treaty. In this sense Article 114 is more devious than Article 352 as a means to deepen the EU's regulatory capacity.

Whatever objectives and techniques drive diverse regulatory action at Member State level become the EU's concern when it addresses that diversity by introducing harmonization legislation. This, the *dual function* of harmonization, shows that the adoption of common rules serves to deregulate and integrate the EU market but, in the unavoidable selection of the *quality* of those rules, it also achieves a re-regulation of the EU market. This is a major reason why Article 114 generates a scope to EU influence which goes far beyond that suggested by its text.

37 See Case C-376/98 note 29, paras 98, 117; Case C-380/03 note 22, para 43; Cases C-154/04 and C-155/04 note 22, para 33.

38 Directive 2001/95 on General Product Safety OJ [2002] L11/1.

39 Directive 2005/29 OJ [2005] L149/22.

Article 114 and its predecessors have accordingly been used as an authorization to harmonize across a wide sweep of the regulatory landscape in the EU. It has been used to harmonize areas of consumer protection law, such as that governing 'timeshare'[40] and the control of unfair terms in consumer contracts.[41] Rules on advertising, suppressing misleading forms, and liberalizing comparative practices have been harmonized in the name of the completion of the internal market.[42] Unfair commercial practices in business-to-consumer transactions are the subject of harmonized control.[43] This in turn empowers the Court, frequently asked to interpret these measures of harmonization and periodically inclined to do so in an expansive manner which strengthens still further the impact of EU law.[44] There are heaps of other examples of the promiscuity of the harmonization programme. Article 114 has been used to set common standards on access to particular types of vehicle for persons of reduced mobility, it being admitted that the 'principal aim' of the measure is to guarantee the safety of passengers.[45] An EU law on disability is thereby shaped alongside the making of the internal market—this is the dual function of harmonization. Directive 98/44 on biotechnology, based on Article 114, reduces regulatory diversity by establishing a common approach to the patenting of human biological material, but this plainly has both an economic and an ethical dimension which, as an exercise in selecting a European norm against background contested diversity in Europe, is immensely sensitive.[46] Here too an incidental effect is *judicial* empowerment: interpretation of this Directive, a measure ostensibly focused on market-making, has led to the Court being asked whether unfertilized human ova whose division and further development have been stimulated by parthenogenesis, and which in contrast to fertilized ova are incapable of developing into human beings, count as 'human embryos' (and so may not be patented) within the meaning of Directive 98/44.[47] So the EU's institutions become engaged in

[40] Directive 2008/112 OJ [2009] L33/10, replacing Directive 94/47.

[41] Directive 93/13 OJ [1993] L95/29.

[42] Directive 2006/114 concerning misleading and comparative advertising OJ [2006] L376/21.

[43] Directive 2005/29 note 39.

[44] Eg Case C-168/05 *Mostaza Claro* v *Centro Móvil Milenium* [2006] ECR I-10421, examined in Chapter 4.5.

[45] Directive 2001/85 OJ [2002] L42/1.

[46] Explored in M. Varju and J. Sándor, 'Patenting Stem Cells in Europe: The Challenge of Multiplicity in European Union Law' (2012) 49 CMLRev 1007.

[47] Case C-364/13 *International Stem Cell Corporation* judgment of 18 December 2014. They do not count.

identifying the limits dictated by human dignity to the rise of biotechnology and genetic engineering. The pursuit of an internal market roams across remote terrain which is little mapped by the explicit terms of the Treaties.

In all these instances—and there are many more—the logic is that national rules in the field vary and therefore the adoption of EU harmonized rules promotes the good functioning of the internal market. And then political judgement and negotiation dictates the content of the regime, supplemented by subsequent judicial interpretation. This is far more than a merely technical matter of finding a common rule.

This means too that the competence to harmonize is dynamic, not static. The fact that there already exists a complete system of harmonization governing a particular product does not deprive the EU legislature of the competence to introduce an amended regime which better reflects evolving information about risks to health or changing social and political preferences about the preferred level or style of legal intervention in the market.[48]

Making a market for Europe, which has been fragmented along unstable political boundaries for centuries, demands an intense commitment to common rule-making. Article 114 is a powerful motor. A risk, however, is that the EU rule tends, through intense political negotiation, to become an accumulation of practices pursued in diverse ways at national level and therefore heavy-handed and, as a centralized rule, a restraint on innovation and in practice hard to change. Moreover, it is an exercise in replacing cultural diversity, propelled by local particularities, with uniformity. It is not necessarily the case that EU legislative intervention wholly displaces national competence in the field—though sometimes it does: see Chapter 5—it is more that the areas in which national law and practice are influenced by EU law are broader than an unsuspecting reading of the Treaty's conferred competences in general and of Article 114 in particular would suggest.

2.8 THE SCOPE OF COMPETENCE ASSERTED BY *SUBSTANTIVE* EU LAW

EU competence is not merely *legislative*: it has a 'negative' dimension too, in the sense that parts of the Treaty operate by forbidding

[48] Eg Case C-491/01 *R* v *Secretary of State ex parte BAT and Imperial Tobacco* [2002] ECR I-11543, paras 77–80.

particular practices. The Treaty *prohibits* obstacles to free movement (of goods: Article 34 TFEU; of services: Article 56 TFEU), it *prohibits* nationality-based discrimination within the scope of the Treaties (Article 18 TFEU), and it *prohibits* particular anti-competitive practices pursued by private undertakings that are economically dominant or acting in collusion (Articles 101 and 102 TFEU).

The provisions that forbid particular practices that are incompatible with the EU's objectives have in common with the provisions that confer legislative competence that they are broad in their reach, that they are not sector-specific, and that they accordingly have a very deep and wide impact on national practices. But in fact the scope of these prohibitions exceeds the scope of the *legislative* competences. The functional breadth of EU law pushes it into some areas of activity that would not be subject (at all or only under strict limits) to the *legislative* competence of the EU. And then, since the relevant Treaty provisions largely lay down prohibitions which are not absolute and which accordingly allow space for justification, it is necessary to devise some sort of 'policy' for embedding respect for the particular concerns and features of the sector in question within the broad framework of application of EU trade law—but this needs to be done without help from the Treaty itself.

The substance of the matter is the subject of examination in Chapter 6: this explains how both judicial and legislative contributions serve to address the place of diverse national measures of market regulation within the wider internal market project. The concern of this chapter is structural. It shows how the principle of conferral must be understood in the light of the broadening of EU law's impact that follows from the application of the Treaty rules which control practices hostile to the internal market.

The Court's ruling in *ex parte Watts* arose out of the refusal by a local health authority in Bedford first to authorize Mrs Watts to receive surgery abroad and then to reimburse her for the costs of a hip replacement operation she had in France.[49] The Court observed that

> ... although ... [Union] law does not detract from the power of the Member States to organise their social security systems and decide the level of resources to be allocated to their operation, the achievement of the fundamental freedoms guaranteed by the Treaty nevertheless inevitably requires Member States to make adjustments to those systems. It does not follow that this undermines their sovereign powers in the field.[50]

[49] Case C-372/04 [2006] ECR I-4325. [50] Para 121.

In consequence the matter fell for assessment in the light of EU law, for what was at stake was an impediment to cross-border provision of medical care. Refusal to allow a patient to receive services in another Member State requires justification, and in a series of cases the Court has set out in detail what this inquiry involves.[51] The structural value of the ruling in *Watts* is that it illuminates the inadequacy of the Treaty as a means to achieve insulation of national practices—even where there is an explicit trend in that direction. Article 168 TFEU concerns public health and its seventh paragraph states that 'Union action shall respect the responsibilities of the Member States for the definition of their health policy and for the organisation and delivery of health services and medical care'; and that 'the responsibilities of the Member States shall include the management of health services and medical care and the allocation of the resources assigned to them'. The comparably worded predecessor to this, Article 152(5) EC, was invoked in *Watts*. But the Court treated that provision as inapt to exclude the possibility that other provisions in the Treaty, including those on free movement, might require adjustment to national systems of social security. An analogy should be drawn with the capacity of *legislative* action designed to promote the internal market pursuant to Article 114 TFEU being used to confine the value of such provisions as means to protect State autonomy. In the second *Tobacco Advertising* case, discussed in Section 2.7.4,[52] the Court refused to allow that same provision, formerly Article 152(5) EC and now Article 168(7) TFEU, to curtail the scope of what was Article 95 and is now Article 114 TFEU.

The quotation from *Watts* extracted at the start of this section encapsulates the Court's approach not only where health care is involved, but also in a number of other fields where EU internal market law sweeps far beyond the limits of EU legislative competence as a basis for controlling Member State practices. Asserting that EU law does not undermine the sovereign powers of Member States but that 'the achievement of the fundamental freedoms guaranteed by the Treaty nevertheless inevitably requires Member States to make adjustments' has become a standard formula in cases where the achievement of economic integration collides with Member States' powers to act in realms where the EU is not competent (at all or only under limited conditions) to act as a substitute *legislator*. Social security is a common example;[53] taxation is

[51] See eg L. Hancher and W. Sauter, *EU Competition and Internal Market Law in the Healthcare Sector* (OUP, 2012), Part II.

[52] Case C-380/03 note 22.

[53] Cf eg Case C-512/03 *J E J Blankaert* [2005] ECR I-7685.

another;[54] and even the maintenance of public order and the safeguarding of internal security have been revealed as matters of national competence that are nevertheless reviewable in so far as their pursuit impedes cross-border trade.[55]

Sport shows how this model may apply also to private practices, which fall within the scope of some of the Treaty provisions on free movement (Chapter 6.2.3) and on competition. At the time of the dispute in *Bosman*, more than twenty years ago,[56] the EU had *no* explicit legislative competence in the field of sport (and even today its competence, introduced in 2009 by the Treaty of Lisbon as Article 165 TFEU, is thin). However, the Court ruled that sport is subject to EU law in so far as it constitutes an economic activity and it found that practices in football associated with the transfer system and the selection of non-national players violated EU law on free movement of persons and non-discrimination. But it shaped an understanding of what may be permissible in sport, to meet its special characteristics, even in the admitted absence of any Treaty guidance. It agreed that 'the aims of maintaining a balance between clubs by preserving a certain degree of equality and uncertainty as to results and of encouraging the recruitment and training of young players must be accepted as legitimate'.[57] It is not for the EU to dictate how football should shape its transfer system. It *is* for the EU—specifically its Court—to rule on how football shall *not* shape its transfer system. It shall not violate EU internal market law. And this forced the Court to engage with the question of what a transfer system is for, even though the Treaty is utterly silent on such matters. The transfer system was duly amended in a less restrictive direction—not by EU legislative act, which would be a constitutional step too far, but by processes internal to football subject to an obligation not to violate EU free movement and competition law.[58]

The Court has a point in *Watts* and its other rulings in this vein when it declares that the achievement of the fundamental freedoms requires an adjustment by the Member States which does not undermine 'their sovereign powers in the field', because core decisions about resource allocation and organizational structure belong at State level. So too in *Bosman*: rule-making authority still ultimately belongs with governing bodies in sport.

[54] Cf eg Case C-446/03 *Marks and Spencer* v *Halsey* [2005] ECR I-10837; Case C-182/08 *Glaxo Wellcome* [2009] ECR I-8591.

[55] Case C-265/95 *Commission* v *France* [1997] ECR I-6959.

[56] Case C-415/93 *Bosman* [1995] ECR I-4921.

[57] Para 106.

[58] There remain open and as yet unlitigated questions about whether the amended system *is* compatible: see G. Pearson, 'Sporting Justifications under EU Free Movement and Competition Law: The Case of the Football Transfer System' (2015) 21 ELJ 220.

The Union cannot set the ground rules for the organization of social security systems or taxation or sport or for preserving public order (and so on). One should not exaggerate the scale of the EU's influence. But one should not lightly set it aside either. Free movement law stops States (and to some extent private parties: Chapter 6.2.3) acting in the absence of justification for chosen practices that impede cross-border trade. So EU law has a type of veto power on national practices, albeit one that is exercised in ad hoc manner, through litigation or sometimes intervention by the Commission. EU law circumscribes the scope of 'sovereign' State choices, and there is a hint of disingenuous camouflage in the Court's claim that EU law does not 'undermine' such State powers. At best this formula offers only an intellectually thin engagement with a more complex reality. It is the shaping of justification under EU free movement and competition law which allows space for important choices about what and is not allowed (as distinct from what is required, which is achieved only by positive EU intervention in the shape of legislation). Sometimes the EU's intervention is unexceptional or benign, but on occasion there is room for more controversial assessment. *Watts* certainly did not require public authorities to pay for every patient that preferred to secure treatment in another Member State, but it did require a more individualized assessment than was at the time undertaken in England, where waiting lists were a routine means to manage finite budgetary resources. EU law required local *adaptation*. EU law acquires legitimating force from its ability to put national practices to the test, but the question is whether its test is unduly imbalanced in favour of individual-driven market-based solutions.[59]

The Court's rulings which are most vulnerable to this line of criticism are *Viking Line* and *Laval*.[60] The cases were not identical but both concerned plans to 'reflag' ships from Nordic countries to Baltic states, in order to take advantage of lower labour and regulatory costs. Trade unions wanted to take action designed to deter this. So EU free movement law came into contact with the pursuit of collective labour rights. The Court found, in line with its long-established case law (examined in Chapter 6), that the union action fell within the scope of Article 43 EC, now Article 49 TFEU, even though private parties, unions, were responsible. The right to strike is explicitly excluded from the scope of EU *legislative* competence in the social policy field (now by Article 153(5)

[59] See eg C. Newdick, 'Citizenship, Free Movement and Health Care: Cementing Individual Rights by Corroding Social Solidarity' (2006) 43 CMLRev 1645.

[60] Case C-438/05 *International Transport Workers' Federation* v *Viking Line ABP* [2007] ECR I-10779; Case C-341/05 *Laval un Partneri* [2007] ECR I-11767.

TFEU), but in the application of free movement law the Court adopted a structurally similar approach to that employed in *Watts*. Member States are free in principle to lay down the conditions governing the existence and exercise of the right in question, but in exercising that competence they must comply with EU law, including free movement law. It then followed that collective action which restricts inter-State trade may be taken only on condition that it meets standards recognized by EU law. But in shaping those standards the Court had no mandate set out in the Treaty. The Treaty contained only the—*in casu* ineffective—exclusion of the right to strike found now in Article 153(5) TFEU. The Court proceeded to adopt a highly controversial approach. It confined the permissible scope of justified action to circumstances where jobs or conditions of employment were under serious threat, thereby excluding longer-term strategic action in so far as it impedes cross-border commercial activity. This is to assert a radical curtailment of the scope of industrial action as commonly understood under national and international law. Internal market law was interpreted in such a way as to call into question hard-won social and political struggles.

EU law acts as a jack-in-the-box: it surprises, it disrupts, its impact is hard to foresee.[61] In part this follows from the Court's often adventurous approach to interpretation and the jack-in-the-box metaphor is apt for many judgments encountered in this book, concerning both substantive and constitutional law, but is also a structural consequence of the Treaty design itself. Free movement and competition law reach far beyond the scope of legislative competence, triggering the jack-in-the-box's spring. The threshold to be crossed before national rules fall within the scope of internal market law is low and the Treaty is not designed to wall off particular national practices from its impact. As with legislative competence, so with free movement law: when one is engaged in economic activity, it is very difficult to construct an argument apt to secure insulation from the application of EU law. This means that an attempt to separate the role of the EU in achieving economic integration from the role of the Member States in choosing patterns of social regulation is fatally undermined. The two come into collision, and need conflict rules to determine which shall prevail. The principal arguments therefore tend to surround the question whether a particular practice is *justified* or not. A general criticism of the structure of EU law holds that the deregulatory grip of free movement

[61] T. Wilhelmsson, 'Jack-in-the-Box Theory of European Community Law' in L. Krämer, H.-W. Micklitz, and K. Tonner (eds), *Law and Diffuse Interests in the European Legal Order* (Baden-Baden: Nomos, 1997).

and competition law is tight and that EU law lacks the constitutional authority and the legislative will to compensate for that shift by adopting regulation at EU level. Chapter 6 explores more fully how forceful this criticism is generally and in that vein it explores more deeply how the Court assesses whether national practices are justified, but *Viking Line* and *Laval* are vivid affirmation of the vigour of this attack in the particular circumstances of free movement and labour disputes.

A complete account would move beyond free movement and competition law to provide a systematic account of the prohibitions imposed by the Treaty which operate beyond the spheres where the EU is equipped with legislative competence. One final illustration will suffice here. The prohibition against discrimination based on nationality (Article 18 TFEU) applies across the whole sweep of the material scope of the Treaty. But such prohibitions are not confined to the explicit terms of the Treaty. In *Mangold* the Court decided that a prohibition against discrimination on grounds of age is a general principle of EU law.[62] Moreover, it is a general principle that is applicable even in cases involving private parties, and is therefore not confined by the constitutional limits that attach to the impact of unimplemented Directives in national court proceedings (Chapter 4.7). This is very much a 'competence creep' judgment. *Mangold* is a jack-in-the-box.

2.9 THE RELATIONSHIP BETWEEN THE FREE MOVEMENT AND COMPETITION RULES, ON THE ONE HAND, AND THE LEGISLATIVE PROVISIONS, ON THE OTHER, IS NOT STATIC

Part Three TFEU is home to a number of Treaty provisions which are sufficiently precisely and unconditionally worded to permit their immediate application in litigation without the need for legislative elaboration. Obvious examples are the provisions on free movement and competition law. Other Treaty provisions are more programmatic in character, and require amplification by legislative action taken at EU level. So, on this model, where the achievement of the EU's objectives cannot be delivered by the application of prohibitions laid down by the Treaty, attention shifts to the exercise of legislative competence. This is sometimes a clean-cut margin: where a pattern of diverse national rules is shown to restrict inter-State trade but in a manner that is justified because of, for example,

[62] Case C-144/04 *Mangold* [2005] ECR I-9981.

the concern to suppress unfair practices or unsafe products, there is a comfortably smooth adjustment from free movement law to legislative harmonization (Chapter 6).

But the allocation of rules to the category of those apt for immediate judicial application or those awaiting legislative amplification is not preordained. This is a matter of interpretation of the Treaty which belongs to the Court of Justice, and it has a tendency to prefer where possible to find that rules are apt for immediate application. This enhances the effective application of EU law, while also reducing the need to rely on the EU's political institutions to provide legislative solutions. So for example in *Reyners* v *Belgian State*[63] a Dutch national resident in Belgium holding a Belgian legal qualification was denied admission as an *avocat* in Belgium because of rules restricting that profession to Belgians. His argument that he had rights to establish himself in Belgium was countered by the submission that Article 52 EEC (now Article 49 TFEU) could not be applied directly by national courts because its implementation was dependent on the issue of specific Directives regulating the professions envisaged by the relevant provisions of the Treaty. The Court rejected this argument, and found that since Reyners was subject to conditions which would not have been applied to an identically qualified Belgian, a clear breach of the unambiguous rule against discrimination on grounds of nationality had occurred. The adoption of secondary legislation facilitates free movement, but the rule of equal treatment is independently enforceable. Such an interpretative choice greatly increases the ability for private parties and the Commission to challenge obstructive national rules, stripping away the discretion of the political process to choose the pace of liberalization of the market (*in casu*, for professional services) by fashioning legislative solutions. The famous *Cassis de Dijon* ruling bears the same stamp.[64] As explored more fully in Chapter 6, the Court for the first time checked non-discriminatory national technical standards against the standards of EU law, in so far as such measures obstructed inter-State trade in goods. States had to justify their regulatory choices in judicial proceedings—and in the case Germany had no good reason to impose minimum alcohol content requirements on blackcurrant liqueurs. The consequence was that weaker French liqueurs could access the German market and this right could be vindicated by litigation before German courts, which were charged with the responsibility to set aside offending national rules once they had

[63] Case 2/74 [1974] ECR 631.

[64] Case 120/78 *Rewe-Zentrale AG* v *Bundesmonopolverwaltung für Branntwein* [1979] ECR 649.

been condemned as unjustified. The vigour of (what is now) Article 34 TFEU as an instrument of market integration was dramatically increased. So was the judicial role at the expense of the legislative role. One final example: in *Defrenne* v *SABENA*[65] the Court found that the requirement that Member States shall ensure men and women shall receive equal pay for equal work, now found in Article 157 TFEU, is capable of direct application by national courts even in cases involving private parties. The consequence was a reduced need for legislative amplification of the principle, whether at EU or at national level, and an increased ability for private parties to challenge discriminatory practices directly, relying on EU law before national courts.

Sometimes a Court decision on free movement or competition so muddies the waters that it stimulates a response from the political institutions. This may take the form of Commission guidelines or the adoption of binding legislation to 'clarify', adjust, or extend the approach chosen by the Court or, most radical of all, it may even prompt Treaty revision. *Cassis de Dijon* promoted the Commission swiftly to publish a Notice stating that goods lawfully manufactured in one Member State are in principle to be admitted to the markets of other Member States, and there is in consequence a much diminished need for legislative harmonization of divergent national standards.[66] The flow of cases on patients' rights of which *Watts*[67] was one led to the subsequent adoption of Directive 2011/24,[68] which is in fact largely a rather pedestrian codification of the Court's position on prior authorization of treatment and reimbursement. The Court, through its typically broad approach to the invocation of free movement and competition law in judicial proceedings, may provoke a political response.

2.10 'EUROPEANIZATION'—AN IMPRECISE TERM FOR AN IMPRECISE CONCEPT

'Europeanization' is a term designed to capture loosely the combined force of the influences considered previously in this chapter. Legislative harmonization is of remarkable functional breadth, and sets common standards that fall for implementation at national level across a wide-ranging patchwork. EU free movement and competition law run beyond the reach of EU legislative competence in exercising influence, though they serve as a restraint on national (public and private) regulatory autonomy rather than requiring the adoption of particular common standards mandated by the

[65] Case 43/75 [1976] ECR 455. [66] OJ [1980] C 256/2.
[67] Case C-372/04 note 49. [68] OJ [2011] L88/45.

EU. In this context EU law induces adaptation at national level—perhaps constructive but arguably disruptive—without having itself any explicit transformative solution to present. There is more, too: decisions such as *Reyners* and *Cassis de Dijon* concern the very relationship between legislative competences and the Treaty prohibitions, but also at a more detailed level judicial decisions interpret often ambiguous Treaty and legislative material, while, as explored in Chapter 3, the EU's legislative output, is not at all confined to the adoption of binding rules but rather embraces also 'soft' law, the 'open method of co-ordination' (OMC), and benchmarking. EU law- and policy-making typically lacks the systematic character of national practice, because of the constitutional constraint of the principle of conferral. But in practice the EU Treaty is structured to bring a very wide range of activities actually or potentially within its scope: seen from the other direction, the Treaty is structurally ill-designed to protect particular areas of Member State autonomy in any absolute principled sense. The EU exercises a wider influence than a formal inspection of the text of the Treaty may lead one to expect, primarily because of the EU's characteristic engagement through functionally driven competences, and this seeps down in diverse ways to affect national practices, with diverse effects in different States and varying too at different times. And so the EU is an agent for change.[69]

'Europeanization' is a calculatedly imprecise term that suggests the plurality of influences exerted on national practice by EU law and policy as distinct from any exaggerated claim that these become areas subjected to direct or, still less, exclusive EU legislative mandate.[70] It is, moreover, a pattern of extraordinary diversity and complexity. The EU's true transformative potential would be missed by an inspection of only Article 5 TEU, containing the principle of conferral, and Articles 2–6 TFEU, the competence catalogue.

One should not be too surprised. Building and maintaining an appropriate regulatory framework for an integrated market is a large challenge, and one that is unavoidably political. In particular making a market in Europe, pock-marked by centuries of accumulated regulatory diversity, demands an intense commitment to common rule-making, supported by other softer initiatives that reflect co-ordination and mutual interdependence. Achieving a free(d) market demands strong institutions and a

[69] U. Sedelmaier, 'Europeanization', ch 57 in E. Jones, A. Menon, and S. Weatherill (eds), *The Oxford Handbook of the European Union* (OUP, 2012).

[70] This is why periodic attempts to determine the percentage of national law that is attributable to 'Brussels' are fruitless, or at least unavoidably imprecise.

strong network of legal rules, backed too by a constitutionalized legal order. The character of EU competence, which is more flexible than rigid, reflects this.

2.11 THE EXERCISE OF A CONFERRED COMPETENCE

The principle of conferral limits EU action to the competences conferred upon it by the Member States in the Treaties. This concerns the *existence* of competences. Article 5(1) TEU adds that the use of Union competences is governed by the principles of subsidiarity and proportionality. This concerns the *exercise* of competences. The EU must act within the bounds set not only by the principle of conferral but also by the principles of subsidiarity and proportionality.

2.11.1 *The aims and the ambiguities of subsidiarity and proportionality*

Article 5(3) TEU sets out the principle of subsidiarity. This provides that

> in areas which do not fall within its exclusive competence, the Union shall act only if and in so far as the objectives of the proposed action cannot be sufficiently achieved by the Member States, either at central level or at regional and local level, but can rather, by reason of the scale or effects of the proposed action, be better achieved at Union level.

So the EU may possess a competence to act in an area, but this shall not entitle it to act in particular case where it cannot (in short) add value to action by the Member States.

The initial clause's reference to 'exclusive competence' is a little less obscure now than it used to be, because the Lisbon Treaty for the first time inserted a definition of the concept of 'exclusive competence' and listed the areas of activity covered by it.[71] But in general the ambiguities of the subsidiarity principle, largely deliberate, have kept writers occupied ever since its endorsement as a general principle in the Maastricht Treaty with effect from 1993, and they live on materially unaltered today despite periodic tinkering as a result of Treaty revision. In particular, the gulf endures between subsidiarity as a rather self-evident if abstract principle of good government on the one hand and, on the other, its status as a formally justiciable principle which is nonetheless very awkward for a court to apply without trespassing in areas of political judgement.

Article 5(4) TEU stipulates that under the principle of proportionality 'the content and form of Union action shall not exceed what is necessary

[71] Arts 2(1) and 3 TFEU.

to achieve the objectives of the Treaty'. As with subsidiarity, so too with proportionality: in the abstract this makes perfect sense and indeed proportionality was devised by the Court as a controlling principle in EU law long before it was embraced in the text of the Treaties, but plenty of questions remain open about how in practice to monitor the application of this controlling principle when the EU exercises its legislative competence.

Both provisions assume that simply because a competence *exists* is an inadequate reason to *exercise* it. Subsidiarity and proportionality are threshold conditions, designed to insert a pause in EU law-making between finding a competence to act and the decision to exploit it. Both principles suggest that restraint should attend the EU's endemic legislative tendency to promote centralization at the expense of State autonomy. But both principles, as a general observation, are of limited value in promoting legislative reflection and still less value in empowering judicial policing. And so both principles, like the principle of conferral considered above, are less virtuous and effective in practice than in principle.

2.11.2 *Subsidiarity*

The principle of subsidiarity holds appeal as a means to help to focus attention on the need for a proper accounting of the costs and benefits of choosing between centralized rules and local autonomy. Centralization may reduce fragmentation and release economies of scale. Preserving local autonomy, by contrast, may allow more sensitive reflection of citizen preferences and may permit regulatory experimentation. There are (different) costs and benefits associated with centralization and with preservation of local autonomy. Drawing up the balance sheet is no exercise in purely objective calculation but rather depends on selection of priorities, and it also demands sector-specific nuance. This tends to suggest that subsidiarity's proper role is to promote the asking of the right sort of questions rather than providing definitive answers. As was drily remarked by the former President of Ireland Mary Robinson, '...the chief advantage of [subsidiarity] seems to be its capacity to mean all things to all interested parties—simultaneously'.[72] The Commission itself has conceded that subsidiarity 'cannot be easily validated by operational criteria'.[73] It has proved easy to add the label of 'compliance with subsidiarity' to a legislative measure's Preamble, but rare is it to see any serious engagement

[72] M. Robinson, 'Constitutional Shifts in Europe and the United States: Learning from Each Other' (1996) 32 Stanford Jnl Intl Law 1, 10.

[73] Commission's annual report on subsidiarity and proportionality in 2010, COM (2011) 344, p 2.

with what is at stake in making that judgement. So, to take a perfectly typical example, Directive 2000/31 on electronic commerce asserts in its Preamble that '... by dealing only with certain specific matters which give rise to problems for the internal market, this Directive is fully consistent with the need to respect the principle of subsidiarity', but not a shred of further elucidation in support of this claim is offered.[74] The same is lamentably true of policy documents, which too often pay mere lip-service to the rigours of subsidiarity.[75]

In this vein it has been remarked that the Commission's eagerness to explain how proposed EU legislative measures conform to the dictates of subsidiarity is not matched by an equal readiness to offer examples of how subsidiarity prompted a decision *not* to advance a proposal.[76] But the target should not be the Commission alone. Subsidiarity is properly part of the practice of *all* the political institutions and of the Member States too. This general problem was helpfully illuminated by Jean-Claude Piris, at the time Director General of the Council's Legal Service, in evidence presented to the Subsidiarity Working Group of the Convention on the Future of Europe.[77] He confessed that the Service had rarely expressed doubts about compliance with the principle of subsidiarity, but pointed out that once it is decided to introduce rules at EU level, the bargaining process typically involves States aiming to secure a result as close as possible to their own pre-existing systems. If EU rules were being adopted on a blank canvas, subsidiarity might be a helpful guideline, but EU rules are typically under consideration in a much denser regulatory environment. The outcome at EU level is commonly cumulative. This provides an insight into how an institutional climate supposedly infused with the spirit of subsidiarity is capable of generating an intensification of rules damaging to expression of local autonomy.

Subsidiarity comes into play only once it has been decided to pursue a particular objective in respect of which the EU possesses a conferred competence. But if the question is framed as 'who should adopt rules in common?', it will be hard to avoid an answer that includes the EU. What

[74] OJ [2000] L178/1.

[75] Eg Council Conclusions on the role of sport as a source and a driver for active social inclusion, OJ [2010] C326/5.

[76] UK Parliament, House of Commons Select Committee on European Scrutiny, Eleventh Report, 2002-03, Part 7. The Commission is not wholly guilty of this sin of omission: a report annexed to the Conclusions of the Presidency at the Edinburgh European Council 1992 cited three proposals withdrawn in the light of the demands of the principle of subsidiarity.

[77] WD-004 WG I 13 July 2002.

is missing is any questioning of the very virtue of taking of the action in the first place: missing is any inquiry into the vice of denying the autonomy of action taken solely at national level.[78] Deeper still there is a compelling argument that subsidiarity has come too *late* to the EU debate, in the sense that the *pre-existing* allocation of competence should be reassessed, not merely future possibilities.[79] A general problem with the EU is that its reverse gear—a contraction in or 'repatriation' of conferred competences—has very rarely been engaged.[80] If one views the problem of excessive centralization in the EU as rooted in the flexibly generous scope of conferred competence and the prevailing institutional culture, then subsidiarity is a feeble antidote. Moreover, appeal to subsidiarity as a reason not to act when the real issue is the contested political merits of a proposal—for example, a debate about the level of intensity of common social policy or labour market regulation that the EU should pursue—is still more apt to deploy subsidiarity in a way that obscures rather than helps.

In truth subsidiarity serves as an invitation to begin a debate rather than the provision of helpfully precise benchmarks apt to conclude that debate. It has become a slogan to capture the perceived problems—'too much EU', 'too little respect for national particularity'—not a means to secure practical resolution. The quest to craft a more concrete context within which to understand the practical application of the principles leads from the Conclusions of the Edinburgh European Council in 1992 and the inter-institutional agreement of 1993 to the Amsterdam Protocol on subsidiarity and proportionality which entered into force in 1999, and which is now found in amended form as the Protocol on the Application of the Principles of Subsidiarity and Proportionality, attached to the Treaties. But catching subsidiarity (and proportionality) on paper is one thing: putting flesh on the bones through the generation of an institutional culture of law- and policy-making which will take a serious and balanced view of the virtue and vice of centralization in the EU is a far greater challenge. This is a concern for all the EU's institutions, in

[78] Cf eg G. Davies, 'Subsidiarity: The Wrong Idea, in the Wrong Place, at the Wrong Time' (2006) 43 CMLRev 63.

[79] Eg E. Carbonara, B. Luppi, and F. Parisi, 'Self-Defeating Subsidiarity' (2009) 5 Review of Law and Economics 742.

[80] The addition of sector-specific competences which serve as a restraint on recourse to Art. 352 TFEU (Section 2.7.3) is one of the few examples, though even that is only indirectly a contraction. On legal means to achieve contraction, assuming political will, see R. Zbíral, 'Restoring Tasks from the European Union to Member States: a Bumpy Road to an Unclear Destination?' (2014) 52 CMLRev 51.

particular those which are supposed to give voice to particular national and local sensitivities—which means the Council but could and should also mean the Parliament, but so too, since the entry into force of the Treaty of Lisbon in 2009, means *national* Parliaments. This is considered further in Section 2.12.

2.11.3 Proportionality

The principle of proportionality is, thanks to the Court's ingenuity, a long-standing principle of EU administrative law,[81] but it was formally admitted to the text of the Treaty only as late as 1993, on the entry into force of the Maastricht Treaty. It is now found in Article 5(4) TEU, which stipulates that under the principle of proportionality 'the content and form of Union action shall not exceed what is necessary to achieve the objectives of the Treaty'. This provision is supplemented by the abovementioned Protocol on the Application of the Principles of Subsidiarity and Proportionality.

Compliance with the demands of proportionality is, like compliance with the demands of subsidiarity, a condition of the legality of EU measures. A measure that imposes burdens which go beyond those necessary to bring about its intended objectives is disproportionate and it is therefore invalid. Proportionality also exerts control over national measures that fall within the scope of EU law, considered more fully in Chapter 4.8.4. Moreover, with particular reference to the building of the EU's internal market, it conditions the compatibility of national measures which restrict inter-State trade. As will be explored more fully in Chapter 6, it is in fact common for the Court to find that a national measure pursues a legitimate objective but that the means used are disproportionately restrictive.

Proportionality, then, offers a means to confine the intensity of EU intervention, and in this sense it shares with subsidiarity the potential to preserve some degree of national and local autonomy against the centralizing tendencies of EU law-making. However, significant though proportionality certainly is in structuring assessment of the legitimate bounds of action taken by public authorities, it also shares with subsidiarity a lack of precision. Proportionality, like subsidiarity, raises questions about the virtues of rule-making without offering a concrete basis for calculating what should and what should not be done. Proportionality, like subsidiarity, asks demanding and politically charged questions about the proper intensity of regulation.

[81] On proportionality generally see P. Craig, *EU Administrative Law* (OUP, 2nd ed, 2012), chs 19, 20.

2.11.4 *Judicial control of subsidiarity and proportionality*

Subsidiarity and proportionality carry evident political resonance but they are legal principles too. Compliance with them is a condition of legality. But the Court has been astutely cautious.

In *R* v *Secretary of State ex parte BAT and Imperial Tobacco*[82] a challenged Directive was found to fall within the permitted (post-*Tobacco Advertising*) scope of what is now Article 114, for it made an adequate contribution to the internal market. It complied with the principle of conferral. It was accordingly in principle open to review for compliance with the principle of subsidiarity, but the Court adopted an approach which makes it difficult to imagine circumstances in which a harmonization measure, or indeed any EU measure setting common rules, will be found to violate the demands of subsidiarity. The Directive's objective—to eliminate the barriers raised by the differences between national laws—could not be sufficiently achieved by the Member States individually. It is the very fact of variety in chosen approaches taken that caused the problem in the first place! The Court concluded that the matter therefore called for action at EU level, in full conformity with the principle of subsidiarity. This is either admirably deft or cynically evasive according to taste. The Court has deftly sustained subsidiarity as a legal principle on paper while evasively conceding much in practice to legislative discretion. Once it is determined that a competence to establish common rules exists, the political decision to exercise that competence seems *in practice* immune from judicial subversion. This has become established as the Court's standard approach.[83] Provided there is a modest indication in a measure's Preamble that political attention has been paid to treating the EU as a better rule-maker in the given circumstances than the Member States acting individually, thereby assuring that the procedural requirement to give reasons for legislative action has been met,[84] it is highly improbable that the Court will ever find that that dictates of the subsidiarity principle have not been met.

It is not difficult to gain the impression that the Court has adopted a calculatedly narrow approach to subsidiarity as a legal concept according to an assumption that it is in the political sphere in which subsidarity concerns are most apt to be aired. In an address in 2002 the then President of the Court, Gil Carlos Rodriguez Iglesias, made precisely this distinction, arguing that 'subsidiarity is a principle of an essentially political

[82] Case C-491/01 [2002] ECR I-11543.

[83] See similarly Case C-103/01 *Commission* v *Germany* [2003] ECR I-5369; Cases C-154/04 and C-155/04 note 22; Case C-58/08 note 22.

[84] Art 296 TFEU.

nature' and asserting a concern to purge the Court's diet of 'political hot potatoes'.[85] The Court has achieved this, in this sphere at least. It may be best to appreciate 'subsidiarity' as the label for a debate in the EU which has echoes of similar debates that take place frequently in any system of divided political power. There is no 'right answer' to the question 'who does what?': preferences and rhythms alter over time in federal and quasi-federal systems. One can understand the Court's reticence to become too heavily involved in these matters. The consequence, however, is that *judicial* supervision of the exercise of legislative competence in the name of subsidiarity is very limited.

The judicial application of the proportionality principle betrays a similar, if slightly milder, anxiety to avoid usurpation of the legislative role. Proportionality is declared to be justiciable according to Point 13 of the Protocol, but this was plain long before the Treaty made such provision. In fact, the Court had no great difficulty in developing the principle of proportionality within the EU legal order, for it is a well-recognized element in national administrative and constitutional law. German law, in particular, has provided inspiration for the Court's development of EU law. It is, however, plain that the application of the proportionality principle depends heavily on the context in which it arises and that it is relatively uncommon for violations to be found, especially where legislative rather than administrative measures are subject to review. The sensitive issue is fixing the proper relationship between power exercised by political institutions and the review function entrusted to judges. This tension is as plain in EU law as it is in any system which is based on the rule of law.

In this vein the Court has long embraced respect for the broad discretion which it thinks proper to grant to the EU legislative process where political, economic, and social choices are at stake and where complex assessment is demanded. The Court tends to accept that only where a measure is manifestly inappropriate in relation to the objective which it seeks will validity be called into question.

Alliance for Natural Health offers an illustration of the Court's typical approach.[86] An EU Directive permitted the marketing of nutrients only where they had received a favourable opinion from the competent scientific authorities. Nutrients that had not been shown to present a risk to human health, but were not in receipt of a favourable opinion, were

[85] 'The Court of Justice, Principles of EC Law, Court Reform and Constitutional Adjudication' (2004) 15 *Euro Business Law Rev* 1115, 1117.

[86] Cases C-154/04 and C-155/04 note 22.

prohibited. It was argued that this 'positive list' system was a more burdensome means of regulating the market than the 'negative list'. The Court agreed, but it did not agree that the burden was disproportionate. The chosen legislative measures were appropriate for achieving their objective and the Court, citing the obligation of the EU legislature to pursue a high level of protection of human health which is now contained in Articles 114(3) and 168(1) TFEU as well as Article 35 of the Charter, concluded that they did not go beyond what was necessary to attain that objective.

Typical too of the Court's approach is its ruling on the 'Roaming Regulation', in *Vodafone, O2* et al v *Secretary of State*, in which the Court conceded a broad discretion to the EU legislature in areas involving political, economic, and social choices in which it is called upon to undertake complex assessments and evaluations.[87] Legality would be called into question only if the measure is manifestly inappropriate having regard to the objective which the EU is seeking to pursue. Such a finding is highly uncommon: the Court is evidently determined to allow the political institutions room to enjoy a sufficiently wide discretionary power in law-making.

2.11.5 *Subsidiarity and proportionality in substantive law*

In EU free movement law, where the principle of subsidiarity is used in the context of scrutiny of national measures rather than EU legislation, it has been similarly pushed to one side as a basis for active judicial intervention. The approach taken in *Bosman* is typical. It was pressed on the Court that the subsidiarity principle dictated that intervention in the name of EU law should be confined to what is strictly necessary, but the Court simply retorted that this could not permit the adoption of sporting rules in Member States that run contrary to the Treaty.[88] Subsidiarity does not serve *in principle* to immunize national autonomy from control exercised in the name of EU law. Proportionality has a more muscular role to play in review of national measures that interfere with cross-border trade. This is elaborated in Chapter 6.3.

2.11.6 *Subsidiarity and proportionality: inadequate restraint on centralization*

The EU has an institutional momentum in favour of legislation. Of course, States too suffer from this malaise, but the anxieties about legitimacy are different in the EU context—especially that centralization

[87] Case C-58/08 note 22. [88] Case C-415/93 note 56, para 81.

may load responsibilities on to institutions that lack the expertise and/or the resources to fulfil them, and that there may anyway be an inadequate store of social legitimacy enjoyed by the EU's institutions when they are asked to address politically contested issues. Clearly one should debate how many of the problems are endemic to the Treaty, how many are attributable to exploitation of the EU level of law-making by the political institutions as a means to circumvent domestic obstacles to reform, and how many are due to slack control exercised by the Court. But the general anxiety asserts that it is not safe to entrust the application of the core principles governing the existence and exercise of EU competence solely to the EU's own institutions.

2.12 REVIEWING COMPETENCE REVIEW

If one lauds the 'harmony' of setting common rules and takes as its antonym 'disharmony', then the impulse for centralization in the EU is clear. But it could be different. If one contrasts harmony with tolerance of diversity then the value of respecting local autonomy becomes more conspicuous. These are debates that deserve political and cultural depth. The debate about centralization in Europe deserves a fuller and richer vocabulary than that which is provided by the principles of conferral, subsidiarity, and proportionality. But as a matter of law those are the framing principles that the Treaty provides. The question is: can a richer basis for inquiry be shaped?

2.12.1 *The reforming dynamic*

The 2001 Laeken Declaration on the Future of the European Union set out three series of questions under the sub-title 'A better division and definition of competence in the European Union.' They were: (a) How to make the division of competence more transparent; (b) Does there need to be a reorganization of competence?; and (c) How to ensure that a redefined division of competence does not lead to a creeping expansion of EU competence, while at the same time ensuring the European dynamic does not come to a halt. The thematic tension is effectiveness versus control: confining the EU to an agenda which can be reliably identified in advance and ensuring the whistle can be blown quickly and uncontroversially if the boundary is crossed is a control-driven agenda, but the problem is that this will diminish the EU's capacity to act effectively in order to address the wide range of objectives assigned to it by its Treaties. It may cause damage worse than the cure, in particular because the imposition of an inflexible division between Union and State competences is likely to harm the EU's capacity to fulfil its mission by denying it an adaptable and efficiently functioning system of governance that properly implicates several levels. Crucially, *competence* and *legitimacy* work together—just as trespass beyond the limits of attributed competence strains legitimacy, so too unduly confined competence undermines legitimacy by diminishing the EU's problem-solving capacity.

The greater one perceives the problem—of ever-expanding EU competence and activity more generally—to be, the more radical the plans for reform. Conversely, those less alarmed or at least more anxious to preserve the EU's flexible powers, even if the price to be paid for that is to leave the door open to 'creep', tend to be content to retain the essence of the pre-existing system. At the Convention on the Future of Europe, attention to the matter of competence control occupied much time.[89] The latter—the conservatives—were broadly in the majority, and this set the path to what ultimately emerged as the modest reforms made by the Treaty of Lisbon with effect from 2009.

What was proposed but *not* embraced included: 'hard lists' governing competence. One could envisage different models of 'hard lists', involving for example exhaustive and tightly defined lists of the areas in which the Union is competent to act or identification of areas off-limits to the Union and therefore remaining within the exclusive competence of the Member States;

(i) the deletion of (what are now) Articles 114 and/or 352 as the principal problem cases in the corrosion of 'competence creep';

(ii) equipping national Parliaments with a veto over proposed EU legislation;

(iii) A freshly minted 'court of competence', comprising members drawn from not only the Court of Justice but also national judiciaries.

What was accepted and what is now the renovated and strengthened 'competence method' involves solutions which are towards the modest end of the scale. First, the clarification and reorganization of the Treaty rules governing competence now found in Articles 2–6 TFEU was designed to promote a more transparent and informed debate about what the EU does, how it does it, and why. That is supplemented by reform of the system for monitoring the existence and exercise of competence by bringing in *national Parliaments* and charging them with the responsibility to monitor legislative 'creep' according to a new *ex ante* monitoring system, the 'early warning system'.

[89] See S. Weatherill, 'Competence Creep and Competence Control' (2004) 23 YEL 1.

2.12.2 *The role of national parliaments—political deliberation and competence review*

Articles 5(3) and 5(4) TEU make explicit reference to mandating the application of the two principles by the institutions of the Union in accordance with the Protocol on the Application of the Principles of Subsidiarity and Proportionality. That, however, is to make no difference of substance: in fact, the perceived problem is precisely that the EU's institutions do a poor job of this. For subsidiarity—but *not* for proportionality—it is also stated that national Parliaments are to ensure compliance with the principle in line with the procedure found in the Protocol.[90] Until 2009 national Parliaments had no explicit voice in the EU law-making process, because it was assumed that their influence would be projected through the Council, composed of representatives of national governments. The reforms in effect concede that the Council is too remote from everyday national parliamentary practice to constitute a genuinely reliable voice of national and local particularity, and so national Parliaments are granted their own distinct institutional identity at EU level.

The Protocol on the role of national Parliaments deals with the distribution of information to national Parliaments. It provides for the submission of a reasoned opinion in cases of suspected violation of the subsidiarity principle, and then an eight-week legislative 'standstill' period designed to give national Parliaments a real practical opportunity to intervene, applicable in all but urgent cases. The Protocol on subsidiarity and proportionality absorbs this procedure and puts flesh on the bones. Where reasoned opinions on non-compliance with subsidiarity represent at least one third of all the votes allocated to national Parliaments, the draft must be reviewed. The Commission may then maintain, amend, or withdraw the draft, giving reasons for this. This is the yellow card. Where reasoned opinions on non-compliance with subsidiarity represent a simple majority of votes cast by national Parliaments, then the Commission must review the proposal and, if it decides to maintain it, must itself present a reasoned opinion dealing with its view why the proposal complies with the subsidiarity principle. These opinions are then made available to the Union legislator and shall be considered in the manner set out in the Protocol. This is the orange card.

There is no veto here—no red card. There is instead an attempt to promote more dialogue about whether particular proposals are valid or

[90] There is a sector-specific reference to this role for national Parliaments in Art 69 TFEU in the Title of the TFEU dealing with the *Area of Freedom, Security and Justice*.

well-intentioned. And the assumption is that national Parliaments, as the voice previously excluded from a process that is suspected to have provoked too much of a centralizing dynamic and at the same time the big losers from exactly that trend, will nudge the institutional balance towards a more critical edge, while, at the same time, leaving intact the basic structure of the EU's law-making process.

The emphasis is on the predominantly *political* nature of subsidiarity. The involvement of national Parliaments does not at all remove the legal requirement that EU acts comply with the principle of subsidiarity. But, as considered in Section 2.11.4, the point is that the Court has in practice placed subsidiarity largely beyond the reach of judicially based control. So this is an attempt to enrich *political* safeguards against centralizing bias. In fact, the Court could help to enliven this political debate. It would not be incompatible with its reticence to use subsidiarity as a basis for *substantive* review to place firm *procedural* obligations on the legislature when they are in receipt of objections raised by national Parliaments.[91] So, without touching an act's political merits, the Court could hold unlawful an act adopted which fails adequately to engage with those objections, which would force the EU's political institutions to take seriously the channel of dialogue envisaged under the early warning procedure and so too to induce national Parliaments actively to participate in developing a critical voice.

How transformative this new political arrangement is capable of proving *in practice* is as yet hard to measure. Pre-existing problems suffered by national Parliaments such as sheer lack of time to turn the gaze away from domestic politics cannot be solved by creating a procedure on paper. And national executives dominate Parliaments most of the time in most of the Member States, so one needs to be cautious in identifying what fresh critical thinking national Parliaments may be able realistically to contribute. But as a minimum this agenda points to the thematic concern of the Lisbon Treaty to raise the profile of *national*-level political processes and controls, and to make thinner the apparent divide between 'Brussels' and national political life. This is virtuous.

The Commission, reviewing practice so far, has strained to maintain an optimistic tone. National Parliaments have 'further enriched the discussions'.[92] In 2012 there were seventy reasoned opinions (on twenty-three different proposals)[93] and in 2013 this rose to eighty-eight reasoned opinions (on thirty-six different proposals).[94] In 2014 the number of

[91] Cf X. Groussot and S. Bogojević, 'Subsidiarity as a Procedural Safeguard of Federalism' in L. Azoulai, *The Question of Competence in the EU* (OUP, 2014).

[92] COM (2011) 344, p 10. [93] COM (2013) 566. [94] COM (2014) 506.

reasoned opinions dropped sharply—only twenty-one were received, on fifteen different proposals—but this was attributed by the Commission to the decrease in the number of legislative proposals it had made as it approached the end of its term of office, not to any diminished desire on the part of national Parliaments to make use of the procedure.[95]

The threshold for the yellow card has been crossed just twice, while that required for an orange card has not been crossed in any case.

The first yellow card was aimed at the Commission Proposal for a Regulation on the exercise of the right to take collective action within the context of the freedom of establishment and the freedom to provide services.[96] This, the so-called 'Monti II' legislative proposal of the Commission, which was (roughly) aimed at making some contribution to clarifying the consequences of the Court's rulings on labour law and free movement of companies in *Viking Line* and *Laval*,[97] was fiercely opposed by some Member States (and the Parliament too). The Commission withdrew the proposal, but it did not admit to violation of the subsidiarity principle. Instead it simply cited absence of adequate political support. The second yellow card dates from autumn 2013 and concerns a Proposal for a Council Regulation on the establishment of the European Public Prosecutor's Office. The Commission noted that the reasoned opinions submitted by national Parliaments ranged over issues of not only subsidiarity but also proportionality and substance, but on this occasion it reviewed the proposal and determined to maintain it.[98] It has not yet been adopted.

It is perfectly possible that the modesty of the system will be revisited and that it will be strengthened through, for example, extension to cover not only subsidiarity but also conferral, proportionality, and, deeper still, the very political merits of a proposal, although inspection of the Commission's Annual Reports reveals that this appears to be occurring de facto in any event.[99] But it is important to grasp that the perceived problem of 'competence creep' is not to be tackled solely or even mainly by reshaping the institutional arrangements at EU level. The point of equipping national Parliaments with the 'yellow card' is to shake domestic political oversight of action taken by ministers in the Council out of its torpor, but one may also expect greater activity within those domestic political processes themselves. Denmark has famously been the State which has

[95] Paras 2.2, 4 COM (2015) 315. [96] COM (2012) 130.

[97] Note 60. [98] COM (2014) 506, pp 8–10.

[99] See D. Jancic, 'The Game of Cards: National Parliaments in the EU and the Future of the Early Warning Mechanism and the Political Dialogue' (2015) 52 CMLRev 939.

for a long time placed strict limits on the mandate granted its ministers when they participate in Council deliberations, and one may expect other Member States to introduce more restraints. The *Bundesverfassungsgericht*'s ruling on the Lisbon Treaty required and extracted changes in domestic political oversight as a precondition to German ratification.[100] The Treaty of Lisbon not only created new rights for national Parliaments at EU level; it also provoked adjustment in scrutiny of EU activities carried out by national Parliaments *at national level*.

2.13 CONCLUSION

It is important to conclude with a balanced view of the issues under scrutiny in this chapter. The argument is *not* that the EU has deviously or in consequence of the structural deficiencies of its Treaty invaded vast terrains of policy-making with the result that national autonomy is ruinously undermined. That would be to go too far. There is a risk of concentrating on what the EU *can* do and ignoring what the EU *cannot* do. The EU does not have a police force or an army; it does not have tax-raising powers; it does not determine the overall shape or budget of systems of social welfare or of education or of health care.[101] It is in important respects an exercise in extending *administrative* capacity to the transnational plane.[102] The sites of primary constitutional responsibility for hugely important areas of deep political saliency to the peoples of Europe remain at national level. Quite properly so, from the perspective of those who doubt the EU is able to bear the load of responsibility for such politically contested policy areas.[103] Moreover, even where the EU affects national autonomy, it does not often exclude it. The majority of areas in which it exercises legislative competence are shared or supporting. Exclusivity claimed by the EU is rare and confined to the matters listed exhaustively in Article 3 TFEU. So national action remains permitted, in so far as it is compatible with any EU legislation that has been adopted and subject to compliance with the general rules of EU law, such as free movement and non-discrimination.

[100] Note 16.

[101] See in particular in this vein A. Moravcsik, 'The European Constitutional Compromise and the Neofunctionalist Legacy' (2005) 12 JEPP 349.

[102] See especially P. Lindseth, *Power and Legitimacy: Reconciling Europe and the Nation State* (OUP, 2010).

[103] Eg G. Majone, 'Europe's Democratic Deficit: The Question of Standards' (1998) 4 ELJ 5.

Even so, and in line with a major thematic argument in this book, the point is a *relative* one: the EU's interventionist influence on national autonomy goes beyond what a strict textual reading of the Treaties might lead one to expect, and it is far deeper than that exerted by any other international Treaty. So the principle of conferral has in practice a dynamic which surpasses the expectations of those who work laboriously to craft small extensions of legislative competence at times of Treaty revision. As explained in reflecting on 'Europeanization' (Section 2.10), the EU exerts a range of influences within its Member States. The model of binding EU rules, applying in common to all Member States and excluding the possibility of Member States taking any different approach, is the most stark, but is in fact relatively uncommon. The EU operates across a broad spectrum of influence, nudging, promoting, and restraining the scope for action by public authorities and private parties at national level. The other extreme, where national autonomy is entirely unaffected by the EU, is also relatively uncommon and hard to pin down.

The principle of conferral, and the associated principles of subsidiarity and proportionality, are in practice more slippery than one would expect of such constitutionally fundamental rules. But many provisions of the EU law are broad, functionally driven, and perhaps vague, but for good reason. It is not feasible that the multi-functional activities of the modern Union, characterized by close interdependence with its Member States, could be reduced to a neat set of legal rules dictating who does what. Sector-by-sector close attention must be devoted to planning the respective contributions of EU and national laws. And although alleged 'competence creep' opens the EU to criticisms rooted in want of formal legitimacy, the more cautious it is about 'competence sensitivity', the more it risks being seen as unresponsive and irrelevant, to the detriment of its ability to gather legitimacy through effective problem-solving on behalf of its Member States. The EU's claims to legitimacy need to be measured and tested by examining the strengths and weaknesses of both the EU and the Member States, and the problem-solving capacity of the EU, as a source of legitimacy, *depends* on institutional autonomy and an embedded degree of risk of competence creep. The reforms of the Lisbon Treaty, placed at the modest end of the range, recognize this trade-off and emphasize process-based remedies, most of all the direct involvement of national Parliaments, rather than the elusive search for rigid rules.

3

HOW DOES THE EU DO IT?

3.1 A UNIQUE SYSTEM OF GOVERNANCE

The EU's system of operation is unique, but in the matter of institutional design the EU is its own worst enemy. The arrangements which govern the preparation, adoption, and enforcement of laws in the EU involve the interaction of the Council, the Parliament, and the Commission, and they are not only fiendishly complicated but also forbiddingly different from any model that would be recognizable within a single State. The shorthand reference to 'Brussels!' is typically used part in scorn but also in exasperation at the sheer intransparency of the EU's institutional set-up. It is hard to treat a system as legitimate when it is scarcely comprehensible.

There is no denying that it is hard going at the level of intricate detail, and this challenge of legitimacy is real. But the trick is to look beyond and above the detail. *Why* is the EU uniquely structured? It is no accident. The system is built on deliberately novel foundations which calculatedly avoid mimicry of State structures. This is because a major purpose of the EU is to manage the interdependence of States without seeking to replace them with a single super-State. It would therefore be utterly counter-productive to draw on the State as direct inspiration. The EU's institutions give voice to the expression of the interests of States—naturally and inevitably so, given the foundational role of States in creating and sustaining the EU—and this is primarily the role of the Council. But the voice of the peoples of Europe is heard directly too—this is the role of the Parliament. And, in the most remarkable instance of institutional creativity in the EU's design, a body has responsibility for proposing and preparing legislation which is in most instances exclusive, yet not only is it not accountable to voters, it is also constitutionally wedded to promoting the EU's interests, not those of individual States. This is the Commission, and its existence is the most powerful illustration of the need to secure the effective management of the interdependence of States by empowering an institution that is not controlled by those States. This autonomy from control, inspired by the quest for effective problem-solving undistorted by partisan pressure, is also visible in the judicial as well as the political context, in the role allocated to the Court of Justice of the EU.

The purpose of this chapter is to use these driving thematic concerns to explain 'governance' in the EU, a term apt to cover the processes of interaction between involved parties leading to decision-making. 'Governance' is distinct from, and wider and more flexible than, 'government', which suggests a more tightly defined system of rule-making typically confined to a State. The EU's system of governance operates beyond the State and it is unique, but there are good and historically deep-rooted reasons why this is so. And from that vantage point the detail, which is admittedly hard to digest at first, begins to fit more readily into the overall aspiration.

3.2 THE INSTITUTIONS OF THE EU—A GENERAL SKETCH OF THEIR NATURE AND PURPOSE(S)

States have incentives to co-operate where action in common is better at getting the job done than action of a unilateral nature. An intergovernmental institutional model would maximize the control which Member States are able to exercise over their creation. The most brutal form of intergovernmentalism would be built on State bargaining and agreement by consensus or not at all. Implementing any agreement struck would then be a national matter. The more ambitious the co-operative endeavour, the less likely that this will be a model apt to satisfy the need to get things done effectively. A secretariat might be set up to facilitate the preparation of ideas and/or the adoption of decisions, perhaps also to supervise implementation. The more flexible its mandate, the looser the grip exercised by the States that set it up, but the more agile it will be in responding to new and unforeseen problems. Participants might be induced to accept that some decisions may be taken without the need for across-the-board consensus. A State might risk being out-voted: it will know that it will in turn have the chance to out-vote others as part of the bargain. Parties might open up their implementation processes to external scrutiny and even accept the possibility of sanction should they be found in default, under an understanding that all other parties accept the same discipline. In this way reciprocity strengthens the credibility of the obligations undertaken. States have incentives to accept a relaxation in their *control* over what may be done through the international organization in order to make more *effective* the discharge of the tasks that have been entrusted to that organization. On the other hand, the more control they cede, the greater the risk that some decisions taken will be contrary to their preferences. And the more politically salient and contested the matters that are being handled in this environment, the more pressure there is for some expression of democratic involvement, so nudging the system beyond focus on State interests alone to accommodate *people*.

Establishing any international organization serves up questions of design of this type.[1] And these are the background questions faced by the EU. It is an international organization based on Treaties, and its design involved and, as it evolves, continues to involve the need to incorporate a number of different, and sometimes conflicting, motivations. The challenges that the EU faces are not unique. But the choices it has made about how to address them are unique.

In short, the EU retains a strong intergovernmental streak, most prominently in the role of the Council and the European Council, but more than any other international institution that has ever existed it also embraces institutional choices which radically undermine the controlling grip exerted by individual Member States. Pursuit of the uniquely ambitious mission of the EU would be hopelessly thwarted were individual State interests to be allowed a dominant profile. The desire to proceed in an *effective* manner has led to a number of innovations which ensure the EU has a momentum and influence which is intended to allow it to act as more than just the sum of its parts. The exercise of State power is curtailed and managed—precisely because of the understanding that membership of the EU allows power to be enhanced because it is exercised collectively. This does not at all mean that the EU lacks a mooring in its Member States—and sometimes veto power is conserved today, most strikingly at times of Treaty revision but also on occasion *within* the system too, where unanimity in Council is exceptionally required for some types of legislative action—but it does mean that the interaction of States in the EU is driven by a dynamic that is a great deal more nuanced than intergovernmentalism. So the Commission is an institution which is formally independent of the Member States, and it is charged with the responsibility to devise and to propose EU legislation (exclusively, in most cases) and to ensure that the law of the EU is enforced. Its autonomy is vital to secure progress by cutting through partisan State interests. But its absence of accountability is the reason why it does not *make* law. The adoption of legislation is the preserve of the Council and the Parliament, today in most instances acting jointly under the so-called ordinary legislative procedure of the EU. The Parliament's existence and role reveals another dimension of the EU's working method that is much deeper than

[1] See eg M. Mazower, *Governing the World: The History of an Idea* (Penguin, 2012). The Commission's *European Governance: A White Paper* COM (2001) 428 was the first attempt to articulate a distinctive vision from within the EU's institutional architecture.

intergovernmentalism. The Parliament, directly elected since 1979, represents the peoples of Europe, and sits and typically votes by party affiliation, not by nationality. Even the Council, correctly understood as the most prominently intergovernmental of the EU's main institutions since it comprises representatives of the governments of the Member States, has features which distance it from a classic instance of inter-State bargaining. Most of all, the fact that it normally—and, over time, increasingly—makes legislative decisions according to a species of qualified majority voting (QMV) means not only that States have no veto but also that they are induced to co-operate in order to piece together coalitions apt to create adequate majorities or blocking minorities.

This architecture is not democratically legitimate in any State-like sense, but *that is the point.* It is specific to the aspirations loaded on the EU. The decision on whether or not to adopt proposed legislation rests on a dual source of legitimacy, via States, in the Council, and via the peoples of Europe, in the Parliament. This catches the notion that the EU is an international organization set up by States but that it also exerts a direct impact on the rights and obligations of citizens. A legitimacy asserted not by representation but by performance exists in the case of the Commission. Its job is to reflect and promote the aims of the Treaties by proposing legislation and by supervising compliance with the rules once agreed. To do that job effectively it is constitutionally insulated from pressure brought to bear by the Council, or by the States more generally, or by the Parliament. That legislation is made both by an institution representing States and one representing people and, moreover, only on the initiative of an independent institution, the Commission, is central to the EU's claim to have established a system that is qualitatively different from that found in a typical international organization. And beyond the political environment stands the Court of Justice, which has its own distinctive position of autonomy and power. It enjoys compulsory jurisdiction and it has a direct channel of co-operation with the national courts via the preliminary reference procedure. This distances the EU's institutional character still further from inter-State bargaining.

It has long been conventional to describe the EU as based on a combination of intergovernmental and supranational features. The Council is the most conspicuously intergovernmental forum, while the Commission and the Parliament (and in a different way the judicial institution, the Court) are supranational, in the sense that their ties reach beyond the structures of individual States. The terms 'intergovernmental' and 'supranational' have become a little tired today, and the EU system has acquired extra layers of complexity, but the basic notion of an interplay between the two concepts is supposed to ensure the successful operation of the EU. So the word 'Brussels', typically spat rather than spoken, commonly aims to depict the EU as something that binds its victim Member States against their will, but this is to miss the very real sense that the Member States too are part of 'Brussels'. There may be no European public space nor a European *demos*, but the EU has intimate connection with national politics and voters, most obviously through the Council, Parliament, and the role of national Parliaments. States get things done through 'Brussels' and although they are not in exclusive control, their hands exert a strong grip.

In the hands of an enthusiast this might sound glowing, even heroic. There are, however, centrally important and enduring tensions that plague this set-up. The idea that the EU benefits from a dual sourced democratic legitimation—Council (States) and Parliament (peoples)—has obvious appeal in articulating just how and why the EU is an international organization, not a State, but one with more a intimate relationship with citizens than any other international organization. Article 10(1) TEU is proudly explicit—'The functioning of the Union shall be founded on representative democracy'—and Article 10(2) insists on the achievement of representation of both citizens in the Parliament and Member States in the European Council and in the Council. So, one might think, the more emphasis is placed on the Council and the Parliament, the more democratic the process. This is a trap. The danger is to use assumptions based on systems found in States and to apply them normatively to the development of the EU. But States have citizens who share a *demos*—or, at least, they are *relatively* homogenous when contrasted with the EU. There is no EU *demos*. There is little sign of its emergence and, in the absence of '*demos*-forming' ingredients such as a European media and European political parties, little likelihood of it either. Pushing more power up to the EU level cannot be justified by claims that the EU thereby becomes more democratic, if the very basis of that concept, the existence of a single *demos*, is lacking. In fact, if one correctly identifies an absence of EU *demos* then such a shift is not merely misguided, but will be counter-productive. It will deepen the sense that the EU's expanding role is not legitimate. In concrete terms this dictates caution when the relationship between EU and Member State competences is under consideration: doing more at EU level cannot simply be adequately justified by a simple claim that Europe's peoples will have their say in the Parliament. So too the Council's claim to legitimacy as the authentic expression of the voice of national political preferences is compromised by the depletion of intergovernmentalist method consequent on the rise of QMV. Decisions taken by a State representative in Council are supposed to be subject to control and review by that State's national Parliament, but the generality of QMV in Council reduces that 'controllability'. In any event the reality is that frequently national Parliaments will lack the energy and resources, as well as the incentives, to track what is occurring at EU level. This fracturing of the control exercised by national Parliaments explains the formal though limited status allocated to national Parliaments under the Treaty of Lisbon (Chapter 2.12 and Section 3.4.5), but more generally the allegation is that the Council operates as a means to accentuate *executive* power in the Member States.

Moreover, appreciation of the unique but delicate balance between the supranational and the intergovernmental elements of the EU's design dictates caution when appeals are made to increase the oversight and accountability of the Commission. The appeal of greater accountability—achieved by, for example, subjecting appointment to the Commission to a vote of the Parliament—is lessened once one appreciates that independence is essential to the effective performance of the Commission's Treaty-mandated tasks. To 'democratize' without awareness of the costs is to make the mistake of assuming the more like a State the EU becomes, the more legitimate it is. Not so, if one cherishes effective problem-solving and recognizes that the EU's genius is to manage interdependence between States but not itself to aspire to acquiring all their features. Equally, however, the assumption is that the problem-solving tasks conferred on the supranational institutions are defined in and legitimated by the Treaty mandate granted by the Member States. This requires a reliable application of the principle of conferral. Chapter 2 tracked the tensions associated with 'competence creep'.

The phrase 'institutional balance' conveys a need to keep each element working as envisaged by the Treaties. It is an enduring debate. Over time Treaty revision and institutional practice has led to the detail being modified. The Council's method of voting has moved steadily towards a wider embrace of qualified majority, with unanimity reserved for exceptional cases. The profile of the Parliament has risen. The European Council, which comprises the Heads of State or Government of the Member States, the President of the European Council, and the President of the Commission, has become more important over time as a site to develop general political directions and priorities. The institutional pattern has been decorated further by inclusion of independent agencies and most of all by the European Central Bank. But what has in the past been referred to as the Community method, and is today found in the EU's ordinary legislative procedure, focused on the Commission's (usually exclusive) right of legislative initiative and then the adoption of legislation by Council (acting by QMV) and Parliament, remains of central importance to much of the EU's law-making, and its essence would not be unfamiliar to those who designed the system in the 1950s.

3.3 THE *LIMITED* POWERS OF THE INSTITUTIONS OF THE EU

Title III of the TEU contains the *Provisions on the Institutions*. The EU's institutional framework 'shall aim to promote its values, advance its objectives, serve its interests, those of its citizens and those of the Member States, and ensure the consistency, effectiveness and continuity of its policies and actions'.[2] And the Union's institutions, listed in Article 13 TEU, are the European Parliament, the European Council, the Council, the Commission, the Court of Justice, the European Central Bank, and the Court of Auditors. There are also two advisory bodies, the Economic and Social Committee and the Committee of the Regions, whose profile is relatively low.[3]

Each institution shall act within the limits of the powers conferred on it by the Treaties, according to Article 13(2) TEU. This matter is different from, but connected to, the limited competence enjoyed by the Union generally according to Article 5 TEU. Article 13(2) relates to the requirement that each institution shall confine its action to that envisaged by the Treaties. The *Union* may be entitled to act in a particular sphere but each institution will possess only particular defined powers, stipulated by whichever Treaty provision serves as the base for the preparation and adoption of a particular legal act. There is, however, an important theme that connects Article 13(2) TEU and Article 5 TEU, which holds that in principle the Treaty mandate conferred by and ultimately controlled by the Member States is not unlimited and may not be altered from within the EU system.

An institution which trespasses beyond the limits of the powers conferred on it by the Treaties may face challenge before the Court. Most of the litigation in this vein has involved *either* States that have been outvoted on a particular proposal in Council trying to show that another legal base should have been used instead *or* institutions (Commission or

[2] Art 13 TEU. [3] Art 300 TFEU.

Parliament usually) trying to show that another legal base should have been used instead of the one chosen. In the former instance typical cases have arisen where a Member State has tried to persuade the Court that a legal base requiring unanimity in Council should be preferred over one allowing QMV, the incentive being retention of a veto in Council.[4] In the latter the incentive is typically preference for a legal base where the applicant institution's powers are stronger. So, for example, the Parliament has pursued litigation in the hope of showing that (what is now) Article 114 TFEU should have been in preference to what is now Article 352 TFEU because it is significantly more heavily involved where the former legal base is used.[5]

The Court is forced to decide these wrangles. This is part of its role in protecting the allocation of competences and powers made by the Treaty from re-allocation according to political preferences asserted by Member States acting within the EU system or by the EU's own institutions. It explicitly asserts the need to protect the 'principle of institutional balance',[6] which means that Member States acting through the Council do not enjoy the flexibility to adjust the procedures foreseen by the Treaty. Nor may concerns of administrative efficiency and rapid action change the allocation of competences and powers set by the Treaty.[7] It is not a matter of 'discretion'.[8] The Court's primary responsibility is to the Treaty, which ranks above passing majoritarian political preferences expressed *within* the Treaty system. After all, the Treaty was the subject of approval by the designated national constitutional processes in all the Member States, and should be changed only through the same processes. In this vein the Court has consistently stated that the choice of the legal basis for a measure cannot depend simply on an institution's conviction as to the objective pursued, but rather must be based on objective factors which are amenable to judicial review.[9] Choice of legal base has 'constitutional significance'.[10]

The Court has in the past often been forced to perform this protective role in circumstances where the Treaty is neither helpful nor precise

[4] Eg Case C-84/94 *UK* v *Council* [1996] ECR I-5755.

[5] Eg Case C-436/03 *Parliament* v *Council* [2006] ECR I-3733.

[6] Eg Case C-133/06 *Parliament* v *Council* [2008] ECR I-3189, para 57.

[7] Eg Opinion 1/08 on GATS [2009] ECR I-11129.

[8] Eg Case C-363/14 *Parliament* v *Council* judgment of 10 September 2015, para 43.

[9] Eg Case C-377/98 *Netherlands* v *Parliament and Council* [2001] ECR I-7079; Case C-338/01 *Commission* v *Council* [2004] ECR I-4829; Case C-94/03 *Commission* v *Council* [2006] ECR I-1.

[10] Eg Case C-370/07 *Commission* v *Council* [2009] ECR I-8917, para 47; Opinion 1/08 note 7, para 110.

in defining exactly what is required. To take a particularly awkward example, it was often hard to decide whether a measure setting common standards was properly treated as associated with the internal market or with the protection of the environment, not least because it typically pursued both aims—yet the choice mattered because of the differing applicable legislative procedures.[11] Happily, this is mostly old news: periodic Treaty revision has *reduced* the likelihood of such litigation by streamlining the EU's legislative procedures and eliminating some of the worst inconsistencies caused by mutually incompatible law-making procedures. Most law-making in the EU is today conducted according to the 'ordinary legislative procedure', as set out in elaborate form in Article 294 TFEU and involving a Commission proposal and adoption jointly by Council (by QMV) and Parliament. It is only on the rare occasions on which there is a possibility of choosing a legal base which demands a different procedure that inter-institutional problems are likely to arise. In such circumstances the Court has a long-standing test, based on examination of the aim and content of the measure, and where a measure pursues two aims it must be founded on the legal base required by the main aim. Where such a priority cannot be established a measure must be founded on more than one legal base, save only where procedures laid down for each legal basis are incompatible with each other. This is today gratifyingly uncommon. It will arise only in relation to niche areas where the Parliament's position is affected by choice of legal base,[12] or where the choice is between a 'mainstream' legal base attracting the ordinary legislative procedure and one from which a State is permitted an opt-out,[13] or where the choice between legal bases determines whether a Member State has room to apply stricter standards than the EU norm.[14] But given the widespread reliance on the ordinary legislative procedure as the norm in the EU, it will be unusual to encounter these problems of mutual incompatibility between legal bases.

A huge amount of relevant institutional detail is spelled out in provisions found both in the TEU and in the TFEU. Title I of Part Six TFEU contains *Institutional Provisions*. This is frankly heavy going. Roughly, however, one needs to come to grips with the general function of each institution, the way it reaches a decision, and the way it

[11] Eg Case C-300/89 *Commission* v *Council* [1991] ECR I-2867 ('Titanium Dioxide').

[12] Eg Case C-490/10 *Parliament* v *Council* judgment of 6 September 2012.

[13] Eg Case C-431/11 *UK* v *Council* judgment of 26 September 2013; Case C-656/11 *UK* v *Council* judgment of 27 February 2014. See further Chapter 5.4.

[14] Eg Case C-512/12 *Octapharma France* judgment of 13 March 2014.

interacts with other institutions. That is—at a general level—not so difficult to grasp. For the purposes of law-making within the Union, the interaction of the Commission, the Council, and the Parliament is central. The Council shares with the Parliament the exercise of legislative and budgetary functions.[15] The Council and the Parliament—normally acting under the 'ordinary legislative procedure'—are the places where legislation is made or rejected. The Commission (contrary to popular myth) does *not* make law. Its function is to prepare and propose legislative initiatives and then, should those proposals be accepted by the Council and the Parliament—the EU's true legislative institutions—the Commission is also responsible for making sure that rules, once agreed, are followed. As already insisted, but sufficiently important to bear repetition, this institutional pattern is not readily comparable to anything that one would find *within* a State. This is entirely unsurprising given the key thematic point that the EU is *not* a State but rather an organization within and through which States seek to manage their interdependence.

3.4 THE EU'S PRINCIPAL INSTITUTIONS

A more detailed account of each EU institution is now required before returning to assess just what is intended by this architecture, and to reflect on what it reveals about power and accountability and most of all democracy in a transnational setting. This follows at Section 3.10, but even that is incomplete. Precisely because the EU does not replace its Member States but rather seeks to manage their interdependence, no serious understanding of how the EU operates can exclude national bodies—courts, especially but not only constitutional courts, and national Parliaments, as well as public authorities charged with the responsibility to apply EU rules more generally. These bodies have formal and hidden means to exert influence on EU law and policy-making. A proper appreciation of the functioning of the EU must break down the artificial divide between 'Brussels' and national practice, not least to use such transparency as a means to deter national politicians for blaming the EU for activities they have in fact supported and/or claiming credit for achievements impossible without resort to the EU. But, as this chapter's opening sentence confessed, it is the EU's institutional density that makes this a tough challenge.

[15] Arts 14(1), 16(1) TEU.

3.4.1 The Council

The Council consists of a representative of each Member State. It is specified that this must be someone 'at ministerial level', able to commit his or her government and to cast its vote.[16] The minister will be the minister responsible for whatever the subject matter under discussion at that particular Council happens to be. Two particular configurations are mentioned explicitly in the Treaty, the General Affairs Council and the Foreign Affairs Council, while for other configurations the Council is to be drawn up by act of the European Council according to Article 236 TFEU.[17] So there is an Economic and Financial Affairs Council (Ecofin), an Agriculture and Fisheries Council, and so on. The Council enjoys democratic legitimacy in the sense that it is composed of individuals who are part of the elected government of a particular Member State, but that legitimacy is sourced from national level. It is an *EU* institution, but it claims no democratic credentials earned *directly* at the European level.

Articles 237–243 TFEU provide more detail, but the key is that the Council, composed of State representatives, is the institution in which State interests are accommodated. It seems to be, and to some extent it is, a familiar type of international institution, of an intergovernmental character.

However, the Council's place as the focal point of State representation in the EU is qualified by three particular features. First, in many areas of EU activity Council decisions are taken not by unanimity but by the species of majority voting known as 'qualified majority'. So the Council is the home of State interests—but in most instances not home to a State veto. Second, the Council has, in consequence of periodic Treaty revision, increasingly come to share its dominance in matters of legislative decision with the Parliament to the point where today, for most purposes, the two institutions work in tandem under the 'ordinary legislative procedure', which is considered more fully in Section 3.7. This is the key to understanding how the Council, though at one level a perfectly orthodox intergovernmental creature, is in fact embedded in a distinctively EU institutional environment. Periodic Treaty revision has increased the scope of qualified majority decision-making in Council while also increasing the involvement of the Parliament, so that the intergovernmental heartbeat of the Council is greatly modified by the desire to enhance effective decision-making (and so the surrender of the national veto) and the rise of

[16] Art 16(2) TEU. [17] Art 16(6) TEU.

a transnational assertion of democracy (manifest in greater power for the Parliament).

The third necessary modification to the depiction of the Council as the focal point of State representation is, as already mentioned in Section 3.2, to admit the partial validity of the allegation that the Council is the site for expression of the interests not of 'States', but of State *executives*. The decline of truly effective Parliaments is endemic at *national* level across Europe: governing parties with an adequate majority do not need to persuade their opponents of the worth of their policies. Executives dominate. Weight of workload, poor resourcing, plus the forbidding intransparency of the EU system make it all the more probable that national Parliaments will have little practical opportunity to restrain executives from exploiting the Council to advance their policies, even in order to circumvent blockages that are stubborn in a purely national context. QMV helps: it provides a perfect cover. So for example a minister may claim to oppose an EU initiative yet explain support for it in Council on the basis that a qualified majority was already in place and so opposition would have been a waste of political capital.

The reforms made by the Treaty of Lisbon which, with effect from 2009, allocate national Parliaments an explicit role in monitoring the application of the principle of subsidiarity (Chapter 2.12) are a partial reflection of the perceived need to provide for a sturdier defence of national political processes than is secured through the Council as an institution. National Parliaments are usefully granted this voice in the EU law-making process, but their best contribution to sustaining a healthy institutional and constitutional balance in the EU would be to devise means to assert a more attentive supervision of the conduct of their representatives in Council.

3.4.2 The European Parliament

Article 14 TEU, amplified by Articles 223–234 TFEU, deals with the Parliament. Members of the Parliament are directly elected by Union citizens for a five-year term. Their total number shall not exceed 751 according to Article 14(2) TEU, which also provides that representation shall be 'degressively proportional', which means that although smaller Member States have fewer MEPs than larger Member States, their citizens are in fact better represented per head. Germany has sixteen times as many MEPs as Malta—96 to 6—but Germany's population is fully 160 times larger than Malta's. Elections are organized nationally, and models of voting and representation vary according to national preference among several forms of proportional representation. Even the day on which the vote is held varies, so the elections span four days, Thursday to Sunday, every five years. A common rule, however, is that a national of one Member State who is resident in another Member State is entitled to vote and stand as a candidate in European elections under the same conditions as locals: this applies by virtue of the rules on Citizenship of the Union.[18] The same parties that are familiar on the national political scene are those which contest the European elections. There are no genuine transnational political parties. But in the Parliament itself the parties do not sit in national blocs. The groupings, if not individual parties, are transnational, loosely arranged according to political families that would be familiar in a national political setting. The largest grouping has usually been based on the centre left, though more recently the centre right has held sway. Fractious groupings on the far left and the far right are more common than in most national Parliaments, though still peripheral.

The Parliament has been the winner at times of Treaty revision. Its power and influence has grown far beyond its original designation as an essentially advisory Assembly. The Parliament's extensive right of co-decision (with the Council) under the ordinary legislative procedure which today dominates EU law-making elevates it high on any list of Europe's most influential law-makers. This suggests that the Member States have felt it necessary to accompany the extension of competences and the rise of 'qualified majority voting' in Council, the other themes that animate periodic Treaty revision, with an added dose of representative democracy of the direct kind, as a supplement to the Council's indirect claim to representative status. However, no clear articulation of such a political vision underpinning the role of the Parliament has ever been adopted.

The level of turnout at elections for the European Parliament has steadily drooped, and in most countries falls far below turnout at elections for national governments. This seems paradoxical. The more powerful the European Parliament as an institution has become, the less interested the voters. There are doubtless a mixture of reasons for this trend, among them a general dissatisfaction with the political process in Europe which is not unique to the EU. But clearly a factor is the sense of remoteness. In the absence of any true pan-European political debate, reflected and accentuated by the absence of a true European media and European political parties, it is no surprise that citizens tend to know little and care less about their directly elected representatives in the European Parliament. There is

[18] Art 20 TFEU: Chapter 7.

no European 'public space'; in the absence of any broad feeling of being part of a 'European people' there is no European *demos*. Many *national* political cultures in Europe are fragmented and contested too, but all have identifiably stronger common bonds than those which exist hesitantly at European level.

This challenges the vitality and legitimacy of the European Parliament. To strengthen the Parliament is plainly to deepen democracy, in so far as one accepts the Parliament as an authentic voice of the peoples of Europe who directly elect its members. If, by contrast, one refuses to accept that an institution with legislative power at the European level which represents people, not States, can be legitimate in the absence of a true European *demos* then equipping the Parliament with extra powers does not address the supposed 'democratic deficit'; in fact, it deepens it. The droop in turnout serves as a tentative empirical support for the latter. So any assessment of the adequacy of the representative character and chains of accountability in the EU's institutional architecture depends on a priori assessments of one's toleration of the legitimacy of siting institutions beyond the State. If there is a way out of this bind, it must lie in recognition that any satisfying understanding of the proper place of the Parliament must, like any satisfying understanding of the EU more generally, treat it as part of the full picture of governance in Europe which insists on the mutually supportive relationship between national and EU institutions. The point is to move beyond choosing either State or EU, but rather to find a role for both—and that applies equally to European Parliament and to national Parliaments. They should not compete. They should do different things and reinforce each other.

3.4.3 The Commission

The Commission's job is to 'promote the general interest of the Union and take appropriate initiatives to that end'.[19] Greater detail is found in Articles 244–250 TFEU. The Commission is not a law-maker.[20] That is the province of the Council and the Parliament. The Commission's role predates and post-dates the legislative moment.

The Commission is responsible for proposing and preparing legislative initiatives. Moreover, with the exception of activity relating to the Area of Freedom, Security, and Justice (AFSJ),[21] it is *only* the Commission which may generate a proposal apt to lead to Union law-making.[22] Although the Parliament may request the Commission to submit a proposal, the

[19] Art 17 TEU.

[20] There are two tiny anomalies: Arts 45(3)(d), 106(3) TFEU.

[21] See Arts 67–89 TFEU: Chapter 5.

[22] Art 17(2) TEU.

Commission is not obliged to comply, though it must give reasons for inaction.[23] Naturally the Commission is not impervious to the political mood: it would waste energy by advancing proposals in which there is no interest among the Member States and/or Parliament and equally it will be minded to think seriously about initiatives that seem likely to encounter a receptive audience. In this vein the agenda-setting ambitions of the European Council are especially salient, especially in high-profile areas such as the management of the Eurozone, which is examined at Section 3.9.2. The Parliament's 'power grab' in the matter of choice of the Commission President in 2014, considered in this section, is doubtless one manifestation of that institution's growing desire to exert influence on legislative trajectory. And of course the Commission is intensively lobbied, not only by political actors but also by industry and civil society. But the formal position remains clear within most areas covered by the TFEU: if the Commission will not start the ball rolling no other foot is allowed to kick it.

The driving assumption is that the Commission's exclusive right of legislative initiative is essential in order to promote proposals that are in the common interest rather than driven by partisan interests, and that a body subject to dictation by Member States and/or other EU political institutions would be deprived of the necessary independence and authority. Once the Commission has chosen to exercise its right of initiative it then rests with the Council and Parliament to decide whether or not to adopt binding rules—though hideously complicated rules and practices govern the to and fro of possible amendment of a proposal once launched by the Commission.

The Council may delegate to the Commission power to implement technical adaptations to existing EU legislation (Article 290 TFEU). This is *not* an exception to the rule that the Commission does not make laws, because the root of the power lies in the Council's delegating act. In practice this power to act, which enables relatively quick law reform at the level of detail, is rather commonly used, if politically very low-profile. Article 291 TFEU creates a distinct though connected procedure for conferring implementing powers on the Commission. These two provisions are successors to the 'comitology' procedure, which involved the delegation of implementing powers to the Commission supervised by committees composed of national officials. Detailed examination of this fearfully complex and constitutionally murky process of negotiation lies beyond

[23] Art 225 TFEU.

the scope of this book,[24] but these arrangements form part of the overall thematic narrative of seeking to confer problem-solving capacity on EU institutions while also asserting Member State control.

The Commission also possesses important powers of supervision over rules once adopted. It can bring Member States before the Court in the event that it considers they are in breach of EU law obligations, whether sourced in the Treaty or in secondary legislation. This is the so-called infringement procedure found in Article 258 TFEU. It can even seek the imposition of financial penalties on egregious defaulters, although, as detailed in Article 260 TFEU, it falls to the Court to decide whether or not this is justified. The Commission also has important powers to secure the observance of the competition rules by private undertakings, including the possibility of imposing sometime large fines on defaulters, and it polices the rules controlling the grant of aid to undertakings by public authorities too.

The Commission has a five-year term of office and members must have an independence which is 'beyond doubt'. Instruction from governments is ruled out.[25] Article 245 TFEU stipulates that members of the Commission 'shall refrain from any action incompatible with their duties' and that they shall undertake no other occupation during their term of office. According to the same provision Member States 'shall respect their independence and shall not seek to influence them in the performance of their tasks'. The logic of the Commission as an institution is that it is the honest broker. Allocating an exclusive right of initiative to the Commission, thereby denying it to the Member States and the European Parliament, is intended to smooth the process of law-making by ensuring that whatever proposal is put on the table is not immediately suspected to be no more than promotion of particular national interests or a plan skewed by party political gain. Equally, the impartial supervisory role of the Commission is designed to ensure a breach of EU law is tackled without bias dictated by the nationality or political clout of the offender. The administration of policy is placed above electoral considerations. Similarly competition law requires impartial judgment which is removed from national politicking, and given that the grant of aid to industries is so politically tempting, there is obvious appeal in shifting responsibility out of national hands and into that of an independent European agency. And so under the Treaty the Commission has the last word on whether aid planned by national

[24] See A. Türk, 'Comitology', Ch 13 in A. Arnull and D. Chalmers (eds), *The Oxford Handbook of European Union Law* (OUP, 2015).

[25] Art 17(3) TEU.

authorities is compatible with the internal market.[26] *All* the Member States are subject to this control: *all* the Member States are in this way protected from the itch to subsidize clever entrepreneurs playing off one jurisdiction against another.

As explained in Chapter 1, the EU can be understood as in part based on the desire of Member States to tie their own hands into the future, thereby to ensure on a reciprocal and mutually reinforcing basis that they avoid harming each other and instead work together to achieve peace and prosperity. Tying hands and keeping them tied has an unavoidable institutional dimension, and the place of the Commission, to which is granted a relatively high degree of autonomy from Member State control, is best understood from this perspective. The very existence and character of the Commission as an institution stands as an expression of the stubborn unfeasibility of a workable EU system that is rooted in pure intergovernmentalism.

The most prominent faces of the institution are the twenty-eight Commissioners (the 'College'), but the Commission also comprises some 30,000 permanent officials based in Brussels, spread across the several Directorates-General that deal with particular policy sectors. Given the sweep of its responsibilities this seems a rather small number: by comparison, Hampshire County Council in the South of England has some 40,000 employees to support a population not a great deal larger than one million. The reason lies in the fact that EU practice generally, and that of the Commission in particular, is heavy on rule-making but very light on practical implementation of agreed policy, since most of EU law is absorbed and applied at national level. Hampshire County Council employs people who clean its streets and who fine people who drop litter on them, whereas the Commission, while involved in rule-making, is not engaged in day-to-day application of the rules it initiates, except in the field of competition law.

At the apex of the Commission is its *President*, whose responsibilities are set out in Article 17(6) TEU. Some Presidents have been more high-profile than others. Jacques Delors, a wily Frenchman, was perhaps the most energetic, and the acceptance of the programme to complete the internal market, captured in the 1985 White Paper (Chapter 6), offered important proof of his political cunning, for that project—presented as motivated by economic reform—was in truth (also) nothing less than a plan of action to rescue the EU from the torpor into which it had slipped by

[26] Arts 107–109 TFEU.

the early 1980s. This is a classic case study in the Commission's potential as the engine of European integration. Other Presidents have been less rambunctious, and some have been downright disastrous.[27] The Portuguese Manuel Barroso, generally rated as careful and competent, was President of the Commission from 2004 to 2014, when he was replaced by Jean-Claude Juncker, a former Prime Minister of Luxembourg and a veteran of EU political activity.

The *High Representative*, appointed by the European Council and charged with the conduct of the Union's common foreign and security policy,[28] is also a member of the Commission. The post of High Representative was created by the Treaty of Lisbon to provide a sharper focus and a clearer identity for the Union's external face. The mandate comes from the Council. The High Representative presides over the Foreign Affairs Council. But he or she shall be a member of the Commission. The post risks creating confusion by bringing together the intergovernmental and the supranational elements of the Union. The Briton Catherine Ashton became the first High Representative in 2009, and was replaced in 2014 by the Italian Federica Moherini.

All the other Commissioners share out portfolios, some of which are high-profile and prized, such as competition and the internal market, while others are more humdrum and sometimes accepted only grumpily. There has always been one Commissioner per Member State but the Lisbon Treaty put in place arrangements to reduce this number.[29] The chief reason was that there are not really enough attractively meaty jobs to go round. However, as part of the package agreed in 2009 to sweeten Irish voters ahead of the second Irish referendum on ratification of the Treaty of Lisbon, it was agreed to abandon this plan and stick to one Commissioner per Member State. Conveniently the relevant provision, Article 17(5) TEU, allows the European Council to alter the number by unanimous vote, and to woo the Irish a commitment was made, and duly fulfilled, to make the switch back to one Commissioner per Member State. It seems that even though Commissioners are supposed to be independent of partisan national concerns there is still a sense of legitimacy instilled at national level by having 'our' Commissioner. And in fact there is no serious pretence that Commissioners are *unfailingly* independent of national pressures. Blatant bias is very rare, but research reveals a degree of

[27] D. Dinan, 'Famous Non-Performers: Franco Malfatti, Gaston Thorn and Jacques Santer', Ch 17 in E. Jones, A. Menon, and S. Weatherill (eds), *The Oxford Handbook of the European Union* (OUP, 2012).

[28] Arts 18, 27 TEU.

[29] Art 17(5) TEU, Art 244 TFEU.

connection between a Commissioner's national affiliation and his or her behaviour.[30] Some are worse than others, but defence of some national interests is periodically part of the job, especially and perfectly rationally in the case of Commissioners with future ambitions to return from Brussels to participate in national political life.

The Commission's President is elected by the Parliament on a proposal by the European Council acting by qualified majority.[31] So the Parliament chooses—but on a 'take it or leave it' basis. The President, the High Representative, and the other members of the Commission are subject 'as a body' to a vote of consent by the Parliament, which then leads to appointment of the Commission by the European *Council*—not the Parliament.[32] The Parliament has, however, been astute to exploit its formal powers to stretch its influence: its dissatisfaction with individual nominated Commissioners has on occasion led to their withdrawal under the threat of withholding approval of the whole package, which is the only formal power granted to the Parliament. Then, according to Article 17(8) TEU and amplified in Article 234 TFEU, the Commission, once in place, is responsible 'as a body' to the Parliament, and the Parliament can force the resignation of the Commission 'as a body'. But the Parliament cannot vote to remove an individual Commissioner (though the Commission President can[33]).

This is all rather delicate and reveals much about the peculiar—and densely opaque—institutional character of the EU. Accountability and external control of the Commission are attenuated, but deliberately so. The Commission is intended to be independent and calls for greater 'accountability' risk compromising that essential prerequisite for fearless discharge of its impartial role in holding the line on the commitments undertaken in the Treaty. This is not to say that no attention needs to be paid to ensure that the Commission really does stick to that impartial role. It is, however, to warn that the claim that because the Parliament is directly elected and the Commission is not then the former's preferences should prevail is not at all respectful of the 'institutional balance' intended by the Treaty. Appeal for 'more democracy' has a different resonance in a State than it does in an organization like the EU, established to manage the interdependence of States which are themselves already democratic but in some respects unable fully to meet their citizens' expectations because of the reality of dense mutual interdependence.

[30] R. Thomson, 'National Actors in International Organizations: The Case of the European Commission' (2008) 41 Comparative Political Studies 169.

[31] Arts 14(1), 17(7) TEU. [32] Art 17(7) TEU. [33] Art 17(6) TEU.

These tensions were stretched intriguingly taut in 2014. Within the Parliament individual 'candidates' for the Commission Presidency were identified as associated with each political grouping. The Parliament claimed that the candidate of the grouping which secured the highest number of seats in the European elections held in May 2014 should then become, as the successful *Spitzenkandidat*, the President of the Commission. This was devoid of constitutional basis, for Article 17(7) TEU does no more than direct the European Council to take into account the European elections. It was in truth an attempt to provide political momentum that would in practice force the proper nominating body, the European Council, to acquiesce in the preferred choice of the Parliament. Indeed, the Parliament argued that this was nothing less than the expression of the will of the peoples of the EU. This was fanciful. Turnout at the elections averaged under 43 per cent across the twenty-eight Member States and dipped below 40 per cent in thirteen of them.[34] Even in the States where campaigning made an attempt to make explicit this link between the European elections and consequences for choice of Commission President, it would have been devilishly difficult to find more than a tiny pool of voters who had even an inkling of this supposed chain of legitimacy. In some States no such link was even aired.

This was more than an instance of the Parliament seeking to use its formal powers to lever extra influence in practice. More seriously, this was an overt attempt by the Parliament to assert its own *democratic* credentials at the expense of the claims of the European Council mapped out in the Treaty, and it was without a doubt a challenge to the foreseen institutional balance. Thematically, effectiveness competes with control: here the Parliament was attempting to assert control, and it was treating the Commission as the holder of a degree of political power over which it, the Parliament, wished and hoped to assert a form of accountability. In line with a thematic claim of this book, this may not simply be misconceived in the unique institutional environment of the EU; it may indeed be counter-productive in so far as it falsely seeks to align the workings of the EU with those that one would expect to find within a State. The risk is that this induces deeper alienation from the EU's pretensions rather than generating any sense of attraction or allegiance.

In the event in 2014 there was a clear reluctance in principle on the part of some Member States to agree to the installation of a candidate of the biggest grouping in the Parliament for fear that too much would have

[34] http://www.results-elections2014.eu/en/turnout.html.

been ceded in practice to the Parliament's agitations. But ultimately there was no sufficient desire to resist and that candidate, Jean-Claude Juncker, *was* selected.

Article 230 TFEU requires the Commission to reply to questions put to it by the Parliament, but the nature of this procedure, and any sanctions, is left wholly undeveloped. Similarly, Article 233 TFEU provides that the Parliament shall discuss in open session the annual general report submitted to it by the Commission, but no detail or direction is added. It is likely that this will evolve. The Parliament will doubtless wish to assert its democratic credentials in seeking to hold the Commission to account but, as suggested previously in this section, the logic of this claim is far from unimpeachable. The Commission's claim to an immunity from detailed accountability, and instead fidelity to the task mapped by the Member States in the Treaties, is based squarely on its intended place within the EU's unique design. The arrangements do not mirror those found in a State, precisely because the EU is *not* a State but rather an arena in which the interdependent interests of States are managed.

3.4.4 The European Council

The European Council 'shall provide the Union with the necessary impetus for its development and shall define the general political directions and priorities thereof'.[35] Further detail is provided in Articles 235–236 TFEU. The European Council consists of the Heads of State or Government of the Member States plus the three most prominent 'faces' of the Union, its President, the Commission President, and the High Representative (although the latter is only to 'take part' in the European Council's work, according to Article 15, and so is not a full formal member). The European Council does not exercise legislative functions: this is made explicit by Article 15(1) TEU. At one level its role is marginal to the detailed business of law- and policy making. On another it is vitally important to tone, trends, and style—especially in the external sphere, where Article 22 TEU provides for it to 'identify the strategic interests and objectives of the Union'. And, as discussed further in Section 3.9.2, the European Council has acquired a very powerful position in handling the troubles of the Eurozone. The European Council is also the site for resolving disputes after the pushing of the 'emergency brake', an important control device where particularly sensitive issues arise,[36] and it is granted defined powers to take 'big picture' binding decisions about, for example, the composition

[35] Art 15 TEU.

[36] See Arts 82(3), 83(3), 86(1), 87(3) TFEU on Judicial Co-operation in Criminal Matters.

of Parliament,[37] the number of Commissioners,[38] and appointment of the Commission[39] and the High Representative.[40] It is also central to the—hitherto unused—procedures aimed at a Member State guilty of serious and persistent violation of the Union's core values.[41]

It is frequently a scene of shameless and shameful grandstanding, featuring the destructive political reflex to acclaim national success alongside the implication, and sometimes even the explicit and gleeful claim, that others have been defeated. The EU is based on a logic that the sum is greater than its parts—it should (often) be win/win, not a zero-sum game. Rarely is nuance or grace on show after meetings of the European Council.

The rising profile of the European Council challenges the 'institutional balance' which has long been found at the heart of the orthodox understanding of the relationship between the trio of Commission, Council, and Parliament.[42] Its emergence in the 1970s represented a push to intergovernmentalism and in particular to more assertive control exercised by the bigger Member States. However, although the European Council has to some extent subverted the Commission's agenda-setting role, much of what it does is associated with the grander matters of 'high politics' which have in recent years become more openly part of the scope of co-operation pursued through the EU and for which the Commission has never had a remit. A great deal of detailed activity within the EU escapes the European Council's gaze completely. There is a 'sub-European Council' hum which is powerful and enduring, and which corresponds to a more supranational dynamic.

The President of the European Council serves a term lasting two and a half years, renewable once. This post was an innovation of the Lisbon Treaty, and he or she shall not hold a national office, whereas pre-Lisbon the President was the head of State or Government of whichever State held the Presidency on its six-monthly rotation among the Member States. The President is elected by the European Council itself. Some detail is supplied in Article 15 TEU but the general idea is to improve continuity and achieve a higher profile by the appointment of a more permanent President. The role is, however, open to shaping over time. It could be treated as essentially managerial, and that model suggests it would be better styled as Chair of the European Council rather than President, or

[37] Art 14(2) TEU. [38] Arts 17(5) TEU and 244 TFEU.

[39] Art 17(7) TEU. [40] Art 18(1) TEU. [41] Art 7 TEU.

[42] Eg U. Puetter, *The European Council and the Council: New Intergovernmentalism and Institutional Change* (OUP, 2014).

it could be much more high-profile, although the risk of that model is that the President might be seen to claim an eminence in circumstances in which he or she would lack the democratic credentials that should attach to such a status. It might moreover cause friction with other aspirants to that role, the High Representative, the Commission President, and, still more awkward, with major national leaders too. And, retaining the pre-Lisbon pattern, there is still a Presidency of the Council existing separately from the office of President,[43] which (other than for the Foreign Affairs Council) continues to rotate between the Member States every six months. Some holders of that position will doubtless feel no qualms about competing for the limelight with the 'true' President and they will, of course, have a rather better democratic mandate, albeit a national one. In fact the President of the Commission, by virtue of an admittedly attenuated claim of legitimacy as a result of appointment by the Parliament, arguably enjoys a better, if contestable, claim than the President of the European Council to democratic accountability. In sum, there is considerable institutional complexity. Who speaks for the EU? Quite a lot of people, and not always with the same voice.

The choice in 2009 of Herman Van Rompuy, a thoughtful but far from flamboyant Belgian, was an expression of a preference for a relatively low-profile politician. Donald Tusk, the Pole who succeeded Van Rompuy in 2014, may emerge as more combative. Political moods and needs change. And choices are not made in isolation. The horse-trading in late 2009 that eventually threw up Manuel Barroso as the (reappointed) President of the Commission, Herman Van Rompuy as the first President of the European Council, and Catherine Ashton as the first High Representative was marked by concerns about balancing the appointments between small and large States, southern and northern States, and the political 'family' with which the individual was associated. The demonstrated expertise and experience of the candidates appeared to be of worryingly slim significance. In fact, Van Rompuy and Ashton, the former a head of government in Belgium for scarcely a year and the latter a Commissioner for a similarly short period, seemed to benefit from being relatively unknown and therefore without enemies, in contrast to other more high-profile contenders. A similar pattern of horse-trading dominated the selections made in 2014, spiced by the additional pressures injected by the Parliament in a (successful) attempt to secure its preferred candidate as President of the Commission. The importance of gender balance—or at

[43] Art 16(9) TEU.

least not too severe gender imbalance—was also more overtly discussed. In the event Jean-Claude Juncker replaced Manuel Barroso as President of the Commission; Donald Tusk, a Polish politician, took over from Van Rompuy as the President of the European Council; and the Italian politician Federica Moherini, relatively inexperienced, succeeded Catherine Ashton as the High Representative.

3.4.5 National Parliaments

Before the entry into force of the Treaty of Lisbon in 2009 the assumption was that national Parliaments played no direct role in the functioning of the EU system. They were left wholly unmentioned in the Treaties. Their role was indirect: in holding to account those ministers who participated in decision-making in the Council. The problem was that national Parliaments could often find it difficult to track what was happening or likely to happen in Council—in remote 'Brussels'. Moreover, national executives eager to exploit the EU level of governance in order to circumvent the orthodox controls of national political cultures would have no incentive to channel information to national Parliamentarians—quite the reverse. And even a national Parliament that keeps its representatives on a short leash—as the Danish *Folketing* is particularly noted for doing—may find its supervision worthless where QMV in Council subverts the reservations of a small number of Member States.

The Treaty of Lisbon made important changes with effect from 2009. Article 12 TEU draws national Parliaments explicitly into an active contribution to 'the good functioning of the Union' by six named routes: receipt of information, including draft Union legislative acts, in accordance with the Protocol; application of the subsidiarity principle in accordance with the Protocol; participation in defined evaluation and monitoring procedures under the TFEU provisions governing the AFSJ; participation in the procedure for Treaty revision; receipt of notification of accession applications; participation in co-operation between national Parliaments and the European Parliament, as foreseen by the Protocol.

How much this will really change *in practice* is open for debate. The everyday obstacles to the active engagement of national Parliaments in EU law- and policy-making—want of time, resources, energy—remain very real. However, as a minimum this agenda points to the thematic concern of the revisions achieved by the Treaty of Lisbon to raise the profile of *national*-level political processes and controls in the development of the EU. This is designed to enrich the debate about the proper allocation of responsibility between national and EU planes of law- and policy-making. A successful transformation of this type will be achieved only if national Parliaments are able not only to exploit the opportunities for influence listed in Article 12 TEU but also to hold their representatives in Council to account with more vigour than has been the norm in past practice. Patterns will doubtless vary greatly across the twenty-eight Member States.

3.4.6 The Court

The political institutions of the EU are interdependent in complicated ways, but the judicial institution stands alone. It used to be known as the European Court of Justice (ECJ) but its post-Lisbon name is the Court of Justice of the European Union (CJEU). Its home is Luxembourg.

In any legal system the more clear and unambiguous the rules, the less significant is the possibility of a creative role allocated to the institutions that apply them. In any legal system the easier it is to change the rules, the less depends on interpretation of them given from time to time. In the EU the Treaty rules are far from clear and unambiguous and are very difficult to change. The consequence is that the Court of Justice enjoys a remarkably powerful position. The balance between judicial and political power which is a necessary point of inquiry in any constitutional system is unusually heavily tipped in favour of the former in the EU. The Treaties, which establish an incomplete contract which is not lightly subjected to amendment because of the need for unanimously approved Treaty revision, delegate much power to the Court. Even EU secondary legislation, though easier to alter through political processes than the Treaties themselves, is *relatively* more difficult to change than typical legislation found at national level, so here too the Court enjoys a high level of autonomy from correction when it makes its interpretative choices. There are viable analogies between the Commission and the Court—both have been established according to a design which grants them a mandate to perform defined tasks while sheltering them from direct accountability for particular decisions taken—but the Court is a legal, not a political, institution. Quite what the key distinction between (permitted) interpretation of legislative texts and their (forbidden) amendment entails, and how the autonomy granted to the Court invites its erosion, is a vital topic of inquiry in any inspection of the role of the Court in the shaping of EU law. And it permeates this book, as it does any account of the EU's legal order.

Article 19(1) TEU provides that the Court of Justice of the Union shall include the Court of Justice, the General Court, and specialized courts. The Court of Justice stands at the constitutional apex of the system; the General Court (formerly known as the Court of First Instance) deals primarily with cases involving competition law and relatively detailed matters of judicial review of EU acts; the 'specialized courts' number just one (so far), the Civil Service Tribunal which deals with EU staff cases.

Article 19(1) TEU directs that the Court 'shall ensure that in the interpretation and application of the Treaties the law is observed'. Article 19(1) TEU adds that 'Member States shall provide remedies sufficient to ensure effective legal protection in the fields covered by Union law', an innovation of the Treaty of Lisbon, the impact of which is not readily understood unless one already knows of the Court's rich and full case law from which this direction is drawn. This is examined in Chapter 4.5.

Article 19(2) TEU covers the judges and the Advocates General of the Court. It is a feature of the practice of the Court of Justice that an Advocate General, having heard the case in precisely the same way as the judges, delivers an Opinion on which the Court may choose to draw in shaping its own ultimate and authoritative judgment. Opinions of Advocates General are commonly, but certainly not always, followed by the Court and tend to be written in a more discursive fashion than Court judgments, which tend to be relatively compressed and sometimes calculatedly opaque because they are required to be delivered as a single collegiate judgment. There are no dissenting judgments in Luxembourg, and some rulings of the Court hint at the strain involved in finding a sufficient level of agreement on a contested point of law. There is no formal system of precedent in EU law, but considerations of legal certainty lead the Court typically to situate its rulings in the context of previous case law, which it regularly cites—but the more ambiguous or terse a ruling, the more malleable it is in future development of the law. More is said of this technique in Chapter 4.2.

Article 19(3) TEU declares that the Court shall, in accordance with the Treaties, rule on actions brought by a Member State, an institution, or a natural or legal person; give preliminary rulings on the interpretation of Union law or the validity of acts adopted by the institutions; and (a rather unhelpfully vague appendix) 'rule in other cases provided for in the Treaties'. This brief list will make little sense to anyone unfamiliar with the Court's role place and it is to the TFEU that one must turn to grasp what is really at stake.

Articles 251–281 TFEU provide extensive detail on procedure and jurisdiction. Article 263 TFEU provides an action to annul EU acts. This is the most important of the direct actions before the Court. Article 265 TFEU provides a complementary action aimed at controlling failure to act. Article 277 TFEU allows a measure to be challenged indirectly in an action brought against another measure. Articles 268 and 340 TFEU allow claims to be brought against the EU institutions for compensation for loss suffered as a result of unlawful action.

Access to the Court is not unlimited. In particular, although the Member States and the three principal political institutions of the EU are treated as privileged applicants that enjoy an unfettered right to bring an action for annulment of an EU legal act before the Court pursuant to Article 263, natural or legal persons are entitled to bring such an action only in the circumstances defined by the fourth paragraph of Article 263. This confines such actions (by private parties or so-called non-privileged applicants) to acts of which the applicant is the addressee, acts of direct and individual concern to that person, and the regulatory act which is of direct concern to the person and which does not entail implementing measures.

The underlying point is that if a private or non-privileged applicant is *not* able to fit him- or herself within one of these categories then he or she does not have standing to seek the act's annulment before the Court in Luxembourg. But the limited availability of the *direct* action for annulment envisaged by Article 263 does not exhaust the individual's legal protection. He or she may instead be able to rely on proceedings before a *national* court coupled to use of the Article 267 preliminary reference procedure as a basis for inviting the Court of Justice to rule on the validity of a challenged EU measure. Provided a national cause of action can be established, it may be possible to claim before a national tribunal that a relevant EU act on which implementing measures adopted by a national body are based is unlawful. This is the significance of the reference to a regulatory act 'which does not entail implementing measures' in Article 263(4): where there *are* implementing measures, the route before national courts is open to provide judicial protection by means of an attack on those implementing measures plus, if necessary, an Article 267 preliminary reference, but absent need for implementing measures, then the direct action before the Court in Luxembourg foreseen by Article 263(4) is available after all. But even this concession, an innovation of the Treaty of Lisbon consequent on contested earlier rulings,[44] leaves open a gap in judicial protection. The 'regulatory act' has been interpreted by the Court to exclude legislative acts.[45] In consequence, as the Court has expressly acknowledged,[46] the existence of a complete system of remedies on which the Court proudly insists does *not* entail

[44] For an account see A. Arnull, 'Judicial Review in the European Union', Ch 15 in A. Arnull and D. Chalmers (eds), *The Oxford Handbook of European Union Law* (OUP, 2015).

[45] Case C-583/11P *Inuit* et al v *Commission* judgment of 3 October 2013.

[46] Ibid, paras 105–106.

that an individual may insist on a right to judicial review of a legislative act. The Court resisted the claim that Article 47 of the Charter mandates such an outcome. In the background is the assumption that the political process deserves a degree of immunity from an individual's complaint pursued before the courts. It is after all not normal at State level for private parties to enjoy an unfettered right to bring direct challenges against legislation before a court. A precise analogy between the EU and State practice in matters of judicial review would not be appropriate, for the EU legislative process is by design different from that found at State level, but there is a shared assumption that *some* matters are best left primarily to the political process, which is typically achieved by a mix of restrictive rules on standing and, even where those rules are satisfied, a light standard of judicial review.

Article 275 TFEU largely excludes the Court's jurisdiction in the area of Common Foreign and Security Policy (CFSP) under the TEU, while Article 276 TFEU places a smaller limitation on jurisdiction pertaining to law and order and internal security under Title V of Part Three TFEU (the AFSJ). These limitations, which have counterparts of sorts within national systems, are vestigial traces of the old and ungainly 'three-pillar' system of the EU which was abolished with effect from 2009 on the entry into force of the Treaty of Lisbon. These persisting limitations aside, the Court's jurisdiction was expanded by the Treaty of Lisbon through the collapse of the third pillar into Title V of Part Three TFEU and the grant of binding force to the Charter of Fundamental Rights.

A central part of the Court's job is plainly to decide on the lawfulness of measures adopted by the political institutions. It polices infractions of the principle of conferral: a measure that goes beyond the competence of the EU should be declared invalid. So too it checks that the EU legislative process is conducted in compliance with respect for fundamental rights and conformity with other principles such as legal certainty, equality, subsidiarity, and proportionality. It checks the validity of action taken by the EU's political institutions against the standards required by the Treaties, in a manner that is readily compared with its national judicial counterparts charged with the defence of national Constitutions. If the Treaties function in some respects like a Constitution for the EU, then the Court of Justice functions in some respects like a Constitutional Court for the EU. But its impact on the political institutions is capable of being considerably more nuanced. In particular, the choices the Court makes about the scope and impact of substantive law may have direct implications for the allocation and exercise of legislative powers. A powerful example, met in Chapter 2.9, is provided by the Court's dedicated willingness in the 1970s in particular to interpret key provisions on free movement of goods[47] and persons[48] as apt for immediate enforcement by national courts even without elaboration by the adoption of secondary legislation. This had the effect of reducing the need for legislative attention to such matters, and in turn, by promoting the directly enforceable deregulatory impact of the Treaty, had a transformative effect on the shape of the internal market, which will be examined further in Chapter 6. Moreover, a trend encountered in Chapter 2.7.5, the Court's interpretation of EU secondary legislation sometimes has the—unexpected—effect of widening the reach of those rules.

3.5 LEGAL ACTS

The legal instruments available to the EU are set out in Article 288 TFEU. In order to exercise the Union's competences the institutions may adopt Regulations, Directives, Decisions, Recommendations, and Opinions. The first three are binding acts; the last two are not. All five have been in the EU's armoury since the inception of the system in the 1950s. Each is defined in Article 288 TFEU. The Regulation 'shall have general application. It shall be binding in its entirety and directly applicable in all Member States'. This characteristic of 'direct applicability' insists on the immediate impact of the EU regulation within the legal orders of the Member States. It does not require implementation at national level. In fact, implementation is in principle forbidden for it would conceal the EU nature of the act, although it is not unknown for a Regulation itself to envisage and authorize national-level implementation. In contrast to the Regulation, the Directive requires action at national level in order to convert it into an operational rule. The Directive binds addressee Member States 'as to the result to be achieved' but leaves it to the implementing process at national level to choose the applicable form and methods. Typically a Directive will include a time limit of perhaps eighteen months or two years within which the Member State can decide how best to put in place a scheme for ensuring the attainment of the Directive's objectives. The Directive, in sharp contrast to the Regulation, is an EU act which will also become a national act as a result of implementation and consequently, even if in principle all the Member States should finish at the same destination, there will be diversity across the twenty-eight Member

[47] Case 120/78 *Rewe-Zentrale AG* v *Bundesmonopolverwaltung für Branntwein* [1979] ECR 649.

[48] Case 2/74 *Reyners* [1974] ECR 631.

States in the way in which the EU objectives are translated into national law and practice. This tends to conceal the common EU source of the rules but permits reliance on established domestic procedures and institutional arrangements in order to achieve the EU objectives expressed through the medium of the Directive. Although some Directives are remarkably concrete and challenge the conceptual divide from the Regulation, in principle the Directive is a legal act which is less conducive to uniformity and centralizing homogeneity than the Regulation.

A vast terrain of EU law and policy is mapped by dense networks of Regulations and Directives. The Common Agricultural Policy, governed by Articles 38–44 TFEU, takes up the majority of the EU's budget, and it is built on a mountain of Regulations. Directives tend to make up the bulk of EU consumer law, social policy, and environmental law, since the Directive, as distinct from the Regulation, permits a degree of flexibility in the digestion of EU objectives by pre-existing national regimes. The Directive tends to be the more transformative legal act, sometimes in ways unforeseen by either EU or national legislator, for embedding the requirements of the EU Directive may require or induce adaptation of national law beyond the scope of the EU mandate, and perhaps beyond the scope in principle of EU conferred competence generally.

The Decision 'shall be binding in its entirety'. This covers two distinct types of measure: the Decision which is essentially administrative in nature, such as a Decision addressed to an undertaking which the Commission considers to be in breach of the Treaty competition rules, and the Decision which sets out a wider policy programme.

Some languages, but not English, distinguish between these two types of act.[49]

Recommendations and Opinions are stated to have no binding force. This seems straightforward, but it is worth noting that in some circumstances the adoption of acts which are formally non-binding may nonetheless have legal consequences. For example where the Commission takes a firm position on a particular matter, even without the sheen of binding legal formality, it may generate legitimate expectations that it will not alter its approach, at least without giving due notice. This may be legally enforceable.[50] Moreover the Court directs that national courts should take recommendations into consideration, in particular where they cast light on the interpretation of national measures adopted in order to implement

[49] In German, Entscheidung/Beschluss.

[50] Eg Case T-282/02 *Cementbouw Handel & Industrie BV* [2006] ECR II-319, para 77.

them or where they are designed to supplement binding EU provisions.[51] It has also given weight to Commission 'impact assessments' in determining the validity of binding acts that emerge from such a process of consultation.[52]

Most of the legal bases scattered throughout the TFEU specify which acts are available to the institutions. This is a question of powers, not competences. So, for example, in the building of the internal market, Article 115 allows the adoption of Directives, whereas Article 114 allows for the adoption of 'measures' and so for this, but not only this, reason it is much broader in scope.[53] In the absence of such explicit provision, the institutions may choose on a case-by-case basis, according to Article 296 TFEU. That provision also states that acts shall state the reasons on which they are based. Article 297 TFEU deals with publication in the *Official Journal*.

3.6 SOFTER AND MORE FLEXIBLE FORMS OF POLICY-MAKING

There has emerged in recent years an increasingly creative approach to law- and policy-making at EU level. The Member States have on occasion been eager to proceed in common, but without fitting themselves into the 'box' of EU law-making, involving the orthodox institutional arrangements and the armoury of legal acts stipulated by Article 288 TFEU. The most spectacular example was the choice for a three-pillar structure for the EU made at Maastricht, which is still partially visible despite its formal abolition on the entry into force of the Lisbon Treaty in 2009, in the sense that the CFSP, the old 'second pillar', is contained in the TEU while the old 'third pillar', though now housed in Title V of Part Three of the TFEU (Chapter 2.9.4), still carries certain marks that distinguish it from 'normal' TFEU practice. The main reason for the Member States' reluctance to follow orthodoxy was and remains an instinct of *control*: they preferred to confine the release of supranational energy in these areas of common activity for fear that they would lose braking power. So, in ways that are different in detail, the role of the Commission and the Court is dampened while that of the Council is enhanced, and State power within the Council is secured by reliance on a voting rule that is frequently unanimity.

[51] Eg Case C-322/88 *Grimaldi* [1989] ECR 4407; Joined Cases C-317/08 to C-320/08 *Rosalba Alassini* [2010] ECR I-2213.

[52] Eg Case C-58/08 *Vodafone, O2* et al v *Secretary of State* [2010] ECR I-4999, Chapter 2.7.4.

[53] See further Chapter 6.4.4.

The rise of the so-called 'OMC'—the Open Method of Co-ordination—suggests a comparable dissatisfaction with the pattern of the EU method. OMC is not strictly a legal act. Rather it is a form of co-operation pursued in preference to orthodox EU law-making. It involves the setting of guidelines which are implemented through national processes which are then the subject of monitoring and review, which, on the most benign interpretation, should then lead to further learning and experimentation. OMC deliberately avoids binding rules and sanctions in the event of breach, although it may interact with more conventional and legally binding types of EU act to create a complex hybrid pattern of governance. More generally benchmarking and mutual learning and consultation and peer review have become ever more conspicuous as the EU gropes its way towards a far wider, richer, and less hierarchical range of modes of governance. This may in turn risk injecting a far higher degree of intransparency into the system.[54]

There are both negative and positive reasons for preferring use of the OMC and other new forms of governance instead of—or at least in supplement to—the orthodox patterns of EU law-making. The principal negative reason lies in a wish to insulate such relatively soft co-operation from the harder binding nature of EU law: the Member States in this sense want to assert thematically important 'control' over the direction taken by matter subjected to the OMC, and to avoid the loss of control that flows from 'Europeanization'. The positive reason holds that the OMC is simply better suited to achieve the ends in view than binding EU laws. The very idea of OMC is 'soft'—to set a framework that will induce learning by choice and example—and so top-down formal rule-making is simply unnecessary, even counter-productive. In this sense OMC is not second-best: it is better than EU orthodoxy, for it is more likely to induce creative and context-sensitive adaptation of laws and practice. The most virtuous interpretation of such trends would hold that they move progressively beyond a model that is focused on the rigid separation between the regulatory choices of the Member States disciplined by free movement and competition law on the one hand and the re-regulatory assumption of responsibility by the EU on the other. Softer forms of governance are based on the claim that it does not have to be, and should not be, a question of action by *either* the Member States *or* the EU but rather

[54] Stressing the heterogeneity of forms (and of critical evaluations), K. Armstrong, 'The Character of EU Law and Governance: From Community Method to New Modes of Governance' (2011) 64 CLP 179; F. Terpan, 'Soft Law in the European Union—The Changing Nature of EU Law' (2015) 21 ELJ 68.

something that melds the two and which may also draw in expertise from beyond the public sphere. The risk, however, is that OMC is used as a way to cover up the lack of consensus that has made political progress on hard rules elusive. OMC's virtue may be its vice—that it is flexible may also mean that it is easily evaded, for there are no defined procedures for implementation; still less are there sanctions in the event of failure to implement. This is especially troubling if OMC is understood as a route to *regulation* of the market which finds itself always outpunched by the constitutionally 'harder' commitments to *liberalizing* the internal market through the application of the free movement and competition rules. So, for example, it has been found that OMC has pushed social inclusion on to the national agenda for the first time in some Member States but evidence of real policy change in consequence is thin, especially where such policy concern is confronted by an antagonistic agenda focused on economic growth achieved through deregulation.[55] Moreover, strategies of co-ordination cannot and do not aspire to establishing common rules of the type presupposed by most forms of binding EU act: instead pressures for reform triggered by soft law initiatives tend to vary enormously across countries and over time.[56]

At a more specifically constitutional level, ticklish questions arise about how to ensure accountability and judicial review as such 'soft' networks emerge and act in such a way as to generate effects that are significant in practice (such as the production of guidelines which are not 'law' but which *are* followed).[57] In principle an act adopted by an EU institution intended to have legal effects is subject to judicial review and cannot survive if the Treaty does not grant the necessary competence or power: hard law may not be adopted under the cover of soft law.[58] But this is not apt in practice to provide an adequately nuanced means to control these trends which break the bounds of EU institutional orthodoxy: it anyway depends on litigation being initiated. The emergence of influentially

[55] M. Dawson and B. De Witte, 'The EU Legal Framework of Social Inclusion and Social Protection: Between the Lisbon Strategy and the Lisbon Treaty' in B. Cantillon, H. Verschueren, and P. Ploscar (eds), *Social Inclusion and Social Protection in the EU: Intercations between Law and Policy* (Hart 2012).

[56] Eg in relation to labour market policies, J. Paetzold and O. Van Vliet, 'EU Co-ordination and the Convergence of Domestic Unemployment Protection Schemes' (2014) 52 JCMS 1070.

[57] Eg M. De Visser, 'Judicial Accountability and New Governance' (2010) 37 LIEI 41; L. Senden, 'Soft Post-Legislative Rulemaking: A Time for More Stringent Control' (2013) 19 ELJ 57.

[58] Eg Case C-57/95 *France* v *Commission* [1997] ECR I-1627; Case T-258/06 *Germany* v *Commission* [2010] ECR II-2027.

involved private actors sharpens the anxiety. One need not impose the *same* rules governing procedure and participation on such new forms of governance as have been the norm in the past, but at the same time one needs to devise methods for achieving *some* degree of oversight of transformative practices that might otherwise become alarmingly untethered to any type of control.

There is a link here to a risk that these trends may generate yet more, albeit softer, 'competence creep' of the type examined in Chapter 2, which is apt to provoke a centralizing imbalance in the EU. This is to some extent inevitable, in the sense that the rise of softer forms of governance is in part motivated by concern to move beyond the limiting rigidity of competence demarcation and instead to accommodate by co-ordination the strengths of both the EU and its Member States. The Lisbon Strategy, agreed in March 2000—which was designed to convert the EU economy into the most competitive and dynamic in the world—and its successor, the Europe 2020 strategy for smart, sustainable and inclusive growth,[59] provide a good example of action taken across a wider range of areas such as social cohesion, education, and research and development which could not feasibly be taken by either the EU or its Member States but rather is better pursued by both. However, a major risk looms that this leads to intransparency, negligible concrete action, and the shifting of blame for failure to an EU that is ill-equipped to deliver and away from lacklustre but cunningly evasive national politicians. The Lisbon Strategy and Europe 2020 are good examples of those pernicious trends too.

OMC has not been granted any constitutionally preordained shape by the Treaties—that would defeat its 'learning by doing' aspiration. But even within the TFEU there are glimpses of a thematically similar acceptance that the EU law-maker may not know best. In the field of social policy there is a long-standing readiness to rely on the 'social partners'. The Union shall facilitate dialogue between them[60] and this may lead to agreements concluded at Union level which then fall to be implemented either in accordance with the procedures and practices specific to management and labour and the Member States or, in matters covered by Article 153, at the joint request of the signatory parties, by a Council decision on a proposal from the Commission.[61] So, for example, this is the basis for Directive 2010/18 implementing the revised Framework Agreement on parental leave which had been concluded by the 'social partners', Business Europe, the European Association of Craft, Small and Medium-Sized Enterprises (UEAPME), the European Centre of Employers and

[59] COM (2010) 2020. [60] Art 152 TFEU. [61] Art 155(2) TFEU.

Enterprises providing Public Services (CEEP), and the European Trade Union Confederation (ETUC).[62]

'Better Regulation' is a slogan that has gained adherents across Europe, not only in the EU, but the Commission has pursued regulatory reform in its name (and that of 'Smart Regulation') with vigour.[63] At one level pursuit of 'Better Regulation' is no more than a glib statement of the blindingly obvious, for no one would champion 'Worse Regulation', but nonetheless at its core is pursuit of a more critical approach to choice of methods for achieving EU objectives. Subsidiarity and proportionality, examined in Chapter 2, are part of the critical inquiry, and so too is pre-legislative impact assessment and wider consultation, but the agenda ranges more broadly to touch the forms of rule-making. Self-regulation and co-regulation have become fashionable. According to this model 'the Commission asks industry to come up with solutions provided these do not contradict EU law and the Commission's policy objectives'.[64] Obvious examples include voluntary standard-setting and the promulgation of Codes of Conduct, which may complement or substitute for formal legislation. The Services Directive offers an easy example: it envisages the adoption of European codes of conduct for professions as a supplement to implementation by the Member States.[65]

Engaging private actors more heavily in the rule-making process has the attraction that their greater expertise may help to create a more sophisticated system of regulation. It may be more quickly adopted and adapted than normal binding legislation, and it may permit sensitivity to local diversity more readily than top-down inflexible EU rules. But it carries with it the risk that powerful private interests may come to dominate a process that is supposed to operate in the wider public interest. Problems of intransparency and friction with the rule of law loom on the road towards such softer and privatized modes of rule-making.[66] The Commission has therefore directed that such 'private law-making' shall proceed on the basis of a balanced involvement of all stakeholders, that oversight by competition authorities shall be maintained, and that enforcement should be properly secured.[67] Easier said than done.

[62] OJ [2010] L68/13.
[63] http://ec.europa.eu/smart-regulation/index_en.htm.
[64] Commission Staff Working Document, SEC(2007) 1518, Instruments for a modernised single market policy, p 11.
[65] Dir 2006/123 OJ [2006] L376, Art 37.
[66] Eg C. Joerges, 'Integration through De-legalisation' (2008) 33 ELRev 291.
[67] SEC(2007) 1518 note 64, p 12.

This is plainly not a debate that is unique to the EU. Inquiry into the rising power of private interests and their privileged access to sources of power is at bottom associated with the health of a democracy and preservation of the rule of law. But in the EU it has particularly awkward dimensions, in particular in consequence of the very fact of the EU's distinctive governance scheme, escaping the orthodox assumptions of accountability found at State level, and its attempt to claim a legitimacy through participation of civil society as an antidote to capture by producer interests.[68]

More generally what is at stake here is a concern to achieve some degree of shelter from an orthodox assumption that EU law is made in a uniform way and binds all Member States in a uniform manner. 'Europeanization', already addressed in Chapter 2.10, is a helpful generic term but evidently, on the basis of the above account, it serves to describe several distinct phenomena. There are many subtle manifestations, stretching beyond the rise of OMC and softer forms of governance, such as restricting the EU to setting minimum rules only and permitting 'opt-outs' of several varieties. This latter debate is of sufficient richness to deserve separate treatment, in Chapter 5.

3.7 THE LEGISLATIVE PROCESS

Article 289 TFEU declares that the EU has two legislature procedures. In most, though not all, areas the EU legislative process operates on the basis of the first of these, the 'ordinary legislative procedure'. The exceptions are covered by the second and less important, a 'special legislative procedure' which exists in several different variants. Article 289 TFEU adds that 'legislative acts' are legal acts adopted by either the ordinary or a special legislative procedure (and so are confined to Regulations, Directives, or Decisions). All acts adopted through other methods are non-legislative.[69]

Article 289 TFEU states that the 'ordinary legislative procedure' consists of joint adoption by the Parliament and Council of a Regulation, Directive, or Decision on a proposal from the Commission. The ordinary procedure is the predominant form of law-making under the TFEU. Much supporting detail is found in Article 294 TFEU, which sets out the processes of first reading, second reading, conciliation, and

[68] See B. Kohler-Koch and C. Quittkat, *Demystification of Participatory Democracy: EU Governance and Civil Society* (OUP, 2013).

[69] So, eg, the 'early warning system' examined in Chapter 2.12.2 is aimed only at draft *legislative* acts.

third reading which are designed to promote dialogue between the responsible political institutions with a view to advancing amendments and securing agreement on a text by a process of iterative negotiation where no immediate agreement is forthcoming. This detail is profoundly important in practice, but the quest for the big institutional picture may excusably be pursued without reciting this line by line. The basic pattern of the ordinary legislative procedure is clear, and it is centrally important to the interaction of the EU's political institutions in the legislative process. And, of particular significance, the ordinary legislative process is recognizably in line with the very system that was put in place in the 1950s, when the Treaty of Rome put down the roots of the modern EU. That the Commission should be exclusively responsible for initiating legislation and that the Council should be the institution responsible for its adoption, with the Parliament (initially the 'Assembly') also involved, was the original plan. True, successive Treaty revision has elevated the Parliament's role from a largely consultative status to the current position where it enjoys a right of co-decision with the Council, and the voting rules in Council have been modified over time too, so today QMV is the norm (among the twenty-eight Member States) rather than the original rule of unanimity (among the six founding Member States). And in small areas under the AFSJ the Commission shares its right of initiative.[70] But the core design—Commission proposes, Council and Parliament dispose—has largely been sustained over sixty and more years.

That the Council and Parliament dominate the adoption stage of the legislative process shows the 'dual sourced' legitimacy on which EU lawmaking is founded—authorization by both States and peoples. That the Commission retains an exclusive right of legislative initiative (in almost all areas) shows the importance attached to impartial power-broking as a means to secure effective action. This is itself an element in the overall claim to legitimacy made on behalf of the EU system. Control (by States) and effective action (by autonomous EU institutions) are blended together.

The adoption of legal acts pursuant to the ordinary legislative procedure requires the support of both Council and Parliament. The applicable voting rules are set out in the Treaty. In the case of the Parliament it is rather straightforward. The rule stipulated by Article 231 TFEU is action by a majority of votes cast (save as otherwise provided in the Treaties, which is rare).

[70] Art 76 TFEU; also Art 289(4) TFEU. See Section 3.9.1.

Determining the applicable voting rules in Council has been much more controversial. What is at stake is—once again—the tension between the effectiveness of action at EU level and the control exercised by the participating Member States. A unanimity rule would preserve the braking power of each Member State, but such a system, permitting a veto, would equally make it very difficult to get things done, especially things of a contested nature. The EU long ago abandoned unanimity as the norm in Council. Periodic Treaty revision, beginning with the Single European Act in 1987, has set aside the national veto in an increasing range of areas, largely because of the perceived need to break logjams as the EU added new Member States and operated across wider fields of activity. But the EU has never taken the radical plunge in favour of simple majority voting. The ordinary legislative procedure operates according to an intermediate model. Article 16(3) TEU is clear: the norm is *QMV* in Council. This means—as is specified in Article 16(4) TEU—at least 55 per cent of the members of the Council, comprising at least fifteen of them and representing Member States comprising at least 65 per cent of the population of the Union, must vote in favour: and a successful blocking minority must include at least four Council members. This formula ensures that the Member States with the largest populations wield the most power, while smaller Member States enjoy more influence than would be on offer according to a system calculated only with reference to size of population. So there is protection for minorities among the Member States, within a set of arrangements which clearly encourages the building of coalitions between States with a view to crossing the threshold to secure qualified majority or piecing together a sufficiently stubborn bloc to constitute a blocking minority.

Only exceptionally does the system specifically provide for a different voting rule in Council: usually where the matter is *so* sensitive that Member States have been reluctant to surrender veto power even in the full knowledge that this will impede decision-making. This is especially apparent in the pursuit of a common foreign and security policy. The relevant provisions are housed not in the TFEU, but rather in Title V TEU, and are considered in Section 3.9.3.

Within the TFEU there are occasional but rare exceptions to use of the ordinary legislative procedure and the consequent reliance on QMV in Council allied to co-decision with the Parliament. These are the special legislative procedures referred to in Article 289(2) TFEU, which are found scattered in haphazard fashion throughout the Treaty as vestigial traces of past political compromise. For example, legislative action by the Council to combat discrimination based on sex, racial or ethnic origin, religion or belief, disability, age, or sexual orientation requires unanimity pursuant to Article 19 TFEU, and the Parliament's 'consent' alone is required. Article 113 TFEU allows for harmonization of some forms of taxation, but subject to unanimity in Council. The enduring use of the unanimity rule reveals just how sensitive States are to fiscal 'sovereignty', but such assertion of State control is unavoidably connected to diminished decision-making capacity at EU level. Therefore, and unsurprisingly, little legislative activity has been achieved via this legal base. Naturally, those who would wish to champion State-level decision-making in such matters, inter alia to promote competition in choice of tax rates, would be entirely satisfied with such a lack of action, whereas those who favour tax harmonization, inter alia to tackle perceived competitive distortion consequent on inter-State variations and as a means to encourage deeper political co-operation, would be dismayed. The point here is not to make a choice between such economically and politically competing visions: the point is only that institutional design, and in particular selection of applicable voting rule in Council, has direct and important implications for the intensity of EU-level rule-making and consequently for the shape of the EU internal market.

The history of voting rules in Council is fiendishly complex, but two main themes explain the alterations made over time, culminating in the current pattern. The first is rather technical. The rules whereby the presence of a qualified majority is calculated became ever more tortuous and intransparent as sensitive compromises about and concession to State power were made, and a major aim of the reforms made by the Treaty of Lisbon was to clarify the system, according to the above-mentioned rule in Article 16(4) TEU, whereby at least 55 per cent of the members of the Council, comprising at least fifteen of them and representing Member States comprising at least 65 per cent of the population of the Union must vote in favour: and a successful blocking minority must include at least four Council members. But even the Treaty of Lisbon did not heal all the past scars. The rules mentioned above applied only from 1 November 2014 and, moreover, a further transitional regime covers the period from then until 31 March 2017. This is covered by Article 238 TFEU and a Protocol on transitional provisions, supported by a Declaration. The calculation of QMV, and the surrounding protective caveats for minorities, are highly complex and deeply intransparent, for it largely follows the old model discarded by Lisbon; but in substance the point is that the threshold figures for achieving a qualified majority are higher during this transitional period, which reveals the lingering desire for retention of Member State control.

The second animating theme explaining the pattern of Council voting over time is of deeper significance. The areas of law-making that are subjected to QMV under the Treaty have been steadily increased on periodic Treaty revision. This drift is explained by the thematic perception that QMV, as distinct from a system with a higher threshold such as one requiring unanimity among the Member States in Council, is more effective at securing the adoption of difficult decisions. Harmonization of laws offers a vivid example. The Treaty has always authorized the harmonization of laws as a means to promote the integration of markets. Until 1987 this was subject to a requirement of unanimity but then, in the amendments made by the Single European Act, an additional provision was inserted, authorizing the adoption of measures by qualified majority in Council. The clear message was that control should be weakened in order to strengthen the effectiveness of collective decision-making regarded as necessary to achieve the economic benefits flowing from an integrated trading space across the territory of the European Union. The relevant provision today is Article 114 TFEU, which employs the ordinary legislative procedure. However, the sensitivity of the matter is revealed by the exclusion in Article 114(2) TFEU of harmonization of fiscal provisions, those relating to the free movement of persons, and those relating to the rights and interests of employed persons. Action to harmonize in these realms must be pursued through other Treaty provisions—such as Article 115 TFEU, which requires unanimity in Council. Here, then, are sensitivities about the perceived need for State 'control' which are reflected in exceptional insistence on a rule of unanimity in Council. That same sensitivity can be spotted in the Treaty provisions on social policy. Article 153(2) TFEU separates out the several relevant fields of social policy listed in Article 153(1) for which the Union has (shared: Article 4 TFEU) competence by subjecting *some* to the ordinary legislative procedure and *others* to a special procedure requiring unanimous support in Council. A similarly messy partition between matters safely left to the ordinary legislative procedure and those kept in the grip of Council unanimity is found in Article 192 TFEU on environmental protection by the Union. Provisions 'primarily of a fiscal nature' fall into the latter category, suggesting a thematic concern to link veto power in Council to spending. The same is found in Article 194(3) TFEU, providing that unanimity in Council shall govern measures of energy policy where they are (same phrase) 'primarily of a fiscal nature'.

This is not an exhaustive list but it shows how on occasion protection of the State veto remains locked into the Treaty. Control over fiscal policy is plainly cherished with particular eagerness. However, one should remember that there has never been a comprehensive overhaul of the Treaties. They are still marked by their incremental development, and even though the Treaty of Lisbon has asserted a priority for the ordinary legislative procedure, there remain eccentricities which defy rational explanation. So, for example, Article 103 TFEU, on giving effect to the competition rules, places law-making power in the hands of the Council, relegating the Parliament to the position of mere consultee. This is explicable only as historical accident. Periodic Treaty revision has typically extended the areas in which the EU is competent, enhanced the powers of the Parliament, and extended the areas in which the Council votes by QMV rather than unanimity, and more broadly still it has served to reduce the messy variation in applicable procedures between different Treaty provisions by prioritizing the ordinary legislative procedure as the dominant method, but it remains the case that the EU does not have a single legislative process from which it never deviates. And that damages transparency.

3.8 LEGISLATIVE PRACTICE

Although the 'ordinary legislative procedure' is based on the approval of the Parliament and the Council operating by QMV, it is *not* the case that States are regularly out-voted in Council. Consensus is a working method deeply embedded in legislative practice. The Luxembourg Accords, struck in 1966 after France had withdrawn from participation in Council business for several months in protest at the Commission's initiatives, involved acceptance that States could raise defence of very important interests as a reason not to put the matter to the vote in Council—a veto, in effect, whatever might be the letter of the relevant Treaty provision. This blockage is no longer visible in Council practice, in part as a result of the reforms made by the Single European Act with effect from 1987, under an assumption that the increase in the number of participating States and the widening of the EU's ambition—in particular the rise to prominence of the 1992 internal market project—made a system which embraced the control of a national veto ineffective.[71] Ever since, the shift towards QMV as the norm in Council has spread functionally ever wider. But it remains tacitly acknowledged that defence of the vital interests of a Member State shall be given due political weight, whatever the formal voting rule. Concessions

[71] On the decline of the Accords, see L. Van Middelaar, 'Spanning the River: The Constitutional Crisis of 1965–1966 as the Genesis of Europe's Political Order' (2008) 4 Euro Const L Rev 98.

are commonly made to reluctant States even where strictly their concerns could be dismissed by resort to voting. So, for example, the notorious Working Time Directive[72] includes a number of concessions designed to placate the reluctant but (at the time of its adoption) politically isolated UK, such as the possibility for a worker to opt out of the maximum stipulated hours.[73] All Member States are sensitive to dissentients, for they know that they too may one day be in a minority. Since the adoption of harmonization legislation by QMV became possible in 1987, there has not been a wave of rule-making adopted in defiance of loudly aggrieved minorities, but there has been a significant acceleration in law-making. On occasion a matter is pushed to a contested vote, and a State may find itself out-voted, and clearly the possibility that this may occur tends to affect the way that a State conducts its bargaining strategy. Under unanimity a State can behave intransigently, aware it needs no allies to thwart a legislative proposal. Under QMV that would be very dangerous. So States are drawn to compromise rather than express fruitless protest, while States in the majority, aware that they may be in a minority on another occasion, are frequently willing to offer accommodating compromise. There is an 'affinity for consensus'.[74] This reduction in unilateral State control enhances the effectiveness of EU decision-making. But it is not cost-free. The extracted compromises may cause adopted rules to be longer, shot through with derogations, and muddled by ambiguity shielding agreement to disagree. The Working Time Directive divides opinion on the political and economic merits of such intervention in labour markets, but from a purely technical drafting view it is a measure which is dense and forbidding as a result of the attempt to accommodate divergent traditions among the Member States on how working time is to be regulated, if at all, and by whom: public act or private bargaining.[75] This is an enemy of the quest for Better Regulation (Section 3.6), and it is far from an isolated example in the EU's legislative *acquis*. Moreover, such messy trends may cause 'competence creep' of the type considered in Chapter 2 and may, given the accumulated intransparency of legislative texts, disable effective control exercised over Council business by national Parliaments.

[72] Dir 93/104, now re-cast as Dir 2003/88 OJ [2003] L299/9.

[73] The UK, motivated by domestic political pressures, ungraciously and unsuccessfully nevertheless challenged the validity of the Directive before the Court: Case C-84/94 *United Kingdom* v *Council* [1996] ECR I-5755.

[74] J. Lewis, 'Council of Ministers and European Council', Ch 23 in *The Oxford Handbook of the European Union* note 44, p 322.

[75] In detail, see C. Barnard, *EU Employment Law* (4th ed, 2012) Ch 11; A. C. L. Davies, *EU Labour Law* (2012), Ch 7.

In fact, a criticism of Council practice is that it is *too* consensual. Article 16(7) gnomically states that 'a Committee of Permanent Representatives of the Governments of the Member States shall be responsible for preparing the work of the Council'. This is repeated in Article 240 TFEU. In practice it is rare for States to be out-voted in Council, but in fact, even more revealing of practice, much Council business is not even the subject of serious debate, and agreement is commonly reached in the above-mentioned Committee—COREPER—the proceedings of which are not open to the public at all, and very hard for national Parliaments to track. Decisions are hidden. Sometimes they are technical and apolitical, but sometimes they are more sharp-edged.

3.9 BEYOND MARKET-MAKING

Most of the EU's legislative business today is conducted according to the ordinary legislative procedure, but some areas remain special, largely because of a disinclination among the Member States to commit fully to the EU's orthodox method in areas that are more sensitive than market-making.

3.9.1 The Area of Freedom, Security, and Justice

The provisions governing law-making in the AFSJ are the most atypical in the TFEU, but they have generated significant blocks of legislative activity. So they deserve attention both because of their practical significance as the source of the EU's mixed record on making sense of the tension between freedom and justice on the one hand and security on the other, and also for the insight they provide into the balance between control and effectiveness.

The AFSJ is dealt with in Title V in Part Three TFEU. It comprises five chapters and, tempting though it is to discard the debris of the EU's erratic interventions in this field prior to the entry into force of the Treaty of Lisbon, it is hard to make more than superficial sense of this Title without at least some knowledge of patterns of past development. The story is, in short, that the Member States agreed in the Treaty of Maastricht to co-operate more deeply in deciding policies on the treatment of people, moving beyond the purely intergovernmental model that had yielded only fragmentary consensus. This, which applied with effect from 1993, was in many respects an unavoidable consequence of the opening of national borders within the EU: if the movement of people across borders is to be unrestricted then a person wishing to gain access to the territory of the Union holds an obvious incentive to target entry on the State with the most permissive regime, even if that may not be his or her true target destination State. So strengthening common approaches to matters associated with movement across the Union's external frontiers (asylum and immigration) held logical appeal, as well as the promotion of more general co-operation between judiciaries in civil and criminal matters and between police forces. But, sensitive to the loss of control that would flow from housing these forms of co-operation within the well-established system instituted in and developed since the 1950s, the Member States chose to craft a new way of working together which was not purely but more overtly intergovernmental. This took shape as the so-called *third pillar* of the European Union, dealing with matters of Justice and Home Affairs. In loose summary it attributed less involvement to the Parliament, the Commission, and the Court than did the orthodox EC system of the time; it made available different legal instruments; and, at bottom, it prioritized action through the Council with a bias towards unanimous voting (hence the ready label 'intergovernmental'). However, by common consent the new procedures worked sluggishly. In the Treaty of Amsterdam, which entered into force in 1999, it was agreed to re-balance the bargain, diminishing control and enhancing the effectiveness of action. So some of the relevant material was transferred out of the third pillar and into the EC Treaty, creating a Title on Visas, Asylum, Immigration and Other Policies related to Free Movement of Persons, devoted to the progressive establishment of an Area of Freedom, Security, and Justice. Traces of the past were retained. The Commission, Parliament, and Court were *more* closely involved in law- and policy-making than before, with a corresponding reduction in the primacy of the Council, but the method was still not quite on all fours with orthodox 'Community method'. In particular, unanimity in Council remained more prominently visible, the Commission's right of initiative was stripped of its exclusivity, and the Court's jurisdiction was curtailed. Moreover, the whole Title was subject to a pair of 'opt out' Protocols placating particularly wary Member States: one for the UK and Ireland, one for Denmark. Meanwhile the institutionally intergovernmentalist third pillar lived on, duly thinned down as Provisions on Police and Judicial Cooperation in Criminal Matters. This was a rather messy set of arrangements, but nonetheless a great deal of legislative activity took place, not least as a result of the bloody stimulus of 9/11.

It was finally decided formally to abandon the three-pillar system in pursuit of a more transparent and operationally efficient system with effect from 2009, on the entry into force of the Treaty of Lisbon. Consequently the third and first pillars are fused in Title V in Part Three TFEU on the AFSJ. But in fact even now the provisions on the AFSJ stand somewhere between TFEU orthodoxy and the TEU. The traces of the 'Maastricht pillars' are still visible. And the chosen arrangements reveal much about the Member State anxieties that dictate that special controls still pervade this Title.

There are five Chapters in Title V of Part Three TFEU AFSJ. They are General Provisions; Policies on Border Checks, Asylum and Immigration; Judicial Co-Operation in Civil Matters; Judicial Co-Operation in Criminal Matters; and Police Co-Operation. Much of the Title matches the pattern found elsewhere in TFEU. The 'ordinary legislative procedure' dominates, though unanimity in Council is exceptionally visible, which shows that occasionally the power to stop is more important than the power to reach agreement. The Court's jurisdiction is largely normal.[76] But the fourth and fifth chapters are the successors to the 'old' third pillar and they are still marked by sharp differences from the TFEU's norm. Article 76 TFEU makes clear that acts adopted under chapters 4 and 5 (plus the special niche case of Article 74 TFEU) shall be adopted either on a Commission proposal or on the initiative of a quarter of the Member States. So the Commission's cherished exclusive right of initiative is withheld. This shows that the Member States wished to retain a degree of involvement in the setting of the legislative agenda in this politically high-profile area. Sensitivity abounds. The opt-outs, for the UK and Ireland and for Denmark, live on too (Chapter 5.4).

There are plausibly good reasons explaining the distinct shape of EU law-making in this area. The rise of criminal law 'beyond' the State is a great deal more challenging than market-making. Its (partial) decoupling from the State cannot be legitimated exclusively according to a logic rooted in the effectiveness of collective action. It demands a much closer assessment of whether a process 'above the State' can command legitimacy when it acts in such a way as to deprive individuals of their liberty. This has attracted theoretical inquiry[77] as well as reflection on the extent to which the EU's rules adequately absorb the type of safeguard that is needed in matters of criminal justice.[78] Not for nothing did the *Bundesverfassungsgericht* in its *Lisbon* ruling place great emphasis on the linkage between the identity of the State and the criminal law:[79] not for

[76] Art 276 TFEU contains the most striking exceptions, concerning policing and internal security.

[77] Eg M. Fichera, 'Criminal Law beyond the State: The European Model' (2013) 19 ELJ 174.

[78] Eg E. Herlin-Karnell, *The Constitutional Dimension of European Criminal Law* (Hart, 2012).

[79] Chapter 4.11.3.

nothing has the EU European Arrest Warrant model for mutual recognition of diverse national systems of criminal justice, itself rooted as a more general model in Article 82 TFEU, provoked some of the most sceptical reactions among national courts to the basic constitutional assumptions of EU law as a system that claims supremacy over State law.[80] The model of conditional mutual recognition which releases French *Cassis de Dijon* on to the German market[81] has been assumed too easily to serve as a sufficient analogy to justify a model that leads to French nationals accused of crime being 'freed' to submit to the German criminal justice system, and so attention has been paid with increasing zeal to the conditionality of the envisaged mutuality, which might justify refusal to surrender, and to the need for supporting minimum standards adopted by EU legislative intervention.[82] A detailed account of this dense legislative *acquis* escapes the scope of this book,[83] but the thematic anxiety to achieve an adequate balance between common EU rule-making and the legitimate concerns of national particularity is central to it.

3.9.2 The Eurozone

The arrangements for the creation and governance of the Eurozone emerge from a long historical trajectory,[84] but they were first crafted in detail by the Maastricht Treaty. Like those governing the AFSJ, they depart from the norm elsewhere in the TFEU, contradicting any notion that the TFEU is home to a single system of rule-making, and in similar vein their detail is forbiddingly dense. The original plan involved commitments made by the Member States to co-ordinate their separate economic and fiscal policies under a system of supervision and agreed budgetary discipline, while also setting in train the creation of a single currency, the Euro. That chosen model, rooted in diverse though co-ordinated economic and fiscal policies pursued at national level alongside a single monetary policy, remains clearly visible today: Articles 5 and 120–126 TFEU cover economic policy, Articles 3(1)(c) and 127–133 TFEU

[80] See eg Case C-303/05 *Advocaten voor de wereld* [2007] ECR I-3633; Case C-399/11 *Melloni* judgment of 26 February 2013.

[81] Case 120/78 [1979] ECR 649; Chapter 6.2.2.

[82] Eg V. Mitsilegas, 'The Limits of Mutual Trust in Europe's Area of Freedom, Security and Justice: From Automatic Inter-State Co-Operation to the Slow Emergence of the Individual' (2012) 31 YEL 319; C. Janssens, *The Principle of Mutual Recognition in EU Law* (OUP, 2013).

[83] More fully S. Peers, *EU Justice and Home Affairs Law* (OUP, 3rd ed, 2011).

[84] See F. Snyder, 'EMU—Integration and Differentiation: Metaphor for European Union' in P. Craig and G. De Búrca (eds), *The Evolution of EU Law* (OUP, 2011).

monetary policy. The separation seemed to reserve core decisions on taxing and spending to national governments, but in reality the deepening interdependence of national economies—indeed, the very decline of a feasible notion of a 'national economy'—allied to the loss of monetary policy as a tool of economic management has put ever increasing strain on the structure. In particular, governments' pursuit of fiscal policies that loaded them with groaning levels of debt was not deterred by the normal sanction of high interest rates charged for risky borrowing, because of misperception and misjudgement among lenders. The crisis that struck in 2008 changed everything, and the EU's single monetary policy has come to be accompanied by an ever denser set of constraints on the exercise of notional national autonomy in setting economic and fiscal policies. And that iterative process of centralization of economic management is certainly not yet complete.

The Euro came into being in 1999 and today the Eurozone covers nineteen of the twenty-eight Member States. The Euro is backed by a commitment to maintain price stability as the primary objective overseen by the national central banks and the European Central Bank, an institution under a strict mandate to act independently of any EU institution or national government.[85] Achieving credibility in commitments undertaken over time through the tying of political hands and the creation of an independent institution has plain associations with the motivations that led to the design of the Commission. The principal template, however, is the German Bundesbank, and the central anxiety to maintain price stability—to prevent inflation—is driven hard by the horrors of the German economic experience in the inter-war years (and the greater horrors that it precipitated from 1939).

This is no more than a brisk summary: the past, present, and future of the Eurozone is worth a book in its own right.[86] Chapter 5.4 deals more carefully with issues of fragmentation within the Eurozone, covering fragmentation both between the States that are part of the Eurozone and those that are not and between the governing legal forms, which cover EU law and international law. The key concern of the current chapter is institutional. The planned institutional design within the Eurozone is basically an intergovernmental model for economic and fiscal policy, which means limited roles for the Court and the Commission and a high level

[85] Now in Arts 130 and 282(3) TFEU.

[86] Economics: P. De Grauwe, *Economics of Monetary Union* (OUP, 10th ed, 2014). Law: A. Hinarejos, *The Euro Area Crisis in Constitutional Perspective* (OUP, 2015); K. Tuori and K. Tuori, *The Eurozone Crisis: A Constitutional Analysis* (CUP, 2014).

of emphasis on State co-ordination both within and *a fortiori* outwith the EU, but also a supranational dimension located in the European Central Bank in the matter of monetary policy. But, in addition to the institutional sketch, at least some reference is required to the substantive tensions, though they will be examined again in Chapter 8, because here, more than anywhere else, the EU's system is under severe strain and how they are—if they are—resolved will determine the future shape of the EU, if it is to survive in recognizable form.

The project of monetary union was underpinned by a political vision of deepened unity, but it also had its perceived economic virtue, most of all in the elimination of the transaction costs caused by the existence of different currencies, the release of potential for productive growth, and the suppression of opportunistic devaluation causing competitive distortion. However, these perceived gains had costs too—in part those associated with the diminution of choice that follows from any centralization of policy-making, but also more particular anxieties that a single monetary policy would not fit diversity of economic performance across the zone, and most of all relative inflexibility and immobility in labour markets. Creating a single currency was a more unstable and speculative project than creating an internal market, because of the unavoidable need for more supporting action in common and because it was clear that gains from monetary union would be unevenly spread to a much higher degree. The process has lurched in new directions: pressure has grown for more central co-ordination, which has been in part delivered, but pressure for more accountability has not yielded similar results. The institutional design is plainly incomplete.

The so-called Stability Pact, first entered into in 1997, was a manifestation of a trend away from decentralized choices about economic and fiscal policies towards ever closer co-ordination. Built on two EU Regulations,[87] it was designed to promote more rigorous surveillance of budgetary discipline by national governments and, in cases of excessive deficit, to provide for the possibility of sanctions for non-compliance, in supplement to procedures envisaged already by the Treaty for co-ordination of Member State economic policies and avoidance of excessive deficits.[88] Its weakness was quickly revealed, as Germany and France (among others) broke the rules, and when the Commission intervened and called on the Council, as foreseen by the Treaty, to impose sanctions, it refused to do so. No doubt some Member States were reluctant to act for fear of losing political capital invested in the two

[87] Reg 1466/97 OJ 1997 L209/1, Reg 1467/97 OJ 1997 L209/6.

[88] Especially what are now Arts 121 and 126 TFEU respectively.

biggest Member States, and some too will have cherished the prospect of preserving their own room for evasion. This prompted the Commission to ask the Court to annul Council decisions *not* to proceed to adopt the formal instruments contained in the Commission's recommendations to impose sanctions. In *Commission* v *Council* the Court found a way to avoid becoming directly engaged in this delicate system for controlling excessive government deficits.[89] The Council could not 'break free'[90] from the rules laid down by the Treaty and by secondary legislation. Here it had incorrectly done so, so the Commission's application was in part successful. But the Court found that the Treaty system placed responsibility for making the Member States observe budgetary discipline essentially with the Council on the basis of the exercise of discretion.[91] The Court did not and could not direct the imposition of sanctions. The scheme was duly revised and made more flexible in 2005,[92] but it retains this driving feature of Council discretion in the imposition of sanctions for breach in preference to a harder, more supranationally directed, model of supervision.

The institutional design is specific to the Eurozone, but the tensions are not. An intergovernmental scheme enjoys the clear advantage that it connects directly to national democratic processes, but that immediately exposes it to the very risk that States will adopt policies that harm their neighbours which has always provided a powerful legitimating force in support of the EU's distinctive institutional character. By contrast, embedding clear and enforceable rules at EU level would make the system more credible and effective, but would ask questions about the adequacy of democratic input into the shaping of policies that are far more politically divisive than the regulation of agricultural markets or the removal of protectionist trade barriers.

This is a very practical case study in institutional design, but its sharp edges were felt most keenly through the tortured dealing that has been conducted since the financial crisis that erupted in 2008. Huge public intervention was required to prevent the collapse of the imprudent financial services sector. Debt mounted: default by one or more States within the Eurozone loomed, with inevitable wider economic implications within the interdependent system. The political will was to hold together the Eurozone, but simple bail-out of indebted States was forbidden by the Treaty.[93] Something more nuanced, yet effective, had to

[89] Case C-27/04 *Commission* v *Council* [2004] ECR I-6649.
[90] Para 81.
[91] Especially paras 76, 80.
[92] Reg 1055/2005 OJ [2005] L174/1, Reg 1056/2005 OJ [2005] L174/5.
[93] Today Art 125 TFEU.

be pieced together. The so-called 'six-pack' of legislative measures was adopted in 2011 according to the method foreseen by the TFEU.[94] It put in place stronger mutually agreed surveillance of economic and fiscal policy which, the Treaty envisaged, was pursued notionally at national level. Within that package there is an obvious sub-division between Member States that are primarily concerned to grant support and Member States that are primarily in receipt of support, which in turn is reflected in the substance of the measures which are concerned both to define the terms on which assistance is provided and to create procedures for oversight of the conduct of the recipients, with associated sanctions that go beyond models of peer pressure and benchmarking to include possible pecuniary sanction.[95] The so-called 'two-pack', adopted in 2013 and also housed within the TFEU, brought about further adaptation of fiscal surveillance, involving submission of a draft annual national budget for inspection by the Commission and Eurozone finance ministers prior to final adoption and intensified Commission review of Member States facing particular difficulties.[96]

The involvement of actors and institutions beyond the individual Member States in economic policy-making reflects the interdependence of choices within which national action is shaped: the avoidance of orthodox 'hard' rules at EU level reflects the concern to locate the ultimate site of authority for such politically salient decisions at national level, under conditions of accountability to voters for decisions on tax and spend. But the deal struck in and sustained since the 1950s was to create an EU that would act in areas of relatively low political salience and would deliver economic growth. The Eurozone is developing in a way that complies with neither feature.

More structurally ambitious plans to deal with the crisis were not the subject of support from all the Member States and, after much political wrangling, are now instead pursued through the European Stability Mechanism, founded on a free-standing international Treaty to which most but not all EU Member States are party (Chapter 5.4), which, though formally outwith the EU legal order, was in substance unavoidably

[94] Reg 1173/2011 OJ [2011] L 306/1, Reg 1174/2011 OJ [2011] L306/8, Reg 1175/2011 OJ [2011] L306/12, Reg 1176/2011 OJ [2011] L306/25, Reg 1177/2011 OJ [2011] L306/33, Dir 2011/85 OJ [2011] L306/41.

[95] See P. Craig, 'Economic Governance and the Euro Crisis: Constitutional Architecture and Constitutional Implications', Ch 2 in M. Adams, F. Fabbrini, and P. Larouche (eds), *The Constitutionalization of European Budgetary Constraints* (Hart, 2014).

[96] Reg 472/2013 OJ [2013] L140/1, Reg 473/2013 OJ [2013] L140/11.

tangled up with the existing rather dense thicket of adjacent EU law, and which also made use of EU institutions. It too was checked by the Court, which, as it had in the earlier case involving the Stability Pact, kept its hands off.[97] The mechanism came into force in 2012 and is loosely known as the 'Fiscal Compact', though strictly this refers only to its Title III. Its content is framed round a 'golden rule' that government budgets be balanced, which the parties are to incorporate into their domestic constitutions. Procedures for monitoring debt reduction, where necessary, and structuring correction are included. Its institutional arrangements are more strongly intergovernmental in character than EU orthodoxy, as one would expect given its formal designation as an instrument operating outwith the EU, although the Commission and the Court are 'borrowed' in limited aspects.

The economic balance sheet of the Eurozone is troubling, but the political and constitutional balance sheet is in deficit to an alarming and probably unsustainable degree. The European Council has become increasingly powerful, not only setting the direction of general initiatives but also becoming heavily engaged in detailed policy preparation. The Commission has become correspondingly less influential. Although the Commission's role was formally to propose the legislation making up the six-pack and the two-pack, in reality it was following the firm lead provided by meetings of the Heads of State or Government of the Eurozone States (the so-called Euro Summits). The European Parliament is little involved. National Parliaments are in practice marginalized because of the speed and remoteness of decision-making at EU level. The use of non-EU routes which are executive-dominated exacerbates intransparency. Crisis management had institutional consequences: this is a genuine break with the model that has served the EU for so long, involving a jolting shift towards a preference for intergovernmentalism. The anxiety holds that the orthodox 'constitutional balance' in the EU's institutional architecture has been sacrificed to the power of the executives of the rich and powerful Member States.[98]

Chapter 8 will assess the routes available to craft an institutional design that responds adequately to the need for an effective system of economic management at EU level which is subject to control by the Member States and which is open to political contestation rather than simply presented as the only medicine available.

[97] Its legality was assured in Case C-370/12 *Pringle* judgment of 27 November 2012: see Chapter 5.4.2.

[98] M. Dawson and F. De Witte, 'Constitutional Balance in the EU after the Euro-Crisis' (2013) 76 MLR 817.

3.9.3 *Common Foreign and Security Policy*

The procedures governing the Union's Common Foreign and Security Policy (CFSP) are housed in Chapter 2 of Title V of the TEU, Articles 23–46 TEU. In summary, they are heavily dominated by intergovernmental patterns of control. The normal voting rule is unanimity in the European Council and the Council,[99] the possibility of qualified majority being reserved for limited and tightly defined circumstances where, even then, the sensitivity at stake has generated a special 'emergency brake' procedure for a State concerned about 'vital and stated reasons of national policy',[100] as well as an exclusion of the possibility of qualified majority touching decisions 'having military or defence implications'.[101] And the possibility allowed to the European Council (unanimously) to shift Council decision-making from unanimity to qualified majority under this Title 'shall not apply to decisions with military implications or those in the area of defence'.[102]

The Commission and Parliament have carefully confined roles. The Court's role is confined to two matters alone: its jurisdiction to monitor compliance with Article 40 TEU (which directs that implementation of the CFSP shall not undermine the operation of the TFEU and vice versa) and to review the legality of decisions providing for restrictive measures taken against natural or legal persons pursuant to Chapter 2 of Title V TEU as provided for by Article 275(2) TFEU.

The external face of the Union is the High Representative of the Union for Foreign Affairs and Security Policy, though he or she has relatively little formal autonomous agenda-setting or decision-making power. The High Representative's mandate comes from the Council and the High Representative shall preside over the Foreign Affairs Council. But he or she shall be a member of the Commission. In truth, as already mentioned in Section 3.4, he or she jostles for visibility with the President of the Commission, the President of the Union, and, in external affairs, most of all with the Heads of State or Government of the major Member States.

The adoption of legislative acts in this area is excluded by Articles 24 and 31 TEU. Softer forms of action—general guidelines, decisions, strengthening co-operation—are envisaged by Article 25 TEU.

In part this model, which in broad shape remains that which was chosen when this area was first brought within the scope of the EU with effect from 1993, reflects the gross imbalance between the Member States which

[99] Arts 24(1), 31 TEU. [100] Art 31(2) TEU. [101] Art 31(4) TEU.
[102] Art 48(7) TEU.

have relatively large and powerful armed forces—most of all the UK and France—and those, the majority, which do not, which also includes some formally neutral countries (such as Ireland and Austria). One could scarcely imagine the UK and France accepting that they might be out-voted in the adoption of binding decisions to unleash armed force, nor indeed that the UK and France would accept being out-voted on a binding decision *not* to do so.

So this area is remote from EU decision-making orthodoxy. But it is also true—though not necessarily for that reason justified—that at national level foreign and security policies are commonly handled through far less open and accountable systems than 'normal' policy-making. A consequence of the structural impediments to finding agreement on EU external action taken in common is that the influence of the States of Europe on the wider world is today thinner than has been the case for several centuries. This may well be a source of relief to the many regions subjected to European colonialist ambition, though a different agenda for the future projection of European values, embracing promotion of the rule of law and the entrenching of human rights, has considerable appeal. But in the matter of external action, as distinct from internal patterns of integration, the Member States have largely preferred 'autonomous decline' over 'collective empowerment', preferring 'the pursuit of narrow national interests over effective multilateral action'.[103]

3.10 BRUSSELS, INTERGOVERNMENTALISM, AND SUPRANATIONALISM

It is the *interaction* between the institutions which reveals the unique method of functioning of the EU. The story rests on the combination of what has long been labelled, and still in many respects can still helpfully be labelled, the supranational and intergovernmental elements of the EU.

There are good reasons why the EU can function successfully only provided its institutions enjoy a degree of autonomy from the Member States. In this vein the independence of the Commission and the Court are most conspicuously required in order to provide an environment within which State commitments can be extracted and enforced on a credible long-term reciprocal basis. The design deliberately suppresses short-term accountability in order to promote long-term commitment. The Treaty, as an

[103] A. Menon, 'Divided and Declining? Europe in a Changing World' (2014) 52 JCMS Annual Review 5, 20.

incomplete contract, could not function without institutions that enjoy a degree of distance from political processes within the Member States. This is the core of the case in favour of the need for 'supranational' elements in the system. But the story is of control too, not just autonomy. 'Brussels' in several respects *is* the Member States—via the Council, as an indirect source of democratic legitimation, and the Parliament, a supplementary direct source of democratic legitimation. And 'Brussels' implements and enforces few of these rules. National authorities do, so the EU operates in many areas via 'indirect rule' in the sense that EU rules become absorbed as national rules applied by national agencies (doubtless in diverse and not always legally correct ways). This (in short) is the intergovernmental 'controlling' aspect to EU policy-making—which exerts a strikingly more powerful influence in the areas beyond the grip of the ordinary legislative procedure, where the Council and/or the European Council are centrally important and where unanimous voting commonly prevails.

There is a lot more to the EU than supranationalism versus (or, better, plus) intergovernmentalism. So, for example, it is wrong to suppose that all officials in the Commission are able or willing to act with scrupulous disdain for partisan State interests.[104] Commissioners in particular typically emerge from national political life and, especially where they plan to return to it, there is an obvious temptation to remain at least sensitive to the home State viewpoint. The Parliament is an odd creature too—there is relatively little 'European politics' which promotes the rise of transnational parties. The Parliament reflects some pretty peculiar interest groups, it has a pretty poor record as a co-legislator (amendments are sometimes swept in erratically with scant regard for the intelligibility of a text[105]), and most of all its claims to act as a 'European Parliament' are undermined by the absence of a European people.

Just as the supranational elements of the Union are not all they may initially seem, the same is true of the intergovernmental elements. There is a misleading tendency to refer to 'Member States' as monoliths. But the 'Member State' can be broken down into a great many different actors, public and private, with distinct interests and incentives. Sometimes political élites in States exploit the EU law-making process to circumvent blockages to reform at national level. This may make the EU particularly

[104] Eg L. Hooghe, 'Images of Europe: How Commission Officials Conceive Their Institution's Role' (2012) 50 JCMS 87.

[105] Directive 2006/123 on Services is a particularly clear example of the Parliament acting as an inhibition to intelligible drafting: J. Flower, 'Negotiating European Legislation: The Services Directive' (2006-7) 9 Camb YELS 217.

appealing as a means to effect change, and it gives national politicians no incentive whatsoever to be open about deliberations taking place at EU level, still less to educate national political cultures on the operation of the EU. Quite the reverse. An agreement in Council may be slipped through beneath the scrutiny radar in a way that domestic change could not be. The very fact that the Council involves collective negotiation (commonly under the shadow of QMV) induces participants to find workable solutions rather than stand uncompromisingly and immovably on national red lines. This is the 'affinity for consensus' mentioned previously[106] and it commonly involves trade-offs being struck across a package of measures, so that States yield on proposals that in isolation they might vigorously oppose in return for acquiescence in proposals they particularly cherish. So the EU, even (and perhaps especially) in its intergovernmental manifestations, may be a means to strengthen executive power rather than to assert State control. Under this critique the EU serves as an extra insulation of national political élites from popular democracy.

These criticisms have substance. But tackling them may expose or generate still worse afflictions. This is a thematic argument of this book: that proposed institutional reform of the EU must be attentive to costs as well as benefits.

The plea for greater accountability is frequently aimed at the supranational institutions, most of all the Commission. There are clearly serious issues to address here, but the risk is assuming the virtue of accountability while neglecting the vice of reducing the EU's capacity as a site for problem-solving and reduction of transaction costs. An 'accountable' Commission would be a more heavily politicized Commission and therefore a Commission less able to perform its designated (and sometimes discharged) function as honest broker. So, for example, placing supervision of state aids under overtly political control would probably result in a higher level of freedom for those public authorities with the loudest voice and the most money. The same would probably be true of enforcement of EU law more generally. And the more 'accountable' the Commission, the greater the 'no *demos*' problem—to whom is this body, operating outside (though created by) the well-established structures of national democracy, to be made accountable? The Parliament might seem the most immediately obvious contender, but that makes some ambitious assumptions about its legitimacy as a representative of a European people, not peoples. To make the Parliament more politically powerful on the basis that it is the

[106] Lewis note 74.

EU's primary democratically legitimated institution must reckon with the plain fact that quantitative patterns of voting demonstrate that *national* Parliaments, not the European Parliament, are the primary site of political allegiance among citizens of the Member States. To push for enhanced powers for the European Parliament according to a prescription of enhanced democracy might in fact be utterly counter-productive, in so far as the shift generates resentment that national political processes have been hollowed out in favour of a remote and little-understood institution that tours between Brussels and Strasbourg. Of course national political processes *are* to some extent hollowed out: one of the EU's purposes is to tackle problems that escape the grip of States acting unilaterally. But the EU operates on the basis of the interaction of (in short) its intergovernmental and supranational dimensions, and the danger inherent in promoting EU-level institutions as the primary sources of law and policy is that it makes assumptions about the virtue of creating at EU level a model that is familiar within the State. This is vice: it is to diminish the EU's unique trajectory to treat it as a State-in-waiting. And so, in concrete terms, the European Parliament's pretensions deserve a sceptical hearing rooted in caution about direct democracy as the only route to legitimacy beyond the State. The EU's failure to conform to the institutional architecture typically found in a State is neither accident nor necessarily weakness, but rather the very point.

A satisfying understanding of the EU treats it as part of the full picture of governance in Europe which insists on the mutually supportive relationship between national and EU institutions. The point is to move beyond choosing either State or EU, but rather to find a role for both. Of course national institutions score better than the EU if judged according to conventional benchmarks of social legitimacy. There is no European *demos*. The absence of a well of legitimacy at EU level adequate to support distributional and politically contested decision-making argues for the whole process to be treated as ultimately a (sophisticated) process of building *administrative* capacity at EU level in the service of the Member States, rather than a more ambitious *constitutionalized* process.[107] This is true up to a point. To seek to contain the bigger constitutional ambition as merely an expression of the 'functional demands of interdependence'[108] is convincingly understood not as a denial of the reality of an EU public law that

[107] See especially P. Lindseth, *Power and Legitimacy: Reconciling Europe and the Nation State* (OUP, 2010).

[108] P. Lindseth, 'Equilibrium, Demoi-Cracy and Delegation in the Crisis of European Integration' (2014) 15 German LJ 529, 540.

has constitutional rhythm but instead as a corrective to any assumption that the true and necessary path is to propel the EU towards Statehood. The EU may not be able to claim democratic credentials in the way that a State does but this does not mean that it lacks legitimate authority, which it is able to find in its role in supplementing the Member States where their own legitimacy runs thin—which applies where they externalize costs and, because of the constraints of unilateral action, fail to solve problems their citizens want solving.

There is no EU *demos*, but there are *demoi*. A focus on the EU as a site of *demoi* is a valiant attempt to portray the EU as a place where transnational rules do not replace, still less suppress, the several different locations of *demos* to be found across the EU but instead lock those locations into a credible set of commitments whereby the promise is made not to assert dominance over—but rather to recognize the equal validity of—those who choose to be different. It is not designed to suppress difference. It aims instead to preclude an insular refusal to acknowledge when the assertion of difference might inflict external costs on neighbours. As Nicolaidis puts it, 'The idea of European demoi-cracy is seductively simple: a Union of peoples who govern together, but not as one.'[109]

Although the particular institutional arrangements found within the EU are unique, the general thematic tension of deciding how much should be placed beyond the rhythms of everyday majoritarian politics and treated as an embedded feature of the system which, if even subject to alteration at all, can be changed only by special procedures such as 'super-majorities' is one that attends the crafting of any constitutional system of government. Few systems are so sanguine about the virtue of power exercised without constraint by a majority in Parliament that they choose to place nothing beyond the power of the government of the day, although there are immense variations on how much is protected and how and for how long. The EU fits into this general narrative of constitutional design, combining foundational rules which create autonomous institutions and adaptive capacity delivered by politically responsive institutions.

3.11 THE NARRATIVE OF 'CONSTITUTIONALISM'

The EU's *institutional* character, examined in Section 3.4, is demonstrably significantly more sophisticated than that found in an orthodox international organization. So too the EU's *constitutional* character is quite

[109] K. Nicolaidis, 'European Demoicracy and its Crisis' (2013) 51 JCMS 359.

different from, and more densely intricate than, the pattern that exists in typical international organizations.

The most obvious sources of EU law are the Treaties and secondary legislation adopted pursuant to the procedures considered in Section 3.7. However, there are other sources of EU law. These cover general principles developed by the Court and other forms of policy direction. Some of these, such as proportionality, have been absorbed into the formal texts at times of Treaty revision. Some, such as equality and the right to an effective remedy, are now contained in the Charter. Others, such as the protection of legitimate expectations, remain partly or wholly unwritten. Their influence is significant in the shaping of EU laws, for they impose limitation on the choices available to the legislative institutions. The adoption of measures which fail to meet the standards mandated by these principles should lead to their invalidation in proceedings before the Court. Most of all, the rise of these general principles reveals much about the extraordinarily creative role of the Court of Justice. It would be grossly misleading to suppose that that Court does no more than passively ensure the proper application of the Treaties and adopted Regulations, Directives, and Decisions. It does much more, not least because of the many textual gaps found in the formal sources of EU law. The Court is not a legislative institution, but it is a law-making institution. And it is a judicial institution which wields considerable political influence.

This is a narrative of 'constitutionalization'. Article 2 TEU commits the Union to respect for the rule of law and human rights. Article 19 TEU declares that the Court shall ensure that 'the law is observed'. The Charter of Fundamental Rights, stretching over fifty-four Articles, commits the Union to recognition of series of rights, freedoms, and principles. It has the same legal value as the Treaties.[110] That is rhetoric-on-paper, but the Court's ingenuity and ambition has long given detailed and sophisticated shape to these aspirations. The Court has engaged in a process of converting a Treaty-based legal order into something significantly richer—one that asserts a constitutional framework within which the exercise of public power is subject to review and control in the name of the rule of law. That public power *is* so confined is central to the claim made by democratic governments across Europe (and beyond) to exercise legitimate power, but it means too a powerful place for courts and, especially where the relevant controlling documents, be they constitutions or charters or rights, are ambiguous, they leave much space for courts to act in politically sensitive

[110] Art 6(1) TEU.

and contested realms. This vision, in part codified in the Treaties and in the Charter, is the EU's particular version of a narrative whereby judges enjoy a degree of autonomy in elucidating the concrete implications of review and control of the exercise of political power.

3.12 GENERAL PRINCIPLES OF THE EU LEGAL ORDER: THE CREATIVE ROLE OF THE COURT

The principles of subsidiarity and proportionality were addressed in Chapter 2.11. The former is a creation of the Treaties; the latter was shaped over time by the Court before a version was admitted to the Treaties. Violation of either principle is fatal to the validity of an EU act. They are general principles of the EU's legal order which carry vertical significance in the sense that they involve an allegation that the EU has acted in a way that improperly confines the scope of action of Member States. There are also other principles that are of more general application, in the sense that they form the basis for an allegation that an EU act is invalid for failure to comply with them. This is not about defending Member State autonomy directly, but rather a matter of controlling the exercise of power by the EU's institutions, in order to protect among others private individuals. Proportionality is in part of this type, but classic examples of general principles which are used to review the legality of EU acts include the protection of legitimate expectations and the principles of equality and of non-discrimination.

There are several routes by which questions about the validity of EU acts may be brought before the Court. Indirectly, the initiation of a challenge before a national court will allow use of the Article 267 TFEU preliminary reference procedure to send to Luxembourg an inquiry as to whether an impugned measure is lawful. Indeed, in pursuit of the uniform application of EU law the Court has insisted that a national court may not hold EU measures invalid and is therefore obliged to make such a reference when doubts prevail about an act's validity.[111] However, the majority of the case law in the field of EU administrative law is made up of challenges to the validity of EU acts brought pursuant to Article 263 TFEU. The issue under Article 263 TFEU, and also under other less frequently used routes to secure direct review of the legality of EU acts, is on what basis the Court should determine legality. It is provided in Article 263 TFEU that the grounds of review are 'lack of competence,

[111] Case 314/85 *Foto-Frost* v *HZA Lübeck-Ost* [1987] ECR 4199. See further Chapter 4.3.

infringement of an essential procedural requirement, infringement of the Treaties or of any rule of law relating to their application, or misuse of powers'. This is evidently a wide-ranging and imprecisely defined collection. In particular, the concept of 'any rule of law' relating to the application of the Treaties is nowhere defined and the Treaty provisions that offer an explicit invitation to the Court to shape general principles are few and sector-specific.[112] There is accordingly considerable scope left to the Court to shape its own pattern of judicial review. It has eagerly seized this opportunity, and it subjects the exercise of public power in the EU to control according to standards which in some instances are not explicitly recognized in the Treaty at all or, at least, were not so recognized at the time the Court broke the ground.

The Charter has absorbed much of this material, but the Court led the way. The elaboration of the general principles of EU law, which bind the EU institutions and in some circumstances the Member States (Chapter 4.8.1), offers another important dimension in the narrative of building a 'constitutionalized' legal order out of textually unpromising materials. And it shows how powerful the Court is. The Member States, acting through Treaty revision, have typically felt impelled to follow, not restrain, the Court's pioneering lead.

Advocate General Mazak put it vividly: the Court's general principles have 'added flesh to the bones' of EU law so that it does not remain based on a framework treaty, 'a mere skeleton of rules, not quite constituting a proper legal "order" '.[113] The Court's explanation for its elaboration of these general principles is unapologetically rooted in its distinctive understanding of the character of EU law and, in particular, its desire to position EU law as a legal order which transcends its Treaty-based roots. Thirty years ago, in *Parti Ecologiste Les Verts* v *European Parliament*, the Court hailed a system 'based on the rule of law, inasmuch as neither its Member States nor its institutions can avoid a review of the question whether the measures adopted by them are in conformity with the basic constitutional charter, the Treaty'.[114] In the case itself this led it to find acts of the Parliament were susceptible to judicial review, even though the relevant provision of the Treaty envisaged only review of 'legality of acts of the Council and the Commission'. This, the Court reasoned, was a gap that needed to be plugged, for otherwise acts that exerted legal effects would be free from judicial oversight. The detail of the ruling in *Les Verts*

[112] A rare example is Art 340(2) TFEU on non-contractual liability.

[113] Case C-411/05 *Palacios de la Villa* [2007] ECR I-8531, para 85 of his Opinion.

[114] Case 294/83 *Parti Ecologiste Les Verts* v *Parliament* [1986] ECR 1339.

is no longer of importance because subsequently the Treaty was amended to reflect the path already cut by the Court. Today the relevant provision is Article 263 TFEU. But this is precisely what is revealing about this decision: it demonstrates the Court's capacity to step beyond the *textual* limitations of the Treaty in pursuit of fulfilment of its vision of the broader objectives of the spirit and system instituted by the Treaty. It referred in its reasoning to a Treaty provision which is today Article 19 TEU, which commits the Court to 'ensure that in the interpretation and application of the Treaties the law is observed', but its pitch is much broader. Most vividly of all, the Court chose to use language redolent of a constitutional legal order, emphasizing 'the rule of law' and labelling the Treaty a 'basic constitutional charter'. This and subsequent (re)interpretations have made *Les Verts* a landmark.[115]

The Court's approach has been praised as an embodiment of its willingness to treat the EU as possessing a living constitution.[116] The other side of that same coin is stamped by anxiety about creative interpretation that borders on judicial 'competence creep' to the detriment of the principle of conferral and the EU's internal institutional balance. Is this ad hoc opportunism rather than principled elaboration? How is it possible to predict the Court's choices? AG Mazak captured it well: 'it lies in the nature of general principles of law, which are to be sought rather in the Platonic heaven of law than in the law books, that both their existence and their substantive content are marked by uncertainty.'[117] Legal uncertainty is no small concern.

True, not everything is a general principle. In *Audiolux* the Court refused to extract a general principle attached to the protection of minority shareholders from existing defined rights and obligations established by Directives on company law. What was missing was 'the general, comprehensive character which is otherwise naturally inherent in general principles of law'.[118] And in *Sonia Chacon Navas* the Court refused to accept that non-discrimination on grounds of sickness counts as a general principle of EU law.[119] In *Fag og Arbejde (FOA) v Kommunernes Landsforening (KL)* the Court decided there is no general principle forbidding discrimination

[115] Cf U. Sadl and Y. Panagis, 'What is a Leading Case in EU Law? An Empirical Analysis' (2015) 40 ELRev 15.

[116] Eg K. Lenaerts and J. Gutierrez-Fons, 'The Constitutional Allocation of Powers and General Principles of EU Law' (2010) 47 CMLRev 1629.

[117] Case C-411/05 note 113, para 86.

[118] Case C-101/08 *Audiolux* [2009] ECR I-9823, para 42.

[119] Case C-13/05 *Sonia Chacon Navas* [2006] ECR I-6467.

based on obesity, though it did find that obesity may fall within the notion of a 'disability', which would be within the scope of the prohibition foreseen by Directive 2000/78 for matters arising in the workplace.[120]

So the Court, invited to 'constitutionalize' the legal order, shows restraint. But not always. In *Mangold* the Court added the principle of non-discrimination on grounds of age to the list of EU law's general principles, and it added that this applied not only to public authorities but even in relationships between private parties (employer and employee, in the case).[121] Assessment of this ruling erodes the (somewhat artificial) divide between this chapter and the next, where EU law's application at *national* level is considered: general principles and the narrative of constitutionalization may apply to control not only EU acts but also (some) public and private practices pursued at national level within the scope of EU law. In *Mangold* the Court referred to 'various international instruments and . . . the constitutional traditions common to the Member States'[122] as inspiration for discovery of this general principle, but it offered no fuller explanation. And in fact the Court's breezy claim is poorly supported by examination of national and international rules governing the scope of protection of discrimination on grounds of age in private relationships.[123]

This is EU law as a jack-in-the-box.[124] The Court stands accused of a mysteriously und unpredictably selective approach, under which it performs an amending function rather than the role of interpretation to which it is in principle limited. *Seda Kücükdeveci* built on *Mangold* by linking this general principle to the right to non-discrimination contained in the Charter of Fundamental Rights[125] and in *AMS* the Court made clear that some but not all provisions of the Charter are capable of horizontal application.[126] Probably the Charter, which was granted binding effect from 2009 by the Lisbon Treaty, will become the Court's showcase: it lends constitutional authority to the Court's mission to embed protection of individual rights within the EU legal order. However, much of the Charter itself is written with little concern for detailed precision, so the Court retains room for adventurous decision-making. A conclusion on the legitimacy of the Court's reasoning cannot sensibly be reached without

[120] Case C-354/13 judgment of 18 December 2014.

[121] Case C-144/04 *Mangold* [2005] ECR I-9981. [122] Para 74.

[123] For a balanced assessment see M. Dougan, 'In Defence of *Mangold*?' in A. Arnull, C. Barnard, M. Dougan, and E. Spaventa (eds), *A Constitutional Order of States? Essays in EU Law in Honour of Alan Dashwood* (Hart, 2011).

[124] Chapter 2.8.

[125] Case C-555/07 *Seda Kücükdeveci* [2010] ECR I-365.

[126] Case C-176/12 *Association de médiation sociale* judgment of 15 January 2014.

more detailed excursion examining the trends in the case law, but it is important to appreciate that judicial law-making of this type stretches the EU's institutional balance of which the Court itself is in other contexts so fond,[127] and, still deeper, it is not readily reconciled with the foundational requirement in Article 5 TEU that the EU shall not act beyond its Treaty mandate.

3.13 THE GENERAL PRINCIPLES

Legal certainty stands as a classic example of the Court's determination to establish general principles that control the exercise of legislative and administrative power. It is not explicitly to be found in the EU's constitutional texts, but the Court has long insisted that it counts as a fundamental principle of EU law. It requires that 'rules should be clear and precise, so that individuals may ascertain unequivocally what their rights and obligations are and may take steps accordingly'.[128] This is not a surprising principle. It is an instantiation of the rule of law. But this is exactly to capture the Court's ambition to transcend the limitations of the Treaty as a basis for supervising acts of the EU's institutions.

The principle of legitimate expectations too is not found in the Treaty. It is the creation of case law, albeit that there are plenty of similar types of protection to be found in national administrative law. The Court has explained that 'any trader on the part of whom an institution has inspired reasonable expectations may rely on the principle of the protection of legitimate expectations'.[129] So where EU rules had compensated dairy farmers for discontinuing milk production, it was found unlawful subsequently to introduce a quota system tied to past production levels without taking account of the position of the farmers whose level was zero.[130] Similarly, where the Commission published a 'Leniency Notice' setting out the concessions on offer to an undertaking co-operating with it during its investigation into a cartel, a legitimate expectation is created that the Commission will stick to the promised deal.[131]

However, policies change and the principle of legitimate expectations does not stifle that dynamic. Where traders are able to foresee the adoption

[127] Section 3.3.

[128] Eg Case C-110/03 *Belgium* v *Commission* [2005] ECR I-2801, para 30; Case C-386/06 *R (International Association of Independent Tanker Owners (Intertanko))* v *Secretary of State for Transport* [2008] ECR I-4057, para 69.

[129] Case C-342/03 *Spain* v *Council* [2005] ECR I-1975, para 47.

[130] Case 120/86 *Mulder* [1988] ECR 2321.

[131] Case T-15/02 *BASF AG* v *Commission* [2006] ECR II-497, paras 487–488.

of the measure which will affect their interests, they cannot claim to be protected from its adoption by the principle of legitimate expectations.[132] So too traders have no legitimate expectation that an existing situation will be maintained indefinitely.[133] So, for example, where the owner of a fishing vessel had his right under a licence issued pursuant to EU rules to catch bluefin tuna in the Mediterranean cut short as a result of the introduction of emergency measures by the EU, the principles of legal certainty and legitimate expectations did not assist.[134] The basic EU measure explicitly envisaged curtailment of the fishing season where serious threats to conservation of tuna stock were found, so traders could foresee the risk. The nature of affection for legitimate expectations is to protect the position of the individual but not irrevocably to tie the hands of political and administrative decision-makers.

The principle of equality, initially developed by the Court, is absorbed by the Charter. Its Title III is entitled simply *Equality*. Article 20 declares that 'Everyone is equal before the law.' Article 21 asserts a prohibition against any discrimination 'based on any ground such as sex, race, colour, ethnic or social origin, genetic features, language, religion or belief, political or any other opinion, membership of a national minority, property, birth, disability, age or sexual orientation' and adds that 'Within the scope of application of the Treaties and without prejudice to any of their specific provisions, any discrimination on grounds of nationality shall be prohibited.' Article 23 directs that 'Equality between women and men must be ensured in all areas.'

The Court's case law has long made clear that comparable situations must not be treated differently and that different situations must not be treated in the same way unless such treatment is objectively justified.[135] The early cases tended to be concerned with relatively technical matters of market regulation, and such matters still form part of the Court's diet today. Beginning in the 1970s a group of cases elaborated EU requirements of gender equality in pay and other employment conditions, and the Court from an early stage insisted that the concern was with both the economic rationale of preventing States obtaining

[132] Eg Case 108/81 *Amylum* v *Council* [1982] ECR 3107; Case C-342/03 *Spain* v *Council* [2005] ECR I-1975; Case C-310/04 *Spain* v *Council* [2006] ECR I-7285.

[133] Eg Case 230/78 *Eridania* [1979] ECR I-2749; Case C-342/03 note 132; Case C-310/04 note 132.

[134] Case C-611/12P *Jean-François Giordano* v *Commission* judgment of 14 October 2014.

[135] Eg Case C-303/05 note 80, para 56; Case C-550/07P *Akzo Nobel Chemicals and Akcros Chemicals* v *Commission* [2010] ECR I-8301, para 55.

advantage by refusing to impose requirements of equality on firms operating within their jurisdiction and also the commitment to social progress.[136] Secondary legislation and a heap of case law has elaborated that task, but the principle of equality has been applied more broadly, beyond the economic sphere as narrowly understood and asserting a basis for proper treatment of people rather than just workers. The relevant legal base today is Article 19 TFEU, and the two main Directives are Directive 2000/43 on racial equality and Directive 2000/78 on employment equality.[137] Once again to elide the division between this chapter and the next, one significance of the *Mangold* judgment mentioned previously[138] is that litigants able to rely on a general principle of EU law are not confined to reliance on the Directives, which are subject to limitation in their application against private parties before national courts in cases where a Member State fails properly to implement the Directive (Chapter 4.7). In this vein the Court's elucidation of the horizontal application of Charter principles, initiated in *AMS*,[139] will have practical and constitutional significance.

3.14 THE HORIZONTAL PROVISIONS: 'MAINSTREAMING' PROTECTIVE REGULATORY INTERVENTION

The general principles considered in Section 3.13 are binding on the EU institutions and, if violated, lead to annulment of the relevant act. The EU legal order also contains a number of other legal principles which are of a softer nature. They are less likely to form the basis for an application by an individual seeking the annulment of a particular act—though that possibility cannot be excluded—and instead their primary function is to structure the choices made about the content of legislative initiatives and to guide the Court's interpretative choices. These are so-called mainstreaming or horizontal provisions, which typically assert that a particular objective shall be embedded across the wide sweep of EU law- and policy-making. They typically have textually similar, though not identical, counterparts too in the Charter.

Article 3(3) TEU and Article 191(2) TFEU provide (in slightly different ways) that the Union shall aim at a high level of protection of the quality of the environment. Article 191(2) supplements this with more concrete

136 Eg Case 43/75 *Defrenne* v *SABENA* [1976] ECR 455.

137 OJ [2000] L180/22, OJ [2000] L303/16 respectively.

138 Case C-144/04 note 121.

139 Case C-176/12 note 126.

policy direction: 'Union policy on the environment ... shall be based on the precautionary principle and on the principles that preventive action should be taken, that environmental damage should as a priority be rectified at source and that the polluter should pay.' Article 37 of the Charter directs that a 'high level of environmental protection and the improvement of the quality of the environment must be integrated into the policies of the Union and ensured in accordance with the principle of sustainable development'. This objective of policy integration is also mandated by Article 11 TFEU.

Article 151 TFEU directs the Union and the Member States to have 'as their objectives the promotion of employment, improved living and working conditions, so as to make possible their harmonization while the improvement is being maintained, proper social protection, dialogue between management and labour, the development of human resources with a view to lasting high employment and the combating of exclusion'. The Charter too contains several references to social provision.

Article 168(1) TFEU provides that 'A high level of human health protection shall be ensured in the definition and implementation of all Union policies and activities.' Article 35 of the Charter contains precisely the same stipulation in its second sentence, while in its first sentence it directs that 'Everyone has the right of access to preventive health care and the right to benefit from medical treatment under the conditions established by national laws and practices.'

Article 169(1) TFEU provides that 'In order to promote the interests of consumers and to ensure a high level of consumer protection, the Union shall contribute to protecting the health, safety and economic interests of consumers, as well as to promoting their right to information, education and to organise themselves in order to safeguard their interests.' Article 12 TFEU requires the integration of consumer protection requirements into other EU policies. Article 38 of the Charter states that 'Union policies shall ensure a high level of consumer protection.'

Slight but eccentric textual variation among these several provisions offers scope for intricate argument about precisely what is at stake, but the similarities far outweigh the differences. The binding thread is that the interests concerned tend to be collective or diffuse in nature and, in general, they are difficult to vindicate on an individual basis, sometimes because they may not be converted into legally recognized rights—a particular concern where environmental issues are at stake—and sometimes because the bearer of rights lacks the resources to pursue their effective vindication—frequently the case where consumers and workers are concerned.[140] In a sense what is visible here is the elaboration of the values expressed in Article 2 and 3 TEU, especially the 'social market economy' referred to in Article 3(3) TEU.

Principles of this type are capable of forming the basis for an allegation that an EU legislative measure is invalid for failure to meet the stipulated requirements of a high level of protection. Admittedly, it would be rare to find such a violation. Were the Court to find a manifest legislative neglect to take into consideration the protective quality of the harmonized rule or a manifest error of appraisal regarding the applicable conditions, then it would be prepared to annul the adopted act,[141] but provided that the Union legislature is sufficiently conscientious to ensure citation of the relevant provisions in the impact assessment and in particular in the Preamble to adopted legislation, it seems improbable that the Court would intervene. This points to the importance for the advocate of protection of diffuse interests and of the weaker party to achieve influence in the political negotiation which fixes the content of the EU rule, since the Court typically allows a generous margin of discretion in selecting the appropriate form of measure in areas involving political, economic, and social choices in which the legislative institutions undertake complex assessments and evaluations.[142] In this vein the Court refuses to interpret the assorted Treaty directions to pursue a high level as an obligation to set EU rules that match the highest level found among the Member States.[143] A degree of political compromise is inevitable, and, in a manner akin to its cautious treatment of alleged violation of the proportionality principle (Chapter 2.11.4), the Court is alert to leave space for its shaping. This makes particular good sense as far as Treaty provisions that in any event leave space for national measures that are stricter than the agreed EU norm are concerned, as is the case for environmental protection measures (Chapter 5.2.2).

The most powerful role played by these horizontal provisions lies in the *interpretation* of the EU's considerable volume of legislative activity in these fields. EU measures—mostly Directives—elaborate in detail the Treaty framework of worker, health, consumer, and environmental protection.

[140] In similar though imperfectly realized vein, their counterparts in the Charter would count as principles, not rights: see Art 52(5) Charter.

[141] Cf Case C-284/95 *Safety Hi-Tech* v *S & T* [1998] ECR I-4301, para 37.

[142] Eg, in application to Art 114 TFEU, Case C-66/04 *United Kingdom* v *Parliament and Council* [2005] ECR I-10553, para 45; Case C-270/12 *United Kingdom* v *Council and Parliament* judgment of 22 January 2014, para 102. See generally on the democratic case for and against judicial review of legislative choices (in the EU and beyond), Arnull note 44.

[143] Case C-233/94 *Germany* v *Parliament and Council* [1997] ECR I-2405.

Pursuit of a high level of protection may not carry much weight as a legal principle apt to trigger annulment of an EU act, but the Court has actively concerned itself to adopt an interpretative approach which seeks to make real the Treaty's policy priorities.

A small collection of examples must suffice to make the point. In interpreting the legislative *acquis* on the regulation of working time, the Court has openly embraced an understanding of the employee as 'the weaker party to the employment contract' and has identified the need 'to prevent the employer being in a position to disregard the intentions of the other party to the contract or to impose on that party a restriction of his rights'.[144] In the interpretation of Directive 2006/12 on waste, the term 'discard' and in consequence 'waste' must be interpreted in the light of (inter alia) the aim of a high level of protection of the environment set by Article 191(2) TFEU, which means it may not be interpreted restrictively.[145] In similar vein the Court has insisted that pursuit of a high level of consumer protection is a reason to avoid a restrictive interpretation of the material scope of Directive 2005/29 on unfair commercial practices.[146] Derogations from EU rules for the protection of consumers must be interpreted strictly.[147] This interpretative approach is common and it is firmly supported by the directions provided by Articles 12 and 169 TFEU and Article 38 of the Charter.

It is plausible to extract from these sources a general principle of protection of the weaker party recognized by EU law, rooted in the Treaty and Charter provisions on 'mainstreaming' and nourished by the case law of the Court.[148] However, this is another area where the Court's sense of adventure has pushed it close to the margin between (permissible) interpretation of legislative texts and (impermissible) amendment and amplification. *Simone Leitner* offers a vivid illustration.[149] The Court ruled that Directive 90/314 on Package Travel, a measure of legislative harmonization, implicitly recognizes the existence of a right to compensation for non-material damage, such as disappointed expectations of an enjoyable

[144] Joined Cases C-397/01 to C-403/01 *Pfeiffer and others v. Deutsches Rotes Kreuz* [2004] ECR I-8835, para 82; Case C-429/09 *Günter Fuß* v *Stadt Halle* [2010] ECR I-12167, para 80.

[145] Eg Joined Cases C-241/12 and C-242/12 *Shell Nederland and Benelux Shell* judgment of 12 December 2013, para 38.

[146] Eg Case C-122/10 *Ving Sverige AB* judgment of 12 May 2011, paras 29, 39.

[147] Eg Case C-203/99 *Veedfald* [2001] ECR I-3569, para 15; Case C-481/99 *Heininger* [2001] ECR I-9945, para 31; Case C-215/08 *E. Friz* [2010] ECR I-2947, para 32.

[148] H. Micklitz (ed), *The Many Concepts of Social Justice in European Private Law* (Elgar, 2011); N. Reich, *General Principles of EU Civil Law* (Intersentia, 2014).

[149] Case C-168/00 [2002] ECR I-2631.

holiday. It explained the Directive's purpose of eliminating disparities between national laws pushed in favour of bringing rules governing compensation for non-material damage within its scope, for otherwise distortion caused by legal diversity would persist. Moreover, compensation for non-material damage arising from the loss of enjoyment of a holiday is of particular importance to consumers. The obvious objection is that the Court thereby extends the reach of harmonization into areas where agreement through the legislature process had not been possible, which is constitutionally troubling as well as perilous to legal certainty, a value which the Court elsewhere (Section 3.13) protects when imperilled by legislative or administrative action. *Sturgeon* offers another example.[150] Regulation 261/2004 establishes common rules on compensation and assistance to air passengers. The Court interpreted the Regulation to cover not only passengers on cancelled flights but also those on delayed flights. This is not expressly foreseen by the Regulation. It was achieved by an interpretative stretch, based on reference to the context and objectives of the legislative scheme, including the aim of a high level of protection for passengers.[151] This is judicial gap-filling, but here not in relation to a relatively spare Treaty text but rather in the extended interpretation of an intricately designed piece of secondary legislation. Chapter 4.5 addresses a related phenomenon, where the Court's concern to secure the objectives pursued by a Directive has prompted it to make demands of national procedural law that reach beyond the Directive's text. The broad thematic questions focus on the legitimacy of the Court's intrusion into the EU legislative arena and into national autonomy.

3.15 FUNDAMENTAL RIGHTS

The protection of fundamental rights provides the most vivid illustration of the Court's approach to the development of general principles. More concretely, examination of the Court's defence of fundamental rights when asked to review the validity of EU measures promises to reveal much about the reality of the EU's commitment to restraining the exercise of political power in the cause of protecting individuals who may suffer prejudice in consequence. This is a heavily constitutionalized narrative.

[150] Joined Cases C–402 and C–432/07 *Christopher Sturgeon* et al v *Air France SA* [2009] ECR I–10923.

[151] See S. Garben, 'Sky-High Controversy and High-Flying Claims? The *Sturgeon* Case Law in Light of Judicial Activism, Euroscepticism and Eurolegalism' (2013) 50 CMLRev 15.

3.15.1 Fundamental rights in the Treaties

The EU's commitment to fundamental rights is written clearly into the text of the Treaties. Article 2 TEU declares grandly that 'The Union is founded on the values of respect for human dignity, freedom, democracy, equality, the rule of law and respect for human rights, including the rights of persons belonging to minorities', and that 'These values are common to the Member States in a society in which pluralism, non-discrimination, tolerance, justice, solidarity and equality between women and men prevail.' Article 6 TEU provides that the Union recognizes the rights, freedoms, and principles set out in the Charter of Fundamental Rights of the European Union. Moreover, Article 6(2) TEU commits the Union to accede to the European Convention for the Protection of Human Rights and Fundamental Freedoms. This, the Court had insisted, lay beyond the scope of EU competence pre-Lisbon.[152] There is also a supplementary Protocol relating to Article 6(2) EU. Accession is to 'make provision for preserving the specific characteristics of the Union and Union law' and it is to be ensured that accession 'shall not affect the competences of the Union or the powers of its institutions'. Accession is therefore conditional and in Opinion 2/13 the Court, stressing the need to protect the autonomy of the EU legal order, found that the arrangements negotiated did not meet the conditions,[153] which will certainly delay and perhaps preclude the realization of the commitment to EU accession to the ECHR.

Article 6 TEU does *not* require a national court to apply the ECHR directly, disapplying any incompatible rule of national law,[154] but it asserts a practical concordance between EU law and the ECHR. Article 6(3) TEU states that 'Fundamental rights, as guaranteed by the European Convention for the Protection of Human Rights and Fundamental Freedoms and as they result from the constitutional traditions common to the Member States, shall constitute general principles of the Union's law.'

Article 7 provides for the suspension of a Member State in circumstances where it is determined that there is a clear risk of a serious breach of the values inscribed by Article 2, although happily the procedures have never been activated.

The EU has had since 2007 its own Agency for Fundamental Rights, charged with the responsibility to provide assistance and expertise.[155]

Compliance with fundamental rights, of which the Charter counts as the most prominent expression, is a condition of legality of measures

[152] Opinion 2/94 [1996] ECR I-1759. [153] Opinion 2/2013 18 December 2014.
[154] Case C-571/10 *Kamberaj* judgment of 24 April 2012.
[155] Reg 168/2007 OJ [2007] L53. See http://fra.europa.eu.

adopted by the EU. Two principal questions arise. First, what is the content of the fundamental rights for which the EU legal order demands respect? Put in more concrete terms, how often has the EU been found to violate fundamental rights? Second, if an EU measure is judged compatible with EU fundamental rights standards, is there room for a Member State asked to apply that EU measure within its jurisdiction to test its validity against *national* fundamental rights standards? This is a question which asks what is the relationship *in principle* between EU law and national law, but it is one which is likely to matter *in practice only* where EU standards are lower than those demanded at State level. In this sense the two principal questions—on the content of EU fundamental rights and on their relationship with national protection of fundamental rights—are connected. However, in this book, the first is examined in this chapter and the second is reserved for the next (Chapter 4.3).

3.15.2 Content

The Charter is the most elaborate instrument in EU law dedicated to the protection of fundamental rights. It was drawn up in a first version in 2000 as a non-binding text but it has exerted binding effect since 2009 as provided for by the Treaty of Lisbon. This is guaranteed by Article 6(1) TEU, which endows the Charter with the same legal value as the Treaties. It is addressed to the EU's own institutions and (examined in the next chapter) to the Member States when they are implementing EU law.[156] The Charter, a free-standing document stretching over fifty-four Articles, deals, to cite its chapter titles, with dignity, freedom, equality, solidarity, rights, and justice. Some of its content is familiar and unsurprising—the right to life, the prohibition of torture, respect for private and family life, freedom of expression, right to property, equality and non-discrimination[157]—while there are some accompanying quirky niches, such as the right of access to a free placement service.[158] The Charter's Preamble expresses a commitment to common values in Europe, and declares that it reaffirms the rights as they result from the constitutional traditions and international obligations common to the Member States, the EU's own Treaties, the European Convention for the Protection of Human Rights and Fundamental Freedoms (a product of the Council of Europe), the Social Charters of the EU and of the Council of Europe, and case law from Luxembourg and Strasbourg. An explicit connection is made to

156 Art 51(1) Charter, *Scope*.

157 Arts 2, 4, 7, 11, 17, 20, 21 respectively.

158 Art 29.

the European Convention on Human Rights (ECHR): Charter rights which correspond to ECHR rights shall have the same meaning and scope, albeit that this does not prevent EU law providing more extensive protection.[159] The organic linkage will be stronger still once the commitment made on behalf of the Union in Article 6(2) TEU to accede to the European Convention for the Protection of Human Rights and Fundamental Freedoms is completed, although, as mentioned, this process was stalled by Opinion 2/13.[160]

3.15.3 Scope: visibility, not creativity

The Charter's Preamble states that 'it is necessary to strengthen the protection of fundamental rights', but adds that this is to be achieved 'by making those rights more visible'. Protocol 30, attached to the Treaties by the Treaty of Lisbon, states unequivocally that the Charter 'reaffirms' existing rights, freedoms, and principles, 'but does not create new rights or principles'. From this perspective the Charter's claim to exercise a transformative effect on the status of fundamental rights in the EU is confined to its acquisition of binding effect. But in fact this conservative tone is strengthened further by several aspects of the Charter which reveal that those drafting it were anxious to *minimize* its impact. Article 6 TEU provides that the Charter 'shall not extend in any way the competences of the Union as defined in the Treaties'. This is no more than a recitation of the principle of conferral contained in Article 5 TEU. But the fact that any recitation was even thought necessary reveals the nervousness about the EU's creeping dynamic. It also trusts the Court to police it. Anxiety to forestall unanticipated extension of the Charter's impact as a result of creative judicial interpretation is visible in Article 51 on *Field of Application*, where it is hammered home that 'The Charter does not extend the field of application of Union law beyond the powers of the Union or establish any new power or task for the Union, or modify powers and tasks as defined in the Treaties.'

3.15.4 Scope and interpretation of rights and principles

Article 52 of the Charter deals with *Scope and interpretation of rights and principles*. Article 52(5) is in this hesitant vein especially significant. It separates rights from principles, and explicitly confines the role of the latter. The Charter provisions which contain principles fall for implementation by Union institutions and by Member States when they are implementing

[159] Art 52(3) Charter. [160] Note 153.

EU law, but it is provided that 'They shall be judicially cognisable only in the interpretation of such acts and in the ruling on their legality.' Principles—as opposed to rights—are to be confined in their effect and influence. And the 'Explanations' attached to the Charter, to which 'due regard' shall be had in interpretation,[161] set out the view that principles, as distinct from rights, do not provide a basis for a direct claim by an individual for positive action by the institutions of the EU or by the authorities of the Member States.

There is, however, clear ambiguity surrounding these provisions. The *political* concern to signal to the Court (but not only the Court) that the Charter should not be used as a springboard to an extensive reading of the reach of the Charter is not matched by *legal* precision. The distinction between rights and principles has counterparts in national constitutional practice,[162] and it is immediately recognizable to legal theorists too,[163] but there is variation in exactly what is intended by the distinction and in the consequences of making it. Moreover, the intent behind Article 52(5), that there may be principles in the Charter that require implementation and are inapt to create subjective rights, is spectacularly different from the Court's approach in some of its heroic cases of the 1970s, in which it found Treaty provisions to create directly effective rights suitable for vindication by private individuals even where the Treaty seemed to envisage a need for elaboration by secondary legislation. *Defrenne* v *SABENA*, considered in Chapter 2.9, addressed the *principle* that men and women shall receive equal pay for equal work, now found in Article 157 TFEU (then Article 119 EEC).[164] This was directly effective to the advantage of individual employees: they did not have to await legislative amplification. The Court aggressively rejected an argument against its direct effect based on the use in this Article of the word 'principle', since, the Court remarked, the Treaty itself employs the word *principle* 'to indicate the fundamental nature of certain provisions', and it was able to note that then—as now, in the TFEU—the heading of the first part of the Treaty is devoted to 'Principles'.[165] The Court added that 'If this concept were to be attenuated to the point of reducing it to the level of a vague declaration, the very foundations of the Community... would be indirectly affected.'[166]

161 Art 52(7) Charter.

162 See S. Peers, T. Hervey, J. Kenner, and A. Ward (eds), *The EU Charter of Fundamental Rights: A Commentary* (Hart, 2014), pp 1505–11.

163 R. Dworkin, *Taking Rights Seriously* (Harvard, 1977); R. Alexy, *A Theory of Constitutional Rights* (Oxford, 2002).

164 Case 43/75 [1976] ECR 455. 165 Para 28. 166 Para 29.

But that is the attenuation pursued by the Charter as far as its 'principles' are concerned.

The Charter itself is not drafted with scrupulous care in this regard. Its Article 23 refers to the 'principle of equality', but this looks more like a right; Article 25 refers to the rights of the elderly, but looks more like a principle. There is slack in the Article 52(5) leash that the Court might choose to exploit. The Charter is *not* the last word on the meaning of rights and principles in EU fundamental rights law.

The Court is biding its time. In *AMS* Advocate General Cruz Villalón spent a lot of time considering the distinction between rights and principles.[167] The Court did not.

In *Glatzel*, however, the Court chose to play the Article 52(5) game.[168] It treated Article 26 of the Charter as creating a requirement to respect and recognize the right of persons with disabilities to benefit from integration measures, but not to require the EU legislature to adopt any specific measure. In the absence of any elaborating specific expression, it did not confer on individuals 'a subjective right which they may invoke'.[169] It (rather cheekily) cited *AMS*.

A narrow view would hold that the Charter collects together the existing body of fundamental rights protection under EU law and stops its growth. A competing wider view would separate out the Charter from the—wider and still vigorously dynamic—body of EU fundamental rights protection derived from general principles elucidated from the constitutional traditions of the Member States and the ECHR. Neither view is precluded by the ambiguous wording of the Lisbon Treaty. The Court remains on a long leash.

3.15.5 Legislative activity and legislative review: the pattern

The EU legislature is responsible for elaborating the scope and impact of fundamental rights both directly, pursuant to for example Article 19 TFEU combating discrimination, and also indirectly, where legislation in a host of areas ranging across migration, policing, broadcasting and competition law, and many others unavoidably involves that attention be paid to the fundamental rights of those targeted by such measures.[170] Modern practice dictates that legislative texts pay scrupulous regard to the need to comply with EU fundamental rights standards in general and

[167] Case C-176/12 *Association de mediation sociale* note 126.

[168] C-356/12 judgment of 22 May 2013. [169] Para 78.

[170] For a taxonomy, see E. Muir, 'The Fundamental Rights Implications of EU Legislation: Some Constitutional Challenges' (2014) 51 CMLRev 219.

with the Charter in particular. So, to select a random but typical example, Directive 2010/13 on Audiovisual Media Services, a measure of harmonization which sets out common rules governing the sector, asserts in its Preamble that 'it enhances compliance with fundamental rights and is fully in line with the principles recognised by the Charter of Fundamental Rights of the European Union, in particular Article 11', which concerns freedom of expression and information.[171]

It is, however, the Court of Justice that is responsible for deciding whether the EU legislative institutions have lived up to their promises. Long before the Charter ever existed—long before the Treaty made mention of fundamental rights, which occurred only with effect from 1993—the Court was alert to the importance of embedding respect for fundamental rights within the EU legal order. This is a story often told, profoundly interesting and yet to some extent, especially at the level of detail, remote from the current Charter-focused challenges. In a short summary confined to a single paragraph: the original Treaties failed to make any provision for the protection of fundamental rights, presumably because in the 1950s it was not readily envisaged that the EU, which in its early years dealt largely with the elimination of tariffs and other trade barriers, would impinge on fundamental rights. Alert litigants quickly dispelled that complacency, although the early cases largely involved alleged infringement of economic rights, such as the right to property, as a result of regulatory intervention in agricultural markets. The modern landscape of the EU, which features significant impact on social and political rights, is much richer. But that was to come later. The early applicants typically won, and yet lost. They won in the sense that they were able to persuade the Court to review the legality of acts against the standards of fundamental rights, even though the Treaty took no explicit account of such concerns. They lost because the Court was routinely unimpressed that any violation had in fact occurred. The landmark case of *Internationale Handelsgesellschaft*, a preliminary ruling made in reply to a German administrative court, concerned alleged interference with principles of German constitutional law as a result of the system of licensing established in the market for cereals.[172] The Court pointed out that to permit (what was then) EC law to be checked against conditions of validity set by national law would damage the 'uniformity and efficacy' of EC law. This was to claim the supremacy of EU law over national law in the event of conflict: Chapter 4.3. On its

[171] OJ [2010] L95/1, Recital 16. [172] Case 11/70 [1970] ECR 1125.

own terms impeccably logical, this ruling was at the same time deeply alarming, for it brutally asserted that technical, even trivial, rules governing cereals should prevail over the constitutional guarantees provided by a State to its citizens. However, the Court astutely packaged its claim to supremacy along with a commitment to protect fundamental rights *as a matter of EU law*. Such rights are, the Court proclaimed in that foundational ruling in *International Handelsgesellschaft*, 'inspired by the constitutional traditions common to the Member States', and respect for fundamental rights 'forms an integral part of the general principles of law protected by the Court of Justice'.[173] So, as a matter of EU law, regulation of the market does not have to comply with national laws on fundamental rights, but it does have to comply with the EU's system of fundamental rights protection. The Court then found that the licensing system was simply the normal consequence of the system for regulating the cereals market envisaged by EU law and it did not violate any right of a fundamental nature.

The entry into force of the Maastricht Treaty in 1993 allowed the system's founding texts to catch up with the pace already struck by the Court. From that time the Treaties have explicitly acknowledged the importance of protecting fundamental rights. Today, since the entry into force of the Lisbon Treaty in 2009, the commitments to fundamental rights are writ large, in Article 2 TEU, the Charter, and the planned but stalled accession to the ECHR.[174] But Article 6(3) TEU's declaration that 'Fundamental rights, as guaranteed by the European Convention for the Protection of Human Rights and Fundamental Freedoms and as they result from the constitutional traditions common to the Member States, shall constitute general principles of the Union's law' still serves as homage to the Court's pathbreaking early contribution.

The Court of Justice has refused, in the name of preserving EU law's cohesion through a claim to its supremacy, to permit the validity of EU law to be brought into question in the light of national conceptions of fundamental rights and, in similar vein, it has refused to permit the adaptation of the EU Treaty system to expose the validity of its measures to review from outside, by the European Court of Human Rights.[175] EU law's conception of fundamental rights alone is the basis for review conducted in the name of EU law. But does EU law in particular, and its Court in particular, deserve to be trusted with this task? That was the

[173] Para 5. See also eg Case C-222/84 *Johnston* v *Chief Constable of the Royal Ulster Constabulary* [1986] ECR 1651 para 18.

[174] Opinion 2/13 note 153.

[175] Ibid.

question raised by *Internationale Handelsgesellschaft* and it is the question that is still raised today, albeit in the light of a more vigorously written tapestry of constitutional commitments to the centrality of fundamental rights in EU law. Such a question can be answered only through engagement with the case law.

In the period between 2000 and 2009, during which the Charter lacked binding force,[176] the Court exhibited an initial reluctance to acknowledge it. Only in 2006 did it mention the Charter for the first time in a judgment, albeit *en passant*, in connection with an unsuccessful application for annulment of a Directive which cited the Charter in its own Preamble.[177] Subsequently it shrugged off its caution and began to decorate its judgments with references to the Charter, even in advance of its acquisition of binding force in 2009.[178] And the deepest and most vigorous instance of the Court's defence of fundamental rights in EU law arrived in 2008, in advance of the entry into force of the Lisbon Treaty, though, since the text had by then been agreed, in its shadow. This is *Kadi and Al Barakaat* v *Council*.[179] The case concerned challenges to the validity of EU measures 'freezing' use of funds by alleged terrorists. The EU was implementing resolutions of the United Nations' Security Council: this was a perfect illustration of how power is exercised in multiple but interacting ways above and beyond the State, with consequent pressing challenges for orthodox understandings of accountability, judicial control, and protection of the rule of law.[180] The Court agreed that it could not review the validity of an act of the Security Council, but it insisted that it could review the EU's implementing measures. It emphasized the importance of fundamental rights protection in the EU as a constitutional guarantee forming part of the very foundations of the legal order.[181] And, finding violation of the applicants' right to be heard, the principle of effective judicial protection, and respect for property, it annulled the EU Regulation. The Court regarded itself as presiding over an 'autonomous legal system which is not to be prejudiced by an international agreement'.[182] *Kadi and Al Barakaat* is

[176] It was 'solemnly proclaimed' by the Parliament, Council, and Commission at the Nice European Council in December 2000: OJ [2000] C364/1.

[177] Case C-540/03 *Parliament* v *Council* [2006] ECR I-5769.

[178] Eg Case C-432/05 *Unibet* v *Justitiekanslern* [2007] ECR I-2271; Case C-303/05 note 80; Case C-244/06 *Dynamic Medien* [2008] ECR I-505.

[179] Joined Cases C-402/05P and C-415/05P *Kadi and Al Barakaat* v *Council* [2008] ECR I-6351.

[180] Cf C. Harlow, 'Composite Decision-Making and Accountability Networks: Some Deductions from a Saga' (2013) 32 YEL 3.

[181] Eg paras 284, 290, 303–305, 316 of the judgment.

[182] Para 316.

significant as a basis for understanding how the Court will treat its role in reviewing the EU's proliferating range of powers to impose targeted sanctions,[183] but more generally it amounts to a statement of the existential significance of the EU legal order's commitment to fundamental rights.

Kadi should not be allowed to breed complacency. For every individual rescued by the Court from the brutal exercise of executive power in the name of preserving 'security' there are doubtless many thousands left stranded in a legal black hole and even, as we have come to learn, subjected to torture. Even in *Kadi* itself, the effects of the contested measures were left in place for three months after the date of the judgment to permit the Council the opportunity to remedy the infringements found[184] and, after rapid extraction of summary reasons from the UN Sanctions Committee, the oppressive measures were duly re-made. But the story did not end there. The freshly made decisions were duly annulled by the General Court and an appeal to the Court of Justice failed.[185] The Court's review, which was relatively intense, dismissed as inadequate the reasons for listing offered by the EU, which were in fact no more than repetition of summaries offered by the Security Council's Sanctions Committee. In a coruscating analysis that flays Western political élites for their determination post-9/11 to rip away fundamental rights in the name of security, Gearty has celebrated the Court of Justice's refusal in the *Kadi* cases to agree to a drift away from open trial to opaque administrative process.[186]

The question arises as to whether this is truly typical of a Court properly attentive to fundamental rights or whether instead this was an exceptional intrusion into the political sphere driven by the Security Council's insensitivity to the precarious position of vulnerable individuals. *Kadi* might even be seen as a rather cynical exercise in protecting EU law and the Court's own power from external standards rather than as a judgment truly committed to the protection of fundamental rights. *Opinion 2/13*, which has structural similarities with *Kadi* in its defence of the autonomy of the EU legal order and its focus on the Court on the sole protector of fundamental rights, invites similar wry appraisal, although preserving the autonomy of the EU legal order is not inevitably incompatible with a genuine and effective commitment to fundamental rights within it.

[183] C. Eckes, 'EU Restrictive Measures against Natural and Legal Persons: From Counterterrorist to Third Country Sanctions' (2014) 51 CMLRev 869.

[184] Paras 373–376.

[185] Case C-584/10P *Commission and UK* v *Kadi* judgment of 18 July 2013.

[186] C. Gearty, 'In Praise of Awkwardness: *Kadi* in the CJEU' (2014) 10 Euro Const LR 15.

3.15.6 Legislative activity and legislative review: the practice

Since it acquired binding force in 2009 the Charter has tended to provide the Court's starting point in testing measures for compliance with fundamental rights, and sometimes it chooses to look no further for sources on which to rely.[187] The Court is plainly intent on locating the Charter at the heart of its decision-making. As the Court put it in *Fransson*, 'The applicability of EU law entails applicability of the fundamental rights guaranteed by the Charter.'[188] The Charter becomes the 'shadow' of substantive EU law.[189]

The Court is steadily accumulating a body of case law which has a pattern in common with the early years—respect for fundamental rights is asserted but violation is rarely found. Regulation of the market is the EU's everyday business. The Charter, in particular its Article 15(1) on the right to engage in work and to pursue a freely chosen or accepted occupation, its Article 16 guaranteeing the freedom to conduct a business, and its Article 17 on the right to property, are increasingly deployed by traders to attack intervention in the market, but largely without success. *Deutsches Weintor eG* v *Land Rheinland-Pfalz* provides a typical example.[190] Regulation 1924/2006 harmonizes rules governing nutrition and health claims made about food. Pursuant to the Regulation, use of the phrase 'easily digestible' in connection with wines was forbidden. In proceedings initiated by an affected trader the Court was asked whether this restriction was compatible with Articles 15(1) and 16 of the Charter. It drew on Article 35 of the Charter, which requires that a high level of human health protection be ensured in the definition and implementation of EU policies and activities. The Court did not also cite Article 38 on consumer protection, though it easily could have done. The Court considered that EU law required a reconciliation of 'the requirements of the protection of those various fundamental rights protected by the Union legal order' and the striking of 'a fair balance between them'.[191] The claim made highlighted *only* the easy digestion of the wine and this was apt to encourage alcohol consumption, with increased risks for consumers' health. The Court was

[187] Eg Case C-199/11 *Otis NV* judgment of 6 November 2012, Case C-396/11 *Ciprian Radu* judgment of 29 January 2013.

[188] Case C-617/10 *Fransson* judgment of 26 February 2012, para 21.

[189] K. Lenaerts and J. Gutiérrez Fons, 'The Place of the Charter in the EU Constitutional Edifice' in *The EU Charter of Fundamental Rights: A Commentary* note 162, p 1568.

[190] Case C-544/10 *Deutsches Weintor eG* v *Land Rheinland-Pfalz* judgment of 6 September 2012.

[191] Para 47.

persuaded that the EU's prohibition was lawful. This legislative regime was based on a reconciliation of the several fundamental rights at stake, striking a fair balance between them. And this has become the Court's orthodox treatment of such attempts to destabilize the regulation of markets in the interests of commercial freedom. So in *Herbert Schaible* a sheep farmer sought to attack requirements laid down by Regulation 21/2004 that he should identify individual animals and ensure electronic identification as violation of Article 16 (freedom to conduct a business) and Article 20 (equal treatment), but the Court briskly responded that the EU's intervention, rooted in concern for health risks, including the spread of foot-and-mouth disease, was lawful.[192] Charter rights are not absolute and the Court is sensitive to the need for careful calculation when invited to endorse aggressively deregulatory claims to commercial freedom. This is in line with its past treatment of the right to property as a general principle of EU law which may be the subject of legislative restriction on its exercise in pursuit of objectives in the general interest.[193] A margin is allowed to the EU legislature. The Charter has not altered that. *Denise McDonough* v *Ryanair Ltd* proves the point.[194] The Court upheld provisions on compensation for air passengers in Regulation 261/2004 as striking a 'fair balance' between, on the one hand, Articles 16 and 17 of the Charter and, on the other, Article 38 on consumer protection. The Court's analysis cited both *Promusicae*,[195] a pre-Lisbon ruling, and *Deutsches Weintor*,[196] post-Lisbon, without suggesting they are cut from a different cloth.

Outside the sphere of general market regulation there are instances of the Court finding EU legislative measures incompatible with the Charter. It is always a risk to focus on and to exaggerate the significance of what are in truth exceptional decisions: most Charter-based claims fail. But, with that caveat in mind, the Charter has bared its teeth. In 2011 in *Association belge des Consommateurs Test-Achats*, the Court relied on the Charter to find invalid a provision of Directive 2004/113 implementing the principle of equal treatment between men and women in the access to and supply of goods and services.[197] Article 5(2) of Directive 2004/113 allowed Member States to permit differences relating to sex in the calculation of insurance premiums and benefits. The Court held this to be invalid for violation

[192] Case C-101/12 judgment of 17 October 2013.

[193] Eg Case C-491/01 *R* v *Secretary of State ex parte BAT and Imperial Tobacco* [2002] ECR I-11543, para 149; Cases C-184/02 and C-223/02 *Spain and Finland* v *Parliament and Council* [2004] ECR I-7789 para 52.

[194] Case C-12/11 judgment of 31 January 2013.

[195] Case C-275/06 [2008] ECR I-271.

[196] Note 190.

[197] Case C-236/09 judgment of 1 March 2011.

of Articles 21 and 23 of the Charter, which forbid discrimination based on sex and require that equality between men and women be ensured in all areas. The Directive itself purported to advance the principle of equal treatment between men and women and included recitals hugging close to the right to equality as expressed in a number of instruments, including the Charter itself, albeit in its pre-Lisbon non-binding form, and so it is hardly surprising that the Court refused to accept a blatant contradiction of the type attempted by its Article 5(2). As a matter of principle, the Court's ruling acts as a strong statement of hierarchy: Charter rights and freedoms come first, and the exercise of EU legislative competence is conditional on respect for the Charter's requirements. In this sense the Member States have agreed to bind the EU legislative process to a higher site of norms.

Claims to privacy are particularly sensitive in so far as they collide with State concern to assert supervision in the name of security. Which prevails? To depict this as a process of 'balancing' has a kernel of truth yet tends to conceal the deeply sensitive choices involved, between values that are not readily measured against each other. It is here that one may inspect the argument that what the Charter does—what *any* constitutionally entrenched text that is not written with utter precision does—is to place judges in a position to thwart the political process. In some decisions the Court has found interference with privacy to be compatible with the Charter;[198] in others it has taken a different view. The latter type tend to be the more high-profile, even if (for that very reason) they should not be taken as wholly typical. In *Google* the Court interpreted relevant provisions of Directive 95/46 on data protection to mean that in some circumstances the operator of a search engine is obliged to remove information from the list of results displayed.[199] This is the so-called 'right to be forgotten', rooted in Article 7 of the Charter (right to respect for private life) and Article 8 (right to the protection of personal data). The Court tried to meet the obvious anxiety that this would shelter the powerful from scrutiny by noting that special circumstances may arise with reference to 'the role played by the data subject in public life', where interference with privacy rights may be 'justified by the preponderant interest of the general public in having... access to the information in question'.[200] This is no easy test to apply, which is an immediate reminder of how awkward is the role a Court plays in such cases of review of legislative compromises.

[198] Eg Case C-291/12 *Michael Schwarz* v *Stadt Bochum* judgment of 17 October 2013; Joined Cases C-446/12, C-447/12, C-448/12, C-449/12 *Willems* et al judgment of 16 April 2015.

[199] Case C-131/12 *Google* judgment of 13 May 2014. [200] Para 87.

The Court's most striking ruling arrived in *Digital Rights Ireland* et al, in which it found Directive 2006/24 on data retention to be invalid.[201] The measure was adopted as a measure of legislative harmonization (under what is now Article 114: Chapter 2.7.4). The Court found that the Directive 'entails a wide-ranging and particularly serious interference with those fundamental rights in the legal order of the EU',[202] and that interference was neither precisely circumscribed to ensure that it was actually limited to what is strictly necessary nor was it accompanied by adequate safeguards against misuse. The Court, which did not permit the legislature the room to act provided it committed no 'manifest error', relied on the Charter but also referred to the ECHR in holding the Directive to be invalid.[203] A thematically similar approach, in which a strict review of intrusion into privacy is asserted in explicit compliance with *Digital Rights*, is visible in *Maximilian Schrems*.[204] The Court decided that Decision 2000/520 on the transfer of data to the United States under the so-called 'safe harbour' arrangements—whereby the US does not meet EU standards but is assumed to meet equivalent standards of data protection—was not valid.

The Court is commonly reluctant to set aside majoritarian political preferences expressed through EU legislative choices. This is plain in the soft standard of review it tends to adopt in circumstances where the legislature has acted in areas involving political, economic, and social choices which demand complex assessment.[205] It is visible too in its minimalist approach to review in the name of subsidiarity.[206] But its credentials as a constitutional court which has crafted a system that protects individual rights are strengthened by rulings such as *Test-Achats*, *Kadi*, and *Digital Rights*, where the Court refused to be swayed by a host of Member States intervening in support of the EU measures. This may be an instrumental means to entrench the supremacy of EU law against review practised by national courts and it may too, in the light of Opinion 2/13,[207] reveal how an autonomous EU legal order must be a fundamental rights-compliant legal order in order to survive, but there is more to it than strategy. The Court is (also) engaged in the protection of fundamental rights against political convenience.

[201] Joined Cases C-293/12 and C-594/12 *Digital Rights Ireland* et al judgment of 8 April 2014. See also Joined Cases C-92/09 and C-93/09 *Volker and Markus Schecke* [2010] ECR I-11063.

[202] Para 65.

[203] Paras 35, 54, 55.

[204] Case C-362/14 judgment of 6 October 2015.

[205] Eg Case C-66/04, Case C-270/12 note 142.

[206] Case C-491/01 note 193; Chapter 2.11.4.

[207] Note 153.

4
WHAT IS THE RELATIONSHIP BETWEEN EU LAW AND NATIONAL LAW?

4.1 THE CONSTITUTIONALIZED LEGAL ORDER

The previous chapter explored the process of 'constitutionalizing' the EU's legal order. The legislative process is characterized by democratic legitimation driven by State representation (Council) and by the representation of peoples (Parliament), while legitimacy through performance is promoted by the Commission's autonomy. The Court of Justice and the Treaties themselves, periodically revised over time, have in combination delivered a set of principles of law which reflect and control the scope of the public power which the EU's political institutions (and, on their behalf, public authorities in the Member States) may exercise. The EU's legal order has grown richer and deeper than orthodox public international law.

This chapter addresses a distinct but complementary dimension of the narrative of the 'constitutionalization' of the EU's legal order: that pertaining to its relationship with the legal orders of the Member States. The Treaties have nothing to say about the question of priority—which prevails in the event of conflict: EU or national law? Nor do the Treaties spell out how, if at all, national courts should apply rules sourced at EU level. The Court of Justice, by contrast, has had a great deal to say on these matters. From the very beginning, in landmark judgments delivered in the early 1960s, the Court has identified EU law as *supreme*—it applies in preference to national law in the event of conflict—and as *directly effective*, which means that rules of sufficient clarity and precision fall to be applied on an everyday basis by the national courts of the Member States. And the Court of Justice and the national courts are organically tied together in a co-operative relationship by a procedure that is foreseen explicitly in the Treaties, the preliminary reference procedure which permits, and in some circumstances requires, awkward points of EU law raised at national level to be transmitted to the Court in Luxembourg for authoritative resolution. The net result is that EU law exerts a much more powerful influence at national level than does orthodox public international law. This, as will become clear, has always been precisely the Court's mission. It presents it as international law—which it certainly is—but *also* as something more, something that directly controls aspects of the course of domestic legal proceedings—as something *new*. EU law is much more deeply *constitutionalized* than anything familiar on the international plane and, in particular in the claim to its supremacy over conflicting national law and in its directions about how EU law should be treated by courts in the Member States, EU law functions *as if* arranging the vertical relationship between tiers of governance in a federal system (of sorts).

4.2 THE PRELIMINARY REFERENCE PROCEDURE

Article 267 TFEU creates a channel of communication between national courts and the Court of Justice. This is the preliminary reference procedure, which empowers the Court to rule on matters concerning the interpretation of the Treaty and the validity and interpretation of acts of the institutions of the Union. National courts may—and in the case of a court against whose decision there is no remedy under national law, *must*—request the Court to provide a ruling. This ruling, once supplied, is then applied by the referring national court to dispose of the case. Without such a procedure, national courts would likely drift far apart in their understanding of EU rules. The existence of the preliminary reference promises a much higher degree of conformity in the interpretation and application of EU law at national level than can be found in the application of the typical international Treaty which lacks any such channel of judicial communication.

The preliminary reference procedure serves as an organic link between the national and the EU legal order. Many of the Court's most heroic judgments which have shaped the character of the Union legal order are preliminary rulings. And this is not at all a connection struck only between courts at the apex of national legal orders and the Court of Justice. Many preliminary rulings have been issued in response to references made by relatively low-level courts in the national legal orders. In fact, references by national constitutional courts in particular are rare and, under what has been astutely diagnosed as the pressure caused by the 'intensification' of the EU legal order,[1] have begun to trickle only recently.[2]

[1] See A.G. Cruz Villalón, para 40 of his Opinion in Case C-62/14 *Gauweiler*.

[2] The first by the Italian *Corte costituzionale* was made in 2008 (Case C-169/08 *Presidente del Consiglio dei Ministri* v *Regione sardegna* [2009] ECR I-10821); by the Spanish *Tribunal Constitucional* in 2011 (Case C-399/11 *Stefano Melloni* judgment of 26 February 2013); by the French *Conseil constitutionnel* in 2013 (Case C-168/13 PPU *Jeremy F* judgment of 30 May 2013); by the German BVerfG in 2014 (Case C-62/14 *Gauweiler* judgment of 16 June 2015).

Most of all, Article 267 TFEU holds out the promise of *uniformity*. Locating the Court of Justice as the authoritative voice in stating the meaning and effect of EU law is intended to promote the uniform application of EU law across the territory of the twenty-eight Member States. As the Court put it at an early stage, the procedure 'is essential for the preservation of the Community character of the law established by the Treaty and has the object of ensuring that in all circumstances the law is the same in all States of the Community'.[3] This is perforce an exaggeration, for no legal system spread across such diversity of tradition and structure can truly be the 'same' everywhere, but this discourse of sameness and uniformity is deep-rooted, and it is persistent. In December 2011 the Grand Chamber loudly proclaimed that 'The main purpose of the jurisdiction conferred on the Court by Article 267 TFEU is to ensure that European Union law is applied *uniformly* by national courts.'[4] In 2014, in Opinion 2/13, it referred to Article 267 as a 'keystone' of the judicial system, having 'the object of securing uniform interpretation of EU law... thereby serving to ensure its consistency, its full effect and its autonomy'.[5]

The claim is best understood in a relative sense, rather than as a frankly implausible model of mirrored perfection: *relative to* orthodox international law, EU law is apt for more uniform treatment by national judiciaries.

Thanks to the preliminary reference procedure, national courts applying EU law are not acting in solitary confinement. Instead they have access to the Court of Justice directly, by making a reference. Moreover, the Court has deepened the vigour of the procedure by holding that national courts should also rely on judgments of the Court which have been provoked by referring courts elsewhere in the Union.[6] This is not a system of binding precedent but it does mean that rulings of the Court radiate beyond the limits of the case at hand: the value for money of a single preliminary ruling is increased. Once again, in explaining this expansion, the Court appealed explicitly to the value of promoting the uniform application of EU law.[7] And the same logic, the quest for 'uniform interpretation', has promoted it to provide rulings even in cases that have no

[3] Case 166/73 *Rheinmühlen-Düsseldorf* [1974] ECR 33.

[4] Case C-366/10 *Air Transport Association of America* judgment of 21 December 2011 para 47 (emphasis added).

[5] Opinion of 18 December 2014, paras 176, 198.

[6] On validity, Case 66/80 *ICC* v *Amministrazione delle Finanze* [1981] ECR 1191; on interpretation, Joined Cases 28, 29, and 30/62 *Da Costa & Schaake NV* [1963] ECR 31.

[7] Case 66/80 note 6, paras 11, 12.

material connection with EU law where relevant national rules have been modelled on EU law.[8]

Exceptionally the Court of Justice declines jurisdiction, most prominently where it finds the question asked purely hypothetical and therefore of no relevance to the resolution of the dispute[9] or formulated in such an inadequate manner that it cannot provide a helpful answer.[10] Less exceptionally it strays beyond the limits promised by the concept of 'interpretation' of the law. Although in its landmark early ruling in *Costa* v *ENEL* the Court declared that the preliminary reference procedure, in contrast to the infringement procedure now found in Article 258 TFEU, granted it 'no jurisdiction either to apply the Treaty to a specific case or to decide upon the validity of a provision of domestic law in relation to the Treaty',[11] practice is more nuanced. This will surprise no one familiar with the slippery distinction between application and interpretation of law. The style in which a preliminary ruling is delivered varies. On occasion the Court makes it unavoidably obvious what shall be the outcome of the litigation pending before the national court. In *Walter Rau* v *de Smedt* the Court, asked to interpret Article 34 TFEU in the context of Belgian rules prohibiting the marketing of margarine other than in cube-shaped packs, observed that EU law is violated by rules demanding that packaging shall have a particular shape, 'for example the shape of a cube', in circumstances in which the consumer may be protected and informed by means which hinder the free movement of goods to a lesser degree.[12] Similarly, asked in *Eventech* whether black cabs and minicabs were in a comparable situation, which mattered for the purposes of EU state aid law since the former but not the latter were permitted to use bus lanes, the Court innocently declared it would offer the referring court 'guidance'—and then made very concrete its view that there was no comparability, given that only black cabs may ply for hire, must be wheelchair-friendly, must be metered, and must have drivers possessing 'the Knowledge [of London's streets]'.[13] Where the Court chooses to be so specific, the formal point that it lacks jurisdiction to rule on the compatibility of national law with EU is displaced in practical effect: the preliminary ruling procedure

[8] Eg Joined Cases C-297/88 and C-197/89 *Dzodzi* v *Belgian State* [1990] ECR I-3763.

[9] Eg Case C-83/91 *Wienand Meilicke* [1992] ECR I-4871; C-186/07 *Club Nautico de Gran Canaria* [2008] ECR I-60.

[10] Eg Cases C-320-322/90 *Telemarsicabruzzo* v *Circostel* [1993] ECR I-393; Case C-299/15 *Daniel Striani* judgment of 16 July 2015.

[11] Case 6/64 [1964] ECR 585 note 20.

[12] Eg Case 261/81 *Walter Rau* v *de Smedt* [1982] ECR 3961.

[13] Case C-518/13 judgment of 14 January 2015.

becomes 'the most important procedure for the enforcement of Union law and for the effective protection of rights conferred on individuals by Union law'.[14] But the Court's grip is not always so tight. It sometimes leaves much to national courts. Inviting the referring court to apply the proportionality principle to decide a case on free movement is a favoured device for achieving this (constitutionally proper) surrender of formal decision-making power. In reality the Court has a range of techniques. A ruling which is tied tightly to the facts of the case might help the referring national judge but exert little influence into the future; a ruling that is pitched in abstract terms might be of little help to the referring national judge and exert little influence into the future (though it will likely prompt more referrals in search of clarification); a ruling which is quasi-legislative in style, a 'blueprint', might or might not help the referring national judge but will certainly be influential into the future. Sometimes the Court's choice between cautious minimalism and more ambitious breadth is dictated by awareness of the room it wishes to leave (or not to leave) to the potential involvement of the EU legislative institutions in the relevant field.

The Court always provides a single collegiate judgment: there is no overt dissent in Luxembourg. This makes a contribution to the distinctive character of the Court's rulings, including those under the preliminary reference procedure. At its best this grants harmonious and vigorous authority to the Court as a single voice. At its worst it ensures the production of a ramshackle compromise, stripped of principle and reflecting no more than the bare minimum on which the several judges could agree. Rulings of the latter type may try the patience of national courts—or they may be greeted with relief because they grant flexible room for manoeuvre at national level.

Some of the Court's preliminary rulings are long forgotten while others are imprinted on the brain of every EU lawyer, and the Court's own drafting choices are a factor in that fate.[15] The margin between (permissible) interpretation and (impermissible) amendment tends to generate most of the inquiry into the Court's methodology (Section 4.10), but its

[14] R Barents, 'EU Procedural Law and Effective Legal Protection' (2014) 51 CMLRev 1437, 1455.

[15] See eg J. Komarek, 'Reasoning with Previous Decisions: Beyond the Doctrine of Precedent' (2013) 61 AJCL 149; D. Sarmiento, 'Half a Case at a Time: Dealing with Judicial Minimalism at the European Court of Justice', Ch 1 in M. Claes, M. De Visser, P. Popelier, and C. Van de Heyning (eds), *Constitutional Conversations in Europe: Actors, Topics and Procedures* (Intersentia, 2012) p 13.

style of reasoning, even when firmly within the sphere of interpretation, varies a lot. In short, in providing preliminary rulings the Court operates on a spectrum of specificity.[16]

Vivid variety attaches not only to the style of questions asked and to rulings delivered but also to the motivation for pursuing a preliminary reference. Interest groups, acting in their own name or in support of astutely chosen individual private litigants, exploit EU law to seek to upset established national practices. The preliminary reference procedure has been immensely fertile as a channel of co-operation for building the substance as well as the constitutional character of the EU legal order.[17] Moreover, national *courts* may enhance their position within the domestic legal order by relying on their possibility for direct contact with the Court in Luxembourg in order to step out from the shadow cast by higher national courts.

The success of the procedure is also its failure: the Court's workload has grown so large that delay in the delivery of rulings has become a real problem. The average length of proceedings has lately been reduced, but still stands at some sixteen months.[18] The Court would doubtless welcome confident application of EU law by national courts, both to contain its own workload and as an expression of the entrenchment of EU law in national judicial practice. However, there is evident tension between the Court's eagerness for national courts to assume more responsibility for the everyday interpretation and application of EU law on the one hand and, on the other, the anxiety that stemming the flow of references by becoming less co-operative will weaken the quest for uniformity by inducing national courts to adopt speculative interpretations of EU measures. Geographic and functional enlargements of the Union have increased this tension. The Court's patterns of internal management have been adjusted in response, evident for example in the rise of decisions taken by its chambers, of which there are now ten, but radical solutions requiring reform from the 'outside' which have been mooted—such as allowing the Court to select its own 'docket'—have not been delivered. The preliminary reference procedure looks much as it did when invented in the 1950s.[19]

[16] T. Tridimas, 'Constitutional Review of Member State Action: The Virtues and Vices of an Incomplete Jurisdiction' (2011) 9 Intl J Con L 737.

[17] See eg R. Cichowski, *The European Court and Civil Society: Litigation, Mobilization and Governance* (CUP, 2007); L. Conant, *Justice Contained: Law and Politics in the EU* (Cornell UP, 2002); H. Micklitz, *The Politics of Judicial Co-operation in the EU* (CUP, 2005).

[18] Statistics are provided in the Court's annual reports: http://curia.europa.eu/jcms/jcms/Jo2_11035/rapports-annuels.

[19] Its paragraph 4, added to deal with urgent cases, is the only main innovation.

Article 267 TFEU provides machinery for judicial co-operation in the EU. But it does not address the constitutional quality of the rules on which the Court of Justice is invited to provide interpretative assistance. Nothing in the Treaties deals with matters as fundamental as choosing which law prevails in the event of a conflict, EU or national, and nothing addresses the role of national courts, if any, in applying EU law. But these basic issues were tackled at a very early stage by the Court. Well within the first ten years the Court had established constitutional ground rules from which it has never deviated. EU law is supreme—it prevails over national law in the event of conflict—and EU law is capable of direct effect—provided its rules are sufficiently clear, they fall to be applied directly by national judges.

4.3 SUPREMACY (OR PRIMACY)

The Treaty does not make any provision for what should happen in the event of a conflict between EU law and national law. This gap invited the Court to its historically bold early judgments asserting the distinctive constitutional character of EU law. The ruling in *Costa* v *ENEL* was a preliminary reference made by a low-level Italian court.[20] The dispute concerned a trivial amount of money. But it allowed the Court to assert a principle of central and enduring importance in EU law: that it prevails over national law in the event of conflict. It has *supremacy*.

But how did the Court reach such a conclusion, in the absence of any explicit treatment of the matter of hierarchy in the founding Treaties? It could conceivably have drawn on orthodox international law: it is well established that a State may not excuse violation of a Treaty by pleading compliance with its own domestic law.[21] But it ostentatiously did not do so. Instead it located the source of authority within the EU legal order. And it openly asserted the *separation* of EU law from international law. So the ruling in *Costa* v *ENEL* ringingly states: 'By contrast with ordinary international treaties, the EEC Treaty has created its own legal system which, on the entry into force of the Treaty, became an integral part of the legal systems of the Member States and which their courts are bound to apply.'

So what is today EU law becomes 'an integral part' of national law simply by virtue of the entry into force of the Treaty—which certainly

[20] Case 6/64 [1964] ECR 585.

[21] Now Art 27 of the Vienna Convention of the Law of Treaties.

is, as the Court remarks, a contrast with the orthodox approach to international treaties, the force of which *within* national legal orders, if any, depends on the domestic constitutional rules governing the matter.

In *Costa* v *ENEL* the Court proceeded to examine the 'terms and spirit' of the Treaty of Rome, which has a 'special and original nature'. It effects 'a limitation of sovereignty or a transfer of powers from the States', albeit within limited fields. And that limitation, the Court added, is 'permanent'. Having accepted such a system on a basis of reciprocity it could no longer be open to Member States to assert a priority for domestic laws, for this would jeopardize the attainment of the Treaty's objectives. So the supremacy of EU law is nothing less than an essential element in the legal basis of the Union.

Union law overrides even national constitutionally protected rights, including fundamental rights. The Court made this clear for the first time in *Internationale Handelsgesellschaft*[22] and it has never deviated from this. The case, encountered already in Chapter 3.15, concerned alleged interference with principles of German constitutional law as a result of the EU's regulation of the market for cereals. The Court pointed out that to permit (what was then) EC law to be checked against conditions of validity set by national law would damage the 'uniformity and efficacy' of EC law. It is only against the standards of EU law that the validity of EU acts falls to be measured. This ruling is logical. Were national legal orders able to designate particular matters as too important to be subjected to the supremacy of Union law then the consequence would be variation in the scope and effect of EU law State by State. This is precisely what the Court in *Costa* v *ENEL* regarded as incompatible with the very nature of the system established by the Treaty.

The enduring vigour of the Court's commitment to EU law's supremacy is manifest in its 2013 ruling in *Stefano Melloni*.[23] This Court was asked whether a Member State (Spain) could make the execution of a European arrest warrant (EAW) subject to conditions intended to secure compliance with fundamental rights recognized by the Spanish constitution but which were *not* allowed under the governing EU measure.[24] Clearly the answer should be 'no', under the supremacy-driven reasoning of *Costa* v *ENEL* and *Internationale Handelsgesellschaft*. But Article 53 of the Charter, newly binding with effect from 2009, declares that nothing in the Charter shall be interpreted as restricting human rights and fundamental freedoms

[22] Case 11/70 [1970] ECR 1125.

[23] Case C-399/11 judgment of 26 February 2013.

[24] EU Framework Decision 2002/584 [2002] OJ L190/1.

recognized by Union law, international law and international agreements, and Member States' constitutions. Had this changed the hierarchy? It had not. The Court held that national law, even national constitutional law, may not be used to test the validity of EU acts, for otherwise this would 'undermine the principle of the primacy of EU law'.[25] The EU measure could be tested only against the standards set by EU law. And, proclaiming continuity, the Court cited *Internationale Handelsgesellschaft*, decided more than forty years earlier.

In December 2014 the Court took the opportunity to apply this logic, rooted in defence of 'a judicial system intended to ensure consistency and uniformity in the interpretation of EU law', to find that the arrangements planned in line with Article 6(2) TEU for the accession of the EU to the European Convention on Human Rights (ECHR) were not compatible with EU law.[26] The Court could not accept 'the bodies given decision-making powers by the ECHR' having the power to bind the EU and its institutions to a particular interpretation of the rules of EU law.[27] 'In particular', the Court added, 'it should not be possible for the ECtHR to call into question the Court's findings in relation to the scope ratione materiae of EU law, for the purposes, in particular, of determining whether a Member State is bound by fundamental rights of the EU'.[28] Then the Court referred to *Melloni*, to insist on a need for a *co-ordination* with the ECHR, in the sense that application of national standards with respect to the rights recognized by the Charter *that correspond to those guaranteed by the ECHR* must ensure the level of protection provided for by the Charter and must not compromise the primacy, unity, and effectiveness of EU law.[29] The point, then, is (in short) to protect the supremacy of EU law from stricter demands imposed either by national law or via the ECHR. And the necessary 'co-ordination' was not secured by the planned agreement on accession. The Court's principled claim was to protect the *autonomy* of EU law; the practical institutional consequence was to protect the exclusivity of the Court's jurisdiction over the meaning of EU law.

Valid EU law takes precedence over conflicting national rules. Moreover, validity is a matter determined exclusively by the Court of Justice. EU measures may be challenged as incompatible with general principles of law, including fundamental rights; EU measures may be challenged for violation of the principle of conferral and the principles of subsidiarity and proportionality. Such challenge is possible directly before

[25] Para 58. [26] Opinion 2/13 judgment of 18 December 2014 para 174.
[27] Para 184. [28] Para 186. [29] Para 189.

the Court of Justice (although restrictive standing rules confront private parties[30]) and it is also possible to direct such challenges through national proceedings, typically against national practices that are based on the EU measure that is open to attack. In such circumstances a national court may decide to uphold the validity of the challenged EU act but it may *not* find it unlawful and refuse to apply it. That, the Court concluded in *Firma Foto Frost* v *HZA Lubeck Ost*,[31] is a matter for the Court itself, and accordingly a national court which entertains doubts about the validity of an EU measure must make a preliminary reference, thereby yielding to the Luxembourg Court the exclusive jurisdiction to rule conclusively on the measure's fate (subject only to the particular case of interim suspension of a prejudicial measure pending final determination of validity[32]). Here too the language of uniformity plays a dominant role. Were authority *not* to reside exclusively in Luxembourg, then divergent views taken by national courts about the validity of EU acts would place in jeopardy the 'very unity' of the EU legal order and 'detract from the fundamental requirement of legal certainty'.[33] The Court badged its ruling in *Foto Frost* with concern to protect 'the necessary coherence of the system of judicial protection established by the Treaty'.[34] It is an enduring concern. When, as mentioned above, the Court in 2011 in *Air Transport Association of America* insisted on the role of Article 267 TFEU in ensuring the uniform application of EU law by national courts, it made this observation in the particular context of a question of validity of an EU Directive raised before a national court—and it explained that the requirement of uniformity is 'particularly vital' in such circumstances, where divergence among courts 'would be liable to jeopardise the very unity of the European legal order and to undermine the fundamental requirement of legal certainty'.[35]

The Court's stance is inspired by a desire to make the system work. Of course the Court is absolutely correct to claim in these foundational cases that the unity of the EU legal order is protected by the twin principles of supremacy and exclusive jurisdiction to rule on the validity of EU measures. The legal order would doubtless quickly fray around the edges were the Court to prefer a less top-down hierarchical model. So the Court's insistence that even the most minor piece of technical EU legislation ranks above the most cherished constitutional norm is remorselessly logical,

[30] Art 263(4) TFEU, Chapter 3.4.6.

[31] Case 314/85 [1987] ECR 4199.

[32] Case C-465/93 *Atlanta Fruchthandelsgesellschaft mbH* [1995] ECR I-3761; Case C-68/95 *T. Port* [1996] ECR I-6065.

[33] Case 314/85 note 31, para 15.

[34] Para 16.

[35] Case C-366/10 note 4, para 47.

because to hold otherwise would, as the Court put it, lead to 'the jeopardizing of the cohesion of the [Union]'.[36] But it is also deeply alarming, for it forces recognition of the stark consequence that technical, even trivial, rules governing cereals should prevail over the constitutional guarantees provided by a State to its citizens. One of the most cherished achievements of the post-Second World War period in initially western Europe and latterly almost the whole of Europe has been the embedding of respect for certain shared European values which are not to be set aside by the normal processes of majoritarian politics. *Internationale Handelsgesellschaft*, after all, was decided in 1970, only a generation since (west) Germany had emerged from the horrors of the exercise of State power unconstrained by respect for the individual.

There is, in truth, a certain selfishness, even arrogance, in the Court's eagerness to promote the efficiency and cohesion of EU law at the expense of national values. However, from the very beginning the Court had packaged its claim to supremacy along with a commitment to protect fundamental rights as a matter of EU law. Such rights are, the Court proclaimed in the foundational ruling in *International Handelsgesellschaft*, 'inspired by the constitutional traditions common to the Member States', and respect for fundamental rights 'forms an integral part of the general principles of law protected by the Court of Justice'.[37] So, as a matter of EU law, the regulation of the market does not have to comply with national laws on fundamental rights, but it does have to comply with the EU's system of fundamental rights protection. And in *Internationale Handelsgesellschaft* it did comply. This means that as long as the standards set and reliably enforced at EU level are at least as high as those preferred at national level then there is no damage done to constitutional guarantees within the Member States by the transfer of competence to the EU effected by the Treaties. National courts need not protect individuals from fundamental rights violations committed by the EU because the Court of Justice will do so.

Stefano Melloni follows the same logic, while sharpening still further appreciation of the magnitude of the Court of Justice's claim and the responsibility it has assumed.[38] The Court's adherence to its insistence that EU law, even EU secondary legislation, has primacy over national law, even national constitutional law, arose not in some esoteric area of agricultural market regulation, which was at stake in *Internationale Handelsgesellschaft*,

[36] Case 44/79 *Hauer* v *Rheinland-Pfalz* [1979] ECR 3727.
[37] Case 11/70 note 22, para 5. [38] Case C-399/11 note 2.

but rather in the heartland of criminal justice and individual protection. The EAW, which triggered the apparent conflict in *Melloni* between Spanish constitutional law and the requirements of EU law, is a device designed to promote mutual recognition by replacing lengthy extradition procedures with quicker procedures for surrender of individuals across borders. The EAW has been criticized for deepening action in common at EU level in a way that circumvents cherished national safeguards for those accused of criminal behaviour. However, in *Advocaten voor de wereld* the Court of Justice tested the validity of the Framework Decision against the requirements of EU law, and upheld it.[39] In particular, the Court insisted that although the EU respects fundamental rights, there was here no violation of them. It mentioned in this regard the Charter, albeit then in its non-binding 2000 version. *Melloni*, dealing with the Charter as a binding instrument, follows the same line. The Court, in defence of the principle of supremacy, refuses to permit Spanish constitutional law to be used to check the validity of the EU's EAW, but it demands that, as a condition of its validity, the EAW meet the standards demanded by EU law, most pertinently EU fundamental rights. It found that it did so comply.

It is exactly here that the claim to supremacy is indissociably connected to the claim that the EU is also a site for respecting values that are integral to the political systems of the Member States. The Court, and latterly the Treaty, has been vigorously active in promoting respect for human rights as a condition of legality also at transnational level: no measure adopted by the EU will be allowed to survive unless it complies with the conditions of legality imposed by EU law. Not the least of the reasons for this is that failure to embed such values in the EU legal order will likely provoke a muscular response from national courts anxious to maintain such protection at national level—if necessary in defiance of the claim to supremacy.

The key to *Melloni* is the Court's reverence for its own history. The rise of the area of freedom, security, and justice and the widening of the EU's role, and with it that of the Court, alter the type of cases which reach the Court, as the esoteric joys of agricultural levies are today replaced by the liberty of the person. Supremacy is a claim made only within the scope of the EU's conferred competence, another reason why the principle of conferral examined in Chapter 2 is so vital, but that scope has been steadily widened over time by revision of the Treaties. Supremacy does not

[39] Case C-303/05 *Advocaten voor de wereld* [2007] ECR I-3633. Other similar rulings have followed. See E.Herlin-Karnell, 'From Mutual Trust to the Full Effectiveness of EU Law: 10 Years of the European Arrest Warrant' (2013) 38 ELRev 79.

change—*Melloni* shows the Court's refusal to make any structural alteration in its approach—but the scope of its implications does. The Court has carefully protected its pre-existing vision of an EU legal order built on protection of fundamental rights inextricably combined with a claim to the supremacy of that legal order, under an assumption that only this model, hierarchically favouring EU law over national law and forbidding EU law to be tested against stricter national standards, could ensure that EU law applied uniformly across the territory of all the Member States. The Court's logic is iron-clad when seen from the perspective of preserving the coherence of EU law. This is but one value, however. The more sensitive question is whether this instrumental reasoning is adequate to justify a leap beyond the text of a Treaty which is barren of treatment of such matters. The quest for uniformity serves as a means to wrest power from national judiciaries into the hands of the EU's own judges. Moreover, as will be seen, it causes instability *within* national judiciaries too. Luxembourg is not the only viewpoint, and the readiness of national courts to dance to this tune even where it risks offending their constitutionally protected values is an intriguing story, best left for later in this chapter (Section 4.11).

The Court's insistence that EU law is supreme and must prevail in the event of conflict with national law provoked a series of preliminary references from national courts which permitted the Court to elaborate the implications of the principle of supremacy. In particular, it rapidly became apparent that national legal procedures might require adaptation in so far as they failed to ensure the logical consequences of supremacy and EU law's thirst for uniform application. In *Simmenthal* the Court instructed that 'every national court must, in a case within its jurisdiction, apply Community law in its entirety and protect rights which the latter confers on individuals and must accordingly set aside any provision of national law which may conflict with it, whether prior or subsequent to the Community rule'.[40]

The background to this decision, another preliminary ruling, lay in Italian rules reserving the setting aside of acts as unconstitutional to certain high courts or to the legislative process. This, the Court of Justice concluded, could not apply to EU law. Restricting the capacity of lower courts in this manner was not compatible with EU law, which requires the national judge to give 'full effect' to EU law, if necessary refusing of its own motion to apply conflicting provisions of national law.

[40] Case 106/77 *Simmenthal* [1978] ECR 629.

In consequence, lower national courts are empowered at the expense of their domestically superior counterparts. EU law destabilizes national judicial hierarchies. Moreover, individuals are able to seek the vindication of EU law-sourced rights in a much more expeditious fashion than would be permitted under a system that forced them to appeal to the designated higher authority. This tends to induce private litigation in a manner apt to promote more effective policing of EU rules. This is thematically familiar: from the perspective of EU law the advantages are clear, from the perspective of maintaining the integrity of national legal orders and judicial hierarchies less so.

In similar vein in *Interedil Srl* the Italian Corte suprema di cassazione held that the Italian courts had jurisdiction to hear bankruptcy proceedings.[41] A local Italian court, the Tribunale di Bari, took the view that this was incorrect as a matter of EU law because Regulation 1346/2000 on insolvency allocated the matter to the courts of the UK. A reference was made to the Court of Justice on the interpretation of the relevant provision of the Regulation but first the Court was asked to address the argument that the Corte suprema's ruling had acquired the force of *res judicata*, and so a dispute no longer existed. The Court held that a national court is not 'bound by a national procedural rule under which that court is bound by the rulings of a higher national court, where it is apparent that the rulings of the higher court are at variance with European Union law, as interpreted by the Court of Justice'.[42] Once again the lesson holds that EU law breaks open matters closed under national law.

The offending national rule does not vanish. EU law does not require that a national court declare it invalid. It is, as the Court remarked in *Simmenthal*, 'inapplicable'. So the national judge's job is to 'disapply that rule'.[43] Some authors prefer to refer to primacy rather than supremacy precisely in order to capture this notion that EU law controls the applicability, not the validity of national law (and indeed primacy is the word normally preferred in the Court's judgments, primauté being the word in French).[44] It falls to the national legislature to amend the legislation to remove the violation of EU law—because even a rule that is routinely judicially disapplied shall not remain in place because of the damage it

[41] Case C-396/09 *Interedil Srl* [2011] ECR I-9915.

[42] Para 39.

[43] Cases C-10-22/97 *Ministero delle Finanze* v *IN.CO.GE* [1998] ECR I-6307 para 21; Case C-314/08 *Krzysztof Filipciak* [2009] ECR I-11049.

[44] See M. Claes, 'The Primacy of EU Law in European and National Law', Ch 8 in A. Arnull and D. Chalmers, *The Oxford Handbook of European Union Law* (OUP, 2015), pp 182–5.

may inflict on legal certainty.[45] The Court pulls a deft trick here: national law is not *invalid* for lack of conformity with EU law, but it is incumbent on the State as a matter of EU law to eliminate it in the name of preservation of legal certainty and effectiveness, which in this sense add something extra beyond supremacy and the obligation of disapplication. This preserves the jurisdiction of the Member State, rather than the Court of Justice, to decide on the constitutional validity of national law: so too it asserts a separation between the EU legal order and those of the Member States. And this is not mere fiction. The law in question is not exterminated by EU law and it may be retained—applied by judges and slimmed down by the legislature—in so far as it applies to situations which lack an EU dimension. Doubtless then it will be the subject of protest that it unfairly discriminates against those who happen not to have crossed a border, but that is a matter to be addressed under domestic law because it is a domestic issue.

In *Factortame*, yet another product of the fertile channel of co-operation provided by the preliminary reference procedure, the Court explained that where a national court considers that the sole obstacle which precludes it from granting interim relief is a rule of national law, then it must set aside that rule.[46] The background here was an English rule precluding the grant of interim relief against the Crown. This, the Court of Justice concluded, obstructed the effective application of EU law, and consequently national courts should as a matter of EU law regard themselves as freed from the bar erected by national law. The Court's point was not that they *must* grant such a remedy (which is in effect the temporary suspension of a statute), but rather that they must be competent so to do, depending on the circumstances. Once again, it is the involvement of claimed EU law rights that triggers change, and it would have been open to the UK to retain the rule precluding interim relief against the Crown in purely domestic proceedings. Subsequently English courts made the convenient finding that in fact the rule in question did not exist even for the purpose of domestic proceedings.[47] EU law requires change within its formal reach but it may induce wider change at national level too.

What is at stake here is the empowerment of national judges by EU law. They were permitted in *Simmenthal* to play a role reserved under national law to higher courts and the legislative process and in *Factortame*

[45] Cf eg Case 167/73 *Commission* v *France* [1974] ECR 359. Case C-367/98 *Commission* v *Portugal* [2002] ECR I-4731.

[46] Case C-213/89 *Factortame* [1990] ECR I-2433.

[47] *M* v *Home Office* [1994] 1 AC 377.

they acquired a role previously reserved to political processes. This is a further demonstration of the distance that the Court of Justice has placed between EU law and public international law. An orthodox understanding of international law would certainly not provide Italy or the UK with any defence simply because their courts were not equipped with the power to correct the legal infraction, but the State's default would be addressed on the international plane. EU law, by contrast, makes more subversive demands of national procedures. Moreover, lower courts are able to exploit the preliminary reference procedures exactly in order to recruit the Court of Justice as an ally in seeking domestic change.

The Court's rulings have become remarkably intricate. *Melki and Abdeli* asked whether identity checks at or within 20 kilometres of the French border constituted 'border checks' within the meaning of the EU's legislative *acquis*, but it also raised a procedural question.[48] At stake was an interlocutory procedure for the review of the constitutionality of national laws. This violates EU law if either before the submission of a question on constitutionality to the responsible national court or after the decision of that court all the other national courts are prevented from making a preliminary reference. Citing inter alia *Simmenthal* and *Factortame*, the Court insisted on the need to protect 'the effectiveness of EU law' and the 'full force and effect' of EU rules.[49] The Court did not only explain what is *not* allowed: it went out of its way to explain what *is* allowed. Such national procedures are permitted on condition that the other national courts remain free to make a preliminary reference at whatever stage of the proceedings they consider appropriate; to adopt any measure necessary to ensure provisional judicial protection of the rights conferred under EU law; and to disapply, at the end of such an interlocutory procedure, the national legislative provision at issue if they consider it to be contrary to EU law. This serves as a good example of the Court's penchant for shaping a preliminary ruling as a quasi-legislative 'blueprint' (Section 4.2). The result is to channel the autonomy of the national court and to structure in a rather detailed way how it shall and shall not treat EU law.[50]

Fransson adds to the store of rulings which amplify the concrete role to be played by national judiciaries in the shadow of the requirements of supremacy.[51] The reference asked whether it was compatible with EU law for national courts to disapply any provision of national law contrary to a fundamental right guaranteed by the ECHR and by the Charter *only*

[48] Joined Cases C-188/10 and C-189/10 [2010] ECR I-5667.

[49] Para 44.

[50] Cf in this area Case C-41/11 *Inter-Environnement Wallonie* judgment of 28 February 2012.

[51] Case C-617/10 *Fransson* judgment of 26 February 2013.

where that infringement is clear from the instruments concerned or the case law relating to them. The Court of Justice replied that such a presumption in favour of the national provision is *not* permitted under EU law. The Court cited *Simmenthal* and *Melki and Abdeli* and repeated its concern to protect the effectiveness of EU law. The national court must not be blocked from being able to assess fully the compatibility of the national provision with EU law.

Long-term consistency is visible in the Court's case law. In 2013, in *Fransson*, it insisted on the obligation placed on a national court to set aside any provision of national law which might impair the effectiveness of EU law in a sentence which *exactly* replicated one used thirty-five years previously in *Simmenthal*, save only for the switch from European 'Community' to 'Union'.[52]

What the Court is doing in these remarkable cases is requiring the setting aside of frequently cherished features of the national legal order on the imprecise basis of pursuit of effectiveness.[53] Especially where the Court empowers lower courts, it disempowers higher courts: it weakens the authority of national constitutional hierarchies. Still, supremacy does not mean that an individual may in all circumstances expect a national court to set aside national measures which are in conflict with EU law. Within any legal order, even at national level, the fact that a particular practice is not compatible with the law does not invariably mean that the point may be taken in particular legal proceedings. Time limits provide a neat illustration. In *Q-Beef* the applicant sought recovery of levies paid to the Belgian state in violation of EU law.[54] But more than five years had elapsed since the claim arose and so the action was time-barred under Belgian law. The Court recognized the role of reasonable time limits in providing legal certainty and would not require that they be set aside unless the conduct of the national authorities combined with the existence of a limitation period resulted in totally depriving a person of the opportunity to enforce rights. So a breach of EU law would go unremedied. But this can happen under national law too. What EU law strikes at is national systems that make *ineffective* the protection of the individual—as in a case such as *Factortame*. There lies a line between impermissible national procedural rules and those which serve an interest that is enough to resist the demands of EU law. This issue, the extent to which national procedural

52 *Fransson* note 177, para 46; *Simmenthal* note 40, para 22.

53 Cf J. Komarek, 'The Place of Constitutional Courts in the EU' (2013) 9 Euro Const Law Rev 420.

54 Case C-89/10 *Q-Beef* judgment of 8 September 2011.

law is subject to adaptation in the name of EU law's demand for effectiveness, deserves separate treatment (Section 4.5).

4.4 DIRECT EFFECT

EU law is capable of *direct effect*, which means that provisions of the Treaty and of secondary legislation which are sufficiently precise and unconditional shall be applied in proceedings before national courts.

This is the Court's doing. As with EU law's supremacy over national law, so too its direct effect within national law: the Treaty makes no such explicit stipulation. Article 288 TFEU refers to the particular attribute of *direct applicability*, which pertains to Regulations (alone) and means that they are law in all the Member States once made. Direct effect is something broader, for it concerns the capacity of any sufficiently precise provision of EU law to be applied in everyday judicial practice at national level. The existence of the Article 267 TFEU preliminary reference procedure *implies* that EU law is capable of being applied by national courts, for otherwise the purpose of that procedure would be weakened. But it is at least arguable that, in conformity with the normal assumption that it is for domestic law to choose how, if at all, to admit rules made at the international level into domestic legal proceedings, there should be no requirements *imposed by EU law* pertaining to the treatment of EU law by national judges.

And, one should be aware, exactly this argument was—unsuccessfully—pressed on the Court when it first addressed this issue, as early as 1962. *Van Gend en Loos*, another preliminary ruling, concerned a customs duty imposed on the importation of ureaformaldehyde from Germany into the Netherlands in breach of EU law on the free movement of goods.[55] Van Gend en Loos claimed reimbursement of the sum before the Dutch courts. A preliminary reference was made in order to discover whether the Treaty could assist a private litigant before a national court. The Belgian government argued that the question of EU law's treatment within national legal orders was, like the treatment of international Treaties generally, a matter of *national* constitutional law, not EU law (and that it would accordingly vary among the Member States). And the Dutch government argued that an alleged infringement of the Treaty by a Member State should be controlled via the Commission-initiated infringement procedure created by the Treaty (today Article 258 TFEU),

[55] Case 26/62 *Van Gend en Loos* [1963] ECR 1.

and that it was inapt also to be brought before the Court via the preliminary reference procedure. Advocate General Roemer was of a similar view in his Opinion in the case. This is to insist on the separation of EU and national procedures.

But this was not the approach chosen by the Court of Justice. It found EU law capable of *direct effect*, which means it may create legally enforceable rights before national courts. And, in parallel with the interpretative approach which discovered the supremacy of EU law, this finding derives from the nature, not the text, of the Treaty.

In this 'heroic' decision of *Van Gend en Loos* the Court reasoned that the Treaty objective of establishing an integrated market of direct concern to interested parties implied that what was at stake was 'more than an agreement which merely creates mutual obligations between the contracting states'. Not only Member States but also their nationals are addressed by EU law; and EU law 'not only imposes obligations on individuals but is also intended to confer on them rights which become part of their legal heritage'. So Dutch courts, not simply the EU's own Court, should as a matter of EU law protect such rights.

The emergence of direct effect mirrors that of supremacy. Undeterred by the absence of any explicit treatment of the matter in the Treaties, the Court prefers instead to extract a view of the nature of EU law from within the system and purpose of the Treaty. Its reasoning—based on drawing consequences from the existence of the Article 267 TFEU preliminary reference procedure and more broadly the place of the individual within the texture of the Treaty—carries weight, but a more modest view was entirely plausible. The Court consciously chose to make a leap. And it is a remarkable leap. The Court frames the Treaty not only as a binding instrument of international law but also as a means for it to assert a loud voice describing how it is applied within the legal orders of the Member States. So *as a matter of EU law* it is not only at inter-State level, in the EU's own institutional architecture, that EU law binds; it is also for national courts to apply EU law as directly effective (and supreme) in domestic proceedings. The Court has actively distanced EU law from orthodox international treaty law—it is, the Court declared in *Van Gend en Loos*, 'a new legal order of international law', in similar vein to its depiction soon afterwards in *Costa* v *ENEL* as a legal system that operates 'by contrast with ordinary international treaties'. EU law is international law, but not only international law: it is transnational law too—and it is (a form of) constitutional law as well. It affects *individuals*—it grants them benefits and it imposes obligations on them.

This determined emphasis on individuals has a very significant practical consequence for the policing of EU law. The Treaty envisages that where a Member State is in breach of EU law, the Commission shall initiate so-called 'infringement proceedings' pursuant to (what is today) Article 258 TFEU, which may, if the Member State fails to comply, result in a judgment of the Court of Justice recording the infraction. If left unremedied, that may subsequently expose the Member State to financial sanctions as a result of a further decision of the Court, as foreseen by Article 260 TFEU. And persistently defaulting States have on occasion been financially penalized. This is a procedure which is *relatively* powerful when compared with most Treaty-based regimes: the Commission enjoys autonomy in selecting which infractions it will prioritize, the Court enjoys compulsory jurisdiction, and there are concrete penalties that may be imposed. But even so the infringement procedure has its weaknesses: unearthing violations may be difficult and proceedings tend to be slow and sporadic. The principle of direct effect carries the practical consequence that, quite independently of action taken at EU level, a defaulting Member State may also find itself the subject of control exercised by its *own* courts, applying directly effective EU law at the behest of an aggrieved individual. This is commonly known as the principle of 'dual vigilance'. Enforcement is both centralized—in the hands of the Commission—and decentralized—in the hands of private individuals. The significance of this in shaping the 'new legal order' is immense. The direct effect of EU law, coupled to its supremacy over national law in the event of conflict, asserts the deep penetration of EU law into national legal orders.

Mancini and Keeling vividly claimed that *Van Gend en Loos* took EU law 'out of the hands of politicians and bureaucrats' and 'gave it to the people': it was, they asserted, a democratizing achievement.[56] One might wish to be sceptical about who these 'people' really are. Most litigation involving assertion of EU law rights is driven by powerful repeat-playing commercial interests, and endowing such trends with the sheen of 'democracy' looks generous. And the deregulatory teeth of EU law are far sharper than the re-regulatory: Treaty provisions that restrain public authorities and in some cases private parties from restricting inter-State

[56] F. Mancini and D. Keeling, 'Democracy and the European Court of Justice' (1994) 57 MLR 175, 183. For an earlier but thematically comparable account see P. Pescatore, 'The Doctrine of Direct Effect: An Infant Disease of Community Law' (1983) 8 ELRev 155; also stressing the place of the individual, D. Halberstam, 'The Bride of Messina: Constitutionalism and Democracy in Europe' (2005) 30 ELRev 775; D. Chalmers and L. Barroso, 'What *Van Gend en Loos* Stands For' (2014) 12 Int Jnl Const Law 105.

trade are typically precise and have been found to be directly effective, whereas many of the rules that elaborate the EU's regulatory policies in the field of consumer, employee, and environmental protection are contained in Directives which are never enforceable directly against private parties (Section 4.7.2) and which, given their character under Article 288 TFEU as measures that set only an objective while leaving detailed choices about implementation to Member States, ought normally to lack the necessary unconditionality required of rules capable of direct effect. But scepticism about such imbalances in the private enforceability of EU law cynicism should have limits, for some significant cases before national courts have involved the promotion of social protection, including *Defrenne* v *SABENA*,[57] and the Court is quicker than one might initially expect to find Directives capable of creating directly effective obligations. Moreover, the 'individual' as lodestone has taken the Court beyond trading rights as a legitimation of EU authority into fundamental rights too.

In any event Mancini and Keeling are absolutely right to insist on the *practical* significance of direct effect as a means of empowering individual applicants in the quest to hold parties to bargains undertaken in the Treaties or in secondary legislation. The sharp edges of these rights, enforceable with vigour, 'legalize' matters that might in a different context be dealt with through more collective politically driven arrangements and the type of dense administrative and enforcement capacity which are simply missing in the EU. One could understand the Court's choices about the constitutionalized vigour of EU law as a means to promote the credibility of Treaty commitments undertaken by the Member States on a reciprocal basis. Absence of any hint that those choices be set aside at times of Treaty revision lends support to such an understanding. Certainly the Court was influenced by the diet of cases fed to it by individual litigants, frequently powerful commercially motivated actors, combined with the Court's broader perception of the need to deepen the integrative process.[58] So, in order to generate the radical changes needed to convert the fragmented chaos of political Europe into a single economic space, the result is intensified litigation—and more lawyers too.[59]

[57] Case 43/75 [1976] ECR 455.

[58] Cf discussion of feedback loops in litigation, A. Stone Sweet, 'The European Court of Justice', Ch 6 in P. Craig and G. De Búrca (eds), *The Evolution of EU Law* (OUP, 2nd ed, 2011).

[59] D. Kelemen, *Eurolegalism: The Transformation of Law and Regulation in the European Union* (Harvard UP, 2011).

Not all EU law is capable of direct effect. There are conditions which pertain to the character of the rule and the type of legal act. In the first instance, a provision must be sufficiently precise and unconditional to merit being found directly effective: it must be 'justiciable', that is, of a type that is apt for judicial application. So, for example, in *Deutsche Lufthansa* v *ANA* the Court refused to allow a charge levied by an airport authority for services provided to an airline to be tested against Treaty provisions listing the EU's activities:[60] they did 'not lay down obligations on Member States or public or private bodies'.[61] Treaty provisions of a programmatic nature are not typically capable of direct effect and depend for their development on the adoption of secondary legislation (which may then be precise enough to be treated as directly effective, if necessary).[62] But the firmer the rule, the more apt it is for application by a national court. And the Court of Justice has frequently been assiduous in finding a sufficiently precise core even to a legal rule which might have appeared too conditional to attract direct effect. This has already been encountered in Chapter 2.9. In *Reyners* v *Belgian State*[63] a Dutch national resident in Belgium holding a Belgian legal qualification was denied admission as an *avocat* in Belgium because of rules restricting that profession to Belgians. His argument that he had rights to establish himself in Belgium was countered by the submission that (what is now) Article 49 TFEU could not be applied directly by national courts because its implementation was dependent on the issue of specific Directives regulating the professions. The Court disagreed. It found that since Reyners was subject to conditions which would not have been applied to an identically qualified Belgian, a clear breach of the unambiguous rule against discrimination on grounds of nationality had occurred. The adoption of secondary legislation facilitates free movement, but the rule of equal treatment is independently enforceable. Such an interpretative choice greatly increases the ability for private parties and the Commission to challenge obstructive national rules, stripping away the discretion of the political process to choose the pace of liberalization of the market (*in casu*, for professional services) by fashioning legislative solutions. Another good example, this time occurring under EU secondary legislation rather than the Treaty itself, is provided by *Francovich*.[64]

[60] Arts 3 and 4 EC, now in adjusted versions Arts 3–6 and 119 TFEU.

[61] Case C-181/06 [2007] ECR I-5903 para 31.

[62] The same question arises in distinguishing between rights and principles under the Charter (Chapter 3.15.4), although it is far from clear that the same answers are appropriate.

[63] Case 2/74 [1974] ECR 631.

[64] Joined Cases 6/90 and 9/90 *Francovich* [1991] ECR I-5357.

A worker who had suffered loss as a result of the insolvency of his employer wished to claim the protection envisaged by a Directive (80/987), but since Italy had failed to transpose that Directive into national law, he could succeed only if able to rely on the terms of the Directive itself in proceedings before the Italian courts. The Directive offered options from which the Member State could choose in determining the operative date from which protection should be available in the case of unpaid wages. But the Court did not consider that this robbed the legal rule of a sufficiently unconditional character, because it was possible to identify a 'minimum guarantee' envisaged by the Directive. There was therefore a directly effective right to claim the sum that would have been due had the State, in implementing the Directive, chosen the model least generous to the worker. This illustrates the Court's creativity in finding even a scheme conferring discretion on the implementing Member State to be capable of generating a minimum protection which is apt to be treated as direct effect by a national court.[65] But there are limits. The Court proceeded in *Francovich* to find that the transposition of the Directive required a choice to be made about the institutional arrangements governing the payment of compensation. There was nothing concrete in the Directive, so on this point the required unconditional legal rule on which the worker could rely was missing. The legal rule was not 'justiciable': it was not directly effective in proceedings before a national court. The claimant failed at this hurdle but, as will be explained in Section 4.6, this was not the end of Francovich's contribution to the 'constitutionalization' of EU law, because the Court proceeded to consider whether even in the absence of direct effect he could seek compensation from the Italian state for its failure to put in place the scheme of legal protection mandated by the Directive. And he could.

The four main types of binding legal rule embraced by EU law are provisions of the Treaty, Regulations, Directives, and Decisions. They need to be kept separate for the purposes of understanding the scope of direct effect. Treaty provisions may be directly effective against the State—that is, they may be vertically directly effective. So, for example, the rules on free movement of goods and services, found in Articles 34 and 56 TFEU, are directly effective. A private party whose trading interests are affected in violation of these Treaty provisions may challenge national restrictions before a national court, asserting the EU rules as directly effective—and therefore apt for application by a national judge—and supreme too, so

[65] See similarly Case C-194/08 *Susanne Gassmayr* [2010] ECR I-6281.

requiring the disapplication of offending national law. There are hundreds of such cases (Chapter 6). Some Treaty provisions are capable of direct effect against private parties too—that is, they are capable of horizontal direct effect. This is true of Articles 101 and 102 TFEU, the Treaty competition rules which forbid particular types of anti-competitive practices and abusive conduct by an economically dominant firm. National courts, in addition to the Commission, are responsible for the application of these rules. And although Article 157 TFEU directs that 'the principle of equal pay for male and female workers for equal work' shall be ensured by each Member State, the Court long ago decided in *Defrenne* v *SABENA* that it is directly effective even in proceedings between individuals.[66] So this core element of social policy can be pursued through private litigation before national courts.

Regulations and Decisions are capable of direct effect too. It depends on the terms of each particular measure. The key is, once again, their character as a sufficiently justiciable norm. Directives, however, seem different. According to Article 288 TFEU they require implementation at national level. Since the Member State chooses the applicable form and methods for converting the Directive into domestic law, there would appear to be no *unconditional* rule at EU level. Nevertheless, the Court has found Directives capable of direct effect in some circumstances, and more generally has found other devices for ensuring they exert an influence on national proceedings where a Member State has failed to carry out the required act of transposition. The special case of Directives in proceedings before national courts deserves separate treatment, which it will be given in Section 4.7.

4.5 RIGHTS AND REMEDIES

Article 19(1) TEU dictates that Member States shall provide remedies sufficient to ensure effective legal protection in the fields covered by Union law. This is supplemented by Article 47 of the Charter, which stipulates that everyone whose rights and freedoms guaranteed by EU law are violated 'has the right to an effective remedy before a tribunal in compliance with the conditions laid down in this Article'. Article 19(1) TEU was an innovation of the Treaty of Lisbon while Article 47 of the Charter owes its binding force to that same Treaty, but, as already mentioned in Section 4.3, the Court has a long-standing commitment to the importance of securing the effective application of EU law at national level. Both Article 19(1)

[66] Case 43/75 *Defrenne* v *SABENA* [1976] ECR 455.

TEU and Article 47 of the Charter are in effect confirmation of the Court's approach, but on their own they are hopelessly inadequate to convey a sense of how the Court has energetically asserted not only that EU law is *supreme* and *directly effective* but also that it makes demands of the procedures and remedies which secure the vindication at national level of the rights it creates. For that, a glimpse into the case law is required.

The Court first articulated its view in 1976. In *Comet* it conceded that in the absence of any relevant EU rules, it is for the national legal order of the Member States to designate the rules and procedures governing the protection of directly effective rights conferred on individuals by EU law.[67] It stated this *national procedural autonomy* to be subject only to two apparently rather limp provisos: first, that the rules be no less favourable than those governing the same right of action domestically, and second that it should not be impossible in practice to exercise those EU law rights. The 'relevant EU rules' to which the Court referred in *Comet* are few and far between—there has been negligible political will to support legislative intervention into national law on remedies and procedures, and EU measures intruding on the law governing remedies are largely confined to niche areas of public contracting, injunctions in consumer cases, competition law, and access to environmental justice.[68] So the matter has devolved to the Court. The first of its provisos in *Comet*, which is basically a requirement of non-discrimination designed to ensure the EU-based litigant is at least as well treated as the litigant relying on national law, is not at all surprising. This so-called principle of equivalence requires that the relevant national rules on procedure and remedies be applied without making any distinction between breaches of EU and national law, in so far as the purpose and cause of action are similar.[69] In the context of the preliminary reference procedure that assessment of similarity would normally belong with the national court. By contrast, the second proviso in *Comet* has proved much more radically transformative. The Court swiftly converted the requirement that it should not be impossible in practice to exercise EU law rights into a more actively expressed formula which insisted on the obligation effectively to protect those rights. In *Simmenthal, Factortame*, and subsequently *Francovich* (examined further in Section 4.6) the Court fastened on to the defence of the 'effectiveness' of EU law as a

[67] Case 45/76 [1976] ECR 2043.

[68] Dir 89/665 OJ [1989] L395/33; Dir 2007/66 OJ [2007] L335/31; Dir 2009/22 OJ [2009] L110/30; Dir 2014/104 OJ [2014] L349/1; Dir 2003/35 OJ [2003] L156/17.

[69] Eg Case C-326/96 *Levez* [1998] ECR I-7835 para 41; Case C-63/08 *Virginie Pontin* [2009] ECR I-10467 para 45.

reason for intervention in national practice.[70] This has become the driving concern. Typically today the Court simply describes national autonomy as conditioned by EU law's principles of equivalence and effectiveness.[71]

This means that simply granting to the EU-based litigant the same protection as that available domestically may not be adequate. As a matter of EU law domestic procedure may need to be upgraded, in so far as it falls below the EU-mandated standard of 'effectiveness'. This is important in understanding the general theme of 'constitutionalization' whereby the Court has actively distanced EU law from orthodox public international law. EU law is unique because it penetrates deeply into national legal orders and makes explicit, concrete, and disruptive demands that national law shall work in the service of EU law.

Cases dealing with limitation periods have been particularly regular visitors to Luxembourg. It is common in all legal systems to provide that legal proceedings may not be initiated once a defined period of time has elapsed after loss has been suffered. Placing such a limit on the initiation of a legal challenge is plainly detrimental to the effective protection of rights held by a party who misses the deadline. At the same time, such procedures, which lift the indefinite threat of litigation from the shoulders of potential defendants, are of obvious value in promoting legal certainty and securing the efficient administration of justice. Where the rights which may not be pursued because of lapse of time are based on EU law, the tension arises: which should prevail? Where does the 'effective' protection of EU law rights yield to other concerns such as legal certainty?

The Court has no objection in principle to use of reasonable limitation periods designed to achieve these objectives, but EU law would require the disapplication of a limitation that is so short as to deny the applicant effective protection of his or her EU law rights.[72] The Court is not shy of providing occasional clarification designed to guide the national court: so, for example, it has suggested that fifteen days seems too short[73] while three years seems reasonable.[74] In the above-mentioned

[70] Case 106/77 note 40, paras 18, 22, 23; Case C-213/89 note 46, paras 20, 21; Cases C-6/90 and C-9/90 note 64, paras 33, 34, 39.

[71] Eg Case C-413/12 *Asociación de Consumidores Independientes de Castilla y León* v *Anuntis Segundamano España SL* judgment of 5 December 2013 para 30; Case C-295/04 *Vincenzo Manfredi* [2006] ECR I-6619 para 62.

[72] Eg Case C-261/95 *Palmisani* v *INPS* [1997] ECR I-4025; Case C-2/06 *Willy Kempter* [2008] ECR I-411; Case C-63/08 note 69.

[73] Case C-63/08 note 69.

[74] Case C-62/00 *Marks & Spencer* [2002] ECR I-6325; Case C-445/06 *Danske Slagterier* [2009] ECR I-2119.

Q-Beef a five-year limitation was found in principle compatible with EU law; moreover, it was found that it is for national law to determine from when time starts to run, subject only to the proviso that this must not totally deprive an individual of an opportunity to enforce his/her rights.[75] This could mean that an intransparent or discretionary time limit would not comply with EU law and might need to be set aside:[76] so too where public authorities have misled the applicant who as a result finds him- or herself out of time.[77] As with the principle of equivalence, so with the principle of effectiveness: the decision on whether particular national rules are compatible with EU law rests ultimately with the national court which is able to consider all the prevailing circumstances, such as the complexity of the issues and the number of persons affected. At a thematic level the key point is that national procedural law becomes subject to the influence of EU law despite the absence of any legislative content to the EU's role. The principle of effective judicial protection is therefore a motor of the phenomenon of 'competence creep' encountered in Chapter 2.

The Court has taken on a sensitive task. When is EU law ready to disturb established national practice in the name of 'effectiveness'? When, and why, will it respect the autonomy of national systems? In *i-21 Germany and Arcor* v *Germany*[78] it found there is *no* requirement that administrative bodies be placed under an obligation to reopen a decision which has become final upon expiry of reasonable time limits for legal remedies or by exhaustion of those remedies. Concern to preserve legal certainty is embedded in EU law, and accordingly a misapplication of EU law may go uncorrected. In similar vein the Court has accepted there is no obligation imposed on national courts to apply EU law of their own motion where this would violate a national (*in casu*, Dutch) rule that an individual bringing an action shall not be placed in a less favourable position than if s/he had not brought that action.[79] This is plainly respectful of national autonomy. But the Court's stance is dependent on the context. In *Mostaza Claro* v *Centro Móvil Milenium* a consumer had failed to argue that an arbitration clause was unfair during the course of the arbitration.[80] She raised the matter only in subsequent proceedings contesting the (adverse) arbitral finding. As a matter of Spanish law this was too late. The European

[75] Case C-89/10 note 54. [76] Eg Case C-445/06 note 74 para 33.
[77] Case C-208/90 *Emmott* [1991] ECR I-4269.
[78] Case C-392/04 and C-422/04 [2006] ECR I-8559.
[79] Case C-455/06 *Heemskerk BV* [2008] ECR I-8763.
[80] Case C-168/05 [2006] ECR I-10421.

Court, called on by preliminary reference to interpret Directive 93/13 on unfair terms, explicitly acknowledged 'that review of arbitration awards should be limited in scope and that annulment of or refusal to recognise an award should be possible only in exceptional circumstances'.[81] But this concern for legal certainty had to compete with the aim of the Directive to protect the consumer as the weaker party to the contract. And the Court prioritized the latter concern, so the national court had to disapply the rule under national law requiring that where the alleged unfairness of the arbitration agreement has not been raised in the course of the arbitration proceedings, it may not be raised subsequently in an action for annulment.

Mostaza Claro reveals how the introduction of the *consumer* into the fact pattern may diminish the Court's willingness to respect national procedural autonomy. The importance of securing finality in arbitration was subordinated to this concern. In a more orthodox commercial setting the Court has typically been more inclined to allow national rules to apply even where they exclude the invocation of relevant points of EU law.[82] The objection to the Court's approach is that it introduces unpredictability. *Some* arbitration agreements may be unpicked despite clear stipulation to the contrary under national law. It is hard to know with confidence just what shall be the reach of the ambiguous but potentially vigorous adaptation required by the dictates of the principle of effective judicial protection. The EU's slim legislative *acquis* reveals attention to the choices involved—for example, it is expressly recognized that commercial certainty may dictate that a contract shall not be set aside even where awarded by a public authority in breach of EU rules, the remedy being confined to a claim for damages[83]—but in the hands of the Court, the decision on which priority shall prevail becomes disturbingly ad hoc. Even the fact that the matter arises in a consumer, rather than a commercial, context is not decisive. In *Mostaza Claro* the consumer had raised the matter of unfairness in proceedings contesting an adverse arbitral finding, whereas by contrast in *Asturcom Telecomuncaciones*[84] the consumer had failed even to challenge the arbitral award within the time limit stipulated by national law, and so the Court of Justice took a tougher approach and accepted that the importance of *res judicata* and ensuring the

[81] Para 34, citing Case C-126/97 *Eco Swiss* [1999] ECR I-3055.

[82] Contrast Joined Cases C-222/05 et al *Van der Weerd* [2007] ECR I-4233 and in particular the discussion of *Mostaza Claro* at paras 39–40.

[83] Directive 89/665, Art 2(6), as amended by Directive 2007/66 note 68.

[84] Case C-40/08 [2009] ECR I-9579.

sound administration of justice should prevail over the consumer interest in re-opening the matter.

The fine margins are colourfully illustrated by *Banco Español de Crédito* v *Joaquín Calderón Camino*.[85] This, another case arising out of Directive 93/13 on unfair terms, concerned a Spanish rule precluding a court before which an application for repayment of a loan has been made against a consumer from assessing whether a term concerning interest on late payments is unfair, where the consumer has not lodged an objection. The Court found the Spanish rule did *not* meet the requirements of effectiveness under EU law, and so had to be set aside—to the evident gain of the consumer. In contrast, Advocate General Trstenjak had proposed the Court find *no* breach of the effectiveness principle and her Opinion stresses the virtue of national autonomy and the rule's capacity to achieve speedy and efficient administration of civil justice. There is no easily identifiable line between respect for national autonomy and expertise and assertion of EU intervention in the name of 'effectiveness'.[86]

The cases on consumer law are unusually rich,[87] but plenty of other areas illustrate the Court's sense of adventure. In *Pfleiderer AG* v *Bundeskartellamt* the customer of undertakings that had been fined sought access to the files of the Bundeskartellamt (German competition authority) in order to prepare a claim for damages against those undertakings.[88] This is not covered by the Treaty nor dealt with under the governing EU Regulation, 1/2003. So it was a matter of national law—subject to the normal EU qualifications. The Court agreed that the Treaty competition rules would be made more 'effective' were private claims for damages facilitated, and that access to files would be accordingly valuable. On the other hand, release of information held in files might dissuade undertakings from co-operating with competition authorities, including in the context of leniency programmes which encourage 'whistle-blowing' from inside cartels. That would damage the 'effective' supervision of the competition rules. So there are competing claims

[85] Case C-618/10 judgment of 14 June 2012.

[86] Precisely the same pattern—Court willing to intrude, A.G. (Wahl) not—is visible in Case C-169/14 *Sánchez Morcillo* judgment of 17 July 2014, another Dir 93/13 case.

[87] On case law under Directive 93/13 see, H. Micklitz and N. Reich, 'The Court and Sleeping Beauty: The Revival of the Unfair Contract Terms Directive' (2014) 51 CMLRev 771; on Directive 2005/29 see J. Stuyck, 'The Court of Justice and the Unfair Commercial Practices Directive' (2015) 52 CMLRev 721.

[88] Case C-360/09 judgment 14 June 2011.

to effectiveness—one that would militate in favour of access to the file, one which would do the opposite. In *Pfleiderer* the Court simply invited the national court to weigh the competing interests on a case-by-case basis, but the dynamic relationship between the judicial and the legislative institutions is well illustrated by the subsequent adoption of an EU Directive which adds to the limited store of legislative direction about the content about national procedures by providing (inter alia) that Member States shall ensure that, for the purpose of actions for damages, national courts shall *not* order the disclosure of leniency statements or settlement submissions.[89] This plainly firms up the common content of national laws beyond that which can be delivered by the more ambiguous control of 'effectiveness'.

Deploying the principle of effectiveness is for these purposes a means to prevent EU law being frustrated by national law.[90] One could view this positively as a process of renovation which forces national systems to upgrade their approach in order to accommodate the interests of new actors empowered by EU law. That, after all, is not so far away from the benign interpretation of the reforming impact of free movement law on national practice (Chapter 6). But in that field a serious objection to EU intervention asks whether assessment under EU law does full justice to the range of interests and motives entangled in national law. Put another way, EU law may be viewed from within its own territory as inevitably benign in its modernizing influence whereas, viewed from a national perspective, it may be regarded as a pernicious destabilizing influence. The same anxiety arises here. National procedural law may conceivably serve to frustrate the unhampered application of EU law, but that is unlikely to have been its purpose when adopted. Instead such rules serve a complex mix of aims, such as legal certainty and the efficient administration of justice. Respect for such expression of national autonomy would be promoted by requiring that EU-based claims be protected in an *equivalent* manner to national claims, while being much less aggressive in insisting that national remedies be *effective* in their (ambiguous) EU sense. The consequence would be diminished intrusion in the name of EU law and enhanced legal certainty before national courts.[91] But the threat posed by EU law should not be exaggerated. In truth the Court's practice has altered over time, but it is not blindly insensitive to such concerns. Initial caution

[89] Dir 2014/104 note 68 Art 6(6).

[90] Eg Case C-119/05 *Lucchini* [2007] ECR I-6199 para 59.

[91] See eg A. Ward, 'Do unto Others as You Would Have Them Do unto You' (2008) 33 ELRev 739.

was followed by a more aggressive, even intolerant attitude to national choices, but lately a more balanced model of assessment has taken shape.[92] The Court has developed a more or less consistent formula whereby it admits that any assessment of national practice conducted in the name of effectiveness shall include assessment of the place of the relevant rule within the overall scheme of the national legal order and its understanding of the proper conduct of proceedings.[93] This points to a case-by-case inquiry which is as flexible as it is unpredictable.

In 2007 in *Unibet* the Court stated that national procedures shall not undermine the right to effective judicial protection guaranteed by EU law, but it insisted that EU law does not mandate the creation of *new* remedies before national courts to protect EU law rights.[94] This is a position to which it has resolutely stuck even after the entry into force of the Lisbon Treaty and the inclusion of Article 19(1) TEU's direction that Member States shall provide remedies sufficient to ensure effective legal protection in the fields covered by Union law, supplemented by Article 47 of the Charter on the right to an effective remedy.[95] But this is not persuasive, or at best it is deeply formalist. Even in *Unibet* the Court adopted a tortured formulation to concede that the 'no new remedies' rule is relaxed where national law contains no remedy which makes it possible to ensure, even indirectly, respect for an individual's rights under EU law.[96] Given the obligation to adapt imposed by the principle of effective judicial protection, the paradigm of national procedural autonomy—the idea that EU law creates rights but national law may select remedies and procedures—creates a false impression.[97] The Court entertains concerns such as preservation of legal certainty and procedural economy as adequate in principle to justify closure under national level even where errors of EU law contaminate the decision taken. But such concessions are made on EU law's terms. In this sense, because any obstructive rule must run the gauntlet of 'effectiveness', there is in truth no national procedural autonomy.

[92] On the trajectory of the case law and academic commentary, see M. Dougan, 'The Vicissitudes of Life at the Coalface: Remedies and Procedures for Enforcing Union Law before the National Courts' Ch 14 in *The Evolution of EU Law* note 58.

[93] Eg Case C-34/13 *Monika Kušionová* judgment of 10 September 2014; Case C-40/08 *Asturcom Telecomunicaciones* [2009] ECR I-9579; Case C-449/13 *CA Consumer Finance SA* judgment of 18 December 2014; Case C-662/13 *Surgicare* judgment of 12 February 2015.

[94] Case C-432/05 *Unibet* v *Justitiekanslern* [2007] ECR I-2271.

[95] Eg Case C-583/11P *Inuit* et al v *Commission* judgment of 3 October 2013 paras 103–4.

[96] Para 41 *Unibet* note 94.

[97] M. Bobek, 'Why There Is No Principle of Procedural Autonomy of the Member States', in B. de Witte and H. Micklitz (eds), *The European Court of Justice and Autonomy of the Member States* (Intersentia, 2011).

4.6 STATE AND PRIVATE LIABILITY

According to taste, the pattern of development covered in the previous section is either remarkably clever or deeply unsettling. Perhaps it is both. The subject of this section is the Court's most dramatic incursion into national procedural and remedial autonomy. It sharpens still further the debate about whether the Court is ingeniously engaged in strengthening the effective protection of EU law rights or whether instead it stands accused of disrupting established national procedures while paying scant regard for the concerns that have shaped them over time. The concern of this section is liability to compensate those suffering loss as a result of a violation of EU law.

The Treaty does not envisage that a Member State could be liable to compensate parties who suffer loss as a result of its failure to comply with the Treaty. Article 340 TFEU provides that in cases of non-contractual liability the Union shall, in accordance with the general principles common to the laws of the Member States, make good any damage caused by its own institutions, which promises an intriguing exercise in applied comparative law in shaping such principles, but the Treaty makes no reference at all to the invocation of such principles before *national* courts in cases against *national* authorities. As already seen, the Treaty goes only so far as to provide in Article 19(1) TEU that Member States shall provide remedies sufficient to ensure effective legal protection in the fields covered by Union law, which is buttressed by the right to an effective remedy stipulated by Article 47 of the Charter. Even those spare texts are innovations of the Lisbon Treaty, and so they date as binding norms from only December 2009. But long before that the Court had already made a far more concrete advance.

Beginning with the landmark *Francovich* case, the Court has insisted that in pursuit of 'the full effectiveness' of the rules of the Treaty it 'is inherent in the system of the Treaty' that a State can be held responsible for damage caused to individuals as a result of breach of EU law.[98] So, whatever may be the state of national law, national courts are *as a matter of EU law* treated as competent to award compensation to parties harmed by breaches of EU law.

Francovich has already been met (Section 4.4). He was a worker in Italy who claimed that he should have been protected from loss suffered

[98] Cases C-6/90 and C-9/90 *Francovich and Others* v *Italian State* [1991] ECR I-5357 paras 34 and 35.

as a result of the insolvency of his employer, but the protection was missing because Italy had failed to transpose the relevant EU Directive (80/987). Because the Directive offered the Member States a wide discretionary choice as to the institutional arrangements designed to govern the payment of compensation, there was no sufficiently unconditional legal rule of the type that is essential to generate directly effective rights. But the Court stepped boldly beyond direct effect as a means of protecting the individual. The Court held that EU law recognized the liability of the State to provide compensation for loss suffered as a result of deprivation of the protection it was intended should be received under the Directive.[99]

Were compensation unavailable in the event of a Member State being responsible for violation of rights granted by EU law, the 'full effectiveness' of EU law would be impaired.[100] This is incontestably true. It is, however, a bold judicial step to rely on the pursuit of 'full effectiveness' as an adequate justification for establishing a principle that is wholly unrecognized in the text of the Treaties. The Court's claim for the authority of the principle whereby a State must be liable for damage caused to individuals as a result of its breach of EU law was that it 'is inherent in the system of the Treaty'.[101]

An individual who is deprived of a right that is intended to be conferred by a Directive (typically because of a failure to implement the Directive properly or at all) may be able to claim damages to compensate for loss suffered in an action brought before the courts of the defaulting Member State. The vigour of reasoning based on pursuit of 'effectiveness' is evident in that the Court's approach does not in any way rely on the application of a principle of non-discrimination, whereby national courts would be required to award damages in a case of violation of EU law if they would do the same in a similar action involving national law. Instead *Francovich* insists that even if national law would *not* offer protection in the circumstances, EU law requires an upgraded level of 'effective' protection.

Francovich concerned the mishandling of a Directive by the Italian authorities, but the principle that there may arise a liability to compensate an individual suffering loss caused by a violation of EU law cannot logically be confined to the case of untransposed Directives alone. *Factortame (no.3)/Brasserie de Pecheur* was the first case in which the Court ruled that a State may be liable to pay compensation where it has violated primary

[99] However, he still lost—he was ultimately found to fall outside the class of persons protected by the Directive: Case C-479/93 *Francovich* v *Italy* [1995] ECR I-3843.

[100] Para 33. [101] Para 35.

Treaty provisions (*in casu*, concerning free movement).[102] *Factortame (no.3)/Brasserie de Pecheur* also permitted the Court to address the question of the necessary level of culpability that must be attributed to the defaulting State, a matter that had not been addressed in *Francovich* where, after all, the breach of EU law—failure to transpose a Directive into national law—could not have been more glaring. It will not always be so clear.

In *Factortame (no.3)/Brasserie de Pecheur* the Court explained that EU law confers a right to reparation where three conditions are met: the rule of law infringed must be intended to confer rights on individuals; the breach must be sufficiently serious; and there must be a direct causal link between the breach of the obligation resting on the State and the damage sustained by the injured parties.[103]

None of these three criteria is particularly surprising. *Factortame (no.3)/Brasserie de Pecheur* could be treated as an exercise of applied comparative law, for each element is a familiar aspect of typical national systems governing the award of compensation in the event of loss. What is striking is the Court's concoction of these rules from a Treaty background which is completely barren of any indication that EU law shall dictate to national courts that they shall be competent to make awards of compensation for breach of EU law, still less what shall be the governing criteria. The liability of the EU's *own* institutions is foreseen by the Treaties in the abovementioned Article 340 TFEU, and the applicable principles have subsequently been fused by the Court so there is now a single stream of law governing the liability of Member States and the EU's institutions in the event of unlawful action causing loss.[104]

The Court has pushed its own creation still further. In *Köbler* it held that a State may incur liability for manifest misapplication of EU law by a court adjudicating at last instance.[105] In *Courage* v *Crehan* it ruled in favour of the possibility that liability may be imposed on *private* parties to compensate those suffering loss as a result of their breach of EU competition law.[106] Here it re-asserted reliance on the logic of enhanced incentives to comply with EU law in declaring that the 'full effectiveness' of what is now Article 101 TFEU would be put at risk if it were not open to any

[102] Joined Cases C-46/93 and C-48/93 *Brasserie du Pêcheur* v *Germany* and *R* v *Secretary of State for Transport, ex parte Factortame Ltd* [1996] ECR I-1029.

[103] Ibid, para 51.

[104] Case C-352/98P *Bergaderm* v *Commission* [2000] ECR I-5291 para 41; Joined Cases C-46/93 and C-48/93 note 102, para 55.

[105] Case C-224/01 *Köbler* [2003] ECR I-10239.

[106] Case C-453/99 *Courage* v *Crehan* [2001] ECR I-6297.

individual to claim damages for loss caused by its violation and that the existence of such a right strengthens the working of the rules and discourages practices in violation of the Treaty.

Neither ruling is uncontroversial. The Court's finding in *Köbler* that liability may even attach to the State because of *judicial* errors calls into question the independence of the judiciary and raises the spectre of legal uncertainty consequent on recycled litigation in the guise of damages claims by parties who have failed in their initial quest to establish they have been wronged. The Court has gone some way to meet such concerns by accepting that since interpretation of provisions of law forms part of the very essence of judicial activity, a judicial decision which turns out to be mistaken will only exceptionally be sufficiently serious as to constitute a breach sounding in damages.[107] A court must have manifestly infringed the applicable law, which one would suppose would be highly uncommon.[108] And *Courage* v *Crehan* is open to the criticism that it is based on a hasty assumption that the very different contexts of liability incurred by private parties on the one hand and public authorities on the other can be swept up in the same net by breezy reliance on 'effectiveness'. A more sector-sensitive approach to assessing the virtue of more aggressive policing through actions for compensation is arguably required.[109] The key thematic point is that, however one judges the desirability of these contextually extended applications of the principle to which *Francovich* gave birth, reasoning built on pursuit of the 'effectiveness' of EU law has proved remarkably powerful in ensuring the ever deeper penetration of national law by the requirements of EU law. The cases discussed in Section 4.5, concerning national time limits and arbitral finality, were remarkable, but the line of case law beginning with *Francovich* and amplified by *Factortame (no.3)/Brasserie de Pecheur* acts as an even more vivid demonstration of how the boundary insulating national law on remedies from the influence of EU law has been significantly eroded.

Whether a breach of EU law is sufficiently serious depends on whether it involves manifest and grave disregard of the limits on its discretion allowed by the law. In particular, the clearer and more precise the rule

[107] Case C-173/03 *Traghetti del Mediterraneo* [2006] ECR I-5177.

[108] But it appears to have happened in Portugal: Case C-160/14 *Ferreira da Silva e Brito and others* judgment of 9 September 2015.

[109] See eg K. Havu, 'Horizontal Liability for Damages in EU Law—the Changing Relationship of EU and National Law' (2012) 18 ELJ 407; D Leczykiewicz, 'Private Party Liability in EU Law: In Search of the General Régime' (2009–2010) 12 *Cambridge Yearbook of European Legal Studies* 257.

breached, the more likely the breach is to be treated as 'sufficiently serious'; conversely the greater the degree of ambiguity, for example because the Commission has not objected to national practice or where a Court ruling has not yet clarified the matter at the time the violation occurred, the less likely that the breach will engage a responsibility to compensate. So for example in *ex parte Synthon BV* the discretion allowed to national authorities in dealing with applications for authorization of medical products pursuant to an EU Directive (2001/83) was minimal, and the procedure, though set out clearly, had been ignored.[110] This was a sufficiently serious breach. By contrast in *R* v *HM Treasury, ex p British Telecommunications* the Court found that the relevant provision of the Directive, on which the UK had relied in excluding particular operators active in the telecommunications sector, was imprecisely worded and was reasonably capable of bearing not only the interpretation preferred by the Court in its judgment, but also the interpretation given to it by the UK, which, the Court accepted, had been adopted in good faith and on the basis of plausible arguments.[111] The UK had violated EU law and would have to alter its practice, but the violation was not 'sufficiently serious' and so those operators suffering loss were not entitled to compensation.

The state of the Court's own case law is plainly relevant. In *N* Dutch tax rules were held unlawful but there was no earlier ruling on the matter at hand, so this was treated as a breach of EU law but not a sufficiently serious breach for the purposes of a claim for compensation.[112] By contrast in *Günter Fuss* v *Stadt Halle*, which involved a Hauptbrandmeister who had been working beyond the limits set by Directive 93/104 on working time, the Court found an obvious disregard of pre-existing case law, and felt it had sufficient information to treat this as sufficiently serious.[113] That a *national* court has chosen to make a preliminary reference on a point must not be taken automatically to show that no sufficiently serious violation has occurred, for otherwise the preliminary reference might be compromised.[114] However, one would suppose that commonly the doubts entertained by the national court about the state of EU law that

[110] Case C-452/06 *ex parte Synthon BV* [2008] ECR I-7681; also Case C-470/03 *A.G.M.-COS.MET* v *Suomen valtio* [2007] ECR I-2749.

[111] Case C-392/93 *R* v *HM Treasury, ex p British Telecommunications* [1996] ECR I-1631.

[112] Case C-470/04 *N* [2006] ECR I-7409.

[113] Case C-429/09 *Günter Fuss* v *Stadt Halle* [2010] ECR I-12167; also Case C-398/11 *Hogan* et al v *Minster for Social and Family Affairs* judgment of 25 April 2013.

[114] Case C-244/13 *Ogieriakhi* judgment of 10 July 2014.

prompted the reference would be doubts reasonably entertained by the actor in question too.

Although only the Court is able to provide authoritative rulings on the meaning of EU law, the Court treats 'the attitude of the Commission' as one relevant factor in the determination of whether the breach is sufficiently serious.[115] A Member State could confidently expect to escape liability should it have acted in conformity with the Commission's view of the law even where the Court subsequently takes a different view, but where a Member State is advised by the Commission that it is acting in violation of EU law it is formally entitled to await final authoritative determination by the Court; however, it needs to be aware that its chances of being found liable in damages should the Court confirm the Commission's view have been increased. So *Francovich* strengthens the Commission's hand in the matter of enforcement of EU law. Indeed, as the Court itself has asserted,[116] this line of case law strengthens the incentives to comply with EU law generally. This is a consistent theme in understanding the Court's plugging of EU law into national legal proceedings: it protects individuals and at the same time it uses them to further the vigorous policing of the rules of EU law agreed to by the Member States. It gives EU law teeth.

In *Francovich* the Court's citation of *Van Gend en Loos*, *Costa* v *ENEL*, *Simmenthal*, and *Factortame* pointedly locates the ruling in the purest waters of EU constitutionalism, washing deep into national legal orders in a way that would not be claimed by orthodox international treaty law. The Court's claim in *Francovich* that it is acting in line with what is 'inherent' in the Treaty is designed to confirm its self-perception as a vigorous actor in making good what the Member States have left unwritten. This reveals the Court's sense of ambition in promoting the right to effective judicial protection before national courts which, though recognized by Article 19(1) TEU and Article 47 of the Charter, has been given much more concrete shape by the Court. The Court's creative elucidation of common principles has won praise as commentators have compared the sensitivities of the judicial process favourably with the less flexible route of legislative intervention in the field.[117] Moreover, the development of such principles at EU level carries a dynamic which will prompt renewed attention to the shaping of such rules within domestic legal orders,

[115] Joined Cases C-46/93 and C-48/93 note 102, para 63.

[116] Eg Case C-453/99 note 106, para 27.

[117] Eg W. Van Gerven, 'Harmonization of Private Law: Do We Need It?' (2004) 41 CMLRev 505; D. Leczykiewicz, 'Where Angels Fear to Tread: The EU Law of Remedies and Codification of European Private Law' (2012) 8 ERCL 47.

doubtless promoting further creative reflection on the role of legal protection of this nature.[118]

So far, so very good. And yet there is a dark side. There are some strong and contestable assumptions here about the relative expertise and legitimacy of judges over legislatures. The case law promises an imbalance in the control of violations of EU law, for those which affect commercial interests with access to deep pockets are in practice a good deal more likely to be sanctioned than those which affect diffuse interests such as consumers or environmental protection. Indeed, the Court's requirement that an identifiable *right* exist in the first place is more readily satisfied by an obstruction to an individual's freedom to trade than by a claim to the collective virtue of regulatory protection. In *Peter Paul* bank account holders were found to have acquired no right in the *Francovich* sense even where the State had mishandled the EU mandate to protect them, because supervision was purely a matter of the public interest.[119] So the fact that the breakthrough case, *Francovich*, was driven by missing protection of a worker is thoroughly misleading.[120] Most cases are driven by corporate interests.

As with direct effect, so with State liability: one might be rather sceptical about just how 'democratic' Mancini and Keeling's discourse of individual rights under EU law truly is in practice.[121] Everyone may dine at the Ritz. Few can afford to do so. Most *Francovich* litigants will be rich. The force of this critique is softened by appreciation that it seems that relatively few cases pursued before national courts are successful.[122] There are plenty of escape routes in the Court's approach for a national court anxious about the damaging effect of slapping a liability to compensate on public or private bodies. In particular, the threshold criterion that demands a 'sufficiently serious' breach serves to insulate the (in short) excusable violation which is remedied by an order requiring reform from costly consequences. This helps to reduce the risk of 'over-deterrence' that may inhibit worthwhile legislative intervention at national

[118] Eg N. Reich, 'Horizontal Liability in EC Law: Hybridization of Remedies for Compensation in Case of Breaches of EC Rights' (2007) 44 CMLRev 705; F. Marcos and A. Sanchez Graells, 'Towards a European Tort Law? Damages Actions for Breach of the EC Antitrust Rules: Harmonising Tort Law through the Back Door?' (2008) 16 Euro Rev Private Law 469.

[119] Case C-222/02 [2004] ECR I-9425.

[120] Even Francovich himself lost: note 99.

[121] Note 56.

[122] T. Lock, 'Is Private Enforcement of EU Law through State Liability a Myth?' (2012) 49 CMLRev 1675; R. Condon and B. Van Leeuwen (eds), 'Bottom Up or Rock Bottom Harmonization? Francovich State Liability in National Courts' LAW 2015/03, EUI Working Papers.

level.[123] Nevertheless, at the level of principle, there are anxieties about the capacity of a Court—especially a transnational court—to develop principles of liability that are sufficiently nuanced to take adequate account of the complex range of interests at stake in such disputes. After all, national rules governing compensation claims are typically the product of long-term evolution, involving the reconciliation of the need for individual protection and the wider public interest. The Court's case law is vulnerable to the accusation that elaboration of principles that promote coherence at *Union* level tend to undermine settled law at *national* level.[124] In particular one must take seriously the anxiety that prioritizing a monetary remedy for those fortunate enough to have the legal and practical means to pursue it with success may severely destabilize the allocation of scarce resources to protection of collective interests within a Member State. Every penny paid to a private litigant is lost to the public purse.

The argument, in short, is that the Court is dangerously promiscuous in its reliance on 'effectiveness'. Reasoning on the basis of what is 'inherent' in the Treaty doubtless offers creative scope for extending the penetration of EU law into national legal orders. But it also strains Article 5 TEU and, the other side of that coin, it erodes varied choices made in the name of national autonomy while concentrating a high level of law-making power on the Court of Justice. The sense that the Court has moved into an area where it lacks the expertise to provide a sufficiently nuanced set of legal principles was taken on to a specifically constitutional plane by the German government in its submissions in *Brasserie du Pêcheur*.[125] It objected that a general right to compensation could be created only by legislation and that its judicial creation would not be compatible with the allocation of competences and powers foreseen by the Treaties. The Court, having already unleashed *Francovich* five years earlier, was unsurprisingly unpersuaded. It simply confirmed that its elucidation of the existence and extent of State liability was an instance of interpretation of the Treaty—which is its job.[126] And it repeated the claim made in *Francovich* that the principle of State liability is inherent in the system of the Treaty.

The German objection was not without force but it was brushed aside by the Court. This offers a bracing reminder of the autonomy enjoyed by the Court of Justice. Its interpretations of the Treaty may be overturned

[123] Eg R. Van den Bergh, 'Francovich and its Aftermath' in M. Poiares Maduro and L. Azoulai (eds), *The Past and Future of EU Law* (Hart, 2010).

[124] A refreshingly sceptical point of view: C. Harlow, 'Francovich and the Problem of the Disobedient State' (1996) 2 ELJ 199.

[125] Joined Cases C-46/93 and C-48/93 note 102.

[126] Para 24.

by revision of the Treaty, but this is possible only when the process of revision is in train and it requires the unanimous support of the Member States. It is for good reason rare. It is not simply that assembling unanimity is awkward: it is that one may readily conclude that the Court's approach is in line with most, perhaps all, Member States' preferences, in the sense that, as explained in Chapter 1, a strong explanation for the acceptance of commitments as a member of the EU is rooted in reciprocity. The costs incurred by being locked into a system that imposes relatively high penalties in the event of default are exceeded by the benefits of knowing that all other participants are equally firmly locked into the long-term plan. Commitments are made credible by the Court's contribution in a ruling such as *Francovich*. And indeed the type of objection advanced by Germany would doubtless be resisted by the Court today with reference to Article 19 TEU and Article 47 of the Charter, which are admittedly not as concrete in their instructions to national courts as *Francovich* and its progeny, but which nevertheless suggest that the Member States, in revising the Treaty, are perfectly content to affirm the grip which EU law has on national autonomy in the matter of procedure and remedies. Indeed, even before the Treaty of Lisbon entered into force the Court had already made great play of Article 47, as if to claim the legitimacy of its own long-established approach.[127]

4.7 DIRECTIVES AS A SPECIAL CASE

Regulations and Decisions, as instruments of EU secondary legislation, are capable of direct effect. It depends merely on their provisions disclosing a norm that is sufficiently clear and unconditional for immediate application by a national judge. But the Directive is a different creature. According to Article 288 TFEU it sets out a result to be achieved, but the way to get to that result is through implementing measures adopted at national level within the deadline specified by the Directive. And these measures will differ State by State. So, although the overall aim of the Directive should be reached in common across all the Member States, the detailed rules will differ State by State according to the choices made about the applicable form and methods for converting the Directive into domestic law. Crucially, then, the very nature of the Directive as a legal instrument is *conditional*—conditional on national implementation. When made at EU level, the Directive is not designed to be law *in that form* at

[127] In particular Case C-432/05 *Unibet* [2007] ECR I-2271.

national level. So—one might suppose—the Directive cannot be directly effective. But one would be wrong.

4.7.1 The direct effect of Directives

The Court has swept beyond both the apparent textual limitations of the Treaty and its own pre-conditions for finding an EU legal act capable of direct effect in national legal proceedings. In 1974 the Court was invited to follow the argument set out in Section 4.7 that the very nature of the Directive as a legal act is to rely on national choices about implementation, and that this conditionality precludes the possibility of attributing direct effect to a Directive.[128] But the Court refused to exclude the possibility that a Directive may be invoked in national legal proceedings. It stated that it would be incompatible with the binding effect attributed to a Directive by the Treaty to exclude in principle the possibility that the obligation which it imposes may be invoked by those concerned. Here the Court's view of the character of EU law dictates its approach. Contrary to the Court's claims, the binding effect of a Directive does *not* require that it be capable of invocation before a national court. Even without such a property the Directive would still be binding—and where a Member State failed to comply it would be subject to pursuit by the Commission and condemnation by the Court pursuant to the Article 258 TFEU infringement procedure. In fact the Court's choice is driven by its concern to ensure that the nature of EU law is such that it is *not only* operative at the transnational level, according to the procedures foreseen by the Treaty, *but also* apt to penetrate national legal orders. The Court's distinctive constitutionalized vision of the EU legal order embraces Directives too, notwithstanding Article 288's apparent assumption that Directives reach national law only where Member States perform the necessary transformative implementation. So a Directive is capable of having direct effect within national legal proceedings, provided its terms are sufficiently justiciable according to the normal tests.

Some Directives lack the necessary precision. So, for example, a provision of Directive 89/105 which required a Member State which imposed a price freeze on medicines to carry out annual review to ascertain whether macro-economic conditions justified the retention of the freeze was held incapable of direct effect because of the absence of any rules governing the basis for adopting price control measures or the criteria governing annual review.[129] But it would be a mistake to assume that the character of the Directive, a legal act that leaves room for choice at national level in

[128] Case 41/74 *Van Duyn* v *Home Office* [1974] ECR 1337.

[129] Joined Cases C-471/07 and C-472/07 *AGIM ASBL* [2010] ECR I-113.

the method of transposition, is incompatible with the pre-conditions of direct effect, because it is far from uncommon for Directives to contain concrete obligations. Directive 73/173 included a number of express provisions concerning the classification, packaging, and labelling of solvents, compliance with which entitled a trader to market his goods in the EU, and the Court in *Ratti* had no difficulty in treating such rules as directly effective.[130] Directives which harmonize laws in order to promote market integration—which was the purpose of the measure in *Ratti*—will tend to achieve that objective more readily the more concrete their terms are, and therefore many Directives are conditional in the sense only that they require implementation. They frequently contain unconditional substantive rules. And, as with direct effect generally, the consequence of attributing direct effect to Directives is both to improve policing of the obligations contained in a Directive and also to create rights vested in individuals. So in *Ratti* the Court ruled that a Member State which has not implemented a Directive by its deadline is disallowed from insisting in proceedings before a national court that an individual shall comply with domestic law rather than the provisions of the (wrongfully unimplemented) Directive.

However, the Court has not brought its treatment of the potential for Directives to infiltrate national legal proceedings wholly into line with the approach adopted in the case of Treaty provisions, Regulations and Decisions. Directives remain different. In part this is because they are incapable of direct effect until the deadline set for their transposition at national level has expired. Until then Member States retain a freedom to choose how to absorb the Directive's requirements into national law, and are subject only to a much weaker obligation not to jeopardize the achievement of the Directive's aims before the deadline has passed.[131] But more so Directives are different because they are not apt to impose obligations directly on *private* parties in proceedings before national courts.

4.7.2 *Directives may not exert horizontal direct effect*

In its earliest decisions, involving the enforcement of provisions of Directives against *public* authorities in national legal proceedings, the Court remarked as part of its reasoning that 'the useful effect' of a Directive is promoted by permitting such invocation.[132] This is true, and would have readily dictated that the same logic should support

[130] Case 148/78 *Ratti* [1979] ECR 1629.

[131] First elaborated in Case C-129/96 *Inter-Environnement Wallonie* [1997] ECR I-7411; see also Case C-144/04 *Mangold* [2005] ECR I-9981.

[132] Case 41/74 note 128.

invocation of an unimplemented Directive against a *private* party too. But the Court hastily abandoned very broad reasoning driven by the Directive's 'useful effect' and instead preferred a narrower explanation for the Directive's penetration of national legal proceedings. In *Marshall* it focused on the obligation of a Member State to perform its obligation to implement a Directive and therefore conceived of the directly effective application of the (justiciable) terms of the Directive as a device to stop the Member State taking advantage of its own failure to comply with its Treaty obligation.[133] It followed from this that a Directive should not be capable of direct effect when the party on which obligations would be thereby imposed was a *private* party, not culpable for the absence of measures implementing the Directive into the national legal order. Put another way, a Directive may not exert *horizontal direct effect* in proceedings before national courts.

The rejection of the 'horizontal direct effect' of Directives places a limit on the legal protection of those intended to benefit from a Directive. *Faccini Dori v Recreb* neatly captures what is at stake.[134] Ms Dori concluded a contract with a seller at Milan Central Railway Station. She bought an English-language correspondence course. But shortly afterwards she changed her mind and told the seller she had decided to withdraw from the contract. Under EU law she had such a right, by virtue of Directive 85/577 which protected consumers who enter into deals away from sellers' business premises. Under Italian law she had no such right, because the Directive had not been transposed into Italian law. Italy was certainly in default of its EU law obligations. But the Court decided that this did not entitle her to rely on the Directive before Italian courts to claim the envisaged right given that her claim was horizontal—that is, against another private party.

The Court adopted a constitutional perspective. Finding a Directive capable of horizontal direct effect would, it stated, 'be to recognise a power in the Community to enact obligations for individuals with immediate effect, whereas it has competence to do so only where it is empowered to adopt regulations'. It is also true that legal certainty would be compromised by embrace of the horizontal direct effect of Directives, for how could individuals easily know of the content of Directives? The Court did not address the point in *Faccini Dori* but subsequently in *Wells*, a case concerning environmental protection, it added this consideration

[133] Case 152/84 *Marshall* [1986] ECR 723 para 47.

[134] Case C-91/92 *Faccini Dori* v *Recreb* [1994] ECR I-3325.

to strengthen its stance against the horizontal direct effect of Directives. It declared that 'the principle of legal certainty prevents directives from creating obligations for individuals. For them, the provisions of a directive can only create rights'.[135]

Unimplemented Directives may be invoked in proceedings before national courts to impose obligations on the State but not on private parties—there is vertical direct effect but, for Directives, no horizontal direct effect. The private party who is intended to be subject to *obligations* pursuant to an EU Directive is protected from such obligations until such time as the State performs the necessary act of transposition of the Directive into national law. The private party who is intended to enjoy *rights* granted by an EU Directive against another private party must also wait. This is no mere technical matter. As explained in Section 4.4, the *Treaty* commitment to equal pay for men and women is directly effective even in proceedings between individuals,[136] but the large majority of the EU's activity in the fields of labour market regulation and social policy is expressed and elaborated through Directives, so the exclusion of their horizontal direct effect in national legal proceedings has the effect that State failure to implement Directives curtails in practice the envisaged scope of the EU's protective rules. The same applies to EU consumer protection and environmental protection, which are largely the product of Directives. Consequently there is ample room to lament the Court's restrictive choice, but, given the weight of repetition in its case law, there is no realistic likelihood of the Court changing its mind.[137]

The full picture is, however, murkier. Even though Directives may not be relied on to impose obligations directly on private parties in proceedings before national courts, there are, beyond their direct effect, other devices which may cause unimplemented Directives to exert an impact in legal proceedings before national courts. And this may lead to a significant disturbance of the insulation which private parties appear to enjoy from the direct effect of EU Directives. The several aspects of this phenomenon are now tracked.

[135] Case C-201/02 *Wells* [2004] ECR I-723, para 56.

[136] Case 43/75 *Defrenne* v *SABENA* [1976] ECR 455.

[137] Eg Case C-192/94 *El Corte Inglés* v *Cristina Blasquez Rivero* [1996] ECR I-1281; Case C-97/96 *Verband Deutscher Daihatsu Händler* [1997] ECR I-6843; Case C-80/06 *Carp Snc* v *Ecorad* [2007] ECR I-4473; Case C-555/07 *Kücükdeveci* [2010] ECR I-365; Case C-508/14 *Česky telekomunikační* judgment of 6 October 2015.

4.7.3 *The extended understanding of the 'State'*

Although Directives are capable of direct effect only against the State, that notion is for these purposes widely defined. This was already clear in *Marshall*, where the Court ruled in principle against the horizontal direct effect of Directives but treated a health authority in the South of England as part of the 'State'.[138] So it was subject to directly enforceable obligations of equal treatment for men and women under a relevant EU Directive. A private employer would not have been. In *Foster* v *British Gas* the Court reached a little further.[139] The Court held that irrespective of legal form, an entity which has been made responsible by a State measure for providing a public service and which has for that purpose special or exceptional powers beyond those which result from the normal rules applicable in relations between individuals may be subjected to directly effective obligations drawn from Directives.[140] This is analytically awkward. If the reason for permitting Directives to exert vertical direct effect is that it prevents the State escaping from the consequences of its own wrongdoing in failing to implement the Directive in accordance with Article 288 TFEU, it seems odd to extend the scope of that vertical direct effect to entities that are remote from the central organs of the State and which therefore neither carry responsibility for the deficiency in the state of national law nor are able to repair it. This suggests that the Court, having excluded the horizontal direct effect of Directives, felt inclined to narrow the field in which that exclusion applied. So the State, and consequently the scope of vertical direct effect of Directives, was pushed ever wider. Even if that was not the Court's strategy, that was plainly the *effect* of its case law. There is, in fact, a thematic instability in this area of the law. Directives *are* different from other EU legal acts, inter alia for want of aptitude to exert horizontal direct effect—but the differences are less clean-cut and less easily explained than one might expect.

4.7.4 *The obligation of consistent interpretation*

This is all the more evident when one examines the obligation cast on national courts to interpret national law in the light of EU Directives. In *Marleasing SA* v *CIA* the Court of Justice stated that a national court called on to interpret national law 'is required to do so, as far as possible, in the light of the wording and the purpose of the Directive in order

[138] Case 152/84 note 133.

[139] Case C-188/89 *Foster* v *British Gas* [1990] ECR I-3313.

[140] See also eg Case C-356/05 *Farrell* [2007] ECR I-3067; Case C-282/10 *Maribel Dominguez* judgment of 24 January 2012; Case C-671/13 *Indeliu* judgment of 25 June 2015.

to achieve the result pursued by the latter'.[141] This, moreover, applies whether the relevant national provisions were adopted before or after the Directive. So where a Member State has not implemented a Directive at all, or has done so inadequately, the Directive still acquires a voice in relevant national proceedings. It falls to the national *judge* to perform this act of interpretation, to reconcile 'as far as possible' existing national law and the Directive that is missing. This is 'indirect effect'—the Directive is not applied directly but it is applied indirectly through the medium of the relevant provisions of national law. In fact, questions associated with the direct effect of a provision of EU law only come into play once interpretation of a relevant provision of national law in a manner compatible with the provision of EU law proves impossible.[142]

Such judicial correction of the failings of the State's legislative or administrative bodies may cause Directives to exert a decisive impact on national legal proceedings even where private parties are involved. The factual situation in which the Court insisted on 'indirect effect' in *Marleasing* involved two private parties.[143] This, then, has the potential to compensate for any lack of protection in national proceedings consequent on the absence of horizontal direct effect. In fact it calls into question the very purpose of withholding horizontal direct effect.

The Court has over time refined, clarified, and extended both the source and the scope of this obligation to interpret national law consistently with EU law. In *Marleasing* itself, it drew on Article 5 EC, which is today in adjusted version Article 4(3) TEU. This (inter alia) imposes an obligation of sincere co-operation on the Member States to assist the Union in carrying out its Treaty-defined tasks, and the Court interpreted this duty to bind all organs of the State, including the judiciary. The Court subsequently made a more existential claim in *Pfeiffer* in which it found the duty to be 'inherent in the system of the Treaty', identifying it as a means whereby the national court may 'ensure the full effectiveness' of EU law.[144] This has become the Court's orthodox rationale[145] and it has repeated this bold claim since the entry into force of the Lisbon Treaty in

[141] C-106/89 *Marleasing SA* v *CIA* [1990] ECR I-4135 para 8. See even earlier Case 14/83 *Von Colson and Kamann* v *Land Nordrhein-Westfalen* [1984] ECR 1891.

[142] Eg Case C-282/10 *Maribel Dominguez* judgment of 24 January 2012, para 23; Case C-306/12 *Spedition Welter GmbH* v *Avanssur SA* judgment of 10 October 2013 para 28.

[143] See also Case C-32/93 *Webb* v *EMO Air Cargo* [1994] ECR I-3567; Case C-185/97 *Coote* v *Granada Hospitality* [1998] ECR I-5199; Case C-350/03 *Schulte* [2005] ECR I-9215.

[144] Cases C-397/01 to C-403/01 *Pfeiffer* [2004] ECR I-8835 para 113.

[145] Eg Case C-212/04 *Adeneler* [2006] ECR I-6057 paras 108–111; Case C-268/06 *Impact* [2008] ECR I-2483 paras 98–101.

2009.[146] The identification of 'indirect effect' as 'inherent' in the system cements a direct connection between the principle of consistent interpretation and the Court's finding in *Francovich* that a State may be liable for damage caused to individuals as a result of breach of EU law, which also locates the principle as 'inherent in the system of the Treaty'.[147] This conforms to the concern, visible as far back as *Van Gend en Loos*, to root the special character of EU law in the structure and purpose of the Treaty itself, not in any particular textual provisions. And there is a substantive link too, for the point that horizontal direct effect is not tolerated in the case of Directives prevents X claiming a right against Y which should be available under a Directive where Y is a private party unless 'indirect effect' comes to the rescue, but the culpable party—the Member State which failed to transpose the Directive—may be brought into the line of fire thanks to the *Francovich* doctrine. X should sue the Member State to recover the loss caused by the State default where the courts cannot help.

The case law reveals a gradual though not always consistent extension in the Court's vision of what is expected of national courts. In *Marks and Spencer plc* v *Commissioners of Customs and Excise* the Court spelled out the logical extension that implementation is an enduring obligation, not exhausted by transposition on paper.[148] Even if national measures correctly implement the Directive it falls to a national court to ensure that national authorities apply those measures in a manner compatible with it. This carries the consequence that the Directive must always be taken into account in the development of national practice. It does not and must not vanish simply because the Member State has put in place an accurate implementing text. This also entails that national judges should be attentive to interpretation of EU Directives delivered by the Court of Justice, for these too should guide their understanding of the meaning of national measures within the field occupied by the Directive. This is especially significant given that the Court's interpretative choices are sometimes not easily predicted. The ruling in *Pfeiffer* et al[149] offers the fullest statement of the extent of the obligation cast upon national judiciaries to achieve the result sought by the Directive, and it is a ruling which the Court has taken to reciting as standard in subsequent case law,[150] including that arising since

[146] Eg Case C-306/12 note 142, para 29, citing *Pfeiffer* and referring to the TFEU.

[147] Cases C-6/90 and C-9/90 note 64, para 35.

[148] Case C-62/00 [2002] ECR I-6325.

[149] Cases C-397/01 to C-403/01 note 144.

[150] Eg Case C-12/08 *Mono Car Styling* SA [2009] ECR I-6653; Case C-378/07 et al *Angelidaki* [2009] ECR I-3071.

the entry into force of the Lisbon Treaty in 2009.[151] This makes clear that the obligation applies to interpretation *in particular* of measures adopted for the purpose of implementing the Directive—but not only such measures. The national court shall consider national law as a whole in order to assess to what extent it may be applied in order to generate a result which is in conformity with that pursued by the Directive. Logically this pushes national judiciaries to interpret all relevant sources of law in the light of any relevant Directive.

The obligation cast on national courts is inherent in the system of the Treaty, so it is not confined to the impact of Directives. A Regulation is directly applicable but may in some circumstances leave room for necessary national implementation (for example in fixing penalties in the event of infringement). In *Rolex* the Court transposed the principle of consistent interpretation from the sphere of Directives to the context of a Regulation of this type, referring to *Marleasing*.[152]

The assumption which drives this ingenious line of case law is that if a Member State has failed to do its job of implementation by legislative or administrative act, with the result that the objectives pursued by the EU Directive are left unfulfilled within the national legal order, then the national judiciary will ride to the rescue. In pursuit of legal certainty and proper compliance with the Treaty it is always incumbent on the Member State to plug the gap by (finally) doing what is required to transpose the Directive into national law, but in the interim the courts of that Member State should be making ad hoc contributions to protecting individual litigants from treatment inconsistent with that envisaged by any relevant Directives.

One may readily object that this is constitutionally unsettling, as well as tending to disturb legal uncertainty before national courts in so far as national law may be adjusted in the light of a lurking EU measure. The pursuit of the full effectiveness of EU law, which the Court has taken as its guiding mission in its explanations for 'indirect effect' in *Pfeiffer* and other cases in the same vein, ignores the damage done by driving EU law so deep and sometimes so unexpectedly into national law. True, the Court envisages some *limits* to the national courts' duty to interpret national law in the light of EU law. It stops (inter alia) where interpretation *contra legem* would be required. In *Impact*, an Irish reference concerning a Directive on gender equality, the Court accepted that the use of the interpretative

[151] Eg Case C-282/10 note 140; Case C-306/12 note 142; Case C-42/11 *Lopes Da Silva Jorge* judgment of 5 September 2012.

[152] Case C-60/02 *Rolex* [2004] ECR I-651, para 59.

duty cast on national courts to secure the 'full effectiveness' of EU law is 'limited by general principles of law, particularly those of legal certainty and non-retroactivity' and so it 'cannot serve as the basis for an interpretation of national law *contra legem*'.[153] And, unusually, the Court went out of its way to accept that the national court would *not* be required to give an Irish statute retrospective effect because that would be a case of *contra legem* interpretation. Similarly, in *Association de médiation sociale* the Court explicitly found that the relevant provision of French labour law was incapable of being interpreted consistently with the requirements of EU law.[154] There is here an analogy with the subjection of national remedies and procedures to the demands of EU law, considered at Section 4.5. National courts must use the principle of effectiveness to adapt national remedies and procedures, but there are limits, most of all associated with the preservation of legal certainty.

Criminal law raises in this context special concerns because of the threat of deprivation of an individual's liberty. The Court accepts that general principles of law, in particular the principles of legal certainty and non-retroactivity, dictate that a Directive cannot, of itself and independently of a national law adopted by a Member State for its implementation, have the effect of determining or aggravating the liability in criminal law of persons who act in contravention of the provisions of that Directive.[155]

Interpretation to meet the demands of the Directive is, according to the Court's consistent formula, required 'as far as possible', and the precise nature of this proviso becomes highly significant in determining where the corrective role of national judges ends. Where the interpretative task demanded of the national judge goes beyond what is 'possible', the individual who is the intended beneficiary under a Directive finds his or her claim blocked. Recourse to a *Francovich* action against the State for compensation is then possible. The bolder the interpreting national judge, the less need for action taken directly against the defaulting State, and the deeper the damage to legal certainty—and the less significant the exclusion of horizontal direct effect in cases where *private* parties are affected by the exercise of the interpretative role cast upon national judges. Cases such as *Impact* and *AMS*, where the Court makes plain what is *not* expected of a national judge, are abnormal, and exactly what is in this context 'possible' as interpretation and ruled out

[153] Case C-268/06 note 145, paras 100–103.

[154] Case C-176/12 judgment of 15 January 2014; Chapter 3.12.

[155] Case 80/86 *Officier van Justitie* v *Kolpinghuis Nijmegen* [1987] ECR 3969; Joined Cases C-387/02, C-391/02 and C-403/02 *Silvio Berlusconi* et al [2005] ECR I-3565.

as impermissible judicial law-making is largely hidden within national practice. Doubtless very different levels of enthusiasm prevail in different Member States—and divergence between different courts, between different judges, within individual States is unavoidable too. Ultimately, however, where national law is wrenched by interpretation into line with a relevant but unimplemented Directive in a case involving private parties, indirect effect goes some distance to compensating the party who is denied the right to rely directly on the Directive in a horizontal situation—but the result is imperilled legal certainty, a key anxiety which serves as a major reason for the Court having refused horizontal direct effect in the first place.[156]

4.7.5 Incidental direct effect (exclusionary effect)

The phenomenon of 'incidental direct effect' of Directives offers further insight into how the Court's rejection of 'horizontal direct effect' of Directives does not tell the full story about the capacity of unimplemented Directives to exert an effect on national legal proceedings involving private parties. A Directive shall not be applied by a national court in such a way to impose an obligation on a private party. But a Directive may nevertheless be applied by a national court in such a way as to prejudice the position of a private party by precluding reliance on another source of legal rights which collide with the requirements of the Directive. In this way, private parties in domestic proceedings are capable of being affected *incidentally* by the exclusionary effect of unimplemented Directives. This sounds gnomic. A couple of concrete examples are helpful in conveying what is at stake.

In *Arcor AG* the German regulatory authorities had approved a funding and connection scheme in favour of Deutsche Telekom.[157] This had been done in plain violation of an EU Directive. But if the approval were set aside by a German court in proceedings brought by Arcor and other telecommunications firms against the German public authorities the consequence would be to prejudice the position of Deutsche Telekom, a private third party. This, the Court of Justice held in a preliminary ruling, is nonetheless what should follow, provided the relevant provision of the Directive was sufficiently unconditional (which it was). There was no question of the Directive imposing an obligation directly on Deutsche Telekom—which is *not* allowed under EU law, for it would entail the impermissible phenomenon of horizontal direct effect attributed to a

[156] Especially in Case C-201/02 *Wells* note 135.

[157] Joined Cases C-152/07 to C-154/07 *Arcor AG* [2008] ECR I-5959.

Directive. Instead Deutsche Telekom's legal position was altered as a result of the invocation of a Directive in proceedings by another private party brought against the defaulting State. Deutsche Telekom was the victim of 'incidental direct effect'; or, to capture the idea that it was the third party harmed by litigation between two other parties (one public, one private), one might label this a 'triangular situation'.

Wells follows a comparable pattern.[158] Wells, a private individual, complained that a quarry was being developed by a private mining company under an authorization issued by the relevant public authority which, pursuant to applicable EU environmental protection legislation, should not have been issued. It was held that the national court was entitled to require the withdrawal of the authorization—even though this would prejudice a third party, the private mining company. This would not be a case of horizontal direct effect, which the Court in *Wells* explained is ruled out because of the principle of legal certainty, for the Directive did not impose an obligation on the mining company. Instead it would involve adverse repercussions for the mining company—an 'incidental' effect consequent on application of the Directive in the proceedings between Wells and the public authority. This is permitted as a matter of EU law.

EU law operates here to *exclude* a rule of national law (*in casu*, the approval decision) because of the State's mishandling of a Directive whereas EU law cannot *substitute* an obligation drawn from a Directive for the existing obligation imposed by national law. It is thematically important that the Court is concerned to enhance the effectiveness of EU law before national courts. This is not an exception to the Court's refusal to extend horizontal direct effect to Directives but it is a legal doctrine, based on exclusion and not substitution of national law by EU law, that pays little heed to the demands of legal certainty which serve as one of the main reasons for the Court's rejection of horizontal direct effect. The private individual in the position of Deutsche Telekom in *Arcor* and the quarry company in *Wells* find that their situation is radically altered by the invocation of EU law. As with indirect effect, considered in Section 4.7.4, so too incidental effect may cause Directives to exert a decisive impact on national legal proceedings even where private parties are involved.

Case law concerning the so-called 'Notification Directive' casts still harsher light on the sense that the phenomenon of incidental direct effect weakens the coherence of the Court's case law governing the effect of Directives in national legal proceedings. Directive 98/34 requires Member States to give

[158] Case C-201/02 *Wells* [2004] ECR I-723.

advance notice of plans to introduce new technical specifications; and they must comply with a 'standstill obligation' for a defined period after notification of draft measures before bringing them into force.[159] The purpose of this 'early warning system' is to forestall the introduction of new measures that will harm the internal market. The terms of the Directive make no mention at all of whether a Member State's failure to comply with the obligations of notification and/or 'standstill' has any effect on the enforceability of the technical rules in proceedings before *national* courts. But, in accordance with the theme of this chapter that enforcement by national courts is vital to the effective policing of EU law, the Court seized its opportunity in *CIA Security International SA* v *Signalson SA and Securitel Sprl*.[160] It held that breach of the procedural obligation to notify robs the measure of enforceability in proceedings before national courts involving third parties. Accordingly a trader was unable to rely on Belgian law to secure a court order against another trader dealing in products (burglar alarms) that were not in conformity with a Belgian technical regulation because it had not been notified to the Commission. The Belgian courts were required to disapply the Belgian technical specification as a result of the procedural default of non-notification.

The applicant, exercising quasi-public powers, could not enforce those powers because the State had mishandled its obligations under the Directive. There is no question here of horizontal direct effect. No obligation was imposed on a private party: only the application of the national rule was *excluded*.

The subsequent ruling in *Unilever Italia SpA* v *Central Food SpA*[161] is more awkward. Unilever had supplied Central Food with a quantity of virgin olive oil. Central Food rejected the goods on the basis that they were not labelled in accordance with a relevant Italian law. This law had been notified to the Commission but Italy had not observed the Directive's 'standstill' obligation. Unilever submitted that the law should not be applied and sued Central Food for the price of the goods. The Court pointed out that were the Italian rules applied they would have the effect of hindering trade in a product not complying with the rules, and it held that for want of notification the Italian rules should *not* be applied. This is incidental direct effect in the sense that State default has an impact on the allocation of risk under a contract between two private parties. It is *not* a case of horizontal direct effect, which is not permitted, because, as the Court put it, the Directive 'creates neither rights nor obligations for individuals'.[162] It

[159] OJ [1998] L204/37.
[160] Case C-194/94 [1996] ECR I-2201.
[161] Case C-443/98 [2000] ECR I-7535.
[162] Para 51.

is an instance of EU law excluding the application of a relevant rule before a national court, leaving the pre-existing contract to determine the rights and obligations of the parties.

In *Unilever* the impact of the unenforceability of the State measure was felt directly in a contractual dispute between private parties. This was new. There was no contract in *CIA Security*. Similarly in *Arcor* there was no contractual relationship between private parties at the core of the litigation. So in *Unilever* the Court extended the scope of 'incidental direct effect' before national courts while correspondingly reducing the terrain in which unimplemented Directives are sealed off from exerting detrimental effects on private parties in national proceedings. The Court maintained its position in favour of 'incidental' direct effect in its subsequent decision in *Sapod Audic*.[163] However, in that decision it suggested a route whereby the impact on private parties might be softened. It ruled that

> the severity of the sanction under the applicable national law, such as nullity or unenforceability of the contract...is a question governed by national law, in particular as regards the rules and principles of contract law which limit or adjust that sanction in order to render its severity proportionate to the particular defect found.[164]

Manifestly, this opens up the likelihood of different approaches in different Member States to the same violation of Directive 98/34.

Unilever is a revealing decision. If one understands the refusal to permit horizontal direct effect to Directives to be based on finding it unacceptable that unimplemented Directives should impose obligations directly on private parties directly in proceedings before national courts, then 'incidental direct effect' is readily digested. It does not *substitute* obligations drawn from a Directive for existing obligations—the unacceptable feature of horizontal direct effect—but rather merely *excludes* certain provisions of national law, those which are incompatible with the Directive.[165] If, by contrast, one understands the rejection of the horizontal direct effect of Directives to lie in a concern for preservation of the legal certainty of private parties against whom potentially unknown obligations rooted in a Directive might otherwise be enforced, then one would oppose the phenomenon of 'incidental direct effect' because it too offends against private parties' legal certainty. After all, preservation of legal certainty is not

[163] Case C-159/00 *Sapod Audic* [2002] ECR I-5031. [164] Para 52.

[165] See eg V. Skouris, '*Effet utile* versus Legal Certainty: The Case Law of the Court of Justice on the Direct Effect of Directives' (2006) 17 European Business Law Review 241.

only a general principle of the EU legal order[166] but also a reason which the Court gave in *Wells*[167] for excluding the horizontal direct effect of Directives. However, in *Unilever*, the Court, ignoring a vigorous Opinion of Advocate General Jacobs which explained why legal certainty should dictate that the consequences of State default under the Notification Directives should not have a detrimental effect on private parties relying on existing national law, preferred instead to embrace 'incidental direct effect' even in litigation involving exclusively private parties.

There is evident tension here between legal solutions that show fidelity to preservation of legal certainty on the one hand and, on the other, those that promote the deeper penetration of national legal orders by EU law. A further manifestation of this tension between competing understandings of the proper reach of EU law into national legal orders, involving embrace of a solution favouring the latter priority, is provided by the Court's discovery of general principles of EU law that operate in horizontal situations. In cases of faulty or non-existent implementation of a Directive by a Member State, the Court's stance denies individuals the right to rely directly on a Directive before a national court in so far as the party on whom an obligation would be imposed is not for these purposes to be equated with the 'State'. The individual will, however, succeed if able to find a general principle of EU law which is enforceable even in horizontal situations. This is one of several reasons why *Mangold*, met already in Chapter 3.12, is so important—and so controversial—for it finds non-discrimination on grounds of age to be not simply a general principle of EU law but also one that operates directly in relationships between private parties.[168]

Werner Mangold, a fifty-six-year-old man, entered into a contract to work for Rüdiger Helm, a lawyer. The contract provided that the employment relationship would start on 1 July 2003 and last until 28 February 2004. The reason for this fixed term was rooted in a statutory provision under German law intended to make it easier to conclude fixed-term contracts of employment with older workers (as defined). But was this lawful under EU law? Both a relevant Framework Agreement and Directive 2000/78 establishing a general framework for equal treatment in employment and occupation were, it was argued, apt to exclude such a national rule that allowed a diminution in the protection of older persons in work when compared with other workers. But Mangold's main

[166] Eg Case C-469/00 *Ravil* [2003] ECR I-5053; Case C-212/04 *Adeneler* [2006] ECR I-6057. See Chapter 3.13.

[167] Case C-201/02 note 135.

[168] Case C-144/04 *Mangold* [2005] ECR I-9981.

problem in advancing this allegation of discrimination before the German courts was that Helm was a private employer, so Mangold's reliance on the Directive was excluded by the Court's refusal to entertain the horizontal direct effect of a Directive.

The Court came to Mangold's rescue. It ruled that Directive 2000/78 'does not itself lay down the principle of equal treatment in the field of employment and occupation'.[169] So what does? The Court found the source of the principle to lie 'in various international instruments and in the constitutional traditions common to the Member States',[170] and from these seeds it extracted a general principle of law forbidding discrimination on grounds of age.

As already noted in Chapter 3.12, the Court's claim that a general principle of this type is widely found at national and international level is unconvincing and, moreover, the ruling adds to the apprehension about the Court's unpredictable willingness to inflate the scope of EU law with meagre textual support. But, of present concern, the significance of the Court's constitutional sleight of hand in *Mangold* was profound in practical terms. It meant that Mangold, seeking to attack the German rules, could rely on this general principle of EU law which was applicable even in relationships between private parties, and in consequence he had no need to trouble himself with limitations of the constitutional reach of *Directives*. True, this is an instance of EU law being used to *exclude* a national rule in the context of a private dispute. It is not a case of imposing an obligation on a private party. So in this sense the doctrinal purity of the Court's case law is not disturbed. Moreover, 'constitutionalizing' private law by injecting standards protecting the individual from discriminatory treatment is not unknown.[171] But, to re-assert the anxiety articulated above in connection with the incidental direct effect of Directives, if concern to preserve legal certainty underpins the Court's entrenched rejection of the horizontal direct effect of Directives, then it is puzzling (and unexplained by the Court) that concern about legal certainty seem to vanish as it embraces the horizontal direct effect of a general principle.

The Charter of Fundamental Rights went unmentioned in *Mangold*, but it offers a possible basis for a more credible rooting of the claim that EU law forbids discrimination on the basis of age. Its Article 21 lists age as one of several prohibited grounds of discrimination. *Seda Kücükdeveci*

[169] Para 74. [170] Para 74.

[171] See eg C. Mak, *Fundamental Rights in European Contract Law: A Comparison of the Impact of Fundamental Rights on Contractual Relationships in Germany, the Netherlands, Italy and England* (Kluwer Law International, 2008).

v *Swedex GmbH & Co. KG* connects *Mangold* to the Charter.[172] This was another employment dispute involving private parties. Under German law, periods of employment completed before the age of 25 were not to be taken into account in calculating the applicable notice period. The Court treated this as discrimination on grounds of age forbidden by EU law. The Court cited *Mangold* and confirmed that non-discrimination on grounds of age must be regarded as a general principle of EU law, to which Directive 2000/78 gives specific expression. The Charter had by now acquired binding effect, so the Court added that that since its Article 21 prohibits discrimination based on age, the full effectiveness of EU law required a national court to disapply any provision of national legislation contrary to the principle of non-discrimination.

The Court is busy developing its case law to require that provisions of the Charter be used to block the application of national provisions that are incompatible with EU law. *Association de médiation sociale* is a Grand Chamber decision which deserves siting among the Court's heroic 'constitutionalizing' judgments.[173] The dispute was between the Association de médiation sociale (AMS, an association governed by private law), which objected to the appointment of a trade union representative on the basis that it, the AMS, was not legally required to take measures for the representation of employees because it had too few employees. And it seemed clear that AMS would succeed under French law, because the threshold number set by the Labour Code was not exceeded. However, it was also clear that French practice was not compatible with Directive 2002/14, because its method of calculation wrongly allowed exclusion of relevant employees, thereby defeating the purpose of the Directive. The key question was therefore a constitutional one. Could EU law exert any influence in a dispute between private individuals before a national court? Plainly the Directive could not confer rights or impose obligations on private parties. The Court then considered the obligation imposed on a national court to interpret national law in the light of EU law, but noted that this cannot serve as the basis for an interpretation of national law *contra legem*.[174] It thought this would be such a case—the French Labour Code was incapable of interpretation in conformity with Directive 2002/14. It contradicted it. This led to Article 27 of the Charter on workers' rights to information and consultation. *Kücükdeveci* had shown how to use Article 21 in a dispute between individuals in order to preclude the application of

172 Case C-555/07 *Kücükdeveci* [2010] ECR I-365.

173 Case C-176/12 *Association de médiation sociale* judgment of 15 January 2014.

174 It cited *Impact* note 145.

a national provision which is not in conformity with a Directive, so the question was whether Article 27 could perform the same function here, and require disapplication of the restrictions set by the French Labour Code. The Court thought not. This was not because Articles of the Charter may not in principle achieve this exclusionary effect—*Kücükdeveci* shows that they may—but rather because the specific text of Article 27 was not sufficiently precise to do the job. All the Court could offer was mention of *Francovich* as a back-stop protection for individuals suffering loss as a result of the French violation of EU law.

It may be that the Court has responded to some of the criticism of *Mangold* by confining the capacity of general principles to exert horizontal effect to those found within the Charter which operate in a sufficiently precise manner. But it is clear that as a matter of law *some* Articles of the Charter are capable of exerting an effect in horizontal cases, and the task now is to separate out those Charter provisions apt for direct application from those requiring legislative elaboration. It remains troubling that the anxiety that this may harm the legal certainty of private parties, a vividly animating theme elsewhere in EU law, is here left unaddressed. The Court's case law in this area is erratic and rough-edged.

4.8 GENERAL PRINCIPLES, FUNDAMENTAL RIGHTS, AND CONSTITUTIONALISM

The content and evolution of EU fundamental rights in particular and general principles of law more broadly was considered in the previous chapter. The question here is the scope of their application to Member States. Member States have their own diverse, but often sophisticated, methods to protect fundamental rights, and all are party to the ECHR and so subject to supervision by the Court of Human Rights based in Strasbourg. How much more does and should the EU add to this coverage?

4.8.1 The scope of the Charter's Application to Member States

Article 51 of the Charter covers *Field of Application* and states that the provisions of the Charter are addressed to the Member States only when they are 'implementing' Union law. So there are limits: Member States clearly enjoy immunity from inspection pursuant to EU fundamental rights outwith such situations. But quite what the notion of 'implementing' encompasses is not spelled out in the Charter. However, well before the Charter acquired binding force in 2009, the Court had *already* insisted that Member State practice must comply with EU fundamental rights in circumstances which reach beyond a narrow notion of implementation. Not only must the Member States ensure that implementing practice associated with EU secondary legislation is consistent with fundamental rights requirements;[175] so too, since fidelity to fundamental rights is an integral part of the general principles of EU law, must national attempts to justify restrictions on cross-border trade themselves be compliant with EU fundamental rights.[176] Any suspicion that Article 51 of the Charter's reference to 'implementing' EU law as the trigger for review of Member State action might change the Court's consistent approach once the Lisbon Treaty came into force in 2009 were dispelled by its ruling in *Fransson*.[177] This was a preliminary reference from Sweden which concerned the *ne bis in idem* principle (the right not to be tried or punished twice for the same offence) which is laid down in Article 50 of the Charter as well as the ECHR. The Court robustly stated that the Charter 'confirms' its own case law on the extent to which actions of Member States must comply with the EU's system of fundamental rights protection.[178] It then found that the case involved the implementation of EU law. The Swedish rules in question were not explicitly designed to transpose the EU's VAT Directive 2006/112, but they were designed to penalize its infringement. They fell within the scope of the obligation imposed on Member States by EU law to impose effective penalties for conduct prejudicial to the financial interests of the European Union, contained specifically in Article 325 TFEU and more generally in Article 4(3) TEU. Admittedly this fact pattern fits within an understanding of 'implementing' EU law which is focused on absorption of EU secondary legislation, but the Court carefully coupled its claim that Article 51(1) of the Charter 'confirms' its case law with reference to the application of EU fundamental rights to national legislation falling within the scope of EU law, and it cited the cases asserting a wider understanding of the notion of implementing, including those pertaining to free movement law.

The Court in *Fransson* vividly declared that 'The applicability of European Union law entails applicability of the fundamental rights guaranteed by the Charter.'[179] This means that a generous reading of the scope of substantive EU law carries with it a correspondingly generous reading of the scope of the Charter. *Mary Carpenter*, a case that will be examined

[175] Case 5/88 *Wachauf* [1989] ECR I-2609.

[176] Case C-260/89 *ERT* v *Dimotiki* [1991] ECR I-2925. See also eg Case C-112/00 *Schmidberger* v *Austria* [2003] ECR I-5659, examined in Chapter 6.

[177] Case C-617/10 judgment of 26 February 2013.

[178] Para 18.

[179] Para 21.

in more depth in Chapter 7.5, makes the point with force.[180] Mr Carpenter was a British national living in the UK, who sought to rely on EU free movement law to defeat a threat to deport his wife, a third country national (from the Philippines). He succeeded, even though the matter seemed remote from the building of an internal market, because the Court noted that part of his job involved contact with buyers of services which he provided in other Member States. Deporting his wife would affect his business, and this brought the matter within the scope of EU law and immediately required that the UK justify its plan in the light of fundamental rights, in particular respect for family life. It could not do so. A string of decisions commencing in 2011 with *Ruiz Zambrano* provides an even more striking example of the extending reach of EU law and consequently of its ever wider engagement with human rights.[181] They too are examined more fully in Chapter 7.5, but their essence is to permit EU law to be used in some circumstances to challenge the threatened expulsion of third country nationals who are part of the family of an EU national even where that EU national has no connection at all with cross-border movement. Once EU law is found to apply, the threatened national action falls to be checked against the right to respect for private and family life provided for in Article 7 of the Charter. In substance, if not in form, the Court is pushing ever closer to asserting a general jurisdiction in matters of human rights when they arise on the territory of the EU, even in cases where the matter appears to be internal to a single Member State.

To some extent this is hardly a surprise: the conferred competences of the EU have been gradually expanded, principally by the Member States themselves at times of Treaty revision, and they are in any event, as detailed in Chapter 2, not designed to wall off particular areas of national practice from the influence of the EU, so it is logical that the impact of fundamental rights in EU law will become ever more profound in spite of the limits nervously expressed here and there in the Charter and in the Treaties.[182] Yet limits there must be, unless the vertical division of competences between the EU and its Member States is to collapse completely, and occasionally they are glimpsed. Chapter 2.6 explained how, as a result of the Treaty's design, cases in which the Court has emphatically refused to find an EU law element do exist, but they tend to be extreme or artificial or transient. *Kremzow*, concerning imprisonment under rules of Austrian criminal law that were not designed to secure compliance with EU law

[180] Case C-60/00 [2002] ECR I-6279.

[181] Case C-34/09 *Ruiz Zambrano* [2011] ECR I-1177.

[182] Especially Arts 5 and 6(1) TEU and Art 51(2) of the Charter.

and which caused a merely hypothetical impediment to free movement, is one;[183] *Grogan*, where the supplier of information about cross-border abortion services, a students' union in Dublin, had no *economic* motivation, is another.[184] Where EU law does *not* apply, then logically the matter is immune from review in the light of the EU's fundamental rights standards (though doubtless may be reviewed pursuant to national law and/or the ECHR).

It is not the case that EU law applies wherever national authorities act within the scope of the Treaties. *Cruciano Siragusa* concerned an order requiring the owner of renovated property in Italy to restore the site to its former state.[185] The Court found that even though an aim of the national legislation was protection of the environment, clearly a matter within EU competence, there was no *obligation* imposed on the Member State by EU law to act in this specific way in the circumstances that had arisen and so this was not a matter of implementation, as foreseen by Article 51 of the Charter. Therefore the Charter did not apply. *Víctor Manuel Julian Hernández* concerned protection of employees in the event of the insolvency of their employer, a matter addressed by EU Directive 2008/94.[186] It ruled that implementation such as to trigger application of the Charter 'presupposes a degree of connection between the measure of EU law and the national measure at issue which goes beyond the matters covered being closely related or one of those matters having an indirect impact on the other'. The Court listed relevant factors—whether the national legislation is intended to implement a provision of EU law; the nature of the legislation at issue and whether it pursues objectives other than those covered by EU law, even if it is capable of indirectly affecting EU law; and also whether there are specific rules of EU law on the matter or rules which are capable of affecting it. In the case itself it found that the relevant Spanish rules pursued objectives different from that of guaranteeing a minimum protection for employees in the event of the employer's insolvency, the aim of the Directive. So even though the national legislation came within an area in which the EU is competent to act (pursuant to Article 153 TFEU), the Charter was not applicable. Room for national autonomy is preserved.

A tighter material connection than the simple fact that national action happens to fall within an area where the EU has been active or where it

[183] Case C-299/95 [1997] ECR I-2629. [184] Case C-159/90 [1991] ECR I-4685.

[185] Case C-206/13 judgment of 6 March 2014. The problem is not new: cf Case C-309/96 *Annibaldi* [1997] ECR I-7493.

[186] Case C-198/13 judgment of 10 July 2014.

may become active is required, though exactly what is at stake seems to require case-by-case examination. But even here the Court in *Fransson* added a caveat. In a situation where Member State action 'is not entirely determined by' EU law, the application of national standards must not compromise the level of protection provided for by the Charter or the 'primacy, unity and effectiveness' of EU law.[187] Precisely what this means will need future elucidation.[188] But it highlights once again that although in principle Member States are not always called to account in the name of EU standards of fundamental rights, it hard to identify confidently just where the line lies beyond which the conditioning influence of EU law evaporates. This is messy and not conducive to legal certainty, and it detracts from claims that fundamental rights deserve universal application, but it flows ultimately from, first, that the EU operates according to the principle of conferral and, second, that the exact contours of that principle are ill-drawn (Chapter 2); and, more deeply, from a concern to preserve and promote a plural vision of rights and cultures in the EU.[189]

4.8.2 Protocol on the UK and Poland

The Charter's application is geographically fragmented. Article 1 of the *Protocol on the UK and Poland* states that:

> The Charter does not extend the ability of the Court of Justice of the European Union, or any court or tribunal of Poland or of the United Kingdom, to find that the laws, regulations or administrative provisions, practices or action of Poland or of the United Kingdom are inconsistent with the fundamental rights, freedoms and principles that it reaffirms. In particular, and for the avoidance of doubt, nothing in Title IV of the Charter [on *Solidarity*, mainly concerning social and employment protection] creates justiciable rights applicable to Poland or the United Kingdom except in so far as Poland or the United Kingdom has provided for such rights in its national law.

Article 2 adds that 'To the extent that a provision of the Charter refers to national laws and practices, it shall only apply to Poland or the United

[187] Case C-617/10 note 51, para 29. See also Case C-399/11 note 2 para 60; Case C-206/13 note 185, para 32; Case C-198/13 note 186, para 47.

[188] D. Sarmiento, 'Who's Afraid of the Charter? The Court of Justice, National Courts and the New Framework of Fundamental Rights Protection in Europe' (2013) 50 CMLRev 167; F. Fontanelli, 'Implementation of EU Law through Domestic Procedures after Fransson' (2014) 39 ELRev 682.

[189] Cf eg M. Cartabia, 'Europe and Rights: Taking Dialogue Seriously' (2009) 5 Euro Const Law Rev 5.

Kingdom to the extent that the rights or principles that it contains are recognised in the law or practices of Poland or of the United Kingdom.'

There is something immediately disquieting about a Charter of Fundamental Rights from which two Member States are allowed an opt-out. What notion of equality is promoted by such a fragmented vision? This, however, is the system to which the Member States, in ratifying the Treaty, have consented: State rights prevail over individual protection.

The *political* aim of the Protocol is clear. It responds to fears that expansionist case law fed by the Charter might upset particular features of British and Polish social and economic life. The *legal* meaning is far more obscure. The most expansive interpretation would hold that in so far as the Court adopts a creative and dynamic pattern of interpretation in Charter cases, in particular those pertaining to its Title IV, that will have no relevance as far as the UK and Poland are concerned. But this seems an unlikely outcome, not least because it is hard to imagine the Court would be prepared to advertise its rulings as extensions in this sense. The narrowest interpretation would hold that what is provided for in the case of the UK and Poland is in fact no more than a statement that anyway applies now and in the future to all the Member States. So the Protocol begins by stating that it does not *extend* judicial powers—but Article 6(1) EU already stipulates this.

The European Scrutiny Committee of the UK Parliament's House of Commons has made strenuous efforts to identify occasions on which the Protocol might have practical bite,[190] but it admitted the Protocol is 'comfort' rather than a safeguard.[191] The Court of Justice will have a role to play in addressing these conundrums. So far, when the Protocol has been raised before it, it has shown no inclination to authorize any divergent approach in cases involving the UK and Poland, although admittedly none yet has raised any plausible claims to such treatment.[192]

4.8.3 The content of the Charter

Once the matter is shown to involve 'implementing' EU law, then the content of the control exercised is dictated by the Charter. The same

[190] *The Application of the EU Charter of Fundamental Rights in the UK: a State of Confusion*, 43rd Report of Session 2013–14, HC 979 (2014), paras 85–88.

[191] Ibid, paras 51, 141.

[192] Joined Cases C-411/10 and C-493/10 *N.S.* v *Secretary of State* judgment of 21 December 2011. The Secretary of State had argued before the High Court that the Charter does not apply in the UK but this absurd argument, not advanced in Luxembourg, is anyway slapped down (paras 118–120).

inquiry is demanded of Member State implementation as applies in the control of EU measures, which was the subject of examination in Chapter 3.15.6. Finding a violation is relatively uncommon. It is not, however, unknown. In *Liivimaa Lihaveis MTÜ* an association of cattle breeders was refused a subsidy by the Monitoring Committee of the Estonia-Latvia Programme, a body set up on the basis of EU Regulation 1083/2006 governing the Structural Funds and the Cohesion Fund.[193] The decision could not be the subject of an appeal before any court. The Committee was found to be implementing EU law within the meaning of Article 51(1) of the Charter and the absence of any remedy against such a rejection deprived the association of its right to an effective remedy, in breach of Article 47 of the Charter.

It was, however, suggested in Chapter 3 that one should not be too quick to assume that use of the Charter as a basis for review of EU acts has brought about any significant change in the Court's willingness to intervene, and the same caution is relevant here too, in assessing the Charter's role in reviewing national practices. The Court in *Liivimaa Lihaveis MTÜ* added that the requirement for judicial review of any decision of a national authority constitutes a general principle of EU law.[194] So a national court should rule on the lawfulness of a disputed national measure and regard an action brought for that purpose as admissible even if the domestic rules of procedure do not provide for this in such a case, and the Court cited one of its own rulings from as long ago as 1992.[195] The Charter frames the analysis, but it does not seem to herald any transformative effect. Its Article 47 simply absorbs existing judicial practice.[196]

It is possible that other provisions of the Charter will perform a more active transformative, rather than merely presentational, role. But there is scant evidence of this. For example, in *Monika Kušionová*, a case arising out of Directive 93/13 on unfair terms, the Court relied on Articles 7, 38, and 47 of the Charter in its interpretation of the demands of 'effectiveness' in the context of the possible loss of a consumer's family home which had been used as security for a loan, but it carefully located its ruling in the mainstream of its long-standing case law.[197] The Charter is likely normally to amount to no more than a re-framing of existing interpretative approaches.

[193] Case C-562/12 *Liivimaa Lihaveis MTÜ* judgment of 17 September 2014.
[194] Para 75. [195] Case C-97/91 *Oleificio Borelli* v *Commission* [1992] ECR I-631.
[196] See similarly Case C-104/13 *Olainfarm AS* judgment of 23 October 2014.
[197] Case C-34/13 judgment of 10 September 2014.

Similarly, in instances that involve more classic competing values it seems improbable that the Charter does anything more than offer a new way to present familiar style of analysis. In *Wachauf*, the case in which the Court first made clear that Member States are held to EU standards when they implement EU legislation, the Court carefully declared that fundamental rights are not absolute, but rather fall to be considered in relation to their social function.[198] This is close to the pattern seen in the previous chapter, where strained attempts to use the Charter to maximize commercial freedom at the expense of regulatory choices adopted at EU level have proved fruitless (Chapter 3.15.6). In *Wachauf*, which concerned EU rules governing milk production, the Court found that the restrictions envisaged under the EU regime left the competent national authorities a sufficiently wide margin of appreciation to enable them to apply those rules in a manner consistent with the protection of fundamental rights of producers. That implied that there is an obligation drawn from EU law to implement in a way that is compliant with fundamental rights, and the Court has subsequently confirmed that. *Promusicae* addressed the implementation of Directives on e-commerce and intellectual property.[199] In the context of breach of copyright, where disclosure of information is sought by a right-holder, it held that Member States, acting to implement the EU measures, must balance relevant fundamental rights—the right to private life on the one hand and, on the other, the right to property and to an effective remedy. The Court drew inter alia on the Charter, albeit in its formally non-binding status. It has, however, subsequently become standard for the Court to rely on the Charter in directing Member States to strike a fair balance between the rights and freedoms protected by EU law.[200] In these cases the Court typically cites *Promusicae*, thereby confirming that the grant of binding force to the Charter by the Treaty of Lisbon has not brought about substantive change.

The non-absolute nature of EU fundamental rights when placed in the hands of national authorities also emerges clearly from cases on free movement. These require adjudication on whether the fundamental but non-absolute right to free movement is superior to the fundamental but non-absolute right of a political or cultural character which forms the basis of the Member State's justification for restricting free movement. The Court insists on fact-specific assessment rather than abstract hierarchies in order to resolve these collisions. Chapter 6.3.4 explores this more fully,

198 Case 5/88 note 175.

199 Case C-275/06 [2008] ECR I-271.

200 Eg Joined Cases C-468/10 and C-469/10 *ASNEF* [2011] ECR I-12181; Case C-70/10 *Scarlet Extended SA* [2011] ECR I-11959.

but *Omega Spielhallen* deserves mention here as an especially rich decision because it has ringingly clear echoes of the Court's original strategy in the fundamental rights cases decided several decades ago.[201] The case concerned the suppression of games involving simulated killing in Germany on the basis that such practices offended against Germany's constitutionally protected standards of respect for human dignity. This restricted the importation of services from the UK. The Court found that EU law 'undeniably strives to ensure respect for human dignity as a general principle of law', a proposition today confirmed by Article 1 of the Charter, and added that accordingly the objective of protecting human dignity is compatible with EU law, 'it being immaterial in that respect that, in Germany, the principle of respect for human dignity has a particular status as an independent fundamental right'.[202] So, as it had done more than thirty years previously in *Internationale Handelsgesellschaft*,[203] the Court refused to defer to national concern to place protection of fundamental rights under domestic law ahead of EU law, but it did not deny the validity of the national court's anxieties about applying an EU law insensitive to the protection of fundamental rights. It reconciled the situation by instead locating protection of fundamental rights within the EU legal order. More recently the Court has placed a heavier emphasis on Article 4(2) TEU and respect for national identity in structuring this balancing process,[204] but the basic point is unaltered: the Court seeks to allay national sensitivities about EU law undermining high-level national values by embedding respect for those values in the EU's own legal order.

4.8.4 Proportionality

As explained in the previous chapter, the principle of proportionality is set out in Article 5(4) TEU, which states that the content and form of Union action shall not exceed what is necessary to achieve the objectives of the Treaty. The principle was actively shaped by the Court as a restraint on the activities of the EU's institutions over time well in advance of its elevation to a principle recognized by the Treaty, and Member States too are subject to the EU principle of proportionality where they act to implement EU law. This, as already discussed, covers both cases where the Member State is implementing EU law in the conventional sense of ensuring that the objectives set out in a measure of EU secondary legislation are met within the national legal order and cases where the Member State

201 Case C-36/02 *Omega Spielhallen* [2004] ECR I-9609.

202 Para 34.

203 Case 11/70 note 22.

204 Eg Case C-208/09 *Sayn-Wittgenstein* [2010] ECR I-13693, examined in Chapter 6.3.4.

seeks to show a justification for practices that interfere with the exercise of fundamental economic freedoms. In short, a barrier to inter-State trade may be justified only on the condition that it is proportionate. This, explored in Chapter 6, means that a Member State choosing between various measures to attain the same objective must choose the means which least restrict free movement.[205]

The more sensitive and sincere the national justification, the less brusque the Court's treatment of it. In some cases the Court modifies its application of the proportionality principle by agreeing that the national regulator is entitled to enjoy a margin of discretion in deciding the appropriate level of intervention. *Omega Spielhallen* is of this type:[206] so, structurally, is *Bosman*, considered in Chapter 2.8.[207] In such cases the Court pushes its control of national measures into a degree of functional alignment with the respectful attitude to EU legislative choices in areas of social or economic complexity explained in Chapter 2.11.4.

4.9 CONSTITUTIONALISM AND COHERENCE

The journey that was begun by the Court of Justice more than fifty years ago with the landmark rulings in *Van Gend en Loos* and *Costa* v *ENEL* has in one sense not deviated at all, while in another sense it has turned into a wildly unpredictable adventure. There has been no deviation from the Court's initial double-footed lunge: EC law then, EU law now, is *supreme*, meaning that it prevails over national law in the event of conflict, and it is capable of *direct effect*, which means that provided it is of a sufficiently clear and unconditional character, it is to be applied by national courts. Those principles in combination grant immense practical significance to EU law. A breach of EU law may attract attention from the Commission, which has important powers of supervision, but the most immediate risk to a public authority or a private party that infringes EU law is likely to be litigation commenced at national level.

Supremacy and direct effect in combination minimize scope for cost-free violation of EU law. Indirect effect adds to the penetration of EU law into national legal orders: in fact, where a national court interprets national law in compliance with relevant EU law, it removes the need to rely on the direct effect of the relevant provisions of EU law. The horizontal direct effect of Directives is excluded, but both indirect and incidental

[205] Case 261/81 *Walter Rau* v *de Smedt* [1982] ECR 3961 para 12; Chapter 6.3.

[206] Case C-36/02 note 201.

[207] Case C-415/93[1995] ECR I-4921.

direct effect go some way to curtailing the full implications of this apparent refusal to allow EU Directives to affect the legal position of private parties in national proceedings. Even where these several devices do not serve to grant a party in national proceedings the protection promised by EU law, the principle of liability fashioned in *Francovich* may be ridden to the rescue. More generally national choices about remedies and procedures are capable of being jolted, sometimes vigorously, by the EU law demands of equivalence and, even more so, of effectiveness. Moreover, national practices that fall within the scope of the notion of 'implementation' of EU law may be reviewed for compliance with the general principles of EU law, most conspicuously today those contained in the Charter.

The consequence of the creation of this constitutionalized legal order is that EU law can be used within the Member States in a way that far transcends the orthodox use of the rules of international law.

EU law, then, can be exploited. Private parties will have strong incentives to seek to rely on EU law where they are faced with intractable obstacles to domestic law reform. This is most prominent in cases involving free movement law and competition law pursued by large commercial operators, but on occasion social policy, especially gender equality, has been advanced through carefully targeted litigation commenced at national level and engaging the Court of Justice via the preliminary reference procedure.[208] Environmental pressure groups are frequent visitors to Luxembourg; cases concerning consumer protection also proliferate.[209] One of EU law's main legitimating claims is rooted in its capacity to generate renovation of practices at national level which are outdated in an environment of interdependence between States and yet which are unlikely to be changed if retained within a purely national political and legal context. The 'constitutionalization' of EU law, and in particular its embedding into national legal practice, supports and advances that process.

However, when one examines the detailed elaboration of the principles governing the infiltration of national legal orders by EU measures, one readily appreciates that some very awkward decisions have been made by the Court of Justice.

More than forty years ago Pierre Pescatore argued that direct effect should be seen as the normal state of the law: absence of justiciability would militate against application by national judges but otherwise there should be no constraint on the direct penetration of national legal

[208] Eg Cichowski note 17; Hoskyns, *Integrating Gender* (London, Verso, 1996).

[209] See eg Micklitz and Reich and Stuyck note 87.

proceedings by EU norms.[210] Simple though this solution might seem, it is adamantly *not* the one that the Court has chosen. The central tension in its case law is between, on the one hand, the promotion of the effective application of EU law before national courts and, on the other, the application of rules and principles that serve legitimate concerns such as preservation of legal certainty yet obstruct EU law. The Court itself accepts that there are proper limits on its penetration of national legal proceedings: the horizontal direct effect of Directives is excluded by the Court for both constitutional reasons associated with the limited vision of the Treaty[211] and for reasons of preservation of legal certainty.[212] Indirect effect shall not reach as far as *contra legem* interpretation and special rules apply to preclude aggravation of criminal responsibility. Moreover, EU law does not insist that all obstructive national rules of procedure be set aside. Reasonable time limits may be maintained, for example, even where errors of EU law contaminate the decision taken. The principle of *res judicata* may exceptionally be displaced—in consumer cases, in state aid cases, and perhaps in other cases provided a sufficiently compelling reason is found—but the Court is careful to insist on the exceptional nature of such intervention.[213] Legal certainty demands closure of litigation at some point. 'Effectiveness' is important but it is not overriding. There is nothing technical about this. Granting the individual a degree of security about his or her legal position is a matter associated with nothing less than the rule of law.

However, in other circumstances EU law appears to jeopardize that safe harbour. The phenomena of both indirect and incidental effects may in some circumstances lead to a significant rearrangement of the pattern of legal obligation that appeared to prevail under relevant rules of national law. The rise of general principles that apply 'horizontally' subverts the careful containment of EU law's reach into private law relationships via unimplemented Directives. *Mangold* as an unexpected lurch in the case law may now have been superseded by the Charter, but the Charter itself is a new arena within which the Court is asked to make choices about content and scope that are by no means fully or carefully defined by the agreed text.

[210] P. Pescatore, 'The Doctrine of Direct Effect: An Infant Disease of Community Law' (1983) 8 ELRev 155.

[211] Case C-91/92 note 134, para 24.

[212] Case C-201/02 note 135, para 56.

[213] Case C-119/05 note 90 on state aid is explained as a 'highly specific situation' in Case C-213/13 *Impresa Pizzarotti* judgment of 10 July 2014 para 61; in Case C-40/08 note 93 the Court found that effectiveness 'cannot be stretched' so far as to help, para 47.

It is therefore open to question whether the evidence of the previous pages shows that the Court has constructed a framework which places a coherent dividing line between the intrusion of EU law into national legal proceedings in defiance of local obstructive rules, on the one hand, and continued respect for the virtue of such rules on the other. In particular, the objection is that each of these clusters of case law is internally consistent but, when one tries to map their inter-relation, the fault lines gape. The cases in which—in short—legal certainty has been allowed to prevail, with the consequence that private parties are immune from the invocation of relevant EU law in national proceedings, make sense when seen from within. The cases in which the effectiveness of EU law dictates that even private parties may find themselves affected by EU rules which their government has failed to transform into the domestic legal order make sense too, when seen from within. The problem arises when one tries to compare the two groups. If legal certainty is important enough to rule out the horizontal direct effect of Directives, why is it important enough to rule out indirect effect in cases involving private parties *only* where what is asked is *contra legem* interpretation or concerns aggravation of criminal liability? The relative weightings attached to the desire to promote the effective application of EU Directives even in proceedings before national courts involving private parties, on the one hand, and anxiety about damage to legal certainty on the other seem to vary according to which particular phenomenon is involved. This seems inconsistent.

Part of the reason for this inconsistency has been skilfully diagnosed as an absence of transparent understanding of just what the basis for EU law's penetration of national law really is (and should be).[214] Some of the case law is best explained according to a model that treats EU law and national law as part of a single unified system, and therefore assumes that EU law is automatically applicable by national courts, without any need for attention to the notion of direct effect, unless there is some particular reason for a limit. Refusing the horizontal direct effect of Directives would be such a limit, based on the need to preserve legal certainty. A less radical model assumes that EU law and national law are separate orders, and that there must be some particular reason or trigger that leads to EU law entering and being applied within a national legal order. That job is

[214] See M. Dougan, 'When Worlds Collide! Competing Visions of the Relationship between Direct Effect and Supremacy' (2007) 44 CMLRev 931; also K. Lenaerts and T. Corthaut, 'Of Birds and Hedges: The Role of Primacy in Invoking Norms of EU Law' (2006) 31 ELRev 287; P. Craig, 'The Legal Effect of Directives: Policy, Rules and Exceptions' (2009) 34 ELRev 349.

done by direct effect. So the former model involves the invocability of EU law before national courts, not simply individual rights, and is obviously broader than the latter. A more theoretical inquiry would use these phenomena to explore whether there is truly a single EU legal system, of which the legal systems in the Member States are subordinate component parts, or whether instead, and probably more plausibly, there are '28 plus 1' distinct but interacting legal systems at work in the EU.[215]

The 'incidental direct effect' cases provide an especially vivid example of why different understandings of why EU law reaches into national legal proceedings may lead to quite different views on whether EU law should be of relevance in a particular piece of litigation. Choosing the exclusion approach makes it perfectly logical that EU law should apply in a case like *Unilever*, because there is no question of—impermissible—reliance on a right created by EU law in substitution for national law, but rather only use of EU law to clear away—to exclude—an obstacle under national law to reliance on a pre-existing right. And this is wholly consistent with *Faccini Dori*, where EU law, the Directive, was not admitted as applicable because that would have led to—impermissible—reliance on a right created by EU law. So on this view horizontal direct effect is correctly treated as different from incidental direct effect. However, if one instead regards the driving concern in the denial of horizontal direct effect to Directives to be rooted in preservation of legal certainty then one would insist that a case like *Unilever* should be decided with that as the paramount concern and one would, preferring a narrower approach, conclude that the Directive should not have been allowed to infiltrate the national action for breach of contract in a way that totally transformed the allocation of risk in a private contractual relationship. This view holds it irrational to treat horizontal direct effect differently from incidental direct effect. The key point is that how one understands the *reason* to draw a line between invocable provisions and those that are not invocable dictates where one locates that line. One's view of whether *Unilever* confirms a key distinction or blurs it depends on one's starting point. And neither the Treaty nor the Court's case law offers any open-and-shut verdict on what is the correct starting point.

In conclusion, there are a lot of individual *trees* in the Court's case law, and some of them are mis-shapen. More than fifty years on from *Van Gend en Loos* and *Costa* v *ENEL* this is surprising and to an extent unsettling.

[215] J. Dickson, 'Directives in EU Legal Systems: Whose Norms Are They Anyway?' (2011) 17 ELJ 190.

But the overall shape of the *wood* deserves emphasis in conclusion. As a result of the Court's choices, EU law is much more deeply *constitutionalized* than anything familiar on the international plane and, in particular in the claim to its supremacy over conflicting national law and in its directions about how EU law should be treated by courts in the Member States, EU law functions *as if* arranging the vertical relationship between tiers of governance in a federal system.

4.10 WHAT HAS BEEN THE REACTION TO THE COURT'S MISSION TO 'CONSTITUTIONALIZE' EU LAW (AND WHY)?

Most of this chapter so far has been about the Court of Justice's heroic interpretation of EU law as a source which is supreme in the event of conflict with national law and, moreover, capable of penetrating deeply into the fabric of everyday judicial practice in the Member States. In *Costa v ENEL* the Court heralded a 'contrast with ordinary international treaties': the EU Treaty 'has created its own legal system which, on the entry into force of the Treaty, became an integral part of the legal systems of the Member States and which their courts are bound to apply'.[216] In *Van Gend en Loos* the Court described EU law as a source of legal rights for individuals which operates 'independently of the legislation of the Member States'.[217]

That EU law becomes 'an integral part' of national law simply by virtue of the entry into force of the Treaty certainly is, as the Court remarked, a contrast with the orthodox approach to international treaties, the force of which within national legal orders depends on the domestic constitutional rules governing the matter. That is, general international law does not oblige States to incorporate treaties into their domestic law and grant them priority over national law in domestic proceedings. International law assumes that its rules are superior to national law and this means that that a claim to comply with national law cannot excuse a failure to meet obligations under international law. But that is dealt with on the international law plane. EU law, by contrast, pushes its supremacy down the throat of national judges.

The notion that a Treaty may be 'self-executing', that is, that its terms may be apt for direct application by a national court, is not unknown, but it is a creature of national, not international, law. Where it is

[216] Case 6/64 note 20.
[217] Case 26/62 note 55.

recognized at national level, it depends on the nature of the terms and, in the background, the intention of the Contracting Parties. The Court of Justice, in establishing the functionally comparable notion of direct effect in EU law, did not look at all to the *travaux preparatoires*, which were in any event not available, but instead steeped its interpretation in its own flamboyant reading of the particular scheme of the Treaty of Rome. So the law of Treaties contains principles which are functionally similar to supremacy and direct effect, the twin pillars of the Court of Justice's 'new legal order' for the EU, but they do not come remotely close to the claims made by the Court of Justice about the detailed quotidian intrusion of EU law into national legal orders. Most of all, the Court's early judgments deliberately avoid the conventional discourse of international Treaties in order to create a founding myth of juristic novelty within the EU.

The 'new legal order' which the Court heralded in *Van Gend en Loos* could not have been new at all. Its source was and is a Treaty, which is a perfectly common type of legal instrument. We know today that the agile shift which the Court achieved, distancing EU law in rhetoric and then in practice from international law, was not at all inevitable, and was indeed in the crucial early years opposed by powerful figures, including some—though a minority—of the judges of the Court itself, most dramatically in *Van Gend en Loos*.[218] The dissent was hardly surprising given the fragility of the novel claim that EU law had been levered by the force of the Court's own reasoning to become the pre-eminent source of legal authority within each of the Member States.

So the alert reader of this chapter will on occasion have wondered how it could be that national courts simply absorbed the Court's extraordinarily, even outrageously, bold readings of Treaty texts which are deficient of any explicit textual support. Are national judges really so passive? What of the *national* rules governing the relationship between international Treaties and domestic law to which the Court of Justice pays not the slightest heed?

This opens up the breadth of the narrative. The Court, like the other institutions of the EU, has no real presence *inside* national legal and political systems, and its impact is felt, if at all, through national institutions, officials, and judges who carry out the decisions made at EU level. Given the absence of coercive powers, it is the national courts *alone* who

[218] See eg (with references) Editorial, 'For History's Sake' (2014) 10 Euro Const Law Review 191.

can convert into practical reality the abstract constitutional claims made by the Court. The question is whether they *do* carry them out, and if so, why.

And the short answer as far as courts are concerned is that they do carry them out, but for reasons that are different from the vision chosen by the Court of Justice in its elaboration of EU law. Instead, national courts have reasons rooted in *national* law for treating EU law as supreme, directly effective, and further adorned by doctrines such as State liability and indirect effect.

Understanding the impact of EU law within national legal orders must take as its starting point the conventional approach taken to the relationship between international law and domestic law. EU law is, after all, rooted in international Treaties. In Europe some States accept that Treaty law, and therefore EU law, may or must be applied by national courts without any need for its transformation into recognizable domestic form (the 'monist' approach), whereas in other States the orthodox approach is to insist that Treaty law, and therefore EU law, must be converted into domestic law by some implementing measure before national courts may or must apply it (the 'dualist' approach). So, for example, in Portugal judges apply EU law because Article 8(3) of the Portuguese Constitution states that 'Rules laid down by the competent organs of international organization to which Portugal belongs, apply directly in municipal law insofar as the constitutive treaties as applicable provide to that effect', whereas in the UK EU law was made part of domestic law by a statute, the European Communities Act 1972, which instructs judges to apply EU law according to the interpretation provided from time to time by the European Court of Justice.

Both traditions—monist, dualist— share the same basic starting point, which is that the 'bridge' across which Treaty law, and therefore EU law, travels in order to enter the national legal order is a bridge created by that State's constitutional arrangements. This is simply not compatible with the explanation given by the Court of Justice in *Costa* v *ENEL*, in which it heralded a 'contrast with ordinary international treaties' in that the EU Treaty 'has created its own legal system which, on the entry into force of the Treaty, became an integral part of the legal systems of the Member States'. There is here no bridge created by national law.

So far, so scandalous. A group of jurists whose sympathies lay with the tendency towards 'constitutionalization' of EU law did not object. Quite the contrary. In fact, EU law—initially EC law—quickly emerged as a distinctive branch of scholarship, as books and journals, as well as developing academic careers, reflected and promoted the separation of EU law from general international law.[219] An empire was built around Luxembourg which largely described and sought to consolidate the achievements of the Court. An occasional sober voice noted that direct effect and supremacy have clear conceptual counterparts in public international law and questioned whether the breakdown of the relationship between EU and international law should be the subject of mediation.[220] But most writers did not explore such analogies and preferred instead to accept the divorce and to promote the vision of the new legal order on the terms proclaimed by the Court. There was no lack of insight or naiveté.[221] Indeed, the scholars concerned, typically motivated by a yearning desire to see States in Europe bound by ties of a deeper and more durable nature than those that had been shattered time and again before 1945, had extraordinarily vivid reason to embrace and promote the Court's vision. Eric Stein was among the more influential: a man who fled Prague in the summer of 1939 and later learned that most of his (Jewish) family had been killed by the Nazis brought an utterly understandable 'emotional (intuitive) impulse' to his normative assessment of EU law's need to mutate away from conventional international law.[222] Writing a review of Gerhard Bebr's book *Development of Judicial Control of the European Communities*, itself a powerful example of painstaking scholarly anxiety to promote the Court's constitutionalizing mission,[223] Stein explicitly endorsed the need for lawyers and interested scholars [to] defend with a firm hand the legal-constitutional 'acquis communautaire', lest 'the unique experiment in institution building ... go the way of the GATT and the traditional intergovernmental organizations'.[224] It took a long time for EU law scholarship to accommodate critical voices. The first significant attack on the Court's audacity arrived in 1986 when Hjalte Rasmussen published *On Law and Policy in the European Court of Justice*, which accused the Court of egregious trespass beyond its job of interpretation, in particular in the direction of expanding the reach of EU law.[225]

[219] See eg A. Boerger and M. Rasmussen, 'Transforming European Law: The Establishment of the Constitutional Discourse from 1950 to 1993' (2014) 10 Euro Const Law Review 199.

[220] D. Wyatt, 'New Legal Order, or Old?' (1982) 7 ELRev 147; O. Spiermann, 'The Other Side of the Story: An Unpopular Essay on the Making of the European Community Legal Order' (1999) 10 EJIL 763.

[221] See eg A. Vauchez, 'The Transnational Politics of Judicialization. Van Gend en Loos and the Making of EU Policy' (2010) 16 ELJ 1.

[222] A. Boerger, 'At the Cradle of Legal Scholarship on the European Union: The Life and Early Work of Eric Stein' (2014) 62 AJCL 859, 892.

[223] Nijhoff, 1981.

[224] Book Review (1984) 78 AJIL 692, 696.

[225] Nijhoff, 1986.

Rasmussen's methodology deserved and received criticism.[226] He was selective and he was sometimes too quick to condemn the legitimacy of genuinely difficult interpretative choices about the meaning of sparely written texts. But Rasmussen deserves huge credit for the change in the intellectual shape of EU law which has bred today a more diverse and critical brand of scholarship, in relation to interpretative techniques in particular[227] and substantive choices more generally.[228] But the decisive choices made by the Court in the 1960s were met at the time by a strategically receptive academic community.

The Member States, acting at times of Treaty revision, could have put the Court in its place by agreeing to alter or wholly dismantle its constitutional creations. Aside from a nibble here and there,[229] they have not done so. Indeed they have commonly not merely left the Court's case law untouched but actively strengthened it by writing it more or less into the text of the Treaty. This is true most prominently of fundamental rights, as examined in Chapter 3.15, but it is visible too in more technical areas such as standing in judicial review[230] and effective remedies before national courts.[231] Such protection of the Court's judgments is partly explicable by reference to the sheer difficulty in assembling the unanimity necessary at times of Treaty revision to upset them, but more positively one can reflect that in the early years when EU law, both primary and secondary, was made only with unanimous support, the Member States probably found appeal in the Court's energetic development of the doctrines of supremacy and direct effect which had the effect of enhancing deterrence of violation of agreed norms.[232] Confirming a causal link between the Court's great

226 Eg M. Cappelletti, 'Is the European Court of Justice "Running Wild"'? (1987) 12 ELRev 3.

227 Eg G. Conway, *The Limits of Legal Reasoning and the European Court of Justice* (CUP, 2012); G. Beck, *The Legal Reasoning of the Court of Justice of the EU* (Hart, 2013). For a helpful review of recent work, see J. Bengoetxea, 'Text and Telos in the European Court of Justice' (2015) 11 Euro Const Law Rev 184.

228 J. Shaw and J. Hunt, 'Fairy Tale of Luxembourg?: Reflections on Law and Legal Scholarship in European Integration', in D. Phinnemore and A. Warleigh (eds), *Reflections on European Integration: 50 Years of the Treaty of Rome* (Palgrave Macmillan, 2009).

229 On the 'Barber Protocol', concerning pensions, see J. Höreth, 'The Least Dangerous Branch of European Governance? The European Court of Justice under the Checks and Balances Doctrine', in B. de Witte, E. Muir, and M. Dawson (eds), *Judicial Activism at the European Court of Justice* (Elgar, 2013).

230 Case 294/83 *Parti Ecologiste Les Verts* v *European Parliament* [1986] ECR 1339, absorbed by what is now Art 263(1) TFEU.

231 Case 45/76 note 67; now Art 19(1) TEU.

232 J. Weiler, 'The Community System: the Dual Character of Supranationalism' (1981) 1 YEL 273.

constitutionalizing judgments and their political environment is close to impossible, but hints exist. Pierre Pescatore, judge at the Court from 1967 and 1985 and a true insider, has drawn attention to the coincidence in time of *Van Gend en Loos* and the retention of unanimity in Council driven by President de Gaulle and culminating in the Luxembourg Accord logjam that, as explained in Chapter 3.8, was loosened only by the rise of qualified majority voting (QMV) achieved by the Single European Act with effect from 1987.[233]

The suppression of State veto power in Council altered the dynamic by opening up possibilities for Member States to be bound by rules to which they had *not* agreed, so more complex reasons to explain the conditions on which the Court depended to advance and protect its innovations have been required, and have been provided;[234] but an important insight remains the thematic awareness of Member States that whatever may be the costs of being held ever more tightly to obligations, the benefits accruing as a result of all the other Member States being equally and reciprocally in the grip of EU law are greater. Much of the Court's constitutionalization of EU law fitted this pattern and so was left untouched. The Court has become powerful and autonomous of political correction to a degree unseen in any other international court.

The academic community and political élites within the Member States had their reasons for accommodating the Court's pretensions. But the sternest challenge to the Court's vision of EU law as a new legal order comes from within national constitutional orders, most of all from national courts charged with the responsibility to protect national constitutions.

4.11 THE REACTION OF NATIONAL COURTS

No Member State judiciary accepts *Costa* v *ENEL* at face value: no Member State judiciary could accept it, without surrendering constitutional authority.

4.11.1 Twenty-nine stories

So as far as the Court of Justice is concerned, the principles of supremacy and direct effect apply within national legal orders as a matter of EU law,

[233] P. Pescatore, 'Van Gend en Loos, 3 February 1963—A View from Within' in *The Past and Future of EU Law* note 123 p 5.

[234] Eg K. Alter, *The European Court's Political Power* (OUP, 2009), especially Ch 6, 'Who are the Masters of the Treaty? European Governments and the European Court of Justice'.

whereas for national courts their acceptance is a consequence of national law, which is (in different ways in different States) opened up to EU law. The logical consequence that must be confronted is that if there is an impediment to the application of EU law within domestic constitutional law then that will be effective to curtail the reach of EU law—in blatant violation of the principle of supremacy as understood by the Court of Justice and to the detriment of the achievement of the Treaty objectives, on which the Court relied in its foundational cases as the basis for its interpretation favouring supremacy and direct effect. One could, as an EU lawyer, airily dismiss the need for inquiry into national reactions—EU law must be uniform. One could observe that any national court that refuses to accept the rules places its State in breach of its EU law obligations, under the orthodoxy of international law's rule that a State may not excuse its default by reference to internal difficulties. And yet this would be entirely to miss the point of the EU. It aims to harness national diversity into a viable system of management of interdependence. International law models are set aside in favour of a much more intimate judicial collaboration between Luxembourg and the national systems. How this is done—if it is done—at national level is not technical detail; it is the very lifeblood of the EU's operating system.

The way in which this apparently irreconcilable gulf in understanding has been handled is a story that requires twenty-nine chapters: one taking account of the EU and twenty-eight covering each Member State.[235] Excepting only the UK, which lacks a written Constitution, each Member State of the EU provides in its Constitution, one way or another, explicitly or indirectly, that EU law shall be applied at national level.[236] The Constitution is the bridge. Moreover, given that the relevant provisions of the several Constitutions are in some cases not EU-specific and in some cases singularly unhelpful on any or all of the questions of how EU law is to be applied, much power is delegated to national supreme or constitutional courts. In Europe there is in general great diversity between models of constitutional review.[237] As far as EU law is concerned, supremacy resolves the problem with perfect simplicity, but it is a different

[235] Eg M. Claes, *The National Court's Mandate in the European Constitution* (Hart, 2005); M. Everson and J. Eisner, *The Making of a European Constitution: Judges and Law beyond Constitutive Power* (Routledge Cavendish, 2007).

[236] M. Claes, 'Constitutionalising Europe at its Source: The European Clauses in the National Constitutions: Evolution and Typology' (2005) 24 YEL 81; P. Popelier, 'Europe Clauses and Constitutional Strategies in the Face of Multi-Level Governance' (2014) 21 MJ 300.

[237] M. De Visser, *Constitutional Review in Europe* (Hart, 2013).

vision at national level, where the starting point is not the EU Treaties as interpreted by the Court of Justice but rather the values asserted by the national Constitution—of which openness to EU law is not necessarily the pinnacle. This is a 'pluralist' inquiry. It would be possible to impose a single narrative only by suppressing diversity. There have been plenty of attempts through history to establish a single source of political authority throughout Europe, or at least most of it. None has succeeded, but tens of millions of people have been slaughtered in the process. It can be done. It has been done in the US. The modern understanding of the relationship between State law and federal law in the USA, in particular that State law may not set aside federal law and that States may claim no right of unilateral secession and, via the Fourteenth Amendment, that fundamental rights protect all US citizens from abridgement by States, was established in the 1860s. This was the product of the Civil War. It cost more than 600,000 lives. So the real question about establishing a single source of political authority is—can it be done *without bloodshed*? It looks unlikely, and the European Union's aspiration is to create a framework within which diversity can be managed, not replaced by forcing one vision's primacy at the expense of all others. This is the challenge—and the appeal—of constitutional pluralism in Europe.

4.11.2 The case of the United Kingdom

In the UK the European Communities Act 1972, which entered into force as the UK prepared for accession in 1973, provided the necessary bridge. It gives EU law effect in the UK by instructing judges to apply EU law according to the interpretation provided from time to time by the Court of Justice. So this provides a permanent connection between everyday judicial practice in the UK and the requirements of EU law. The Act also provides a statutory basis for the adoption of secondary legislation designed to implement EU laws in the UK.

In the UK the orthodox understanding is that what Parliament has given, Parliament can take away, so it is possible simply to repeal the European Communities Act and, as a matter of domestic law, thereby to rupture the statutory connection made between judges in the UK and EU law. In one sense this makes EU law peculiarly vulnerable to government whim in the UK, since on this orthodox understanding it can be deprived of effect before domestic courts simply by the enactment of a statute like any other; in another sense it shows the ease with which EU law may be embedded within the domestic legal orders of the UK, because a simple statute does the job. Elsewhere, such as in Germany (Section 4.11.3), if the Constitution, protected by the *Bundesverfassungsgericht*, blocks the application of EU law there is nothing that the government of the day can do about it, short of attempting to alter the Constitution itself.

The European Union Act 2011 added to the statutory ground rules. It includes the so-called 'referendum lock': that the UK shall not consent to further transfer of competences to the EU unless that has been approved by a referendum. In detail, the conditions for triggering the requirement are shot through with ambiguity.[238] More generally, what is clearly an attempt to trumpet the sovereignty of Parliament over strengthened EU centralization is itself undermined by the sovereignty of Parliament simply to repeal the commitment to a referendum whenever it so chooses.

The early case law in the UK did not speak with one voice but there emerged a readiness to interpret domestic legislation that is ambiguous in such a way as to ensure it complies with obligations undertaken under EU law.[239] This, however, is not an EU-specific approach: it is an orthodox presumption in circumstances where domestic rules are intended to give effect to international law obligations.[240] In this way judicial interpretation will rescue UK law from being applied in a manner incompatible with EU law. But even though 'interpretation' was in some instances stretched by English courts to its very furthest edge,[241] it has limits, and cannot always save the day. What happens where a domestic statute is irremediably in contradiction to the demands of EU law—are UK courts able to intervene by reviewing a statute? The famous *Factortame* case provided an opportunity for rigorous exploration of the special demands of EU law. The House of Lords (today the Supreme Court), equipped with the Court of Justice's preliminary ruling that it possessed the power to grant interim relief in proceedings against the Crown,[242] then had to decide whether to exercise that power on the facts of the case before it. Their Lordships considered the case appropriate for the grant of relief in favour of Factortame, pending the final ruling.[243] The point was that before, the Court of Justice's ruling courts in the UK had not considered themselves equipped with any such power, and the ruling in Luxembourg

[238] P. Craig, 'The European Union Act 2011: Locks, Limits and Legality' (2011) 48 CMLRev 1915.

[239] Eg *Macarthys Ltd* v *Smith* [1981] 1 QB 180; *Garland* v *British Rail Engineering* [1983] AC 751.

[240] Eg *R* v *Lyons* [2003] 1 AC 976.

[241] Eg *Litster* v *Forth Dry Dock Co* [1990] 1 AC 546; cf *Robertson* v *Swift* [2014] 4 All ER 869, 876–877.

[242] Case C-213/89 *R* v *Secretary of State for Transport, ex parte Factortame* [1990] ECR I-2433.

[243] [1991] AC 603, [1990] UKHL 13.

was greeted with attention and, in some quarters, outrage for its alleged invasion of British—specifically Parliamentary—sovereignty.[244] Lord Bridge, however, chose in his speech directly to confront such attacks:

> there is nothing in any way novel in according supremacy to rules of Community law in those areas to which they apply and to insist that, in the protection of rights under Community law, national courts must not be inhibited by rules of national law from granting interim relief in appropriate cases is no more than a logical recognition of that supremacy.

This would be astonishingly radical were he to source such an obligation *in EU law itself*, but he did not. He sourced it in domestic law, the 1972 Act. The approach taken, however, is *in practice* protective of EU law. Lord Bridge treated the 1972 Act as directing that a UK court should override any rule of national law found to be in conflict with any directly enforceable rule of EU law. This is accepted not simply because the Court of Justice so insists, but instead because the ECA 1972 says that the English courts shall follow what the Court of Justice insists. The presumed site of ultimate legal authority is Parliament, not the EU Treaties. The effect, however, is that not only will judges interpret even subsequently adopted statutes according to an imported assumption that all are to be read as intended to meet the obligations imposed by EU law, but also that national rules, even statutes, will be disapplied in so far as they conflict with EU obligations.

In this sense the 1972 Act is treated as reaching into the future, to condition the impact of subsequently adopted acts that conflict with EU law obligations. The orthodox principle of implied repeal, according to which an inconsistency between two statutes is resolved in favour of the approach mandated by the later in time, is set aside. This identifies the ECA 1972 as constitutionally superior to the norm, for it is insulated from any possibility of being treated as repealed by implication by a later inconsistent statute. In January 2014 the Supreme Court's ruling in *HS2* engaged with this debate.[245] The case itself involved questions about the compatibility of the government's plans to develop HS2 (high speed railway) through a 'hybrid bill', involving debate in Parliament, with requirements imposed by EU environmental law. No incompatibility was

[244] See eg Hansard, HC Debs, vol 174, 20 June 1990: Teddy Taylor MP, 'Any law that we enacted last week, that we will consider today or that we enact next week can be repealed in a flash by the judges in Luxembourg... There is no point in our going ahead with passing laws when we have no guarantee that those laws will prevail.'

[245] *R (on the application of HS2 Action Alliance Limited)* v *The Secretary of State for Transport and another* [2014] UKSC 3.

found and no preliminary reference was made. But of longer-term significance, the distinction between ordinary statutes and higher-ranking 'constitutional instruments' was asserted. Such 'constitutional instruments' include ancient pre-Union instruments from England (the Magna Carta, the Petition of Right 1628, the Bill of Rights) and from Scotland (the Claim of Rights Acts 1689, the Act of Settlement 1701, and the Act of Union 1707), and now the European Communities Act 1972, the Human Rights Act 1998, and the Constitutional Reform Act 2005. But not texts alone: also within the scope of the constitutional instrument are 'fundamental principles, whether contained in other constitutional instruments or recognised at common law, of which Parliament when it enacted the European Communities Act 1972 did not either contemplate or authorise the abrogation'.[246]

It seems these constitutional instruments can be changed only by express primary legislative act; they are too important to be repealed by implication. So in the UK not all laws are of the same type. As far as EU law—but not only EU law—is concerned, an express statutory direction to prefer a domestic statute over conflicting EU law should be followed by the courts, and the consequences that would follow from defiance of EU law should be addressed in the political sphere and not in proceedings before English courts. But *express* statutory provision is required. There is, for all the accusation that *HS2* involves constitutional innovation built on meagre intellectual foundation (*why* are these particular instruments 'constitutional'? How many are there?), a highly agreeable implication of the claim that the ECA (and other constitutional instruments) may not be repealed by implication. It forces Parliament to use express words, making transparent the magnitude of the change, and thereby ensuring the necessary direct political engagement with the step proposed. In this sense such an overt violation of EU law would immediately reveal the incendiary political implications.

In sum, although *in principle* the statutory basis for reception of EU law in the UK does not meet the Court of Justice's vision of the reasons why EU law is supreme, in practice a pragmatic accommodation is secured by statute and judicial receptivity. The refusal to countenance the ECA's implied repeal by a later conflicting statute means that there is partial entrenchment of the ECA. And in practice this gets to the position the Court of Justice expects. Only in the event of an express repeal of the ECA would the matter become awkward. But such a politically dramatic

[246] Para 207.

step would not be awkward merely or even mainly in the context of litigation before the English courts.

4.11.3 The case of Germany

Germany offers a fascinating and influential case study. Its supreme constitutional court, the *Bundesverfassungsgericht* (BVerfG), has delivered several judgments in which it has *always* found the demands of EU law to be acceptable according to the German constitution but in which it has *frequently* raised the alarm about what it would not accept, should the EU demand it. The *Bundesverfassungsgericht* court barks—but it has not yet bitten.

Its concerns are directed *both* at the practice of the EU's institutions within the arrangements established by the Treaties *and* at the ability of Germany to participate in revision of the Treaties. Its concerns in the former case are rooted in anxiety about the EU taking over functions that were not authorized by the German political process at the time the Treaty was revised. In the latter case its concerns are more nebulous, but are tied to fears about undermining the vitality of domestic political processes.

Article 24(1) of the German Basic Law (*Grundgesetz*) provides that 'The Federation may by a law transfer sovereign powers to international organizations.' This provision 'opens up' German law to the application of law emanating from a different source. This has been readily treated as providing the necessary bridge between German law and EU law. This was supplemented with effect from 1992 by Article 23, which makes provision for the particular case of the EU. Article 23(1) provides that:

> With a view to establishing a united Europe, the Federal Republic of Germany shall participate in the development of the European Union that is committed to democratic, social, and federal principles, to the rule of law, and to the principle of subsidiarity, and that guarantees a level of protection of basic rights essentially comparable to that afforded by this Basic Law. To this end the Federation may transfer sovereign powers by a law with the consent of the Bundesrat.

But the *Grundgesetz* contains a great deal more than merely openness to the EU.

The first flashpoint was generated by concern to protect fundamental rights. The logic of EU law's supremacy is that it shall prevail over national law in all circumstances—even if the national law in question protects fundamental rights of the citizen. This, as already suggested in Section 4.3, is an audacious claim which makes extraordinary demands of national legal orders which have embedded protection of fundamental rights as an existential element of the post-Second World War settlement.

In a decision known as *Solange I* the BVerfG described the protection of fundamental rights as an inalienable, essential feature of Germany's Basic Law.[247] This is exactly to *refuse* the Court of Justice's claim that once competences have been conferred on the EU, judicial control exercised at national level pursuant to national standards is terminated. *As long as—solange*, in German—the EEC (as it then was) fails to provide reliable protection of fundamental rights at a level secured by the *Grundgesetz*, the BVerfG cannot recognize EU law's claim to supremacy. So *German* standards condition readiness to apply *EEC* law on German territory. But there was no violation found in the case itself.

The core of this reservation has *never* been abandoned. In this sense supremacy, as preached by the Court in Luxembourg, has been rejected in Germany. But *as long as* the EU does provide sufficient protection of fundamental rights, there is no practical problem—as the BVerfG knows and, once *Solange I* had been decided (and probably before then), as the Court of Justice knew too. And this dynamic is the key to the subsequent elaboration of the case law.

Thirteen years later, in *Solange II*, the BVerfG found that fundamental rights protection at EU level had attained a reliably comparable standard to that secured by the German Basic Law.[248] It referred at length to the Court's case law, including the rise of fundamental rights protection, and to political commitments in the field made by the Parliament, the Council and the Commission, and the European Council. This does not set aside the 'as long as' proviso. Quite the contrary: it endures. But it diminishes any practical possibility of the trigger being pulled. In fact, the proviso is inverted. No longer will the BVerfG intervene as long as the EU fails to secure adequate protection, but rather the BVerfG will *not* intervene so long as there *is* effective protection of fundamental rights. In the subsequent *Bananas* ruling the BVerfG insisted that any allegation of a gap between EU and German standards of fundamental rights protection 'must state in detail that the protection of fundamental rights required unconditionally by the Basic Law is not generally assured in the respective case'.[249] The judgment, which emphasizes the rise of fundamental rights protection at EU level and includes warm remarks about the quality of protection secured by the Court of Justice, is written in a tone sceptical that any such gap will be found. Nor was there one in the *Bananas*

[247] [1974] 2 CMLR 549. The breadth of academic, public, and political interest surrounding the ruling has been exposed by B. Davies, *Resisting the European Court of Justice: West Germany's Confrontation with European Law, 1949–1979* (CUP, 2012).

[248] [1987] 2 CMLR 225. [249] 7 June 2000, 2 BvL 1/97.

litigation itself. This is not to surrender a power of review in principle, but it vastly reduces the likelihood of its exercise in practice.

It is here that a fuller appreciation of the Court of Justice's shaping of fundamental rights as general principles *of EU law* is acquired. This, tracked in Chapter 3.15, was not a development that occurred in isolation. There is an intimate relationship between the Court's case law on supremacy and that on fundamental rights. It is not simply that German judicial resistance pushed the Court to act in defence of its creation—after all, *Internationale Handelsgesellschaft*[250] pre-dates *Solange I*. The story is more nuanced than that. One would hope that the Court of Justice would have been inspired by the growing impact of EU law on individuals to shape protection in the name of fundamental rights within the EU legal order, but the fact is that such a trend to connect fundamental rights to the claim to EU law's supremacy was also influenced and provoked by anxiously militant national courts.

It is not the protection of fundamental rights alone that has generated reservations about the unleashing of a supreme EU legal order in Germany. Supremacy is a claim made for EU law under conditions set by what Article 5(1) TEU today calls the 'principle of conferral': that is, EU law prevails over national law in the event of conflict but only in areas to which the national political process has consented, at the time of Treaty revision. It follows that this bargain is broken if the EU acts beyond the areas in which it enjoys conferred powers. The Court of Justice ought to invalidate any such trespass. But is there a role for national courts to police it?

Brunner was a constitutional complaint which was directed, in short, at preventing German ratification of the Maastricht Treaty on the basis that this was incompatible with the Basic Law.[251] It failed, but the BVerfG set out what could not be done by Germany in the name of EU integration, while finding that no such offending action was envisaged by the Maastricht Treaty. *Brunner* therefore shares with the cases concerning fundamental rights a thematic readiness to bark but not to bite, while also setting up the possibility for a form of indirect dialogue with the Court in Luxembourg. The BVerfG's loudest bark was its assertion that 'the Union Treaty as a matter of principle distinguishes between the exercise of a sovereign power conferred for limited purposes and the amending of the Treaty, so that its interpretation may not have effects that are equivalent to an extension of the Treaty', and it added that such an interpretation

[250] Case 11/70 note 22. [251] [1994] 1 CMLR 57.

of enabling rules 'would not produce any binding effects for Germany'.[252] Although the basic idea that the EU operates on the basis of conferred powers and that the EU may not 'self-authorize' an expansion of its competences is in principle not controversial, the claim that the BVerfG may police these rules plainly contradicts the stance of the Court of Justice, which includes also a claim to exclusive jurisdiction in ruling EU measures invalid.[253] However, after examination of the provisions of the Treaty, the BVerfG concluded that the limits of the EU were 'reliable'.[254] So ultimately this is a judgment that is generously inclined to the EU's pattern of development—*over*-generous, some would complain, for the story told in Chapter 2 of this book is not of firmly 'reliable' limits.

The ruling in *Brunner* concludes with the gloriously opaque instruction that what is vital in future is that 'the democratic bases of the Union will be built up in step with the integration process, and a living democracy will also be maintained in the member-States as integration progresses'. This type of grand but wildly imprecise control figures prominently in *Lisbon*, the decision of the BVerfG which approved German ratification of the Lisbon Treaty in 2009.[255] The detail of this judgment is not identical to those that preceded it, but thematically the similarities are clear and close. The BVerfG makes plain that despite the constitutional 'openness' to European integration to which it is explicitly committed,[256] some things may *not* be done in the name of the EU, while it avoids making plain exactly what it is that may not be done. However, and familiarly, it found that what was proposed to be achieved by the Lisbon Treaty was *not* beyond the pale as far as Germany was concerned, save only that the BVerfG directed that adjustments be made to strengthen domestic oversight of legislative resort to Article 352 TFEU (Chapter 2.7.3).

Lisbon is not written with economy or precision. The BVerfG declares that European integration may not violate 'the Member States' constitutional identity which is not amenable to integration'.[257] What is at stake is not simply the structural issue of the terms on which the EU may be empowered, but a line beyond which no empowerment, however reliably it may be drawn, is permitted because of damage done to Germany's constitutional identity. However, quite what this blocking notion of 'identity' entails is left calculatedly obscure. It is sketched

[252] Para 99. [253] Case 314/85 note 31. [254] Para 94.

[255] Judgment of 30 June 2009, *Bundesverfassungsgericht*, BVerfG, 2 BvE 2/08: available at http://www.bundesverfassungsgericht.de/entscheidungen/es20090630_2bve000208en.html.

[256] *Europarechtsfreundlichkeit*, paras 225, 240. [257] Para 239.

in different ways in different parts of the judgment.[258] An exhaustive list of its elements is never provided. *Lisbon*'s ambiguities are doubtless calculated, leaving room for manoeuvre by the BVerfG in future and room too for astute German politicians to refer to the risk of a veto cast by the BVerfG as a device to repel politically unpalatable proposals at EU level.

The BVerfG remains busy. In *Honeywell* it was pressed to find that the Court of Justice's controversial ruling in *Mangold* amounted to a step beyond the (permitted) task of interpreting EU law and instead to constitute a shift in the allocation of competences made by the Treaty.[259] In conformity with previous practice, the BVerfG did not rule out the possibility in principle of conducting such a review. But any such '*ultra vires* control' must be exercised in a spirit of 'openness' to EU law, which means more concretely that it must be restrained. To be so condemned, a ruling in Luxembourg would have to involve a sufficiently serious and manifest transgression leading to a structurally significant shift in the allocation of competences to the detriment of the Member States. This is an imprecise threshold, but it is certainly a calculatedly high one and it will rarely, if ever, even be approached, let alone crossed. *Mangold* was on this approach *not* an *ultra vires* judgment. *Francovich*, which, as mentioned in Section 4.6, was subsequently attacked by the German government before the Court of Justice as an impermissible extension in the scope of EU law, would on this approach probably also receive a green light were it to be attacked *before German courts* as an *ultra vires* judgment. The pattern of control is readily compared with that applied in fundamental rights cases: a rhetoric of intervention is coupled to a conditional promise that it is unlikely to occur in practice.

In 2014 the BVerfG made its first ever preliminary reference to Luxembourg. The case arose in the context of the scramble to find arrangements suitable to stabilize the crisis in the Eurozone, in particular the Outright Monetary Transactions (OMT) programme (Chapter 3.9.2). The BVerfG made plain that it had serious doubts that the rules could possibly be compatible with EU law, expressing particular concern about perceived infraction of Article 123 TFEU's prohibition of monetary financing and of the mandate in respect of monetary policy with which Article 127 TFEU equips the European Central Bank (ECB). The BVerfG's readiness to fulfil the promise it had made in *Honeywell* to engage with the Court of Justice when addressing such matters of validity provides

[258] Paras 235, 298, 351.

[259] Judgment of 6 July 2010, 2 BvR 2661/06.

welcome recognition that any decision could not feasibly be treated as having repercussions only in Germany. On the other hand, the BVerfG rather aggressively set out how it expected the Court to answer the questions it referred, under a far from concealed threat that unless its concerns were met, in particular through a narrow interpretation of OMT's valid scope, the programme would be treated as not binding in Germany. This departs from the more constructive and conciliatory tone of *Bananas* and *Honeywell* in which readiness to accept and accommodate different judicial views was secured by insisting on a high threshold before the BVerfG would find any violation. The Court of Justice's response, a deft and carefully drawn preliminary ruling, addressed some though not all of the concerns expressed: it held the measure compatible with EU law provided it be implemented in particular ways in the future.[260] The Court stressed the broad discretion of the ECB under the Treaty, although it used the principle of proportionality in particular to assert control over the exercise of that discretion. Whether this will satisfy the BVerfG remains to be seen. An approach closer to its ruling in *Honeywell* than its reference in *Gauweiler* would be superior as a means to leave space for reasonable disagreement between courts.

An important element in the assessment of this story is that where the German court declares that it is protecting German constitutional values and therefore controlling the application of EU law on German territory, it is in effect asserting a jurisdiction that will have effects that certainly will not be confined to German territory. The EU itself claims as one of its foundational legitimating motivations the concern to arrest the capacity of States to inflict harm on their neighbours as a result of choices that are insensitive to their external effects: this is also the context against which the deliberations of the BVerfG in such cases takes place. Preservation of the rule of law means this cannot be a reason for restraint where a clear violation of constitutional law is evident, but awareness that a decision taken nationally will be felt transnationally is a reason for restraint and deference to political processes where the matter is more legally ambiguous. Anxiety about the weakness of a judicial claim rooted in protection of German democracy where this would lead to 'incalculable consequences for the operating currency of the eurozone' led Justice Lübbe-Wolff, dissenting in the BVerfG's decision to make a reference in the OMT case, to want to treat the complaint as inadmissible. The majority of the judges of the BVerfG are more interventionist, but not—yet—to the point of

[260] Case C-62/14 *Gauweiler* judgment of 16 June 2015.

finding a violation of a sufficient magnitude to bring the house of cards crashing down.

4.12 JUDICIAL DIALOGUE

The national constitution provides the bridge across which EU law travels in order to become embedded in national legal orders, but that bridge is not only constructed of openness to EU law; it also comprises (in different ways in different Member States) potential *blockages* to EU law. So, it seems, supremacy on the terms expressed by the Court in *Costa* v *ENEL* is a myth. Supremacy is in fact in the gift of national constitutional tradition. And it is a gift that could be withheld. But it is a gift that is not withheld.

This in turn points to the most deeply intriguing dimension of this narrative. To what extent have national courts been able to provoke a response from the Court of Justice in consequence of their claimed, but not exercised, capacity to 'close' national law to the demands of EU law where EU law contradicts particular (sometimes ill-defined) values cherished under national law? The inquiry is into the presence of a form of judicial dialogue between courts in Europe.

Each Member State has its own narrative, but the BVerfG seems the most influential among courts in the Member States. There are three distinct but thematically connected types of review that the BVerfG views itself as competent to perform: reviewing compliance of EU law with fundamental rights, review of EU law accused of stepping beyond the competence conferred by the Treaties, and review of EU law in defence of the admittedly ambiguous notion of constitutional identity.[261] Each of these three *German* concerns has an EU reaction—and this is not an accident. Fundamental rights have been developed at EU level by the Court of Justice hand in hand with its claim to supremacy, and the necessary association between the scope of the EU's objectives and its commitment to fundamental rights in their pursuit has been taken over by the Member States in the shape of ever firmer commitments made at times of Treaty revision, now culminating in the Lisbon Treaty's grant of binding force to the Charter and (subsequently stalled) accession to the ECHR (Chapter 3.15). Control of the limited grant of competence made by the Treaties to the EU is part of the job of the Court, and it has found EU measures invalid

[261] See M. Payandeh, 'Constitutional Review of EU Law after *Honeywell*: Contextualising the Relationship between the German Constitutional Court and the EU Court of Justice' (2011) 48 CMLRev 9.

for want of competence—albeit rarely. The first *Tobacco Advertising* case was examined in Chapter 2.7.4.[262] Here too the Treaty has been revised to give greater prominence to the principle of conferral and the corollary that any matter in respect of which the EU lacks competence belongs with the Member States. Chapter 2.2 described these changes as cosmetic in the sense that they did not change the law, but their true significance is best understood as attempts to address the corrosive *perception* of competence creep. So too, in this controlling vein, national Parliaments have been allocated a role in checking the rhythms of centralization through the early warning system applicable to subsidiarity (Chapter 2.11). Defence of (a form of) constitutional identity is recognized by Article 4(2) TEU, a beefier version than previously applicable as a result of the Treaty amendments made with effect from 2009 by the Treaty of Lisbon, and the Court has relied on Article 4(2), inter alia to show respect for national measures imperilled by the pressures of trade integration driven by free movement law.[263] True, the defence of such matters through *German* law, as assumed but not practised by the BVerfG, does not meet the pure version of EU supremacy proclaimed by the Court of Justice. Neither fundamental rights, nor review of conferral, nor Article 4(2) constitute an acceptance of the BVerfG's claim that *Germany* has particular concerns that justify it setting a limit on the reach of EU law within Germany; rather, the EU has in these several different ways attempted to load the same concerns *into EU law* as a means to meet national anxieties.

In the background is concern to take seriously such sensitivities lest national courts intervene unilaterally. EU law is opened up to national constitutional concerns while still laying formal claim to the supremacy of EU law over national law, in balance with the *Bundesverfassungsgericht*'s concern to open up German law to EU law, while still placing limits on its subjection to EU law in the name of German constitutional law. This is a narrative of pluralism.

One can take a more muscular approach: this is an expression of a reality. EU law *is* limited by national constitutional values, in the sense that national courts will not apply it in the absence of the necessary respect. This, then, is not EU law achieving supremacy in a rigid top-down hierarchical sense. Instead EU law's supremacy is *conditional* on acceptance by national courts, which in turn involves a conditionality rooted in inspection of EU law's fidelity to core systemic values. By responding to these concerns and

[262] Case C-376/98 *Germany* v *Parliament and Council* [2000] ECR I-8419.

[263] Eg Case C-208/09 *Ilonka Sayn-Wittgenstein* [2010] ECR I-13693. See further Chapter 6.3.4.

embedding them in EU law, the Court and the Treaty build the EU legal order and push into the realms of the improbable the practical collision between claims to authority that is in principle unavoidable.

Is this really happening or is this making sense of accident? One of the most vividly positive accounts of the nature of the relationship between different courts in Europe is provided by the President of the BVerfG, Andreas Vosskuhle, in a paper published in 2010.[264] He describes a European association of constitutional courts,[265] based on co-operation within a 'triangle of jurisdiction' with corners in Karlsruhe, Luxembourg, and Strasbourg. At one level the paper is openly dismissive of the Court of Justice's pretensions. He states that 'The Federal Constitutional Court has recognised the primacy of Union law from the perspective of national constitutional law'; 'such primacy is neither absolute nor based on Union law, but anchored in national constitutional law and therefore also limited by it'.[266] But this resistance is coupled to the positive mood of openness to EU law—*Europarechtsfreundlichkeit*—which he hails as a constitutional *obligation* imposed on German judges.[267] The BVerfG, he explains, strives to conform to what is required under EU law as interpreted by the Court of Justice, while, as part of a two-way process, he stresses the importance of the Luxembourg Court's restrictive approach to the scope of EU legislative competence (where he cites the first *Tobacco Advertising* case[268]) and its developing respect for Member State identities (especially where that may be endangered by the law of the internal market law).

This is spectacularly selective. It would not be hard to find examples from the Court's case law which strain the plausibility of this presentation of a cautious and respectful jurisprudence in Luxembourg. The first *Tobacco Advertising* case looks exceptional in the light of subsequent rulings such as *Tobacco Advertising II*, examined in Chapter 2.7.4, which are far more generous to the permissible scope of legislative action undertaken in the name of market-making harmonization.[269] And whereas a ruling such as *Faccini Dori* might fit a narrative of restraint, for one of the Court's reasons for refusing to embrace the horizontal direct effect of Directives was expressly based on the constitutional limits of the Treaty, the appraisal of EU law's effects on individuals before national courts demands a much wider perspective than the particular instance of horizontal direct

[264] A. Vosskuhle, 'Multilevel Cooperation of the European Constitutional Courts' (2010) 6 European Constitutional Law Review 175.

[265] *Der Europäische Verfassungsgerichtsverbund*.

[266] Page 190.

[267] Pages 179–80.

[268] Case C-376/98 note 262.

[269] Case C-380/03 *Germany* v *Parliament and Council* [2006] ECR I-11573.

effect of Directives and cases such as *Pfeiffer*, *Unilever*, and *Mangold*, examined in Sections 4.7.4 and 4.7.5, all challenge Vosskuhle's depiction of judicial modesty in Luxembourg. *Francovich* too is hardly a ruling showing restraint at the murky outer edges of EU competence, and the Court's ungainly dalliance with a very wide understanding of when Member States are 'implementing' EU law for the purposes of subjection to the Charter (Section 4.8.1) is another instance where exorbitant reading might be thought likely to provoke resistance from national judges. Another judge of the BVerfG, Peter Huber, adopted sterner language than Vosskuhle to criticize the Court's 'poor performance' in policing the principle of conferral.[270] However, while the debate is plainly fluid, it is significant that Vosskuhle chooses an emollient tone. He wears a velvet glove, but in it always lurks a fist, and a warning to the Court of Justice of the European Union (CJEU) not to press ahead with ambitious rulings without full awareness of the gaze cast upon it from national level. Underlying the account is an understanding that each participant in the dance could stop the music, but that each knows that and has incentives not to do so.

Academic writing makes strong claims to have uncovered wider evidence of such judicial sensitivity. The idea is that the relevant actors are outward-looking: they know they exist in an environment in which their claims are not unquestioningly accepted and therefore have to be reasoned and made palatable. So for example Sabel and Gerstenberg show how national (constitutional) courts, the European Court of Justice (ECJ), the ECHR, and other international tribunals defer to each other's decisions on the condition that (*solange*) respect is shown for certain mutually agreed foundational concerns.[271] Courts in different jurisdictions seem able to assess and accommodate these overlapping sources of legal authority rather skilfully. In similar vein, Theil's inquiry into practice of constitutional courts in Germany, France, the Czech Republic, and Poland finds 'informal dialogue' between courts and a 'cross-border migration of constitutional ideas'.[272] All parties involved have incentives to sustain

[270] P. Huber, 'The Federal Constitutional Court and European Integration' (2015) 21 Euro Public Law 83.

[271] C. Sabel and O. Gerstenberg, 'Constitutionalising an Overlapping Consensus: The ECJ and the Emergence of a Coordinate Constitutional Order' (2010) 16 ELJ 511. See also M. Claes, M. De Visser, P. Popelier, and C. Van de Heyning (eds), *Constitutional Conversations in Europe: Actors, Topics and Procedures* (Intersentia, 2012); G. Martinico and O. Pollicino, *The Interaction between Europe's Legal Systems: Judicial Dialogue and the Creation of Supranational Laws* (Elgar, 2012).

[272] S. Theil, 'What Red Lines, If Any, Do the Lisbon Judgments of European Constitutional Courts Draw for Future EU Integration?' (2014) 15 German Law Jnl 599.

'an atmosphere of cooperation between the courts, where each side has an incentive to strive to respect the position and tradition of the other'.[273]

This is conditional, or co-operative, or mediated supremacy. It is to understand the relationship between national courts and the Court of Justice as one of mutual respect and accommodation rather than one rooted in hierarchy. This may not be the vision of *Costa* v *ENEL*—but it is a more appealing vision precisely because it informed by a plurality of voices, which tend to ensure a wide range of interests and values become part of the evolution of EU law. In fact, making practical sense of 'supremacy' needs the Court of Justice to be pragmatic, not dictatorial, because it has no coercive means to enforce its view on national courts. Supremacy in an absolute sense is in this sense a brittle claim. Conditional supremacy is more stable and realistic.

It is not simply a vertical dialogue. There are horizontal aspects to it too. National constitutional courts listen to each other. They expect to be listened to: it is not simply a desire to preen that prompts the BVerfG to make available its major judgments in English as well as German. It wants to influence the debate *between* national courts as well as that conducted with Luxembourg, and it does so. In its *HS2* ruling in 2014 the UK's Supreme Court referred explicitly to the BVerfG's reluctance to read Court of Justice decisions in a way that places in question the identity of the national constitutional order,[274] thereby strongly suggesting an aligned rejection in principle of the purity of *Costa* v *ENEL*, while at the same time it also drew explicitly on the BVerfG to assert 'the cooperative relationship' which exists between the Luxembourg court and a national constitutional court 'such as the Bundesverfassungsgericht or a supreme court like this',[275] thereby suggesting a desire to engage with a process of dialogue that will avoid conflict in practice. Something similar in relation to anxiety that the Court of Justice might go beyond the limits of the competences conferred by the Treaties animates the Supreme Court's ruling in *Pham*, where again reference is made to 'the spirit of co-operation of which both the Bundesverfassungsgericht and this court have previously spoken', as well as to the expectation that it 'will be a very rare case indeed where any problem arises in this connection'.[276] One of the Supreme Court judges in *HS2* has extra-judicially explicitly mentioned Article 4(2) TEU in the context of such co-operation.[277]

[273] N. Barber, 'Legal Pluralism and the European Union' (2006) 12 ELJ 306, 329.

[274] Note 245 para 111. [275] Para 202.

[276] [2015] UKSC 19, para 91 (Lord Mance).

[277] Lord Reed, 'EU Law and the Supreme Court', The Sir Thomas More Lecture for 2014, p12 http://www.lincolnsinn.org.uk/index.php/education/euro-programme/events

There is clear evidence of horizontal cross-referral among the supreme courts of Europe as they shape their view of the relationship between national law and EU law.[278] Judges of national constitutional courts meet and communicate with each other: judicial visits by national judges to Luxembourg are far from uncommon.[279] In part the messages to Luxembourg carry a more credible note of defiance or, perhaps better, persuasion if delivered in harmony, but that is an inadequately nuanced account of what is at stake. The process of cross-reference is a bit ad hoc, perhaps selective and opportunistic, typically sparked by particular flash-points such as the EAW and ratification of the Lisbon Treaty, but it deserves to be seen as an increasingly dense pattern of constructive communication about the proper development of the EU's constitutionalized legal order which is not composed of EU law alone but necessarily also embraces national law. National courts are *warning* the Court about what may be the fate at national level of rulings which are seen to go too far while also *encouraging* the Court (therefore) to take seriously their concerns. And the fact is that national courts do not rebel against the Court's rulings. They may express periodic disquiet about their quality and they may use the flexibility provided by the preliminary reference procedure's division of function between interpretation (performed by the Court in Luxembourg) and application (the job of the national court) to modify their domestic impact, but they are prepared in principle to apply them.[280] On the most optimistic reading, this is a breeding ground for a common European understanding of constitutional law(s) to which a wide range of judges are entitled to contribute. Supremacy in particular and EU law in general is not in practice as 'top-down' as *Costa* v *ENEL* might lead one to imagine— and a good thing too.

It is, in conclusion, well worth recognizing that the obstacles placed by national courts in the way of EU law's entry into national law on terms

[278] Eg M. Wendel, 'Comparative Reasoning and the Making of a Common Constitutional Law: EU-related Decisions of National Constitutional Courts in a Transnational Perspective' (2013) 11 Int J Con Law 981. The comparative reflex is not confined to treatment of EU law: M. Bobek, *Comparative Reasoning in European Supreme Courts* (OUP, 2013).

[279] Lord Reed note 277, 11–12; also M. De Visser and M. Claes, 'Courts United? On European Judicial Networks' in A. Vauchez and B. De Witte (eds), *Lawyering Europe* (Hart, 2013).

[280] The one exception, rejection by the Czech Constitutional court of the ruling in Case C-399/09 *Landtová* [2011] ECR I-5573 as *ultra vires*, is explained by internal Czech judicial quarrels: see eg A. Capik and M. Petscko, 'Slovak Pension Cases before the CJEU and Czech Courts' (2013) 9 Croatian YELP 61.

of unconditional supremacy have much in common with the obstacles the Court of Justice itself has placed in the way of EU law's subjection to external sources of law. In fact, the Court of Justice has itself borrowed the BVerfG's reasoning when it comes to addressing the external boundary of EU law, its relationship with *international* law. As already observed in Chapter 3.15.5, in *Kadi and Al Barakaat* v *Council*,[281] which concerned challenges to the validity of EU measures imposing restrictions 'freezing' use of funds by alleged terrorists pursuant to relevant resolutions of the United Nations' Security Council, the Court agreed that it could not review the validity of an act of the Security Council, but it insisted that it could and must review the EU's implementing measures. It is easy to see the inspiration behind the applicants' (successful) argument in *Kadi* that '*So long as* the law of the United Nations offers no adequate protection for those whose claim that their fundamental rights have been infringed, there must be a review of the measures adopted by the Community in order to give effect to resolutions of the Security Council.'[282] Decisions of German courts are open but potentially closed to the application of EU within the German legal order: *Kadi* is closed but potentially open to the application of international law within the EU legal order. The Court found that, at UN level, there were no adequate 'guarantees of judicial protection',[283] and in doing so doubtless prompted and intended to prompt reconsideration of Security Council practice.[284]

The Court did something structurally similar in *Opinion 2/13*.[285] It found that the planned arrangements for complying with the obligation imposed on the EU by Article 6(2) TEU (an innovation of the Lisbon Treaty) to accede to the ECHR were *not* compatible with EU law. It referred to 'the autonomy enjoyed by EU law in relation to the laws of the Member States and in relation to international law'.[286] Concern to preserve this characteristic led the Court to assert pre-conditions which had not been met associated with safeguarding 'the essential character' of the Court's powers, thereby to prevent an 'adverse effect on the autonomy of the EU legal order'—and it cited *Kadi*.[287] The Court has been flayed for a perceived arrogant desire principally to protect its own autonomy, more than that of the EU more generally, and the ruling was certainly a surprise. But

[281] Joined Cases C-402/05P and C-415/05P *Kadi and Al Barakaat* v *Council* [2008] ECR I-6351.

[282] Para 256, emphasis added. [283] Para 322.

[284] On the general international law context see A. Tzanakopoulos, *Disobeying the Security Council: Countermeasures against Wrongful Sanctions* (OUP, 2011).

[285] 18 December 2014. [286] Para 170. [287] Para 183.

appreciation should be conditioned by the limits of the Court's power: just as it is able in this way to resist the claims of the Security Council and the ECHR, so too it knows that its own claims to legal authority may be resisted from within national legal orders. The result of Opinion 2/13 might be to encourage the Court itself to pursue more assiduous protection of human rights, not least because national courts are likely to look hard at whether the Court can live up to the monopoly power it claims in *Melloni*[288] and in Opinion 2/13. The theme is judicial interaction.

4.13 PLURALISM

To speak today of 'the law of a State' in Europe is to mislead. What is really at stake is 'the laws in a State'. The density of legal regulation has increased. There is national law, but there is EU law too—and there are other sources too that, one way or another, penetrate the landscape. 'Constitutional pluralism' is a broad church.[289] However, in the EU context, its rise is most closely associated with Neil MacCormick's idea of pluralism in the sense of 'interactive' legal orders.[290] This is suggestive of the creativity involved in depicting the relationship as something other than hierarchical. Instead of a vertical understanding of authority, with EU law at the top, what emerges is a horizontal pattern, whereby both EU and national legal orders (and other systems too, such as the ECHR) make claims to authority that are perfectly convincing on their own terms but not consistent with that of the other level. And—indirectly, through forms of dialogue—they share their concerns with each other, to induce co-operation. This builds towards pluralism: that there are in Europe independent claims to constitutional authority which are incapable of being reconciled with each other, and yet which need no such reconciliation as long as the competition is not pursued to destructive finality.

It is a demanding model. For it to succeed, all engaged actors must be sensitive to each other's values and anxieties. In concrete terms it means that the EU national supreme and constitutional courts must 'submit controversial issues to the ECJ rather than solve them solely according to their own preferences'; and the Court of Justice must 'in turn [show] willingness

[288] Case C-399/11 note 2.

[289] Eg M. Avbelj and J. Komárek, *Constitutional Pluralism in the European Union and Beyond* (Hart, 2012).

[290] Initially in 'Beyond the Sovereign State' (1993) 56 MLR 1, then in *Questioning Sovereignty* (OUP, 2000).

to listen to the constitutional concerns of its national interlocutors'.[291] And willingness must be accompanied by expertise and deft sensitivity.

And yet there is ample evidence that it is happening. It is not merely good fortune. All relevant actors possess incentives to avoid a direct collision. Threats can be productive in so far as they may generate concessions or, more constructively, a re-balancing of a relationship. Once a threat is executed things may never be the same again, both as between the (judicial) parties to the dispute and, by a process of spillover, in application to other interested parties as well. What is at stake here is—to borrow the splendid phrase of Mireille Delmas-Marty—ordering pluralism.[292] EU law and ECHR law lay claim to exercise a supervisory jurisdiction with respect to national law, and in the case of EU law the claim has a still deeper constitutional arrogation too, in the guise of the principles of supremacy and direct effect. But part of this pluralism—the *ordering* element—is a tolerance of diversity infused by a readiness to respect at EU and ECHR level the particularities of national law too, and so to avoid a ruthless streak demanding only uniformity. ECHR law does this most of all through its 'margin of appreciation', whereas EU law is shaped by respect for national law and culture as an *EU* legal value while national law itself, as part of its own *national* constitutional identity, is willing to accommodate adaptation dictated by the reality of economic interdependence to which EU law reacts while also promoting it.

Part of the pluralist claim is that this does happen. And then the constitutional pluralist 'seeks to make a virtue out of necessity'.[293] An extra element of the pluralist claim is that this *should* happen, in order to instil a degree of respect and mutuality into a relationship that otherwise could be conflictual. Pluralism can lead to an arena for defusing potential conflicts by promoting communication, so that all courts involved understand and are sympathetic to the claims made by others lying outwith their sphere of formal authority and, on a reciprocal basis of toleration, ensure that potential collision becomes instead constructive engagement. They should pursue 'integrity'—whereby autonomy must be infused by awareness of and openness to mutual solidarity.[294] This would not set aside

[291] B. De Witte, 'Direct Effect, Primacy and the Nature of the Legal Order' in *The Evolution of EU Law* note 58, p 357.

[292] *Ordering Pluralism: A Conceptual Framework for Understanding the Transnational Legal World* (Hart, 2009).

[293] N. Walker, 'Constitutionalism and Pluralism in Global Context' in *Constitutional Pluralism in the European Union and Beyond* note 289, p 18.

[294] S. Besson, 'From European Integration to European Integrity: Should European Law Speak with Just One Voice?' (2004) 10 ELJ 257.

the deep-rooted irreconcilability which locates the ultimate source of legal authority in different places (the EU Treaties/the national constitution). But it would ensure a functioning EU legal order built on distinct legal *orders*. And it would reflect the wider case for an EU that compensates for its Member States' deficiencies in legitimacy without seeking to replacing them.

An element in the normative case favouring pluralism is exactly that it promotes dialogue about what should be done, rather than seeking to impose a single solution from above—or from below. It assumes too a need for judges able and willing to explore conscientiously where reason and principle should take them. This invites association with general and often abstract theories of judicial adjudication, but in fact in Europe this is an intensely practical and concrete matter (too).[295] The debate in this vein about fundamental rights is familiar and long-standing, and it continues: *Melloni*,[296] *Fransson*,[297] and Opinion 2/13[298] are simply the latest chapter. Article 4(2) TEU looks likely to offer the platform on which to test the ability of the judicial actors involved to accommodate the several different concerns associated with supremacy and identity that motivate both EU and national constitutional courts.[299] Article 4(2) locates respect for national identities as a *Union* value. The really awkward questions ask what it is that national systems seek to defend against the incursion of EU law—or, better, to have respected by, and as a matter of, EU law. If it is simply the desire to do whatever national law provides, then the whole EU project smashes into the brick wall of national obstinacy. This would not be the conditional supremacy of EU law; it would be the absolute supremacy of State law. But too cramped an approach to the threshold shaped by national identity would strip it of any useful role in mediating the competing claims of EU law as a renovating force apt to manage interdependence among States in Europe and national law as an expression of autonomy and local preference.[300] There must, to make pluralism virtuous, surely be a *quality* check on what defence of national identity entails, not least because some aspects of what has been claimed as expression of 'national

[295] Eg M. Kumm, 'The Moral Point of Constitutional Pluralism' in J. Dickson and P. Eleftheriadis (eds), *Philosophical Foundations of EU Law* (OUP, 2012).

[296] Case C-399/11 note 2. [297] Case C-617/10 note 51. [298] Note 285.

[299] Eg A. Von Bogdandy and S. Schill, 'Overcoming Absolute Primacy: Respect for National Identity under the Lisbon Treaty' (2011) 48 CMLRev 1417; M. Dobbs, 'Sovereignty, Article 4(2) TEU and the Respect of National Identities: Swinging the Balance of Power in Favour of the Member States?' (2014) 33 YEL 298.

[300] Of particular value in this vein are the Opinions of AG Maduro in C-213/07 *Michaniki* [2008] ECR I-9999 and AG Cruz Villalón in Case C-62/14 *Gauweiler* note 1.

identity' in European history have involved embrace of vile ethnic, racial, or religious disdain for the 'other'. This can and should be achieved by linking Article 4(2) TEU, as an EU—not a unilaterally national—understanding of national identity to the EU *values* expressed in Article 2 EU. So this means a State could not claim to rely on Article 4(2) as a basis to protect national identity in circumstances that would in substance contradict the EU's *values*.[301] Article 4(2) will be shaped by dialogue between national courts and the Court of Justice, and the fundamental rights cases which stretch all the way back to *Internationale Handelsgesellschaft* are not the worst model.

The constitutional orders of the EU and of the Member States are in this sense interlocked. For some it is 'multi-level constitutionalism': an attempt to understand how and why rule-making stretches above and below the State and is not confined to public authorities nor to orthodox binding norms. It provokes a need to achieve some kind of accommodation of these several fragmenting influences. The debate, fiercely contested, stretches far beyond the EU,[302] but in its specific EU manifestation it fits the thematic concern to manage interdependence, thrust into a specifically *constitutional* context.[303] National courts apply EU law because their constitutional tradition so directs, so there is both a total refusal to accept the core of the reasoning that animates *Costa* v *ENEL* and a vigorous determination nevertheless to make the relationship work. The Court of Justice, for its part, respects constitutional sensitivities expressed at national level by incorporating them into EU law (fundamental rights, competence restraint, identity), so there is both a total refusal to accept the core claims of national constitutional authority and a vigorous determination to make the relationship work as a co-operative, not a hierarchical endeavour, and one which is revealed as a dynamic *process*.

True, this is to accept—even to champion—the possibility that individuals may have to look to two (or more) sources to understand their legal position. This plural vision is open to criticism as incompatible with

[301] S. Rodin, 'National Identity and Market Freedoms after the Treaty of Lisbon' (2011) 7 CYELP 11: as an example he cites reserving a vote to men only. See also on how it is shaped, and who shapes it, M. Claes, 'Negotiating Constitutional Identity, or Whose Identity Is It Anyway?', Ch 8 in *Constitutional Conversations in Europe: Actors, Topics and Procedures* note 15.

[302] Eg F. Fabbrini, 'The Constitutionalization of International Law: A Comparative Federal Perspective' (2013/14) 6 Euro Jnl Legal Studies 7.

[303] Eg I Pernice, 'Multi-level Constitutionalism in the European Union' (2012) 27 ELRev 511; P. Popelier and W. Vandenbruwaene (eds), 'Special Issue: The Constitutional Adulthood of Multilevel Governance' (2014) 21 MJ.

the rule of law, to which the EU itself as well as its Member States are committed.[304] Inability to locate ultimate authority seems to obstruct holding rule-makers accountable for their choices and to blur methods of effecting change. And yet appeal to more dedicated respect for the rule of law cannot solve the problem any more readily. Pluralist co-existence of legal orders in Europe is not only possible, it is appealing in that, though imperfect to the dedicated positivist, it is as good as it gets.[305] There is no perfect model in the interdependent pattern of States in Europe. To impose one could be deeply damaging, in so far as it ignites a dispute over where the true source (or sources) of supreme legal authority in the Union really lie. Anxiety associated with perceived need to 'resolve' the issue about competing claims to the source of legal authority is an invitation to find winners—and therefore also losers. Europe has a history of battles about winning and losing, which would be very good to reserve for the past, not the future. And even if that battle were fought and won (though quite *how*?), the result would be either to strip away the pretensions of EU law and restore the centrality of State power in a way that would harm the management of independence which is the EU's core mission or to confer ultimate authority on the EU as the 'State' that would replace its Member States, creating immense problems of legitimacy. What is at stake here is not a single hierarchically clean legal order but rather a European legal system that comprises a large number of legal orders, law-makers, and other jurisgenerative forces.[306] In so far as this is an attempt to shape the EU as an arena within which law and politics can co-exist in a mutually reinforcing way, it is inevitably characterized in Europe by a certain imprecision—for, after all, what is at stake is nothing less than a challenge to the hegemony of national constitutional law. In fact the system works precisely because each participant is able to rest its consent to involvement on different bases, which may be constitutionally irreconcilable in a purely formal sense but which do not generate any practical need to choose which is 'right'. That choice is what is to be avoided, and that is what, one way or another, courts avoid. The current constitutionally pluralist pattern permits this. And that reflects bigger claims about

[304] Eg J. Baquero Cruz, 'The Legacy of the Maastricht-Urteil and the Pluralist Movement' (2008) 14 ELJ 389.

[305] M. Maduro, 'Europe and the Constitution: What If This Is as Good as It Gets?' in J. Weiler and M. Wind (eds), *European Constitutionalism beyond the State* (CUP, 2003); S. Douglas-Scott, 'Justice and Pluralism in the EU' (2012) 65 Current Legal Problems 83.

[306] Eg K. Tuori, 'Transnational Law: On Legal Hybrids and Perspectivism', Ch 1 in M. Maduro, K. Tuori, and S. Sankari (eds), *Transnational Law: Rethinking European Law and Legal Thinking* (CUP, 2014).

the proper understanding of the relationship between European Union and the Member States. It is not about either/or.

4.14 CONCLUSION: CONSTITUTIONALISM—WHAT IT IS (AND WHAT IT IS NOT)

Chapters 3 and 4 share a common theme: the development of *constitutionalism* in the EU. *Constitutionalism* captures the idea that the EU legal order is *not only* a sub-species of international law *but also* a system with an intimate relationship to the individual and deeply embedded within national legal orders. And this is largely the product of the work of the Court of Justice. Article 19(1) TEU directs that the Court 'shall ensure that in the interpretation and application of the Treaties the law is observed', but this hopelessly understates the creative role played by the Court in the elaboration of the EU legal order. The Court deals with texts which are ambiguous and material that is shot through with gaps. It makes interpretative choices which are often bold and most of all it does it in conditions of a high level of autonomy from correction through the political process, though under the less obvious but real constraints formed by the need to persuade national judges.

Chapter 3 showed how the EU legislative process has an institutional sophistication which is more profound than any other international organization ever established by an international Treaty. It is underpinned by the input legitimacy of the peoples (the Parliament) and of the States (the Council) and also by the output legitimacy which is provided by the fulfilment of tasks mandated by the Treaties (the Commission). And the Court has embroidered this system by insisting that principles that protect the individual from the oppressive exercise of public power shall be part of it and shall provide the basis for judicial review of the validity of EU legislative and administrative acts. Much of the constitutionalized character of EU law is today recorded in the Treaties and the Charter of Fundamental Rights, but the Court was the pioneer of evolutionary constitutionalism.

The current chapter has mapped the three principal aspects to the narrative of EU constitutionalism as it applies within national legal orders. The first concerns the relationship between EU and national law, where the Court has imposed a hierarchy in favour of EU law despite the absence of any explicit treatment of the matter within the Treaty. This is *supremacy* or *primacy*. The second aspect concerns the penetration of national legal orders by EU law. The practical implications of supremacy or primacy would be limited were there no or only limited opportunity to rely on EU law in proceedings before national courts and they would vary if the matter was left solely to *national* constitutional law, but the Court has chosen, again without explicit support in the Treaty, to fashion a powerful set of rules which thrust EU law deep into everyday national legal practice in all the Member States. This is most prominently the notion of the *direct effect* of EU law, widened in recent years to embrace a range of other phenomena which require national judges to apply EU law, including the obligation to interpret national law in the light of EU law and the principle of liability to compensate in the event of causing loss in violation of EU law. The Court has also specified with increasing precision just how courts in the Member States should deal with EU law, a process which has driven the influence of EU law deep into national law governing remedies and procedure. This goes beyond the assumption under international law that it is for domestic systems to deal with the way in which its rules should be applied (if at all) within domestic systems. These features of EU law make non-compliance with its requirements no easy option, and sometimes an expensive one. The third aspect to the EU legal order as a 'constitutionalized' regime involves its dedication to certain general principles which confine the exercise of power not only by the EU's institutions (Chapter 3.15) but also (to a more limited extent, hinged on the concept of 'implementation' of EU law) by the Member States (Section 4.8). Taken together these three elements ensure EU law prevails over national law in the event of conflict and that it is for national courts to apply EU rules directly in many circumstances, if necessary protecting those holding rights under EU law against the public authorities of that very State; in addition, they place judicially enforced checks on the exercise of public power. This is 'constitutionalism': the use of the word is designed to convey a flavour of the conversion of a Treaty-based legal order into one that in important respects (also) functions *as if* it is arranging the relationship between different levels of governance within a polity.

The *constitutionalized* legal order is sufficiently powerful to be difficult to evade when it is not to the short-term taste of public or private actors and it is granted the necessary qualities that constrain the exercise of public power that entitle it to deserve respect as an expression of the rule of law, respect for which is written into Article 2 TEU. The Court has in the same vein moved beyond its original depiction of a 'new legal order' of international law[307] to describe the Treaty as a 'basic constitutional

[307] Case 26/62 *Van Gend en Loos* [1963] ECR 1.

charter'.[308] Opinion 2/13 treats the EU as a new legal order, 'the nature of which is peculiar to the EU', and it insists too on the need to protect the Treaties as the 'basic constitutional charter'.[309]

However, one should not exaggerate the vigour or the coherence of EU law's *constitutionalism*.

At EU level the restrictive standing rules applicable to private parties which are contained in Article 263(4) TFEU and the relatively light judicial application of the general principles of the EU legal order, especially where review of EU legislative choices in complex areas are at stake (Chapter 3.14), serve to ensure a degree of insulation for the political process. 'Constitutionalism' emphatically does not mean aggressive subordination of political decision-making to judicial supremacy.

Moreover, although the penetration of national law by EU law, combined with the EU law requirement that effective judicial protection be provided, do much to confine the scope for evasion of the agreed rules, there remains more scope for public and private actors to elude its grip than would be available in a purely national context. This is true for constitutional reasons—for example, the absence of horizontal direct effect attributed to Directives—but also for practical reasons associated with the nature of EU law. Its texts are quite often adopted as compromises or as broad programmes and are therefore inapt to create individual rights. Even *Francovich*, which heroically slid individual protection beyond the confining concept of direct effect, is daunting: it is neither easy nor cheap to sue the State.

Moreover, the role of national courts in the preliminary reference procedure is also a means for them to mediate the intrusive effects of EU law within national legal orders. Article 267 TFEU empowers the Court, as the authoritative source of interpretation of EU law, but it also empowers national courts. They can—lawfully and sometimes creatively on the edges of legality—choose *not* to make a reference, thereby to soften the impact of EU law on cherished national structures. The Court's own recommendations to national courts accept that the necessity to make a reference is missing where a national court considers that sufficient guidance is given by the case law of the Court of Justice.[310] Even though the Court has long counselled national courts against over-confidence in their own assessment of the correct meaning of EU law, not least given its linguistic variations, the need for contextual assessment, and the fact that

[308] Case 294/83 *Parti Ecologiste Les Verts* v *European Parliament* [1986] ECR 1339.

[309] Note 285, paras 158 and (citing Case 294/83 *Les Verts* v *Parliament*) para 163.

[310] OJ [2012] C338/1, para 13.

the same word found in an EU act and a national act may not carry the same meaning,[311] there is plainly room for national courts acting in line with EU law to decline to call on the Court's interpretative assistance. And even if the national court refuses to refer in the grey zone, where its choice is at least questionable as a matter of EU law, the individual who is not able to secure redress at national level has no direct right of action in Luxembourg. *Köbler* notwithstanding,[312] national courts enjoy flexibility. The issue arises *ex post* too. Tools are available to national judges who wish to curtail the impact at national level of a Luxembourg ruling that they mistrust. Outright defiance based on denial of the constitutional authority of the Court of Justice to make such a judgment (for, most obviously, want of competence or violation of fundamental rights) is very rare,[313] but there are more subtle and effective techniques available for confining the impact of a ruling at national level by, for example, reading it in a narrow fact-specific way. It is, as a general observation, remarkably difficult to know how EU law is *really* applied at national level.[314] There may be virtue in this: it leaves space for reasonable disagreement and avoids outright conflict. The Court itself can enrich this collaborative process, by keeping its own rulings on hotly sensitive issues more abstract than concrete (Section 4.2).

The argument, then, is *relative*: EU law is capable of much more vigorous enforcement at the behest of the individual than orthodox public international law. It is relatively more influential as a constitutionalized system operating at transnational and still more so at national level than is orthodox public international law; and part of the story too is the relative autonomy from direct *political* control and correction enjoyed by the Court of Justice. But the constitutionalized legal order of the EU still contains within it one critically important feature which distances it from the legal order which one would find within a single (federal) State: the reason given by the Court of Justice for EU law's meaning and impact within national legal orders is not accepted by the courts of the Member States. The Court's original and persisting claim to deal in a *new legal order*, accompanied by deliberate use of unfamiliar words for concepts which are familiar in international law, acted as a signal that the Court wanted to

[311] Case 283/81 *CILFIT* [1982] ECR 3415. [312] Case C-224/01 note 105.

[313] Note 280.

[314] Cf M. Bobek, 'Of Feasibility and Silent Elephants: The Legitimacy of the Court of Justice Through the Eyes of National Courts' in M. Adams, J. Meeusen, G. Straetmans, and H. de Waele (eds) *Judging Europe's Judges: The Legitimacy of the Case Law of the European Court of Justice* (Hart, 2013).

position EU law somewhere other than in international law orthodoxy. But none of this would have had any deep practical effect unless it was accepted and applied by *national* courts. What was truly 'new' about EU law was how national courts treated it. EU law *became* 'new'. It therefore remains crucial that EU law cannot operate without the active support of the national courts. This is constitutional pluralism that survives only through willing and active judicial sensitivity. The EU legal order, like the EU itself, functions successfully only if it is understood as encompassing the management of interdependence of both transnational and national dimensions.

5

DOES EU LAW APPLY UNIFORMLY?

5.1 INTRODUCTION

The zeal for uniformity in EU law has already been met in Chapter 4.2, where the preliminary reference procedure was identified as an instrument which allows the Court of Justice to promote a uniform interpretation of EU laws across the territory of all the Member States. Supremacy too is closely associated with the credo of uniformity: that EU law is supreme prevents a Member State acting unilaterally to diminish the impact of EU law on its territory. The concern in this chapter is uniformity in the scope of application of *substantive* EU law—the question to be addressed is whether EU rules must bind all the Member States in the same way at the same time or whether instead a differentiated application may be tolerated, or even promoted. What room is there for *flexibility* in the scope of application of EU law?

This is a question which arises in connection with EU secondary legislation—once adopted, do EU rules ensure a uniform regulatory environment or are Member States granted flexibility to select their own adornments? It also arises at the level of the Treaty superstructure: the Treaty both envisages the pursuit of common policies by some but not all the Member States (the so-called process of enhanced co-operation) and accommodates the possibility of a motley bunch of opt-ins and opt-outs, whereby some States are permitted to stand aside temporarily or permanently from whole areas of common policy-making. The more Member States the EU acquires, the greater the diversity of economic performance, social structures, and political preferences, and so the greater the pressure to accommodate divergence.

The pressing issues that are examined in this chapter focus on the extent to which the basic common core framework that is undoubtedly needed for the Union to function effectively is capable of accommodating divergence without tumbling towards disintegration and destruction. That in turn requires some appreciation of just how compelling the virtue of uniformity truly is.

In the early years the driving assumption was plainly that uniformity was desirable—indeed that it was the ultimate aim. A Treaty commitment to 'lay the foundations of an ever closer union among the peoples of

Europe' was inscribed in the Preamble to the Treaty of Rome that established the EEC with effect from 1958, and that same phrase appears today in the Preamble to the TFEU, while the TEU's Preamble resolves 'to continue the process of creating an ever closer union among the peoples of Europe'. On the face of it, uniformity is therefore central to the whole project. Gerhard Bebr wrote in 1981 of 'the responsibility of the Court under the Treaties to establish a rule of law and preserve the efficacy and unity of the Community legal order against any centripetal tendencies whenever and wherever manifested'.[1] No doubt it was unity in interpretation, of the type examined in the previous chapter, that was his major animating concern, but also part of this vision of the proper state of EU law was uniform scope of application. Even today this type of discourse is readily visible, if often left undefined. The Court's Opinion 2/13 refers to 'the implementation of the process of integration that is the *raison d'être* of the EU itself'.[2]

In the context of economic integration, the appeal of uniformity in the application of legal rules is obvious. Establishing rules that apply in common is a means to create the common conditions for the regulation of an internal market which is not split by diversity in practice State by State. But even so, despite the deep roots of uniformity as a leitmotif in the EU, things have changed. Uniformity is today less apt as a *description* of EU law-making than it used to be and, in more contested and elusive vein, it is vulnerable to criticism as an inappropriate normative aspiration for the modern EU.

In part these changes are simply the product of the political difficulty in agreeing common rules in an EU that is functionally and geographically expanded far beyond its origins as a project largely focused on eliminating trade barriers and pursued initially by just six Member States in Western Europe. Agreeing opt-outs and analogous flexible devices is an inevitable middle ground between complete consensus and deadlock. But there is a much more positive narrative that may be applied to this rising tide of variation. One size does not fit all. A State with short, fast rivers will not have the same environmental concerns as one with long, slow rivers, a maritime State has a more pressing concern for conservation of fish stocks than a landlocked State, and so on across a whole sweep of regulatory choices. The challenge is to find an appropriate balance between the virtues of uniformity—such as predictability, transparency,

[1] G. Bebr, *Development of Judicial Control of the European Communities* (Nijhoff, 1981) p 6.

[2] Opinion of 18 December 2014, para 172.

and solidarity—and the virtues of variation—local choice, sensitivity to local conditions, and room for experimentation. The debate has evident association with that centred on subsidiarity, encountered in Chapter 2.11, but it is in an important sense much richer. Subsidiarity, stripped down to its core, asks whether the EU should act or not, whereas the debate about flexibility asks whether some but not all of the States in the EU should act in common, and if so, when and according to what conditions. Once viewed from this perspective the inquiry is transformed from a set of technical questions about the design of legal rules into a much more profound assessment of whether the EU is built on assumptions about convergence or whether instead it is and should be tolerant of diversity. The early years of the EU were, after all, enthused by an understandable desire to build concrete uniformity out of the ruins of a devastated continent, but viewed according to a longer historical perspective there is something unsettling about models for Europe that insist on sameness, even if, unlike forces for evil in the past, the EU strains to act by consensus rather than by force of iron and blood. Europe has some scar tissue that will never heal.

5.2 DIVERSITY: THE SCOPE OF APPLICATION OF SECONDARY LEGISLATION

Chapter 2 tracked the diverse range of legislative competences conferred on the EU. The question addressed here asks what effect the adoption of EU legislation has on national competence.

5.2.1 *Exclusive competence*

Article 3 TFEU declares that the Union possesses exclusive competence in five areas: customs union, the establishing of the competition rules necessary for the functioning of the internal market, monetary policy for the Member States whose currency is the euro, the conservation of marine biological resources under the common fisheries policy, and, finally, the Common Commercial Policy. It is moreover stated in Article 3(2) TFEU that the Union possesses exclusive competence 'for the conclusion of an international agreement when its conclusion is provided for in a legislative act of the Union or is necessary to enable the Union to exercise its internal competence, or in so far as its conclusion may affect common rules or alter their scope'. The meaning of exclusive competence is spelled out in Article 2(1) TFEU, which stipulates that 'When the Treaties confer on the Union exclusive competence in a specific area, only the Union may legislate and adopt legally binding acts, the Member States being able to do so themselves only if so empowered by the Union or for the implementation of Union acts.'

There is no question here of allowing national action subject to conformity with the principles of the EU. Action by the Member States is simply impermissible within the fields in which the Union is exclusively competent. In federal jargon, which is admittedly not the norm in the Court of Justice's vocabulary, State powers are 'pre-empted' and the Union has 'occupied the field'. Questions of competence are close to supremacy and have many of the same practical consequences for the ranking of EU law above national law. But they are not the same thing. National action is precluded not because the rules of EU law apply in the field and override in the event of conflict with national provisions, but instead where, even though there are no EU rules with which national rules can come into conflict, the national action is impermissible. Pre-emption in this sense logically precedes supremacy. It is more clean-cut and it is more dramatic in its exclusionary effect on national powers. There is no room for flexibility here.

It probably makes sense to exclude the possibility of Member States being allowed any flexibility in the construction of matters such as a customs union and a common commercial policy. These are foundation stones of the common economic project to which the Member States are committed. It is at first glance harder to grasp why the EU enjoys exclusive competence over the conservation of marine biological resources under the common fisheries policy, but not in other policy areas, and the reference in Article 3(2) TFEU to the conclusion of an international agreement is abstruse too. And to list 'monetary policy for the Member States whose currency is the euro' as an exclusive EU competence is vulnerable to challenge on the basis that clearly the EU does not have exclusive competence for monetary policy on its territory: rather, it shares it with the States whose currency is not the euro. In truth, the list of exclusive competences, which was inserted into the Treaty for the first time with effect from 2009 by the Treaty of Lisbon, is imperfect, largely the product of ad hoc decisions over the Court over time, as it claimed particular areas as exclusive to (what is now) the EU despite an absence of concrete Treaty specifications.[3] The Court's dynamic rulings in this vein are largely from as long ago as the 1970s, when, for example, it ruled that the power to implement the Common Commercial Policy was held exclusively by the

[3] Cf. R. Schütze, 'Lisbon and the Federal Order of Competences: A Prospective Analysis' (2008) 33 ELRev 709.

Community (as it then was).[4] The Lisbon Treaty was mainly concerned to assemble the (limited) status quo pertaining to exclusive competences, rather to think afresh about the matter. Accordingly, it is improbable that the Court will adjust its stance.[5]

5.2.2 Shared and supporting competence

The EU's exclusive competences are few, and they are not the norm. Shared competence is a different matter. In the areas in which competence is shared between the EU and the Member States, listed in Article 4(2) TFEU, plainly the assumption is that both have a role to play. This is all the more so in the case of the third and weakest of the EU's categories of competence, supporting competence, covered in Article 6 TFEU. The question here is what effect the adoption of EU rules exerts on residual national competence to act in the relevant area. Most pertinent of all, may a Member State add stricter or otherwise more wide-ranging rules on top of the agreed EU rule?

Some Treaty provisions make plain that EU legislative measures adopted pursuant to them do *not* exclude State competence to act in a more interventionist manner. Several of the Treaty provisions governing supporting competences provide examples. According to Article 6(c) TFEU the EU enjoys a supporting competence in the matter of culture. This is amplified in Article 167 TFEU, which limits action by the Union to 'encouraging cooperation between Member States and, if necessary, supporting and supplementing their action' in defined areas, and ties legislative action to the adoption of incentive measures by the Council and Parliament, which expressly excludes any harmonization of laws, and to Council recommendations. Clearly Member States have a largely free hand in the field of culture even where the EU has acted. The EU is similarly placed in a deliberately subordinate role in the regulation of sport. Article 6(e) TFEU lists (inter alia) sport as a supporting competence enjoyed by the EU, and the amplifying Article 165 TFEU confines action to incentive measures adopted by the Parliament and Council, excluding any harmonization of laws, and to Council recommendations. There is plenty of flexibility, and little uniformity, even after the EU has acted. Sport is mainly the business of public authorities in the Member States and sports' own governing bodies, which are typically private associations in form.

[4] Opinion 1/75 [1975] ECR 1355.

[5] Eg Case C-114/12 *Commission* v *Council* judgment of 4 September 2014.

Areas of shared competence typically grant the EU the possibility of a rather higher profile and stronger legislative presence, but still commonly carefully define the limits of EU action, and therefore as a corollary preserve areas of State autonomy. Consumer protection is listed as a shared competence in Article 4(2)(f) TFEU. Article 169(2)(b) TFEU adds that in order to promote the interests of consumers and to ensure a high level of consumer protection, the Council and Parliament may adopt measures which 'support, supplement and monitor the policy pursued by the Member States'. Article 169(4) TFEU adds that such measures 'shall not prevent any Member State from maintaining or introducing more stringent protective measures', although it is added that such measures must be compatible with the Treaties, which means inter alia that they must not be unjustified barriers to inter-State trade, and that the Commission shall be notified of them. Article 168 TFEU applies a comparable regime to the matter of public health, albeit adding an explicit exclusion of harmonization of laws in its fifth paragraph. Here too there is a great deal more flexibility than uniformity even after the EU has made use of these legislative powers. In fact, it has made little such use, not least because of the restricted reach of this Treaty authorization, and most EU legislative activity in these fields has been pursued under Article 114, where even though the decisive factor in the legislative choice may be consumer protection or public health, the EU is free to act provided an adequate contribution to the making of the internal market exists.[6]

Some Treaty provisions grant the EU legislative powers which are rather less tightly circumscribed, yet still preserve space for stricter national rule-making even after the EU has made its choice. Environmental protection is a shared competence.[7] The scope of EU legislation is rather broadly drawn according to Articles 191 and 192 TFEU—certainly these provisions are less crabbed than Articles 168 (public health) and 169 (consumer protection). Article 193 TFEU states that 'The protective measures adopted pursuant to Article 192 shall not prevent any Member State from maintaining or introducing more stringent protective measures.'[8] This is to locate the EU as a maker of *uniform* rules which also serve as *minimum* rules, in so far as they grant flexibility to the Member States to adopt a

[6] Eg Case C-380/03 *Germany* v *Parliament and Council* [2006] ECR I-11573, examined in Chapter 2.7.5.

[7] Art 4(2)(e) TFEU.

[8] On the notion of more stringent measures of environmental protection pursuant to what is now Art 193 TFEU, see eg Case C-6/03 *Deponiezweckverband Eiterköpfe* [2005] ECR I-2753; Case C-100/08 *Commission* v *Belgium* [2009] ECR I-140

higher level of protection, although, as in the case of consumer protection under Article 169, the Treaty adds that such national measures must be compatible with the Treaties, and that they shall be notified to the Commission. Social policy is a shared competence, and in similar vein Article 153(4) TFEU provides that EU legislative intervention 'shall not prevent any Member State from maintaining or introducing more stringent protective measures compatible with the Treaties'. Member States may not go below the standard mandated by the EU measure but they may choose to go higher. The EU sets the floor but not the ceiling.

The model varies in detail, sector by sector, legal base by legal base. It is poorly captured by the definitions in the Treaty, especially that of shared competence. In fact on this point Article 2(2) TFEU, which declares that in areas of shared competence 'The Member States shall exercise their competence to the extent that the Union has not exercised its competence' and that 'The Member States shall again exercise their competence to the extent that the Union has decided to cease exercising its competence', is so condensed that it is in truth downright misleading. Clearly in some circumstances, as explained previously in this section, Member States may exercise their competences even where the EU has exercised its, albeit that the precise detail varies depending on the subject matter at stake and, at bottom, on the detail of the applicable legal base.

These assorted provisos are all best understood as devices for expressing Member State *control* over the trajectory of EU legislative intervention as its scope in principle deepens. It is illuminating in this vein that they are the product of carefully negotiated Treaty revision. The Environment title was a creation of the Single European Act (SEA); Consumer Protection was added as an explicit EU legislative competence with effect from the entry into force of the Maastricht Treaty in 1993. The Member States, revising the Treaty, were persuaded of the virtue of granting the EU an explicit competence to act in an area previously left unmentioned by the Treaties, but they were fastidious in the drafting: no competence *carte blanche* was conferred on the EU. Norbert Reich captured the theme as it emerged: 'the more competences the [Union] is acquiring, the less exclusive will be its jurisdiction.'[9]

This model of *minimum* rule-making preserves room for national choice even after the EU has legislated. Allowing stricter rules to be adopted by Member States leaves room for a regulatory

[9] N. Reich, 'Competition between Legal Orders: A New Paradigm of EC Law' (1992) 29 CML Rev 861, 895.

laboratory—learning, regulatory emulation, innovation. There are multiple impulses to the shaping and re-shaping of regulatory standards in the EU. To lock the entire EU into a single agreed standard from which any deviation is forbidden would over-emphasize uniformity and a levelled playing field at the expense of regulatory protection and its periodic improvement. This cautions against clean-cut lines of exclusivity consequent on the EU's legislative entry into a particular field. Minimum rule-making stands for flexibility, pluralism, and multi-level governance.

But does this apply also to the internal market?

5.2.3 Harmonization in the internal market

Article 4(2)(a) lists the internal market as an area of shared competence. This, however, presents a different set of questions. Article 114 TFEU is the key Treaty provision dealing with the harmonization of laws in the service of the creation of an internal market. It is different from the batch of sector-specific Treaty provisions considered above in the sense that, as already elaborated in Chapter 2.7, it is driven by the functional logic of market-making and so it is of much broader scope than the carefully written legal bases on consumer protection, public health, environmental protection, and so on. It is different too in the effect its use has on residual national competence to act. Article 114 does not explicitly allow Member States to adopt stricter rules than the agreed EU rule. All it contains is a limited procedure under Article 114(4)–(9) whereby States may be permitted to apply stricter standards than are envisaged by the agreed EU rule, but only under defined and carefully limited pre-conditions and only after securing Commission approval. Article 114(4) allows a request to the Commission to maintain existing national provisions on the basis of major needs referred to in Article 36, or relating to the protection of the environment or the working environment. Article 114(5) concerns a request to introduce new national provisions, and by contrast it confines Member States to invocation of 'new scientific evidence relating to the protection of the environment or the working environment on grounds of a problem specific to that Member State arising after the adoption of the harmonisation measure'. So here the available grounds for setting rules that differ from the agreed EU standard are significantly narrower than those envisaged by Article 36 TFEU.

Article 114(4)–(9) endorses persisting regulatory fragmentation even after the EU has supposedly acted to harmonize the area in question. So a Member State may find that it is outvoted in Council and unable to prevent the adoption of a measure of harmonization, because Article 114 provides for use of the ordinary legislative procedure and therefore qualified majority voting (QMV) in Council, but it is allowed to apply to the Commission to exploit the safety valve granted by Article 114(4)–(9).

This procedure reveals clearly the thematic tension between control and effectiveness. The provisions were first inserted into the Treaty, albeit in slightly less flexible versions, by the SEA with effect from 1987. Before then, under the Treaty of Rome, legislative harmonization was possible under what is today Article 115 TFEU, but crucially it required and still requires unanimity in Council. Largely for that reason it has fallen into disuse, replaced in practice by Article 114 TFEU. The bargain struck at the time of the SEA was precisely to authorize the EU legislative process to become more agile, by embrace of QMV in Council for harmonization, but as compensation to offer space for managed derogation from the chosen harmonized standard. So what is today Article 114(4)–(9) reveal a reluctance on the part of Member States to accept complete surrender of their regulatory autonomy in consequence on EU legislative action (which they are unable to block unilaterally). Article 114(4)–(9) mediates the tension inherent in facilitating effective decision-making at EU level in a way that heightens fears that national concerns might be subordinated to the EU interest perceived by a majority. It sets aside a pure vision of pre-emption whereby the EU, once it has legislated, eliminates Member State competence to act in the field. More positively, it is a reflection of the importance of accommodating more than simply free trade on a level playing field within the framework of Union law.

These provisions were so sensitive that they were drafted to close the deal at the level of the Heads of State and Government,[10] and at the time fears were expressed that they represented a damaging backward step in the pattern of a uniform legal order. They were the subject of a savage attack by Pierre Pescatore, who would readily count as one of the most influential of the early community of EU lawyers; indeed, he was a judge of the Court from 1967 to 1985. He complained of 'enlarged possibilities of unilateral protective measures by Member States under Article 36…to which elusive notions such as safety, protection of the environment and protection of the working environment have been added' and warned of 'a new era of protectionism'.[11] This is in a sense ancient history but it reminds us of how strongly driven the EU was by the thirst for 'uniformity' as a

[10] C.-D. Ehlermann, 'The Internal Market following the Single European Act' (1987) 24 CMLRev 361, 389–98.

[11] P. Pescatore, 'Some Critical Remarks on the Single European Act' (1987) 24 CMLRev 9, 12.

guiding virtue. In the event there are relatively few recorded instances of Member States invoking this procedure and fewer still of the Commission granting approval,[12] and so the procedure has turned out to lack real practical bite. Its principal significance is the insight that uniformity is a contested virtue, and one that generates political anxieties about loss of national control and choice.

There is no generally applicable 'minimum' formula found in Article 114 to compare with that found in Article 169(4) (concerning consumer protection) or Article 193 (environmental protection). *Octapharma France* illustrates why this matters in practice.[13] The ruling concerns plasma products used in transfusions. There were two potentially relevant Directives, one adopted under Article 114 governing medicinal products, which the supplier argued applied, and the other adopted under Article 168 governing blood and blood components, which France argued was applicable. The incentive to litigate was that measures adopted under Article 168 leave space for Member States to adopt stricter rules, whereas measures adopted under Article 114 allow only the more cramped and managed derogation foreseen by Article 114(4)–(9). The detailed outcome is of no general interest—the Court in fact found that the Article 168 measure applied, and so stricter rules were allowed in the case of collecting and testing (but not processing, storage, and distribution). What matters is to realize that the landscape of EU law is itself not uniform in dictating what shall be the effect of EU legislative action on residual national competence.

5.2.4 *'Minimum harmonization' as oxymoron? The constitutional and policy debate*

The awkward question is whether individual measures of secondary legislation adopted under Article 114 may include a minimum formula, allowing stricter national rules in defined and limited circumstances. Pursuit of the level playing field as a rationale for harmonization would seem to dictate that States are required to abide by the EU rule and to refrain from any further regulation in the sector subjected to harmonization pursuant to Article 114, save only for the possibility of resort to its paragraphs (4)–(9). Aggressive promotion of the internal market would reject 'minimum harmonization' as an oxymoron—a technique that cannot harmonize rules precisely because it accepts national variation. This would characterize Article 114 as a source of maximum, not minimum, EU rules.

[12] Eg (approval) Dec 2004/1 [2004] OJ L1/20; (rejection) Dec 2001/571 [2001] OJ L202/46.

[13] Case C-512/12 judgment of 13 March 2014.

Some individual EU measures of secondary legislation are openly wedded to this maximum model. Directive 2005/29 on unfair commercial practices[14] takes as its legal base Article 95 EC, which is today in amended form Article 114 TFEU. The harmonization of national laws on unfair commercial practices which prejudice consumers' economic interests is firmly rooted in the economic project of market integration. The Directive requires that, in short, fair practices be permitted throughout the EU and that unfair ones be prohibited, according to a common EU-wide definition of unfairness elaborated in the Directive. Article 4 contains the so-called *Internal market* clause: 'Member States shall neither restrict the freedom to provide services nor restrict the free movement of goods for reasons falling within the field approximated by this Directive.' As expressed in the Preamble, this maximum model of harmonization 'will considerably increase legal certainty for both consumers and business [by creating] a single regulatory framework based on clearly defined legal concepts regulating all aspects of unfair commercial practices across the EU'.[15] And in case law providing an authoritative common interpretation of the Directive, which is pivotally important if the ambition to establish this level regulatory playing field is to be fulfilled, the Court has gone out of its way to confirm that stricter national intervention in the market within the material scope of the Directive is *not* permitted.[16] Indeed—for exactly the same reason of achieving regulatory predictability in the internal market—the Court has an important job in defining precisely what *is* the material scope of the Directive.[17]

The EU's legislative process does not always generate the adoption of unequivocal rules. Compromise along the way causes gaps. The matter of pre-emptive effect intended by a particular piece of secondary legislation then becomes a question of interpretation. So, for example, in *Firma Eau de Cologne & Parfümerie-Fabrik Glockengasse* v *Provide* the Court ruled that a Directive on the approximation of laws relating to cosmetic products occupied the field which it covered, with the consequence that Italian rules that required the provision of information on product packaging that went beyond that envisaged by the Directive were incompatible with EU law.[18] Such requirements had led to importers being forced to alter

[14] OJ [2005] L149/22. [15] Recital 12.

[16] Eg Case C-261/07 *VTB-VAB NV* [2009] ECR I-2949. Case C-206/11 *Georg Köck* judgment of 17 January 2013.

[17] Eg Case C-122/10 *Ving Sverige AB* [2011] ECR I-3903; Case C-428/11 *Purely Creative Ltd and others* v *OFT* judgment of 18 October 2012.

[18] Case C-150/88 [1989] ECR 3891.

packaging for the Italian market, thereby impeding trade, which was precisely the economic cost that the Directive was designed to eliminate. The case was initiated by a German producer with an obvious commercial incentive to have the Italian restrictions set aside. The adoption of a rule of this type at EU level in furtherance of the free movement of goods has the constitutional point that it disables *as a matter of principle* a Member State's capacity to apply stricter rules by invoking the interests referred to in Article 36 TFEU. So in the 'Dim Dip' case, *Commission* v *UK*,[19] the UK had introduced a requirement that all new vehicles should carry dim-dip lights. Such devices were not listed in a relevant Directive, and the Court held that the UK rule unlawfully excluded cars made in other States not equipped with such lights; crucially, it determined that because the matter was covered by the Directive, it was not even open in principle to the UK to try to justify the requirements as safety measures which allowed a reduction in the brightness of headlights to make them less likely to blind oncoming drivers. The alleged merits of the dim-dip device were simply irrelevant to the Court's examination. Action by the Member State was pre-empted by EU intervention.

It is quite common for the Court to reach this conclusion, even where it is not made explicit on the face of the EU measure (usually a Directive).[20] In such circumstances, each legislative act bites off an area previously within national competence and, by pre-empting national action in the area concerned, it creates a defined area of exclusive EU competence. Harmonization has as a major motivation the creation of a common economic area in which producers are able to use a single production line to service the whole EU. This permits the realization of economies of scale and, in a competitive market, the fruits should be enjoyed by consumers. National-level variation is excluded: the protective concerns previously addressed (in divergent fashion) by Member State laws are absorbed in the EU measure, backed by Articles 12, 114(3), and 169 TFEU and Article 38 of the Charter, which are addressed to the development of the content of the EU norm. The State eager for alteration of the regime must press for change at EU level, rather than acting unilaterally in a way that will harm the internal market. This, of course, accentuates the importance of investing political effort in negotiating the content of the harmonized regime.

[19] Case 60/86 [1988] ECR 3921.

[20] Eg Case 190/87 *Oberkreisdirektor* v *Moormann* [1988] ECR 4689; Case C-44/01 *Pippig Augenoptik* v *Hartlauer* [2003] ECR I-3095; Case 148/78 *Ratti* [1979] ECR 1629; Case C-374/05 *Gintec International* [2007] ECR I-9517; Case 246/80 *Broekmeulen* v *Huisarts Registratie Commissie* [1981] ECR 2311.

Neglect of the debate about how to construct the EU regime—rigorous or mild regulation, detailed or flexible—carries the penalty that a State may find itself locked into a regime from which it may not depart unilaterally and which is hard to alter at EU level.[21]

The constitutional force of pre-emption according to this model is aggressive. This model of 'maximum harmonization' promotes market-making at EU level, but it also stands for savage curtailment of national regulatory autonomy. It was explained in Chapter 2.7 that Article 114, functionally driven by the imperative of internal market-making, has a very wide scope and resort to it does much in practice to undermine the limitations placed on the EU's reach into national autonomy by other sector-specific Treaty provisions. So Article 114's alignment with a model of maximum harmonization is apt to unleash a vigorously centralizing and homogenizing dynamic. But Article 114 does not always generate maximum rules.

As a matter of empirical observation the EU's legislative *acquis* is home to a great deal of *minimum* harmonization, where the EU harmonized standard sets the floor but it is open to each Member State to choose to raise the ceiling. Like the safety valves found in Article 114(4)–(9), this model reflects the notion that harmonization need not involve the automatic subordination of national choices about market regulation to the dictates of trade liberalization. But minimum harmonization is still more flexible in the leeway offered to States than the relatively tightly defined provisions of Article 114(4)–(9), which set out exhaustively the available grounds for setting rules that differ from the EU standard and which moreover specify a supervisory management process involving the Commission. Neither restriction applies to the more agile phenomenon of minimum harmonization.

Much of the harmonized *acquis* pertaining to the protection of the economic interests of consumers is built on an assumption that minimum harmonization shall be the norm.[22] So, for example, the constitutional basis for Directive 93/13 on Unfair Terms in Consumer Contracts is Article 100a, today in amended form Article 114 TFEU.[23] Several Member States have legislation in the field, but these reveal very different techniques. This diversity distorts the development and functioning of the internal market. The Directive is designed to put

[21] Though the procedures for delegation and implementation conferred by Arts 290 and 291 TFEU may help: see Chapter 3.

[22] See S. Weatherill, *EU Consumer Law and Policy* (Elgar European Law, 2012) Ch 3.

[23] Directive 93/13 OJ [1993] L95/29.

in place a common EU standard for testing the fairness of terms that have not been individually negotiated which are found in consumer contracts. However, it is expressly by Article 8 of the Directive that 'Member States may adopt or retain the most stringent provisions compatible with the Treaty in the area provided by this Directive, to ensure a maximum degree of protection for the consumer.' Directive 99/44 on consumer sales and guarantees includes a functionally equivalent minimum proviso to the effect that Member States 'may adopt or maintain in force more stringent provisions, compatible with the Treaty in the field covered by this Directive, to ensure a higher level of consumer protection'.[24] Minimum Directives do not set a single rule as both floor and ceiling, but rather only a floor. Member States may maintain stricter rules, up to the ceiling set by primary law; in particular, the Treaty provisions on free movement.

This legislative practice pursuant to (what is today) Article 114 TFEU aligns the harmonized consumer law *acquis* with practice in the sphere of environmental protection, where the Treaty base itself contains a constitutional direction that minimum rule-making is the EU norm. More pertinently still, it also aligns the EU's activities in the consumer field driven in the name of market-making harmonization with the (little used) consumer-specific Treaty base found in Article 169(4) TFEU which, as mentioned in Section 5.2.2, also locates in the Treaty an explicit preference for minimum rule-making by the EU.

A minimalist explanation for this convergence may be found in the suggestion that the areas in which minimum harmonization has achieved a high profile are areas that are not really at the core of the integrative process. Allowing diversity in levels of consumer protection directed at economic interests and standards of environmental protection may have some incidental distortive effect on trade patterns, but such rules do not directly affect the composition of products. A connected explanation holds that some of the relevant EU measures date from before the conferral of an explicit legal base governing environmental protection (which occurred in 1987 by virtue of the SEA) and consumer protection (1993, the Maastricht Treaty). The EU legislature borrowed the Treaty-conferred competence to harmonize laws (and sometimes the predecessor to Article 352 TFEU; Chapter 2.7.3) in order to express a unanimous political preference for the development of a legislative programme of environmental and consumer protection at a

[24] OJ [1999] L171/12.

time when the Treaty conferred no relevant or adequate competence in that field. And the inclusion of a 'minimum' clause was part of the political deal: Member States acquiesced in a stretching of EU legislative competence on the condition that they were granted scope to maintain stricter rules under the minimum formula. So one could see minimum measures as apt where the harmonized rules do not affect methods of production. By contrast, measures dealing with product specifications—as in *Dim Dip*—are located in the heartland of economic integration and must maintain the classic approach whereby EU rules pre-empt national rules, subject only to (the rarely invoked) managed derogation procedure in Article 114(4)–(9).

This is an *ex post facto* rationalization of the legislative practice. This perspective—that 'minimum harmonization' has no place where a genuine market-making ambition underpins the legislation—has, however, provided the Commission more recently with the propulsion to advance a policy preference hostile to minimum harmonization and fixed instead on the supposed superiority of maximum harmonization as a means to improve the predictability of the regulatory framework underpinning the internal market.

The Commission's Consumer Policy Programme for 2002–2006 stated a need 'to review and reform existing EU consumer protection directives' in order 'to minimise variations in consumer protection rules across the EU that create fragmentation of the internal market to the detriment of consumers and business'.[25] The preferred method to achieve this was a shift from minimum to maximum harmonization, so effecting a complete transfer of regulatory responsibility from Member States to the EU in the field covered by the measure in question. In the February 2007 Green Paper on the *Review of the Consumer Acquis* the orthodox model of minimum harmonization was not even entertained as a possible option for the future.[26]

Briefly, the Commission's policy preference appeared to enjoy a supportive constitutional dimension. In the first *Tobacco Advertising* case the Court criticized the annulled Directive for failing to 'ensure free movement of products which are in conformity with its provisions'.[27] The annulled measure was replaced by the more tightly drawn Directive 2003/33 which duly included an explicit market access clause, and which survived challenge before the Court in *Tobacco Advertising II*, in which the Court expressly noted with approval the presence of that market access

25 OJ [2002] C137/2. 26 COM (2006) 744.

27 Case C-376/98 *Germany* v *Parliament and Council* [2000] ECR I-8419, para 101.

clause.[28] This case law is capable of being read as insisting that it is a condition of the validity of a measure of harmonization that it excludes the possibility of States making stricter demands of imports than are envisaged by the EU measure itself (excepting only recourse to Article 114(4)–(9)). But this case law does not deserve to be taken at face value. There were other good reasons in *Tobacco Advertising* for annulling the Directive, most of all the weak connection between market-making and the regulation of advertising on media such as ashtrays and parasols, and other good reasons in *Tobacco Advertising II* and in *BAT* to treat the measures as valid, given their adequate contribution to the functioning of the internal market. So the style of harmonization was not centrally important to the Court's analysis. In particular the radical interpretation, which would rule out minimum harmonization in principle, deserves a sceptical reception precisely because the Court has frequently in the past *accepted* harmonization measures that appear to permit stricter rules to be applied even to imports.[29] Moreover, since *Tobacco Advertising*, it has taken exactly the same permissive approach and has offered no objection at all to national rules on advertising[30] or the marketing of goods[31] and services[32] that are stricter than required by a relevant EU Directive, while simply ignoring its own apparently contradictory comments in *Tobacco Advertising*. It takes a strategically selective and frankly meretricious reading of the case law to insist on rejecting the constitutional feasibility of minimum harmonization pursuant to Article 114. The best interpretation of this erratic case law is that the Court has not excluded *in principle* the possibility that Article 114 may be used as the basis for the adoption of a harmonization measure which insists on only minimum standards. In fact a measure-by-measure investigation is required: on occasion, as in *Tobacco Advertising*, this will reveal that an absence of a market access clause serves as one element leading to the conclusion that the measure is lacking an adequate contribution to the internal market, but more commonly the introduction of minimum rules brings the position closer to that which would prevail in an internal market than that which obtained previously under a completely unharmonized pattern, and it leaves space too for the Member States to top up

[28] Case 380/03 *Germany* v *Parliament and Council* [2006] ECR I-11573, paras 73–74; also Case C-491/01 *R* v *Secretary of State ex parte BAT and Imperial Tobacco* [2002] ECR I-11543, para 74.

[29] Eg Case 382/87 *Buet* [1989] ECR 1235.

[30] Eg Case C-71/02 *Herbert Karner GmbH* [2004] ECR I-3025 (Dir 84/450 on advertising).

[31] Eg Case C-322/01 *DocMorris* [2003] ECR I-14887 (Dir 97/7 on distance selling); Case C-441/04 *A-Punkt Schmuckhandels GmbH* [2006] ECR I-2093 (Dir 85/577 on distance selling).

[32] Case C-593/13 *Rina Services* judgment of 16 June 2015 (Dir 2006/123 on services); Case C-212/11 *Jyske Bank Gibraltar* judgment of 25 April 2013 (Dir 2005/60 on money laundering).

the chosen degree of regulatory protection, should they so wish. So there is no *constitutional* objection to minimum harmonization.[33] It is a matter of policy preference and sensitivity to the particular sector at stake.

At the level of policy, the Commission's record in persuading the Council and Parliament of the virtues of a shift away from the minimum and towards the maximum model in matters pertaining to harmonization of rules affecting the economic interests of consumers is mixed. Directive 2005/29 on unfair commercial practices, mentioned previously in this section, is a measure of maximum harmonization, so Member States must suppress practices that are unfair within the meaning of the Directive but they must *not* block the use of practices that are fair. Here the Commission successfully piloted the maximum model of harmonization through the legislative process, using as its main propulsion the benefits that would flow in the creation of the internal market from stamping out room for stricter national rules that would fragment the market along national lines. By contrast Directive 93/13 on unfair terms and Directive 99/44 on sales and guarantees apply only minimum rules. The Commission's attempt to convert those two Directives into measures of maximum harmonization, under an assumption that this would improve the functioning of the internal market, ran into insuperable political opposition precisely because of unwillingness to surrender national autonomy in matters of consumer protection. In October 2008, as a result of its review of the consumer *acquis*, the Commission adopted a proposal for a Directive on Consumer Rights which would have replaced Directives 85/577 (doorstep selling), 97/7 (distance selling), 93/13, and 99/44 with a single measure which would have pursued what the Commission described as *targeted full harmonization*—maximum rules.[34] This, it was argued, would have provided a simplified and more consistent regulatory framework apt to realize the advantages of the internal market while also achieving a high level of consumer protection. Perhaps it would have, but the Member States and the Parliament were not prepared to accept such a radical vertical transfer of regulatory responsibility away from the national level in favour of the EU. The finally adopted and slimmed-down Directive 2011/83 on consumer rights transforms only Directives 85/577 on doorstep selling and 97/7 on distance contracts from minimum to maximum harmonization,

[33] Light may be cast on the Court's position in challenges pending to the validity of Dir 2014/40, which replaces Dir 2001/37 and which in its Arts 24(2) and (3) envisages scope for restrictions on imports which go beyond the harmonized norm (Case C-358/14 *Poland* v *Council and Parliament*, Case C-477/14 *Pillbox 38*, and Case C-547/14 *Philip Morris*, pending).

[34] COM (2008) 614.

thereby precluding stricter national rules in those areas.[35] The minimum character of Directives 93/13 on unfair terms and 99/44 on consumer sales, which are substantively far more important, is left intact: despite the Commission's efforts, Directive 2011/83 scarcely touches them. Political fear of the loss of State autonomy that flows from the creation of an area of law placed beyond national adaptation and open to reform by the EU alone was too strong.[36] Maximum harmonization, unpalatable in this instance, asserts a single notion of consumer protection when in fact consumer preferences, tastes, and capabilities differ in Europe.[37]

Directive 2006/123 on Services in the internal market offers another powerful example.[38] The Commission's original proposal, unveiled in 2004, would have put in place maximum harmonization, so that service providers would have been free to operate throughout the EU without hindrance, provided only that they complied with the standards set by the Directive and implemented locally. This exercise in vertical re-allocation of regulatory competences proved politically unpalatable. In fact the ferocity of the response, built around angry rhetoric and anxieties about the 'Polish plumber' undercutting local providers, clearly exposed the sensitivity of what might at first seem a technical matter associated with regulatory design and style of harmonization.[39] The Directive as finally adopted is more modest. It does not go so far as the Commission's 2004 proposal in limiting 'host State' regulatory competence to simple implementation of the common EU standards, but it goes further than Article 56 TFEU by limiting 'host State' regulatory competence to the list of interventions in the services market which are expressly foreseen by the Directive. That is, the standard and broad 'public interest' justification available to a State that restricts free movement is here disabled in favour of a more focused set of justifications. Article 16 of Directive 2006/123 provides that Member States shall respect the right to provide services in a Member State other than that in which the provider is established, but limitations imposed by 'host states' are permitted provided they respect

[35] OJ [2011] L304/64.

[36] See S. Weatherill, 'The Consumer Rights Directive: How and Why a Quest for "Coherence" has (Largely) Failed' (2012) 49 CMLRev 1279.

[37] Cf S. Weatherill, 'Maximum or Minimum Harmonisation—What Kind of "Europe" Do We Want?' in K. Boele-Woelki and W. Grosheide (eds), *The Future of European Contract Law* (Kluwer, 2007); V. Mak, 'Review of the Consumer Acquis: Towards Maximum Harmonisation?' (2009) 17 European Review Private Law 55.

[38] OJ [2006] 376/36.

[39] See eg J. Loder, 'The Lisbon Strategy and the Politicization of EU Policy-making: The Case of the Services Directive' (2011) 18 JEPP 566.

stated principles—non-discrimination, necessity, and proportionality—and 'necessity' within Article 16 covers justification 'for reasons of public policy, public security, public health or the protection of the environment': a narrower formulation than Article 56 TFEU. The main point here is that a pure model of 'maximum harmonization', ruthlessly stripping away any room for diverse local choice, was exposed as politically toxic. The Services Directive is not maximum harmonization, but it is harmonization that improves the functioning of the internal market by curtailing the permitted scope of justified national restrictions to a more narrow range than would be allowed without harmonization, while also regulating the EU's services market according to both the common rules found in the Directive and the national measures that may be introduced in the light of its Article 16.

5.2.5 *Policy and priorities*

The Commission's driving concern behind its push to prioritize maximum harmonization in the field of consumer law is the improved functioning of the internal market. It is clearly right to assert that the minimum model of harmonization damages the unity of the internal market. Member States may and do set stricter national rules within the scope of the EU measure, and this denies a 'level playing field' for trade. But the maximum model of harmonization has disadvantages too. Stricter national rules are disallowed, which prevents national choice and flexibility. Consumer protection is set at the level chosen by the EU—it cannot be raised by national law, but rather only by the laborious processes of reform at EU level, and, moreover, if the EU maximum is *lower* than existing national standards, then in those States the EU causes a reduction in protection from market failure and/or market inequities, as well as, more generally, depriving them of room to express local preference. Put another way, the Commission's aim to achieve 'a significantly higher degree of coherence in European contract law'[40] would be achieved *at EU level* under a model wedded to maximum harmonization, but *at national level* the consequence would likely be much less coherence, because established rules that are found to fall within the material scope of the EU measure must be set aside unless they are precisely in line with the EU system (on paper and as interpreted by the Court), to the detriment of accumulated local

[40] D. Staudenmayer, 'The Place of Consumer Contract Law within the Process on European Contract Law' (2004) 27 JCP 269, 277. The author was a Commission official closely involved in the project.

preferences. The more 'coherent' the EU regime, the less coherent and the less autonomous national systems become.

So the issue is whether the costs outweigh the benefits, or vice versa, and that calculation cannot be made without placing some price on competing values. Ruling out space for stricter national rules brings benefits consequent on the uniformity promoted at EU level, leading to a simplification of the regulatory landscape. That is doubtless the 'harmony' seductively located within the discourse of harmonization. But equally, a shift to maximum harmonization involves a priority for market-making under a single centralized rule to the exclusion of local regulatory autonomy. Within the field occupied by the EU measure, maximum harmonization switches off the competence for Member States to pursue any goals other than those chosen by the EU. The Commission is open to the accusation that it is using the discourse of internal market-driven 'coherence' to disguise the sensitive political implications of its policy preferences. This is in many ways the lesson of the shrunken Consumer Rights Directive, 2011/83, explained in Section 5.2.4.

The alternative vision prefers minimum harmonization as not merely a tolerance but indeed an embrace of diversity and differentiation as in themselves valuable within an EU dedicated to more than economic growth and consumer empowerment, and inapt for reduction to a 'one size fits all' model. Minimum harmonization stands for regulatory pluralism. The 'minimum or maximum' debate is evidently important in the development of EU contract law and its place within the internal market,[41] but it is but one manifestation of a much deeper political and cultural inquiry into the preferred relationship between the EU and its Member States—how much should be done in common; how much diversity should be tolerated, even encouraged?[42]

Minimum harmonization deserves a more tolerant appreciation than the Commission allows, in relation to consumer contract law and more generally. Mr Cruz Villalón is one of the most perceptive Advocates General ever to grace the Court, and his Opinion in *European Air Transport SA* supplies a fascinating assembly of interpretative techniques *against* maximum harmonization.[43] The case turned on the definition of

[41] F. Gomez and J. Ganuza, 'An Economic Analysis of Harmonization Régimes: Full Harmonization, Minimum Harmonization or Optional Instrument?' (2011) 7 ERCL 275.

[42] See eg N. Boeger, 'Minimum Harmonisation, Free Movement and Proportionality' in P. Syrpis (ed), *The Judiciary, the Legislature and the EU Internal Market* (CUP, 2012); S. Weatherill, 'Maximum versus Minimum Harmonization: Choosing between Unity and Diversity in the Search for the Soul of the Internal Market' in N. Nic Shuibhne and L. Gormley (eds), *From Single Market to Economic Union: Essays in Memory of John A Usher* (OUP, 2012).

[43] Case C-120/10 *European Air Transport SA* judgment of 8 September 2011.

'operating restrictions' which may be imposed (at Brussels airport) in conformity with the requirements concerning noise imposed by Directive 2002/30, and the Court's ruling goes no further than that particular point. However, Advocate General Cruz Villalón also asked whether scope was left for national measures that are stricter than those mandated by the Directive, and this drew him into an engagement with the need to balance transport policy and environmental protection. He was highly sceptical of the virtue of maximum harmonization in such circumstances. His Opinion expresses wariness about an interpretation that would cause a 'paralysis of state action' to do anything beyond that mandated by the EU. He also referred to fundamental rights associated with protection of the environment, specifically Articles 7 and 37 of the Charter, which are clearly promoted more effectively by a model of minimum rather than maximum rule-making at EU level. Minimum harmonization represents a realistic attempt to accommodate diverse national tradition and to promote scope for dynamic regulatory innovation within the process of integration. In fact, the stakes are high enough to justify reliance on Article 4(2) TEU as a provision that favours minimum over maximum harmonization, for only by foreclosing the pre-emptive effect of EU law is space left for the expression of national identity in its many diverse forms across the Member States. So there is a strong case to be made for regarding maximum harmonization as applicable only exceptionally, where its use has been carefully justified in prevailing sector-specific conditions.

This debate is of immense practical significance in the detail of law-making, but it also reveals much about the choices to be made about the vertical distribution of competences within the EU and, wider still, it illuminates the values of the EU, seeking to accommodate a balance between market-making uniformity and homogenization and variety across a wide sweep of multi-functional activity.

5.3 LEGISLATIVE FLEXIBILITY: MATERIAL SCOPE, DEROGATIONS, AND THE LAW AND PRACTICE OF IMPLEMENTATION

Maximum harmonization offers the maximum promise of uniformity. But even where a measure in principle excludes stricter national rules it is still not uncommon to discover that the EU legislative process has left more space for persisting diversity among national practices than the label 'maximum harmonization' would lead one to anticipate. First, an EU measure frequently does not fully harmonize the area which it addresses, and it is not uncommon for the exact reach to be in any event left unambiguous under a compromise legislative formula. This is a matter of material scope. Second, even within a measure's undoubted material scope, room may be left for derogations, options, and exceptions. This is a reflection of the 'affinity for consensus' in Council, noted in Chapter 3,[44] as well as the need to accommodate the concerns of the Parliament, which may mean that dissenting views are apt to shape, sometimes to mis-shape, the text of agreed measures. Third, the practice of implementation at national level—of Directives, most obviously—is inevitably destructive of pure EU-level uniformity, as Member States, deliberately or without calculation, lawfully or unlawfully, select their own preferred route to give local effect to the EU's objectives as expressed in a measure of harmonization.

These features combine to challenge the reality of the discourse about 'uniformity' in the internal market and in the EU more generally. In fact the very word 'harmonization' tends to exaggerate the true effect of an EU measure once it is absorbed into the national legal orders of the twenty-eight Member States.

5.3.1 *Material scope*

A measure may be maximum in its pre-emptive effect, but it may not amount to full harmonization of the area in question, because its material scope is limited. Terminology is not always used with precision in these contexts, but the concepts need to be kept distinct: an EU measure exerts some kind of effect on national regulatory competence in the field which it occupies (maximum or minimum is the most obvious choice) but that implies a need to define its precise material scope, a separate inquiry which is sometimes expressed as an investigation into whether the measure offers full or partial harmonization.

A measure of harmonization which excludes important but sensitive matters makes a contribution to the uniform regulation of the matter at EU level that is considerably less significant than might be expected. Directive 2006/123 on services in the internal market is a fine example.[45] It would be more accurately called the Directive on *some* services in the internal market. It excludes (inter alia) gambling and health care services from its material scope; similarly, contracts for gambling and health care services are explicitly placed beyond the reach of Directive 2011/83 on consumer rights.[46] Such exclusions reveal the controlling reflex which Member States inject into the law-making process, and are doubtless in

[44] J. Lewis, 'Council of Ministers and European Council' Ch 23 in E. Jones, A. Menon, and S. Weatherill (eds), *The Oxford Handbook of the European Union* (OUP, 2012), p 322.

[45] Note 38. [46] Note 35.

part explicable with reference to the influence of powerful lobbying interests. The result is that harmonization covers a narrower material scope than first impressions suggest, and often this is a narrower scope than the Commission had first proposed. It should, however, be remembered that such painstaking sectoral exclusion from secondary legislation is not apt to immunize such practices from the impact of primary EU law. Both gambling and especially health care have been the subject of transformative rulings pursuant to the Treaty free movement rules.[47]

Directive 2005/29 on unfair commercial practices provides another good example.[48] The Directive, according to its Recital 7, 'does not address legal requirements related to taste and decency which vary widely among the Member States'. It is there stated that commercial practices such as solicitation in the streets may be undesirable in Member States for cultural reasons. A ban may be maintained. Precisely where this limit between unfair practices, regulated by the Directive, and practices apt to cause offence or shock, left for treatment under national law, will fall is elusive,[49] but the political refusal to acquiesce in a fully comprehensive EU measure is instructive. Here too national requirements related to taste and decency, though excluded from the Directive, could be attacked as restrictions on free movement, but it would be open to Member States to show justification for their choices, which would not be true had they been brought within the material scope of this measure of maximum harmonization.

A distinct aspect of the 'all is not what it may seem' understanding of the maximum character of Directive 2005/29 is that in some acutely sensitive areas the legislative negotiation led to the imposition of only minimum rules, contrary to the maximum model so prized by the Commission. Article 3(9) of Directive 2005/29 excludes financial services from the maximum harmonization regime and states instead that Member States are allowed room to choose to apply more restrictive rules, which then fall to be tested against the orthodox standards of justification in so far as they impede cross-border trade.[50] So the Directive is on close inspection a hybrid: mainly maximum, partly, in response to particular sectoral sensitivity, minimum.

The more imprecise the provisions detailing a measure's material scope, the more power is delegated to the Court to determine what is truly at

[47] Chapters 2.8, 6.3.1. [48] Note 14.

[49] Cf B. Keirsbilck, *The New European Law of Unfair Commercial Practices and Competition Law* (Hart, 2011), pp 265–7.

[50] Eg Case C-265/12 *Citroën Belux* judgment of 18 July 2013.

stake. This is true of any provision of primary or secondary EU law, but it carries extra bite in the context of maximum harmonization because locating a matter within the material scope of such a measure requires Member States not only to regulate according to the EU standard but also ruthlessly to set aside any aspect of national law and practice within that material scope which applies a divergent standard. Given the unavoidable compromise nature of some EU legislation, squeezed through the intricacies and eccentricities of Commission, Parliament, and Council inquiry, coupled too to the multilingual challenge of EU texts, the Court is frequently asked to resolve ambiguities. This is where its principles of interpretation examined in Chapter 3.14—such as that in favour of a high level of consumer protection[51]—may come to play a decisive role.

5.3.2 Derogations

A related phenomenon, which also serves to reflect the demand for flexibility and the unavoidable need to compromise, is found in the pattern of derogations, options, and exemptions allowed to Member States from aspects of initiatives with which they are uncomfortable. A matter that falls within a measure's material scope may be subject to varying treatment even where the headline boast is of maximum harmonization. Were the EU wedded to a pattern of a single homogenous legal order, this would be anathema. In times of an enlarged, multi-functional Union, the inevitability, and to some extent the desirability, of this route, has become increasingly apparent. The risk lies in the possibility that the compromises made may fragment a measure to such an extent that the final text's claim to provide a source of uniform rules for the Union is a sham.

A neat example of the tensions and the associated institutional implications, both horizontal and vertical, is provided by Directive 85/374.[52] It is commonly referred to as the 'Product Liability Directive'. Harmonization of national provisions concerning the liability of the producer for damage caused by defectiveness of products is explained by the need to address the distortions in competition in the EU and the impact on the movement of goods which are caused by divergences between the laws of the different Member States. It is an internal market measure, but it falls to the EU to make its own choice about what shall be the content of the EU's own harmonized regime. That choice is liability without fault on the part of the producer of a defective product. So in principle the producer of a defective product should not escape liability simply because he or she failed

[51] Eg (Dir 2005/29) Case C-122/10, Case C-428/11 note 17.

[52] OJ [1985] L210/29, as amended by Dir 1999/34 OJ [1999] L141/20.

to appreciate the product's character because of, for example, want of full understanding of the problem that emerged. However, this model was the subject of sustained attack during the preparation of the measure by interest groups and some Member States who argued that adopting such a model, on the face of it advantageous to the consumer harmed by a defective product, would diminish incentives for producers to innovate, while also increasing insurance costs that would be passed on to consumers in the form of higher prices. Whether or not one accepts these criticisms, they were strong enough to wrest a concession in the text of the Directive, and it is one that has remained part of the regime ever since, despite periodic Commission reviews. The system of strict liability on which the Directive appears to be based is diluted by the inclusion of a so-called development risk defence in Article 7(e). A producer of a defective product is able to escape liability by proving 'that the state of scientific and technical knowledge at the time when he put the product into circulation was not such as to enable the existence of the defect to be discovered'. And, crucially, this defence, applicable where the flaw is loosely interpreted, unknown, and unknowable, is optional. Article 15(1)(b) permits Member States the option of extending liability even to defects of this type. So in some States the 'development risk' defence will be available to traders faced with claims by consumers harmed by the supply of defective products, but in other States, where different choices have been made, no such protection can be relied on.

One may readily have predicted that relatively few States would choose to exercise the option foreseen by Article 15(1)(b) and thereby deny their traders the protection of the defence, for this would impose costs on them from which their competitors elsewhere in the EU would be immune. So it has proved. The Commission reported in 2000 that among the (then) fifteen Member States the defence had been set aside only by Luxembourg and Finland, and in part by Spain, France, and Germany.[53] In 2011 it referred to only Luxembourg and Finland.[54]

The inclusion of this option in the Directive provides an insight into the difficulty of achieving harmonization of each and every aspect of a matter which is the subject of EU intervention. It is possible to view the Directive as containing at its heart a fundamental failure to agree a core liability rule. Marketing a product that has been exhaustively tested, yet which is later discovered to be defective, will attract potentially vast liability in States that have excluded the defence, but no liability at all in

[53] COM (2000) 893. [54] COM (2011) 547, p 8.

States that retain it. Firms that are sued will have powerful incentives to endeavour to make tactical use of the rules of private international law in order to establish that the rules under which they are properly sued are those of a State that has retained the defence. The choices may affect their decision on where to locate in the first place. Consumers in States that offer the defence are likely to be much worse off than their fellow Citizens of the Union in States that have rejected the inclusion of the defence, unless they too are able to exploit the rules of private international law to find the most favourable forum.

It remains contentious how far options granted in Directives constitute an acceptable recognition of national peculiarities and/or distinct national preference and how far instead they undermine the whole notion of harmonization of laws and equal conditions of competition and protection across the territory of the EU. But, simply to make a descriptive point, they form part of the landscape, and all these tensions have been multiplied by the EU's pattern of geographical and functional expansion over time.

There are many other examples that could be collected from a traverse of the EU's legislative *acquis*. The Working Time Directive, Directive 93/104 (working time), later re-cast as Directive 2003/88,[55] was adopted as a measure aimed at improving health and safety in the working environment. It was touched on in Chapter 3.8 as a particularly powerful example of how an EU measure can finish up forbiddingly dense. It is complex and in some respects rigid, not least because of the attempt to accommodate divergent traditions on how working time is to be regulated, if at all, and by whom: public act or private bargaining. Articles 17–19 of the Directive are all concerned with detailed derogations, with special provision for, for example, managing executives or other persons with autonomous decision-taking powers; family workers and workers officiating at religious ceremonies in churches and religious communities; and cases where there is a foreseeable surge of activity, particularly agriculture, tourism, and postal services. Article 20 adds special rules for mobile workers and offshore work; Article 21 deals with workers on board seagoing fishing vessels. Article 22 allows Member States an option not to apply the weekly maximum for working time where an employer has obtained the worker's agreement to work longer—though the provision is a good deal more complicated than is captured by this brief summary.

[55] OJ [2003] L299/9.

Periodic rulings of the Court, usually favourable to the position of employees, have added to the impression that this regime is messier and more unpredictable than it needs to be.[56] But surprise would be naïve. Common rule-making is not a technical exercise. It is deeply political. If the EU can truly create uniformity out of the diverse practices found across twenty-eight Member States, it is unlikely that the matter subject to regulation is very important.

5.3.3 *Implementation*

Even where one is dealing with an EU measure that asserts a common standard according to the maximum model and admits of no derogation, one must reckon with the likelihood that uniformity as a paradigm for EU law will be challenged by patterns of implementation and enforcement at national level. A starting point is appreciation that although the Court employs an orthodox formula which conventionally insists on the need for an autonomous EU meaning of concepts contained in EU legal instruments in order to preclude the unevenness that flows from diverse national understandings,[57] the practical reality is hard to map systematically, and it is probably common for national preconceptions to infect the way in which concepts and terms drawn from EU law come to be applied locally.[58] And so is bred divergence, often unwittingly. Even a Regulation, which is directly applicable, is likely to be handled in different ways according to local administrative and juridical culture in the different Member States, but the Directive, in particular, is not apt to generate a uniform pattern State by State. According to Article 288 TFEU it is explicitly envisaged that Member States shall choose the form and methods that they deem most suitable to achieve the result intended by the Directive. This fully envisages diversity. This is the Directive's vice, but it is also its virtue, for Member States are permitted to absorb EU requirements into their legal and administrative culture in the way that they judge most appropriate. It allows them to use measures, procedures, and institutions to implement EU Directives which already exist to perform analogous tasks at national level: a whole new 'EU-fit' bureaucracy does not need to be created within the Member States.

[56] In detail, see C. Barnard, *EU Employment Law* (4th ed, OUP, 2012); Ch 11; A. Davies, *EU Labour Law* (Elgar, 2012), Ch 7.

[57] Eg Case C-276/14 *Gmina Wrocław* v *Minister Finansów* judgment of 29 September 2015, para 25.

[58] Eg S. Prechal and B. Van Roermund, *The Coherence of EU Law: The Search for Unity in Divergent Concepts* (OUP, 2008).

The nature of EU law generally, but especially Directives, is that it depends on effective national application. Few EU measures mandate the adoption of specific procedures or penalties. The obligation cast on Member States is as flexible as it is abstract. Implementing measures shall have unquestionable binding force and they shall display the specificity, precision, and clarity necessary to satisfy requirements of legal certainty.[59] This entails that a measure must be properly publicized, so persons concerned may ascertain the scope of their rights and obligations. An administrative practice, understood internally but not made transparent to the public, would not suffice. As far as enforcement and sanctions are concerned, the Court has referred airily to a general obligation to adopt practices that are sufficient to be effective and dissuasive, while also limited by the requirement that they be proportionate.[60] But this is imprecise and allows huge diversity between the Member States. That is admittedly the whole point of the Directive as a legal instrument, but the risk is that this model allows room for States—calculatedly or inadvertently—to minimize costs involved in faithful implementation. 'Creative compliance' refers to the ability to exploit the flexibility at stake. For example, the State may appear willing to conform to EU obligations and may put the law in place on paper, but it may decline adequately to resource enforcement agencies, so the law on paper has little significance in practice. This may or may not be unlawful: the standard of effective enforcement does not put numbers on the budgetary commitment that must be made at national level to give teeth to an implementing regime. The State may even 'creatively' trim away some of the (to it) more objectionable aspects of the Directive when it implements it on paper—or, worse and harder to track, when it administers it on the ground. Such tactics lie close to the margin of the State's obligations of fidelity to the Union's objectives, and sometimes they may trespass beyond them. But alleged infractions are hard to root out, for they will frequently be concealed deep in national or local practice. The Commission may pursue the matter, but this is likely to be time-consuming. Private actions are possible. Both direct effect and *Francovich* offer routes to challenge such arguably illegal action and to deny States any advantage from unlawfully creative compliance. However, such actions require a substantial investment of time

[59] Eg Case C-441/02 *Commission* v *Italy* [2006] ECR I-3449; Case C-415/01 *Commission* v *Belgium* [2003] ECR I-2081.

[60] Eg Joined Cases C-362/13, C-363/13, and C-407/13 *Fiamingo* judgment of 3 July 2014; Case C-348/04 *Boeringer Ingelheim KG* [2007] ECR I-3391; Case 326/88 *Hansen* [1990] ECR I-2911.

and money. *Francovich*, it should be recalled, was an 'easy' case for the litigants and for the Court, because there was a total failure to implement a Directive, already recorded by the Court of Justice.[61] This is not what is at stake in more nuanced resistance to EU rules that are perceived to be unduly inflexible. And subtle misapplication of measures in fields such as environmental protection will be challenged only if sufficiently alert and well-resourced activist groups exist. The loss suffered is spread thinly among a large number of individual litigants, none of whom is likely to have an obvious right or an adequate incentive to sue.

The existence of minimum standards and opt-outs, which detract from uniformity, may be particularly apt to undermine the ability of a national court to identify a justiciable right for the purposes of direct effect or a *Francovich* claim. The rise of the 'Framework Directive', promoted as part of the Commission's agenda of improved governance[62] and which has much appeal in maximizing flexibility in locating routes to best practice in achieving designated objectives, carries with it difficulty of oversight. The looser the legal regime, the harder it is to enforce according to classical models. The Court has nibbled at the edges of this problem. It has taken steps to adapt its jurisprudence in order to secure the effective enforcement of the option-ridden Directive. In *Francovich* itself the Directive allowed States to select from options in deciding the length of the period in respect of which workers who were the victim of a collective redundancy would be compensated, but the Court was able to identify the minimum guarantee envisaged by the Directive and ruled it capable of forming the subject of an enforcement action pursued by the individual worker. This is clever stuff. But there does need to be an identifiable minimum and the more compromise is written into a legislative text, the less likely this will be to find. And most of all, litigation is ad hoc, unreliable, and selective. It is endemic to the whole EU system that rule-making occurs at EU level but rule enforcement is almost exclusively the province of authorities in the Member States. The risks and incentives to evade full compliance with EU law in its local application, which are immense, are structurally loaded into the EU's working system.

The flight from uniformity must reckon with the criticism that it hinders effective enforcement and, more broadly, that it deepens intransparency which itself is corrosive of the EU's legitimacy. On the other hand, sensitivity to local peculiarity is a valid counter-concern and models

[61] Cases C-6, C-9/90 [1991] ECR I-5357; Chapter 4.6.

[62] Initially in *European Governance: A White Paper*, COM (2001) 428.

that respond to deficiencies in national-level enforcement by urging a higher level of centralized oversight are likely to generate a hostile reaction which might itself tarnish the EU's legitimacy. The tension is inescapable, and no model can satisfactorily resolve it. Choices must be made.

5.4 TREATY-SANCTIONED DIVERSITY

The case against uniformity is in part negative. It is unfeasible to insist on uniform rules in a Union that is geographically and functionally expanded far beyond the shape of the early years when the discourse of uniformity was at its most militant. But it is also positive. It is not desirable to impose a uniform model, especially one rooted in a transfer of exclusive competence to the Union, which risks stifling local preference, experimentation, and innovation and tends to provoke alienation from—even resentment to—the EU's centralizing pretensions. This suggests an attraction in loosening the shackles of uniformity. And, as explained in Section 5.1, in a number of respects—directly and indirectly, calculatedly and incrementally—the EU has retreated from the classic pre-emption model of occupation of the field involving transfer of exclusive competence into EU hands consequent on the adoption of secondary legislation.

This narrative of loosened commitment to 'one size fits all' deserves to be traced at the higher level of the Treaty itself. There are several manifestations of the flight from uniformity. But the basic idea holds that Member States are offered room for manoeuvre. What is at stake is in part the inevitable adjustments to the notion of uniformity demanded by an EU structure that is supporting an ever-increasing number of Member States and an ever-increasing range of functions and in part the insight that the EU can be a more agile and responsive regulator if it is able to enjoy a wider choice than to act in the name of all twenty-eight Member States or not to act at all. Yet lurking behind such potentially creative shifts lies the fundamental threat that what may be lost is the common constitutional and institutional structure within which the EU's mission to manage the interdependence of States has long been pursued.

This controlling instinct has already been met and discussed in Chapter 2. In this chapter the concern is not about the way in which common practices are agreed but rather about whether all the States participate. The Maastricht Treaty, which entered into force in 1993, set up the 'three pillars' of the EU, which were in their own right manifestations of use of different institutional and constitutional models to shape co-operation and which, though formally abandoned with effect from 2009 on the entry into force of the Lisbon Treaty, are still visible to the constitutional archaeologist, as will be noted in Section 5.4.1. But it was also the Treaty which most strikingly introduced 'variable geometry' into the EU.

Some manifestations were slight in effect, if heavy in symbolism. Denmark extracted a Protocol which provides that 'Notwithstanding the provisions of the Treaties, Denmark may maintain the existing legislation on the acquisition of second homes.' Restrictions, which favour Danish buyers, plainly contradict basic assumptions of non-discrimination on the basis of nationality, and could be protected only by such a proviso written into primary EU law. The Social Policy Protocol crafted as part of the negotiation of the Maastricht Treaty authorized the eleven Member States other than the UK to act in areas wider than the explicit scope of the then existing Treaty provisions dealing with social policy. This was the way found to bridge the gap in Treaty negotiation between the eleven Member States' determination to widen the scope of common policy-making and the UK's implacable opposition.[63] This was a very visible two-speed structure, and qualitatively different from a device such as minimum harmonization, because it involves a refusal by one State to participate in the common pattern at all. But it mattered little in practice: few measures were in fact adopted under the new channel and once political attitudes changed after the change of government in the UK in 1997 the tear in the fabric of uniformity was repaired; with effect from 1999, on the entry into force of the Amsterdam Treaty, the two speeds became one, and social policy is today contained in the uniformly applicable Title X of Part Three TFEU, comprising Articles 151–161 TFEU.

But in other areas the rejection of functional and geographic uniformity was of wider and more enduring significance.

5.4.1 *Justice and home affairs—the area of freedom, security, and justice*

The evolution of the EU's area of freedom, security, and justice (AFSJ) reveals a troubled story of Treaty revision over the years scarred by testy compromises, intricate detail, and curmudgeonly opt-outs, so an account that is abbreviated and confined to the main themes is provided here.[64] In short, it was agreed under the Maastricht Treaty to bring matters pertaining to justice and home affairs within the scope of the EU, but, betraying the nervousness felt by Member States about submitting such sensitive matters to the system's institutional and constitutional orthodoxy shaped

[63] See J. Kenner, *EU Employment Law: From Rome to Amsterdam and Beyond* (2003), Ch 6.

[64] More fully S. Peers, *EU Justice and Home Affairs Law* (OUP, 3rd ed, 2011).

by the original Treaties agreed in the 1950s, a novel system was crafted that placed heavy reliance on inter-governmental co-operation at the expense of the Parliament, Commission, and Court. It was the EU, but it was not the E(E)C: this was the so-called 'third pillar' of the EU. It covered co-operation in matters such as asylum policy, immigration policy, and policy regarding nationals of third countries; judicial co-operation in both civil and criminal matters; and aspects of police co-operation. With effect from the entry into force of the Amsterdam Treaty in 1999 the third pillar was slimmed down, and its narrower remit reflected by its re-naming as Police and Judicial Co-Operation in Criminal Matters. Meanwhile material on visas, asylum, immigration, and some other policies related to free movement of persons was transferred to the first pillar, the traditional EC, according to a method that accepted a much stronger, though still not perfectly orthodox, involvement for the Parliament, Commission, and Court. The shift in favour of the first pillar revealed a political readiness to abandon *some* of the institutional and constitutional caution that had gripped the negotiation of the Maastricht Treaty, largely in order to improve and accelerate effective rule-making by embracing a more orthodox model. The stated focus was on the progressive establishment of a newly minted concept, an 'area of freedom, security, and justice'. The Treaty of Lisbon, which entered into force in 2009, abandoned the vestigial third pillar entirely and fully transplanted the Treaty provisions on the creation of the AFSJ into the TFEU, where they now constitute the five Chapters of Title V of Part Three of the TFEU, covering policies on border checks, asylum and immigration, judicial co-operation in civil and criminal matters, and police co-operation. Its provisions, Articles 67–89 TFEU, remain visibly different, revealing their historical special character, in that they do not follow *precisely* the law-making method observed across most of the rest of the TFEU's landscape. They are, however, far closer to the orthodox model today than they ever have been in the past. However, that distinctive, albeit today much reduced, institutional specificity is not the only price which has been paid for the steady deepening of co-operation in this area. Not all Member States participate to the same extent in the patterns of common policy-making which govern the AFSJ, as envisaged by Title V of Part Three of the TFEU. The EU's AFSJ is not geographically homogenous.

The agreement to re-locate much of the relevant material from the 'third pillar' to the first in 1999 included as part of the deal special arrangements in connection with the place of the UK, Ireland, and Denmark. This shattered uniformity was first visible as a result of the creation of the 'Schengen area', a reference to Schengen, a town in

Luxembourg where agreements on the gradual abolition of checks at common borders were signed by some but not all EU Member States in 1985 and 1990. The Schengen deal is the reason why still today ordinary people—though not the high-flying élite politicians who purport to act on their behalf—travelling between the UK and the majority of the Member States find themselves forced to endure sullen passport checks. Inside the core of the AFSJ, which is smaller than the whole EU, there are no such checks. This is plainly not a uniform EU. The rules of the Schengen agreements, initially not EU law, were absorbed into the EU system with effect from 1999 on the entry into force of the Amsterdam Treaty, but only on a basis that protected the UK, Ireland, and Denmark from full binding effect. The EU's legislative *acquis*, which since 1999 has developed considerably beyond the Schengen *acquis* to establish a range of common standards for the regulation of matters of common concern within and at the external borders of this AFSJ, is equally subject to uneven application across the territory of all twenty-eight Member States.

Today, in the relevant Protocols which are attached to the Treaties, arrangements which are in detail infernally complicated ensure that the UK, Ireland, and Denmark are kept separate from the mainstream of law- and policy-making governing the AFSJ. The UK and Ireland are not bound by, but have an opportunity to opt in to, rules adopted by the majority of the Member States. Denmark's position is if anything even more peculiar—a result, as the current governing Protocol makes plain, of the deal struck in late 1992 to induce the Danes to vote 'yes' in a referendum on the country's ratification of the Maastricht Treaty, and envisaging that matters agreed by the other Member States may bind Denmark but as a matter of international, not EU, law. This, then, is the 'area of freedom, security, and justice', which, as a result of the arrangements made under these Protocols, is an *uneven* area.

On occasion the friction caused by these rough edges between uniformity and opting-out trouble the Court. So, for example, in *UK* v *Council* the UK argued that that a measure dealing with social security rights for nationals of European Free Trade Association (EFTA) States should have been pursued under Article 79 TFEU rather than Article 48 TFEU.[65] This sounds an abstruse matter, but the point underlying the UK's application was that were Article 79 used, its opt-out would be preserved since Article 79 is within Title V, whereas Article 48 simply attracts

[65] Case C-431/11 judgment of 26 September 2013.

the ordinary legislative procedure which offers no special protection for unwilling participants. The Court, which formally excludes the relevance of such background politically sensitive twists and instead seeks to extract the aim and content of the measure, found the matter fitted properly into Article 48, and so the UK's application was dismissed.[66]

Under the Lisbon Treaty transitional arrangements were made to permit the UK to choose to opt out of acts of the Union in the field of police co-operation and judicial co-operation in criminal matters which had been adopted before the entry into force of the Treaty of Lisbon. This transitional opportunity ended on the fifth anniversary of the entry into force of the Lisbon Treaty—1 December 2014. The UK was also able, under this special deal negotiated at Lisbon, selectively to opt back in to those measures which it picked. Given the common nature of so many problems faced, it is hard to imagine that the UK would gain more than it loses by choosing not to enjoy the benefits of collaboration with its neighbours according to the well-established mechanisms; and, moreover and more practically, in any event the *acquis* is not a set of isolated measures but rather a package marked by a high level of interconnection.[67] In the event, after contorted debates, the UK chose to opt out of 133 measures and then to opt back into thirty-five of them,[68] including the European Arrest Warrant, amid chaotic scenes in the House of Commons in November 2014 as the government offered bewildered MPs a vote on some, but not all, of the thirty-five.[69]

5.4.2 The Eurozone

The arrangements that govern the 'Eurozone' are fragmented along two axes. Most Member States participate, but some do not. Moreover, the governing rules are a combination of EU law and laws introduced by way of free-standing international treaties. There are understandable reasons of political expediency and crisis management that explain the chosen model, but it is in many respects an ad hoc design and certainly it is forbiddingly intransparent. Much of the EU's pattern of development is élite-driven, but the Eurozone is more vulnerable than most sectors to the accusation that minimal attempt has been made to inform citizens what is

[66] For a similar context and result see Case C-656/11 *UK* v *Council* judgment of 27 February 2014; Case C-81/13 *UK* v *Council* judgment of 18 December 2014.

[67] A. Hinarejos, J. Spencer, and S. Peers, 'Opting out of EU Criminal Law: What Is Actually Involved?' CELS Working Paper (Cambridge), 2012.

[68] The list is recorded at OJ [2014] C430.

[69] http://www.publications.parliament.uk/pa/cm201415/cmhansrd/cm141110/debtext/141110-0002.htm#column_1223.

being done and why, and still less to seek popular approval for the exercise of public power in politically contested domains. This has been addressed in Chapter 3.9.2 and it is pursued further in Chapter 8. The concern here is the absence of a *unified* pattern to the EU in matters of monetary, economic, and fiscal policy.

The Maastricht Treaty introduced the provisions which set in train the process. Part of the deal was to allocate a special position to the UK and to Denmark, set out in Protocols. Today the UK has a special status in relation to the euro, under a Protocol which begins by recognizing 'that the United Kingdom shall not be obliged or committed to adopt the euro without a separate decision to do so by its government and parliament'. Denmark has a similar, but not identical, protected position, by virtue of another Protocol. Sweden too has a de facto opt-out. The Eurozone, of which nineteen Member States are members, is built on deep and long-term, perhaps permanent, cleavage within the wider EU of twenty-eight. It is an 'Economic Schengen'.[70]

The tortured negotiations that have been conducted since the financial crisis erupted in 2008 have placed yet further pressure on the Union model. The so-called six-pack was followed by the two-pack—a group of Regulations and Directives adopted under the TFEU (Chapter 3.9.2). Within that package there is an obvious sub-division between Member States that are primarily concerned to grant support and Member States that are primarily in receipt of support. However, more structurally ambitious plans were not the subject of support from all the Member States. The UK in particular was opposed to the idea of adopting new Treaty arrangements designed to enhance the EU's competence in the field, while Germany in particular was not content with the adoption of secondary rules of EU law and demanded the security of binding Treaty commitments. The consequence was the establishment of the European Stability Mechanism (ESM), which was achieved by ratifying a free-standing international Treaty which, though formally outwith the EU legal order, was in substance unavoidably entwined with the existing and rather dense thicket of adjacent EU law and which also made use of EU institutions. The UK and the Czech Republic chose not to be party to this Treaty: they simply stood aside. A challenge was brought before Irish courts by a private party to the legality of what had been concocted. A preliminary reference was made to the Court of Justice, seeking its view

[70] N. De Sadeleer, 'The New Architecture of the European Economic Governance: A Leviathan or a Flat-Footed Colossus' (2012) 19 MJ 354, 369.

on whether what was done was compatible with EU law. This is *Pringle*.[71] Among several arguments advanced before the Court, probably the most important was the question as to whether what was envisaged as a set of binding obligations under international law amounted to an unlawful undermining of obligations already undertaken as EU Member States. It did not. The Court found that the design had negotiated a perilously narrow course which allowed it to escape condemnation for interrupting the state of existing obligations undertaken pursuant to EU law. In particular, the Court adopted a shrewdly narrow reading of existing EU competences on monetary policy in order to find they did not bar the Eurozone countries from agreeing the ESM Treaty.

The ruling is of intricately detailed importance to the particular circumstances at stake, and will be pored over by those planning the use of EU institutions outwith the EU legal framework more generally[72]—but, of broader significance, the judgment reads EU competence *narrowly* in order to preclude its influence looming as a shadow that prevents the ESM, whereas, as seen in Chapter 2, the Court typically takes a *broad* view of the scope of EU competence, and often, on inspection of the Treaty texts and structures, justifiably so. The flavour of *Pringle* is judicial receptivity to the extraordinary lengths to which the majority of Member States, responding to economic conflagration, felt impelled to stretch in order to put in place common rules which nevertheless do not reach so far as to cover all twenty-eight Member States.

In a constitutional order committed to the rule of law it cannot be acceptable that the Court should decline to exercise its proper function of review simply because a matter has intense political and economic sensitivity. In this vein *Pringle* has been condemned as based on reasoning that is implausible, even underhand, gifting too much autonomy to hasty political fixes that collide with the fundamentals of the Treaty order.[73] It has, however, been defended as a decision in which the Court's ruling is rooted in sufficiently ambiguous legal material to allow it to be acquitted of the charge of getting it *legally* wrong;[74] and moreover it has been hailed as a pragmatic means to leave space for Member States to reach

[71] Case C-370/12 judgment of 27 November 2012.

[72] S. Peers, 'Towards a New Form of EU Law? The Use of EU Institutions Outside the EU Legal Framework' (2013) 9 European Constitutional Law Review 37.

[73] Eg G. Beck, 'The Court of Justice, the Bundesverfassungsgericht and Legal Reasoning during the Euro Crisis: The Rule of Law as a Fair-Weather Phenomenon' (2014) 20 European Public Law 539; M. Everson, 'An Exercise in Legal Honesty: Rewriting the Court of Justice and the Bundesverfassungsgericht' (2015) 21 ELJ 474.

[74] P. Craig, 'Pringle and the Nature of Legal Reasoning' (2014) 21 MJ 205.

agreements outside the sphere of exclusive EU competence while also asserting the primacy of EU law and the importance of the Court's own supervisory jurisdiction (inter alia in checking that the correct *procedure* for Treaty revision has been used, even if the *content* of a Treaty revision may not be checked).[75] *Pringle* is certainly best *explained* as an instance of the Court wishing to leave room for political engagement with sensitive choices, and probably, given the calculatedly murky character of the Treaty rules on which the Court was asked to base its judgment, it is justified in that light too.

To observe that the development of the Eurozone presents huge political and economic challenges is as banal as it is incendiarily true. The Court so far gives the impression that it wishes to find ways to provide a legal shelter to what emerges from the tortured political negotiation. The several political and economic conundrums have their legal ramifications, and repeated litigation seems probable. A system that involves some Member States but not all will doubtless come under strain, inter alia in so far as the interests of the non-participants come to be prejudiced—as they surely will. A system that draws on more than one legal order—national, EU, and international—will generate boundary disputes and conflicts. Minorities—those States participating in the internal market but not the Eurozone—will need protection, but, as explored in Chapter 8, it may not be feasible to achieve both a workable deepening of common decision-making of a nature that is apt to stabilize and democratize the Eurozone while also protecting those States that simply aspire to participation in an internal market and no more.

Regulation of the financial services sector, where the UK is strong, is an obvious likely point of friction. The Single Supervisory Mechanism serves as a centrepiece of the EU's banking union, ensuring supervision of banks in the Eurozone under a scheme in which the European Central Bank (ECB) is pivotal.[76] It stands as a demonstration of how the 2008 crisis provoked a pressure to centralize supervision of the integrating market, rather than to rely on the distribution of competences between home and host States to enforce harmonized EU rules according to the orthodox model pursued previously under EU Directives. So the friction will arise in so far as the banking union focused on the Eurozone develops in a way that threatens the integrity of the wider internal market for financial services.[77] Cases of

[75] B. De Witte and T. Beukers, 'Annotation' (2013) 50 CMLRev 80.

[76] Reg. 1022/2013 OJ [2013] L287/5; Reg 1024/2013 OJ [2013] L287/63.

[77] N. Moloney, 'European Banking Union: Assessing Its Risks and Resilience' (2014) 51 CMLRev 1609, esp at 1661–9.

this type have already reached the Court. So for example the General Court decided the ECB lacks the competence to lay down location requirements that central counterparties shall be located inside the Eurozone.[78] This is but one example of how the mismatch between the size of the Eurozone and the size of the EU causes problems of institutional and constitutional design, and the political and legal problems seem likely only to deepen as the Eurozone becomes more closely integrated and tightly regulated. States on the outside will doubtless seek to negotiate a system of rules setting priorities or (perhaps more likely *and*) a system of process involving weighted voting protection or even veto, but will be confronted by the disinclination of the core States to make concessions likely to weaken the effectiveness of their own plans.

5.5 ENHANCED CO-OPERATION

All the arrangements so far considered have been more or less ad hoc in nature, either strapped on to the Treaties at times of revision in the face of political disagreements among the Member States that simply cannot be resolved other than by conceding some form of opt-out to minority dissentients or, in the case of the ESM, allowed to emerge alongside, but not within, the EU legal order and involving most but not all of the Member States. In the former case, it seems that whatever harm is done to the uniform face of EU law, there can be no constitutional objection to such opt-outs and opt-ins, provided only that the correct *procedure* for revising the Treaties, now covered by Article 48 TEU, is followed. A long time ago the Court, finding the system of judicial supervision proposed under the draft EEA Agreement to be incompatible with the EEC Treaty (as it then was), went so far as to comment that even an amendment of the Treaty could not cure that incompatibility and thereby offered the tantalizing hint that the Court stands ready to review even the constitutionality of substantive Treaty revision in so far as it might violate the existential character of EU law.[79] But it has never repeated this exorbitant claim, and it seems correct as a matter of Treaty law that if the Member States at times of Treaty revision choose to put in place a staggered system, involving oddly shaped layers of participating States in different sectors, then they may stand accused of distorting the accumulated expectations of uniformity and coherence associated with the EU legal order, but that they are acting as Masters

[78] Case T-496/11 *UK* v *ECB* judgment of 4 March 2015.

[79] Opinion 1/91 on the draft EEA [1991] ECR I-6084 paras 71–72.

of the Treaties and may do so if they so choose. *Pringle* shows that the Court, given the opportunity, will check whether EU law obligations have been violated when Member States strike agreements *outwith* the EU system, but it also suggests a judicial willingness to work quite hard to find reasons to approve such political devices.[80]

The incremental drift away from uniformity is firmly established as part of the EU's evolution, even if it appears to contradict some of the more cherished features and aspirations of the system. What is at stake is much more visible in the most remarkable attempt to locate *within* the Treaty a means to manage these tensions. These are the provisions on enhanced co-operation. Unlike the essentially ad hoc, brutally political arrangements sketched in Section 5.4, enhanced co-operation represents an attempt to put in place a more durable framework for permitting some but not all Member States to deeper their collaborative endeavours and, as part of that, it involves careful enumeration of what EU law will *not* permit when some but not all Member States attempt to forge ahead in a manner antagonistic to the uniformity of the twenty-eight.

In effect, Member States wishing to establish enhanced co-operation between themselves, but without the involvement of all the Member States, are permitted to make use of the EU's institutions and law-making processes. The provisions were introduced by the Treaty of Amsterdam with effect from 1999, and have been lightly amended since. Rigorous criteria must be satisfied before 'enhanced co-operation' is permitted. The governing provisions, which concern controls rooted in both substantive criteria that must be satisfied by enhanced co-operators as well as carefully drawn procedural requirements, are contained in Title IV TEU, *Provisions on Enhanced Co-Operation*, which is Article 20 TEU, and in Title III of Part Six TFEU, *Enhanced Co-Operation*, which contains Articles 326–334 TFEU.

In rough summary, the substantive elements require that enhanced co-operation shall aim to further the objectives of the Union, protect its interests, and reinforce its integration process;[81] it shall not undermine the internal market or economic, social, and territorial cohesion, nor shall it constitute a barrier to or discrimination in trade between Member States, nor shall it distort competition between them;[82] and enhanced co-operation shall respect the competences, rights, and obligations of non-participating Member States.[83] The procedural aspects seek to manage the

[80] Case C-370/12 note 71. [81] Art 20 TEU.
[82] Art 326 TFEU. [83] Art 327 TFEU.

application of these controlling criteria. A Commission proposal pursuant to a request by Member States is required, but it is the Council that authorizes enhanced co-operation, when it has established that the objectives of such co-operation cannot be attained within a reasonable period by the Union as a whole.[84] The consent of the Parliament is also required.[85] At least nine participating Member States are required at the outset, but Article 331 TFEU suggests an expectation of momentum, for it provides for the possibility of a Member State joining in existing enhanced co-operation, albeit that Commission must consider that the conditions of participation have been fulfilled.

Special rules apply to enhanced co-operation in judicial co-operation in criminal matters and in police co-operation pursuant to Chapters 4 and 5 of Title V of the TFEU and to common foreign and security policy. And, by definition, enhanced co-operation in the (small) field of exclusive EU competences is unfeasible.

The symbolic importance of these provisions is profound. They mark a decisive break with the orthodoxy of uniformity, not in a sector-specific context but much more generally.[86] The EU can run at two or many more speeds. But the repugnance of such a prospect to long-standing assumptions is clear from the very high hurdles carefully written into these provisions. Plainly the concern to open up this model of differentiated integration was accompanied, and to some extent exceeded, by deep fear about its potentially disintegrative effect. The direction that enhanced co-operation shall not undermine the internal market or distort competition between Member States appears forbidding, given how broadly these notions are typically understood in substantive EU law. How can common action by some, but not all, Member States do anything other than distort competition? As was noted at the time of their creation, the 'controlling' devices would, if applied with a scrupulously literal eye, seem to block use of these provisions in almost any circumstances.[87] This draws attention to exactly the key tension between allowing co-operative acceleration beyond the speed of the slowest members and controlling the damage done by fragmentation.

[84] Art 20 TEU. [85] Art 329 TFEU.

[86] G. Majone, 'Unity in Diversity: European Integration and the Enlargement Process' (2008) 33 EL Rev 457; D. Thym, 'The Political Character of Supranational Differentiation' (2006) 31 EL Rev 781.

[87] Eg S. Weatherill, '"If I'd wanted you to understand I would have explained it better": What is the Purpose of the Provisions on Closer Co-operation introduced by the Treaty of Amsterdam?' in D. O'Keeffe and P. Twomey (eds), *Legal Issues of the Amsterdam Treaty* (Hart, 1999).

The provisions on enhanced co-operation have so far been little used. It was as late as 2010, over a decade after their insertion into the Treaties, before they were first formally invoked. The product was Decision 2010/405, which, with delicious appropriateness, authorized enhanced co-operation in the law applicable to divorce.[88] Then Decision 2011/167 authorized enhanced co-operation in the creation of unitary patent protection.[89] In all, fourteen Member States requested the former and twenty-five the latter. Plainly the impact of enhanced co-operation is not to be judged merely by counting the small number of times it has been triggered. It is at least plausible, though hard to measure with certainty, that Member States uneasy about a particular legislative initiative might have engaged in compromise precisely because they knew that if they simply doggedly remained opposed the matter might have been pushed forward through the medium of enhanced co-operation: that is, the availability of enhanced co-operation may have loosened resistance to use of the 'normal' EU legislative route. But so far enhanced co-operation seems more interesting on paper than in practice.

It is however striking that both Decisions so far adopted offer only brief explanation of how and why the apparently strict Treaty pre-conditions are met. One might, for example, suppose that the creation of unitary patent protection by some, but not all, Member States would inevitably destabilize and re-direct existing patterns of and demand for patent protection in the EU, but Decision 2011/167 simply asserts that the Treaty pre-conditions are satisfied, adding blandly that the creation of unitary patent protection on the territories of the participating Member States does not affect the availability or the conditions of patent protection on the territories of non-participants.[90]

This was tested before the Court. Spain and Italy, the only two Member States which had not joined in requesting the Commission to propose this venture into enhanced co-operation, challenged the Council's authorization Decision. They failed.[91] The Court found the matter, concerning intellectual property rights within Article 118, to be a shared competence which is open in principle to enhanced co-operation. This is entirely unsurprising. It added that the Council's view that this instance of enhanced co-operation was, as the Treaty requires, a last resort would not be set aside. This too is no surprise, for this is at heart a political assessment that is scarcely apt for judicial contradiction. The judgment

[88] OJ [2010] L189/2. [89] OJ [2011] L76/53. [90] Recitals 13, 14.

[91] Joined Cases C-274/11 and C-295/11 *Spain and Italy* v *Council* judgment of 16 April 2013.

then found no damage to uniformity, to the internal market, or to cohesion in the EU, in short because by definition the co-operation occurred within the bloc of participating States only. That, for the Court, is the very nature of enhanced co-operation—that it does not involve all Member States. One might plausibly argue that the impact of enhanced co-operation must be felt at least indirectly by non-participants, for example because of the likely alteration in the attraction of the legal regime available in the participating States relative to that which exists in the non-participating jurisdictions, and that accordingly the operation of the internal market is disrupted, but any such suggestion is absent from the Court's rather superficial and fundamentally permissive analysis. Under the Court's chosen approach, the political decision to pursue enhanced co-operation will rarely, if ever, be constitutionally vulnerable to claims that it violates the Treaty pre-conditions pertaining to the integrity of the internal market.

This chosen approach feels very similar to the Court's artfully reticent attitude to subsidiarity review.[92] It also has a common feel when placed alongside the *Pringle* judgment, which adopts a narrow reading of existing EU competences on monetary policy in order to find they do not bar the Eurozone countries from agreeing the ESM Treaty.[93] The thematically common thread is judicial disinclination to cut across majoritarian political preferences. This means in turn that the minority is pushed to find political, not legal, protection for any anxieties. The consequence of the Court's chosen approach is that whether to invoke enhanced co-operation is largely a political choice and little constrained by constitutional controls. It could be that what will really count is that an objecting minority of Member States knows that resort by the majority to enhanced co-operation is constitutionally plausible and unlikely to be tripped up judicial intervention, with the consequence that the minority objectors might feel their best bet is to seek legislative compromise among all twenty-eight Member States rather than watch powerless from the sidelines as splinter groups of enhanced co-operators spin off. That is, the Court, having offered a generous interpretation of the permitted scope of enhanced co-operation, may in fact have provoked its diminished use, which in turn will help to maintain the integrity of the EU as a bloc of twenty-eight participants. Probably, though, a sober sector-specific appreciation of the future possibilities is required.

[92] Case C-491/01 note 28 paras 177–185; Chapter 2.11.4.

[93] Case C-370/12 note 71.

5.6 DIFFERENTIATED OR VARIABLE INTEGRATION MORE BROADLY

Some highly insightful commentators have pressed the case for a much warmer embrace of the potential of differentiated or variable integration within the EU. After all, the point is not simply that it is politically awkward to find models that suit all twenty-eight Member States across the wide geographical and functional terrain on which the EU acts; it is that this may well be in any event thoroughly unwise. To release some degree of diversity may offer greater scope for reflecting local preference and particularity. It may make policy-making more agile and targeted.

Jean-Claude Piris has advocated embrace of a two-speed EU, whereby a group of States would press ahead with deepened common policies and activities while the others could join as and when they were willing and/or able.[94] This is not a new notion—and indeed part of Piris's argument is that this is happening already—but he wishes to argue that it *should* be more fully accepted as normatively desirable. It is of pressing topicality, given the rupture already made by the rise of the euro, the need for action to preserve it, and, more broadly, the sense of popular alienation from the EU.

Giandomenico Majone has argued for increased capacity to reflect and pursue differentiation in policy formulation and execution. He advances the idea of 'clubs', which would be joined by States with similar needs and preferences in particular areas.[95]

There is much value in such vigorous prescription, and in fact it is a rough-and-ready description of some of what is already happening in the EU. Such models might add energy and purpose to policy formation and development. But they also make the very concept of the EU still more tangled and intransparent. Piris hopes his model will offer a more 'coherent' scheme, attractive to citizens.[96] This is optimistic. Moreover, it must be admitted that the practical obstacles to radically innovative adaptation, however attractive the plans, are, as these authors are aware, formidably high. Writing on a blank sheet of paper (or computer screen) is a luxury unavailable to those directly engaged in imagining the EU's future: the EU is to a significant extent locked into existing patterns which can be overturned only by the assembly of a dauntingly high level of consensus

[94] J.-C. Piris, *The Future of Europe: Towards a Two-Speed EU?* (CUP, 2012).
[95] G. Majone, *Europe As the Would-Be World Power: The EU at Fifty* (CUP, 2009), esp Ch 8.
[96] Pages 103, 120.

among the EU institutions and the Member States. The hesitancy associated with enhanced co-operation is a strong pointer to the obstacles. Both its design in the Treaty and its use in practice reveal controlling instinct and caution. There are very high transaction costs to be incurred in seeking radical change. Something similar can be said of subsidiarity. It correctly encourages that attention be paid to choosing the level of governance, but it is apt to call into question pre-existing choices only if a heap of legal and political cards happen to fall into line. This confines its transformative vitality,[97] and much the same must be said (with regret, even dismay) about the feasibility of prescriptions towards the more radical end of attempts to strip away or at least diminish the strength of assumptions about the EU's need for geographical and functional uniformity. Ad hoc opting-out tends to form the line of least resistance in brokering the resolution of political deadlocks and therefore it tends to emerge as the most common form of flight from uniformity in the EU. However, the development of the Eurozone, and especially the rise of a nascent European economic government to which not all Member States wish to commit, is most likely to test (further) the adhesiveness of common institutional structures and common policy-making (Chapter 8).

5.7 CONCLUSION

It should be clear from this chapter that the grinding process of achieving tortured political compromise means that the EU legal order today is far from uniform, and there is no purity of vision about what is and should be accommodated as legitimate, as opposed to unacceptably opportunistic differentiation. In this sense the EU's 'unity in diversity' has not been shaped according to any sophisticated blueprint and, as this chapter has made clear, it takes many forms. Writing in 1984, Claus-Dieter Ehlermann uncovered a number of instances in which what was then Community law accommodated diversity by offering particular Member States special treatment.[98] His prescription was that economic and social differences could in principle justify differentiation, but that purely political phenomena could not. So, he argued, British (governmental or political) opposition to joining the European monetary system would not be a valid argument for differentiation, whereas showing that the British pound was

[97] E. Carbonara, B. Luppi, and F. Parisi, 'Self-Defeating Subsidiarity' (2009) 5 Review of Law and Economics 742.

[98] 'How Flexible is Community Law? An Unusual Approach to the Concept of "Two Speeds"' (1984) 82 Michigan Law Rev 1274.

in a special position compared with other currencies would be a basis for extending a derogation in favour of the UK.[99] The picture today is a lot messier than that.

Maastricht was the Treaty which brought the matter to the surface. That the decline of uniformity in application of EU law should become most visible at the same time as the principle of subsidiarity entered the lexicon as a generally applicable legal rule is no coincidence. What was at stake was a sense of anxiety about the deepening and broadening and centralizing impact of EU law: what was sought, falteringly and uncertainly, was some means to balance the competing concern for national diversity and autonomy.

Deirdre Curtin, surveying the agreement that became the Maastricht Treaty, offered a famously withering critique.[100] She lamented the intransparency of the process, the concessions made 'capriciously' by national executives acting collectively to special interest group pressure, and the exclusion of the individuals who are supposed to give EU law its special character. She found the three-pillar structure a denial of a coherent overall plan, and she attacked the abandonment in the uniformity of application of EU law as a result of the Danish second-home protocol, the so-called 'Barber protocol', the Irish abortion protocol, and also the Social Policy Agreement. So: 'It must be said, at the heart of all this chaos and fragmentation, the unique *sui generis* nature of the European Community, its true world historical significance, is being destroyed.'[101]

We should not wearily conclude that that was then and this is now—that the battle is lost. Plainly geographical and functional expansion in the EU is an explanation for many departures from uniformity, but that cannot of itself serve as a completely satisfying justification for all the practices collected together for examination in this chapter. Similarly, it cannot satisfy simply to observe that unleashing heterogeneity in the EU is the way to avoid deadlock (or even to induce Member States not to take their problem-solving outwith the EU system). Something clearly is lost when the EU abandons a common stance and the question is whether the price is worth paying, not simply to shrug it off as a sunk cost.

What sort of 'Union' scatters rights and freedoms in an uneven manner? One answer is—any sort of Union that leaves room for expression of local autonomy. So the question is how much uniformity should be beyond

[99] Page 1289.

[100] D. Curtin, 'The Constitutional Structure of the Union: A Europe of Bits and Pieces' (1993) 30 CMLRev 17.

[101] Page 67.

negotiation in the EU—if there is a core value of uniformity, in what areas does it run? This demands a case-by-case reflection. Allowing flexibility in the treatment of the hours of workers on board seagoing fishing vessels[102] is scarcely comparable with the existence of a Charter of Fundamental Rights from which two States have extracted a (partial and oddly written) opt-out[103] or with the existence of an AFSJ that has differently constituted freedom, security, and justice depending on which Member State one inspects. It would strain credibility to imagine that the bloc of twenty-eight States is optimal for all areas of policy-making: it would strain credibility at least as much to suppose that the EU system can survive an uncontrolled pick-and-mix approach to policy-making. It is for these reasons that enhanced co-operation exists but also has safeguards for those States choosing not to join and opportunities guaranteed to join at a later date. The ESM is at one level a quite different set of arrangements and in formal terms it is not EU law at all, but there are similarities in the explicit and implied constraints which the Court attached to the deployment of extra-EU arrangements in its *Pringle* judgment. Here too the position of non-participants, both pre- and post-establishment of the new system, has to be addressed. This chapter shows there is no simple broadly applicable model and the fragmentation of the scope of application of EU law is to an extent an ad hoc process, but there are some common themes of this nature.

The EU's legal order was in truth never as uniform as some of the early clarion calls insisted.[104] However, it has today become formidably complex and immensely varied. So it has been calculated that, looking across patterns of 'instrumental differentiation', largely driven by temporary sensitivities about the consequences of the widening of the EU's geographical scope, and 'constitutional differentiation', built on permanent expression of scepticism about deepening the EU's functional reach—and factoring in policy area, timeline, and identification of which Member States are involved—there were in 2012 a grand total of 194 distinct forms of differentiation that can be isolated, 82 of them the result of Treaty revision, 112 of them consequent on accession.[105] This depicts a remarkably loose and contingent set of arrangements, not at all consistent with any sense of uniform central authority.[106]

102 Art 21 Dir 2003/88 note 55.

103 Chapter 4.8.2.

104 Ehlermann note 10; R. Bieber, 'On the Mutual Completion of Overlapping Legal Systems: the Case of the European Communities and the National Legal Orders' (1988) 13 EL Rev 147.

105 F. Schimmelfennig and T. Winzen, 'Instrumental and Constitutional Differentiation in the European Union' (2014) 52 JCMS 354.

106 Cf J. Zielonka, *Europe as Empire: The Nature of the Enlarged European Union* (OUP, 2007).

Article 4(2) TEU is referred to elsewhere in this book as a pivotal provision[107] and it deserves to close this chapter's interrogation of the growth of differentiation and variation. National identity, for which Article 4(2) commands respect, is a value, but so is uniformity. Finding a way to balance the competing concerns needs to be addressed in an iterative manner, sector by sector, without any expectation that a magic formula exists apt to resolve disputes. In this sense this chapter's interrogation of the tension between uniformity and diversity has much in common with Chapter 2's discussion of the scope of EU competence and of State autonomy under the competing pressures of effectiveness and control, an animating theme also plain in the institutional inquiry conducted in Chapter 3.

[107] Chapters 4.13, 6.3.4.

6

WHAT IS THE EU'S INTERNAL MARKET?

6.1 THE AMBIGUITIES OF INTERNAL MARKET LAW

Article 3(3) TEU commits the Union to the establishment of an *internal market*. The internal market is defined in Article 26(2) TFEU as an 'area without internal frontiers in which the free movement of goods, persons, services and capital is ensured in accordance with the provisions of this Treaty'. In economic terms the territory occupied by the twenty-eight Member States of the EU shall be a single space.

In principle it is easy to provide a broad summary of the scope of internal market law. Article 28 TFEU provides that the EU comprises a customs union. Customs duties on imports and exports between Member States are prohibited between Member States by Articles 28 and 30 TFEU. Article 100 TFEU forbids discriminatory systems of internal taxation. State A cannot tax wine or beer produced on its own territory at a lower rate than wine or beer imported from State B. In these areas litigation today is very infrequent. This, however, cannot be said of the core Treaty provisions dealing with free movement between the Member States of goods, persons, services, and capital. The free movement of goods is addressed by Articles 34–36 TFEU; the free movement of workers by Articles 45–48 TFEU; the right of establishment, comprising rights for the self-employed and for companies, by Articles 49–55 TFEU; the free movement of services by Articles 56–62 TFEU; and the free movement of capital, its significance today reduced by the rise of monetary union in the Eurozone, by Articles 63–66 TFEU. Each provision is worded differently in its detail but each follows a similar model of a basic prohibition against obstacles to inter-State trade supplemented by permitted scope for justifying such choices. And each, written with striking economy, has been the subject of important elaboration by the Court in the vast number of cases which have reached it seeking interpretative assistance on the nature, purpose, and scope of EU free movement law. Something similar can be said of Articles 101 and 102 TFEU, the Treaty provisions on competition law, which supplement the free movement rules which are largely (though not entirely) concerned with the actions of public authorities, by ensuring supervision also of the actions of private parties which may harm the internal market. Article 101 addresses bilateral and multilateral activities (cartels and restrictive practices), while Article 102 prohibits abuse of a position of economic dominance by a single firm. Both are explicitly tied to the internal market. Article 101 targets practices which are 'prohibited as incompatible with the internal market'; Article 102 forbids abuse of a dominant position 'as incompatible with the internal market in so far as it may affect trade between Member States'. Article 107 uses that same phrase 'incompatible with the internal market' in asserting a control over aid granted by a Member State. And the final landmark on the map of the internal market is the legislative contribution provided by the EU's political institutions, of which by far the most conspicuous element is the competence to adopt harmonized rules to replace divergent national measures which restrict inter-State trade and therefore fragment the internal market along national lines. This is the preserve of Article 114 TFEU.

Taken together, the provisions comprise a formidable set of legal rules which restrain action that is hostile to the creation and maintenance of an internal market stretching across the territory of all twenty-eight Member States. The core idea is that markets should not be artificially partitioned along national lines. Moreover, apart from the necessary numerical adaptation, these provisions have survived essentially unscathed since the 1950s. The law of the internal market has deep roots and, unlike so many of the detailed institutional and legislative rules governing the EU's expanding activities, it has not been tinkered with at times of periodic Treaty revision.

In *FA Premier League* et al v *QC Leisure* et al, *Karen Murphy* v *Media Protection Services Ltd*, the Court stated that completion of the internal market is 'the fundamental aim of the Treaty'.[1] This is not true. The project of economic integration is and always has been prominent among the EU's endeavours and much of the TFEU's detailed content is composed of legal rules aimed at securing the integration of markets, but constitutionally it is not and never has been the paramount concern. The original Treaty of Rome declared in Article 2 EEC that the Community (as it then was) would use the *means* of establishing a common market and progressive approximation of economic policies to achieve wider political *ends*, including an increase in stability, an accelerated raising of the standard of living, and close relations between the Member States. This was not altered by the Single European Act (SEA), which with effect from 1987 first introduced the concept of the 'internal market', which has since the

[1] Joined Cases C-403/08 and C-429/08 *FA Premier League* et al v *QC Leisure* et al, *Karen Murphy* v *Media Protection Services Ltd* judgment of 4 October 2011 para. 115.

entry into force of the Lisbon Treaty in 2009 completely superseded the now abandoned notion of a 'common market'. Economic integration was the route chosen in the 1950s by the founders of the system to promote interdependence among participating States: it was the concrete project on which agreement could be readily reached in order to grant initial momentum to the process. But the deeper purpose was to use that process as a vehicle for increasing interdependence—'ever closer Union', as the Treaty Preamble stated and still states. Over time the material at the beginning of the Treaties has been padded and, especially as a result of the Lisbon Treaty, reorganized. The simplicity of Article 2 EEC has been lost. But it remains clear that economic integration, and the project of creating an internal market for the EU, is only one element in the EU's endeavours. Article 3(3) TEU today directs that the Union shall establish an internal market, but this is located *beneath* Article 3(1) TEU, which identifies the EU's aim as to promote peace, its values (as listed in Article 2 TEU), and the well-being of its peoples.

And yet the economic dimension of the project has a high profile. As a simple empirical observation, market integration has always been central to the EU's motivation, and melding a more competitive EU market out of the pattern of previously fragmented national markets has always fuelled the EU's claim to legitimacy: economic prosperity is what it claims to deliver more effectively and sustainably than can its Member States acting without the support of the EU's rules. In the 1980s, as the EU groaned sluggishly in search of new momentum, it was economic integration that came to the rescue. The plan unveiled in the 1985 White Paper on *Completing the Internal Market* was designed to re-energize the original vision and to complete the single or internal market by the end of 1992.[2] In an echo of the 1950s, economic aims had been placed at the forefront of a deeper political ambition: the project to complete the internal market was strongly motivated by an attempt to wrench not simply the EU's economy but the EU itself out of the sclerotic condition into which it had sunk. The constitutional adaptation required to achieve this surge, especially the rise of qualified majority voting to replace unanimity in Council, was pressing enough to generate the first major formal revision of the Treaties, the SEA, which entered into force in 1987. For States emerging from military dictatorship, most prominently Greece, Spain, and Portugal, embedding nascent democracy was the major reason for joining the EU, but economic growth was an ambition too. Indeed, in an echo of the 'means to an end'

[2] COM (85) 310.

thinking of the 1950s, economic success could fend off any risk of slippage away from democratic commitments. Moreover, after the collapse of the Soviet Union in 1989 and the re-emergence of true 'Europe' the EU was a site for democratic renewal and for protection from the Russian bear, but it was also the stimulus to reform of economies suffering from inflexible centralized planning. As the wider political ambitions pursued through the EU have become ever more contested and as it has become plain that there is no automaticity in deepened common action, but rather a frequent need for bold political leadership and concrete Treaty revision, the project of creating an internal market has remained a site of relatively reassuring consensus. So, if one confines review to the descriptive without paying scrupulous attention to the Treaty, the Court was not so far wrong in stating that completion of the internal market is 'the fundamental aim of the Treaty'.[3] It exposes a certain truth—that in practice much of the EU's activity has been dedicated to the achievement of economic integration among the Member States.

The internal market continues to serve as one of the EU's best claims to have transformed the relationship between the States of Europe. Securing the free movement of goods, persons, services, and capital between Member States should, as a matter of economic theory, generate an intensification of competition, the release of economies of scale, and patterns of industrial restructuring stimulated by achievement of comparative advantage, thereby causing improvements in quality of goods and services and a reduction in price. Trade should no longer be distorted by the chance fact of crossing a political border. Ultimately the consumer should win. Lawyers are not trained to provide deep critical appraisal of these assumptions, and must take some of these virtuous claims on trust, while certainly remaining open to more critical concerns about, for example, the potential disregard for sustainable growth that may flow from this economic energy. As a minimum, however, lawyers should be able to reflect on whether legal rules are designed and interpreted in order to meet the economic expectations underpinning the internal project.

The construction of the EU's internal market remains a dynamic project. In 2002 the Commission declared that it will never be 'completed' and that 'The effort to maximise its performance is a process, not an event.'[4] In 2007 it added that 'The single market is evolving, it will never be finalised', and reminded that it is 'a means; it is not an end'.[5] The internal

[3] Joined Cases C-403/08 and C-429/08 note 1.

[4] Commission's Internal Market Scoreboard No 11, 11 November 2002.

[5] A Single Market for Citizens, the interim report to the Spring 2007 European Council, COM (2007) 60, February 2007, pp 3, 10.

market is not 'complete' in any absolute sense. Some sectors, such as those for most manufactured goods, are much more intensively integrated than others, such as the services sector. In part this is because a great deal of the practical management of the internal market depends on administrative co-operation between agencies charged with the regulation of the market across the territory of the twenty-eight Member States, and the required dense networks of co-operation cannot be invented or wished into existence from above, but rather will take a great deal time to evolve, within the frameworks set by EU law. But the dynamic nature of the internal market is also explained by its legally *ambiguous* character.

There are two principal ambiguities at the heart of the internal market, and they provide the thematic frame for this chapter. The first concerns the reach of intervention into the practices of public and private actors—what is subject to review in the name of the internal market? This is a vertical issue: it concerns the extent to which the EU exercises control over the exercise of autonomy within the Member States. It involves defining the scope of application of the so-called 'negative law' provisions of the Treaty, those that prohibit practices hostile to the construction of an internal market, most prominent among them those pertaining to free movement and competition. It also involves defining the permitted scope of the legislative competence to harmonize (and other competences). This is 'positive law', where the EU sets its own common rules rather than simply controlling rule-making at national level. It does not follow that the creation of an internal market requires bland homogeneity. This is plain from a glance at the UK or Germany or the US, which are all 'internal markets' with plenty of local regulatory diversity. But it does entail that a threshold must exist above which local regulatory diversity becomes a problem in the construction of the internal market. The second ambiguity asks how, in circumstances where the threshold is crossed and Member State autonomy is accordingly subjected to review in the name of EU internal market law, it is decided whether the Court resolves the matter (and how) or instead whether the matter falls for legislative treatment (and how). This is a horizontal issue: it goes to the relationship between the EU's judicial and political institutions. An obstacle to inter-State trade could be treated as unjustified after inspection by a court, in which case it may not be applied to obstruct imports; or such an obstacle could be treated as justified after judicial inspection, on the basis that it serves a regulatory objective which is more important than economic integration, with the consequence that it can be eliminated only by the adoption of EU legislative rules which put in place a common regime for the whole of the EU's internal market within which the regulatory objectives pursued in diverse ways at Member State level can be advanced (in common) by the EU itself. The space allowed for justification of national practices is here central. The more eagerly the Court refuses to find a justification for national practices, the greater the reduction in national regulatory autonomy and the less space is left for legislative intervention. By contrast, where national practices are found to be justified, attention turns to legislative action as the means to convert an economic space fragmented by diverse national regulatory choices into an internal market—which in turns makes demands of the regulatory priorities and techniques favoured by the EU law-maker.

The legal framework of the internal market *found in the Treaty* is now essentially static, but there are many open and dynamic questions about its interpretation and application. Most of all, although the internal market is defined in Article 26(2) TFEU as an 'area without internal frontiers in which the free movement of goods, persons, services and capital is ensured in accordance with the provisions of this Treaty', that definition does not commit to any particular combination of the deregulatory impetus achieved through judicially applied negative law and the re-regulatory dynamic provided by politically generated positive law. The true nature of the EU 'internal market' is not spelled out by the Treaty and has instead emerged over time under the combined and dynamic influence of legislative action and the Court's case law. To re-assert the two ambiguities sketched above and developed below, it is necessary to determine the location of the threshold at which State regulatory choices become 'an internal market problem' (Section 6.2); it is then necessary to determine whether, provided they cross the threshold, they are justified despite their obstructive effect on inter-State trade (Section 6.3); and then, under an appreciation that if they *are* justified then attention turns to their removal and replacement through the adoption of EU-level legislation, it is necessary to address the scope and content of such re-regulatory initiatives (Section 6.4). The choices made at each stage determine the shape of the internal market, but they are not unambiguously settled by the Treaties. The purpose of this chapter is to reveal the EU's internal market as a contested concept.

6.2 THE SCOPE OF INTERNAL MARKET LAW

The concept of the 'internal market' both *empowers* and *limits* the EU. The several Treaty provisions which make up the pattern of negative law and positive law are driven by pursuit of the internal market: this is the empowering dimension of the internal market. But there must be limits too: this follows from the principle of conferral set out in Article 5 TEU, which was examined in Chapter 2. The limits are reached where national practices do not affect the project of creating an internal market in the EU. At this point national regulatory autonomy reigns. The problem, however, is that the internal market has a very broad reach—its empowering function is much more conspicuous than its limiting function—and it is hard to identify precisely where its influence stops.

There are three distinct issues that require investigation. First, the internal *market*; second, the *internal* market; third, the personal scope of the provision. In each instance the issue is that there are limits—but that they are broadly drawn, sometimes ambiguous, and sometimes frankly hard to treat as wholly rational. And although the same *questions* arise in connection with each of the freedoms and, in modified guise, in connection with competition law too, the same *answers* have not always been provided by the Court. There is a law of the internal market, but it is neither smooth-edged nor homogenous. This is an extra element to its ambiguous character.

6.2.1 *The internal* market

The pursuit of an internal market assumes there is a 'market' element to the national provision under challenge. Absent any such necessary economic dimension, the matter escapes the scope of application of EU law. The 'market' is not defined by the Treaties, but clearly it is broad in its reach. All sectors are in principle covered. So, for example, the notion of 'goods' covers waste.[6] After all, disposing of waste has a price and so any restriction on its cross-border movement interferes with commercial activity. The concept of 'worker' protected by Article 45 TFEU has an autonomous meaning specific to EU law and, moreover, given its role in defining the scope of a fundamental freedom it is interpreted broadly.[7] Pursuant to a similar thematically broad interpretation, 'services' cover not only those purchased directly but may also cover those for which the user does not make direct payment, so that medical treatment provided by a hospital is a 'service' within the meaning of the law of the internal market where it is funded by sickness insurance schemes.[8] In competition law the 'undertaking' to which Articles 101 and 102 are addressed is any entity that is engaged in an economic activity, regardless of its legal

[6] Eg Case C-2/90 *Commission* v *Belgium* [1992] ECR I-4431.

[7] Eg Case 66/85 *Lawrie-Blum* [1986] ECR 2121; Case C-413/01 *Ninni-Orasche* [2003] ECR I-13187; Case C-507/12 *Saint Prix* judgment of 19 June 2014.

[8] Eg Case C-157/99 *Smits and Peerbooms* [2001] ECR 5473.

status or the way in which it is financed.[9] So, for example, the Court in *Wouters* treated rules of the Dutch Bar prohibiting multi-disciplinary partnerships as within the scope of the competition rules on the basis that members of the Bar provide services for a fee while bearing the financial risks attaching to the performance of those activities, and that the Bar itself was acting as the regulatory body of a profession, the practice of which constitutes an economic activity.[10] The Court's finding was not affected by the 'complexity and technical nature of the services they provide and the fact that the practice of their profession is regulated',[11] a view which corresponded to that already adopted in relation to medical practitioners.[12] The point is not that national practices of this type are inevitably incompatible with EU law: rather the point is that they must be justified according to the standards recognized by EU law (Section 6.3).

In fact it took a revealingly long time for cases to reach the Court in which there was any serious doubt about the existence of an economic context, and the cases that have arisen are rare and ad hoc. The small group of exceptions, where EU law is found *not* to apply, tend to emphasize the force of the general rule that it normally does.

In *SPUC* v *Grogan* action was taken pursuant to highly restrictive Irish laws to prevent students' unions in Dublin from providing information about abortion services available in London.[13] The Court refused to allow the Irish intervention to be tested against the rules governing the free movement of services because the students' union involved had no commercial motivation in providing the information. The fragility of this protection afforded to the Irish regime is plain when one appreciates that had the students' union accepted even a token payment by a clinic in London in return for providing the information in Dublin, then the Court would have been denied its escape route. *Marc Michel Josemans* v *Burgemeester van Maastricht* addressed the licensing of 'coffee shops' in Maastricht, where only fourteen are allowed and they are restricted to residents.[14] The rule's aim was to restrict 'drug tourism', but in doing so it impeded inter-State trade (in drugs and in drug tourists).

[9] Eg Case C-41/90 *Höfner and Elser* [1991] ECR I-1979; Case C-205/03P *FENIN* v *Commission* [2006] ECR I-6295; Case C-327/12 *Ministero dello Sviluppo economic* v *SOA* judgment of 12 December 2013.

[10] Case C-309/99 *Wouters* [2002] ECR I-1577.

[11] Para 49.

[12] Joined Cases C-180/98 to C-184/98 *Pavlov and Others* [2000] ECR I-6451.

[13] Case C-159/90 [1991] ECR I-4685. See Chapter 2.6.

[14] Case C-137/09 [2010] ECR I-13019.

The Court denied that there was any lawful trade in such products, so the free movement and non-discrimination provisions of the Treaty simply did not apply—a finding which borders on the absurd given that the rule had been enacted precisely because there was a lot of such (tolerated) trade in soft drugs. Both rulings suggest a Court eager to find a convenient way to evade adjudicating a thoroughly awkward collision between cross-border commercial freedom and local social and moral choices: but neither ruling asserts any *principled* basis for the excavation of space for national regulatory autonomy unaffected by internal market law. The internal market gets *almost* everywhere. Similarly, activities which fall within the exercise of public powers which are not of an economic nature escape the application of the Treaty rules of competition, so that the Court treated Eurocontrol's function to establish and collect charges levied on users of air navigation services in accordance with an international agreement as connected with the exercise of powers relating to the control and supervision of air space which are typically those of a public authority, and so they were not of an economic nature such as to fall within the competition rules.[15] So too the Court has been willing to treat the management of the public social security system as an activity which does not belong to the sphere of economic activity.[16] But such cases are unusual.

It is normally a low threshold to insist that EU economic law applies only where there is an internal *market* element. Just occasionally the limits to the reach of internal market break the surface of the case law, but these rarities tend to highlight rather than contradict the claim that EU internal market law is extraordinarily broad—that it is more empowering than limiting. So regulatory autonomy practised within the Member States is respected in principle, but not reliably in practice.

And, as explored in Chapter 2.8, the matter is taken further by the point that the free movement and competition provisions are not confined in their scope of application by the limits of the Union's legislative competence. There is no protection for national regulatory autonomy where its exercise contradicts the demands of the internal market, even if the EU is disabled (in part or completely) from intervening through a *legislative* act. So, to remind us of a decision examined in Chapter 2.8, in *Watts* the Court subjected restrictions on the cross-border provision of medical care to inspection and demanded that they be justified, while

[15] Case C-364/92 *SAT* v *Eurocontrol* [1994] ECR I-43; Case C-113/07P *SELEX Sistemi* [2009] ECR I-2207.

[16] Eg Joined Cases C-159/91, C-160/91 *Poucet and Pistre* [1993] ECR I-637.

acknowledging that the EU lacks the legislative competence under the Treaty to assert any role in replacing the Member States as the principal source of decision-making on the organization and financing of their systems of social welfare.[17] This has in turn demanded that the Court become rather creative in filling out the content of the justification that determines whether the national practice passes the test set by internal market law, given that by definition the Treaty is deficient in clear articulation of policy in such areas where the EU's legislative competence is thin or non-existent. The point is structural—the Treaty itself does not place particular sectors of economic activity beyond the reach of its basic rules, so there is little scope for arguing that EU law does not apply *at all*. The power of the market as a means to confer competence on the EU—a negative sort of competence, reaching beyond positive legislative competence—is here vividly seen.

6.2.2 The internal *market*

There must be a cross-border element: a situation that is 'purely internal' to a single Member State falls outwith the scope of the rules of the internal market. Article 34's purpose 'is to eliminate obstacles to the importation of goods and not to ensure that goods of national origin always enjoy the same treatment as imported or reimported goods'.[18] For workers too, the Treaty rules governing freedom of movement cannot be applied to cases in which all elements are purely internal to a single Member State. In *Hans Moser* v *Land Baden-Württemberg*, Moser had been refused access to post-graduate training required for entry to the teaching profession because of his membership of the German Communist Party.[19] He claimed that he might in future wish to work in another Member State, but the Court found this to be a claim based on a 'purely hypothetical prospect of employment in another Member State'.[20] Otherwise put, the matter had no adequate connection with cross-border activity. Any discrimination fell to be tackled under German law, if necessarily supplemented by the European Convention on Human Rights. Competition law is in similar vein confined to practices which exert an effect on inter-State trade patterns.

The story of the *internal* market has similarities with that told in Section 6.2.1 of the internal *market*: there are limits in principle and on relatively rare occasions they loom into view in case law of the type mentioned in

[17] Case C-372/04 [2006] ECR I-4325.
[18] Case 355/85 *Michel Cognet* [1986] ECR 3231 para 10.
[19] Case 180/83 [1984] ECR 2539. [20] Para 18.

the previous paragraph, but in practice the threshold to trigger the application of EU internal market law is crossed a good deal more readily than one would initially suppose. In part this is because it is perfectly logical that the process of eliminating the economic significance of national frontiers should reduce matters that are of truly local significance alone. But more so it is because the Court does not limit the scope of internal market law to a requirement that a host State treat imports in the same way as it treats domestic goods, people, and services. Instead it focuses on the *effect* of national measures.

Article 34 TFEU, the provision of central importance in the law governing goods, states that 'Quantitative restrictions on imports and all measures having equivalent effect shall be prohibited between Member States.' This is absolutely typical of the spare style in which all the relevant free movement provisions are written, and it delegates wide interpretative autonomy to the Court. Of enduring thematic significance, the Court in *Dassonville* chose to emphasize the *effect* of the national measure on the market, not its form. The Court brought 'all trading rules enacted by Member States which are capable of hindering, directly or indirectly, actually or potentially, intra-Community trade' within the scope of Article 34 TFEU.[21] The significance of this so-called '*Dassonville* formula' is best appreciated as a calculated wrench away from a mere anti-discrimination norm. It was and remains a major choice with immense implications for the shape of the internal market.

The next big step was the application of the law governing the free movement of goods to national technical standards even in the absence of any explicit reference on the face of such measures to the origin of goods. This was when the Court's interpretative choice as a surge beyond anti-discrimination became glittering. This was the ruling in the famous 'Cassis de Dijon' case—more properly, *Rewe-Zentrale AG* v *Bundesmonopolverwaltung für Branntwein*.[22]

The litigation involved Cassis de Dijon, a blackcurrant fruit liqueur made in France with an alcohol content of between 15 and 20 per cent. It could not be sold in Germany because it did not comply with German law, which required that such products should have a minimum alcohol content of 25 per cent. The case would have been entirely straightforward had Germany applied a different standard to French-made products than it applied to products made in Germany: practices that discriminate against imports are obviously an obstruction to the completion of the

[21] Case 8/74 [1974] ECR 837.

[22] Case 120/78 [1979] ECR 649.

internal market.[23] But Germany did not target its rules against imports at all. A German-made product with the same relatively low level of alcohol as the French-made product would equally have been excluded from the German market. The problem here was simply that German product standards were *different* from French standards. And the consequence was an obstacle to the free movement of goods and the fragmentation of the internal market along national lines. Diversity between national technical rules has the effect of impeding inter-State trade.

The German rules, treated as antagonistic to the creation of an internal market, could survive only if they could be shown to be justified. But they were not justified, principally because the Court could simply not accept that consumers needed protection from an admittedly unfamiliar product through the imposition of a prohibition on liqueurs that were made according to a slightly different recipe. Germany created a delight for the ages when it tried to claim that suppressing weak, but not strong, alcoholic drinks was a sensible regulatory choice designed to avoid consumers being lured down a dangerous path. The Court treated this with the contempt it deserved. The intervention in the market went too far.

Cassis, which examines the *effects* of a national measure as a basis for the invocation of Article 34 TFEU, is a logical application of the *Dassonville* ruling, delivered five years earlier. Nevertheless, *Cassis* was the first case to deal directly with inter-State divergence among technical standards as a barrier to trade in goods and it was the first case to set out with clarity the test which is still used in judgments more than thirty years later. Technical standards do not escape scrutiny pursuant to the free movement rules simply because they apply equally on their face to all products irrespective of origin; and the judicial process assesses the acceptability of such trade-restrictive measures and, in the absence of adequate justification, requires that they be set aside in so far as they impede imports. There is no need to await the adoption of common EU technical standards. Court-led integration drives forward the construction of the internal market: the legislative process is required only in the event that national rules survive as justified barriers to trade. And in very concrete terms French Cassis could be sold in Germany, providing competition in the market and wider choice for German consumers.

A similar model applies to national rules governing professional qualifications. Refusal to recognize a local qualification simply because its holder is of a different nationality is obviously discrimination,[24] but

[23] Eg Case 192/84 *Commission* v *Greece* [1985] ECR 3967; Case C-405/98 *Konsumentombudsmannen* v *Gourmet International Products* [2001] ECR I-1795.

[24] Case 2/74 *Reyners* [1974] ECR 631, examined in Chapter 2.9.

refusal to recognize qualifications obtained in *another* Member State is also a barrier to the inter-State mobility of people on the same model as *Cassis de Dijon*. The very fact of difference between qualification procedures among the Member States acts as a fragmentation of the internal market. A State must investigate whether the qualification obtained in another Member State is equivalent to that required locally.[25] This opens up the market for services, unless refusal to recognize is shown to be justified. In fact the Court had already deployed language close to that used in *Cassis* in an earlier case arising in the services sector, *Van Binsbergen*,[26] and the approach was readily extended to technical rules affecting the provision of services. *Commission* v *France* illustrates the same preference for market solutions over public regulation.[27] France required tourist guides to hold a local qualification as a pre-condition of offering their services. In principle anyone could secure the qualification: in practice it plainly favoured locals over those qualified elsewhere. As in *Cassis*, the restrictive effect on inter-State trade of diversity between technical rules cast an obligation on France to justify its rules; as in *Cassis*, it could not do so. The Court observed that competition between tour operators would ensure the hiring of competent guides and that accordingly a State licensing regime governing access to the profession could not be justified. 'It also prevents tourists taking part in such organized tours from availing themselves at will of the services in question.'[28] Choice was maximized by opening up the French market to new entrants from other Member States. EU internal market law transfers the decision about use of a particular product or service away from the national regulator to the consumer; and at the same time it promotes choice between providers instead of awaiting legislative action which would impose homogenous rules at EU level.

Regulation of companies differs State by State and in *Centros* the Court used an analogous model to put national practices to the test where they impede the right to set up a branch in another Member State.[29] Centros was a private limited company registered in England. It had never traded in the UK since its formation. Its existence was entirely the result of its two shareholders, Danish nationals resident in Denmark, realizing they

[25] Eg Case C-340/89 *Vlassopoulou* v *Ministerium fuer Justiz, Bundes- und Europaangelegenheiten Baden-Wuerttemberg* [1991] ECR I-2357. The matter is placed on a footing firmer than ad hoc litigation by secondary legislation, especially Directive 2005/36 on professional qualifications OJ [2005] L255/22.

[26] Case 33/74 [1974] ECR 1299.

[27] Case C-154/89 *Commission* v *France* [1991] ECR I-659.

[28] Para 13.

[29] Case C-212/97 *Centros* [1999] ECR I-1459.

could take advantage of the favourable provisions of company law applicable in the UK, most of all the absence of any requirement relating to a minimum paid-up share capital. They sought to register a *branch* of Centros in Denmark, but the Danish authorities objected and refused the registration, insisting that the reality of the matter was attempted evasion of the Danish rules concerning, in particular, the paying-up of minimum capital for a company *established* in Denmark. But the refusal was found to violate EU free movement law. Centros was making a strategic choice 'inherent in the exercise, in a single market, of the freedom of establishment guaranteed by the Treaty'.[30] And the Court simply treated it as 'of little consequence' that company law was not harmonized across the EU. This, firmly in line with the *Cassis* model of scrutiny, is to promote a form of inter-jurisdictional competition and choice (here, in matters of company law) by upholding access to the wider EU market in reliance on home State (here, UK) rules, excepting only circumstances where a host State (here, Denmark) is able to show a coherent and sincere justification for insisting on the application of its own local rules.

The Court has elaborated the Treaty rules into a subtle, flexible, and intrusive set of instruments for advancing market integration while seeking to take account through the 'safety valve' of justification of legitimate national interests in regulatory protection. A State may not simply insist on conformity with its rulebook: it must explain and justify its rulebook. Free movement law is on this model a basis for review of national practices which, had the Court chosen to be more restrained in its understanding of the reach of the Treaty rules by confining their reach to an attack on discrimination, would have been capable of elimination only by EU legislative action—the homogenizing process of harmonization.

That the legal rules are interpreted with reference to the harm caused by fragmentation of the internal market along national lines is visible too in competition law. One of the Court's earliest judgments in the field, *Consten and Grundig* v *Commission*, delivered in 1966, addressed the jurisdictional divide between national and EU competition law.[31] The Court, dealing with the reach of what is now Article 101 TFEU, focused on 'whether the agreement is capable of constituting a threat, either direct or indirect, actual or potential, to freedom of trade between Member States in a manner which might harm the attainment of the objectives of a single market between States'. *Dassonville* lay eight years in the future! The

[30] Para 27.

[31] Joined Cases 56 and 58/64 [1966] ECR 429. See also Case 56/65 *STM* v *Maschinenbau Ulm* [1966] ECR 235.

Court's approach meant that even where sales across borders increased as a result of the deal, the application of EU law was triggered. This set EU competition law on a relatively interventionist road and, in particular, it shaped it as apt to intervene in deals involving territorial separation within the EU. In fact practices isolated to a national market alone are rare—all the more so as the project of market integration in the EU deepens. Even where the matter is on its face confined to the territory of a single Member State, it is still possible to treat this as a deception. *Cooperative Stremsel- en Kleurselfabriek* v *Commission* involved a co-operative of producers in the dairy sector which required all its members to buy exclusively from each other.[32] All the members were Dutch. They accounted for more than 90 per cent of Dutch cheese output. But the Commission held that an effect on inter-State trade had been established, and the Court agreed. The inquiry into the agreement's liability to affect trade between Member States required a determination on whether it was 'possible to foresee with a sufficient degree of probability that it may have an influence, direct or indirect, actual or potential, on the pattern of trade between Member States'.[33] The echo of *Consten and Grundig* mediated through the '*Dassonville* formula' is certainly no accident. The point, when this test was applied in the case, was that practices which tied up the Dutch market in this way tended to confine opportunities for other parties to trade into the Netherlands. They tended 'to reinforce the partitioning of markets on a national basis, thereby holding up the economic interpenetration which the Treaty is designed to bring about'.[34] The thematic concern which drives the analysis of whether the EU is able to claim jurisdiction under both free movement and competition law is isolation of national markets. And this threshold that must be crossed before the EU claims jurisdiction is low.

One can understand the Court's *Cassis* approach as rooted in a desire to attack protectionism. The effect of such technical rules is to isolate the regulated market from competition from beyond its borders and to reduce consumer choice within those borders. However, an attack on protectionism practised at national level is necessary but not sufficient to eliminate obstacles to the creation of an internal market for the EU. A complete ban on a product or service is also caught. Here the issue is not a protectionist effect in favour of local economic activity, because there is no such activity. Rather, a complete ban on access to the regulated market has the consequence that the internal market is fragmented

[32] Case 61/80 [1981] ECR 851. [33] Para 14. [34] Para 15.

along national lines. So the Court has explained that a complete ban on a category of goods imposed in a Member State would simply amount to the most extreme version of the quota and certainly falls within the scope of Article 34.[35] A requirement to obtain permission from the authorities of a State as a pre-condition to establishing a business in that State or providing services on its territory would apply to *all* traders, but its very existence as a restriction is enough to bring free movement law into play.[36] What rules happen to apply in *other* Member States does not matter for these purposes. EU free movement law requires that such measures be shown to be justified. In *Bosman* a footballer's movement across a border—from a Belgian club to a French club—was prevented because of the restrictive effect of the transfer system in the sport.[37] He would have been faced by exactly the same problem had he been trying to join another *Belgian* club, so his problem was not that practices differed between Member States. They did not differ. His problem was the very existence of the system which prevented him gaining access to the employment market in France (or anywhere else), and this was enough for the Court to treat the matter as a restriction on free movement within the meaning of Article 45 TFEU. To assert that the problem here is an impediment to access to the market of the regulating State comes close to capturing what is at stake, albeit that several subtly distinct circumstances are involved, but the overwhelmingly important point holds that just as *Van Gend en Loos* and *Costa* v *ENEL*[38] assert a distinctive strain to EU law as a constitutionalized system built on the platform of an international Treaty, so too *Dassonville*, *Cassis*, and *Bosman* shape internal market law as a system apt to intrude on national autonomy more aggressively than according to a simple and relatively limited demand that imported goods, people, and services be treated the same as locals. The EU digs deeper. And the direct effect of the relevant provisions before national courts means that (in particular) cross-border traders, whose commercial interests are the subject of interference by national measures of market regulation, can pursue litigious activity before national courts, which in turn empowers the Court of Justice of the European Union (CJEU), fed preliminary references of the fertile magnitude of *Dassonville*, *Cassis*, and *Bosman*.

[35] Eg Case 34/79 *Henn and Darby* [1972] ECR 3795, para 12.

[36] Eg Joined Cases C-570/07 and C-571/07 *Blanco Pérez and Chao Gómez* [2010] ECR I-4629; Case C-217/09 *Polisseni* [2010] ECR I-175.

[37] Case C-415/93 *Bosman* [1995] ECR I-4921.

[38] Case 26/62, Case 6/64; Chapter 4.

However, just as the thunderously important decisions on the constitutional character of EU law left enduring loose ends and generated rough edges (explored in Chapter 4), so too the proper reach of internal market law has produced troublingly imprecise and elusive lines of demarcation.

Some matters that are the subject of regulation within a Member State are not caught. The purely internal situation, with no connecting factor to the internal market, is not touched. This follows from the foundationally important principle of conferral found in Article 5 TEU. It is not enough that national laws differ for free movement law to bite.[39] The real problem is determining exactly when it does bite.

Keck and Mithouard is the ruling which stands as the Court's most ambitious attempt to provide a principled statement of the margin between national regulatory autonomy on the one hand and, on the other, the claims of EU internal market law to put national measures to the test of justification.[40] The case concerned national (French) legislation imposing a prohibition on resale of certain goods at a loss. The Court, adopting the classic *Dassonville* formula, found no direct or indirect, actual or potential, hindrance to trade between Member States 'so long as those provisions apply to all relevant traders operating within the national territory and so long as they affect in the same manner, in law and in fact, the marketing of domestic products and of those from other Member States'.[41] Here lie the limits of Article 34—and here lies the start of State regulatory autonomy. The point about cases such as *Cassis de Dijon*, *Centros*, and *Bosman* is that the rules made no distinction according to the origin of the economic activity and yet nevertheless they caused an obstacle to cross-border trade. By contrast, in *Keck* the Court's point is that some rules which make no distinction according to origin do not create any such obstacle to cross-border trade. The rules in *Keck* were of this type. The prohibition against resale at a loss did not appear to partition the French market from the rest of the EU. The impact of *Keck* is most vividly grasped by contrasting it with earlier rulings which it (by implication) over-ruled. In the so-called *Sunday Trading* cases EU law was deployed to attack eccentric rules which restricted the types of goods that could be sold on Sundays in England and Wales. The Court correctly identified that this was a qualitatively different type of obstacle to commerce from that addressed in *Cassis* and its progeny, for the marketing of products

[39] It is surprising (and perhaps revealing) how rarely the Court makes this point in explicit terms; for an example see Case C-565/08 *Commission* v *Italy* [2011] ECR I-2101, para 49.

[40] Cases C-267 and C-268/91 *Keck and Mithouard* [1993] ECR I-6097.

[41] Para 16.

imported from other Member States was not made more difficult than the marketing of domestic products.[42] At stake was a restriction on commercial freedom (on a Sunday) but not an obstacle to the construction of an integrated European economic space. But the Court nonetheless foolishly required that the rules be justified against standards recognized by EU law and although it ruled that in the circumstances they *were* justified,[43] its approach meant that the limits of national regulatory autonomy had become blurred, if visible at all. What sort of national rules would *not* need defending? *Keck* was a necessary correction. Indeed, soon after *Keck*, the Court decided that rules dictating the opening hours of petrol stations needed no justification because they did not count as barriers to inter-State trade.[44] The point is that EU law should not be so wide as to force review of any rule that affects commercial freedom: instead it should be focused on rules that damage the construction of the internal market. Constitutionally this follows from Article 5 TEU and Article 26 TFEU.

The problem at stake—understanding the reach of the free movement rules and, as corollary, the space allowed for national regulatory autonomy—is not confined to goods. *Keck*, however, was about goods and the Court has never tried directly to extend the reasoning deployed in that case beyond that sphere. It has, however, developed functionally similar—perhaps functionally identical—vocabulary destined to address the problem when it arises outside the context of goods. In *Mobistar and Belgacom Mobile* the applicants, mobile telephone operators established in Belgium, complained that taxes imposed on transmission pylons, masts, and antennae were violations of their right to provide services protected by what is today Article 56 TFEU.[45] This went too far. It would have subjected all regulatory initiatives introduced by a Member State to review. The Court decided instead that measures which do no more than create additional costs in respect of the service in question and which affect in the same way the provision of services between Member States and within one Member State do not fall within Article 56's scope. This is a '*Keck*-like' sense of restraint. But the Court avoided any explicit embrace of a convergent approach between the freedoms. *Volker Graf* v *Filzmoser Maschinenbau* is another case where the Court could have propelled *Keck* across the freedoms but chose not to do so explicitly.[46] The case concerned

[42] Case 145/88 *Torfaen BC* v *B&Q plc* [1989] ECR 765 para 11.
[43] Case C-169/91 *Stoke on Trent and Norwich City Councils* v *B & Q plc* [1992] ECR I-6635.
[44] Cases C-401 and C-402/92 *Tankstation 't Heukste & JBE Boermans* [1994] ECR I-2199.
[45] Joined Cases C-544/03 and C-545/03 [2005] ECR I-7723.
[46] Case C-190/98 [2000] ECR I-493.

Austrian rules which denied a worker entitlement to compensation where he or she chose to terminate a contract of employment, whereas compensation was payable where the contract ended without the termination being at the worker's own initiative. Graf had been offered a job in Germany and complained that the Austrian rule deterred his readiness to take up the offer. But his position would have been exactly the same had he been offered a job in Austria. The Court decided that the rule did not deter a worker from ending a contract of employment in order to take a job with another employer, because the entitlement to compensation on termination of employment was dependent on a future and hypothetical event, namely the subsequent termination of his contract without such termination being at his own initiative. This, the Court ruled, was an event 'too uncertain and indirect a possibility for legislation to be capable of being regarded as liable to hinder freedom of movement for workers'.[47] It also noted that, unlike in *Bosman*, the rule did not cause an obstruction to access to the (labour) market. The Court evidently used a species of remoteness test, and in fact it cited *Krantz* v *Ontvanger der Directe Belastingen*, a case concerning goods which also relies on a test which excludes national rules from review where they exert effects which are uncertain and indirect.[48] But in *Graf* the Court avoided *Keck* altogether, even though *Keck* could well be seen as a more sophisticated version of the remoteness test used in *Krantz*.

Explicitly, then, the scope of the several freedoms is not interpreted in a convergent manner. However, the Court seems to have found several functionally similar routes to reach the same destination—namely, that free movement law shall not be inflated into a basis for general review of Member State choices about economic regulation. Its reach is instead confined to the project of creating an internal market.

Exactly where that line lies remains hard to map in precise fashion. The Commission comically claimed in the immediate aftermath of *Keck and Mithouard* that the Court 'has completed its case law'.[49] That is far from the truth. The Court, periodically asked since *Keck* by national courts to address new twists advanced by traders eager to exploit EU law to undermine restrictions on their commercial freedom, has fallen back on some troublingly imprecise threshold tests. Bright lines are elusive, not least because the very concept of the internal market, and in particular its vertical and horizontal foundations, are ambiguous. National rules which restrict the *use* of a product offer a stern but illuminating challenge. In

[47] Para 25. [48] Case C-69/88 [1990] ECR I-583. [49] OJ [1993] C353/6.

Åklagaren v *Mickelsson, Roos* the Court was asked to consider the application of Article 34 TFEU to Swedish rules restricting the use of (inter alia) jet-skis on particular waterways.[50] This was a measure of environmental protection—but that, a potential justification, was irrelevant unless the restriction on use counts as an inter-State trade barrier in the first place. The rule did not discriminate in favour of Swedish producers of jet-skis. Nor did it require any technical adaptation of the product as a pre-condition of entry on to the Swedish market—the rule's effect was not like that met by *Cassis de Dijon*. So, in *Keck* terms, the rule appeared to apply equally in law and in fact to all products. The Court did not stop there. It stated that such a restriction on use 'may, depending on its scope, have a considerable influence on the behaviour of consumers, which may, in turn, affect the access of that product to the market of that Member State'.[51] So if the national measure has a *considerable* influence on the behaviour of consumers, it falls in principle within the scope of Article 34 TFEU (and requires justification). If the influence is not considerable, the measure escapes the scope of application of Article 34 TFEU. So the adjective *considerable* carries heavy constitutional weight. What is *roughly* at stake is concern to identify when a measure harms access to the regulated market in a way that will cause the fragmentation of the internal market, but definitional precision remains elusive and case-by-case application at national level is inevitable.[52] The Court shows a proper concern not to allow a formalist reading of *Keck* to roll back the potency of EU internal market law's review of national practices, but the opposite risk, the undoing of *Keck* itself and consequently excessive review, also looms. Traders are invited to show that a ban on re-selling products at a loss or restrictions on Sunday trading exert a considerable influence on the behaviour of consumers. So the fear is that *Keck*'s astute re-balancing of the vertical allocation of competence in favour of State autonomy is precarious.[53]

The weight placed on *considerable* influence as the vital jurisdictional threshold which separates review of national measures in the name of the building of the internal market from areas of regulatory autonomy reserved to the State is not an isolated instance. The Court has a predilection for the adoption of vague yet constitutionally vital threshold tests. This

[50] Case C-142/05 [2009] ECR I-4273. [51] Para 26.

[52] Eg J. Snell, 'The Notion of Market Access: A Concept or a Slogan?' (2010) 47 CMLRev 437; G. Davies, 'Understanding Market Access: Exploring the Economic Rationality of Different Conceptions of Free Movement Law' (2010) German Law Journal 671.

[53] Eg I. Lianos, 'In Memoriam Keck: The Reformation of the EU Law on the Free Movement of Goods' (2015) 40 ELRev 225.

reflects the awkward distinctions it is asked to make with little explicit help from the governing Treaty provisions, and yet it leaves a sense of unease about the slippery character of the vertical division of competence between the EU and the Member States. So for example the Court has ruled that where a national measure is liable to cause a *serious inconvenience* to an affected person, it falls in principle within the scope of Article 21 TFEU (and requires justification).[54] If the inconvenience is *not* serious, then, as the Court has on occasion made explicit, the measure escapes the scope of application of Article 21 TFEU.[55] So the adjective *serious* carries heavy constitutional weight. Competition law too illuminates what is at stake. The Commission's 'Guidelines on the effect on trade concept contained in Articles 81 and 82 of the Treaty' declare that EU competition law 'is not applicable to agreements and practices that are not capable of appreciably affecting trade between Member States'.[56] The required threshold of an *appreciable* effect has been shaped by the Court's case law and it is granted fuller expression in the Commission's Notice on agreements of minor importance which do not appreciably restrict competition, the so-called 'De Minimis Notice'.[57] This, then, is a limit to the intrusion of EU law into national autonomy. The pivot is the slippery notion of *appreciable* effect.

In sum, free movement law is *less* than a basis for review of any restriction on commercial freedom imposed in a Member State but it is *more* than an anti-discrimination norm. It is defining with precision the threshold beyond which the legitimate zone of national regulatory autonomy is lost which provides the toughest challenge. A test is needed which leaves space for recognition of the dynamic process of market integration (the empowering dimension of the internal market) while also showing respect for Article 5 TEU's principle of conferral (the limiting dimension). At a general level the Court captured the right tone when it identified the type of measure subject to review as one that forces undertakings entering the market of a regulating Member State 'to re-think their business policy and strategy',[58] but its more detailed formulae are operationally imprecise. This is the terrain of *considerable* influence, *serious* inconvenience, an effect that is not *indirect* or *remote* or *uncertain*, an obstacle that is not *hypothetical*, an effect that is *appreciable*, and so on. The evasion of convergence between the freedoms is troubling too, given that the basic issue to be addressed

[54] Eg Case C-353/06 *Grunkin, Paul* [2008] ECR I-7639; Case C-148/02 *Garcia Avello* [2003] ECR I-11613.

[55] Eg Case C-391/09 *Runevic-Vardyn* [2011] ECR I-3787, para 76, 78, 81.

[56] OJ [2004] C101/81, para 12.

[57] OJ [2014] C291/1.

[58] Case C-577/11 *DKV Belgium* judgment of 7 March 2013 para 36.

certainly applies in common irrespective of which economic freedom is at stake: it asks what is the threshold at which national regulatory autonomy becomes subject to review for its prejudicial effect on the EU's internal market, which in turn has constitutional and institutional consequences that are both vertical and horizontal. More broadly what is under examination here is the limits of the EU's legitimate claim to override national authority, for to bring the matter within the scope of EU law typically empowers commercially powerful actors unable otherwise to induce deregulatory change at national level. An absence of connection to the internal market deprives the EU of its legitimating claim to intervene.[59]

The 'negative law' of the internal market should be built on control of discriminatory and physical barriers, technical standards which cause market fragmentation along national lines simply because they are different, and other rules which act as a direct or substantial hindrance to access to the regulated market.[60] This does not solve the problem of deciding precisely what 'direct' and 'substantial' means for these purposes—it is admittedly simply to place a heavy constitutional load on (yet) more adjectives—but it ensures the right questions are being asked about how to navigate a course between the internal market as an empowering and a limiting concept.

6.2.3 The personal scope—Convergence?

The provisions on competition law are clearly written in such a way as to bind private parties. The free movement provisions are, by contrast, written with less clarity and the matter has therefore been delegated to the Court. Certainly they apply to the acts of public authorities in the Member States. The Court has decided that most of the provisions on free movement are also apt to impose obligations on private parties, whereas some, most of all those concerning goods, are not. There are plausible reasons for this difference in treatment. The problem, however, is that the Court has never chosen to provide any. The consequence is that this area of internal market law is unsatisfyingly uneven.

Walrave and Koch concerned discrimination on the grounds of nationality practised according to the governing rules of an international (cycling) sports federation—doubtless a powerful body, but not a public authority.[61] The Court decided that the bloc of relevant rules—those dealing with

[59] A. Somek, 'The Argument from Transnational Effects' (2010) 16 ELJ 315 and 375.

[60] This is the test proposed in S. Weatherill, 'After *Keck*: Some Thoughts on How to Clarify the Clarification' (1996) 33 CMLRev 885.

[61] Case 36/74 *Walrave and Koch* [1974] ECR 1405.

nationality-based discrimination and the free movement of workers and services, which are today Articles 18, 45, and 56 TFEU respectively—'does not only apply to the action of public authorities but extends likewise to rules of any other nature aimed at regulating in a collective manner gainful employment and the provision of services'.[62] It supplied two principal reasons for this finding. First, because the Treaty objective of tackling obstacles to inter-State trade would be 'compromised if the abolition of barriers of national origin could be neutralized by obstacles resulting from the exercise of their legal autonomy by associations or organizations which do not come under public law';[63] second, because given the diversity between Member States on the scope of and relationship between public regulation and private agreements, limiting the Treaty provisions 'to acts of a public authority would risk creating inequality in their application'.[64] And it has sustained this logic over time. The Court has in this way subjected trade unions to obligations imposed by the Treaty rules on free movement, so collective labour action must comply with standards of justification recognized by EU law in so far as its exercise obstructs cross-border corporate mobility.[65] On sporadic occasions the Court has even subjected private parties acting unilaterally, such as employers, to the obligations created by the Treaty provisions on free movement of workers and services, although its rulings in this vein are not consistent enough to support the view that private action of a unilateral nature is always subject to the discipline of these provisions of EU free movement law.[66]

Both the Court's arguments advanced in *Walrave* have force. Extending the free movement rules into the private sphere does indeed make more effective the objective of tackling obstacles to inter-State trade and, moreover, it does ensure an equality of application unaffected by the varying scope of the public and private sectors among the Member States. But these are surely reason for extending *all* the free movement provisions into the private sphere, and yet the Court has obstinately refused to impose obligations associated with the free movement of *goods* on private parties. In *Schmidberger* v *Austria*, which involved private parties obstructing the passage of goods through the Brenner Pass in protest at the environmental damage done by such traffic, the Court found that Article 34 TFEU was in principle apt to form the basis for review of the

[62] Para 17. [63] Para 18. [64] Para 19.

[65] Case C-438/05 *International Transport Workers' Federation* v *Viking Line ABP* [2007] ECR I-10779; Case C-341/05 *Laval un Partneri* [2007] ECR I-11767.

[66] Case C-281/98 *Angonese* [2000] ECR I-4139; Case C-94/07 *Andrea Raccanelli* [2008] ECR I-5939; Case C-379/09 *Maurits Casteels* v *British Airways* judgment of 10 March 2011.

Austrian public authorities' failure to intervene to suppress the protests—but Article 34 TFEU would not apply directly to the private parties themselves.[67] In *Sapod Audic* the Court insisted that an obligation arising out of a private contract cannot be regarded as a barrier to trade for the purposes of (what is now) Article 34 TFEU 'since it was not imposed by a Member State but agreed between individuals'[68]—and for support it reached back to that icon of free movement law, *Dassonville*, in which it had confined the reach of the law governing the free movement of goods to trading rules 'enacted by Member States'.[69] This does not mean that a creature of private law is never bound by Article 34 TFEU: the Court is not blinded by form. In *Commission* v *Ireland* it treated a campaign designed to persuade consumers to 'Buy Irish' as a measure falling within the scope of what is now Article 34 even though it was fronted by a private company and did not entail the imposition of binding obligations, because the scheme had been initiated by and initially funded by the Irish government.[70] The potential effect on imports 'is comparable to that resulting from government measures of a binding nature'.[71] Similarly in *Fra.bo SpA* the Court treated a body that was in form a creature of private law according to German law as subject to the obligation to comply with Article 34, given that it had been granted a power to certify that products complied with German law which restricted the opportunity to market products, including imported products, which were not so certified.[72] The core of the Court's inquiry remained whether the true regulatory context revealed that a formally private law body was in fact acting in a way that has the effect of restricting the free movement of goods in the same way as would measures adopted by public authorities.[73] Normally this can occur only if the State has transformed the capacity of the formally private body. In *Fra.bo* it had, because by law it was in effect able to stand guard over entry of copper fittings originating in Italy on to the German market. Absent any such special features, private practices that interfere with cross-border trade in goods have always been treated as the province of competition law, in contrast to private practices affecting people, which are assessed from the perspective of both competition law and free movement law.

[67] Case C-112/00 *Schmidberger* v *Austria* [2003] ECR I-5659. See similarly Case C-573/12 *Alands* v *inkraft AB* judgment of 1 July 2014.

[68] Case C-159/00 [2002] ECR I-5031 para 74.

[69] Case 8/74 note 21, para 5.

[70] Case 249/81 [1982] ECR 4005.

[71] Para 27.

[72] Case C-171/11 *Fra.bo SpA* judgment of 12 July 2012.

[73] Paras 26, 31–32.

This distinction is hard to understand. The application of the several freedoms to private parties could be justified, as the Court has indeed justified it, with reference to enhancement of the effective and equal application of EU law. A *refusal* to extend the personal scope of the freedoms to bind private parties could be justified as a means to show respect for private autonomy—a concern missing from the Court's orthodox analysis. However, finding a reason to grant binding effect within the private sphere *to some but not all* of the Treaty provisions on free movement is much harder to justify. Possibly one may tentatively argue that where people, rather than goods, assert free movement rights then the human dimension of the claim is enough to inflate the range of parties against whom the claim may properly be vindicated beyond public authorities to embrace also private actors, at least where they exercise collective power. But this is no overwhelmingly powerful argument, not least because it prioritizes one set of private actors over another, those against whom such free movement claims are vindicated. The Court, strikingly, has never even hinted at any rationalization of the odd state of its case law in this area. New vistas may be imagined,[74] but the current uneven pattern seems now too deeply entrenched to be readily altered.

6.3 JUSTIFICATION

Where a measure does not constitute a barrier to inter-State trade, national regulatory autonomy is preserved. There is no need to justify the measure. Where a measure is treated as a barrier to inter-State trade, it is by no means inevitable that the State will be disentitled from applying it, but it must show that it is justified. So where a trade barrier exists in the sense examined in Section 6.2, national regulatory autonomy is therefore *conditional*—conditional on showing an adequate justification for placing the local regulatory choice ahead of the momentum of cross-border trade.

The core finding of the previous section is that it is relatively easy to find the necessary triggering event which places the regulatory body under an obligation to show a justification for its practices. In consequence a heavy load is carried by the safety valve of justification and by the adjudicative

[74] Eg (with different views) S. Prechal and S. De Vries, 'Seamless Web of Judicial Protection in the Internal Market' (2009) 34 ELRev 5; G. Davies, 'Freedom of Movement, Horizontal Effect and Freedom of Contract' (2012) 20 ERPL 805; H. Schepel, 'Freedom of Contract in Free Movement Law: Balancing Rights and Principles in European Public and Private Law' (2013) 21 ERPL 1211.

choices of courts. It is here that the incisive force of EU law's deregulatory edge falls to be measured.

Just how *generous* EU law is in assessing justification has consequences for the vertical allocation of competences between the EU and the Member States. The more cramped the room allowed for justification, the more deregulated the EU's internal market. Also at stake is the horizontal allocation of powers between the judicial and the legislative process. The more national measures are condemned as unjustified trade restrictions, the less need for the EU to adopt legislative solutions to replace varied national rules: conversely, the retention of national measures on the basis that they are treated as justified despite their trade-restrictive effects thrusts the emphasis on the need for legislative action at EU level to introduce common rules. The internal market, as a site of shared competence,[75] is built on both national and EU rules, but just as rulings such as *Cassis de Dijon*, *Keck*, *Centros*, and *Bosman* reveal how choices about the reach of the basic prohibition intimately affect the shape of the internal market being created, so too these choices about the generosity of justification applied to trade barriers in turn dictate how regulated or deregulated shall be the EU's internal market.

6.3.1 The structure of the inquiry

Article 36 TFEU allows room to justify national measures affecting goods 'on grounds of public morality, public policy or public security; the protection of health and life of humans, animals or plants; the protection of national treasures possessing artistic, historic or archaeological value; or the protection of industrial and commercial property'. It adds in its second paragraph that such national action shall not 'constitute a means of arbitrary discrimination or a disguised restriction on trade between Member States'. For persons, Article 45(3) TFEU envisages that rights may be limited where that is justified 'on grounds of public policy, public security or public health' and Article 45(4) excludes the matter of 'employment in the public service'. Grounds of 'public policy, public security or public health' are also cited in Article 52(1) as reasons to treat foreign nationals in a special way in relation to the right of establishment, and this caveat is extended into the sphere of the free movement of services by Article 62. The burden of demonstrating justification is placed on the regulator.[76]

[75] Art 4(2)(a) TFEU.

[76] Eg Case 227/82 *Van Bennekom* [1983] ECR 3883; Case C-14/02 *ATRAL SA* [2003] ECR I-4431.

The scope of justification is not confined to the matters recognized explicitly by these Treaty provisions. In *Cassis de Dijon* the Court not only embraced variation between technical standards as a reason to engage EU law, thereby casting its net beyond a discrimination-only focus (Section 6.2.2); it also accepted that a wide range of justifications in the public interest may be advanced by a regulating authority, stretching beyond the specific and limited list found in the Treaty. In *Cassis de Dijon* it referred unhelpfully to 'mandatory requirements' as a means to capture this breadth,[77] a phrase which has endured but to no good effect, because it is little more than a poor translation into English. A better rendition would be something like 'compelling interests'[78] and in fact later in the judgment itself the Court offers a more satisfying formulation: the true question is whether the purposes pursued by the national measure that restricts inter-State trade 'serve a purpose which is in the general interest and such as to take precedence over the requirements of the free movement of goods'.[79] This general public interest test means that in principle the Court has long been prepared to admit to the examination of whether a national measure is justified a wide range of values that are left unmentioned in the Treaty. So integration of product, labour, and services markets may collide with national initiatives to protect the economic interests of consumers—the purported justification advanced in *Cassis* itself—but also measures designed to protect the environment,[80] to secure respect for human dignity,[81] to protect children,[82] to promote concern for animal welfare,[83] to promote the distinctive features of sport,[84] and to protect workers and the right to take collective action.[85] This is a non-exhaustive list. As with the notion of a barrier to trade, so too here with the notion of justification: the Court, while remaining faithful to the structure contained in the Treaty, has elaborated a complex and sophisticated set of principles that reach beyond the Treaty text as a basis to adjudicate between the competing interests at stake when the lust for inter-State trading freedom clashes with regulatory choices at national level. This is a quasi-legislative approach of the

[77] Case 120/78 note 22, para 8.

[78] *German*: Zwingenden Erfordnisse; *French*: exigences imperatives.

[79] Para 14.

[80] Eg Case 302/86 *Commission* v *Denmark* [1988] ECR 4607; Case C-379/98 *Preussen Elektra* [2001] ECR I-2099.

[81] Eg Case C-36/02 *Omega Spielhallen* [2004] ECR I-9609.

[82] Eg Case C-244/06 *Dynamic Medien* [2008] ECR I-505.

[83] Eg Case C-219/07 *Nationale Raad* v *an Dierenkwekers en Liefhebbers* [2008] ECR I-4475.

[84] Eg Case C-415/93 note 37.

[85] Eg Case C-438/05 note 65.

type met in Chapter 4.2. By adopting this approach the Court has actively interpreted free movement law to make it *porous*.

The Court has performed a structurally and functionally similar adjustment to the competition rules. Article 101 forbids restrictive practices as defined by its first paragraph but allows for carefully confined exemption pursuant to its third paragraph, and yet the Court has, in effect, written into Article 101(1) an opportunity to justify practices that are undeniably restrictive of competition where they serve a wider interest of sufficient importance. *Wouters* is the landmark.[86] The Court found that a Dutch rule forbidding the creation of multi-disciplinary partnerships involving barristers and accountants restricted competition, because it suppressed the possibility to offer a wider range of services and it was liable to limit production and technical development. But the Court then added that the context and the objectives of the restriction matter in determining the application of Article 101(1). The Court asked 'whether the consequential effects restrictive of competition are inherent in the pursuit of those objectives'.[87] And that led it to accept that the motivation for prohibiting partnerships between barristers and accountants, which was to guarantee the independence and loyalty to the client of members of the Bar as part of a broader concern to secure the sound administration of justice, was sufficient to prevail over the finding that the prohibition exerted effects restrictive of competition, and that the rule did not go beyond what was necessary in order to achieve these virtuous ends. There was no breach of EU competition law. In similar vein the Court in *Meca-Medina and Majcen* found that a doping ban imposed on swimmers by a sports governing body did not necessarily constitute a forbidden restriction of competition within the meaning of (what is now) Article 101 TFEU, since they were 'justified by a legitimate objective', that of (in short) clean sport.[88] This approach represents a readiness, also visible in *Cassis de Dijon* and its progeny, to place the economic objectives of EU internal market in their wider social and economic context.

Doubtless the rise of the 'horizontal' provisions in the Treaty and the Charter of Fundamental Rights provide legitimation of the Court's approach. Article 11 TFEU, considered in Chapter 3.14, stipulates that 'Environmental protection requirements must be integrated into the definition and implementation of the Union's policies and activities, in particular with a view to promoting sustainable development', and the

[86] Case C-309/99 note 10. [87] Para 97.

[88] Case C-519/04P *Meca-Medina and Majcen* v *Commission* [2006] ECR I-6991.

construction of the internal market is one such activity into which environmental protection falls to be embedded. Article 12 TFEU does a parallel job for consumer protection; Article 165 TFEU for the 'specific nature of sport'. Moreover, since 'The applicability of EU law entails applicability of the fundamental rights guaranteed by the Charter',[89] the application and interpretation of the free movement and competition rules must be informed by Charter rights and principles, including Articles 22 (culture), 35 (health), 37 (environment), and 38 (consumer).

There are, however, two salient points. First, this is *not* transformative. The Treaty's 'horizontal' provisions coupled to the Charter simply *confirm* the long-standing readiness of the Court to interpret and apply EU internal market law with reference to the wider impact of national rules which it checks for justification. Environmental protection pursued at national level has long been part of the Court's assessment conducted in the name of free movement;[90] sporting bodies were always able to make a case that their legitimate concerns should mitigate the application of free movement law to their practices even before sport became formally recognized by the Treaties with effect from 2009;[91] and culture too has long ago been woven into the determination of whether national measures that restrict trade are justified.[92] In *Pfleger*, a post-Lisbon ruling, the Court treated controls on gambling as a restriction of the freedom to provide services within the meaning of not only Article 56 TFEU but also Articles 15–17 Charter, but, in line with the orthodox approach taken in case law dating back more than a decade,[93] it accepted that in principle concerns such as consumer protection and the prevention of both fraud and incitement to squander money on gambling could constitute adequate justifications for the national choices.[94] The Charter has acquired presentational prominence but it has not changed the structure or substance of free movement law.

The second salient point is that the assessment is neither easy nor uncontroversial. Chapter 3.14 explained that the 'horizontal' provisions and their counterparts in the Charter tend to be 'soft' in legal character: they guide policy-making but do not provide a justiciable basis for

[89] Case C-617/10 *Fransson* judgment of 26 February 2012; Chapter 3.15.

[90] Eg Case 302/86, Case C-379/98 note 80.

[91] Case C-415/93 *Bosman* note 37, para 106.

[92] Eg Case C-250/06 *United Pan-Europe Communications Belgium SA* [2007] ECR I-11135; Case C-531/07 *Fachverband/ LIBRO* [2009] ECR I-3717.

[93] Eg Case C-124/97 *Läärä and Others* [1999] ECR I-6067; Joined Cases C-338/04 et al *Massimiliano Placanica* [2007] ECR I-1891.

[94] C-390/12 *Pfleger* judgment of 30 April 2014.

review of legislative choices. Much the same is true in this matter of review of national choices. The horizontal provisions and the Charter structure the pattern of inquiry conducted in the name of justification, but they do not provide cut-and-dried answers. A fact-sensitive examination of the compatibility of national measures with internal market law is required.

6.3.2 Public health

The availability *in principle* of a rich vein of justification does not at all mean that *in practice* a regulating authority is likely to find success in persuading the Court that its particular choices are justified. There are generally applicable principles which assert a hostility to opportunistic use of the room allowed by EU for justification of trade-restrictive measures. Article 36's second sentence cautions against 'arbitrary discrimination' and the Court has fastened on to this as a basis for refusing to accept that a Member State may justify repressive measures against imports where it is more indulgent to local products or services. So too a Member State which has a choice between various measures to attain the same objective is required to choose that which least restricts free movement. Otherwise the choice is disproportionately restrictive.[95] Competition law operates in an analogous fashion: a doping ban imposed on an athlete would not elude the grip of Article 101 if it imposed disproportionately heavy sanctions.[96]

Many of the early free movement cases focused on the justification recognized by Article 36 whereby States may act to protect the health and life of humans, animals, or plants. And many of these cases involved the exposure of quite ludicrous arguments designed to conceal the aim of the regulator to protect local industry, in flagrant violation of the foundational assumptions of the internal market. In *Commission* v *UK* British restrictions on the importation of turkeys from France were defended as necessary to prevent the spread of contagious poultry disease.[97] The Court was not impressed. It noted that the UK government had been subject to pressure from British poultry producers to block the imports and that the policy had been introduced hurriedly, with the result that French Christmas turkeys were excluded from the British market for the 1981 season. This was not 'part of a seriously considered health policy'.[98] It was

[95] Eg Case 261/81 *Walter Rau* [1982] ECR 3961; Case C-189/95 *Harry Franzén* [1997] ECR I-2471.

[96] Case C-519/04P note 86. [97] Case 40/82 [1982] ECR 2793.

[98] Para 38.

commercially motivated—it was an attempt to protect British farmers from competition at the expense of cross-border traders and British turkey consumers.

Klas Rosengren addressed the Swedish retail monopoly over alcohol as a blockage to importation of goods bought by a consumer in Spain.[99] The justification advanced was public health. But the system did not reduce consumption—it simply increased costs. The Court did not rule out that a system targeted on the particular need to protect young people might be justified, but nothing in the system was so targeted. In the absence of any such targeting the control was treated as disproportionately restrictive of cross-border trade. *Commission* v *Portugal* involved a measure which prohibited the affixing of any type of tinted film designed to filter light to the windscreen and the windows alongside the passenger seats in motor vehicles.[100] In classic *Cassis de Dijon* fashion, this constituted a technical standard that tended to exclude imported products. Portugal argued that its rule enabled seatbelt use by a passenger to be checked by means of a simple observation conducted from outside the vehicle, but the good sense of this initiative was wholly subverted by Portugal's admission that in any event it allowed the marketing of motor vehicles fitted *from the outset* with tinted windows. So the Court concluded that the 'ban must be regarded as being excessive and, therefore, disproportionate with respect to the objectives pursued'.[101] The laughable attempt made by Germany in *Cassis de Dijon* to persuade the Court that a ban on weak alcoholic drink was a justified measure of public health protection when it cheerfully allowed much stronger alcoholic drinks on to the market is typically treated as the very height of absurdity observable in the Court's case law, but the sad truth is that over the years plenty of regulating authorities in the EU have run it close by wasting the Court's time, and that of traders and consumers, by trying to rely on shoddy arguments to protect worthless trade restrictions.

But there are more sincere cases. In *Eyssen* the Dutch authorities were sufficiently anxious about the danger to human health presented by the use of a particular type of preservative in cheese that they introduced a ban.[102] Other less cautious Member States were prepared to allow such additives. The Dutch ban impeded trade in cheeses manufactured in more permissive States, but the Court accepted that regulatory attitudes could legitimately vary in such circumstances and did not find the Netherlands

[99] Case C-170/04 [2007] ECR I-4071.
[100] Case C-265/06 [2008] ECR I-2245.
[101] Para 47.
[102] Case 53/80 [1981] ECR 409.

to have acted unlawfully even though they had intervened in the market more vigorously than the norm elsewhere. The 'precautionary principle' tends to be used to capture this approach today.[103] And a great deal of the necessary assessment of risk in the shadow of precaution has been transplanted from national level to EU level by the increasingly complex and dense network of secondary legislation in the fields of medicines, pharmaceuticals, foodstuffs, and cosmetics.

Commission v *France* provides a helpfully vivid demonstration of the Court's willingness to be persuaded that there is a genuine divergence in regulatory tradition among the Member States which justifies blockage to the integration of markets.[104] France refused to accept woodworking machines that were freely available and used in Germany because it claimed they were unsafe. This plainly restricted inter-State trade. France did not seek to claim it had higher standards of protection than did Germany. Rather, and more subtly, it claimed that techniques of protection differed between the two States. The French rules were based on the aim of protecting users from their own mistakes and therefore curtailed scope for intervention in the machine's functioning by the user. Germany preferred to train users so they were able to deal with any malfunctioning. France demanded machines be foolproof under an expectation that operators were likely to be fools, whereas Germany trained its operators not to behave like fools. Given this demonstrated factual heterogeneity, the release of German machines on to the French market would cause a genuine risk of harm. The French rules restricted trade, but they were justified.

EU internal market law puts national measures that impede inter-State trade *to the test*: it is not a charter for remorseless deregulation. The insistence on articulated and coherent justification is equally visible in connection with the free movement of services. The *Loi Evin* required that television broadcasts in France by French broadcasters of sports events occurring in other Member States should not feature advertisements for alcohol. This plainly restricted the free movement of services, by requiring interference with broadcasts in the case of games taking place in jurisdictions outside France where shirt or poster advertising of alcoholic drinks was permitted. The Court found the rules to be a justified contribution to the protection of public health.[105] The Commission and the UK

[103] Eg Case C-192/01 *Commission* v *Denmark* [2003] ECR I-9693; Case C-387/99 *Commission* v *Germany* [2004] ECR I-3751.

[104] Case 188/84 [1986] ECR I-419.

[105] Case C-429/02 *Bacardi* v *TF1* [2004] ECR I-6613; Case C-262/02 *Commission* v *France* [2004] ECR I-6569.

had pressed on the Court that because the rules concerned only television advertising and did not extend to advertising for alcoholic drinks visible in the background on film sets, and moreover did not extend to advertising for tobacco, they should be regarded as inconsistent and therefore unworthy of being treated as a justified expression of public health policy. The Court was not so strict. Such choices fell within the discretion permitted of the regulating Member State.

6.3.3 The protection of the economic interests of consumers

Case law involving inspection of national measures that purport to offer protection to the economic interests of consumers provides another helpful testing ground within which to understand how far the Court will go in insisting on deregulation in the name of market-making. Once again the crucial element is the quality of the justifications advanced by the regulator.

In *Cassis de Dijon* justification rooted in the protection of public health was dismissed with contempt, as mentioned in Section 6.3.2, and the claim that the introduction of French Cassis on to the German market would cause harm to the economic interests of consumers fared little better. The Court did not deny that consumers might be confused by the appearance on the (German) market of a new and unfamiliar product, but any necessary transparency in the market could be achieved by requiring the disclosure of information about alcohol content on the product packaging. It went too far to fix a minimum level of alcohol content which, if not met, led to the complete exclusion of the product from the (German) market and the suppression of (German) consumer choice. In the same vein the German beer purity laws (*Reinheitsgebot*), which confined use of the name 'Bier' to products brewed using only malted barley, hops, yeast, and water, unlawfully restricted the commercial opportunities in Germany of producers brewing elsewhere according to different recipes and traditions.[106] The Court did not exclude that Germany could require that products be labelled in order to make clear to consumers their properties, but it did exclude a rule so rigid as to have the effect of keeping differently constituted beers off the market altogether. The result was not that production according to traditional German methods was no longer viable, but rather that such production would be—at long last—vulnerable to out-of-State competition. The Court was explicit: consumer preference may evolve over the course of time and trade

[106] Case 178/84 *Commission* v *Germany* [1987] ECR 1227.

integration is 'one of the factors that may play a major contributory role in that development'.[107] It is a dynamic, not static process: internal market law puts to the test the legislation of a Member State that tends to 'crystallize given consumer habits so as to consolidate an advantage acquired by national industries concerned to comply with them'.[108]

There is a strong deregulatory impetus in this case law, infused by a preference for the private autonomy of traders and consumers in the market over public regulation. *Commission* v *France*, the 'Tourist Guides' cases considered in Section 6.2.2 applies exactly this model to the market for services.[109] Competition between tour operators would ensure the hiring of competent guides. Accordingly a State licensing regime governing access to the profession, which would exclude those qualified according to different standards prevailing elsewhere, could not be justified. It is not that consumers have to buy or use unfamiliar imports, but rather that they can choose to do so. Aspects of competition law, forcing a shift from the interests of producers to open cross-border competition, have a similar stamp.

The judges in Luxembourg must have been perplexed and frustrated as their time was taken up with attempts to argue that consumers need to be protected by rules which require margarine to be packed only in a cube,[110] that Edam cheese be regulated according to strict minimum fat rules,[111] that bleach must cross a defined threshold of strength,[112] and that advertising medical treatment be banned on national television networks but permitted on local television networks.[113] The Court will not tolerate a measure which a 'reasonably circumspect consumer' would regard as an unnecessary intervention in the market.[114]

EU internal market law draws some legitimating force from its cleansing of Member State rulebooks, and the fact that Member States troubled to make the trek to Luxembourg to defend such absurdities is solid proof that leaving the matter to be resolved through national political processes would have been fruitless. The approach taken in *Cassis de Dijon* is immensely helpful to those seeking to challenge the thickets of regulatory intervention that have accumulated over the centuries in Europe. Some

[107] Para 32. [108] Para 32. [109] Case C-154/89 note 27.

[110] Case 261/81 *Walter Rau* [1982] ECR 3961.

[111] Case 286/86 *Deserbais* [1988] ECR 4907.

[112] Case C-358/01 *Commission* v *Spain* [2003] ECR I-13145.

[113] Case C-500/06 *Corporación Dermoestética SA* [2008] ECR I-5785.

[114] Eg Case C-470/93 *Verein gegen Unwesen in Handel* v *Mars GmbH* [1995] ECR I-1923 para 24.

of these rules might have had some conceivable virtue as means of standardization designed to achieve transparency when adopted in the context of national markets. But they are woefully anachronistic in the context of the restructuring momentum to build an internal market spanning the territory of all twenty-eight Member States. In truth such rules, defended as measures of consumer protection, were simply measures of protection which operate to the benefit of producers in the regulated territory. Some respite has been provided by legislative requirements imposed on Member States to notify planned technical standards and other product-specific interventions to the Commission with a view to promoting a screening process apt to prevent trade barriers rather having to cure them through litigation,[115] and the regime has been strengthened further by the Court's astute finding that unnotified measures are unenforceable before national courts.[116] But this regime is not comprehensive and a heavy weight still rests on reactive litigation to achieve the intended widening of the choices available to consumers beyond local products and services.

This deregulatory tendency also has an important institutional consequence. Free movement law exerts a prodigious effect on trade-restrictive technical standards, far beyond a discrimination-only focus. Legislative harmonization can therefore be confined to national laws having an impact on the functioning of the internal market which are shown to be justified. This is a vivid insight into how the Court's interpretation of the scope of free movement law is capable of affecting the allocation of institutional power within the EU. This in turn has an impact on the shape of the internal market. Free movement allows circulation of diverse products, and success is dictated by consumer preference, whereas legislative harmonization entails regulatory centralization and uniformity in the composition of bread, beer, pasta, and so on. *Cassis de Dijon* favours choice and diversity over the 'Europroduct'.

But none of this precludes national measures that are justified. The statement of principle that 'the fact that one Member State imposes less strict rules than another Member State does not mean that the latter's rules are disproportionate and hence incompatible' with EU law has been endorsed by the Court with equal application to both the free movement of goods and services.[117] Given that States differ in matters of moral or

[115] Dir 98/34 OJ [1998] L204/37 as amended.

[116] Case C-194/94 *CIA Security International SA* v *Signalson SA and Securitel Sprl*; see Chapter 4.7.5.

[117] Eg Case C-294/00 *Deutsche Paracelsus Schulen* [2002] ECR I-6515 (goods); Case C-3/95 *Reisebüro Broede* v *Gerd Sanker* [1996] ECR I-6511 (services).

cultural choice and given diversity in prevailing social circumstances, the Court avoids an aggressively intolerant attitude to justification which would lead to regulatory standards being forced down to the level of the lowest common denominator found among the Member States. To assume market solutions are always superior would be to neglect a long and rich history of regulatory intervention at national level aimed at curing market failure and correcting market inequities, and EU internal market law is not so crude. So traders have no absolute right to access the entire EU market simply because they meet the standards demanded by their 'home' State.

Buet concerned a French rule which went beyond giving consumers the right of cancellation required by the so-called 'Doorstep Selling' Directive (85/577), which mandated only minimum rules.[118] France prohibited canvassing at private dwellings for the sale of educational material. The Court treated this as an obstacle to inter-State trade by a firm that sold English-language teaching material which earned most of its turnover by such canvassing at private dwellings.[119] Was the French rule justified? It protected consumers against hasty purchases to a degree that surpassed the level that the EU legislature had thought necessary and, moreover, it was more restrictive than the choices made in most of the other Member States. The Court, however, noted the greater risk of an ill-considered purchase where educational material is involved, because such consumers tend to be seeking to catch up, and so are 'particularly vulnerable'.[120] It noted too that the French ban had been enacted 'as a result of numerous complaints caused by such abuses, such as the sale of out-of-date courses'.[121] And it added that 'since teaching is not a consumer product in daily use, an ill-considered purchase could cause the purchaser harm other than mere financial loss that could be longer lasting'.[122]

In the light of this analysis, the Court resisted the opportunity to deploy free movement law in such a way as to deregulate the (French) market. Instead it granted respect to the local regulatory choice designed to protect particularly vulnerable consumers.

A-Punkt Schmuckhandels GmbH v *Claudia Schmidt* has a similar flavour.[123] Parties in the home where jewellery was offered for sale were banned in

[118] Case 382/87 [1989] ECR 1235. The Directive is today replaced by Dir 2011/83, which converts the relevant rules into maximum harmonization: see Chapter 5.2.4.

[119] Para 2. Today there would arise a question whether this is enough to bring the matter within the scope of Art 34 TFEU as interpreted in *Keck*; Section 6.2.2.

[120] Para 13. [121] Para 13. [122] Para 14.

[123] Case C-441/04 [2006] ECR I-2093.

Austria. If this was found to be a barrier to inter-State trade, a matter for the national court to determine,[124] then the Court of Justice was open to the possibility of finding it be justified despite its restrictive effect on commercial freedom. The Court noted that the rule was apt to:

> take account of the specific features associated with the sale of silver jewellery in private homes, in particular the potentially higher risk of the consumer being cheated due to a lack of information, the impossibility of comparing prices or the provision of insufficient safeguards as regards the authenticity of that jewellery and the greater psychological pressure to buy where the sale is organised in a private setting.[125]

The same theme is found in the services sector. *Citroën Belux* concerned a commercial practice consisting of a free offer of comprehensive insurance for six months on the purchase of a Citroën vehicle.[126] This was treated under Belgian law as a prohibited 'combined offer'. The matter fell within the material scope of Directive 2005/29 on unfair commercial practices, which applies a regime of maximum harmonization (Chapter 5), and so would normally provide a complete answer to the question of whether the practice is fair or not, to the exclusion of Belgian preference. But Article 3(9) of Directive 2005/29 excludes financial services from the maximum harmonization regime and states instead that Member States are allowed room to choose to apply more restrictive rules, because, as its Preamble makes explicit, financial services engage 'complexity and inherent serious risks'. This already suggests a receptivity to the virtue of supplementary protection in this sector, should a Member State choose to provide it. The Court was responsive to the legislative nudge. It found stricter Belgian rules to be justified. It displayed a sector-specific sensitivity, and accepted that 'financial services are, by nature, complex and entail specific risks with regard to which the consumer is not always sufficiently well informed'.[127] A combined offer of which one component is a financial service tends to lack transparency as regards the conditions, the price, and the exact content of that service. So there was a sufficiently high risk that consumers might be misled to justify the retention of the rule, despite its trade-restrictive effect.

The principal objection to the rules condemned as incompatible with EU law in *Cassis de Dijon* and the other cases of regulatory absurdity just considered is that they claim that all consumers need protection from some deeply unconvincing source of confusion which at most would

[124] Another *Keck* question: cf note 119.
[125] Para 29.
[126] Case C-265/12 judgment of 18 July 2013.
[127] Para 39.

affect a very small group of breathtakingly unwary consumers (and even then only to the extent of making one false small-scale purchase). By contrast, *Buet* involved a class of consumers vulnerable for want of education, *A-Punkt* concerned consumers who may be vulnerable in a particular setting (at home), and *Citroën Belux* addressed the complexity of financial services. These rules were targeted at particular sensitivities and particular product and service markets. Article 12 TFEU and Article 38 of the Charter of Fundamental Rights both assert a constitutional commitment to the protection of the consumer, but, given a context of regulatory sincerity at national level, the Court has long used the device of justification to restrain pursuit of aggressive deregulation in the name of free movement law.

Centros fits this narrative too.[128] The Court accepts that in principle a targeted control on fraud or related pernicious practices could be lawfully applied by Denmark even where a restriction to corporate free movement follows, but the blanket refusal to admit branches on to Danish territory simply because of non-compliance with host State rules went too far. Abundant case law has clarified just when restrictions on corporate mobility in these type of circumstances are treated as justified.[129] Where the national regulator has identified a particular need for protection and crafted a law that is appropriately nuanced and specific, the Court responds by judging with due respect for that nuance. EU law in fact provokes better—more astutely targeted—regulation at national level under an assumption that its effects on the wider internal market must also form part of the inquiry.

6.3.4 Fundamental rights and free movement

The wider the scope of the justification invoked, the more intricately challenging becomes the Court's job of adjudication. This is in part the consequence of the Court's deliberate choice to pitch the scope of matters that may be advanced as justification for practices that restrict inter-State trade far beyond that envisaged by the explicit terms of the Treaty, but it is also the structural consequence of the Treaty system itself, which uses free movement and competition law as functionally broad instruments to build an internal market in a way that slices into national autonomy far more deeply than does the EU's legislative competence. This, as noted in Chapter 2.8, forces the Court to devise its own understanding of the worth of particular practices pursued at national level in order to concoct a workable test of justification, and to do so in circumstances where by definition the Treaty, deficient in legislative authorization, offers little or

[128] Case C-212/97 note 29.

[129] See *Wyatt and Dashwood's European Union Law* (6th ed, 2011), pp. 649–58.

no policy direction. The shaping of an understanding of the legitimate reach of protection of the economic interests of consumers, considered in Section 6.3.3, is one chapter in a longer story. If national practices that ration the supply of health care services impede a patient from choosing to receiving services in another Member State, then it falls to the Court to develop an understanding of the nature and purpose of systems for the allocation of finite resources in health care as it seeks to craft a framework for understanding whether EU law treats such measures as justified.[130] If sporting bodies act in a manner that is antagonistic to the internal market, then the Court must devise some sort of benchmark against which to judge what is permitted and what is not—and it gets precious little help from the Treaty, and none at all from the free movement provisions themselves.[131] This is the incremental drift of 'policy-making' through litigation. EU law acts as a jack-in-the-box: it surprises, it disrupts, its impact is hard to predict.[132] This structure means that an attempt to separate the role of the EU in achieving economic integration from the role of the Member States in choosing patterns of social regulation is fatally damaged. In the absence of viable rigid demarcation, the two come into collision, and the pivotal role played by justification is exactly the arena in which priorities come to be chosen. Justification, if satisfactorily demonstrated, slams shut the lid of the jack-in-the-box which is free movement and competition law.

The cases pitting differently motivated fundamental rights against each other provide the richest environment for exploration of these tensions. In recent years the Court has been asked to decide cases that pit claims to free movement, which the Court has described as among the 'fundamental rules' of the EU,[133] against national action taken in defence of fundamental social and political rights and freedoms. The emergence of fundamental rights principles as a basis for seeking to curtail the application of EU legislative measures was explored in Chapter 3.15, but here the challenge is to adapt review of national practices in the name of internal market law to accommodate interests which lie beyond the economic sphere.

Schmidberger v *Austria* presented the Court with a perfect model of economic rights clashing with political rights.[134] The Austrian authorities had permitted a protest to block the movement of transport through the

[130] Case C-372/04 *ex parte Watts* [2006] ECR I-4325.

[131] Case C-415/93 *Bosman* [1995] ECR I-4921.

[132] T. Wilhelmsson, 'Jack-in-the-Box Theory of European Community Law' in L. Krämer, H. Micklitz, and K. Tonner (eds), *Law and Diffuse Interests in the European Legal Order* (Baden-Baden: Nomos, 1997). Jack was also met in Chapters 2.8, 3.12.

[133] Eg Case 120/78 note 22, para 14.

[134] Case C-112/00 [2003] ECR I-5659.

Brenner Pass, high in the Alps. The protesters themselves were beyond the personal scope of Article 34 (Section 6.2.3) but the Austrian authorities' failure to intervene was in principle capable of falling within the scope of what is now Article 34 TFEU because it led to an obstacle to trade in goods (for almost thirty hours, while the protest continued). But it was motivated by a concern to protect the freedom of assembly and freedom of expression of those wishing to draw attention to the environmental damage caused by such trade. Nothing in the Treaty offers any helpful means to resolve this clash. The Court stated that both the EU and its Member States 'are required to respect fundamental rights' and so 'the protection of those rights is a legitimate interest which, in principle, justifies a restriction of the obligations imposed by...a fundamental freedom guaranteed by the Treaty such as the free movement of goods'.[135] This entails that the law governing free movement encompasses fundamental rights which conflict—the economic versus the political. One or the other must prevail: these are fundamental rights, but they are not absolute rights. The Court proceeded to require that 'the interests involved must be weighed having regard to all the circumstances of the case in order to determine whether a fair balance was struck between those interests' and added that 'The competent authorities enjoy a wide margin of discretion in that regard.'[136] The Court then proceeded actively to assess the balance. Noting a range of factors,[137] it made plain that the Austrian (lack of) action against those conducting the protests, rooted in respect for freedom of expression, constituted no violation of EU law, despite the restrictive effect on cross-border trade in goods.

The more sensitive and the more remote from commercial considerations the matters advanced in the context of justification of trade barriers, the more generous the Court to the available scope for justification and also to the breadth of the margin of appreciation enjoyed by the regulator. It has, for example, accepted not only that restrictions on trade may be justified where they serve to promote freedom of expression, but also that justification is likely to be particularly favourably assessed where the expression is of a political rather than merely a commercial character.[138] This reveals how the Court, having immersed free movement law in a deep pool of conflicting values and interests, is then drawn into ever more intricate explanation of which priorities shall prevail.

[135] Para 74. [136] Paras 81–82. [137] Paras 81–94.

[138] Case C-71/02 *Herbert Karner GmbH* v *Troostwijk GmbH* [2004] ECR I-3025.

'Balancing', after all, is awkward: if values are incommensurable, what business is or should it be of judges to decide which prevail? This imperils the separation of powers and, deeper still, the rule of law. This explains why the Court is fond of avoiding open embrace of 'balancing' by instead ruling that a protected value is in principle recognized by EU law but that the State has crafted a particular system of protection which is unduly restrictive. Proportionality conveniently allows EU law to condemn the means chosen rather than the ends pursued by a national regulator. From the other—more permissive—direction, the wide margin of discretion allowed to a regulator enables the Court to withdraw from making a direct choice between competing but differently motivated interests. But 'balancing' also involves locating respect for competing values within EU law, rather than treating this as a clash of EU economic freedoms versus national protection of social and political rights. *Omega Spielhallen* provides the best illustration.[139]

Omega Spielhallen involved a ban on a game involving simulated killing, 'Laserdrome', imposed by the Bonn police authority on the basis that such practices offended against standards of respect for human dignity that were constitutionally protected in Germany. This was a restriction on the free movement of services (from the UK). The Court had 'no doubt that the objective of protecting human dignity' was compatible with EU law and added that it was 'immaterial in that respect that, in Germany, the principle of respect for human dignity has a particular status as an independent fundamental right'.[140] In this way the Court deftly avoided constructing the matter as EU free movement law versus German protection of human dignity, instead setting it up as EU free movement law versus EU protection of human dignity. Today it could confirm this approach by citing Article 1 of the Charter, which declares human dignity 'inviolable', but in *Omega*, fully five years in advance of the grant of binding effect to the Charter, the Court showed how even though other Member States at the time were less fastidious than Germany, its treatment of justification could ensure that German anxieties about the damaging effect of trade integration on fundamental rights were accommodated as EU anxieties. This technique has much in common with the development of a common judicial understanding about the need for protection of fundamental rights where the EU itself acts, propelled in part by fear that national judiciaries may disobey the Court in Luxembourg if unpersuaded that adequate protection of fundamental rights is on offer at EU level, a story explored in

[139] Case C-36/02 [2004] ECR I-9609. [140] Para 34.

Chapter 4. The Court added explicitly and in thematically familiar vein that the competent national authorities must 'be allowed a margin of discretion within the limits imposed by the Treaty'.[141]

Schmidberger and *Omega Spielhallen* show how national constitutional sensitivities form part of the assessment of whether trade-restrictive practices are justified—not because they are *national* constitutional sensitivities but because they are constitutional sensitivities. They are absorbed at EU level. The Treaty provision which best captures what is at stake is not found among the provisions on free movement. It is Article 4(2) TEU, which directs that 'The Union shall respect the equality of Member States before the Treaties as well as their national identities, inherent in their fundamental structures, political and constitutional, inclusive of regional and local self-government….' This is a much elaborated successor to Article 6(3) TEU which pre-Lisbon provided merely that 'The Union shall respect the national identities of its Member States', but *Schmidberger* and *Omega Spielhallen* show how, even pre-Lisbon, the Court was appropriately sensitive to the place of such concerns in the application of internal market law. It was predicted in Chapter 4.13 that Article 4(2) TEU would play an increasingly prominent role in framing the management of the tension between uniformity and diversity within the EU and this chapter highlights its role in the particular context of free movement law, where finding a justification for a national practice protects local choice whereas refusing to find justification strips it away. *Ilonka Sayn-Wittgenstein* v *Landeshauptmann von Wien* offers a neat post-Lisbon example.[142] The dispute arose out of a difference dating back to 1919 between Austria, which forbids use of noble titles, and Germany, which does away with privileges but allows parts of the noble title to be retained in the surname. The applicant, known in Germany as Ilonka Fürstin von Sayn-Wittgenstein, was advised that in Austria her name had to be stripped down to Ilonka Sayn-Wittgenstein. This constituted serious inconvenience to her commercial activity: she was a seller of castles. The Court was receptive to the Austrian concern, expressed at a constitutional level, to abolish titles in the service of equality of citizens before the law, but, as in *Omega Spielhallen*, it converted this appeal to justification into an EU concern. The Court, permitting national authorities a 'margin of discretion',[143] referred to Article 20 of the—now binding—Charter which concerns equality. It then observed that in accordance with Article 4(2) TEU the Union is to respect the national identities of its Member States, and that it did not appear disproportionate for a

[141] Para 31. [142] Case C-208/09 [2010] ECR I-13693. [143] Para 87.

Member State to seek to attain the objective of protecting equal treatment by prohibiting use of titles of nobility.[144]

Article 4(2) TEU acts as the gateway through which national concerns pass and are transformed into specifically EU concerns. It is not that EU law defers to Austrian law as a superior norm. Rather it is that EU law has within it an EU conception of constitutional values. These need not be uniform. Article 4(2) TEU does not assert a single brand of national identity. This cannot mean automatic subjection to a State's appeal to its constitutional values, for such a softened test of justification would surrender the aim of constructing an internal market. This diversity must be constrained by the demands of EU law: as discussed in Chapter 4, a State could not claim to rely on Article 4(2) as a basis to protect national identity in circumstances that would in substance contradict the EU's own values.[145] The Court needs to be rigorous in forestalling the transformation of feeble economic and social justifications into a bogus claim to protect identity, but, used with sincerity by both national courts and the Court of Justice, Article 4(2) TEU has immense potential as a means to open up EU law to national constitutional concerns while still laying formal claim to the supremacy of EU law over national law.

These cases are a long stretch from blackcurrant liqueur and the madness of pretending that banning weak alcoholic drinks is a coherent public health policy. Structurally the fundamental rights cases follow the orthodox model of finding a trade barrier and then assessing whether it is justified, but the Court builds in embrace of a margin of discretion granted to the regulator in order to reflect the far more sincere and contextually sensitive arguments advanced in order to justify the national choices. Free movement law has become a more texturally rich landscape not because the Court has changed, but rather because the diet of cases changed. The law of the internal market is revealed as not exclusively concerned to lever open national restrictions on cross-border trading freedom. Indeed, if one is prepared to accept the good faith of the Court in these cases which engage a margin of discretion and balancing, it is not *mainly* about cross-border trading freedom.[146] 'Balancing' is a delightfully dignified notion,

[144] Paras 92–93. See also Case C-391/09 *Runevic-Vardyn* judgment of 12 May 2011.

[145] Especially S. Rodin, 'National Identity and Market Freedoms after the Treaty of Lisbon' (2011) 7 CYELP 11.

[146] Cf eg N. Nic Shuibhne, 'Margins of Appreciation: National Values, Fundamental Rights and EC Free Movement Law' (2009) 34 ELRev 230; F. De Witte, 'Sex, Drugs and EU Law: The Recognition of Moral and Ethical Diversity in EU Law' (2013) 50 CMLRev 1545; D. Damjanovic, 'The EU Market Rules as Social Market Rules: Why the EU can be a Social Market Economy' (2013) 50 CMLRev 1685.

but a stern test in practical adjudication, and it is the room allowed for justification of national measures that prevents internal market law causing a deregulatory bloodbath. But a pair of cases haunt the claim that the Court has struck a plausible balance: they challenge it as complacent.

The rulings of December 2007 in *Viking Line* and *Laval* were met already in Chapter 2.8.[147] They concerned plans to 'reflag' ships from Nordic countries to Baltic States, where the cost of labour and regulatory compliance was lower. This, a claim to free movement, came into collision with the opposition of trade unions, who relied on their right to act in defence of their members' interests. Chapter 2.8 explained that this generated a form of 'competence creep': the right to strike is explicitly excluded from the scope of EU legislative competence[148] but where its exercise restricts free movement, the Court is forced to make a judgment on its proper role and scope in order to decide whether industrial action which harms free movement is justified. The concern in this chapter is more with the substance than the structure. Normally, as explained previously in this section, the Court is sensitive to the damage that may be done by deregulatory aggression inadequately informed by respect for the virtues of challenged practices. Not so here. The Court excluded from the permissible scope of justified practices action taken where 'jobs or conditions of employment were not jeopardised or under serious threat'.[149] So collective action which lacks an intimate connection with the nuts and bolts of a particular labour dispute and which instead has a more long-term strategic and political objective would appear to be unjustifiable in so far as it impedes cross-border commercial activity. The critical question is why should EU law, and the Court of Justice in particular, dictate to organized labour what falls within its permissible range of interests? An answer of sorts is because of the damage done to the internal market by industrial action, but the structural anxiety holds that the Court, weighing matters of social constitutional law against economic considerations, made a clumsy and ill-informed choice which prioritized free movement. It thereby subverted hard-won protection of collective labour rights at national level.[150] The careful 'balancing' of the Court's previous case is here abandoned: the market reigns supreme. Moreover, the Court left wholly

[147] Case C-438/05 *International Transport Workers' Federation* v *Viking Line ABP* [2007] ECR I-10779; Case C-341/05 *Laval un Partneri* [2007] ECR I-11767.

[148] Art 153(5) TFEU. [149] Para 81.

[150] See eg L. Azoulai, 'The Court of Justice and the Social Market Economy: The Emergence of an Ideal and the Conditions for Its Realisation' (2008) 45 CMLRev 1335; C. Joerges and F. Rödl, 'Informal Politics, Formalised Law and the "Social Deficit" of European Integration: Reflections after the Judgments of the ECJ in *Viking* and *Laval*'

out of account any margin of appreciation apt to permit recognition of local circumstances.

This focuses attention on how the Court's extended understanding of the reach of internal market law makes pivotal the judicial understanding of what is and is not justified: the Treaty offers little guidance.

These rulings are a serious threat to the legitimacy of the Court's case law. The criticism that EU law has a deregulatory cutting edge which cannot be fully compensated for by re-regulation because of constitutional asymmetry between negative and positive law, and because of political blockages to the exercise of such competences as do exist, is met by an orthodox EU internal market lawyer's insistence that EU law guards against excessive deregulation by, first, asserting that the reach of EU law has its limits, and second (and frankly more operationally significant), that there is always space to justify obstructive rules and, where justification is polycontextual, an open-textured standard of review which embraces a margin of discretion is applied. *Viking Line* and *Laval* cannot be explained in this way. Inter-jurisdictional competition has been released, as in *Cassis de Dijon* and *Centros* (Section 6.2.2), but it is not ill-focused over-regulation of the market that is condemned as unjustified; rather it is politically highly salient protection of collective labour rights.

Decisions of the Court which interpret primary law—such as *Viking Line* and *Laval*—are not easily shifted, because unanimity at the time of Treaty revision needs to be assembled. This is difficult and highly unusual. Political adjustment through the adoption of secondary legislation is not straightforward either, and in fact the Commission's proposal for a clarifying Regulation in the wake of the judgments ran into the sand as there was no adequate consensus among the Member States and the EU institutions about which priorities should prevail.[151] In such circumstances it may be only the Court that can save the Court from itself. Most of all, the mis-step made in *Viking Line* and *Laval* could be corrected by reliance on the reforms made subsequently by the Treaty of Lisbon, including the grant of binding effect to the Charter, Article 28 of which provides that workers have the right to take collective action to defend their interests, including strike action. Moreover, Article 3(3) TEU now commits the

(2009) 15 ELJ 1; A. Davies, 'One Step Forward, Two Steps Back? The Viking and Laval Cases in the ECJ' (2008) 37 Industrial Law Journal 126.

[151] See the now withdrawn 'Monti II' legislative proposal of the Commission, COM (2012) 130, explained by The Adoptive Parents, 'The Life of a Death Foretold: The Proposal for a Monti II Regulation', Ch 5 in M. Freedland and J. Prassl (eds), *EU Law in the Member States: Viking, Laval and Beyond* (Hart, 2014).

Union to inter alia a 'social market'. Two Advocates General—Cruz Villalón and Trstenjak[152]—have already tried to push the Court in the direction of re-balancing priorities with consequences more sympathetic to social protection, so far without success. However, the point is not that *Viking Line* and *Laval* deal with a different (pre-Lisbon) time and a different set of values: the point is that the decisions at the time they were made were out of line with an internal market law that is normally more sensitive to values other than trading freedom. They are aberrations.[153] As such they remind us of how much depends on judicial choices about whether restrictions shall be treated as justified. Where they are, the internal market is a site of regulatory diversity within which cross-border trade in products and services is blocked. Attention then turns to the legislative route to advancing the internal market, the subject of the next section.

6.4 THE LEGISLATIVE DIMENSION

The Treaty provisions on free movement and competition law sweep away a host of public and private practices that are incompatible with the aim of creating an internal market. Their deregulatory momentum is however not absolute. One way or another there is room to justify practices that leave the market fragmented along national lines. The building of an internal market therefore demands also a supplementary role played by EU legislation. This entails the adoption of common EU rules, which may replace diverse but justified practices pursued at national level in order to level the regulatory playing field or which, under a broader understanding of the necessary scope of the internal market's regulatory underpinning, may be understood as a means to respond to the potential for market failure or inequity. Here, as so often, lurks ambiguity: nothing in the Treaties commits the internal market as a legal concept to any particular model or intensity of regulation.

6.4.1 The scope of conferred competences

The Treaty on the Functioning of the European Union contains a number of bases for the adoption of legislation in particular areas that are explicitly or by (ambiguous) implication associated with the internal

[152] Case C-515/08 *Santos Palhota and Others* (5 May 2010), Case C-271/08 *Commission* v *Germany* (14 April 2010) respectively.

[153] See S. Weatherill, '*Viking* and *Laval*: The EU Internal Market Perspective', Ch 2 in *EU Law in the Member States: Viking, Laval and Beyond* note 151.

market. These include Article 81, which grants the EU a competence to develop judicial co-operation in civil matters having cross-border implications, which is available particularly—though not exclusively—when necessary for the proper functioning of the internal market; Article 113, which provides for harmonization of indirect taxation to ensure the establishment and functioning of the internal market; Article 118 TFEU, which provides that in the context of the establishment and functioning of the internal market, measures may be adopted to create European intellectual property rights; Article 168 TFEU, providing for Union action relating to public health (which includes an explicit exclusion of power to harmonize national laws); Article 169 TFEU, providing for Union action relating to consumer protection (which is confined to measures which support, supplement, and monitor the policy pursued by the Member States); and Article 194 TFEU, providing for Union action on energy in the context of the establishment and functioning of the internal market.

This is a breathless summary of a mixed bag. Some of these legal bases have generated a modest stream of legislative activity, others—such as Article 113, because of its requirement of unanimity in Council, and Article 169, because of its extraordinarily narrowly drawn formulation—have been of negligible significance. The characteristic of each is a sector-specific grant of legislative competence. Of these, only what is now Article 113 was present from the beginning. The others have been added incrementally at times of periodic Treaty revision, in line with the assembly of a political consensus that the Member States would benefit from some degree of co-ordinated action to tackle problems in the sectors concerned.

EU policies that do not immediately suggest an intimate connection with the internal market project are in some instances nevertheless politically part of the package. The Structural Funds and the Cohesion Fund, addressed today in Articles 174–178 TFEU which comprise Title XVIII on *Economic, Social and Territorial Cohesion* in the TFEU's immense Part Three, were added to the Treaty system in 1987 by the SEA as part of an understanding that although the internal market project was intended to create growth for all, the benefits would doubtless be unevenly spread, and that accordingly a political commitment to effect a degree of distribution in favour of less advantaged regions was required.

Environmental protection and labour market regulation are EU competences that grew from an initial focus on the functioning of the internal market to achieve a much broader independent—albeit contested—function. They deserve separate treatment.

6.4.2 *Environmental protection*

There is an evident connection between environmental protection and the internal market. In the first instance national measures are capable of acting as barriers to inter-State trade. Cases have reached the Court in which national measures governing, for example, the recycling of products,[154] transport of waste,[155] and obligatory use of sustainable forms of energy[156] have been found to impede cross-border trade and have therefore been subject to inspection to determine whether they are justified. Coherent schemes have been treated as justified. The presence of such justified inter-State regulatory divergence, which is capable of being viewed not only as a trade barrier but also as a distortion of competition as a result of the different costs imposed on traders in different Member States, readily provides a basis for the adoption of common EU rules as a means to promote the integration of markets. In particular, States with tough laws, Germany most of all, have strong incentives to promote EU-level rules, to avoid competitive disadvantage while also seeking to improve the quality of the environment. And the earliest measures adopted in the field of environmental protection by the EU were adopted explicitly in the name of market-making, based on what was Article 100 (now 115 TFEU), sometimes coupled to Article 235 (now 352 TFEU; Chapter 2.7.3).[157] In 1987, on the entry into force of the SEA, the EU acquired a competence to legislate to promote environmental protection in its own right, and this has been made more elaborate and extensive over time, pursuant to periodic Treaty revision. Today Articles 191–193 TFEU are barren of explicit reference to the internal market and direct that EU policy on the environment shall contribute to the preservation, protection, and improvement of the quality of the environment; the protection of human health; the prudent and rational utilization of natural resources; and the promotion of relevant measures at international level to deal with inter alia climate change. This may readily be understood as a basis for action to deal with the environmental consequences of economic growth released by the internal market project. Sustainable development is key.[158]

6.4.3 *Labour market regulation*

Labour market regulation is also attached to the internal market project, although its proper aim and scope is illuminatingly ambiguous

[154] Case 302/86 note 80. [155] Case C-2/90 note 6.

[156] Case C-379/98 note 80.

[157] The Court confirmed that environmental measures might be based on what was Art 100, now Art 115, in Case 91/79 *Commission* v *Italy* [1980] ECR 1099.

[158] Arts 2(3), 3(5), 21(2)(d), 21(2)(f) TEU; Art 11 TFEU; Art 37 Charter.

and politically contested. In the original Treaty crafted in the 1950s, Article 119 EEC provided that 'Each Member State shall during the first stage ensure and subsequently maintain the application of the principle that men and women should receive equal pay for equal work.' Its modern form, stripped of reference to the first stage (which ended in 1962), is unchanged in substance: it is Article 157 TFEU, which provides that 'Each Member State shall ensure that the principle of equal pay for male and female workers for equal work or work of equal value is applied.' The motivation here was anxiety that a Member State with relatively strong rules designed to secure gender equality would suffer as a result of undercutting pursued by Member States with less interventionist (or no) regimes, although here, in contrast to environmental protection, it was France that was the relatively progressive State that pushed successfully for an EU commitment to gender equality in matters of pay.[159] That commitment was strengthened by the Court's landmark ruling in *Defrenne* v *SABENA* which found the provision was directly effective, so required no legislative amplification before it could be relied on before national courts, and moreover that this was true even in horizontal cases, so it could be relied on before national courts by an employee against a discriminatory private employer.[160] The Court also took the opportunity in *Defrenne* to express its view on the purpose of the equal pay rule. It is not only designed to avoid a situation in which undertakings established in States which have implemented the principle of equal pay suffer a competitive disadvantage as compared with undertakings established in States which have not so legislated, but also aimed at the advance of the social objectives of the EU, which embrace social progress and the constant improvement of living and working conditions.[161] So the EU pursues 'a double aim, which is at once economic and social'.[162]

So the internal market project was understood to require a common set of rules apt to curtail competitive distortion consequent on legislative diversity among the Member States, while it was also imbued with a wider social understanding of the role of the EU. The original Treaties allowed little scope for amplification of this concern through the adoption of secondary legislation: explicit competence was wanting. However, in the

[159] See J. Kenner, *EU Employment Law: From Rome to Amsterdam and Beyond* (Hart, 2003), esp Ch 1.

[160] Case 43/75 [1976] ECR 455. Chapters 2.9, 4.4.

[161] Paras 8–10.

[162] Para 12. That duality appears in far less happy context in para 79 of *Viking Line* note 65 and para 105 of *Laval* note 65.

wake of the politically transformative Paris Summit of 1972, which aimed to put a more 'human face' on the process, legislative activity occurred pursuant to what were then Articles 100 and 235 EEC; today, in amended form, Articles 115 and 352 TFEU. Neither had—has—any explicit connection to social policy, but by asserting that social policy counts as part of the process of creating an integrated market and features among the EU's objectives the EU unleashed a social dynamic, with particular emphasis on labour markets. So for example Directive 77/187 on safeguarding of employees' rights in the event of transfers of undertakings was adopted according to an assertion in its Preamble that differences between Member States' protection of employees can have a direct effect on the functioning of the market, and that accordingly harmonization is required while pursuing improvement in working conditions.[163] The Court actively embraced this double aim, in this vein echoing *Defrenne* when asked to interpret the Directive.[164] It has now been replaced by Directive 2001/23, which takes the same—amended—legal base: Article 94 EC, now Article 115 TFEU, which makes explicit connection to the internal market.[165] This is to locate social policy as part of, not separate from, the internal market.

This is politically contentious. An alternative vision would champion exactly that legislative diversity as a basis for regulatory competition between Member States, allowing local experimentation and diverse preference to prevail ahead of EU-level homogenization of policy. The UK, and its Conservative governments in particular, has fought doggedly against an internal market characterized by an intensified degree of labour market regulation and, wider still, social policy, and this bitter disagreement about the virtue of the EU as a site for common policy-making reached its most conspicuous eruption between 1993 and 1999, when, as a result of an agreement to disagree in negotiating the Maastricht Treaty, a fiendishly complicated, though in substance little used, deal was struck allowing all the Member States excluding the UK to deepen common policy-making in the area.[166] The provisions that deal with social policy are today found in Title X and stretch from Article 151 to Article 161 TFEU. They are the assembly of incremental and frequently tortuously negotiated compromises at times of periodic Treaty revision. Both the scope and the applicable legislative procedure betray the increasing

[163] OJ [1977] L61/26.

[164] Case C-382/92 *Commission* v *United Kingdom* [1994] ECR I-2435.

[165] OJ [2001] L82/16.

[166] Kenner note 159, Ch 6. See also Chapter 5.4 of this book.

difficulty in securing agreement among all the Member States. Article 151 TFEU directs that the Union and the Member States

> shall have as their objectives the promotion of employment, improved living and working conditions, so as to make possible their harmonisation while the improvement is being maintained, proper social protection, dialogue between management and labour, the development of human resources with a view to lasting high employment and the combating of exclusion.

It also states in its third paragraph that they 'believe that such a development will ensue not only from the functioning of the internal market, which will favour the harmonisation of social systems, but also from the procedures provided for in the Treaties and from the approximation of provisions laid down by law, regulation or administrative action'. Article 153(1) then provides a list of areas in which the Union shall support and complement the activities of the Member States with a view to achieving the objectives of Article 151. Article 157 TFEU's commitment to equal pay, the modern successor to the provision that provided the platform for *Defrenne*, is locked into the Treaty, but most of the relevant protective rules that apply in common across the territory of the EU are found in secondary legislation, mostly Directives. The legislative *acquis* itself is a peculiar mixed bag—the product, like the Treaty superstructure itself, of political opportunity rather than coherent structural planning. This is also an area where, as explained in Chapter 3.6, the EU has actively pursued strategies that reach beyond the limited toolkit of legal acts contained in Article 288 TFEU.

Overall, the internal market as a legal and economic construct is supported by a regulatory platform of social policy in areas where the Member States have chosen to act in common in order to improve the quality of the working and social environment in the EU rather than to diverge and compete. This is easily associated today with Article 3(3) TEU's embrace of the 'social market economy' and with Article 9 TFEU's direction that 'In defining and implementing its policies and activities, the Union shall take into account requirements linked to the promotion of a high level of employment, the guarantee of adequate social protection, the fight against social exclusion, and a high level of education, training and protection of human health.' The Charter too, especially its Title IV on *Solidarity*, forms part of this background. On the other hand, there is nothing systematic or comprehensive about EU social policy. It is rather fragmented. It is largely, though not exclusively, related to employment. Much is missing: the core of the commitment to social welfare and, most obvious of all, the attached budget, is not delivered by the EU. A range of—sometimes competing, sometimes of rising or falling prominence—explanations motivate the EU's patterns of intervention.[167] *Viking Line* reminds us that the deregulatory power of the free movement and competition law provisions exceeds that of the provisions that shape social policy, but one of the understandings in favour of EU commitments to social protection is precisely as an antidote to the perceived aggressive deregulation that is calculatedly part of the EU's endeavours to create an integrated trading space, and the legislative *acquis* is not negligible in scope or ambition. But one of the most persuasive rationales for the very existence of the EU lies in its capacity to solve problems that confront the Member States in common in a fashion that is more effective than unilateral State action and the problem here, as reflected in the muddle of Treaty competences, is an absence of consensus as to what the problem really is to which the EU offers a solution. Whether the internal market is primarily a site of regulatory competition or of common social policy-making is a political debate conducted against an ambiguous legal background.

6.4.4 Harmonization

Because the Treaty provisions on free movement are not absolute prohibitions, but rather leave space for justification of national practices, they admit the possible persistence of fragmentation in the internal market. And so the necessary supplementary route to achieving a unified trading space within the EU is based on legislative harmonization of national laws. In this way the two routes to eliminating barriers to trade may be seen as complementary: once the judicial route, which requires the setting aside of restrictive rules that are not capable of being justified, is exhausted as a result of the presence of justification, attention turns to the political process and the adoption of EU standards that apply in common in preference to diverse national rules. And so is levelled the regulatory playing field of the internal market.

The Treaty has always conferred a competence to harmonize laws in the service of market-making. The relevant provision, now more than fifty years old, is today Article 115 TFEU, but since it requires unanimity in Council it has fallen into disuse. The key Treaty provision today is Article 114 TFEU, which was inserted into the Treaty by the SEA with effect from 1987.[168] Since it employs the ordinary legislative procedure it requires only a qualified majority vote (QMV) in Council. Article 114

[167] See eg A.C.L. Davies, *EU Labour Law* (Elgar, 2012) Ch 1; C. Barnard, 'EU Social Policy: From Employment Law to Labour Market Reform' in P. Craig and G. De Búrca (eds), *The Evolution of EU Law* (2nd ed, 2011).

[168] It used to be Art 95 EC, and before that Art 100a.

TFEU provides for 'approximation'—harmonization is the more commonly used synonym—of national laws and practices 'for the achievement of the objectives set out in Article 26'. So this competence is driven explicitly by the internal market.

Any national laws may be subjected to the discipline of harmonization provided only that the establishment and functioning of the internal market is promoted thereby. The EU is competent to intervene to establish harmonized standards pursuant to Article 114 'where there are differences between national rules which are such as to obstruct the fundamental freedoms and thus have a direct effect on the functioning of the internal market...or to cause significant distortions of competition' or where 'the aim is to prevent the emergence of such obstacles to trade resulting from the divergent development of national laws', provided the emergence of such obstacles is likely and the measure in question is designed to prevent them.[169] The threshold is low—this is a vast menu! There is no limit to the subject matter of laws that may be harmonized by the intervention of the EU legislature, excepting only fiscal provisions, provisions relating to the free movement of persons, and provisions relating to the rights and interests of employed persons, which are cut out of the scope of Article 114 TFEU by its second paragraph. This does not at all deny the relevance of these matters to the construction of the internal market. It is simply a political refusal to open up their sensitivities to intervention by QMV. Article 115 is capable of being used to harmonize such rules, but would require unanimity in Council.

Harmonization has a prodigious functional potential. Driven by a logic which treats regulatory divergence among the Member States as a propulsion to introduce replacement common rules at EU level, legislative harmonization has swept broad and deep across the regulatory landscape of the EU. Chapter 2.7 has examined this structural tendency in the EU's competence catalogue. At the constitutional level, it brings into question how realistic it is *in practice* to talk *in principle* about the limits of the EU's conferred competences. In particular, the Court's ruling in *Tobacco Advertising I*,[170] making plain that there are limits to legislative reliance on Article 114 TFEU, has been largely drowned out by subsequent rulings which make plain how easy it is for the EU legislature to skip over those confining limits.[171] In fact the Court's threshold tests, that Article 114

[169] Case C-58/08 *Vodafone, O2* et al v *Secretary of State* [2010] ECR I-4999, paras 32, 33; Chapter 2.7.4.

[170] Case C-376/98 *Germany* v *Parliament and Council* [2000] ECR I-8419.

[171] Eg Case C-58/08 note 169; Case C-380/03 *Germany* v *Parliament and Council* [2006] ECR I-11573, Chapter 2.7.4.

may be used where divergence between national laws exerts an *appreciable* effect or where diverse national action is *likely*, are every bit as slippery as those it has concocted to define the reach of the free movement provisions (Section 6.2.2). However, the main point of this chapter is the shape and density of the pattern of regulation within the internal market which is generated by the springboard that is Article 114.

Harmonization has a dual function. This was explained in Chapter 2.7.5. When diverse national rules governing widgets are harmonized in order to promote an integrated market for widgets across the whole EU, the process necessarily involves a choice about the quality and style of the harmonized standard. Harmonization is deregulatory—on the simplest model, twenty-eight rules become one—but it is also re-regulatory, in the sense that the character of the 'one'—the EU rule—demands to be shaped. So an EU programme of legislative harmonization affecting matters such as consumer protection, environmental protection, or public health is aimed at improving the functioning of the internal market but it *also* involves a vertical transfer of responsibility from State level to EU level (in whole or in part: Chapter 5.2). Through harmonization the EU becomes a site of regulatory responsibility. The EU sets (common) standards of consumer protection, environmental protection, and so on.

There is nothing surreptitious about this. It is inevitable. And it is recognized by the Treaty. In principle, the creation of a unified economic area requires only that the rules apply in common, and it does not matter whether the rules are interventionist or light-touch in nature. However, State regulation of the market in Europe has developed incrementally for centuries, under a variety of motivating forces, and it would be surprising were States to allow the EU's market-making project simply to roll back the accumulated patterns of rule-making designed to protect groups such as consumers and workers from the imperfections and inequities of unregulated markets. And the Treaty therefore ensures that the EU, in adopting harmonized rules, does *not* simply pursue common rule-making. It must also pay attention to the content of the rules which are being set at EU level in partial or total replacement for national rules. This is mandated by Article 114 itself, which in its third paragraph provides that 'The Commission, in its proposals envisaged in paragraph 1 concerning health, safety, environmental protection and consumer protection, will take as a base a high level of protection, taking account in particular of any new development based on scientific facts' and that 'Within their respective powers, the European Parliament and the Council will also seek to achieve this objective.' Commitment to connect the market-making project to the protection of affected interests is entrenched in the EU's constitutional superstructure. Articles 11, 12, 167(4), and 168(1) TFEU and Articles 37, 38, 22, and 35 of the Charter direct that environmental protection, consumer protection, culture, public health, and consumer protection respectively shall inform the definition and implementation of other EU policies. Creating an internal market through harmonization is one such policy. The Court has accordingly embraced this dual function of harmonization. Provided that the conditions for recourse to Article 114 TFEU as a legal basis are fulfilled, the EU legislature 'cannot be prevented from relying on that legal basis on the ground that public health protection is a decisive factor in the choices to be made'.[172] The same is surely true of any other value subject to regulation at national level: it may serve as a 'decisive factor' in EU rule-making provided those EU rules improve the functioning of the internal market.

Article 114 (and its predecessors) have accordingly been used as an authorization to harmonize across a wide sweep of the regulatory landscape in the EU. Chapter 2.7.5 contains vivid illustration. The landscape mapped there is composed of both the relatively dense legislative *acquis* and the contribution of the Court. As explored in Chapter 3.14, it is improbable that a measure would be held invalid for failure to set sufficiently high standards provided the legislative process has addressed questions pertaining to regulatory technique.[173] Coming from the other direction, it is improbable that the Court would find that a measure of harmonization over-regulates the internal market to the detriment of property rights and the freedom to pursue a business, covered by Articles 15 and 16 of the Charter, given (most of all) the Charter's commitments to regulatory values such as public health and consumer protection. The Court charges itself with the task to examine the balance struck between the requirements of the protection of the several fundamental rights protected by the Union legal order and has typically approved the 'balancing' performed by the legislature in setting the harmonized terms of market integration.[174]

Commitments to a high level of protection have also played a prominent role in the Court's interpretation of relevant legislative texts. *Simone Leitner* was met in Chapter 3.14: the Court took an extended view of the reach of the Package Travel Directive (90/314) in order to strengthen protection of the consumer.[175] *Mostaza Claro* v *Centro Móvil Milenium*,

[172] Eg Case C-380/03 note 171, para 39.

[173] Case C-233/94 *Germany* v *Parliament and Council* [1997] ECR I-2405.

[174] Eg Case C-544/10 *Deutsches Weintor eG* v *Land Rheinland-Pfalz* judgment of 6 September 2012; Chapter 3.15.5.

[175] Case C-168/00 [2002] ECR I-2631.

examined in Chapter 4.5 and dealing with Directive 93/13 on unfair terms, required a national court to re-open arbitration proceedings in favour of a consumer even where under national law they were final.[176] Just as national laws on consumer protection have generated a heap of entertaining insights into the Court's application of the free movement rules (Section 6.3.3), so too the rather elaborate harmonized *acquis* on consumer protection has offered the Court plenty of opportunities to demonstrate its attitude to the virtue of regulation at EU level in defence of a value such as consumer protection to which the EU is committed according to its Treaties and the Charter. A comprehensive account is not needed: examples suffice.[177]

Article 6(1) of Directive 93/13 requires the Member States to provide that unfair terms shall not bind the consumer, which the Court has described as a mandatory provision which aims to replace the formal balance which the contract establishes between the rights and obligations of the parties with an effective balance which re-establishes equality between them.[178] This is a harmonized regime constitutionally tied to the internal market but *also* motivated by concern to tackle the imbalance that flows from permitting contractual freedom free rein in the relationship between the trader and the consumer. Intervening in freedom of contract is readily rationalized in national law on the basis that preserving freedom of contract in imbalanced relationships is not freedom at all but rather licence for the powerful to impose on the weak, and harmonization transplants this protective concern to EU level. This policy orientation has concrete consequences when the Court is invited to interpret the Directive. For example, *Árpád Kásler* concerned the interpretation of Directive 93/13 in the context of a challenge to a term dealing with the exchange rate applicable to repayment of a loan denominated in a foreign currency.[179] Article 4(2) of the Directive directs that assessment of the unfair nature of terms shall relate neither to the definition of the main subject matter of the contract nor to the adequacy of the price 'in so far as these terms are in plain intelligible language'. This, the Court reasoned, imposes a 'requirement of transparency' which, given the consumer's 'position of weakness', must be interpreted broadly.[180] Therefore the requirement that a contractual

[176] Case C-168/05 [2006] ECR I-10421.

[177] See S. Weatherill, *EU Consumer Law and Policy* (Elgar European Law, 2012).

[178] Eg Case C-168/05 note 176, para 36; Case C-618/10 *Banco Español de Crédito* v *Joaquín Calderón Camino* judgment of 14 June 2012, para 40; Case C-415/11 *Aziz* judgment of 14 March 2013, para 45.

[179] Case C-26/13 judgment of 30 April 2014.

[180] Paras 71–72.

term must be drafted in plain intelligible language covers not only formal grammatical intelligibility but also a transparent explanation of how the term shall operate, as a means to ensure the consumer is in a position to evaluate the economic consequences on the basis of clear criteria.[181] So, in the particular circumstances, the contract should set out transparently exactly how the mechanism of conversion for the foreign currency shall operate. If it does not, the relevant term does not escape review by a court pursuant to Article 4(2) of the Directive.

Directive 99/44 on consumer sales and guarantees, another measure of legislative harmonization,[182] formed the background to *Froujke Faber.*[183] The Court held that a national court must determine whether an individual counts as a 'consumer' even if the buyer has not relied on that status in the proceedings, for otherwise the rights intended to be conferred by the Directive would be jeopardized. The Court explicitly cited case law dealing with Directive 93/13, and stressed the common rationale of using EU measures of harmonization to address the consumer's relatively weak position while also seeking to advance the internal market. The *quality* of the harmonized landscape is constitutionally significant.

6.5 CONCLUSION

There is a broad band of possible 'internal markets', ranging from one which is radically decentralized as a result of a choice in favour of unrestricted inter-jurisdictional competition to, at the other extreme, one which is radically centralized in the sense that law-making competence has been completely stripped away from the constituent units in favour of the central authority. The EU lies somewhere in between. Its internal market is based on a sharing of competences between the EU and its Member States, as is made plain by Article 4(2)(a) TFEU,[184] but precisely what this entails is not spelled out by the Treaty. Article 26 TFEU itself defines the internal market as an 'area without internal frontiers in which the free movement of goods, persons, services and capital is ensured in accordance with the provisions of this Treaty'. The relevant 'provisions of this Treaty' are of two distinct but complementary types: those that stop public and private actors from impeding cross-border trade and those which grant competence to the EU to adopt its own common rules which

[181] Para 75. [182] OJ [1999] L171/12.

[183] Case C-497/13 judgment of 4 June 2015.

[184] The only exception is the establishing of the competition rules necessary for the functioning of the internal market, which is an exclusive EU competence (Art 3(1)(b) TFEU).

will govern the terms of that cross-border trade. This is negative and positive law. But two particular ambiguities are left unsettled by the Treaty, and these have formed the core of this chapter's examination of the law of the internal market. It is left unclear what is subject to review in the name of the internal market. This is the vertical issue: it concerns the extent to which the EU exercises control over the exercise of autonomy within the Member States. It involves defining the scope of application of the free movement and competition rules and also the reach of the EU's legislative competences. These are thresholds that are demonstrably difficult to fix. The second ambiguity asks how, in circumstances where the threshold is crossed and Member State autonomy is accordingly subjected to review in the name of EU internal market law, it is decided whether the matter is resolved by the Court, or instead whether the matter belongs to the legislative process. This is a horizontal issue: it goes to the relationship between the EU's judicial and political institutions.

The choices are decisive in determining the—centralized, deregulated, or re-regulated—shape of the EU's internal market, but they are not pre-ordained by the Treaties. The Court's case law in particular has been hugely influential in the allocation of regulatory competence over goods and services in the EU. The Court is not afraid to take decisions that have major consequences for the vertical distribution of competences and the horizontal allocation of powers. *Cassis de Dijon* is of this type. The cases which are most vulnerable to criticism are those where it neglects just how much competence it is undermining at national level and how little can be corrected by the exercise of legislative power at EU level. This is why *Viking Line* attracts so much attention for over-pressing the capacity of internal market law to subvert national autonomy in matters of social welfare.

The skeletal nature of the Treaty provisions ensures heavy reliance on the interpretative role of the Court. The Commission's observation that the internal market will never be 'completed'[185] has not only an economic but also a legal dimension.

[185] Commission's Internal Market Scoreboard No 11, note 4.

7
WHO IS THE CITIZEN OF THE UNION?

7.1 INTRODUCTION

Articles 9 TEU and 20(1) TFEU provide that every national of a Member State shall be a Citizen of the Union. And the Court has ringingly asserted that 'Union citizenship is destined to be the fundamental status of nationals of the Member States.'[1]

The question is what this really means. Citizenship of a modern European State brings with it a range of well-recognized rights and duties, such as voting, paying tax, access to social welfare, and performance of military service. All States have different detailed patterns, but the broad idea of the individual citizen's intimate connection with and expected (if not inevitably forthcoming) allegiance to his or her State is largely or wholly missing at EU level. Citizenship of the Union must have a different meaning and content. But what? And why? Articles 9 TEU and 20(1) TFEU also provide that Union citizenship 'shall be additional to and not replace national citizenship'. Citizenship of the EU is no more intended to replace citizenship of the State than the EU is intended to replace the Member States. It supplements it and, on an optimistic reading, it strengthens it to provide a set of entitlements and protection that reach beyond that which can be provided at national level—just as the EU supplements its Member States and, on an optimistic reading, strengthens their capacity to deliver what their citizens demand in an age of mutual interdependence. But, to repeat, what does this actually entail?

The attributes of Citizenship of the Union which are listed in the Treaties are less extensive than those that accrue at State level. There is, by way of vivid example, a right conferred on a national of a Member State resident in another Member State to vote in local but not in national Parliamentary elections in that host State. Here lies a wall between the citizenship of the State and that of the EU. Citizenship as a status conferred by the EU has been built up incrementally by the economic freedoms set

[1] First in Case C-184/99 *Rudy Grzelczyk* v Centre public d'aide sociale d'Ottignies-Louvain-la-Neuve [2001] ECR I-6193 and frequently since.

out in the Treaty, supplemented by the Citizenship provisions created at Maastricht, amplified by legislative intervention, and interpreted creatively by the Court, but there are clearly rights and duties that apply to citizens of a State that do not extend to migrant Citizens of the Union. And the entitlements of Citizens of the Union are themselves subject to sub-division: some people are more favoured than others. This is in part the vestigial trace of the trans-frontier *economic* focus of EU law concerning persons which pre-dates the arrival of Citizenship in the Treaty with effect from the entry into force of the Maastricht Treaty in 1993, and so too it is in part attributable to the notion that EU law rights are triggered only where there is a cross-border dimension: otherwise the matter rests with the internal arrangements preferred by the Member State. It is also the consequence of the creative but, in detail, unpredictable willingness of the Court to amplify both the personal and material scope of protection for the migrant and sometimes the non-migrant, extending too to confer derivative rights on their family members, whether EU citizens or third country nationals. There is some coherence to the sliding scale—the more closely integrated into the host State the migrant, the more generously he or she is protected—but there are inevitably some accumulated ad hoc eccentricities as well as bright lines which, when crossed, make dramatic changes to the migrant's entitlements. And some of the lines are not bright at all.

This area of law is, kindly described, in flux. Less charitably, it is a mess, and one caused by the Member States choosing in the negotiation of Maastricht Treaty to create a status, Citizenship of the Union, which was loosely envisaged as an inducement to the peoples of Europe to treat the EU as something more attractive than simply an economic engine and yet which was left thoroughly ambiguous and ill-shaped in its detail. The Court too, even though required to sift complex and ill-planned material, must shoulder some responsibility for the erratic deployment of the status of Citizenship to achieve ad hoc deepening of the rights enjoyed by some individuals in the EU.

Describing the state of the law in this area is to describe something quite different from that which prevailed twenty years ago and quite probably something quite different from that which will prevail in twenty years' time. EU law governing Citizenship in the Union and, more broadly, people is a moody creature. The aim of this chapter is accordingly to supply some detail but, of greater importance to understanding, to show how, where, and why the scope of protection granted by EU law, and its relationship with national law, is dynamic and contested.

7.2 CITIZENSHIP IN THE TREATIES

The attributes of Citizenship of the Union are listed in the Treaties. Introduced with effect in 1993 by the Maastricht Treaty and lightly amended since, they are now dictated by Articles 18–25 TFEU in Part Two of the TFEU which is entitled *Non-Discrimination and Citizenship of the Union*. A full understanding of EU law's engagement with people would necessarily require analysis also of the provisions on the free movement of persons (Chapter 6) and the increasingly vital contribution of the Charter of Fundamental Rights (Chapters 3 and 4), but the core governing the status of Citizenship of the Union stretches today over these eight articles.

Article 18(1) prohibits any discrimination on grounds of nationality. This is plainly apt for direct application by courts. Article 18(2) grants a supplementary legislative competence to adopt rules designed to prohibit such discrimination, which has not been used, and Article 19 adds a further wider legislative competence to take appropriate action to combat discrimination based on sex, racial or ethnic origin, religion or belief, disability, age, or sexual orientation. This, or more precisely its predecessor before the revisions made by the Lisbon Treaty, has been used. It was relied on in the adoption of Directive 2000/43 on the principle of equal treatment on the basis of racial or ethnic origin,[2] Directive 2000/78 on equal treatment in employment and occupation,[3] and Directive 2000/113 on the principle of equal treatment between men and women in access to goods and services.[4]

Article 20(1) declares the establishment of Citizenship of the Union. Article 20(2) adds that Citizens of the Union shall enjoy the rights and be subject to the duties provided for in the Treaties, of which a non-exhaustive list is provided: (a) the right to move and reside freely within the territory of the Union; (b) the right to vote and to stand as candidates in elections to the European Parliament and in municipal elections in their Member State of residence, under the same conditions as nationals of that State; (c) the right to enjoy, in the territory of a third country in which the Member State of which they are nationals is not represented, the protection of the diplomatic and consular authorities of any Member State on the same conditions as the nationals of that State; and (d) the right to petition the European Parliament, to apply to the European Ombudsman, and to address the institutions and advisory bodies of the Union in any of the Treaty languages and to obtain a reply in the same language.

[2] OJ [2000] L180/22. [3] OJ [2000] L303/16. [4] OJ [2004] L373/37.

The following Articles confirm these rights and permit their legislative amplification. So Article 21(1) confers on Citizens of the Union the right to move and reside freely within the territory of the Union, which serves as mere confirmation of what is already contained in Article 20(2), but also provides a supplementary legislative competence to adopt provisions with a view to facilitating the exercise of relevant rights. Article 22 performs a similar job, setting out a statement of principle coupled to the grant of legislative competence, in relation to the right conferred on Union citizens to vote and stand at municipal and European Parliament elections in the Member State in which he or she resides under the same conditions as nationals of that State. Article 23 deals in parallel with diplomatic or consular protection and Article 24, with cross-reference to Article 11 TEU, deals with the citizens' initiative, as well as the right to petition the European Parliament, to apply to the Ombudsman, and to write to the institutions and agencies of the EU. Article 25 imposes a reporting requirement on the Commission on the application of the provisions of this Part of the Treaty, and allows for a legislative competence to strengthen the rights listed in Article 20(2), albeit that, in line with a thematic anxiety about extension in the profile of EU law rights and obligations driven from within the system and so escaping direct Member State control, the pre-conditions for resort to this legislative competence are highly restrictive. In particular the requirement of Council unanimity plus a requirement of Member State approval in accordance with their respective constitutional requirements means that, unsurprisingly, no legislation has been adopted.

Title II of the TEU, *Provisions on democratic principles*, forms part of the Citizenship landscape. Its Article 10(2) TEU states that citizens are directly represented at Union level in the European Parliament. Article 10(3) adds, as optimistic as it is gnomic, that citizens 'shall have the right to participate in the democratic life of the Union'. Article 11(4) gifts a special bauble: not less than one million citizens who are nationals of a significant number of Member States may petition the Commission to submit a proposal for a legal act designed to implement the Treaties. Corporate interests and extremist groups with particular grudges will probably be able to cross this threshold. Citizens with a general aspiration that the EU shall improve their lives obtain no obvious benefit from it.

It is easy to conclude that Citizenship of the Union is not quite as exciting as it might initially sound. What is excluded is at least as striking as what is included. Most striking of all, the voting rights are carefully written to exclude what is surely the most significant aspect of the franchise: the right to vote in *national* elections to form the government. Migrant EU citizens pay their taxes in their host State, but they do not obtain a right to choose the government that sets the State's tax rates. In this particular and highly important sense, the migrant EU citizen is not treated as a valid member of the national community. One can make a cogent case that opening up voting rights also in national elections to resident nationals of other Member States would represent a proper reflection of their political status, economic contribution, and connection to and involvement with the host polity,[5] but so far this is a step that is constitutionally too far for the Member States to agree to take.

Matters such as access to consular protection and the right to petition the Ombudsman are doubtless of value from time to time but they are far from the essence of civic responsibility. Such benefits do not come close to inflating Citizenship of the Union to anything that seriously resembles the rights of citizenship that accrue at State level. There are other pieces of evidence elsewhere in the Treaty which reveal the enduring perception that migrants are never to be fully assimilated to the status enjoyed by nationals of their host State. These include Article 45(4) TFEU, which excludes employment in the public service from the reach of the rules governing the free movement of workers, and Article 51 TFEU, which similarly separates activities connected with the exercise of official authority from the rules on freedom of establishment. Moreover, according to a logic of calculated evasion which seems to have underpinned the crafting of the status of Citizenship, the Treaty provisions themselves are written conditionally. Article 18's prohibition of discrimination on grounds of nationality applies 'within the scope of application of the Treaties, and without prejudice to any special provisions contained therein'. All the rights listed in Article 20 fall to be 'exercised in accordance with the conditions and limits defined by the Treaties and by the measures adopted thereunder'. The right of free movement and residence created by Article 21(1) is explicitly declared subject to 'the limitations and conditions laid down in the Treaties and by the measures adopted to give them effect'. In strict constitutional terms this does not even need saying. The foundationally important principle of conferral found in Article 5 TEU dictates that the EU operates only on the basis of the competences conferred on it by its Treaties. So in this sense the explicit references to limits found in the provisions pertaining to Citizenship are mere repetition. Accordingly, in one of the Court's first decisions on the impact of Citizenship after

[5] See A. Lansbergen and J. Shaw, 'National Membership Models in a Multi-level Europe' (2010) 8 Intl Jnl Constl Law 50.

the entry into force of the Maastricht Treaty, *Land Nordrhein Westfalen* v *Uecker, Jacquet*, it ruled that German nationals who resided and worked in Germany and had never exercised the right to freedom of movement across borders within the EU could not rely on EU law to protect the position of their family members faced with discriminatory treatment.[6] The matter was purely internal to Germany. The referring national court had asked teasingly whether 'the fundamental principles of a Community moving towards European Union' permitted the retention of such a law that discriminated against a State's own nationals, because after all a migrant EU national in Germany would certainly have enjoyed protection under EU law provided he or she was economically active, but the Court was unmoved. Citizenship of the Union, it explained, was 'not intended to extend the scope of ratione materiae of the Treaty also to internal situations which have no link with Community law'.[7]

This dustily dismissive ruling already contained the seeds of temptation. Citizenship as a legal status does not help in 'internal situations which have no link' with EU law, but, even if in *Uecker, Jacquet* the Court saw no such link, there is scope for creative interpretation of just when an adequate 'link' exists as a means to trigger the material scope of protective effect of EU law. Moreover, the national court was on to something as it trailed suggestively the notion of 'a Community moving towards European Union'. By agreeing to the reforms of the Maastricht Treaty, which created the European *Union* and its associated status of Citizenship with effect from 1993, the Member States had changed the prevailing constitutional rhetoric, and even if the substantive changes were in detail relatively unremarkable, they could hardly have expected that the Court, given its track record and in particular its commitment to the EU legal order as a source of *individual* rights, would remain interpretatively conservative. Citizenship of the Union was 'a futures' market'.[8]

Most of all, Citizenship is plainly not a status that is written on a blank slate. The rights of people guaranteed by EU law have been built up by the development of the economic freedoms set out from day one in the founding Treaties, most of all the free movement of workers, the self-employed, companies, and providers and recipients of services. The principles of direct effect and supremacy granted them transformative power apt to be wielded by persons (both natural and legal). Such provisions confer rights on economically active migrants and form a core

[6] Cases C-64/96 and C-65/96 [1997] ECR I-3171. [7] Para 23.

[8] H. U. Jessurun D'Oliveira, 'Union Citizenship: Pie in the Sky?' in A. Rosas and E. Antola (eds), *A Citizen's Europe* (Sage Publications, 1995), p 82.

part of the legal structure and economic motivation of the EU's internal market. So even in advance of the arrival in the Treaties in 1993 of the status of Citizenship of the Union, there were already citizenship rights *of a sort*—rights belonging to the 'market citizen'. How much more than a 'market citizen' EU law envisaged the migrant as, and how more it should so envisage the migrant, was a live topic of discussion before the Member States took their ill-defined leap at Maastricht, and engaged not only the governing provisions on free movement but also important supporting secondary legislation, which amplified the rights and protection enjoyed by the economic migrant plus, as is thematically unavoidable, the accumulated case law of the creative Court.[9] The attribution of the status of Citizenship of the Union to nationals of the Member States sent the cycle of creativity and inquiry spinning ever more vigorously. How much more than an internal market is the EU—how much more than a market citizen is the Citizen of the Union? Articles 18–25 TFEU, the key provisions entitled *Citizenship*, stand in ill-defined combination alongside the long-standing provisions on free movement, and it is a tough inquiry to pin down exactly who may enter and reside in another Member State, what their entitlements may be once there, and the extent to which EU law has wider effect on persons where they are not economically active and/or have not migrated from one Member State to another. This chapter maps contested terrain.

7.3 DIRECTIVE 2004/38 ON THE RIGHTS OF MOVEMENT AND RESIDENCE OF CITIZENS IN THE UNION

Directive 2004/38 gathers together the conditions governing the exercise of the right of free movement and residence which are enjoyed by Union citizens and their family members, and also covers limits which may exceptionally be imposed on grounds of public policy, public security, or public health.[10] It applies only to Union citizens who move to or reside in a Member State other than that of which they are a national and to family members (as defined in Article 2) who accompany or join them. This does not mean that other lesser forms of movement, nor indeed situations involving no cross-border movement at all, inevitably fall outside the scope

[9] See eg M. Everson, 'The Legacy of the Market Citizen' in J. Shaw and G. More (eds), *New Legal Dynamics of European Union* (OUP, 1995). Cf N. Nic Shuibhne, 'The Resilience of EU Market Citizenship' (2010) 47 CMLRev 1597.

[10] OJ [2004] L158/77.

of EU law; only that they are outside the scope of Directive 2004/38. (This wider reach is examined at Section 7.5.)

The rules set out in the Directive are complex and beset by provisos and derogations, and the conditions governing administrative formalities are dense. But, stripped down to their essence, the core scheme separates out the migrant's presence in the host Member State into three distinct categories: presence for up to three months, presence for between three months and five years, and presence for more than five years.

Article 6 grants Union citizens the right of residence on the territory of another Member State for a period of up to three months without any conditions or any formalities other than the requirement to hold a valid identity card or passport. Family members, even if not nationals of an EU Member State, enjoy a right to accompany or join the Union citizen.

Article 7 deals with a right of residence for more than three months. This is subdivided according to the category into which the individual falls. Migrant workers or self-employed persons (and certain family members) enjoy the right by virtue of their status. And Article 7(3) protects workers and the self-employed person who lose that status in defined circumstances, including illness or accident, and involuntary unemployment. Others—including the self-funding migrant and students—acquire the right *only* provided they have sufficient resources not to become a burden on the social assistance system of the host Member State and have comprehensive sickness insurance cover in the host Member State. What is visible here is the attempt to craft a general system of rights for Union citizens which nevertheless cannot be, or at least has not been, detached from the pre-existing focus on special privileged status accorded to the economically active, including the 'worker' within the meaning of Article 45 TFEU and the self-employed person covered by Article 49 TFEU. Article 7 of Directive 2004/38 therefore provides a concrete illustration of the persisting superior status for some purposes of the 'worker' in EU law.

Chapter IV of Directive 2004/38 deals with the right of permanent residence. According to Article 16 the general rule is that Union citizens (and certain family members) who have resided legally for a continuous period of five years in the host Member State shall have the right of permanent residence there. Article 17 provides that the right may accrue before completion of a continuous period of five years of residence to (inter alia) particular types of workers or self-employed persons who have reached retirement age or who have stopped working as a result of permanent incapacity to work.

The Directive envisages that a Member State may be entitled to expel a migrant EU national from its territory, but the circumstances in which this is justified are carefully circumscribed and, moreover, detailed procedural safeguards are inscribed in Chapter VI of the Directive. Beyond that detail and beyond Articles 41 and 47 (in particular) of the Charter of Fundamental Rights, a right to be heard is anyway inherent in respect for the rights of the defence, which is a general principle of EU law.[11]

The migrant is protected. Clearly missing, however, is any absolute right to move to and reside indefinitely in another Member State vested in any Citizen of the Union irrespective of status or activity.

7.4 SOME CITIZENS ARE MORE EQUAL THAN OTHERS

Directive 2004/38, as explained in the previous sub-section, establishes three distinct categories of migrant. Their entitlements are graded according to the intimacy of the association with the host State. Moreover, the Treaty itself, pursuant to both the provisions on free movement and those on Citizenship, creates rights, but these too vary according to both material and personal scope. Gradation here is partly the consequence of clear Treaty steer, especially in favour of the economically active migrant, and partly the consequence of painstaking and sometimes opportunistic adjudication by the Court, especially in the name of Citizenship of the Union. There is nothing simple and transparent about EU law governing people.

Clearly it is those who are economically active who are able to enjoy rights at the most generous level. The 'worker' has long been interpreted broadly by the Court.[12] The Court has adopted a similarly generous interpretation of scope of the Treaty provisions governing the self-employed and the free movement of services. For example, it long ago decided that the right to migrate in order to provide services is accompanied by a right to migrate in order to receive services.[13] The Court has on occasion broken ground that has subsequently been covered more thoroughly by the legislative process. That the person genuinely seeking work is covered by the Treaty provisions was originally decided by a creative and purposive interpretation of the Treaty supplied by the Court.[14] The Court led, Directive 2004/38 follows: the

[11] Eg Case C-166/13 *Sophie Mukarubega* judgment of 5 November 2014; Case C-249/13 *Khaled Boudjlida* judgment of 11 December 2014.

[12] Eg Case C-53/81 *Levin* [1982] ECR 1035; Case C-139/85 *Kempf* [1986] ECR 1741. Case C-507/12 *Saint Prix* judgment of 19 June 2014.

[13] Joined Cases 282/82 and 26/83 *Luisi and Carbone* v *Ministero del Tesoro* [1984] ECR 377.

[14] Case C-292/89 *Antonissen* [1991] ECR 745.

Union citizen who entered the territory of another Member State in order to seek employment shall not be expelled 'for as long as the Union citizens can provide evidence that they are continuing to seek employment and that they have a genuine chance of being engaged'.[15] So the status of the jobseeker is recognized by Directive 2004/38 but the duration of that person's right to keep looking for work is not measured in months or years (which means in turn that a Member State may not impose a bright line cut-off[16]).

In similar vein, providers and recipients of services enjoy the basic rights of entry into and residence on the territory of the Member State in which they wish to be economically active which are guaranteed by the Treaty. Moreover, the rights are supplemented by a body of long-standing secondary legislation which amplifies the rights and protection enjoyed by the economic migrant, under a double assumption that labour mobility will only emerge as a significant reality in the EU if relatively generous inducement is provided and also that people, as distinct from goods, should be treated with more dignity than simply as motors of the more competitive internal market. So Regulation 492/2011 on freedom of movement within the Union is the key text as far as workers are concerned, being the latest codified iteration of a set of legislative provisions designed to protect and promote migrant workers first enacted in the 1960s.[17] It is supported by Directive 2014/54 which is designed to promote and strengthen the effective exercise of the rights conferred by primary and secondary Union law.[18] The core aim is the prohibition of discrimination on grounds of nationality. Equal treatment with nationals of the host State is mandated in matters of access to jobs, working conditions, dismissal, and access to training. That right to equal treatment extends to 'social and tax advantages',[19] where there may be no direct connection to the work performed by the migrant but where denial of such equal treatment would diminish incentives to cross borders and also shove the migrant into an inferior second-class social ghetto. The legislative *acquis*, typically interpreted by the Court in a manner that is generous in the light of such motivations, has long tended to strengthen the migrant EU national's position: its insistence on a wide understanding of 'social and tax advantages' stretches back over forty years.[20] Family members too, whether EU nationals or third country nationals (TCNs), enjoy legislative rights of entry, residence, and non-discrimination on the territory of

[15] Art 14(4).

[16] Cf Case C-67/14 *Jobcenter Berlin Neukölln* v *Alimanovic* judgment of 15 September 2015.

[17] OJ [2011] L141/1. [18] OJ [2014] L128/8. [19] Art 7(2) Reg 492/2011.

[20] Case 32/75 *Cristini* v *SNCF* [1975] ECR 1085; see also eg Case C-46/12 *L.N.* judgment of 21 February 2013.

the host Member State, albeit not in their own right, but rather as rights that derive from the worker. Here too the logic is that a worker will readily move across borders and enjoy a status higher than a mere economic instrument only if able also to enjoy the security of the family unit. The self-employed and service providers enjoy protection under comparably structured and motivated secondary legislation.

The generosity of equal treatment guaranteed to the economically active is more limited as one moves down the migrant hierarchy envisaged by the Treaty and secondary legislation and shaped further by the Court. Moreover, there are hierarchical gradations *within* the charmed circle of the economically active. This is tough going.

Article 24 of Directive 2004/38 covers *Equal treatment*. It provides that subject to specific provision made by the Treaty and secondary law, 'all Union citizens residing on the basis of this Directive in the territory of the host Member State shall enjoy equal treatment with the nationals of that Member State within the scope of the Treaty'. This extends to family members who have the right of residence or permanent residence. But, contrary to initial appearance, this does not strip away the privileged status of the economically active and extend equal treatment rights to all Citizens of the Union. Article 24(2) reveals a legislative nervousness about financial burdens shouldered by the host State. It attaches a derogation. A host Member State shall

> not be obliged to confer entitlement to social assistance during the first three months of residence or, where appropriate, the longer period provided for in Article 14(4)(b), nor shall it be obliged, prior to acquisition of the right of permanent residence, to grant maintenance aid for studies, including vocational training, consisting in student grants or student loans to persons other than workers, self-employed persons, persons who retain such status and members of their families.

The broad aim of this reservation is clear. Although Article 6 of Directive 2004/38 provides that Union citizens (and certain family members) are entitled to the right of residence on the territory of another Member State for a period of up to three months without any conditions or any formalities other than the requirement to hold a valid identity card or passport, Article 24(2) makes clear that this confers no right to social assistance during this three-month period. Moreover, the right of residence is anyway lost if the citizen becomes an unreasonable burden on the social assistance system of the host Member State,[21] although action taken against

[21] Art 14(1).

a migrant pursuant to this protection of national autonomy must meet EU law requirements of proportionality.[22]

The restriction envisaged by Article 24(2), whereby social assistance and maintenance aid for studies need not be extended to migrants who are not workers, self-employed persons, persons who retain such status, and members of their families, has been the subject of interpretation by the Court. Its precise scope is plainly of direct relevance to understanding just how much better off is the Citizen of the Union when he or she is (in short) economically active; or, seen from the opposite direction, how strategically helpful it might be for an EU national to play the hierarchical game by finding a way to elevate him- or herself into one of the privileged categories (by becoming—more—economically active and/or by crossing a border).

Vatsouras addressed the withdrawal of benefits from those looking for a job.[23] Article 39(2) EC, now Article 45(2) TFEU, insists on no discrimination on the basis of nationality in the grant of benefits intended to facilitate access to the labour market. The Court in *Vatsouras* then held that the derogation in Article 24(2) of Directive 2004/38 must be interpreted in accordance with the intent of this Treaty requirement, so benefits intended to facilitate access to the labour market cannot be 'social assistance' within Article 24(2) of the Directive. This suggests an anxiety on the part of the Court to adopt a relatively narrow view of the scope of the denial of equality rights envisaged by Article 24(2) of the Directive. But ultimately some situations will fall within the scope of Article 24(2) and the right to equal treatment will then be excluded. Much depends on precisely where the line is drawn between those benefits covered by Article 45(2) TFEU as devices for facilitating access to the labour market and those instead subject to derogation from the principle of equal treatment by virtue of Article 24(2) of Directive 2004/38 as mere social assistance or maintenance aid lacking an adequate tie to employment. The sense of uncertainty is compounded when one appreciates that it is constitutionally conceivable that the Court might decide that the limits envisaged by Article 24(2) of Directive 2004/38 are overridden by direct reliance on the Treaty provisions themselves. After all, a Directive cannot take away rights granted by the Treaty. But the exact scope of rights granted by the Treaty is plainly ambiguous, and the Court seems minded to adopt a cautious approach according to which it interprets the Treaty

[22] Case C-413/99 *Baumbast* [2002] ECR I-7091; Case C-398/06 *Commission* v *Netherlands* [2008] ECR I-56.

[23] Joined Cases C-22/08 and C-23/08 [2009] ECR I-4585.

as no more favourable to the migrant than the Directive. *Vatsouras*, by insisting that benefits intended to facilitate access to the labour market cannot be 'social assistance', serves to confine the restrictive effect of Article 24(2), but there is judicial reticence to use the *Treaty* to achieve a more aggressive destabilization of the legislative compromise struck in Article 24(2).[24] In fact, the Court has on occasion applied restrictions envisaged by the Directive by analogy to cases beyond its reach where only the Treaty is in play.[25]

Given the legitimacy challenges associated with an adventurous reading of obligations imposed by primary law which is apt to curtail the scope for legislative adjustment, there is much to be said for judicial restraint. There is a good argument in this area for preferring careful legislative development as the principal route of law reform ahead of the ad hoc eccentricities of judicial decisions, and a good argument too that the Court has latterly shifted into this more cautious gear, at least on occasion.[26] This, however, does not mean that the Court has abdicated a leadership role in cases that fall *outside* the scope of Directive 2004/38, some of which are encountered in Section 7.5. And if Article 24(2) were amended to be even *less* generous to the individual as a result of shifting political moods about the worth of migration, an intriguing challenge would confront the Court were it asked, as it certainly would be, to use the Treaty to subvert such legislative retreat.

In understanding the thematically central point that entitlements vary, the important point to grasp is that Article 24(2) of the Directive's restrictions melt away where a *worker* is concerned. Were the national court to have concluded that Vatsouras was a 'worker' it would have been required to grant the right to the relevant benefits in accordance with Article 24(1) of Directive 2004/38.[27] More broadly, as explained in this section, Regulation 492/2011 provides that the migrant worker may not be treated differently from national workers by reason of his or her nationality in respect of a much wider scope of matters, stretching beyond conditions of employment and work to social and tax advantages and access to training. The purpose is to root out any disincentive to inter-State labour mobility

[24] Eg Case C-158/07 *Förster* [2008] ECR I-8507.

[25] Eg Case C-456/12 *O, B* judgment of 12 March 2014.

[26] Eg M. Dougan, 'The Bubble that Burst: Exploring the Legitimacy of the Case Law on the Free Movement of Union Citizens', Ch 5 in M. Adams, H. De Waele, J. Meeusen, and G. Straetmans (eds), *Judging Europe's Judges: The Legitimacy of the Case Law of the European Court of Justice* (Hart, 2013).

[27] Para 32.

but the consequence is to place a strong legal grip on national welfare choices. The benefits are to be extended to migrants.

The 'worker' is for these purposes not a homogenous category. In *Brian Francis Collins* v *Secretary of State for Work and Pensions* the Court ruled that persons who have already entered into the employment market in another Member State—and who are working or who have worked but are no longer working—are 'workers' who may rely on the applicable secondary legislation to claim the same social and tax advantages as national workers.[28] By contrast, persons who are merely looking for work in another Member State are 'workers' but benefit from the principle of equal treatment only as regards access to employment. Collins, a migrant jobseeker whose previous presence in the UK was remote in time and wholly unassociated with his new quest for work, fell into the latter category and accordingly enjoyed a diminished range of protection when compared with what he could have expected as a currently active worker. In *Vatsouras* the Court explained that a Member State may confine the grant of allowances to cases where 'it has been possible to establish a real link between the jobseeker and the labour market of that State'.[29] That 'real link' could be found (in particular but not exclusively) by establishing that the migrant has for a reasonable period genuinely sought work in the Member State in question. A residence requirement imposed by a State as a condition of access to a benefit is plainly likely to discriminate indirectly on the basis of nationality, because in practice nationals of the State will meet it more commonly than migrants, but it is not directly discriminatory on the basis of nationality, since it can in principle be met by a migrant who is a national of another Member State. As a matter of EU law, the point is that indirect—but never direct—discrimination is open to objective justification, and in such circumstances the residence requirement is capable of justification as a means to check the existence of that legally significant 'real link' between the applicant for the benefit who is seeking work and the national employment market. It is however also clear as a matter of EU law that a threshold requirement such as a minimum residence requirement must be based on criteria that are clear and known in advance and, moreover, that the period must not exceed what is necessary in order for the national authorities to be able to satisfy themselves that the person concerned is genuinely seeking work in the employment market of the host Member State.

[28] Case C-138/02 [2004] ECR I-2703.

[29] Para 38, citing Case C-224/98 *D'Hoop* [2002] ECR I-6191.

Migrant students, like jobseekers, live in this intermediate world: unable to eat at the top table, reserved to workers, the self-employed, and those engaged in the provision and receipt of services, but able to lay claim to some degree of equal treatment with students holding the nationality of the Member State to which they have moved in order to further their education. In *Rudy Grzelczyk* the applicant, a French national studying in Belgium, had been denied the 'minimex', a minimum subsistence allowance paid in Belgium.[30] It was well established under existing case law that payment of the minimex was a 'social advantage' to which a migrant worker would have been entitled on the same terms as locals, but Grzelczyk was not a migrant worker. He was a migrant student. The Court proceeded step by step. A student of Belgian nationality in precisely the same situation as Grzelczyk would satisfy the conditions of access to the minimex. So refusal to grant it to Grzelczyk was straightforward discrimination on the ground of nationality. And this, the Court continued, was discrimination that is certainly forbidden, by what is now Article 18 TFEU—*provided* the matter falls within the scope of application of the Treaty. In the 1980s the Court had concluded that assistance given to students for maintenance and training fell in principle outside the scope of EU law.[31] But now it decided that things had changed. The Court relied on the Maastricht Treaty's creation of Citizenship of the European Union and its addition of a new chapter in what is now the TFEU devoted to education and vocational training to rule that the matter of student support that arose in *Grzelczyk* now fell within the material scope of EU law. And so the applicant was entitled to be treated in the same way as locals: he was entitled to the minimex.

The Court is doing more than tamely following the instructions set out in the Treaties. The Maastricht amendments on which it relied did not *explicitly* foresee the changes it was now making in ruling on the protective reach of EU law. But the Court was justified in drawing attention to the fact that the scope of EU law *had* been changed— consensually, by the Member States, and in a way that could not be supposed to be without consequence. Once the applicant had been brought within the personal scope of EU law—as a migrant lawfully resident in another Member State—the combined force of the status of Citizenship and the rule of non-discrimination on grounds of nationality required by Article 18 took over to grant him a right to equal treatment, and then reference

[30] Case C-184/99 note 1.

[31] Case 197/86 *Brown* [1988] ECR 3205, cited in *Grzelczyk*.

to the Treaty provisions granting the EU a (limited) competence in the field of education placed the matter within the material scope of EU law. So if a Belgian student got the minimex, so must he. *Grzelczyk* allowed the Court to project its approach on to a wider plane: 'Union citizenship is destined to be the fundamental status of nationals of the Member States, enabling those who find themselves in the same situation to enjoy the same treatment in law irrespective of their nationality, subject to such exceptions as are expressly provided for.'[32] This strongly suggests a desire to abandon ad hoc decision-making involving the grant of particular rights to particular groups of (economic) actors and instead promotes a vision of universal protection of individual rights benefiting Citizens of the Union. That in turn suggests a desire to avoid taking the twists and limitations of the Treaty and the secondary legislation *too* seriously: and yet the Court, even at its most creative, may not ignore its legal environment. And in concrete terms the *Grzelczyk* formula places heavy practical emphasis on discovery of just when equal treatment in law irrespective of nationality may be withheld: what *are* the exceptions?

Dany Bidar concerned a French national who had moved with his mother to the UK.[33] He was granted assistance with tuition fees but he was refused a student loan to support his maintenance costs in pursuing a course in economics at University College London. This was because he was not 'settled' in the UK. Bidar contended that this British practice constituted unlawful discrimination on grounds of nationality, forbidden by what is now Article 18 TFEU. The Court agreed that he was able to enjoy rights under EU law to move to another Member State to reside and to study there, and it agreed too that assistance for students, whether in the form of a subsidized loan or a grant intended to cover his maintenance costs, fell within the material scope of the Treaty, noting the significant extension in EU competence in the field of education brought about by Treaty revision. It then treated the rules of which Bidar had fallen foul as indirect discrimination on the grounds of nationality: the threshold requirement of 'settlement' in the UK could be satisfied by a national of any Member State but would typically be satisfied more readily by a British national. So the question was whether the British rules were objectively justified. The Court relied once again on a test based on a real or a genuine link between the migrant applicant and the host Member State from which a benefit was being claimed. The host Member State may demand a 'certain degree of integration into the society of that State'.[34] But—and

[32] Para 31. [33] Case C-209/03 [2005] ECR I-2119. [34] Para 57.

on this point the case of the student differs from that of the person seeking work—it cannot be required that a link be established with the host State's employment market. The 'certain degree of integration' into the host State's society could be assessed in conformity with EU law by reference to the student's residence in the host Member State for a certain length of time. A requirement that the student be 'settled' in the host State might similarly serve to demonstrate the necessary degree of integration. But the particular British rules challenged in *Bidar* did not survive such scrutiny. The problem was that they admitted no possible circumstances in which a national of another Member State could acquire the necessary 'settled' status as a student. So a student from another Member State who had a genuine link with British society was prevented from ever qualifying for a loan on the same terms as a British national. This was not compatible with EU law.

The Court's approach leaves it open to Member States to confine allocation of scarce resources in matters such as support for student maintenance costs to recipients who are integrated into local society. They must, however, strip out the unacceptably restrictive and indirectly discriminatory elements that contaminated the unlawful British scheme in *Bidar*. In *Jacqueline Förster* the Court agreed that tying a maintenance grant to support studies to a requirement of prior residence of five years in Germany was compatible with EU law.[35] It was indirectly discriminatory, because German nationals would typically comply more frequently than nationals of other Member States, but it was open to be met by nationals of other Member States, provided only that they served their five years' residence time. And it was objectively justified by the objective of ensuring that students in receipt of the grant were to a certain degree integrated into German society. The Court approved the five-year rule as a proportionate restriction with reference to Directive 2004/38's use of that same threshold, even though the Directive did not explicitly apply to the facts of the case. This is further evidence of the Court's cautious readiness to conduct creative interpretation of the Treaty with an eye to avoiding any incompatibility with the detailed choices made in particular areas by the EU's legislative process.

A *worker* who undertakes a course of education would be better treated. So, for example, in *L.N.* the applicant was entitled to access to a maintenance grant to support his education provided he was engaged in genuine and effective, albeit part-time, employment and even where

[35] Case C-158/07 [2008] ECR I-8507.

his main reason to enter the Member State in question, Denmark, was to study.[36] The use of the Citizenship provisions coupled to the rule of non-discrimination on grounds of nationality and a wide approach to the material scope of EU law reduces the significance of the dividing line between true 'workers' and individuals such as jobseekers and students, but it does not remove that dividing line—and in fact the applicability of the 'genuine link' test reasserts, while re-locating, the dividing line. It is clearly always strategically desirable for an applicant to be treated as a true worker for these purposes.

The importance of the Court's case law on Citizenship is that even where the individual does not fall within one of the favoured categories of economically active migrant recognized by the Treaty, the assistance of EU law is not exhausted. However, much will depend on exactly how far the host Member State may go in denying benefits on the basis that a 'genuine link' is missing. The broader this notion, the more autonomy is conditionally returned to the Member States. And the more ambiguous the test, the less likely that common approaches will emerge at national level.

It is characteristic of a judicially developed test such as that requiring a 'real link', which represents an attempt to negotiate a route between, on the one hand, placing migrant EU nationals on the same footing as locals and, on the other, respecting Member States' autonomy to favour particular limited groups of recipients of benefits, that it has led to frequent invitations in preliminary rulings to clarify in concrete cases what is at stake. What constitutes objective justification for refusal to grant a benefit that falls within the material scope of EU law to an EU national lawfully resident in the host Member State? Austrian motorway tolls were not payable by disabled persons—provided they were resident in Austria.[37] The Court adopted its orthodox approach in finding that what is now Article 18 TFEU applies in all cases falling within the scope of EU law, and therefore a disabled German on holiday in Austria could challenge the measure. The question was whether such a residence requirement, indirectly discriminatory on grounds of nationality, was objectively justified. The measure was designed to promote the mobility and social integration of disabled persons: the residence requirement reflected the integration of the recipient of free travel into Austrian society. The measure was lawful provided it was proportionate, a matter ultimately for the national court.

[36] Case C-46/12 *L.N.* judgment of 21 February 2013.

[37] Case C-103/08 *Arthur Gottwald* [2009] ECR I-9117.

In another illustrative decision the Court also left the final decision in the hands of the referring national court, but it was plainly unpersuaded that a Belgian 'tideover' allowance for young people leaving education and looking for their first job could be made conditional on having pursued a period of education in Belgium.[38] This was, once again, indirect discrimination on grounds of nationality and so could in principle be objectively justified, but the problem was that the rigidity of this criterion excluded the possibility of showing a 'real link' with Belgium such as to merit access to its social largesse through other pieces of relevant evidence, such as residence, marriage, or active jobseeking.

Illustrative cases have arisen in the converse situation, where a migrant *leaves* his or her Member State only to find that he or she is then ineligible to receive benefits payable only to those resident in the State he or she has quit. The Court has adopted a comparable approach which permits the State to withdraw support from the non-resident, but only where there is an objective justification for the residence rule. So, for example, where Dutch nationals resident in Spain were refused payments due to civilian war victims, the Court treated the refusal as a consequence of exercise of the right granted by what is now Article 21(1) TFEU to move and reside freely within the EU and therefore a breach of EU law unless objectively justified.[39] It considered that payments could properly be targeted at those who had links with the population of the Netherlands during and after the war, but the imposition of a rigid Dutch residence requirement could not be objectively justified. German rules making the award of an education grant for studies in another Member State for a period of more than one year subject to the condition that the applicant must have had permanent residence on German territory for at least three years prior to commencing those studies plainly constituted a restriction on the right to freedom of movement and residence promised by Article 21 TFEU.[40] Germany defended its rules on the basis that the condition ensured recipient students demonstrated a sufficient degree of integration into German society. The Court agreed that this was legitimate, noting that without a power to apply such a criterion to incoming and to migrating students a State might face a financially 'unreasonable burden'.[41] But it concluded that the proof required to demonstrate the genuine link was here unduly exclusive in nature: it disallowed other possible means to show the necessary

[38] Case C-367/11 *Deborah Prete* judgment of 25 October 2012.

[39] C-192/05 *Tas-Hagen* [2006] ECR I-10451.

[40] Joined Cases C-523/11 and C-585/11 *Prinz and Seeberger* judgment of 18 July 2013.

[41] Para 36.

connection, which might be as persuasive as uninterrupted residence for three years, such as connection through family, employment, language skills, or the existence of other social and economic factors.[42]

The Court has come a long way since its landmark ruling in *Maria Martinez Sala* v *Freistaat Bayern* in which, relying innovatively on the Treaty provisions on Citizenship, it ruled that a national of a Member State lawfully residing in the territory of another Member State falls within the personal scope of the Treaty and is accordingly entitled to, inter alia, protection from discrimination on grounds of nationality within the material scope of application of the Treaty.[43] This created 'a feeling of amazement',[44] for it reduced the gap between the entitlements of the economically active migrant and other migrants, but appeal to 'Citizenship' was not powerful enough to close it up altogether, and Directive 2004/38, in particular its Article 24(2) and the Court's own case law envisaging that Member States may withhold benefits from people lacking a 'real link' with their society, has marked out where inability to climb up the ladder into the privileged category of the economically active ('market citizen') forces individuals to reckon with such restraints. *Sala* was a substantive breakthrough and *Grzelczyk* gave it rhetorical punch, and since then the case law has become abundant, as the Court has been asked to elucidate how far protection reaches. The thematic tension is between treating EU migrants on a par with locals and respecting national budgetary control in matters of social provision. Where workers are concerned, preference for the former is readily informed by a productive economic logic, but where migrant individuals who are not economically active call on welfare provision a different logic is engaged, one of claimed social solidarity between migrants and locals. This plainly challenges deep-rooted assumptions about the connection between State and nationality.[45] More concretely, to load a State with the obligation to accept non-nationals within the safety net of its social welfare system is to undermine local choices about priorities in the allocation of finite resources, and may lead

[42] Cf Case C-220/12 *Thiele Meneses* v *Region Hannover* judgment of 24 October 2013; Case C-359/13 *Martens* judgment of 26 February 2015.

[43] Case C-85/96 [1998] ECR I-2691.

[44] D. Thym, 'Towards Real Citizenship? The Judicial Construction of Union Citizenship and its Limits', Ch 6 in *Judging Europe's Judges* note 26, p 156.

[45] See eg A. Somek, 'Solidarity Decomposed: Being and Time in European Citizenship' (2007) 32 EL Rev 787; D. Thym, 'The Elusive Limits of Solidarity: Residence Rights of and Social Benefits for Economically Inactive Union Citizens' (2015) 52 CMLRev 17; A. Hoogenboom, 'In Search of a Rationale for the EU Citizenship Jurisprudence' (2015) 35 OxJLS 301.

to reduction in per capita budgetary allocation. To push in favour of the individual's equality rights protected by EU law despite the financial consequences for collective social support provided by national governments is to strain the legitimacy of the EU project.

Attacks on the phenomenon of 'benefit tourism' within the EU are typically imprecisely explained and short of quantitative empirical support, but they are rooted in a depiction of domestic systems of welfare support being accessed illegitimately. This is an unsettlingly divisive political debate, but it has a legal context too. The rights of the economically inactive migrant EU national require definition. In *Elisabeta Dano* the Court decided that such a person (*in casu*, a Romanian in Germany) whose period of residence is more than three months but less than five years[46] may be refused access to subsistence benefits and social allowances.[47] The judgment focuses explicitly on the *unreasonable burden* of providing support as a threat to which the host State may respond. That the migrant shall not amount to an 'unreasonable burden' is a threshold inspired by use of the phrase in Directive 2004/38, but here it is used in a broader context to separate out the deserving from the undeserving. The tone, focused on the defence of State resources, not the rights of the individual to be treated equally irrespective of nationality, is not typical of much of the Court's past practice, as surveyed in this chapter. It may infect the future. Doubtless the Court will be asked to rule on more cases which involve making difficult demarcations,[48] but central to *Dano* was the finding, which the Court repeatedly emphasized, that she had neither worked nor even looked for work.[49] Such migrants are probably rare and litigious migrants of such a type seeking to rely on EU law will be rarer still, because the judgment invites the concoction of *some* economic dimension in order to strengthen the claim. The enduring story is the—imprecisely defined—hierarchy of protected persons under EU law.

7.5 THE CROSS-BORDER ELEMENT

In crude summary, the previous section showed how the more economically active the person claiming to rely on EU law, the more generous the scope of the right to be treated as well as the national of the Member State in which he or she is resident. In similar vein, injecting a cross-border element into the factual situation is of immense benefit to the person

[46] The key thresholds in Arts 24(2) and 16(1) Dir 2004/38.

[47] Case C-333/13 *Elisabeta Dano* judgment 11 November 2014.

[48] Eg Case C-67/14 note 16.

[49] Paras 39, 40, 66.

seeking protection against repressive measures by the State in which he or she is resident. This has been of particular practical significance in the several illuminating cases in which individuals have attempted to stretch EU law to grant them protection against their *own* State's unwillingness to allow TCN family members to live with them. It is plain that the migrant EU national enjoys rights to be accompanied in his or her State of residence (the 'host State') by a category among his or her family members which is defined in Directive 2004/38, even where they are a national of a third country beyond the borders of the EU, and to this extent the autonomy of Member States to decide their immigration policy is constrained by EU free movement law. But this applies too where the claim is against the economic migrant's home State, provided that an adequate cross-border element can be confected.

Chapter 6.2 showed how relatively easy it commonly is to demonstrate a cross-border element which is apt to trigger invocation of EU law. The law governing the free movement of persons provides some of the most vivid examples of how easy and yet how valuable it frequently is to find a way to invoke free movement law. In *Mary Carpenter* Mrs Carpenter, a national of the Philippines, had entered the UK on a six-month visa, stayed after its expiry without receiving any extension, and then married Peter Carpenter, a UK national.[50] She was subsequently served with a deportation order. EU law is not barren of protection for the residence rights of TCNs, but the threshold conditions are relatively high and in any event the key Directive was adopted only after Mrs Carpenter's difficulties arose.[51] So in the circumstances Mrs Carpenter's EU law rights, if any, were not free-standing but rather derived from her husband. But he was a national of the UK living in the UK. So what role did EU law have? Mr Carpenter ran a business selling advertising space in medical and scientific journals and offering various administrative and publishing services to the editors of those journals. The business was established in the UK, but a significant proportion of the business was conducted with advertisers established in other Member States. Mr Carpenter sometimes travelled to other Member States for the purpose of his business. It was argued that his wife's deportation would require him to go to live with her in the Philippines or separate the members of the family unit if he remained in the UK. In both cases his business would be affected. The Court agreed this

[50] Case C-60/00 [2002] ECR I-6279.

[51] Dir 2003/109 concerning the status of third-country nationals who are long-term residents, OJ [2004] L16/44.

was enough to bring the matter within the scope of EU free movement law. And once it did that, the restrictions—the intended deportation of Mrs Carpenter—had to be justified. The Court referred to the right to family life and cited the European Convention on Human Rights (ECHR). The Court focused on the importance of ensuring the protection of the family life of nationals of the Member States. Deportation was not justified.

The ruling explicitly finds that there is a 'free movement problem':[52] but it finds it very easily. The Court makes minimal effort to establish a connection between the threatened deportation and the perceived impediment to trade. On this logic the individual who shops at a website hosted in another Member State becomes a cross-border trader. Once EU free movement law applies, national restrictions must be justified and, where people are concerned, protection of fundamental rights readily becomes part of the assessment. Today in such a case the Court would doubtless draw the Charter of Fundamental Rights into the assessment of justification, which casts light on how the direction in its Article 51(2) that the Charter does not extend the field of application of EU law tends to conceal that an extended interpretation of the scope of Treaty provisions has the consequence that the Charter is itself correspondingly of extended significance. Article 51(2) is aimed at the wrong target. So in *Carpenter* his right protected her against his State's intervention, and although ECHR law might have been available (too), immediate reliance on the directly effective provisions of EU law before the English courts was a great deal more convenient for the individuals concerned. So too in *R* v *IAT and Singh, ex parte Secretary of State* a British national was able to rely on EU law to protect an Indian spouse when returning to the UK after working in Germany.[53] The driving logic, that without such protection on returning home the objectives of EU law would be thwarted because of reluctance to take up economic activity in another Member State in the first place, has been used creatively by the Court in a group of cases in order to determine just when the migrant has spent enough time outside his or her home jurisdiction in order to be entitled to rely on EU law to claim derivative rights in favour of a TCN when he or she comes home.[54] Protecting the effective enjoyment of free movement rights and thereby avoiding frustrating the objectives of the Treaty is the driving thematic concern.

[52] Paras 29, 30, 37. [53] Case C-370/90 [1992] ECR I-4265.

[54] Case C-456/12 *O and B* judgment of 12 March 2014; Case C-457/12 *S and G* judgment of 12 March 2014.

In *Garcia Avello* the Court decided that EU law forbids discrimination based on nationality where a national of one Member State is resident in another, even where the person has in fact always resided in the Member State in question of which he or she is not a national.[55] *Physical* crossing of a frontier is not required in such circumstances. This meant that children born and resident in Belgium, but holding Spanish (as well as Belgian) nationality, could rely on Articles 18 and 20 TFEU to challenge Belgian rules that denied them the right to have their surname registered according to the Spanish tradition (combining father and mother's name). It is not for the EU to set rules on surnames but it is for the Member States not to violate EU free movement law in setting rules on surnames (Chapter 2.8), and the Court found no justification for the Belgian authorities' refusal. So EU law requires adaptation in national practice to accommodate claims of migrants which are judged to be legitimate.

The Court in these rulings has not at all subverted its classic insistence that a situation that is purely internal to a Member State with no link to EU law escapes the scope of application of EU law, and falls to be addressed under national law. The point of these cases is precisely that an adequate, if sometimes tenuous or peripheral, cross-border element was identified to the Court's satisfaction. That was enough to constitute the required link to EU law.

Lately the Court has made use of the status of Citizenship of the Union to expand still further the triggering notion of the 'link' to EU law, thereby to thrust EU law even into some situations where there plainly and unarguably is no cross-border element to the fact pattern nor even, as in *Garcia Avello*, a State of residence different from the State of nationality. The status of Citizenship does not demolish the idea that a Member State may treat its nationals as it sees fit, unfettered by the demands of EU law in the internal situation that lacks a link to EU law, but it does make that space even more cramped than had previously been understood. The principal beneficiaries are TCN family members of EU nationals: the principal losers are those jealous of the autonomy of States to govern immigration from beyond the EU's territory.

The transformative ruling, delivered early in 2011, is *Ruiz Zambrano*.[56] A Colombian national was resident in Belgium with dependent children who held Belgian nationality and who had never left Belgium. The question was whether the Colombian acquired a right of residence in Belgium, and this mattered because the Belgian authorities proposed to deport her.

[55] Case C-148/02 [2003] ECR I-11613. See also Case C-353/06 *Grunkin and Paul* [2008] ECR I-7639.

[56] Case C-34/09 judgment of 8 March 2011.

Could EU law help? The case law examined so far in this sub-section shows that it is frequently easy to find the cross-border element that converts the apparently internal situation into one which engages free movement law. *Carpenter* has the glow of a case where the Court was eager to intervene to combat injustice, but it explicitly relied on the existence of a cross-border element and indeed there was one, even if it had little to do directly with the particular harm the British authorities wishes to visit upon the Carpenters. In *Ruiz Zambrano* there really was no such trigger. The matter concerned Belgium and Belgium alone. And the Court did not pretend otherwise: in *Ruiz Zambrano* the Court acknowledged that it had had pressed on it the absence of any cross-border element to the case and consequently the inapplicability of the free movement provisions.[57] But it was not deterred. Directive 2004/38 did not help, because it is expressly targeted at cases involving movement between Member States, but the Court turned to the Treaty provisions on Citizenship. Article 20 TFEU, it declared, precludes national measures which have the effect of depriving Citizens of the Union of the genuine enjoyment of the substance of the rights conferred by virtue of their status as Citizens of the Union. This, it ruled, was such a deprivation. A refusal to grant a right of residence to the Colombian would mean the children, who were Citizens of the Union, would have to leave the territory of the Union—and as a result they would be unable to exercise the substance of the rights conferred on them by virtue of their status as Citizens of the Union. So EU law offered protection—there was a 'link' to EU law, one created by the driving concern to protect the genuine enjoyment of the substance of the rights conferred by virtue of the status of Citizen of the Union.

The judgment is astounding and was greeted with amazement and, in some quarters, complete dismay: 'A Supreme Court should behave more responsibly.'[58] The Court claimed it was drawing its test based on protecting the genuine enjoyment of the substance of the rights conferred by virtue of the status of Citizen of the Union from paragraph 42 of its 2010 ruling in *Rottmann*.[59] But the relevant paragraph of *Rottmann* was written much more economically and modestly, and in any event that ruling addressed a much narrower (though itself constitutionally troubling[60]) issue,

[57] Para 37.

[58] K. Hailbronner and D. Thym, 'Annotation' (2011) 48 CMLRev 1253, 1259.

[59] Case C-135/08 [2010] ECR I-1449.

[60] Puzzlement about the true basis of the Court's competence to address questions of nationality in *Rottmann* runs through *Pham* [2015] UKSC 19, the UK Supreme Court decision mentioned in Chapter 4.12.

that of loss of nationality suffered by a national of a Member State. So, in truth, *Ruiz Zambrano* struck out in a new direction, offering a new test for determining when deportation (or in principle any other kind of repressive measure aimed at a TCN family member of an EU national) falls to be reviewed in the light of EU law rather than resting as a matter of national policy autonomy.

The 'purely internal' situation lives on. But it is a slimmer category. What lies within it? In *Ruiz Zambrano* the Court held that Article 20 TFEU precludes national measures which have the effect of depriving Citizens of the Union of the genuine enjoyment of the substance of the rights conferred by virtue of their status as Citizens of the Union. If the deprivation relates to the substance of rights other than those conferred by virtue of that status or to the rights conferred by virtue of status as Citizen of the Union, but not to their substance, then the national measure escapes the scope of application of Article 20 TFEU. Subsequent case law has gone some way to make more concrete just what the Court has in mind. It is only *exceptionally* that appeal to Article 20 TFEU will transform a case in which a Member State is taking action against a TCN who is a family member of one of its own nationals who has never been 'cross-border active' into one in which EU law provides assistance. Denial of the genuine enjoyment of the substance of the rights conferred by virtue of the status of citizenship occurs where the Union citizen in fact has to leave the territory of the Union as a result of the refusal to grant a right of residence to the family member, typically because the Union citizen is dependent on the TCN, but by contrast protection is not available where an individual simply wants to have a TCN family member live with him or her for economic reasons or in order to keep a family together in the territory of the Union, in circumstances where a refusal would not force the individual to leave the territory of the Union.[61] So in *Shirley McCarthy* the applicant, a dual Irish/UK national who was born and had always lived in the UK, married a TCN—a Jamaican—who had no leave to remain in the UK.[62] The Court found that in this instance there was no deprivation of the genuine enjoyment of the substance of rights conferred by the status of citizenship, because 'By contrast' with *Ruiz Zambrano*, the UK measure did not oblige her to leave the territory of the EU.[63] This does, of course, signal to 'internal' applicants precisely how they should structure their case in order to exploit the Court's interpretation of the control

[61] Case C-256/11 *Dereci* judgment of 16 November 2011; Case C-40/11 *Iida* judgment of 8 November 2012; C-87/12 *Ymeraga* judgment of 8 May 2013.

[62] Case C-434/09 judgment of 5 May 2011.

[63] Para 50.

exercised over national immigration practices in the name of citizenship of the Union.

This leaves open awkward questions about when someone is really being 'forced' to leave Union territory. Such questions are fact-dependent, though this is not to trivialize their significance in cases which are by definition dealing with individuals in a precarious position. The Court has declined to limit dependency to blood relationships.[64] A deeper concern is that the Court has left open just what the reasons underlying this specially protected status might be. The matter seems somehow loosely connected with the importance of citizenship and the Court's approach could plausibly be driven by the widened aims of the EU and deepened commitments to fundamental rights accepted under the Lisbon Treaty and now contained in Articles 2 and 3 TEU. Advocate General Sharpston, in her Opinion in *Ruiz Zambrano*, asked whether the time was right to accept that EU fundamental rights should apply to Member State action in all circumstances where the EU has (shared or exclusive) competence even if it has not been exercised—that would mean even where there is no obstacle to free movement. This was calculated provocation. She took care to withhold the suggestion as a basis for resolving the litigation at hand, but she clearly was attracted by the notion that the Lisbon Treaty could be read as a political statement by the Member States which would be apt to trigger such a large leap once an opportunity presented itself subsequently. It would, as she observed, cause a 'federalising effect'.[65] There was an echo here of the invitation offered by the referring court in *Uecker, Jacquet* to use the Maastricht Treaty as a springboard to adopt a wider understanding of the personal scope of EU law even in internal situations.[66] The Court in *Ruiz Zambrano*, as in *Uecker, Jacquet*, was not so bold. But in *Ruiz Zambrano* it clearly chose to slim down the scope of the 'purely internal' situation which has no link with EU law and so falls to be resolved under national law. It simply declined to articulate *why*.

Rulings such as *Carpenter* and the stream initiated by *Ruiz Zambrano* suggest the Court, even if not willing to make the explicit jump proposed by AG Sharpston, is eager to find an adequate connection to EU law precisely so it can offer protection in supplement to that which might be available under national law or the European Convention, but which, as evidenced by the very fact that the matter has reached Luxembourg, has presumably fallen short of the applicant's aspirations. The cases suggest

[64] Cases C-356/11 and C-357/11 *O, S & L* judgment of 6 December 2012.

[65] Para 173 of her Opinion.

[66] Note 6.

the Court is nudging towards treating the right to move as having a 'converse... right *not to move* without being unduly penalized'.[67] Another way to frame such incursion into the apparently 'internal situation' would be to argue that where EU law creates legal rights for the migrant, EU law should not be blind to the ripple of discrimination against non-migrants which it has thereby caused within the national order.[68] But should *EU law* really make such inflated claims? Should it really have so little trust in other sources of protection within the Member States? The tension is between sensitivity to individual rights and sensitivity to the limits of EU competence; between the empowering force of the concept of the internal market combined with that of EU citizenship and preservation of national autonomy. The Court teeters on the brink of treating itself as a court with general human rights jurisdiction, which is not what Article 5 TEU mandates.

7.6 HOW FAR BEYOND 'MARKET CITIZENSHIP'?

EU law governing people has a legacy of 'market citizenship', whereby rights are granted to migrants primarily because of their instrumental market-making function. Social solidarity, a feature of national understandings of citizenship, is missing from such a model of individualized market citizenship. However, the rise of citizenship of the Union has helped to ease EU law beyond a narrow conception of the market citizen. The personal scope of EU law goes beyond the economically motivated cross-border migrant and the material scope of EU law goes beyond matters associated with facilitating direct access to labour markets: EU law comes to the rescue more readily than one may expect.

There is, however, no sophisticated understanding of citizenship traceable in EU law. Its insertion into the Treaty with effect from 1993 was a political gesture unattached to careful explanation and, partly as a result, its exploitation by the Court has been ad hoc. The Court has been immensely creative in this area—or, according to taste, it has been egregiously unwilling to allow legislative solutions to be developed in a systematic manner and has instead intervened in a thoroughly unpredictable

[67] A Dashwood, M Dougan, B.Rodger, E Spaventa, and D Wyatt, *Wyatt and Dashwood's European Union Law* (6th ed, Hart, 2011), p 491.

[68] Cf. M. Maduro, 'The Scope of European Remedies: The Case of the Purely Internal Situations and Reverse Discrimination', Ch 5 in C. Kilpatrick, T. Novitz, and P. Skidmore (eds), *The Future of Remedies in Europe* (Hart, 2000).

manner. Citizenship, in a normatively durable sense, needs much more than ad hoc judicial amplification.

'Citizenship' as a concept attached to a State has attracted a wealth of theoretical and philosophical analysis, stretching back to Plato and Aristotle, but none of this was in the minds of those engaged in the crafting of Citizenship of the European Union. Citizenship is by its nature a means not only to include but also to exclude. Its EU variant operates against a fluctuating background which involves some breaking down of the sharp edges of a citizen's exclusive connection to his or her State through place of birth or tie of blood. The EU goes some way to taking off the harsher edges of the consequences of such rigid categorization, by requiring the assimilation of the non-national to the national for many purposes, under the influences of the rights of the 'market citizen' and the Citizen of the Union. But at the same time the protection of EU law is mainly extended to those who are mobile, who possess resources and are economically active—and to some extent too to those willing and able to get to court to vindicate their rights.[69] This is something less dense and sophisticated than citizenship as an expression of collective identity and social solidarity. Citizenship of the Union lacks any clear blueprint of its own. Certainly EU law is not driven by a philosophically deep sense of justice based on the individual—even to invite such a quest is to bring to mind the very variety of Member State traditions which militate against a single vision of 'Europe's justice'. And, in its detail, the law is unsettlingly fragmented and far from predictable in its scope.[70] Neither Treaty nor secondary legislation are comprehensive, and the case law is driven by varying features—different types of migrant, different types of benefit, different types of devices chosen by Member States to check the existence of a 'genuine link' for these purposes. So the rights to move, reside, and enjoy non-discriminatory access go some way to obliterating the 'other' status of a migrant EU national. To an extent, residence requirements reflecting a real link, which are not nationality-dependent, have pushed State practice beyond exclusive loyalty to nationals. Equal treatment is a norm that is not contingent on sameness of nationality. This hollows out or tames some aspects of the exclusive nature of State power—just as the EU more generally does. EU law allows the migrant to stand tall

[69] Cf A. Jose Menendez, 'Which Citizenship? Whose Europe?—The Many Paradoxes of European Citizenship' (2014) 15 German Law Journal 907.

[70] Eg C. O'Brien, 'I Trade, Therefore I Am: Legal Personhood in the European Union' (2013) 50 CMLRev 1643; N. Nic Shuibhne, 'Limits Rising, Duties Ascending: The Changing Legal Shape of Union Citizenship' (2015) 52 CMLRev 889.

alongside the national of the Member State—but only up to a (sometimes hard to discern) point. It does not put the migrant on a wholly equal footing with his neighbour who is a national of the migrant's host State, and movement in that direction risks a backlash from locals fearful of such imposed equality. Still less does the EU take over responsibility to provide or define citizenship. This is in many respects the 'person-specific' manifestation of the general unsettled question about what is to be the destiny of the relationship between EU and Member States, and the proper limits of the EU's role and competence and ambition.

Ultimately it is easy to conclude that citizenship of the EU is quite different from citizenship of a State—and easy but glib to add the observation that this is no more than one would expect given that the EU is not a State and does not command the same relationship within 'its' peoples. The EU *should not* have a status of citizenship which replicates the rights and duties that one finds at State level, for, if so, the EU loses its unique mission as a means to manage the interdependence of States and is reduced to the unworthy status of an aspirational State and, given the absence of a European public space or *demos*, an unwanted State. EU citizenship should complement citizenship of the Member States. And in some ways it does—most of all by using an equal treatment rule to take off the rough edges of a rigid demand that nationality is the exclusive gateway to residence and welfare rights. This is to use the EU to lever open up rights to a wider pool of beneficiaries than nationals of the grantor State alone. It suggests multi-level citizenship.

8

WHAT ARE THE EU'S VALUES?

8.1 THE EU'S VALUES

The original Treaty of Rome, which created the EEC in 1958, contained inspiring aspiration in its Preamble and included a determination to lay the foundations of an 'ever closer union'. However, by contrast, the vision on offer to a reader plodding through its full length from Article 1 to Article 247 was mundane. Article 1 simply proclaimed the establishment of the European Economic Community; Article 2 set out its tasks, and fastened onto establishing a common market and progressively approximating the economic policies of the Member States as the means to achieve them; Article 3 listed its objectives, eleven of them, (a) to (k). The most conspicuous theme is economic activity. There was no values-driven vocation. This basic pattern remained untouched until December 2009. Admittedly, the name was changed along the way, to European Community in 1993, as one pillar within a wider three-pillar European Union; the listed tasks were widened in scope and the means to achieve them were supplemented by the establishment of an economic and monetary union and reliance on a more generous range on common policies and activities; and Article 3's list of objectives had mushroomed to cover twenty-one of them, (a) to (u), buttressed by a direction in Article 3(2) to eliminate inequalities and promote equality between men and women and by specific provisions on economic and monetary policy contained in Article 4. Part of the landscape too was mapped by the objectives stated in Article 2 TEU, located in the non-EC EU, stretching to a Common Foreign and Security Policy (CFSP) and creation of the Area of Freedom, Security, and Justice.

The Treaty of Lisbon altered this completely. With effect from its entry into force on 1 December 2009 the European Union has *values*, and they are written into the Treaties in advance of any engagement with objectives and activities.

Article 1 TEU continues to perform naming rites. This is a European Union, on which the Member States confer competences to attain objectives they have in common. Article 2 TEU then locates the EU as a project driven by *values*. It provides that:

The Union is founded on the values of respect for human dignity, freedom, democracy, equality, the rule of law and respect for human rights, including the rights of persons belonging to minorities. These values are common to the Member States in a society in which pluralism, non-discrimination, tolerance, justice, solidarity and equality between women and men prevail.

As its second sentence makes explicit, the intent here is to align the European Union's values with those that animate and legitimate States in Europe. The EU is firmly and calculatedly tied to commitments that are regarded as foundational in modern European democratic States. The prominence of the *economic* ambitions of the project has gone missing, and this sense of adjusted priority is accentuated by Article 3 TEU. It too insists on the force of *values* in guiding the Union's trajectory. According to Article 3(1) TEU, the Union's aim 'is to promote peace, its values and the well-being of its peoples'. Only lower down the list, tucked away without fanfare in Article 3(3), does the instruction to the Union to 'establish an internal market' emerge, and this is accompanied by directions to work for 'the sustainable development of Europe based on balanced economic growth and price stability, a highly competitive social market economy, aiming at full employment and social progress, and a high level of protection and improvement of the quality of the environment', as well as to (inter alia) combat social exclusion and discrimination; promote social justice and protection, equality between women and men, solidarity between generations, and protection of the rights of the child; and respect Europe's rich cultural and linguistic diversity. Article 3(5) turns the EU's face outwards, and insists that in its relations with the wider world 'the Union shall uphold and promote its values and interests and contribute to the protection of its citizens' and shall contribute to (inter alia) peace, security, free and fair trade, and the protection of human rights.

According to the Court, the system

> is based on the fundamental premiss that each Member State shares with all the other Member States, and recognises that they share with it, a set of common values on which the EU is founded, as stated in Article 2 TEU. That premiss implies and justifies the existence of mutual trust between the Member States that those values will be recognised and, therefore, that the law of the EU that implements them will be respected.[1]

Article 6 TEU makes a concrete addition to this agenda of preserving and promoting *values*. It directs that the Union recognizes the rights, freedoms, and principles set out in the Charter of Fundamental Rights, which shall have the same legal value as the Treaties, and that fundamental rights,

[1] Opinion 2/13 on accession to the ECHR 18 December 2014 para 168.

as guaranteed by the European Convention for the Protection of Human Rights and Fundamental Freedoms and as they result from the constitutional traditions common to the Member States, shall constitute general principles of Union law. So, as the Court has framed it, 'The applicability of European Union law entails applicability of the fundamental rights guaranteed by the Charter.'[2] The EU's activities are in every respect conditioned by respect for fundamental rights, as enshrined in the Charter, and this commitment was intended to be granted extra organic force by planned accession of the EU to the European Convention on Human Rights (ECHR), as mandated by Article 6(2) TEU. That, however, has been stalled and perhaps precluded by the appeal to the EU's values and most of all to the autonomy of its legal order which led the Court in December 2014 to rule that arrangements planned for accession were incompatible with EU law.[3] Article 7 TEU supplements protection of the values inscribed in Article 2 TEU by providing a procedure whereby their breach to a (defined) sufficiently serious degree may lead to the imposition of sanctions on an offending Member State. This procedure has not (yet) been invoked. The Treaty proceeds in Article 10(1) TEU to state that 'the functioning of the Union shall be founded on representative democracy' and in Article 10(3) TEU that 'every citizen shall have the right to participate in the democratic life of the Union'. Article 13(1) TEU provides the Union with 'an institutional framework which shall aim to promote its values' and Article 49 TEU, which structures the procedure for new applicant States, begins by confining the path to European States which respect the values referred to in Article 2 and are committed to promoting them.

8.2 VALUES AND THE PURPOSE OF THE EU

To crown the EU with *values* is on the face of it transformative. The original European Communities were heavily focused on achieving economic reform and growth in part because of the vital need to reshape and re-energize shattered Europe, or at least, as the Iron Curtain was drawn from north to south across Mitteleuropa, a chunk of the western part of it. For some involved, that was of itself quite enough: for them, there was no desire for any more radical transformation of State structures. For others, by contrast, the expectation was that the institutions and rules that were designed to achieve economic reform through co-ordinated activity would spill over

[2] Case C-617/10 *Fransson* judgment of 26 February 2013 para 21.

[3] Opinion 2/13 note 1.

and promote an ever deeper and ever wider pool of common action, as the economic slid inexorably into the social and the political domains. States, choosing to manage their interdependence through the EU, would accelerate that very interdependence and with it would come an ever more prominent and powerful EU.[4] Either way, the model involved the deliberate concealment of the revolutionary potential of the EU as a reorganization of the very notion of the State post-1945. This was 'integration by stealth':[5] the focus of the early years on economic integration provided a narrative of sorts and a legitimation through prosperity. Unlike States, which tend to come into being through dramatic revolutionary events and/or have founding myths attached to them which explain and legitimate the exercise of political authority,[6] the EU has no popular or populist sheen, and much of the point is that, as an exercise in structuring multi-level governance and performance of defined tasks, it does not and should not.[7]

In this vein Chapter 1 of this book argued that the purpose of the EU is the management of interdependence. This embraces both States and people. It puts in place a process whereby States give up power to act unilaterally so that they may participate in the exercise of a collective problem-solving capacity that is a great deal more effective. Resources of power are not finite: acting through the EU the sum of State powers is expanded so it becomes greater than its parts. The EU 'adds value' to its Member States' capacity to achieve the expectations of their citizens. Moreover, the EU, a place for States to address in common the demands of economic reform and also matters such as climate change, migration, security, and technological change, also serves as a forum through which to impose constraints on States, to 'tame' their historically notorious capacity to cause harm to each other. The EU does this through a relatively dense set of legal rules, adopted on the foundation of international Treaties, and, as a system actively 'constitutionalized' by its Court in

[4] This is obviously a highly compressed account of a rich store of literature. Highly influential was E. Haas, *The Uniting of Europe: Political, Social and Economic Forces 1950–1957* (Stanford, 1968). More recent landmark inquiries include A. Moravscik, *The Choice for Europe* (Cornell, 1998); J. Gillingham, *European Integration, 1950–2003: Superstate or New Market Economy?* (CUP, 2003). For a survey, see N. Walker, 'The Philosophy of European Union Law' in A. Arnull and D. Chalmers (eds), *The Oxford Handbook of European Union Law* (OUP, 2015).

[5] Eg G. Majone, *Dilemmas of European Integration: The Ambiguities and Pitfalls of Integration by Stealth* (OUP, 2005).

[6] Cf eg B. Anderson, *Imagined Communities* (London, Verso, 1991).

[7] Eg V. Della Sala, 'Political Myth, Mythology and the European Union' (2010) 48 JCMS 1.

alliance with national judiciaries (examined in Chapters 3 and 4), striking a course beyond the founding texts according to a vivid and calculated determination to fashion the EU legal order as creative of and legitimated by a discourse of individual rights, not simply State interests. The EU legal rules examined in Chapters 6 and 7 serve to control the infliction of costs externally, by imposing certain justificatory requirements on national practices that have cross-border effects, to check them for anachronism or worse. Without this, States are democratically deficient: 'they cannot include all those Europeans who will be affected by their decisions in the electoral processes, and—vice versa—citizens cannot influence the behaviour of those political actors who are taking decisions on their behalf'.[8]

Part of the legitimating story is therefore to give citizens of one Member State a voice of sorts in the choices made by other Member States. The EU is a force for correcting democratic failure at State level. *Cassis de Dijon* shows how EU free movement law makes louder the voice of out-of-State producers and by proxy German consumers in the pattern of rule production within Germany.[9] Dany Bidar, the French student living in England who had been denied a loan to support his maintenance costs, has a louder voice in the State of which he is a resident but not a national, thanks to EU law.[10] More broadly, primary EU law protects the disadvantaged: Mrs Carpenter could not be removed to the Philippines because her husband, as a cross-border provider of services, was able to rely on EU law,[11] and Ms Defrenne could not be treated worse simply because she is a woman.[12] More broadly this is an agenda of economic reform built on constitutionally entrenched legal rules. Trading freedom and restraint on State intervention counts as an element within a wider political understanding of individual liberty.[13]

EU law pulls such matters out of the exclusive grip of politics and negotiation and subjects them to a system of integration-through-law, embedded also into national everyday legal practice. 'The constitutionalisation of justificatory requirements changes the mode of representation from preferences and power to arguments and reasons and this transforms

[8] C. Joerges, 'What Is Left of the European Economic Constitution?' (2005) 30 ELRev 461, 488.

[9] Case 120/78 [1979] ECR 649; Chapter 6.2.2.

[10] Case C-209/03 [2005] ECR I-2119; Chapter 7.4.

[11] Case C-60/00 [2002] ECR I-6279; Chapter 7.5.

[12] Case 43/75 [1976] ECR 455; Chapters 2.9, 4.4, and 6.9.3.

[13] Eg E. Mestmacker, 'On the Legitimacy of European Law' (1994) 58 RabelsZ 615: the German-language literature is much fuller. Beyond the EU, see eg U. Petersmann, 'International Trade Law, Human Rights and Theories of Justice' in S. Charnovitz, D. Steger, and P. Van den Bossche (eds), *Law in the Service of Human Dignity* (CUP, 2005).

intergovernmental bargaining into transnational deliberations.'[14] It is about making public authorities and sometimes also private parties grasp and justify the consequences of their actions.

The Court's interpretative choices have deep consequences of a vertical and a horizontal nature. The vertical consequences focus on the confinement of State autonomy. The Court's chosen model pulls a very wide range of practices within the scope of internal market law and so places a heavy burden on questions associated with justification. Absence of justification leads to a deregulatory dynamic, but the case law, tracked in Chapter 6, is littered with national rules that are indefensibly protectionist and/or anachronistic and which have no sensible place in an integrating EU market: the obstinately rigid product standard addressed in *Cassis de Dijon* is a perfect example. The Court does, however, plainly recognize limits to market liberalization. There is receptivity to values other than the market in the Court's case law dealing with more sincere forms of justification which has also been described in Chapter 6.[15] EU law is not good at offering insulation *in principle* from the pressures of market-making, but free movement law is not only about free movement: it is not exclusively deregulatory because the room allowed to justify national practices ensures it is porous to non-market values. This is the route to arguing that the social consequences of internal market law are not the collateral damage of its deregulatory thrust but rather embedded centrally within it, a process reinforced by the Lisbon Treaty's grant of binding effect to the Charter and the rise of the commitment to a 'social market economy'.[16] Respect for justified diversity is a value in EU internal market law.

At the horizontal level the Court's choices increase the judicial role in building the internal market at the expense of the political process. *Cassis de Dijon* again captures the core: the use of free movement law to review non-discriminatory technical standards asserts active judicial control of national choices without the need to await tortured negotiation on legislative harmonization at EU level. This has direct consequences for the sort

[14] J. Neyer, 'Justice, not Democracy: Legitimacy in the European Union' (2010) 48 JCMS 903, 918.

[15] Eg D. Damjanovic, 'The EU Market Rules as Social Market Rules: Why the EU Can Be a Social Market Economy' (2013) 50 CMLRev 1685; O. Gerstenberg, 'The Justiciability of Socio-Economic Rights, European Solidarity and the Role of the Court of Justice of the EU' (2014) 33 YEL 245.

[16] Cf eg D. Schiek, 'The EU Constitution of Social Governance in an Economic Crisis: In Defence of a Transnational Dimension to Social Europe' (2013) 20 Maastricht Journal of European and Comparative Law 185; V. Hatzopoulos, 'A (More) Social Europe: A Political Crossroad or a Legal One-way? Dialogues between Luxembourg and Lisbon' (2005) 42 CMLRev 1599.

of market that is being created. It stands for a more decentralized and deregulated market than would emerge were matters reserved for the legislative process. Under the Court's approach the internal market offers consumers a choice of diverse types of blackcurrant liqueur—and beer, and tourist guides, and so on—whereas, had the Court restricted free movement law to a mere non-discrimination norm, the internal market would have been advanced only by EU legislation and the production of a single centralized standard. The internal market is a site of diversity. The choice which it releases is available too to undertakings which wish to select among regulatory regimes at State level. The ruling in *Centros* insists on EU free movement law as a means to promote interjurisdictional regulatory competition in corporate law, since companies may shop around for a favoured regime, albeit that it is not excluded that suppression of particular targeted pernicious practices at State level may be shown to be justified.[17] *Centros* is, as the Court made explicit, another ruling in which the Court makes important decisions about the scope and deregulatory vigour of free movement law without there being any need to pause until common EU legislative standards have been adopted. Such an approach reduces the need for centralization and homogenization.

The incomplete and sparely written character of the Treaties delegates to the Court much room to choose. The judicial choices might sometimes surprise—this is the jack-in-the-box met in Chapters 2.8, 3.12, and 6.3.4—but once made, they are entrenched far more deeply than they could be at national level. The Court's interpretation of primary law may be overridden only by unanimously agreed Treaty revision. Even EU secondary legislation is changed only provided that the Commission submits the necessary proposal and secures adequate political support in both Council and Parliament. This is why the Court's interpretative methodology, famously described by Eric Stein as having been shaped 'tucked away in the fairyland Duchy of Luxembourg',[18] has very direct practical consequences for shaping and foreclosing political choices about the nature of the market and the functionally broad pattern of the EU more generally.[19]

[17] Case C-212/97 *Centros* [1999] ECR I-1459; Chapter 6.2.2.

[18] 'Lawyers, Judges and the Making of a Transnational Constitution' (1981) 75 AJIL 1.

[19] See eg P. Caro de Sousa, 'Negative and Positive Integration in EU Economic Law: Between Strategic Denial and Cognitive Dissonance' (2012) 13 German Law Jnl 979; A. Saydé, 'One Law, Two Competitions: An Inquiry into the Contradictions of Free Movement Law' 13 *Cambridge Yearbook of European Legal Studies* (2010–11) 365; J. Snell, 'Varieties of Capitalism and the Limits of European Economic Integration' 13 *Cambridge Yearbook of European Legal Studies* (2010–11) 415.

Where the EU itself is called on to adopt common rules rather than simply to subject national rules to the test, it does so according to an institutional model that melds effective planning—achieved by immunizing the Commission from direct accountability—with democratic control, achieved under the double legitimation of peoples (Parliament) and States (Council). How to mediate the tension between promoting effectiveness of action at EU level and preserving control exercised by actors at State level has been a central theme of this book. The surrender of the obstinacy of State veto power in the Council in favour of qualified majority voting in most areas of EU activity (Chapters 3.4.1, 3.7) is among the most powerful examples of the force of the former concern; it is illuminating that devices to promote the latter, such as the voice allocated to national Parliaments under the reasoned opinion procedure (Chapter 2.12), are a good deal less vigorous.

Even though the core functions and design of the Council, Parliament, and Commission have much in common today with those put in place in the 1950s, the dynamic pattern of detailed change over time is striking. The aspiration of some of the founders that the system would generate unstoppable momentum in the direction of ever tighter co-operation was proved false. Prognosis of smooth evolution was quickly jolted, most startlingly by the refusal of France in the mid-1960s to adapt to the shift away from unanimous voting in Council which was planned by the Treaty as a means to accelerate decision-making on sensitive issues. This led to the so-called Luxembourg Accords. At the *political* level overt steps were required to induce the system to pursue a path of deepening and widening—there, it became plain, could be no inevitability in that transition. But the necessary impulses were forthcoming, as the pressures of managing interdependence promoted a regular round of Treaty revision, beginning with effect from 1987 when the Single European Act entered into force, travelling via Maastricht (1993), Amsterdam (1999), and Nice (2003), and culminating in the entry into force of the Lisbon Treaty in 2009, which jettisoned the European Community and the three-pillar European Union in favour of a (more or less) unified European Union, committing the Union to a dominant working method involving the dual sourced legitimacy for law-making, composed of States (Council) and people (Parliament).

Each fresh iteration widened the scope of the competences conferred in the EU, adapted the voting rules in Council to open up ever wider scope for qualified majority action (the very problem that had caused such obstruction back in the 1960s), and enhanced the power and influence of the Parliament, the EU's only directly elected institution.

And—in general—the powers of the Commission and the Court were preserved and in some respects enhanced. Moreover, functional growth and institutional sophistication were accompanied by geographic expansion. Democratic renewal came to the Iberian peninsula and to Greece, and later to central and eastern Europe, and was locked in by commitment to EU membership. Established democracies, most of all in the north and north-west of Europe, sought the economic and social advantages of EU membership. The EU was an anchor and a magnet. The original six Member States have swelled to twenty-eight.

In consequence the substance of the EU's commitment to legislative regulation of the market is functionally and geographically wide-ranging. The common policies to which the TFEU commits the EU, which have been extended in scope over times as a result of periodic Treaty revision and which are mapped in Articles 2–6 TFEU and elaborated in detail throughout the TFEU, have been developed through the adoption of much secondary legislation. Most of these are competences that are shared, so that EU law combines with national rules to produce a complex pattern of multi-level governance. The result is that a great deal of activity in areas such as environmental protection, labour market regulation, consumer protection, energy, and so on is governed by an often complex mix of national and EU measures, soft and hard: this is the multi-faceted phenomenon of 'Europeanization' (Chapters 2.10, 3.6). Harmonization is the legislative competence that is widest in its influence. As explained in Chapters 2.7.4 and 6.4.4, harmonization not only puts in place the common regulatory foundation of the internal market; it also, by replacing national regulatory diversity with a single EU model, carries a profound re-regulatory potential. The EU is identified as a social market economy by Article 3(3) TEU and this is given concrete shape by a wide range of measures which preclude the project being treated as purely de-regulatory in aspiration.

Here too the Court has played a major role. This system was rooted in a constitutional character marked by direct engagement with the individual through the conferral of rights and protection against the unjustified exercise of power by States or the EU. The Court's constitutionalizing judgments make the rules far harder to evade: policing is sharpened, under the claim to have created a system of individual protection. This is supremacy and direct effect, supplemented by State and private liability and imbued with principles of good administration and fundamental rights, enforceable not only against the EU but also against the Member States where they implement EU law. The Court has also intruded on national autonomy in matters of procedure and remedies through reliance on the principle of effective judicial protection, now mandated by Article 19(1) TEU and Article 47 of the Charter but in fact, as is explained in Chapter 4.5, stretching back to 1976. So, for example, consumers can expect national courts to crack open the finality of arbitral awards guaranteed under national law where protection envisaged by EU Directives would be denied.[20] Generous judicial interpretation of the scope of secondary legislation adds to the picture: for example, passengers on delayed flights can enjoy rights to compensation even where the EU legislation fails explicitly to envisage such redress.[21]

The EU is an international organization—it is also much *more* than any other international organization. It is in important respects embedded within the legal and political structures of its Member States, under the pattern of multi-level governance assessed in Chapter 4.

But the EU is less than a State. The Court itself has gone out of its way to communicate this. In Opinion 2/13 it stated that 'the EU is, under international law, precluded by its very nature from being considered a State'.[22] The EU helps to supplement the claims of its Member States to be effective democratic and legitimate actors in an interdependent world, by taming them, to prevent the infliction of external harm, and by helping them solve problems their citizens expect to see solved. It seeks not to deny—still less to replace—the varying aspirations of peoples in Europe, but rather to accommodate that diversity within a managed framework.

In an interdependent world, democracy needs to be 'organised transnationally, as a democracy of many *demoi* that crosses the borders between them and organises inquiry and deliberation into the conditions for ongoing cooperation and collaborative problem solving'.[23] Transnational rules do not replace, still less suppress, the several different locations of political authority to be found across the EU, but instead lock those locations into a credible set of reciprocally undertaken commitments designed to make real promises not to externalize costs and to seek collective solutions to problems that are faced in common. There is no federal State 'which does not presuppose the supreme authority and sovereignty of its federal *demos*', but in Europe by contrast 'that presupposition does not

[20] Case C-168/05 *Mostaza Claro* v *Centro Móvil Milenium* [2006] ECR I-10421; Chapter 4.5.

[21] Joined Cases C-402 and C-432/07 *Christopher Sturgeon* et al v *Air France SA* [2009] ECR I-10923; Chapter 3.14.

[22] Opinion 2/13 note 1, para 156.

[23] J. Bohman, 'From *Demos* to *Demoi:* Democracy across Borders' (2005) 18 Ratio Juris 293, 312.

exist'.[24] So EU law is supreme: higher level defeats lower level—but the source of normative authority and of real power comes instead from the lower level, State and peoples. This, as Weiler astutely pointed out, would seem likely to 'result in perennial instability',[25] but the EU has (so far) survived by retaining pursuit of—as the Preamble has always put it—an 'ever closer union among the peoples of Europe' within which diversity is preserved and managed. Nobly so, in Weiler's inspiring and influential vision. He has captured this in the 'principle of constitutional tolerance', whereby a minority in the EU accepts constitutional discipline and periodic subjection to the decisions of a majority even though the connecting factor is not that of a State, where such choices flow from the assumption that the majority and the minority are one people. That is missing in the EU, but still there is agreement—tolerance—to be bound by the decisions taken on that wider (constitutionalized) plane. The practice of qualified majority voting in Council is of course a very concrete manifestation, but it is much more and it is much deeper—it rests in the 'habits and practices' of public administration: immigration officials treating EU nationals in the same way as their own nationals, customs officials, housing officers, and judges too.[26] Long-standing constitutional distinctions rooted in nationality are set aside, not in the name of a single European people but rather in this notion of constitutional tolerance of diversity. Pursuit of a single European *demos* is not the plan: instead this is respect for *demoi* placed within a constitutionalized system of governance. It is not designed to suppress difference, but rather to suppress insular refusal to acknowledge when the assertion of difference might inflict external costs on neighbours.

So the EU does not and should not aspire itself to become a State, because it suffers from serious flaws when judged from the perspective of democratic legitimacy. Most of all there is negligible sense that citizens are part of a single European polity. Any allegiance to the EU is not comparable to that found (albeit imperfectly and unevenly) across Europe at national level. There is a risk of blessing the EU as a transformatively progressive force and disdaining critics as petty nationalists but this, though sometimes valid, risks taking insufficiently sensitive account of the limits of acceptance among the peoples of Europe that politically charged and culturally sensitive decisions belong outwith the confines of national

[24] J. Weiler, 'Federalism without Constitutionalism: Europe's *Sonderweg*' in K. Nicolaidis and R. Howse (eds), *The Federal Vision: Legitimacy and Levels of Governance in the United States and the European Union* (OUP, 2001), p 57.

[25] Page 57. [26] Pages 68–9.

democratic processes. There has been an emergent if inchoate concept of 'Europe' as a political project based on certain common features and aspirations for several centuries,[27] but most people in Europe do not think of their political identity as primarily 'European', still less as tied to the 'European Union'. The relationship of solidarity between a relatively poor region of Germany and a relatively prosperous one is not the same as the relationship between Germany and Greece. It is not that this *should* be so, nor that it can never change: it is simply an observable fact that it is.[28] The absence of a single European public space and the absence of a European people—the absence of a *demos* at EU level—is a strong reason for excluding the EU from acting in politically contested areas, especially where distributional consequences stretching across borders are at stake. Chapter 2 examined the formal limits imposed by the principle of conferral, but the absence of a European *demos* apt to generate allegiance to decisions taken with distributional consequences in particular serves as a deeper reason for restraint on the EU's institutional ambition and on the scope of its competence. This means, to take one concrete instance, that to inflate the powers of the Parliament under a quest to enhance the EU's democratic credentials may not only miss the point, but may in fact prove *worse* than useless in so far as it deepens the sense of alienation from popular political support and associated illegitimacy. The institutional design explored in detail in Chapter 3 does not meet the expectations of democratic Statehood in Europe, but it is not meant to! Its detail is the manifestation of the general perception that States must surrender a degree of power to act unilaterally in order to obtain the compensating benefits of managed action in common. To treat it as simply one stage in 'progress' towards a true European State is to defy the absence of popular support for such a shift. Worse, it assumes that the choice lies between nation States and a European State. That betrays the EU's unique genius in offering a third way—to manage the interdependence of States without itself becoming one.

This does not mean that the EU is not meant to be democratic, but it does mean that it is not meant to be democratic *like a State is democratic*. Both descriptively and normatively it displays a 'democratic ambiguity'.[29] A different lexicon of institutional accountability is required.

[27] See eg A. Pagden (ed), *The Idea of Europe: From Antiquity to the European Union* (CUP, 2002).

[28] Cf T. Risse, *A Community of Europeans? Transnational Identities and Public Spheres* (Cornell, 2010).

[29] D. Chalmers, 'The Democratic Ambiguity of EU Law Making and its Enemies' in *The Oxford Handbook of European Union Law* note 4, pp 303–26.

The key to the modern European Union is that it should not be understood as a means to replace States, but rather as a means better to manage their interdependence. The prescription holds that the EU and its Member States are deficient as fully satisfyingly legitimate actors in different ways: the Member States because of their capacity to inflict external costs and to fail to solve transnational problems, the EU because it cannot act as the government of a *people* of Europe. But put the two together—so the EU helps to curb the infliction of external costs and to solve problems while the Member States remain in place as the primary source of democratic legitimation—and a case for a multi-level system bound together by an artfully constitutionalized legal order emerges. Put another way, testing the EU against the standards of democratic governance expected of a State leads to one inevitable conclusion—failure. Testing the Member States against the standards of effective problem-solving and permitting a voice in local political processes to all affected interests leads to one inevitable conclusion—failure. But the choice is not *between* EU and States. The one reinforces the other.

And the commitment to *values* acts as an underpinning. The Treaty of Lisbon, though not at all aimed at converting the EU into a State in its own right, chose transformatively to recognize that much of the power and responsibility exercised by the EU is State-*like* in character, and has evolved far beyond any narrow preoccupation with economic reform and integration, and therefore requires not only the legitimation delivered by the EU's familiar institutional architecture, extended by the modest reforms of the Lisbon Treaty to include a voice for national Parliaments, but also that it must therefore be tethered to the *values* which reflect the best of European virtues. These, to repeat the first sentence of Article 2 TEU found on this chapter's first page, are of respect for human dignity, freedom, democracy, equality, the rule of law, and human rights, including the rights of persons belonging to minorities. As a result of the generous conferral of competences made over time by the Treaties, the EU has an influence—if not a predominant one—across a vast range of activities performed at State level, but even these are overshadowed by the commitment to values written into the Treaties. So the EU 'does not only *strive* for particular future deliverables, it also *stands* for certain values'.[30]

[30] J. Larik, 'On the Changing Role of the Objectives of the European Union' (2014) 63 ICLQ 935, 958.

8.3 TAKING VALUES SERIOUSLY

A tart response to the breathlessly frothy optimism of the previous section might be: this is *toweringly complacent nonsense*!

The EU—runs a sharply sceptical retort—might express a rhetorical commitment to such values, but the means to hold it to account are risibly inadequate. Judicial control in the CFSP, where some of the most serious infractions of values are liable to occur, is very limited.[31] The EU's commitment to ensuring that its legislative initiatives across the wide sweep of its activities do not violate fundamental rights may be laudable (Chapter 3.15), but its legislative competence to act *directly* to promote fundamental rights is thin, and is simply not capable of making concrete the commitment to values plastered over the first few Articles of the TEU. Moreover, the Court has even gone so far as to block EU accession to the ECHR unless concessions to preservation of the autonomy of the EU legal order and of the jurisdiction of the Court itself are made that would evacuate accession of any real content, value, or meaning.[32] And in any event—asserts the critic—even the rhetoric is wholly misleading: the EU is in truth based on *market* values. The lofty assertions found in Articles 2 and 3 TEU should not dazzle anyone who looks closely at the detailed reality of EU engagement with national social and political practice. It is the economic sphere where the EU has exercised a truly transformative effect. It embeds its rules into national political culture, backed by institutionally powerful rule-makers and enforcers supported by EU 'individuals' who are in truth usually powerful commercial operators. It would be a stretch to treat the Court's nurturing of principles of good administration such as proportionality and protection of legitimate expectations as reflecting 'values', and even claims to fundamental rights tended to arise in the heartland of economic activity: rights to property in the market for cereals are remote from human dignity.[33] Even direct effect was primarily a means to economic ends, placing EU law in the quotidian service of traders in chemicals, meat products, and financial services. So the EU holds its Member States to observe fundamental rights *only* where they are implementing EU law (Chapter 4.8.1) and, in Article 7 TEU, it has a tightly confined and never used competence to intervene where a Member State flouts its values, yet it freely intervenes with non-discriminatory national rules

[31] Art 275 TFEU. [32] Opinion 2/13 note 1.

[33] Case 11/70 *Internationale Handelsgesellschaft* [1970] ECR 1125; Chapters 3.15.5, 4.3.

governing the composition of blackcurrant liqueur, beer, and cheese. The Citizen of the Union has the heart of a consumer. Trade is the EU's business.

This is economic liberalism, not social solidarity: indeed, the former (at EU level) may subvert the latter (at State level). The deregulatory dynamic of which *Cassis de Dijon* serves as such a vivid illustration may be welcomed in the woefully silly circumstances of that particular litigation, but it stands for a wider unleashing of a power under EU law whereby commercial interests are able to seek aggressively to deter or to set aside locally determined regulatory choices. From this perspective *Centros*, as a (conditional) release of regulatory competition in corporate law, shows how a State's views of the limits of market freedom may be fatally undermined if they are treated as unjustified by the Court. Mobile patients are able to exploit EU law to undermine local allocation of finite budgetary resources to the provision of health care.[34] *Viking Line*, which applies the *Centros* model of shopping around for a favoured regime as the core of internal market freedom, stands out as the most direct assault of all launched in the name of the internal market against social values.[35] This has been condemned as neo-liberal slippage, according to which exaggerated embrace of the virtues of intervention in the name of the internal market has led to its legal rules being pushed too hard and too far, to the detriment of responsibilities to deliver social protection within national political systems.[36] The subordination of collective action in defence of workers to the interests of cost-cutting corporate mobility is a betrayal of the claim that internal market law, as a balance between diverse interests, is safe in the Court's hands. Fritz Scharpf, among the most powerful critics of the EU's deregulatory tendency to undermine settlements hard won over time at national level, comments that there is a 'legitimate diversity' of socio-economic institutions and policies across the Member States, 'shaped by intense political conflicts and historical compromises'. They are highly politically contested and 'they need to be defended in public debates by governments facing the sanctions of political accountability. Instead the supremacy of European law allows for judicial

[34] Case C-372/04 *ex parte Watts* [2006] ECR I-4325; Chapter 2.8.

[35] Case C-438/05 *International Transport Workers' Federation* v *Viking Line ABP* [2007] ECR I-10779; Chapter 6.3.4.

[36] A. Somek, 'The Darling Dogma of Bourgeois Europeanists' (2014) 20 ELJ 688. See also D. Schiek, U. Liebert, and H. Schneider (eds), *European Economic and Social Constitutionalism after the Treaty of Lisbon* (CUP, 2011); D. Nicol, 'Europe's Lochner Moment' [2011] Public Law 308; A. McCann, 'The CJEU on Trial: Economic Mobility and Social Justice' (2014) 22 Euro Rev Private Law 729.

interventions that may short-circuit these political processes.'[37] A key element in the anxiety is that the EU's vigorous deregulatory bite dramatically overshadows its much more slender (re-)regulatory reserves. For reasons of constitutional competence, political feasibility, institutional resources, and budgetary capacity the EU simply cannot aspire to intervene to achieve the balance between market deregulation and socially motivated market re-regulation which in States has been pieced together over decades of political struggle.

The correction of markets that work imperfectly and/or unfairly is not a task that can be adequately achieved by the EU, but the Member States are disabled by EU law from performing the full scope of the necessary correction. Almost all political systems choose to place certain matters beyond alteration by everyday majoritarian whim, but the anxiety is that the EU goes too far in entrenching certain (deregulatory) choices. On this account States have been tamed by the EU *too much*. This is what is dangerous in 'the totalization of the process of integration'.[38]

That the EU is doing too much and imposing too high a level of centralization is a further part of the critique. Harmonization pursuant to Article 114 TFEU is the legislative competence that is widest in its influence, as explained in Chapters 2.7.4 and 6.4.4. It is a deceptively unthreatening concept. Who would champion *dis*harmony? Yet in fact the impulse to harmonize tends to disable and disturb national practice. The choice about minimum *versus* maximum harmonization, tracked in Chapter 5.2.4, is the sharpest element of the debate, but *any* kind of harmonization, even if pitched in the form of minimum rules, involves a degree of 're-regulatory' centralization at the expense of local autonomy. It may make *economic* sense to prefer harmony over disharmony in the pursuit of an internal market, but the wider the functional reach of the EU's rules, the more sensitive the political and cultural consequences. One would not quickly question harmonization if its antonym is disharmony, but the depth of the concern is better expressed and laid bare by treating

[37] F. Scharpf, 'The Asymmetry of European Integration, Or Why the EU Cannot Be a Social Market Economy' (2010) 8 Socio-Economic Review 211, 241. See also A. José Menéndez, 'A Proportionate Constitution? Economic Freedoms, Substantive Constitutional Choices and *Dérapages* in European Union Law', Ch 4 in E. Chiti, A. José Menéndez, and P. Gustavo Teixeira (eds), *The European Rescue of the European Union?* (ARENA Report No 3/12, RECON Report No 19); and emphasizing the historical resonances, M. Höpner and A. Schäfer, 'Embeddedness and Regional Integration: Waiting for Polanyi in a Hayekian Setting' (2012) 66 International Organization 429.

[38] L. Azoulai, 'The "Retained Powers" Formula in the Case Law of the European Court of Justice: EU Law as Total Law?' (2011) 4 EJLS 192.

the alternative to harmonization as preservation of diversity and local autonomy. Harmonization can be intolerant of such values. If the EU is an exercise in balancing unity and diversity, harmonization offers an instructively contested test department.

The Court's reliance on 'effectiveness' as a basis for review of national practices, examined in Chapter 4.5, deserves to be assessed from this perspective too. Effectiveness, like harmonization, carries a deceptively unthreatening sheen. Who would plead for ineffective rules? However, it is, like harmonization, a centralizing concept. It stands for invasion of the autonomy and coherence of national settlements: a direction under EU law to adapt national law because it is ineffective immediately causes harm to legal certainty. Making EU law more effective may make national law less so. Again, the root question is about the balance between the virtues of centralization and uniformity and the virtues of protecting and preserving local autonomy and diversity.

And—the critical voice asserts—it is getting worse. The Eurozone sharpens the anxiety that the EU is doing too much and doing it according to a particular contested economic vision.

8.4 FROM STEALTH TO EVASION

Chapter 3.9.2 explained that the Eurozone is based on an apparently neat separation between monetary policy, which is allocated exclusively to the EU (for the States that use the euro), and economic and fiscal policies, which remain the preserve of Member States. This, when devised and installed in the EU system by the Maastricht Treaty in 1993, was hard to square with any durable economic design and in truth it represented a short-term political trick.[39] Its fragility has been exposed now. The story told in Chapter 3.9.2 was of ever increasing co-ordination of economic and fiscal policies, to the point where it is an illusion to talk seriously of national *autonomy* in these fields. EU law closes off many options in economic and fiscal policy. The Stability Pact, first entered into in 1997 and adapted in 2005,[40] promotes more rigorous surveillance of budgetary discipline by national governments and, in cases of excessive deficit, provides for the imposition of sanctions, in supplement to existing Treaty

[39] Eg M. Dawson, 'Economic and Monetary Union: Maastricht's Great Failure' in M. De Visser and P. Van der Mei (eds), *The Treaty on European Union 1993–2013: Reflections from Maastricht* (Intersentia, 2013).

[40] Reg 1466/97 OJ [1997] L209/1; Reg 1467/97 OJ [1997] L209/6; Reg 1055/2005 OJ [2005] L174/1; Reg 1056/2005 OJ [2005] L174/5.

procedures aimed at co-ordination.[41] Since the eruption of the financial crisis in 2008, the political will to hold together the Eurozone rather than allow individual States to sink beneath a rising tide of unserviceable debt collided with the prohibition of 'bail-out' contained in the Treaty.[42] This has promoted a still more vigorous 'co-ordination' of national economic and fiscal policies, involving the setting of concrete rules on how support shall be made available and the terms on which recipients shall receive that support. The so-called six-pack was adopted in 2011;[43] the two-pack in 2013.[44] Such hardening of the rules leads to diminution in the autonomy of the Member States' scope for unilateral action to the point where what is in form 'co-ordination' is in substance much closer to centralized policy-making. The European Stability Mechanism (ESM; Chapters 3.9.2 and 5.4.2) was founded on a free-standing international Treaty to which most but not all EU Member States are party rather than on EU law, but it shares a concern to deepen the control exercised transnationally over national choices about economic and fiscal policy. The golden rule of balanced budgets established by the ESM allied to the conditions attached to provision of financial support under the six-pack and two-pack have the effect of placing certain key policy decisions beyond the reach of political contestation at national level. Startlingly concrete decisions have been directed at particular States pursuant to Treaty procedures designed to avoid excessive deficit and to strengthen budgetary discipline. So for example Greece has been required to adapt its tax and pension systems (including reduction of Christmas bonuses paid to civil servants and elimination of such bonuses paid to pensioners), increase excise duties, change the statutory retirement age, reform—meaning reduce—employment protection, including the facilitation of a greater use of temporary contracts, and a great deal more detail besides.[45]

In the Eurozone the abolition of the tool of monetary policy, now exclusively pursued at EU level, pushes States to adjust—this means to reduce—welfare support and labour market protection, over which they retain a degree of formal autonomy, in order to promote competitiveness, while their supposed autonomy in economic and fiscal policy has become

[41] Especially Arts 121 and 126 TFEU respectively.

[42] Today, Art 125 TFEU.

[43] Reg 1173/2011 OJ [2011] L 306/1; Reg 1174/2011 OJ [2011] L 306/8; Reg 1175/2011 OJ [2011] L 306/12; Reg 1176/2011 OJ [2011] L 306/25; Reg 1177/2011 OJ [2011] L 306/33; Dir 2011/85 OJ [2011] L 306/41.

[44] Reg. 472/2013 OJ [2013] L140/1; Reg 473/2013 OJ [2013] L140/11.

[45] Council Dec 2010/320 OJ [2010] L145/6, adopted pursuant to Arts 126(9) and 136 TFEU, and addressed to Greece. Much more has followed in this vein since 2011, and not only in application to Greece.

an illusion, replaced by ever tighter 'co-ordination'. Part of the very point of the EU is to embed long-term policy commitments and to withdraw some matters from everyday politics and opportunistic selfishness, but the mandate to adopt this model in the Eurozone has been created in a rush and with minimal democratic approval. The commitments made are all of a particular political type: austerity. This is a long way from blackcurrant liqueur and a long way from mutually beneficial consensual deals entered into from a position of formal equality. Were the prevailing institutional and constitutional arrangements of the orthodox EU type, they would be unlikely to be thought legitimate given the politically contested and distributive nature of the choices that have been shifted out of national hands to the transnational level, but in fact what is in place is not even that. It is something thinner, where the Commission and Parliament are marginalized, and, wrenched free of space for contestation, something frighteningly technocratic.[46] The rule-making capacity crafted 'above the state' follows neither the orthodox EU model nor even, in the case of the ESM, the EU model at all. Most of all, the European Council has become increasingly powerful, not only setting general initiatives but also becoming heavily engaged in detailed policy preparation and projection. There is damage to 'constitutional balance' in the EU: the problem is rising executive power expressed transnationally through largely intergovernmental methods with reduced accountability and transparency, especially to the advantage of the bigger and richer Member States, allied to the diminution in the input of national political processes.[47]

A torrent of law- and policy-making is driven and *for the time being* legitimated by the imperative of crisis management. Deep historical scars risk being re-opened by this trend towards executive power.[48] Where integration-through-law is replaced by integration-through-power, the EU's claim to have moulded a unique consensual model of management based on benevolent co-operation and institutional sophistication

[46] See eg G. Majone, 'From Regulatory State to a Democratic Default' (2014) 52 JCMS 1216.

[47] See eg M. Dawson and F. De Witte, 'Constitutional Balance in the EU after the Euro-Crisis' (2013) 76 MLR 817; D. Chalmers, 'The European Redistributive State and a European Law of Struggle' (2012) 18 ELJ 667; D. Curtin, 'Challenging Executive Dominance in European Democracy' (2014) 77 MLR 1; E. Chiti and P. Texeira, 'The Constitutional Implications of the European Responses to the Financial and Public Debt Crisis' (2013) 50 CMLRev 683; N. Scicluna, 'Politicization without Democratization: How the Eurozone Crisis is Transforming EU Law and Politics' (2014) 12 Intl Jnl Const Law 545.

[48] Cf C. Joerges, 'Europe's Economic Constitution in Crisis and the Emergence of a New Constitutional Constellation' (2014) 15 German Law Jnl 986.

is corroded. Perhaps most vividly, the Treaty 'no bail-out' rule, an expression of the *limits* of solidarity and burden-sharing, obstructs deeper integration, but its constraining effect has been reduced by arrangements (under both EU rules and the ESM) which provide support to indebted States but on terms which are not strictly bail-outs, but instead provide that the recipient remains in principle responsible for the commitments made to creditors. It is a *functional* bail-out—a classic example of incrementalism. It also involves the need to skate on precariously thin legal ice, although so far the Court has chosen not to disturb the load-bearing surface.[49]

The EU's economic government seems neither to work very well nor to give voice to those prejudiced by it who might wish to change it. In the summer of 2012 Mario Draghi, President of the European Central Bank (ECB), declared that 'Within our mandate, the ECB is ready to do whatever it takes to preserve the euro.'[50] This was designed to persuade markets that States would not default and it did so, but it did nothing to reassure citizens, because the mandate is exactly the problem. It is price stability without any reference to what that might mean for education, health, social welfare, and public services generally. And 're-politicization' at EU level is missing. Where the interests that are privileged are those of the rich and powerful then the dark fear is that the fight for proper democratic accountability and the subjection of raw power to control by representative political institutions, won hard and bravely over the nineteenth and twentieth centuries, has been quietly lost. This is the *Viking Line* reading of free movement law translated to a much wider and frightening plane. In ever wider fields across the EU national political contestation is robbed of its very point, because key decisions have been spirited away—to the European Council, to the markets. Governments do not have to explain and justify to their electorates what has happened: they can claim their hands are tied. The Court's ruling in *Pringle* has its critics, exposed in Chapter 5.4.2, but it is the very structure of the EMU/ESM system rather than judicial reticence to intervene that is the deepest problem.

From these standpoints, the *values* inscribed in the TEU seem exposed as tawdry window-dressing. The titles alone of two critical analyses are

[49] Case C-62/14 *Gauweiler* (Chapter 4.11.3), Case C-370/12 *Pringle* (Chapter 5.4.2), and Case C-128/12 *Sindicato dos Bancários do Norte* Order of 7 March 2013 show (in different ways) the Court's reticence to disturb politically sensitive arrangements. See A. Hinarejos, *The Euro Area Crisis in Constitutional Perspective* (OUP, 2015), Ch 8. *National* constitutional courts may prove more assertive.

[50] http://www.ecb.europa.eu/press/key/date/2012/html/sp120726.en.html

suggestive enough to capture the perils of intransparent managerial arrogance: 'Saving the Euro at the Cost of Democracy?'[51] and 'The Specter of Authoritarian Liberalism'.[52] Article 2 TEU declares the value of respect for the rule of law: the challenge is to animate this by insisting on 'the accountability of power, and correlative emphasis on freedom and equality'; to treat the slide of the Eurozone into a pattern of conditions imposed by and favouring the dominant parties as a case of the rule of law 'corrupted'—and to correct it.[53]

But *how*?

There are two *simple* antidotes to this poisonous brew.

The first is *simply* to redeploy the EU's orthodox method to create a true fiscal union at EU level—to transfer some powers to tax and spend to EU level and, as part of the deal, to provide for transfer of resources from economically strong to weak regions, just as happens within a State. This would herald the emergence of a single economic government for the EU, built on the orthodox foundations of the Commission (to deliver effective policy-formulation) and the Council and Parliament (to provide dual sourced legitimacy).

The second solution is *simply* to relocate monetary, economic, and fiscal policies at national level, thereby to achieve the necessary clean-cut democratic tether accompanied by transparency which is missing from the current tortured and misshapen system of governance in the Eurozone.

Both models are *simple* but they are at best inadequate and at worst unfeasible. The first design is based on a claim to effective management of the Eurozone, but it makes unrealistic assumptions about willingness to authorize the transfer of the location to make such politically sensitive decisions under the cover of EU governance. It would be highly unlikely to gain the consent of voters or of national constitutional courts. The most powerful proponent of this type of reform is Habermas, whose zeal for the opening up of a European public sphere is highly influential and is persuasively driven by appreciation of the limits of the State's capacities acting unilaterally.[54] But the counter-arguments are strong. Grimm, a regular sparring partner of Habermas, has objected that the EU is *already*

[51] B. Crum, 'Saving the Euro at the Cost of Democracy?' (2013) 51 JCMS 614.

[52] M. Wilkinson, 'The Specter of Authoritarian Liberalism: Reflections on the Constitutional Crisis of the European Union' (2013) 14 German Law Jnl 527.

[53] S. Douglas-Scott, 'The Problem of Justice in the European Union', Ch 16 in J. Dickson and P. Eleftheriadis (eds), *Philosophical Foundations of European Union Law* (OUP, 2012), 436, 442.

[54] See eg J. Habermas, 'Democracy in Europe: Why the Development of the EU into a Transnational Democracy is Necessary and How It Is Possible' (2015) 21 ELJ 546.

'over-constitutionalised' and 'de-politicised' and that given the unfeasibility of generating a fiercer level of political contestation through empowering the European Parliament, because of its want of legitimacy as a result of the absence of a European '*demos*', the scope of primary EU law should be reduced, and in particular that the locking power of the Court should be opened up much more to contested and corrective legislative activity.[55] One does not have to agree with this preference for retreat to understand that Habermas's call to advance lacks popular support. Less structurally ambitious proposals to pursue a commitment to common social protection which matches the commitment to economic policy co-ordination—such as a social compact to balance the fiscal compact[56]—have plenty of normative appeal as a means to rebalance the EU away from its neo-liberal lurch but they crash hard into the existing constitutional deficiencies of the EU's competence toolkit, and are anyway backed by no more than pockets of support among political élites.

The second design makes wholly unrealistic assumptions about the ability of States to operate such policies unilaterally. The price paid for better accountability to citizens would be drastic loss of effectiveness in the execution of policy. In fact to re-emphasize the virtue of unilateral State action would quickly generate pressures to act bilaterally and multilaterally, because of the deep levels of economic interdependence which require management. So abandoning the single currency and abandoning any pretence to a single social model has some appeal as a means to use diversity to counter the alienating effect of over-centralization and to restore national level decision-making. So too it would release lost political options such as currency devaluation.[57] But it would risk denuding States of effective control over activities that do not respect frontiers. The rise of the Euro has exacerbated the problem, but it is not the root cause: the power of mobile capital supplies that. In fact, here one can flip Habermas and Grimm round: Grimm's call to reduce the scope of primary EU law is vulnerable to the insight of Habermas that this expects too much of the effectiveness of unilateral State action.

The heavily incremental and short-term nature of the measures so far taken to stabilize the Eurozone led Tuori and Tuori to conclude their

[55] Eg D. Grimm, 'The Democratic Costs of Constitutionalisation: The European Case' (2015) 21 ELJ 460.

[56] C. Barnard, 'EU Employment Law and the European Social Model: The Past, the Present and the Future' (2014) 67 CLP 199. See also N. Countouris and M. Freedland (eds), *Resocialising Europe in a Time of Crisis* (CUP, 2013).

[57] Cf C. Joerges, 'Europe's Economic Constitution in Crisis and the Emergence of a New Constitutional Constellation' (2014) 15 German Law Jnl 986, esp 1023–1027.

book-length treatment of the Eurozone with the observation that 'we are not very optimistic'.[58]

8.5 WHAT IS THE FUTURE OF EUROPEAN INTEGRATION?

This is a question that is easy to answer. It is completely assured. The interdependence between States in Europe for which the word 'integration' stands as shorthand cannot be unravelled. Without the EU, States would need to piece together a series of sectoral bilateral and multilateral deals and they would need some kind of institutional structure to complete it. Even those who urge their State to quit the EU fully envisage negotiation of bilateral deals with the bloc, even if they implausibly assume how easy it will be to strike them. The EU itself may collapse or lose members: but the motivating force of interdependence as a stimulus to co-operation is not going away. In fact it will likely intensify. 'Europeanization', as explored in Chapter 2.10, has many transformative manifestations,[59] and for that very reason it is not about to be unravelled even if the EU itself were to be terminated or vastly reduced in scale and ambition.

8.6 WHAT IS THE FUTURE OF THE EU?

This is a more tricky question. The EU offers a forum within which to manage interdependence. The internal state of the continent of Europe has over the past sixty years become peaceful, prosperous, and democratic as never before in its history. And although it would plainly be an exaggeration to place all or even most of the credit for this on the EU, it is nevertheless *through* the EU that much of this economic and political transformation has been routed. It does not follow that the current model will endure, nor that it should. That collapsing it would force States to re-imagine ways to manage their interdependence does not at all show that some or all of them will not take that step; it shows only that there are incentives not to. In fact, the major questions that confront the EU do not ask *whether* the States of Europe require frameworks within which to manage their mutual interdependence. They clearly do. The questions surround *how much* should be done in common rather than left to State autonomy; whether the institutional and constitutional patterns for doing

[58] K. Tuori and K. Tuori, *The Eurozone Crisis: A Constitutional Analysis* (CUP, 2014), p 266.

[59] C. Bickerton, *European Integration: From Nation-States to Member States* (OUP, 2012).

whatever is decided should be done in common which were established in the immediate post-War period remain suitable; and whether thirst for uniform application remains the proper model for a geographically and functionally expanded EU. Most of this book has been dedicated to explaining that the system, though still recognizable as that created in the 1950s, has adapted and is under pressure to adapt further under the impulses generated by its geographical and functional expansion. But missing is any coherent blueprint for the scope and pattern of necessary adaptation.

In 2001 the European Council issued its Laeken Declaration on the Future of the European Union. It set out a series of questions designed to frame a debate about the reform of the Union. It included the observation that 'Citizens often hold expectations of the European Union that are not always fulfilled. And vice versa—they sometimes have the impression that the Union takes on too much in areas where its involvement is not always essential.' The Laeken Declaration was driven by an anxiety to rebalance the trajectory of the EU's activities and to engage citizens more closely. But those drafting it didn't know how lucky they were.

Achieving prosperity and entrenching peace may have served as adequate reasons for insulating the EU from the messy pattern of political accountability and contestation that we find at State level, but that cannot hold when the EU is engaged in so much more than technocratic activity. There is a need to determine what the EU really can do better than its Member States—and a need too to determine what the peoples of Europe will tolerate being done in their name at EU level. This is a dynamic inquiry. The contrasting accounts provided in Sections 8.2 and 8.3 both have their truths—deregulation may have its economic benefits and it may be recognized too as a means to compensate for representative malfunctions in the production of rules at national level, but so too EU law may be driven too deep in its scope and may be inadequately sensitive to virtuous regulatory choices at national level. Commitment to *values* is contested terrain.

The really tough cases of design arise where the EU is better at doing the job than the Member States individually but where there is a popular view that the matter should be handled at State level because of its politically contested character. The EU is in a state of existential crisis precisely because it is engaging with issues associated with the management of interdependence that raise this tension. Social policy has long been right on this fault line (Chapter 6.4.3); migration too is increasingly pushed into this sensitive area, first of all in the matter of handling of refugees but so too in relation to the basic issues of free movement of people within the EU (Chapter 7.4). But the Eurozone is probably the most pressing issue of all. Explaining the EU as a means to tame the capacity of States to impose costs on their neighbours and to provide an arena for collective problem-solving tends to underplay just how the insulation from normal patterns of accountability that is a feature of the EU is under strain as it acts in ever more politically salient areas. This is accentuated by the economic crisis that erupted in 2008, both in the sense that it has increased the distributional choices made and in that it has led to institutional choices that limit still further scope for accountability. Tighter agreement on economic and fiscal policy within the Eurozone seems inevitable—but so too, given that what is at stake is not technocracy, does greatly improved accountability and political contestation, unless authoritarianism is to prevail. Only those with a short memory of European history can avoid the sense of chill. The street protests of Athens are protests against injustice and, most of all, disempowerment and absence of voice, and in this they fit into a longer narrative of struggle to break down limits on political participation defined by matters such as property ownership, gender, religion, and race.

The more the EU does, the less adhesive is the legitimation achieved through brilliant but undermined notions such as the EU as a site of *demoi* or of constitutional tolerance; the greater the pressure to break out of the model of integration through stealth. And yet that break-out is itself ever more difficult to achieve. In the background is the rise of 'veto players'—voters who delayed the ratification of the Maastricht and Nice Treaties, forced the abandonment of the Treaty establishing a Constitution, and briefly delayed the Lisbon Treaty too, and national constitutional courts who similarly performed a delaying function though not yet a blocking one. In fact, the refusal of the Dutch and French electorates in 2005 to approve ratification of the Treaty establishing a Constitution was significant, but far more serious has been the response to that jolt, which has been a ruthless determination to keep any future reform out of sight and most of all out of control of voters. The Treaty of Lisbon was largely a re-packaging of the Treaty establishing a Constitution, trimmed of some of its sillier adornments such as an EU flag and anthem, but it was kept carefully out of the reach of voters in France and the Netherlands, where a referendum had been held on the Treaty establishing a Constitution, and in the UK too, where one had been promised. This was grubby. The Laeken Declaration, under a sub-title *The democratic challenge facing Europe*, had identified that 'the European institutions must be brought closer to its citizens'. And yet the story of the Lisbon Treaty is exactly the reverse, one of a desperate desire to keep citizens out. The rising profile of veto players—voters, courts—is mainly met by trying to avoid their claim to speak.

The story of the failure of the Treaty establishing a Constitution and the success (of sorts) of the Lisbon Treaty offers a glimpse of a nightmare: the EU has become too complicated and intransparent for voters to understand and, as a reaction, they reject the texts handed down for their approval by political élites, and so the texts are then converted into legally binding instruments through means that carefully avoid those voters (except the Irish). So deepens the lack of understanding; so grows popular resentment to an authoritarian sense of 'we know best'. And in the Eurozone, which shares a similar narrative of evading popular explanation let alone approval, the 'we know best' claim is demonstrably not convincing anyway to many Europeans. An EU which is imposed on the peoples of Europe contains the seeds of its own destruction.

8.7 CONCLUSION

The EU has come a long way on the basis of a logic of managing interdependence, rooted in the legitimation of taming States and solving problems in common, achieved according to a unique institutional design (Chapter 3) supplemented by a boldly developed constitutional legal order (Chapter 4). A major theme of this book has been the pressure imposed on this design by the EU's geographical and functional expansion. Fragmentation is one response to the tensions caused by pressure of centralization within a geographically and functionally expanded Union. Chapter 5 shows that this has several dimensions. The rise of subsidiarity and national Parliaments (Chapter 2.11) and the increasing interest in the protection of identity promised by Article 4(2) TEU—a proper concern of both national and EU courts (Chapters 4.12, 6.3.4)—are part of this narrative. So is the wider story told in Chapter 4 of managing *conditional* supremacy, which serves as the specifically constitutional version of the sociological observation that there is no European *demos*.

These are classic questions of federalism, but in the EU at no stage can a centralizing tendency be legitimated by appeal to a *demos*. The EU needs to be sustained through its model of constitutional tolerance and as a site of *demoi*-cracy and not through a shift to the super-State that would risk the majoritarian excess and disrespect for local preference that taints too many aspects of Europe's past. It is exactly here that the zeal to 'Europeanize' in the name of effective management collides with entrenched social resistance to hollowing out the State as a site of political authority. But the travails of the Eurozone in particular make the pattern unstable.

Any deeper 'Europeanization' requires a jolt that will move public support further away from attachment to the imagined but exaggerated virtues of the State. The austerity that blights the Eurozone may be that jolt, though not for all twenty-eight Member States. There are other mobilizing candidates too: climate change, migration, an aggressive Russia, a retreating US, an increasingly powerful China. The logic underpinning collective action is strong. However, if the EU is the site for solving such problems but is seen not to do so, its legitimacy is imperilled. Its alienation from popular support is likely to be exacerbated if national politicians shift the blame for policy failures to it—which, acting rationally and exploiting the endemic intransparency of the EU, they will. This may lead to a tipping point, at which citizens do not simply see the EU as a failed problem-solver but rather as the problem-causer. This will tilt the momentum back to the apparently safe haven, and certainly better recognized site, of national-level politics—and nationalism—but it will not make solving the problems any easier. It will make blaming and causing harm to other Europeans easier. This is a road too often travelled by Europeans through history. I am not very optimistic.

INDEX